United States History

by
John Napp
Wayne King

American Guidance Service, Inc.
Circle Pines, Minnesota 55014-1796
800-328-2560

Contents

How to Use This Book: A Study Guide xx

| Unit 1 | **Three Worlds Meet: Beginnings to 1607** . . . . **10** |

Chapter 1   The First Americans: Beginnings to 1400 12
    Section 1   The Earliest Americans 13
    Section 2   The Peoples of Mesoamerica 16
    Section 3   The Southwestern Peoples 20
    Section 4   The Adena-Hopewell
       Mound Builders 24
    Section 5   The Mississippi, Plains, and
       Northwest Civilizations 26
       Chapter Summary and Review 31

Chapter 2   Exploration: 1400–1607 34
    Section 1   Ideas of Exploration Begin 35
    Section 2   Other Explorers Follow 38
    Section 3   England and France Start Colonies . . . 43
       Chapter Summary and Review 47

| Unit 2 | **Colonization and Settlement: 1607–1763** . . . . **52** |

Chapter 3   English Colonies Are Established: 1607–1733 . . . 54
    Section 1   The Jamestown Colony 55
    Section 2   The Pilgrims and the Puritans 59
    Section 3   English Colonies Grow in Number . . . 64
    Section 4   The Colonies Grow Larger 69
       Chapter Summary and Review 73

Chapter 4   A Struggle for Power: 1700–1763 76
    Section 1   Independent Trade in the Colonies . . . 77
    Section 2   Triangular Trade in the Colonies 79
    Section 3   The Move Westward 81
    Section 4   The French and Indian War Begins . . . 84
    Section 5   The War Ends 86
       Chapter Summary and Review 89

Unit 3	Revolution and the New Nation: 1763–1815 94

Chapter 5	A New Nation Begins to Grow: 1763–1775 96
	Section 1 The Proclamation of 1763 97
	Section 2 The Townshend Acts 100
	Section 3 The East India Trading Company 104
	Section 4 The First Continental Congress: 1774. 107
	Chapter Summary and Review 111

Chapter 6	The American Revolution: 1775–1783 114
	Section 1 Americans Respond 115
	Section 2 Congress Takes Action 117
	Section 3 Fighting Spreads 120
	Section 4 The Revolutionary War 123
	Section 5 The Turning Point of the War 126
	Section 6 The British Are Defeated 129
	Chapter Summary and Review 133

Chapter 7	A Government Is Formed: 1783–1791 136
	Section 1 A New Nation Faces Problems 137
	Section 2 A Demand for Change 140
	Section 3 A Need for a New Start 143
	Section 4 The Great Compromise 145
	Section 5 State Conventions Are Organized 148
	Chapter Summary and Review 153

Chapter 8	Political Parties Develop: 1788–1809 156
	Section 1 The First Administration 157
	Section 2 The Government's Progress 160
	Section 3 Adams Becomes the Next President . . 163
	Section 4 The Country Under New Direction . . 168
	Section 5 Valuable Explorations 171
	Chapter Summary and Review 175

Chapter 9	The Young Nation Goes to War: 1809–1815 178
	Section 1 President Madison Takes Office 179
	Section 2 The War Draws Closer 181
	Section 3 The War of 1812 184
	Section 4 The War Ends 188
	Chapter Summary and Review 191

Unit 4　　**Expansion and Reform: 1816–1850** **196**

Chapter 10　A New Spirit of Expansion: 1816–1824 198
　　　　　Section 1　Westward Expansion 199
　　　　　Section 2　The Era of Good Feelings 203
　　　　　Section 3　More Problems With Europe 208
　　　　　　　　　　Chapter Summary and Review 213

Chapter 11　Political Changes Take Place: 1825–1838 216
　　　　　Section 1　An Unpopular President 217
　　　　　Section 2　Growing Tension in the South 219
　　　　　Section 3　Jackson's New Style of Government . . 221
　　　　　Section 4　Texas Gains Independence
　　　　　　　　　　From Mexico 224
　　　　　Section 5　The Election of 1836 226
　　　　　　　　　　Chapter Summary and Review 229

Chapter 12　America Becomes More
　　　　　Democratic: 1825–1858 232
　　　　　Section 1　Industries Develop Slowly 233
　　　　　Section 2　Improving Transportation and
　　　　　　　　　　Communication 235
　　　　　Section 3　The Population Grows 240
　　　　　Section 4　The Early System of Education 242
　　　　　Section 5　American Literature Develops 244
　　　　　　　　　　Chapter Summary and Review 249

Chapter 13　The Country Grows Larger: 1841–1850 252
　　　　　Section 1　The Election of 1840 253
　　　　　Section 2　Ongoing Trouble With Mexico 258
　　　　　Section 3　New Challenges in 1848 261
　　　　　　　　　　Chapter Summary and Review 265

Unit 5 Civil War and Reconstruction: 1850–1877 270

Chapter 14 The Slavery Problem Grows: 1850–1854. 272
    Section 1 The Debate Over Slavery. 273
    Section 2 Slavery Issues Continue. 276
    Section 3 The Kansas-Nebraska Act 279
    Chapter Summary and Review. 283

Chapter 15 The Country Separates:1854–1861 286
    Section 1 A Land Rush in Kansas 287
    Section 2 Fighting in Congress 289
    Section 3 The Lincoln-Douglas Debates 292
    Section 4 The Election of 1860 294
    Chapter Summary and Review. 297

Chapter 16 The Civil War: 1861–1865 300
    Section 1 The North Tries to Compromise 301
    Section 2 Confederates Attack Fort Sumter. . . . 304
    Section 3 The Civil War Begins. 307
    Section 4 The War Continues 312
    Section 5 The Final Chapters of the War 316
    Chapter Summary and Review. 321

Chapter 17 Reconstruction: 1865–1877 324
    Section 1 The Beginning of Reconstruction . . . 325
    Section 2 Johnson's Conflict With Congress
               Continues 328
    Section 3 Reshaping the South 332
    Section 4 Reconstruction Ends 336
    Chapter Summary and Review. 341

| Unit 6 | **Development of Industrial America: 1862–1900 . . . 346** |

Chapter 18 Settling the Western Frontier: 1862–1890 348
    Section 1 The Great Plains 349
    Section 2 Frontier Life 352
    Section 3 The Plains Indians 356
    Section 4 Congress Aids American Indians 360
    Chapter Summary and Review 363

Chapter 19 Becoming an Industrial Giant: 1870–1900 366
    Section 1 The Nation Enters
              the Industrial Age 367
    Section 2 Rockefeller and the Oil Industry 371
    Section 3 Other Major U.S. Industries 375
    Chapter Summary and Review 381

Chapter 20 A Nation of Cities: 1882–1900 384
    Section 1 American Cities Grow Rapidly 385
    Section 2 Immigrant Problems and
              Discrimination 388
    Section 3 City Living 392
    Section 4 Problems of the Cities 395
    Chapter Summary and Review 399

Chapter 21 A New Spirit of Reform: 1872–1897 402
    Section 1 The Gilded Age 403
    Section 2 Reformers Challenge Political
              Practices 405
    Section 3 Labor Unions Are Formed 409
    Section 4 Reformers Start a Political Party 412
    Chapter Summary and Review 417

| Unit 7 | The Emergence of Modern America: 1898–1929. . . **422** |

Chapter 22 America Becomes a World Power: 1898–1913 . . 424
Section 1 Problems With Spain. 425
Section 2 The "Splendid Little War". 427
Section 3 The Nation Increases Its Power 430
Section 4 New Leadership for a New Century. . 433
Section 5 Roosevelt's Other Achievements 437
Section 6 "As Strong as a Bull Moose" 441
Chapter Summary and Review. 445

Chapter 23 World War I: 1913–1920. 448
Section 1 The War Begins in Europe 449
Section 2 The United States Stays Neutral. 453
Section 3 America Enters the Great War 456
Section 4 Wilson's Plan for a
Permanent Peace 460
Chapter Summary and Review. 465

Chapter 24 The Roaring Twenties: 1920–1929. 468
Section 1 Americans Want to Return to
Normal Times 469
Section 2 Society Changes: Fords, Flappers,
and Radios 473
Section 3 The Spirit of the Jazz Age 477
Section 4 Social Problems in the 1920s 480
Section 5 American Confidence Rises
and Falls 482
Chapter Summary and Review. 485

Unit 8	**Depression and World War II: 1930–1945** **490**

Chapter 25 Depression and the New Deal: 1930–1939 492
    Section 1 The Great Depression 493
    Section 2 A New Deal for the Nation 496
    Section 3 The New Deal
                 Changes Government 500
    Section 4 Leisure and Literature of
                 the Depression 504
                 Chapter Summary and Review...... 509

Chapter 26 World War II: 1939–1945 512
    Section 1 Preparation for War............. 513
    Section 2 Steps Toward a Second World War .. 517
    Section 3 World War II Begins 521
    Section 4 War in Asia 525
    Section 5 The Home Front 528
    Section 6 The War Ends................... 530
                 Chapter Summary and Review...... 535

Unit 9	**Postwar United States: 1946–1968** **540**

Chapter 27 A Time of Challenge and Change: 1945–1957 .. 542
    Section 1 The Search for Peace 543
    Section 2 The Cold War Begins............. 547
    Section 3 War in Korea................... 552
    Section 4 Challenge and Change in the 1950s.. 555
                 Chapter Summary and Review...... 561

Chapter 28 Support for Freedom: 1958–1968 564
    Section 1 New Challenges 565
    Section 2 Supporting Freedom Abroad 568
    Section 3 Struggles at Home 571
    Section 4 The Johnson Administration 575
    Section 5 New Movements Try to
                 Change America................... 579
    Section 6 The Politics of Protest 583
                 Chapter Summary and Review...... 587

Unit 10   **Contemporary United States: 1968–Present** **592**

Chapter 29 America in a Changing World: 1968–1980 594
     Section 1   A New Course for the Nation 595
     Section 2   Nixon's Foreign Relations 598
     Section 3   The Watergate Scandal 601
     Section 4   The Ford Administration 605
     Section 5   A New Voice, a New Leader 608
     Section 6   International Problems Continue . . . 613
     Chapter Summary and Review 617

Chapter 30 The 1980s: 1980–1989 620
     Section 1   The Reagan Presidency 621
     Section 2   Reagan Faces International Issues . . . 625
     Section 3   A New President Takes Office 632
     Chapter Summary and Review 637

Chapter 31 The 1990s: 1990–Present 640
     Section 1   Communism Falls 641
     Section 2   The Persian Gulf War 645
     Section 3   The Clinton Administration 648
     Section 4   Foreign Issues 651
     Section 5   Problems and Changes at Home 655
     Chapter Summary and Review 661

Biographies

Juanita, the Maiden of Ampato 19
Montezuma II 40
Margaret Brent 64
James Oglethorpe 80
Phillis Wheatley 103
Benjamin Banneker 122
John Fitch 151
Miguel Hidalgo y Costilla 173
Mother Elizabeth Seton 183
John Ross 204
Sarah Moore Grimké and Angelina Emily Grimké 227
James Fenimore Cooper 245
Samuel F. B. Morse 254
George Catlin 280
Harriet Tubman 288
Lucy Stone 303
P. B. S. Pinchback 334
Cochise 351
Horatio Alger 379
Rose Schneiderman 386
Jane Addams 411
Matthew Henson 442
Jim Thorpe 450
Marcus Garvey 479
Marian Anderson 497
Eleanor Roosevelt 515
Margaret Chase Smith 556
Cesar Chavez 581
An Wang 606
Maya Lin 625
Maya Angelou 654

History in Your Life

Careers   Rosie the Riveter and the Women
                       of World War II 528

Consumer Science   The Earliest Bowling 56
                          The Sewing Machine 274

Fine Arts   Architecture From the Anasazis 22
                       The First Theater in America. 109
                       Spirituals 219
                       Ragtime and the Music of Scott Joplin 432
                       The Music of Irving Berlin. 455

Geography   The Eruption of Mount Saint Helens 623

Health   A Smallpox Vaccine. 165
                       The American Red Cross 396
                       Salk and the Polio Vaccine 554

Industrial Technology   The Nail-Making Machine. 125

Literature   Sequoyah and a Different Form of Writing 209
                       The Works of Edgar Allan Poe. 257
                       The Works of Mark Twain 333
                       The Works of Emily Dickinson 415
                       The Works of Langston Hughes 478

Math   The U.S. Census 149
                       The Advent of Credit Cards 584

Science   The Work of Benjamin Franklin 82
                       John James Audubon 244
                       The Development of Nylon 507
                       The Hale-Bopp Comet 657

Technology   Robert Fulton's Steamboat. 179
                       Otis and the Elevator 289
                       Barbed Wire. 355
                       The Brooklyn Bridge. 369
                       The Microwave Oven 612

Source Readings

An Osage Belief. 30
Cabeza de Vaca's Journal 46
The Mayflower Compact. 72
Poor Richard's Almanac 88
The Stamp Act 110
"Common Sense" 132
The Northwest Ordinance. 152
Prevention of Slave Trade 174
Speech by Tecumseh 190
The Monroe Doctrine 212
A Message From the Alamo 228
"Slavery As It Is" 248
Seneca Falls Declaration. 264
Daniel Webster's Speech to the Senate. 282
The Dred Scott Decision. 296
Lee's Surrender 320
Advice to African-American Students 340
"The Laws" 362
Queen Liliuokalani's Statement on Hawaii. 380
Blanche Bruce's Speech to the Senate 398
Declaration of Woman's Christian
Temperance Union. 416
Speech of Booker T. Washington 444
Suffragette Letter. 464
James Weldon Johnson. 484
Breadline 508
Roosevelt's Four Freedoms Speech 534
The Crisis at Central High School. 560
"I Have a Dream" 586
This Is the America We Want 616
"Women Shooting for the Stars" 636
"Favor Positive Themes" 660

Media in History

The Father of Modern Advertising 68
The Press and the American Revolution. 119
Noah Webster: A Household Name 139
Frontier Newspapers: How the West Was Won 182
The Penny Press. 221
A Person of Many Contradictions. 246
Uncle Tom's Cabin Ignites Slavery Issue 281
Mathew Brady, Civil War Photographer. 309
Magazines Gain Popularity 335
The Pen Is Mightier Than the Sword 370
Edison's "Talking Machine" 394
Radio Makes It Into Prime Time. 458
The Silent Years 472
"War of the Worlds" 504
World War II Songs. 524
The Golden Age of Radio. 551
The Vietnam War 578
Cable TV: The Wired Nation 604
Movies at Home 633
Internet: The Information Superhighway 644

Then and Now

Maps 39
Dentistry 85
Lodging 106
Submarines 118
Handwriting 144
Political Parties 167
Public Education 226
Transportation 239
Immigration .262
Campaigning Methods 292
Military Intelligence 313
Subways 338
Airplanes 378
Child Labor 387
Bicycles 407
Medicine 437
Automobiles 475
Plastics 526
Computers 558
Space Exploration 565
HIV/AIDS 631
Population 659

Writing About History

Research Report 28
Writing Your Opinion 44
Writing a Business Letter . . 63
Writing a Personal Letter . . 77
Research Report 102
Writing an Article 126
Writing an Essay 150
Writing a Speech 172
Letter to the Editor 188
Writing an Advertisement 201
Writing Your Opinion 222
Writing a Poem 247
Research Report 259
Research Report 281
Writing Your Opinion 291
Writing a Short Story or Poem 306
Writing a Song 331
Writing a Speech 359
Research Paragraph 378
Writing a Short Play 390
Letter to the Editor 408
Writing an Essay 429
Research Report 459
Research Report 476
Research Report 495
Writing Your Opinion 529
Writing an Essay 553
Writing an Article 573
Writing a Public Service Advertisement 609
Research Report 628
Writing Your Opinion 658

Skills Lessons

Timeliness 50
Maps 92
Graphs and Charts 194
Fact and Opinion 268
Cause and Effect 344
Using Reference Materials 420
Compare and Contrast 488
Population Growth Table 538
Political Cartoon 590
Voting 664

Maps

Migration Routes Into the Americas 14
Adena-Hopewell Settlements 25
Main Mississippian Settlements 26
The Continents Between Europe and Asia 36
Columbus's Voyages 37
Early European Explorers 41
The Thirteen Colonies 70
French and British Forts 87
Major Battles of the Revolutionary War 131

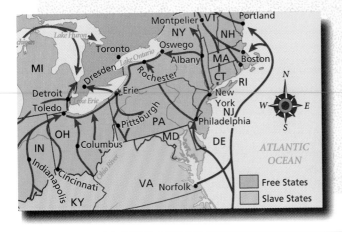

Maps continued

The Annapolis Convention, 1786 140
The Louisiana Purchase, 1803 170
Louisiana Purchase Explorations. 171
Battles of the War of 1812. 186
The Missouri Compromise, 1820 207
The Republic of Texas, 1836. 225
The Cumberland Road and the Wilderness Road 235
The Maine Boundary Settlement, 1842 255
The Treaty of 1846. 256
The Mexican War, 1846-1848 260
The Underground Railroad 276
The Secession of the Southern States 295
The War in 1862 311
The War in 1863 314
The War in 1864 318
Military Districts and Readmission to the Union 329
The First Transcontinental Railroad, 1869. 350
American Indian Reservations, 1890 358
The Spanish-American War in the Caribbean, 1898. 427
Pacific Territories of the United States, 1900 430
The Panama Canal 439
Europe During World War I 452
Europe Before World War I 461
Europe After World War I 461
Europe, 1938-1939 520
Japanese Expansion in Asia and the Pacific 527
World War II in Europe 531
Cold War Divides Europe and Asia. 549
The Cuban Missile Crisis 570
Southeast Asia, 1964. 577
The Camp David Peace Treaty, 1979. 611
The Middle East 627
Russia and the Commonwealth of Independent States. 642
Former Soviet-Occupied Countries. 643

Appendices

Appendix A The Declaration of Independence 670

Appendix B The Constitution of the United States . . 678

Appendix C Amendments to the Constitution 701

Appendix D Presidents of the United States 718

Appendix E The Fifty United States 725

Appendix F World Atlas 738

Glossary 750

Index 768

Alaska

Capital: Juneau
Organized as a territory: 1912
Entered Union: January 3, 1959
Order of entry: 49th state
Motto: North to the Future.
Geographic region: West
Nicknames: The Last Frontier, Land of the Midnight Sun
Origin of name Alaska: Misinterpreted Aleut word, meaning "great land" or "that which the sea breaks against"
State flower: Forget-me-not
State bird: Willow ptarmigan
Largest city: Anchorage
Land area: 570,374 square miles
Land area rank: Largest state
Population: 604,000
Population rank: 49th largest state
Postal abbreviation: AK

How to Use This Book: A Study Guide

*W*elcome to a study of United States history. You may be asking yourself, "Why do I need to know about people, places, and events that happened a long time before I was even born?" When we study the past, we can have a better understanding of why some things happened the way they did. We can learn from the mistakes and the successes of the past.

This book is a story of the United States. As you read the units, chapters, and sections of this book, you will learn about the important people and events that shaped United States History.

How to Study

- Plan a regular time to study.

- Choose a quiet desk or table where you will not be distracted. Find a spot that has good lighting.

- Gather all the books, pencils, and paper you need to complete your assignments.

- Decide on a goal. For example: "I will finish reading and taking notes on Chapter 1, Section 1, by 8:00."

- Take a five- to ten-minute break every hour to keep alert.

- If you start to feel sleepy, take a short break and get some fresh air.

Before Beginning Each Unit

"*This land is very delightful, and covered with an infinite number of green trees and very big ones that never lose their foliage . . . . [They] yield the sweetest . . . perfumes and produce an infinite number of fruits . . . .*"
—Amerigo Vespucci, *The Four Voyages of Amerigo Vespucci*, 1506

Three Worlds Meet

Beginnings to 1607

Unit 1

Try to think what North America looked like 3,000, 1,000 or just 500 years ago. How might America have looked before cities, railroads, and highways covered the land? Consider what the first people on the continent may have been like. How did they get here? Think about what the first European explorers saw.

In this unit you will learn what life may have been like for American Indians. You will learn why European explorers came to an unknown place. You will learn about our nation's earliest beginnings.

Chapter 1: The First Americans: Beginnings to 1400
Chapter 2: Exploration: 1400–1607

Each unit covers a period of time in United States history.

- Read the title and the dates the unit covers.

- Read the opening paragraph.

- Study the picture. Do you recognize anything in the picture?

- Read the quotation. Try to connect the ideas to the picture.

- Read the titles of the chapters in the unit.

- Look at the headings of the sections and paragraphs. They will help you locate main ideas.

- Read the chapter and unit summaries to help you identify the key ideas.

Before Beginning Each Chapter

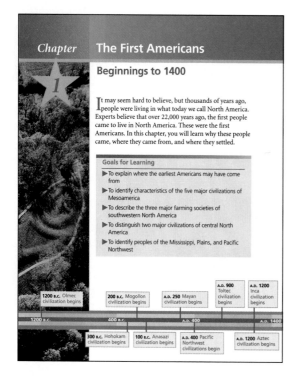

- Read the chapter title and the dates.

- Study the goals for learning. The chapter review and tests will ask questions related to these goals.

- Study the timeline.

Using the Timelines

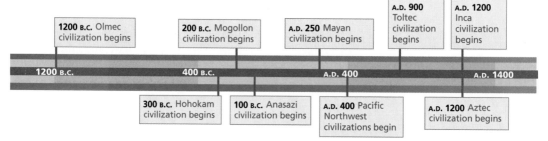

- Timelines help you see the order in which events occurred.

- Look at the beginning and ending dates to identify the time period.

- Key events will be listed on the timeline.

- As you read the chapter, take note of the events listed on the timeline.

Before Beginning Each Section

Read the section title and rephrase it in the form of a question. For example:

Section	1	The Earliest Americans

Write: *Who were the earliest Americans?*

Look over the entire section, noting . . .

- pictures
- graphs
- maps
- boldface words
- text organization
- timelines

Adena-Hopewell Settlements

MAP STUDY

Are there more burial mounds in the Adena or Hopewell area? Near what city is Serpent Mound located?

Adena
Hopewell
• Burial mound

The Hopewell made stone figures. This figure is a Hopewell medicine man.

JUANITA, THE MAIDEN OF AMPATO: c. A.D. 1400s

Juanita was a fourteen-year-old Inca girl whose body was found in the Peruvian Andes in 1995. Researchers found her perfectly frozen body near the heart of the ancient Inca Empire. The researchers nicknamed her "Juanita." Her body was refrigerated to prevent decay and for further study. By studying her remains, researchers have been able to learn about the ancestry, health, lifestyle, and diet of the ancient Incas. Her remains were surrounded by miniature statues, corn, and leaves of the coca plant. Thus researchers believe Juanita was sacrificed to a mountain god in the 1400s. She was four feet ten inches tall and had long black hair and perfect teeth. She was dressed in fine, colorful wool garments and leather slippers. She most likely wore a plumed headdress. The researchers hope to learn more about the lives of the Incas through further respectful study of Juanita.

Architecture From the Anasazi

Anasazi people built large homes on ridges of river canyon walls or the sides of mesas. Many families lived in buildings made up of dozens of cubelike apartments.

Anasazi farmed the flat land below their homes. The Pueblos, Anasazi descendants, continued to live in this manner until the 1500s. Then Navajos took over the Pueblo land and dwellings.

The unique architecture and placement of the Anasazi rock and clay dwellings made them durable. Many are still fairly intact. You can see them in Mesa Verde National Park in southwestern Colorado. These remnants of an ancient American Indian culture have strongly influenced southwestern architecture.

Fine Arts

History in Your Life

As You Read the Section

- Read the major headings. Each subhead is in the form of a question.

- Read the paragraphs that follow to answer the question.

- Before moving on to the next heading, see if you can answer the question.

- If you cannot, reread the section to look for the answers. If you are still unsure, ask for help.

- Answering the questions in the section will help you see if you know the key ideas in the section.

Words to Know
bold type   *Words seen for the first time will appear in bold type*
glossary   *Words listed in this column are also found in the glossary*
★ **red stars**   *Words that may appear on tests*

Using "Words to Know"

Knowing the meaning of all the boxed words will help you understand what you are reading.

These words will appear in **bold type** the first time they appear in your text and will be defined in the paragraph.

a **blockhouse**, or fort, to be built for better protection

Remember, all of the words in the side column are also defined for you in the **glossary**.

Governor — Person chosen to lead a group of people within a given area, such as a colony or a state (p. 56)

The words with the **red stars** (★) identify important words. These words may appear on tests.

What to Do With a Word You Do Not Know

When you come to a word you do not know, ask yourself these questions:

- **Is the word a compound word?**
  Can you find two words within the word? This could help you understand the meaning. For example: *blockhouse*.

- **Does the word have a prefix at the beginning?**
  For example: *unconstitutional*. The prefix *un-* means 'not,' so this word refers to something that does not follow the Constitution.

- **Does the word have a suffix at the end?**
  For example: *voter, -er*. This means one who votes.

- **Can you identify the root word? Can you sound it out in parts?** For example: *dis able*.

- **Are there any clues in the sentence that will help you understand the word?**

Look for the word in the margin box, glossary, or dictionary.

If you are still having trouble with a word, ask for help.

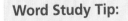

Blockhouse

Chapter 4
Building used for
protection from
attack; fort

Word Study Tip:

- Start a vocabulary card file with index cards to use for review.

  - Write one word on the front of each card. Write the chapter number and the definition on the back.

  - You can use the flash cards in a game by yourself or with a study partner to test your knowledge.

Taking Notes in Class

As you read, you will be learning many new facts and ideas. Writing these key ideas down will help you remember. Your notes will be useful when preparing for class discussions and studying for tests.

There are many ways to take notes. You may want to try several methods to decide which one works best for you.

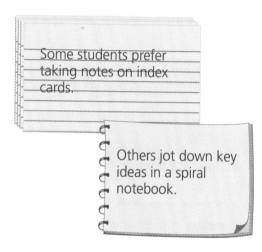

Some students prefer taking notes on index cards.

Others jot down key ideas in a spiral notebook.

- Always write the main ideas and supporting details.
- Using an outline format will help save you time.
- Keep your notes brief. You may want to set up some abbreviations to speed up your note-taking. For example: *with=w/ and=+ dollars=$ United States=US, government = gov't.*
- Use the same method all the time. Then when you study for a test, you will know where to go to find the information you need to review.

Using an Outline

You may want to outline the section using the subheads as your main points. An outline will help you remember the major points of the section. Here's an example of an outline for Section 1.

Section 1: The Early Americans

I. What was the oldest discovery of human life in America?
    A.
    B.

II. What was the Clovis Point?
    A.
    B.

III. What happened to the land bridge?
    A.
    B.

Listening in Class

- Plan to listen to remember.

- Concentrate on the topic. Do not allow your mind to wander.

- If you do not understand, raise your hand and ask a question.

- Listen for these key phrases: this is important..., do not forget..., the first reason..., because of this..., in conclusion..., you need to know this... .

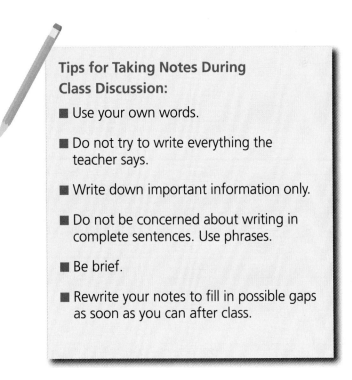

Tips for Taking Notes During Class Discussion:

- Use your own words.

- Do not try to write everything the teacher says.

- Write down important information only.

- Do not be concerned about writing in complete sentences. Use phrases.

- Be brief.

- Rewrite your notes to fill in possible gaps as soon as you can after class.

Getting Ready to Take a Test

The Summaries and Reviews will help you get ready to take tests. Getting information about the test ahead of time and having a study plan will help you do well on the test.

- Ask what type of test it will be. For example: true/false, multiple choice, short answer, matching, essay.

- Keep current on your reading assignments. Do not put off reading the chapter until the night before the test.

- A couple of days before the test, gather all of your notes, vocabulary lists, corrected worksheets, answers to questions in the book, and your textbook.

Use the Summaries

- Read the summaries from your text to make sure you understand the main ideas that you will be reviewing.

- Make up a sample test of items you think may be on the test. You may want to do this with a classmate and share your questions.

- Review your notes and test yourself on vocabulary words and key ideas.

- Practice writing about some of the main events from the chapter.

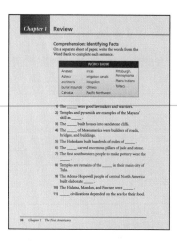

Use the Reviews

- Answer the questions under Identifying Facts.

- Answer the questions under Understanding the Main Ideas.

- Write what you think about the questions under Write Your Opinion.

Use the Test Taking Tip

■ Read Test Taking Tips with each Chapter Review from your text.

Test Taking Tip	Avoid waiting until the night before a test to study. Plan your study time so that you can get a good night's sleep the night before a test.

When Taking a Test

■ Arrive well rested and alert.

■ Look over the entire test before you start.

■ Plan so you will have time to complete each section.

■ If you have trouble with a question, mark it and come back to it later. This will save you time.

■ Proofread your essay answers for errors. Double-check to see that you answered the question that was asked.

■ If time allows, read over all of your answers. Make sure your writing is readable.

Remember to save your corrected test when it is returned. Use it to study for future tests. Identify the type of errors you made. For example: Were most of your errors in a certain section? Perhaps you could study ways to improve in that area.

This introduction has been included as a study tool that you can refer to later. You are now ready to begin your journey into the history of the United States.

"This land is very delightful, and covered with an infinite number of green trees and very big ones that never lose their foliage . . . . [They] yield the sweetest . . . perfumes and produce an infinite number of fruits . . . ."

–Amerigo Vespucci, *The Four Voyages of Amerigo Vespucci*, 1506

Three Worlds Meet

Beginnings to 1607

Try to think what North America looked like 3,000, 1,000 or just 500 years ago. How might America have looked before cities, railroads, and highways covered the land? Consider what the first people on the continent may have been like. How did they get here? Think about what the first European explorers saw.

In this unit you will learn what life may have been like for American Indians. You will learn why European explorers came to an unknown place. You will learn about our nation's earliest beginnings.

Chapter 1: The First Americans:
Beginnings to 1400
Chapter 2: Exploration:
1400–1607

Beginnings to 1400

It may seem hard to believe, but thousands of years ago, people were living in what today we call North America. Experts believe that over 22,000 years ago, the first people came to live in North America. These were the first Americans. In this chapter, you will learn why these people came, where they came from, and where they settled.

Goals for Learning

▶ To explain where the earliest Americans may have come from

▶ To identify characteristics of the five major civilizations of Mesoamerica

▶ To describe the three major farming societies of southwestern North America

▶ To distinguish two major civilizations of central North America

▶ To identify peoples of the Mississippi, Plains, and Pacific Northwest

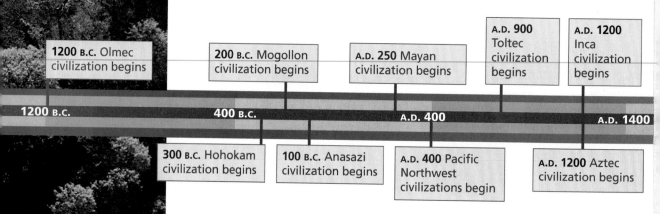

1200 B.C. Olmec civilization begins

200 B.C. Mogollon civilization begins

A.D. 250 Mayan civilization begins

A.D. 900 Toltec civilization begins

A.D. 1200 Inca civilization begins

1200 B.C.   400 B.C.   A.D. 400   A.D. 1400

300 B.C. Hohokam civilization begins

100 B.C. Anasazi civilization begins

A.D. 400 Pacific Northwest civilizations begin

A.D. 1200 Aztec civilization begins

★**Archaeologist**
One who studies the remains of past human life

★**Beringia**
A thousand-mile–wide land bridge that connected Siberia to Alaska

Caribou
Large deer that lives in arctic regions

Culture
The same values, attitudes, and customs of a group

★**Ice Age**
A period of time when much of the earth and the earth's water was frozen

★**Nomads**
People who do not live in one place

Theory
A best guess

Most of what is known of the early inhabitants of North America comes from the work of **archaeologists.** Archaeologists study the remains of past human life. They have dug up things left behind from many different **cultures**. Scientists have helped to find out the age of many things the archaeologists found. Unlike the later history of the people of North America, the early records were not written down. Much of what we know of the first Americans are **theories,** or "best guesses."

There are signs that show that people lived in Siberia (in Asia) as early as 35,000 B.C. During the **Ice Age,** much of Earth and Earth's water was frozen. The level of the oceans was much lower than it is today. A thousand-mile–wide land bridge, known as **Beringia,** connected Siberia to Alaska. Most experts believe that hunters from Siberia crossed the land bridge to North America beginning in 20,000 B.C. They may have been following herds of **caribou.**

What Was the Oldest Discovery of Human Life in America?

Traces of the earliest human life in what is now the United States have been found at the Meadowcroft Rock Shelter, near Pittsburgh, Pennsylvania. Remains of trash uncovered at this site are believed to have been left there between 16,000 and 13,500 B.C. The route the Asian **nomads** may have taken to arrive at this site is still unclear. Nomads are people who do not live in one place.

Experts believe the first Americans traveled down the Pacific coast. Some moved eastward over the Rocky Mountains and down into south central America. Others moved east across what is now Arizona and New Mexico. Many of them continued down the Pacific coast into present-day Central and South America.

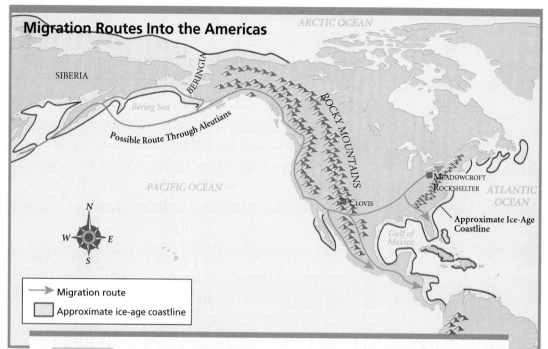

Migration Routes Into the Americas

ARCTIC OCEAN

SIBERIA

BERINGIA

Bering Sea

Possible Route Through Aleutians

ROCKY MOUNTAINS

PACIFIC OCEAN

MEADOWCROFT ROCKSHELTER

ATLANTIC OCEAN

CLOVIS

Approximate Ice-Age Coastline

Gulf of Mexico

N W E S

Migration route
Approximate ice-age coastline

MAP STUDY

What route did the nomads travel? Near which bodies of water did they travel?

★Clovis point
 A finely flaked stone spearhead
★Glacier
 A large body of ice

What Was the Clovis Point?

Early American hunters began using spear points for hunting tools about 11,000 B.C. Named for the area of New Mexico in which it was found, the **Clovis point** was a finely flaked stone spearhead. When attached to a wooden pole, the Clovis point was a powerful tool for killing animals. It was also used for gathering and building. Clovis points have been found near bones of mammoths or bison. Its use is believed to have been limited to North America.

What Happened to the Land Bridge?

By 18,000 B.C., the gradual melting of **glaciers**—large bodies of ice—caused the seas to rise. The land bridge from Asia to North America was covered with water. People could no longer travel to North America on foot. At this time, however, hunters had already spread to the southern tip of South America.

The remains of Meadowcroft Rockshelter include traces of the earliest human life in North America.

Casts of original spearheads found in Meadowcroft Rockshelter.

SECTION 1 REVIEW On a separate sheet of paper, write the word from the Word Bank to complete each sentence.

1) _____ was a thousand-mile–wide land bridge that connected Siberia to Alaska.

2) The _____ was a finely flaked stone spearhead.

3) _____ are people who do not live in one place.

4) _____ study the remains of past human life.

5) Much of the earth and the earth's water was frozen during the _____.

WORD BANK
Archaeologists
Beringia
Clovis point
Ice Age
Nomads

What do you think **?**

What can be learned from studying ancient cultures ?

★**Architect**
A person skilled in designing buildings

★**Astronomy**
The study of space and the planets

★**Civilization**
A high level of cultural development

★**Cultivate**
To grow crops

★**Hieroglyphic**
A system of writing that uses picture-like symbols

★**Mesoamerica**
The area of land that includes what is now Mexico and other countries south through Costa Rica

★**Settlement**
A place or region newly settled

Many of the first people in the Americas settled in **Mesoamerica.** This area includes what is now Mexico and other countries south through Costa Rica. Based on the findings of archaeologists, the people in this region had the earliest advanced **civilizations.** Civilization is a high level of cultural development. Archaeologists believe that the first corn was **cultivated,** or grown, in Mexico as early as 5000 B.C. There were five main civilizations of Mesoamerica.

Who Were the Olmecs?

The strongest **settlement** of early Americans was established in Mexico by the Olmecs between 1200 B.C. and 100 B.C. A settlement is a place or region newly settled. Archaeologists have learned a good deal about the Olmecs from digs in La Venta and San Lorenzo, two of their cities near the Gulf of Mexico.

The Olmecs carved in jade and stone. The remains of their world include pillars, stone heads, figurines, pottery, and mirrors. An Olmec **hieroglyphic** slab, with a date matching 31 B.C., is thought to be the oldest piece of writing in North America. A hieroglyphic is a system of writing that uses picture-like symbols.

What Kind of Civilization Did the Mayans Have?

From about A.D. 250, the Mayans built a huge civilization in Mesoamerica. It covered the area which is now Belize and parts of Guatemala, Honduras, El Salvador, and Mexico. For at least 600 years, the Mayans were a major force in Mesoamerica.

The Mayans were masters of **astronomy**—the study of space and the planets—and of arithmetic. They were the first people in the Americas to develop an advanced form of writing. The ruins of their great cities also show us that they were skilled **architects** and artists. An architect is a person skilled in designing buildings. Long after the fall of

The people of Mesoamerica built large civilizations such as this one in Monte Alban, Mexico.

the Mayans, the ruins of their temples and pyramids remained as examples of some of the finest building in Mesoamerica.

Who Were the Toltecs?

Beginning in A.D. 900, the Toltecs ruled a strong civilization in the Mexican highlands. The ruins of their main city, Tula, includes remains of several temples. One of these temples honored Quetzalcoatl, a great feathered serpent, who the Toltecs believed had founded the city. Experts believe that nomads took over the Toltecs about A.D. 1200. They went on to form the Aztec civilization.

Why Did the Aztecs Have a Powerful Civilization?

The Aztec civilization took shape about A.D. 1200. It is thought to be the result of 3,000 years of improvements and growth by the people in Mesoamerica. From their main city of Tenochtitlán (now Mexico City), the Aztecs ruled a large kingdom in much of central and southern Mexico. By the time of the fall of the Aztecs in A.D. 1521, 100,000 people were living in Tenochtitlán.

The government and **military** forces of the Aztecs were strong and well run. They built roads, **canals,** bridges, and many buildings. A canal is a human-made waterway. People worked as farmers, weavers, or **artisans.** An artisan is a skilled worker. The Aztecs worshiped gods of the sun, the rain, and the wind as well as Quetzalcoatl.

Who Were the Incas?

Experts believe that nomads from Asia settled in the area now known as Peru as early as 10,000 B.C. The Chavin and the Chimu were among the groups to develop this South American civilization. About A.D. 1200, the Incas started a kingdom in southern Peru. The Incas were very good builders, lawmakers, and warriors. They learned about astronomy. Within 200 years, the Incan civilization had grown to include all of present-day Peru. It also included parts of Ecuador on the north and Chile and Argentina on the south.

Civilizations of Mesoamerica

Civilization	Location	Date Started
Olmecs	Mexico	1200 B.C.
Mayans	Central America, Mexico	A.D. 250
Toltecs	Mexico	A.D. 900
Aztecs	Central and southern Mexico	A.D. 1200
Incas	Peru	A.D. 1200

JUANITA, THE MAIDEN OF AMPATO: c. A.D. 1400s

Juanita was a fourteen-year-old Inca girl whose body was found in the Peruvian Andes in 1995. Researchers found her perfectly frozen body near the heart of the ancient Inca Empire. The researchers nicknamed her "Juanita." Her body was refrigerated to prevent decay and for further study. By studying her remains, researchers have been able to learn about the ancestry, health, lifestyle, and diet of the ancient Incas. Her remains were surrounded by miniature statues, corn, and leaves of the coca plant. Thus researchers believe Juanita was sacrificed to a mountain god in the 1400s. She was four feet ten inches tall and had long black hair and perfect teeth. She was dressed in fine, colorful wool garments and leather slippers. She most likely wore a plumed headdress. The researchers hope to learn more about the lives of the Incas through further respectful study of Juanita.

SECTION 2 REVIEW Choose the name in parentheses to complete each sentence. Write your answers on a separate sheet of paper.

1) The (Toltecs, Olmecs, Incas) worked with hieroglyphics.

2) The (Mayans, Aztecs, Incas) were the first people in the Americas to develop an advanced form of writing.

3) The (Mayans, Olmecs, Incas) started a kingdom in southern Peru.

4) A major city of the (Olmecs, Toltecs, Aztecs) was Tenochtitlán.

5) The (Olmec, Toltec, Incan) city of Tula includes remains of several temples.

What do you think **?**

What might lead you to believe that the civilizations of Mesoamerica were advanced?

★Cotton
A plant used to make cloth

★Irrigation
A system of watering crops that uses canals or ditches of water

★Kiva
A large underground room used for ceremonies

Mesa
A flat-topped height

Ritual
The actions that take place during a ceremony

Village
A small settlement

Three farming societies developed around A.D. 1000, in what is now the southwestern United States. The Hohokam lived in what is now Arizona. The Mogollon built their civilization in southeastern Arizona and southern New Mexico. The Anasazi built where Arizona, New Mexico, Utah, and Colorado meet. They also built along the Rio Grande and upper Pecos valleys of New Mexico.

What Happened to the Hohokam?

Archaeologists believe that the Hohokam developed from local peoples and from Mesoamericans who had moved northward. Their civilization began about 300 B.C. The Hohokam were farmers. They were skilled at controlling the land. From A.D. 800 until 1000, the Hohokam built hundreds of miles of **irrigation** canals for watering crops.

Snaketown was a major Hohokam civilization. This city was one of a few large cities that ruled smaller **villages,** largely through control of the canals. The Hohokam built courts in their villages. These were used for sport and for **rituals.** Mounds found within the remains of Hohokam villages may have been dance platforms or places on which their leaders' homes were built. Hohokams weaved **cotton** goods. Cotton is a plant used to make cloth. By about A.D. 1450, most people had abandoned the Hohokam area. This most likely was because of a lack of water and failed irrigation system.

Who Were the Mogollon?

The Mogollon area was much larger than that of the Hohokam. This group is believed to have begun about 200 B.C. There was more rainfall where they lived. The Mogollon were farmers. They built small villages of about twenty houses on bluffs, **mesas,** or on other high grounds. Their communities included underground "pit houses" believed to be the earliest southwestern **kivas.** Kivas were large underground rooms used for ceremonies.

The Anasazi built dwellings in cliffs.

Burial
The act of burying the dead

Dwelling
A home

Religious
Relating to a belief in a higher being

The Mogollon were the first southwestern people to make pottery. Using ways of painting learned from the Anasazi, the Mogollon created their own designs. Their pottery was used throughout their lives and for **burial** offerings to cover the heads of the dead.

What Were the Chaco Canyon Anasazi Like?

The Anasazi civilization began around 100 B.C. They grew corn and hunted. By A.D. 900, the main settlement of the Anasazi was Chaco Canyon in what is now north central New Mexico. The Anasazi were called "Cliff Dwellers" because they built houses into cliffs. The **dwellings** were made of the same copper-colored sandstone of the cliffs. The largest dwelling had more than 650 rooms.

The Anasazi farmers relied on rainfall and their system of catching water runoff from the cliffs. They also kept a calendar by watching the sun and moon. The Anasazi sun priests were able to plan for planting cycles and **religious** ceremonies.

The period of the Chacoan Anasazi lasted fewer than 300 years. From A.D. 1130 to 1180, a drought forced people to leave. The Anasazi continued to live at Cliff Palace and Spruce Tree House at Mesa Verde in Colorado and at Keet Seel in Arizona.

Who Were the Mesa Verde Anasazi?

The Mesa Verde Anasazi lived on the sides of high mesas in southwestern Colorado and southeastern Utah. About A.D. 700, they moved from their pit houses to dwellings aboveground. They built thousands of dams on small streams. On Chapin Mesa, the Anasazi built a stone-lined **reservoir** that could hold almost two million gallons of water. A reservoir is a large place used to store water.

Architecture From the Anasazi

Anasazi people built large homes on ridges of river canyon walls or the sides of mesas. Many families lived in buildings made up of dozens of cubelike apartments.

Anasazi farmed the flat land below their homes. The Pueblos, Anasazi descendants, continued to live in this manner until the 1500s. Then Navajos took over the Pueblo land and dwellings.

The unique architecture and placement of the Anasazi rock and clay dwellings made them durable. Many are still fairly intact. You can see them in Mesa Verde National Park in southwestern Colorado. These remnants of an ancient American Indian culture have strongly influenced southwestern architecture.

Fine Arts

History in Your Life

Who Were the Kayenta Anasazi?

Another group of Anasazi known as the Kayenta lived from A.D. 1100 to 1300 in small villages in northeastern Arizona. They were masters of pottery making and weaving.

Around A.D. 1250, the Kayenta Anasazi began building larger cliff dwellings. Experts believe that the move was made for protection from enemies. Just before 1300, the Anasazi left the Southwest completely. There was warfare among Anasazi groups. A drought and lack of good land for farming caused the wars. Some of the Anasazi moved down into the Rio Grande area where many of their **descendants,** the Pueblos, live today.

Southwestern Civilizations

Civilization	Location	Date Started
Hohokam	Arizona	300 B.C.
Mogollon	Arizona, New Mexico	200 B.C.
Anasazi	Arizona, Colorado, New Mexico, Utah	100 B.C.

Pueblos carved a picture of a Kachina dance (right) on a sandstone cliff in New Mexico. Hopi Eagle Kachinas (below) are still used in rituals.

★Kachina
Spirits of an ancestor

During the time when the Pueblo culture was formed, Navajos moved near the Pueblos from Canada and Alaska. The Navajos learned farming from the Pueblos. One group of today's Pueblos, the Hopi of northeastern Arizona, are known for their **kachina** rituals. Kachinas are spirits of ancestors. Today, Pueblo men act and dress like kachinas in rituals to bring success to the Pueblo people.

SECTION 3 REVIEW On a separate sheet of paper, write *True* if the statement is true or *False* if the statement is not true.

1) Snaketown was a major Hohokam civilization.

2) The Mogollon were hunters.

3) The Anasazi were called "Cliff Dwellers" because they built houses into cliffs.

4) The Kayenta Anasazi built a large reservoir.

5) The Pueblos are descendants of the Anasazi.

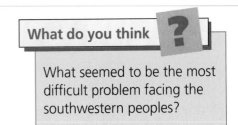

What do you think **?**

What seemed to be the most difficult problem facing the southwestern peoples?

Tobacco
*A plant that some
people smoke or
chew*

About 700 B.C. one group of American Indians began
building burial mounds in the Ohio River Valley to honor
their dead. These people are known today as the Adena.
Many of the burial mounds were as large as 300 feet across.
With great respect, the dead were put in small log rooms.
The rooms were filled with stone tablets, **tobacco,** and
pipes for smoking the tobacco.

Who Were the Hopewell?

The Hopewell peoples were direct descendants of the
Adena. They thrived for several hundred years until about
A.D. 300. Unlike many other people who lived during this
time, the Hopewell never built great cities. Their largest
settlements had fewer than 400 people. Instead, they built
mounds of far greater detail than those the Adena built.

The Hopewell people often built mounds in the shape
of animals. Serpent Mound near present-day Hillsboro,
Ohio, is a perfectly preserved example of a Hopewell
mound. It is a huge mound shaped like a snake.

The Hopewell were known to build mounds in the shapes of
lizards, birds, panthers, and even human beings. They held

The Hopewell made
stone figures. The
figure above is a
Hopewell medicine
man.

Serpent Mound
(right) near present-
day Hillsboro, Ohio, is
an example of a
Hopewell mound.

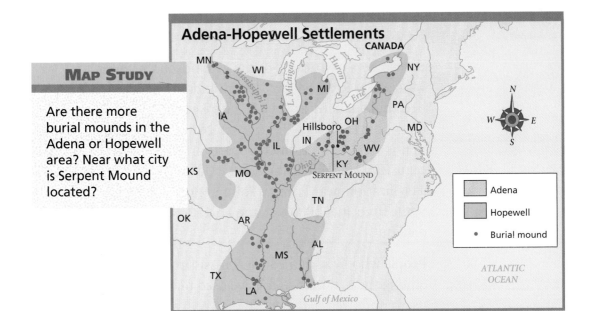

Adena-Hopewell Settlements

burial services and spent much time honoring their dead. However, many experts believe that the Hopewell were more concerned with celebrating life, nature, and rebirth.

Many Hopewell began to trade with settlements throughout the areas east of the Mississippi River. Other peoples adopted Hopewell customs and rituals. The Hopewell respect for rebirth and nature became a part of the beliefs of people from the Great Lakes to the deep South. Some groups of Hopewell continued to live throughout these areas for many years after the original Ohio settlement fell around A.D. 300.

SECTION 4 REVIEW Write the answers to these questions on a separate sheet of paper using complete sentences.

1) What did the Adena build?

2) What were Hopewell settlements like?

3) What is Serpent Mound?

4) What did the Hopewell celebrate?

5) Who did the Hopewell begin to trade with?

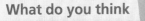

What do you think ?

Why do you think the Hopewell built mounds in the shape of people and animals?

Researchers have found burial grounds in the lower Mississippi River Valley. The grounds are believed to have been built as early as 4500 B.C. Between 1500 and 1000 B.C., one of the earliest civilizations in North America developed in this area. It was formed in parts of present-day Mississippi, Louisiana, and Arkansas. Several different peoples formed a civilization near Poverty Point in northeastern Louisiana. Some time after 1000 B.C., the Poverty Point civilization died out.

People who lived in the lower Mississippi River Valley were among the first known to have used plants. For example, they used sunflower, marsh elder, pigweed, and barley for food. By A.D. 800, corn and squash farming from Mesoamerica changed the lives of many people in this area. Populations increased as people started corn farming. The Mississippians became the most advanced civilization in eastern North America.

MAP STUDY

In which present-day states did the Middle Mississippians live? Which area shown on the map is farthest north?

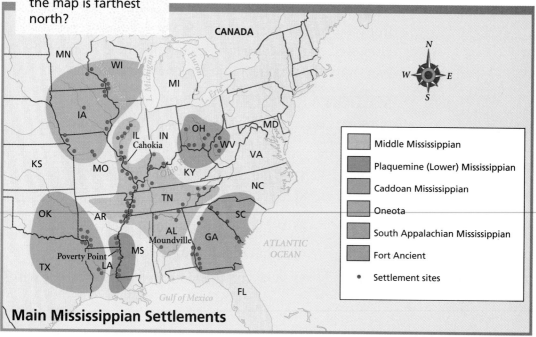

Main Mississippian Settlements

Legend:
- Middle Mississippian
- Plaquemine (Lower) Mississippian
- Caddoan Mississippian
- Oneota
- South Appalachian Mississippian
- Fort Ancient
- • Settlement sites

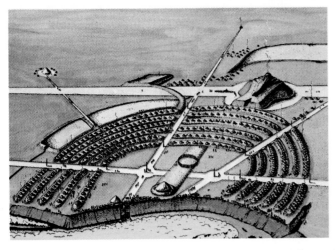

Poverty Point, as shown in this diagram, was a large, well-planned civilization.

What Were Cahokia and Moundville?

Near present-day Collinsville in western Illinois, Middle Mississippians built Monks Mound at Cahokia. This 100-foot–high mound covered sixteen acres of land. It is the largest object built of earth north of Mesoamerica. Cahokia was a major trade center for the Mississippians near the Mississippi River. Perhaps as many as 40,000 people lived there at one time. By A.D. 1500, Cahokia was completely abandoned.

Moundville, Alabama, was built about A.D. 1050 by Middle Mississippians in the southern region. It was the largest settlement in the Eastern Woodlands. By the middle of the 1500s, however, only small groups of people remained in Moundville and in the other settlements.

Who Are Descendants of the Mississippians?

Many present-day peoples such as the Cherokees are descendants of the Mississippians. Although they adopted many European customs, they still keep some traditions of their ancestors from Moundville. For example, every year the Cherokees celebrate the Green Corn Ceremony in honor of the people of Moundville.

The Iroquois also are believed to have descended from Mississippian roots. Northern Iroquois lived in what is now upper New York state. Five tribes—the Oneida, Mohawk, Onandaga, Cayuga, and Seneca—later joined the Tuscarora. They formed a group that stretched 200 miles across New York state. They lived in houses with several families. Although they never numbered more than 22,000, the Iroquois were the strongest force north of Mesoamerica when the Europeans arrived.

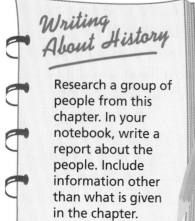
Today, other descendants of the Mississippians such as the Mohawks, the Chippewa, and the Natchez carry on the ways of these earliest ancestors.

Who Were the Plains Indians?

The Plains Indians have been called nomadic peoples. However, they developed villages, too. Beginning about 250 B.C., traders carried stones and metals back to the Hopewell centers. Hopewell ideas caught on with the Plains people. They began making pottery, building burial mounds, taking part in long-range trade, and growing corn.

The Hidatsa and Mandan of North Dakota were not very interested in farming. However, they did grow some food. They also fished and hunted. Along the Knife River, thirteen or fourteen villages have been found. Each one is believed to have had between 2,000 and 3,000 people living there. Villages were set four to six miles apart so that they could keep track of one another. If an enemy burned a village, the people in the neighboring village saw the smoke and prepared to defend themselves.

Unlike many of the people to the North and West, Pawnee people living in present-day Nebraska keep and practice some beliefs of their Mississippian ancestors. For example, the Pawnees believe that the use of ceremonial bundles filled with objects from nature can bring good luck to a village.

Mississippi, Plains, and Northwest Civilizations

Civilization	Location	Date Started
Mississippian	Mississippi River Valley	4500 B.C.
Plains Indians	North American Plains	250 B.C.
Pacific Northwest	Northwestern America, Canada, Alaska	A.D. 400

★Totem pole
A tall, colorful carved object that had a certain religious meaning

As with many other tribes, the Pawnees today are connected to the religious and cultural ways of the Southwest and of Mesoamerica.

Who Were the Peoples of the Pacific Northwest?

By A.D. 400, the Pacific Northwest civilizations began. These peoples include the Tlingit, Haida, Tsimshian, Kwakiutl, and Nootka. In most cases, they built shoreline villages. They depended heavily on the sea for their food and trade. The Nootka, for example, were whalers. Some built **totem poles.** These tall, colorful carved objects had a religious meaning to some of these people.

North of the Pacific Northwest civilizations lived the Eskimo, or Inuit as they are called today. These people are believed to have come from Asia. They settled near the Bering Sea coast in what is now Alaska and along the coasts of Canada and Greenland. They got clothing, food, oil, and tools from sea mammals, fish, and caribou. Today, about 63,000 Inuit still live in America and Canada.

SECTION 5 REVIEW On a separate sheet of paper, write *True* if the statement is true or *False* if the statement is not true.

1) Cahokia was a major trade center for the Mississippians near the Mississippi River.
2) Moundville was the largest settlement in Mesoamerica.
3) The Hidatsa and Mandan were experts in farming.
4) Pacific Northwest civilizations depended on the sea for food and trade.
5) American Indians today still practice many ancient beliefs.

Totem poles had religious meaning for some Pacific Northwest people.

What do you think **?**

Why do you think burial mounds were so important to the first Americans?

An Osage Belief

The Osage are a people who once roamed freely in Missouri, Arkansas, and Oklahoma. Now most of them live on a reservation in Oklahoma. Like the Mayans of Mesoamerica, the Osage believe that their people were descended from the sun and the moon. This passage is an explanation of how Osage people came to live on the earth.

"Way beyond, a part of the Osage lived in the sky. They desired to know their origin, the source from which they came into existence. They went to the sun. He told them that they were his children. Then they wandered still farther and came to the moon. She told them that she gave birth to them, and that the sun was their father. She told them that they must leave their present abode and go down to the earth and dwell there. They came to the earth, but found that it was covered with water. They could not return to the place they had left, so they wept, but no answer came to them from anywhere. They floated about in the air, seeking in every direction for help from some god; but they found none. The animals were with them, and of all these the elk was the finest and most stately, and inspired all the creatures with confidence; so they appealed to the elk for help. He dropped into the water and began to sink. Then he called to the winds, and the winds came from all quarters and blew until the waters went upward as in a mist.

At first rocks only were exposed, and the people traveled on the rocky places that produced no plants, and there was nothing to eat. Then the waters began to go down until the soft earth was exposed. When this happened, the elk in his joy rolled over and over on the soft earth, and all his loose hairs clung to the soil. The hairs grew, and from them sprang beans, corn, potatoes, and wild turnips, and then all the grasses and trees."

From: *The Omaha Tribe*, translated by Alice Fletcher and Francis La Flesche, 1905–1906

Source Reading Wrap-Up

1) Where did the Osage live at first?

2) What relation to the Osage were the sun and the moon?

3) Who did the Osage appeal to for help?

4) When the waters went down, how did vegetables, grasses, and trees begin to grow?

5) Which part of the Osage legend do you like the best? Why?

★ Hunters who crossed a land bridge from Siberia to North America around 20,000 B.C. may have been the earliest Americans. The Asian hunters may have migrated across North America and into South America along several routes.

★ People who settled in Mesoamerica between 1200 B.C. and A.D. 1521 had early advanced civilizations. The Olmecs carved enormous pillars and altars from jade and stone. Arithmetic, astronomy, an advanced form of writing, and architecture were Mayan achievements. The Aztecs had strong government and military forces and built elaborate structures. Incas were builders, lawmakers, warriors, and astronomers.

★ The Hohokam, Mogollon, and Anasazi were three major farming societies in southwestern North America. The Hohokam built hundreds of miles of irrigation canals between A.D. 800 and 1000. The Mogollon grew crops. The Anasazi, or Cliff Dwellers, lived in cliffs, grew corn, and hunted.

★ The Pueblo and Navajo civilizations developed in the Southwest after the Anasazi civilizations declined.

★ Beginning about 700 B.C., the Adena people lived in the Ohio River Valley. They built elaborate burial mounds in many shapes. The Hopewell descended from the Adena. Hopewell civilizations existed until A.D. 300. Their lifestyle influenced people in settlements from the Great Lakes to the South.

★ Civilizations may have been in the Mississippi River Valley as early as 4500 B.C. Corn farming was central to the Mississippian culture starting around A.D. 800.

★ The Plains Indians were nomadic. They did not farm but grew needed food and fished and hunted. The Hidatsa, Mandan, and Pawnee were among the Plains peoples.

★ The Pacific Northwest civilizations developed around A.D. 400. They depended on the sea for food and trade. The Tlingit, Haida, Tsimshian, Kwakiutl, Nootka, and Eskimo, or Inuit, are among the northwestern cultures.

Comprehension: Identifying Facts

On a separate sheet of paper, write the words from the Word Bank to complete each sentence.

WORD BANK		
Anasazi	Incas	Pittsburgh, Pennsylvania
Aztecs	irrigation canals	
architects	Mogollon	Plains Indians
burial mounds	Olmecs	Toltecs
Cahokia	Pacific Northwest	

1) The _____ were good lawmakers and warriors.

2) Temples and pyramids are examples of the Mayans' skill as _____ .

3) The _____ built houses into sandstone cliffs.

4) The _____ of Mesoamerica were builders of roads, bridges, and buildings.

5) The Hohokam built hundreds of miles of _____ .

6) The _____ carved enormous pillars of jade and stone.

7) The first southwestern people to make pottery were the _____ .

8) Temples are remains of the _____ in their main city of Tula.

9) The Adena-Hopewell people of central North America built elaborate _____ .

10) The Hidatsa, Mandan, and Pawnee were _____ .

11) _____ civilizations depended on the sea for their food.

12) The largest earthen structure built north of Mesoamerica was Monk's Mound at _____ near the Mississippi River.

13) The earliest traces of human life in what is now the United States were found near _____ .

Comprehension: Understanding Main Ideas

On a separate sheet of paper, write the answer to each question using complete sentences.

1) How did the first people get to the North American continent?

2) How do we know that the people of Mesoamerica had early advanced civilizations?

3) What evidence shows that the southwestern peoples were farming societies?

4) How did the Anasazi control water supplies?

5) What evidence shows that the Adenas and Hopewells had much respect for their dead?

Critical Thinking: Write Your Opinion

1) The earliest Americans were inventive people. Do you think today's Americans are as inventive as the earliest peoples? Why or why not?

2) Many of the earliest civilizations died out completely. Explain whether you think that could happen to any civilization on Earth today.

Test Taking Tip Avoid waiting until the night before a test to study. Plan your study time so that you can get a good night's sleep the night before a test.

Chapter

2

Exploration

1400–1607

For many years, people in Europe knew of a distant land to the east called Asia, or the Far East. They wanted to explore routes to the Far East. In this chapter, you will learn about these explorations and how they affected world history.

Goals for Learning

▶ To describe the importance of new technology in early navigation and exploration

▶ To identify the major European explorers and the areas they explored

▶ To describe how England's and Spain's power in Europe changed after the Spanish Armada was defeated

▶ To identify the first European colonies and who started them

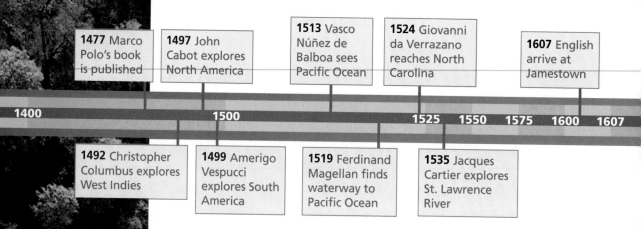

1477 Marco Polo's book is published

1497 John Cabot explores North America

1513 Vasco Núñez de Balboa sees Pacific Ocean

1524 Giovanni da Verrazano reaches North Carolina

1607 English arrive at Jamestown

| 1400 | 1500 | 1525 | 1550 | 1575 | 1600 | 1607 |

1492 Christopher Columbus explores West Indies

1499 Amerigo Vespucci explores South America

1519 Ferdinand Magellan finds waterway to Pacific Ocean

1535 Jacques Cartier explores St. Lawrence River

★**Compass**
Device used to show direction

★**Globe**
Model of the Earth

Merchant
Buyer and seller of goods

★**Monarch**
Person who rules a kingdom or territory

★**Noble**
Someone who is part of a society's upper or ruling class

Publish
To print something, such as a book, newspaper, or magazine

★**Territory**
Land belonging to a country or government

For many years, Arab traders brought jewels, fine silks, perfumes, and spices by land from the Far East. These goods were sold to **merchants** in Italy who then carried them along the Mediterranean Sea to other Europeans. **Monarchs,** people who rule kingdoms or **territories**, and **nobles,** people of the upper class, were eager to buy these goods. The routes traders used were long and dangerous. People soon began to think about finding a route to the Far East by sea.

How Did Exploration Begin?

During the 1400s, several events had a great effect on exploration. One event was the development of the **compass.** The compass had markings and a pointer that showed the direction of north. The compass helped sailors to know what direction they were going. Water travel became much safer.

The second great development was in mapmaking. Maps were being drawn more correctly. Maps helped people to accept that the Earth was round.

A third event was the production of an improved **globe.** A globe is a model of the Earth. Unfortunately, early globes showed only one ocean separating Europe from Asia. They also did not show North America. At that time, people believed that the world was much smaller than it really is.

In 1477, a book was **published** about the experiences of Marco Polo, who explored the Far East during the thirteenth century. The book described China as a land of great wealth. This excited the people in Europe. They began to dream of finding a safer and shorter route to Asia and its riches. The lands in Asia were given the name "Indies" because they included India, China, and the Spice Islands.

★Continent
Large land mass on Earth; for example, North America or Africa

★Voyage
The act of traveling, especially by sea

Who Explored the West Indies?

A man from Italy named Christopher Columbus wanted to find an all-water route to the Indies. He was one of many who believed that since the Earth was round, he could reach the Indies by sailing west.

Columbus did not have enough money to make his dream come true. He tried to get help from the kings of Portugal and England, but they both turned him down. The king and queen of Spain also refused to help at first. Finally, just as he was about to give up hope of making his journey, Queen Isabella of Spain agreed to pay for his **voyage.** He set sail in August 1492 with three small ships— the *Niña*, the *Pinta*, and the *Santa María*.

Columbus did not know that between Europe and Asia lay two great **continents,** or masses of land. When his crew sighted land on October 12, 1492, he thought he had reached the Indies. He called the natives he found on the island "Indios." This word later became "Indians" in English.

Queen Isabella of Spain agreed to pay for Columbus's voyage. He explained his plan to Isabella and her Royal Court before she agreed.

MAP STUDY

Why did Columbus think he could sail directly to the Far East? In which direction would Columbus need to sail to reach Asia?

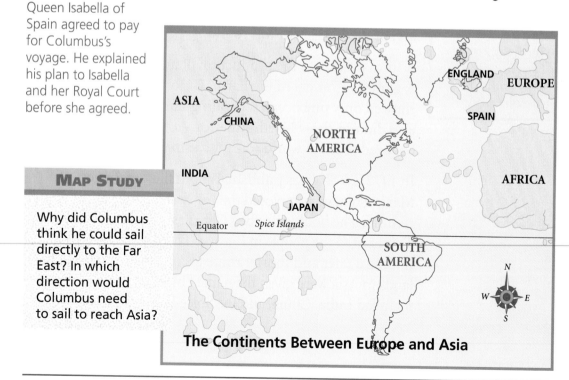

The Continents Between Europe and Asia

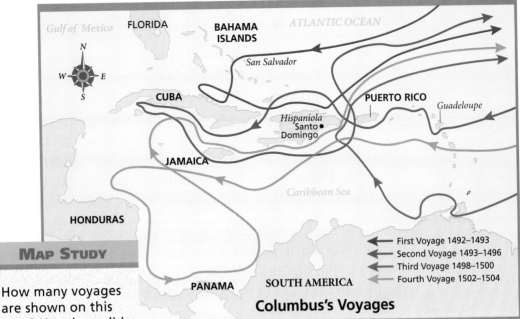

Columbus's Voyages

Map legend:
← First Voyage 1492–1493
← Second Voyage 1493–1496
← Third Voyage 1498–1500
← Fourth Voyage 1502–1504

MAP STUDY

How many voyages are shown on this map? How long did Columbus's fourth voyage last?

Columbus made three more voyages across the Atlantic Ocean. He explored other islands, still believing them to be the East Indies. Because of his mistake, this group of islands is now called the West Indies.

Columbus started the first Spanish colony at Hispaniola on his second voyage to the Indies. Soon there were many Spanish settlements on the islands of Hispaniola, Cuba, and Puerto Rico.

SECTION 1 REVIEW Write the answers to these questions on a separate sheet of paper.

1) Why did Europeans want to find a water route to the Far East?

2) Who paid for Christopher Columbus's first journey?

3) How did the compass aid in exploration?

4) What effect did the development of maps have on most people?

5) How were goods from the Far East brought to Europe?

What do you think ❓

There were many reasons why the Europeans wanted to find a water route to the Far East. What do you think was the main reason? Why?

Other countries soon learned of Columbus and his voyages. In 1497, England sent John Cabot to explore. Cabot was an Italian from Venice who lived in England and had taken an English name. Like Columbus, Cabot thought he could reach the East Indies by sailing west. Cabot set sail farther north. He had one small ship and a crew of eighteen. Cabot reached what is now Newfoundland after one month. He claimed much land for England.

Cabot made a second trip to explore the east and northeast coasts of North America. He was disappointed he had not found the rich cities of China. He still believed he had been just off the coast of the Asian continent.

The mystery of the two continents that lay between Europe and the Far East had not been solved. Columbus and Cabot were sure they had reached Asia. The map on page 41 clearly shows that Cabot was no closer than Columbus.

America got its name from the Italian explorer Amerigo Vespucci.

In 1499, an Italian named Amerigo Vespucci made several voyages to explore the northeastern coast of what is now South America. Vespucci's letters and records described what he found. He called it a new land. People in Europe were so impressed with his descriptions that they named the continent "America." People also called it the "New World."

Who Explored on Land?

One of the first Spanish explorers to go to the New World after Columbus was Juan Ponce de León. In 1513, he led a group in search of gold and the "Fountain of Youth." According to legend, water from the Fountain of Youth made people young again. Ponce de León reached the

southeastern tip of the **mainland,** or main part of the continent. Because of the beautiful flowers and trees there, he named the place "Florida," the Spanish word for flower.

Also in 1513, Vasco Núñez de Balboa led a group of men in search of gold and silver. They became the first Europeans to see the Pacific Ocean from its eastern shore. One of the men with Balboa was Francisco Pizarro. During this trip, Pizarro heard about the rich **empire** of the Incas. An empire is a large amount of territory under one ruler. Pizarro was determined to **conquer** the rulers and take their land and riches for Spain.

By the year 1533, the Incas had been defeated and forced into **slavery.** Their rights were taken away and they were forced to work for the Spanish. Slaves removed huge amounts of gold and silver from mines in the Andes Mountains and shipped it to Spain. Pizarro was later killed by men who worked for Pizarro's former partner, Diego De Almagro.

What Did Ferdinand Magellan Do?

Ferdinand Magellan, a Portuguese captain, was **commissioned** to sail in search of the Far East in 1519. He crossed the Atlantic Ocean and reached the coast of South America. He then journeyed south to the southern tip of South America. The stormy waters led from the Atlantic to the Pacific Ocean. Magellan had found the water route around the New World.

Have you seen a photograph of Earth from space? You can see from one that the world is round. Europeans in the early 1400s could not even imagine a photograph, much less one taken from space. Many of them still believed that the world was flat. They did not know the Western Hemisphere existed. Ferdinand Magellan's trip in 1519 proved that the world is round. Still, many areas of the world were unknown to Europeans. Their maps and globes were far from complete. Now every area of Earth has been explored. You can find a map for any part of it you want to see.

Magellan never completed his journey to the Far East. He was killed in the Philippines. Only one of his five ships and eighteen of his 270 men finally reached the Far East before returning to Spain. It took them three years to complete the trip around the world.

Magellan's voyage was very important. It proved the Earth was really round and provided Europeans with valuable information about the great land that separated Europe and Asia.

Ferdinand Magellan

Who Was Hernando Cortés?

Also in 1519, Spanish explorer Hernando Cortés landed on the coast of what is now Mexico. He was searching for gold and silver. Two years later, his army was equipped with cannons, armor, and sixteen horses. They defeated the Aztec king, Montezuma, and captured his empire in central Mexico.

What Was the Northwest Passage?

An Italian by the name of Giovanni da Verrazano set sail from France in 1524. Some people in Europe believed there was a northern route to the Far East.

MONTEZUMA II: c. 1480–1520

Montezuma II was the king of the Aztec Empire that stretched from the Gulf of Mexico to the Pacific Ocean. His father had founded the empire. Like his father, Montezuma expanded the kingdom. He built beautiful temples and hospitals. The capital of the empire, Tenochtitlán, was set on an island in the middle of a lake. In 1519, the Spanish explorer Hernando Cortés marched on Tenochtitlán, the present Mexico City. Montezuma thought that Cortés was a god who had been expected to return to Earth that year. Because of that, Montezuma sent Cortés rich gifts. Cortés wanted more treasure, however, so he attacked Tenochtitlán. Montezuma died from wounds he got during the attack.

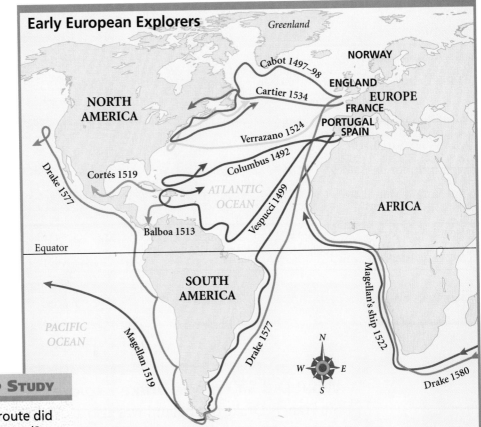

Early European Explorers

Greenland

Cabot 1497–98

Cartier 1534

NORWAY

ENGLAND

EUROPE

FRANCE

PORTUGAL
SPAIN

NORTH
AMERICA

Verrazano 1524

Columbus 1492

Drake 1577

Cortés 1519

ATLANTIC
OCEAN

Vespucci 1499

AFRICA

Balboa 1513

Equator

SOUTH
AMERICA

Magellan's ship 1522

PACIFIC
OCEAN

Magellan 1519

Drake 1577

N

W   E

S

Drake 1580

MAP STUDY

What route did
Drake travel?
How long did
Magellan's trip
take?

This became known as the Northwest Passage. Verrazano carried the French flag to the New World in search of the Northwest Passage. After a stormy voyage of some fifty days, Verrazano reached the American coast of what is now North Carolina. From North Carolina, he sailed north to Newfoundland. His records of the voyage greatly added to Europe's growing knowledge of this new continent.

In 1534, France sent Jacques Cartier in search of the Northwest Passage. He explored the St. Lawrence River in Canada. He thought this great river was the true way to the East. After three voyages to its shores, he finally realized he was mistaken. Cartier was very disappointed with his failure to find the waterway. The lands he claimed for France would later be of great value.

Explorer	Explorations Began	Sponsoring Country	Places Explored
Christopher Columbus	1492	Spain	West Indies
John Cabot	1497	England	Newfoundland, North America
Amerigo Vespucci	1499	Italy	South America
Juan Ponce de León	1513	Spain	Florida
Vasco Núñez de Balboa	1513	Spain	Panama, Pacific Ocean
Ferdinand Magellan	1519	Portugal	South America, Pacific Ocean
Hernando Cortés	1519	Spain	Mexico
Giovanni da Verrazano	1524	France	North Carolina, Newfoundland
Jacques Cartier	1534	France	St. Lawrence River, Canada
Sir Francis Drake	1577	England	South America, Washington, Pacific Ocean

What Did Sir Francis Drake Explore?

Sir Francis Drake of England was also an important explorer. His **expedition,** or journey, began in 1577. Drake sailed to the New World and around the southern tip of South America. He traveled up the Pacific coast as far as what is now the state of Washington. Then he crossed the Pacific Ocean and returned to England by 1580. His expedition was the second to sail around the world.

*Expedition
Journey made by a person or group for a certain purpose

SECTION 2 REVIEW Write the answers to these questions on a separate sheet of paper.

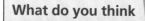

What do you think

Many early explorers fought with or conquered native peoples. Why do you think the explorers did this? What more peaceful actions could the explorers have taken?

1) How did America get its name?

2) What was Ponce de León searching for in the New World?

3) List the countries that sent explorers.

4) Where did Magellan find the water route around the New World?

5) Who searched for the Northwest Passage?

★Armada
Fleet of warships

★Charter
Written agreement granting power in the name of a state or country

★Colony
Group of people living in a new area under rule of their native land

Loot
To take or damage things by use of force

Spain began to benefit from the great treasures and contributions of the New World. Other countries grew jealous of these treasures. French, Dutch, and English ships began seizing Spanish ships on the high seas and **looting** Spanish towns along the coast of America. King Philip II of Spain was very angry with England for these attacks. He sent a fleet of ships in 1588 to crush the English and overthrow Queen Elizabeth I of England. Much to his disappointment, however, the more skilled English sailors defeated this fleet, called the Spanish **Armada**. Spain's power began to weaken after this defeat. England's power increased.

What Was Roanoke?

In 1578, Queen Elizabeth granted an agreement, or **charter,** to Sir Humphrey Gilbert to begin a **colony.** A colony is a group of people living in a new area. Gilbert wanted to establish a colony in the New World. However, Gilbert died during his second attempt at establishing a colony. Sir Walter Raleigh, Gilbert's half brother, received the charter.

English ships defeated the Spanish Armada in the English Channel.

Writing About History

What do you think may have happened to people at the Roanoke colony? Think of some things that could have happened. In your journal or notebook, write two or three paragraphs explaining what you think happened to the colony.

Between 1584 and 1587, Raleigh sent three different expeditions to the New World. The first group was sent to explore and gather information. The second group was sent to live in the new colony. The colony did not do very well, and many people died. Others returned to England.

Raleigh would not give up his plan to start a colony. He asked John White to lead a third and final group. They settled on Roanoke Island off the coast of North Carolina. White returned to England in 1587 to get more supplies. He was unable to return to Roanoke until 1590. No trace could be found of the settlers when he returned. The group had simply disappeared. For that reason it is called the Lost Colony. The only clues were the letters "CRO" carved on one tree and the word "CROATOAN" carved on another. No one knew what the word meant. Included among the missing were White's daughter and granddaughter, Virginia Dare, the first English child born in America.

What Other Colonies Were Started?

The French had shown some earlier interest in starting colonies in America, but little came of it. Seventy years had passed since Cartier discovered the St. Lawrence River and claimed much of Canada for France. The first French colony was started on the St. Lawrence River in the early 1600s. The leader of this small colony, Samuel de Champlain, named the settlement Quebec.

France's territories in America were later called New France. New France never attracted many settlers. The population remained very small for over 100 years. Although Spain, Portugal, and France had claimed large areas of land, only a few scattered colonies were successful.

King James I of England

What Other Colonies Did England Start?

Major changes took place when King James I took the English throne in 1603. He had strict religious rules. He had little patience with those who disagreed with him. English people started to look for a new place to live. The faraway lands of the New World were appealing. These people were looking for religious and **political** freedom.

Two groups of wealthy nobles and merchants formed the Virginia Company of London. They were interested in making money from trade. King James granted them a charter for land within the region of Virginia in 1606. A second charter was granted in the same year to the Plymouth Company. It included land farther to the north in what is now New England.

Three small ships and about 100 men reached the shores of Virginia in April 1607. The place where they landed was named Jamestown in honor of their king.

SECTION 3 REVIEW Write the answers to these questions on a separate sheet of paper.

1) Which country defeated the Spanish Armada?

2) What was the name of the first English colony?

3) What happened to the Roanoke colony?

4) Where was the first French colony started? Who was its leader?

5) Why did the people of England dislike the way King James I ruled?

What do you think ❓

What did the defeat of the Spanish Armada do to England's and Spain's power in Europe? Why do you think this was important?

Cabeza de Vaca's Journal

In 1527, Spanish explorer Álvar Núñez Cabeza de Vaca set out to colonize what is now Florida. In 1528 after shipwrecking off the Texas coast, he and his crew explored Mexico and what is now the southwestern United States. They traveled over American Indian trails and had much contact with Indians. Here is part of Cabeza de Vaca's journal.

"I ordered . . . our strongest man to . . . find any worn trails. . . . We had begun to worry what . . . happened to him, so I detailed another two men to check. They met him shortly and saw three Indians with bows and arrows following him. . . . Later 200 bowmen . . . reinforced the first three. . . . They looked like giants to us in our fright. . . . We gave them beads and bells, and each . . . gave us an arrow as a pledge of friendship. . . .

The next morning, the Indians [brought] . . . fish and . . . roots. . . . Provided with what we needed, we . . . embark[ed] again. . . . We had rowed . . . from shore when a wave . . . capsized the boat. . . . We lost everything. . . .

At sunset the Indians, not knowing we had tried to leave, came again with food. When they saw us looking so strangely . . . I explained . . . that our barge had sunk and three . . . drowned. . . . The Indians, understanding our full plight, sat down and [wailed] . . . When the cries died down, I conferred . . . about asking the Indians to take us to their homes. Some . . . who had been to New Spain warned that the Indians would sacrifice us. . . . But . . . I . . . beseeched the Indians. They were delighted. . . .

In the morning, they brought us fish and roots and acted in every way hospitably. We . . . somewhat lost our anxiety. . . ."

From: Álvar Núñez Cabeza de Vaca's journal in *Adventures in the Unknown Interior of America,* translated by Cyclone Covey.

Source Reading Wrap-Up

1) Why were Cabeza de Vaca and his men frightened of the Indians?

2) What were some kindnesses the Indians showed the explorers?

3) What caused the American Indians to sit down and wail?

4) Why did the explorers ask to go to the Indians' homes, even though they thought they might be killed?

5) How did you react to the way the Indians treated Cabeza de Vaca and his men?

CHAPTER SUMMARY

★ In the 1400s, the development of the compass and improvements in mapmaking and globes helped exploration.

★ In 1477, Marco Polo's book describing the Far East excited the people of Europe and encouraged exploration.

★ Christopher Columbus made his first voyage in search of the Far East in 1492. He explored what was later called the West Indies.

★ John Cabot explored North America in 1497. He claimed much of northeastern North America for England.

★ Amerigo Vespucci made several voyages to South America beginning in 1499. Later, the continent he explored was named America after him.

★ Juan Ponce de León searched for gold and the Fountain of Youth in 1513. He named the land he explored Florida.

★ Vasco Núñez de Balboa led a voyage in 1513 in search of gold and silver. He and his crew were the first Europeans to see the Pacific Ocean.

★ Ferdinand Magellan led a voyage around the world in 1519.

★ Hernando Cortés conquered the Aztecs in 1521.

★ Giovanni da Verrazano searched for the Northwest Passage in 1524. He later reached North Carolina and Newfoundland. Jacques Cartier searched for the Northwest Passage in 1534. He explored the St. Lawrence River in Canada.

★ Sir Francis Drake led the second expedition around the world between 1577 and 1580.

★ The English defeated the Spanish Armada in 1588.

★ Sir Walter Raleigh led three expeditions to the New World between 1584 and 1587. Under Raleigh, John White formed a colony in Roanoke, North Carolina. The colony later disappeared.

★ The first French colony was started on the St. Lawrence River in the early 1600s.

★ In 1606, King James I granted charters for land in the New World. The Virginia Company settled a colony in Jamestown, Virginia, in 1607.

Comprehension: Identifying Facts

Match each sentence below with an explorer from the Word Bank. Write your answers on a separate sheet of paper.

WORD BANK	
Amerigo Vespucci	Hernando Cortés
Christopher Columbus	Jacques Cartier
Ferdinand Magellan	John Cabot
Francis Drake	Juan Ponce de León
Francisco Pizarro	Vasco Núñez de Balboa
Giovanni da Verrazano	

1) Explored the West Indies.

2) Searched for the "Fountain of Youth" in Florida.

3) Led the second expedition around the world.

4) Led an expedition that became the first group of Europeans to see the Pacific Ocean.

5) England sent him to explore. His search for the East Indies failed, but he reached Newfoundland.

6) Explored the St. Lawrence River.

7) Sailed to North Carolina and Newfoundland in search of the Northwest Passage.

8) Defeated the Aztecs.

9) His expedition was the first to sail around the world, though he was killed during the journey.

10) America is named after him.

11) Worked for Vasco Núñez de Balboa before becoming interested in conquering the Incas.

Comprehension: Understanding Main Ideas

On a separate sheet of paper, write the answers to the following questions using complete sentences.

1) How did the globe, compass, and map improve exploration?

2) What happened when other countries became jealous of Spain's discoveries in the New World?

3) Why was defeating the Spanish Armada important for the English?

4) What was Roanoke colony? Who started it?

5) What was the first French colony? Who started it?

6) Why did many people want to leave England when James I became king?

Critical Thinking: Write Your Opinion

1) Do you think the Europeans would have found the New World as quickly if Columbus had not made his voyages? Why or why not?

2) Who do you think was the most important explorer? Why?

3) Many people left England because they were searching for political or religious freedom. Do you think these rights are important in the United States today? Why or why not?

Test Taking Tip When studying for a test, write facts and definitions on index cards. Use them as flash cards with a partner to practice remembering the items.

Timelines display dates and events on a line. They may show key events for a region. They also may list events during an individual's life. Timelines can span thousands of years or cover only a few months.

Timelines show time relationships between events. Timelines help you think of events in the order they occurred. They show when an event occurred. They also show what took place before and after the event.

Always look at the beginning and ending dates to understand the time period.

Each chapter in this book begins with a timeline. These timelines will help you focus on key events and ideas from the chapter. Remember, creating your own timeline of events as you read a chapter can help you study.

This timeline gives important dates in the life of explorer Hernando Cortés. Study it. Then answer the questions.

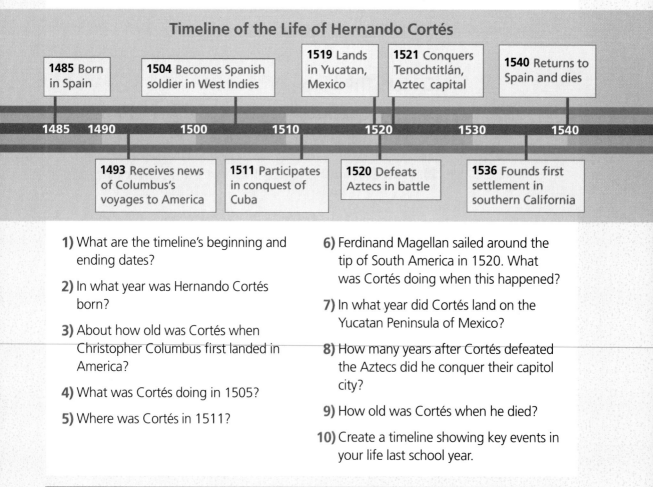

Timeline of the Life of Hernando Cortés

1485 Born in Spain

1504 Becomes Spanish soldier in West Indies

1519 Lands in Yucatan, Mexico

1521 Conquers Tenochtitlán, Aztec capital

1540 Returns to Spain and dies

1485   1490   1500   1510   1520   1530   1540

1493 Receives news of Columbus's voyages to America

1511 Participates in conquest of Cuba

1520 Defeats Aztecs in battle

1536 Founds first settlement in southern California

1) What are the timeline's beginning and ending dates?

2) In what year was Hernando Cortés born?

3) About how old was Cortés when Christopher Columbus first landed in America?

4) What was Cortés doing in 1505?

5) Where was Cortés in 1511?

6) Ferdinand Magellan sailed around the tip of South America in 1520. What was Cortés doing when this happened?

7) In what year did Cortés land on the Yucatan Peninsula of Mexico?

8) How many years after Cortés defeated the Aztecs did he conquer their capitol city?

9) How old was Cortés when he died?

10) Create a timeline showing key events in your life last school year.

★ Hunters crossed a land bridge from Siberia to North America about 20,000 B.C. These earliest Americans may have migrated across North America and into South America.

★ People who settled in Mesoamerica between 1200 B.C. and A.D. 1521 had early advanced civilizations.

★ The Hohokam, Mogollon, and Anasazi societies were in the North American Southwest. The Pueblo and Navajo civilizations developed in the Southwest after the Anasazi society declined.

★ Between 700 B.C. and A.D. 300, the Adena and Hopewell people lived in the Ohio River Valley. Civilizations may have been in the Mississippi River Valley as early as 4500 B.C.

★ The Pacific Northwest civilizations began around A.D. 400.

★ In the 1400s, the compass, mapmaking, and globes helped exploration.

★ Columbus made his first voyage in search of the Far East in 1492.

★ John Cabot explored North America in 1497. He claimed much northeastern land for England.

★ Amerigo Vespucci made voyages to South America beginning in 1499. Later, the continent he explored was named America after him.

★ In 1513, Vasco Núñez de Balboa and his crew were the first Europeans to see the Pacific Ocean.

★ In 1519, Ferdinand Magellan led a voyage around the world and Hernando Cortés conquered the Aztecs.

★ Giovanni da Verrazano searched for the Northwest Passage in 1524. Jacques Cartier searched for the Northwest Passage in 1534.

★ Sir Francis Drake led the second expedition around the world between 1577 and 1580.

★ The English defeated the Spanish Armada in 1588.

★ Sir Walter Raleigh led three expeditions to North America between 1584 and 1587.

★ The first French colony was started on the St. Lawrence River in the early 1600s.

★ In 1607, King James I granted charters to the Virginia Company of London and the Plymouth Company. The Virginia Company settled in Jamestown in 1607.

"Being thus arrived in good harbour, and brought safe to land . . . [the Mayflower Pilgrims] fell upon their knees and blessed the God of heaven, who had brought them over the vast and furious ocean, and delivered them from all the perils and miseries thereof, again to set their feet on the firm and stable earth . . . ."

William Bradford, *Bradford's History 'Of Plimouth Plantation'*, 1630–1651

Colonization and Settlement

1607–1763

Think of yourself as a European living in the 1600s. You are unhappy with the way your government rules. You are unhappy about being unable to worship as you choose. You have heard about a "new land" across a wide sea. Will you be among those who choose to leave home for the new land? Will you be brave enough to sail for three or four months to get to an unknown place? How will you want your government and religion to be different in a new country? Will you be able to brave many hardships to have a better life?

In this unit you will learn why the first European settlers came here and how they made a life. You will learn which countries established settlements and claimed land. You will learn about their very first struggles for freedom.

Chapter 3: English Colonies Are Established:
1607–1733

Chapter 4: A Struggle for Power:
1700–1763

RUDY

Chapter 3

English Colonies Are Established

1607–1733

Early exploration paved the way for colonization in the New World. Many people in England and other parts of Europe were looking to leave their homelands. Businesses were eager to take advantage of what the New World had to offer. In this chapter, you will learn how the first English colonies were established.

Goals for Learning

▶ To describe how the Jamestown colony became a successful settlement

▶ To identify the Pilgrims and the Puritans and where they settled

▶ To explain how each English colony came into being

▶ To describe what life was like in colonial times

▶ To recognize which colonies made up the New England, middle, and southern regions

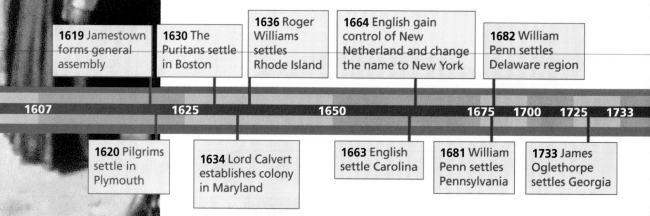

1619 Jamestown forms general assembly

1630 The Puritans settle in Boston

1636 Roger Williams settles Rhode Island

1664 English gain control of New Netherland and change the name to New York

1682 William Penn settles Delaware region

1607   1625   1650   1675   1700   1725   1733

1620 Pilgrims settle in Plymouth

1634 Lord Calvert establishes colony in Maryland

1663 English settle Carolina

1681 William Penn settles Pennsylvania

1733 James Oglethorpe settles Georgia

It took English settlers four months to make the trip from England to Virginia. English settlers arrived in Virginia in April 1607. They explored the region for one month to find a proper place for a colony. Jamestown was finally established in May 1607.

The colonists spent a lot of time searching for gold and silver. The settlers wanted to find the route to the Far East. Thus, little attention was paid to growing crops. Poor leadership and disease were already taking a toll. The region was swampy and did not have good drinking water. Steadily, the number of colonists decreased to nearly half the original number. Because they had come for adventure or gold, some of the men did not want to work. The food supply got smaller as winter approached. There were also many American Indian attacks.

Jamestown was established in 1607. Conditions were difficult for these colonists at first.

How Did Conditions at Jamestown Improve?

Changes needed to be made quickly if the colony was to succeed. A leader had to be found. Fortunately, among the settlers was an experienced military man by the name of Captain John Smith. Captain Smith was made the new leader. He set up a rule that each person had to work.

If a person did not work, then he or she would get no food. Smith tried to get along with the Powhatan tribe. He also ordered a **blockhouse,** or fort, to be built for better protection of the settlement. The Powhatans supplied corn to the starving colonists and proved to be helpful. In spite of this and all of Captain Smith's efforts, the situation was very difficult. Captain Smith was hurt in a gunpowder explosion and had to return to England for proper care. Without him as leader, the colony was in even more trouble.

An English ship arrived at Jamestown in 1610. Conditions had become so bad that the settlers decided to abandon Jamestown. They wanted to go back to England. The settlers went on board, and the ship set sail for open waters. Just as the vessel neared the mouth of the James River, three more English ships were sighted. They were coming to Jamestown. They had new supplies and about 300 more men. This gave the colony new hope. The settlers turned around and went back to Jamestown.

The Earliest Bowling

Our modern bowling began in Europe during the Middle Ages. German players rolled or threw a ball at nine wooden clubs that stood upright. The clubs were weapons commonly carried for protection. The game was called "ninepins."

The first recorded game of ninepins in America was in 1732. Dutch settlers played on a green in New Amsterdam, later named New York. This was called the "bowling green," as that area of New York is still known. When bowling attracted gamblers in America, some states made "bowling at ninepins" illegal. In the 1840s, resourceful bowlers added a tenth pin to evade the ruling. Since then, bowling has become one of America's most popular sports.

Consumer Science

History in Your Life

What Happened When the Settlers Came Back?

Three important events took place after returning to Jamestown. First, Lord Delaware was made **governor** of the colony. This noble proved to be a strong and fair leader. Second, John Rolfe planted tobacco. Jamestown now had a crop of value. Third, Rolfe married an American Indian woman named Pocahontas. She was the daughter of Powhatan, the chief of the Powhatan tribe. This further improved the colonists' relationship with the Powhatans. In a few years the colony was well on its way to becoming a growing and lasting settlement.

Tobacco became very popular in Europe. Colonists needed more land to keep up with the demand for tobacco. The Virginia Company gave the colonists more land. Colonists built large farms called **plantations.** The farmers soon needed more land. They began to use American Indian land for their crops.

Several things affected Jamestown in 1619. The Virginia Company gave settlers permission to form a **general assembly.** This group was known as the House of Burgesses. It met with the governor to make laws for the colony. The settlers chose their own **representatives** to serve in the House of Burgesses. This was the beginning of a representative government in America.

The first general assembly in America was formed in Jamestown, Virginia, in 1619.

The Virginia Company also realized many of the men wanted to leave Jamestown after they made their fortune. This would have hurt the tobacco farming. The Virginia Company would lose money. To prevent this, they brought ninety single women to Jamestown to get married and settle in this new land.

During this same year, the captain of a Dutch ship sold twenty Africans to the colonists. These African slaves worked in the tobacco fields. It was difficult to keep American Indian slaves.

WORD BANK

blockhouse
general assembly
governor
representatives
tobacco

SECTION 1 REVIEW Complete the sentences below using words from the Word Bank. Write your answers on a separate sheet of paper.

1) John Smith ordered the colonists to build a _____ for defense.

2) John Rolfe planted _____.

3) Lord Delaware became _____ of Jamestown in 1610.

4) A _____ was formed in Jamestown in 1619.

5) The Jamestown colonists elected _____ to serve in the House of Burgesses.

What do you think **?**

Why was forming a general assembly an important step for the Jamestown colonists?

★Investor
Person who lends money to a company; the investor hopes to receive more money back when the company makes money

★Share
Certificate bought from a stock company that represents a certain part of ownership of the company

★Stock company
Company that is owned by people who own the company's stock

A kind of company called a **stock company** helped colonization. These companies were owned by people who owned the company's stock. Stock companies were interested in trade and profit. They rewarded **investors** for the risks involved in settling a new colony. People who invested their money hoped to earn a profit. However, they could also lose money.

The Plymouth Company was a stock company. Its charter granted the company the rights to settle in Virginia. However, they settled in what is now called New England. The company's first attempt to establish a colony was a disaster. Poor planning and the cold winter forced the colonists to return to England.

Who Were the Pilgrims?

Religious problems increased in England under the rule of James I. The king was very unhappy with the group of people who did not share his religious ideas. Members of this group were known as Separatists, or Pilgrims. They wanted to break away from the Church of England completely. James I did not accept this group and treated them very harshly. Many of them fled to Holland in Western Europe. Holland, or the Netherlands, as it is called today, was Dutch. The Pilgrims were not comfortable in this setting. The Dutch people had a different language and way of life. Many Pilgrims thought about going to the New World, but they didn't know how to get there. Ships and supplies were expensive and beyond their ability to afford them.

What Plan Did the Pilgrims Make?

A determined group of Pilgrims formed a stock company and bought as many **shares,** or parts of a company, as they could. Much more money was needed. The Pilgrims were able to get the additional money from wealthy investors of the London Company. Many of the members were interested in setting up a new colony.

*Democratic
Government in
which the power is
held by the people

Destination
*Place where one is
going*

Majority
*A number greater
than half of the
total*

The investors were willing to pay for the ships and all the supplies. However, the Pilgrims had to agree to certain conditions:

1. The Pilgrims could settle on land that belonged to the London Company in Virginia.

2. The settlers would have to work for seven years and give all the profits back to the investors.

3. After the seven-year period was over, the settlers would be on their own and free to do as they wished.

The small group of Pilgrims, plus a large number of other people, set sail on the Mayflower. After a sixty-four day voyage across the Atlantic Ocean, the small crowded vessel reached the shore of what is now Cape Cod in 1620. The ship had blown off course. Scouts were sent out to explore the region. A month later, the Pilgrims sailed to their new site, which they called Plymouth.

What Was the Mayflower Compact?

While the Mayflower was anchored in the water off of Cape Cod, a meeting was held in the cabin of the ship. They had landed outside of their chartered **destination.** They were not bound to their charter this far north. They seized the opportunity to set up their own rules of government.

The group elected John Carver as their leader. Choosing a leader was very important. The passengers agreed that laws passed by the **majority** of the group would be obeyed. They wrote the Mayflower Compact to represent this idea. Rule by majority is still a main part of our **democratic** government, which is a

The *Mayflower* was blown off its original course. It eventually anchored off Cape Cod.

Signing the Mayflower Compact was an important event. It was the beginning of democracy in America.

government ruled by the people. A great historical event had taken place. This was the first time European Americans had set up their own government and agreed to obey the laws that the majority made.

The Mayflower Compact could not solve all the problems of the colony. The poor soil, cold winters, heavy debt, and strict religious practices were difficult problems to solve. Because of their strong religious views, the Pilgrims were not able to attract more settlers. However, in time, the settlement was a success.

Who Were the Puritans?

The Puritans were another religious group. Like the Pilgrims, they were unhappy with the way the king treated them. When Charles I became king in 1625, problems increased. He did not approve of their religious ideas. It was difficult for the king to deal with the Puritans. Many of them held government office. They were well educated. The king could not ignore the Puritans or force them to obey.

Charles I took strong measures to keep the Puritans under control. Officials were removed from government positions, and ministers were not allowed to be part of the Church. Many Puritans were put into prison.

In 1629, wealthy Puritans decided to go to America. They obtained a charter in the name of the Massachusetts Bay Colony. The one thousand colonists included teachers, doctors, lawyers, ministers, merchants, and well-to-do country gentlemen. The Puritans spent a great deal of time planning, organizing, and gathering **provisions.** They were well aware of the dangers and problems that lay ahead.

Provisions
Supplies needed for a trip or voyage

The group of Puritans set out for America with a fleet of fifteen ships. They landed in Boston, Massachusetts, in 1630. John Winthrop became the governor of the new settlement. Within a few years, nearly ten thousand colonists came to this settlement. Because the expedition was well managed, it was a success.

The Puritans formed a successful settlement in Boston, Massachusetts.

Writing About History

Write a business letter to a stock company as if you were living in England in the 1600s. Ask for money to start a colony in the New World. Include who you are and why you would like to start a colony.

The Puritans had very strong religious ideas. They had journeyed a great distance to worship as they pleased. Because they had suffered under a cruel king, it was very important for them to have religious freedom. However, they did not grant this freedom to others.

All laws dealing with religion, trade, business, and government were made according to the Puritans' beliefs. Every colonist was expected to follow these laws. Stern measures were taken to make sure people would obey.

SECTION 2 REVIEW Decide if each statement below tells about the Pilgrims or the Puritans. Write *Pilgrims* or *Puritans* beside each number on a separate sheet of paper.

1) Religious group that formed a new colony in Boston.

2) Religious group that formed a new colony in Plymouth.

3) Wrote an agreement called the Mayflower Compact.

4) John Winthrop became governor of their settlement.

5) Elected John Carver as their leader.

What do you think ?

Why do you think the Puritans wanted religious freedom but did not want to grant that freedom to others?

Boundary
A real or imaginary marker that shows what land a person owns

Clergy
Person given the power by the church to perform religious tasks

Equality
Having the same rights as others

★**Proprietor**
One who owns a colony

A new kind of colony was started under Charles I. A wealthy noble could receive a charter with clearly defined **boundaries.** The landowners, called **proprietors,** would have the right to govern their colonies as they wished.

The first such colony was Maryland. King Charles I made George Calvert the proprietor of the Maryland colony in 1632. Calvert died before the charter became official. His son, Cecilius Calvert, received the charter in his place and became proprietor. A colony was established in what is now St. Marys City, on the shores of the Chesapeake Bay, in 1634. Although Lord Calvert was a Roman Catholic, he wanted all religious groups to worship as they wished. Maryland passed the Toleration Act in 1649. The law allowed everyone to enjoy religious freedom. The act was of major importance. It established an **equality** of rights for people of all religions.

When Were Rhode Island and Connecticut Settled?

The strict policies of the Puritans soon brought about problems. Roger Williams, a member of the **clergy,** spoke out against the policies. He fled from the colony in order to avoid prison. Williams made his way to what is now Rhode

MARGARET BRENT: 1600–1671

Margaret Brent has been called one of America's first promoters of women's rights. She came to the Maryland colony from England in 1638. She became a landowner at a time when few women had that privilege. Margaret did well, becoming one of the largest landowners in her state.

Shortly after hiring soldiers to fight a Protestant uprising, Lord Calvert died in 1647. Margaret Brent managed his estate after his death. Unpaid and hungry, the troops threatened trouble. Brent acted quickly. She sold Lord Calvert's estate to pay the soldiers and imported corn to feed them. The Maryland Assembly later praised Brent, saying that the colony was safe in her hands.

Island. The Narragansett tribe helped him. He called his settlement Providence, which meant "God's **guidance**." Soon, some of his followers came to the new settlement. A true democratic colony was formed for the first time in 1636. Roger Williams went to England and got a charter to protect the settlement. He established complete freedom of religion in Rhode Island.

Another group of people was interested in migrating west to the Connecticut Valley. The valley had rich farmland. Thomas Hooker, a **pastor,** was the leader. He started a settlement in Connecticut in 1636. The people were excited about the new opportunity. Like the settlers of Rhode Island, they had a great desire for religious freedom.

What Other Colonies Were Settled?

The region that extended south of Virginia to Florida was available for colonies. It was possible that the Spanish in Florida would move northward. This would be a serious problem for English settlements in that area.

Carolina

In 1663, several English nobles approached Charles II, then king of England, and requested a charter to settle that region. The king recognized the advantages of settling in this area. Different crops could be grown in the warmer climate. The charter was granted. The region was called Carolina. As settlers arrived, Charleston, named in honor of Charles II, became an important port.

Political quarrels developed in Carolina. They were continually a source of trouble. The proprietors finally gave up and sold their interest to the British Government. They in turn divided Carolina into North Carolina and South Carolina in 1729.

New York

New York's original name was New Netherland. It began in 1609 as a Dutch colony. The colony grew very slowly because of its strict land-ownership **policy.** The Dutch landlords, or **patroons,** kept a tight hold on available lands for settlers.

Guidance
Direction or leading

Pastor
Member of the clergy

★**Patroon**
Dutch landowner

Policy
Set of rules or an action plan set forth by a person or group

The English were uncomfortable with this Dutch settlement. King Charles II declared that all lands of the region belonged to his brother, James, Duke of York. An English fleet forced the Dutch governor, Peter Stuyvesant, to give up the Dutch claim. The English took over the colony in 1664 and renamed it New York.

New Hampshire

Another colony was New Hampshire. This colony was part of Massachusetts for 39 years. New Hampshire was sold to the king of England in 1679. The king made New Hampshire a royal colony. It did not have an elected government. The king chose the governor.

Pennsylvania

William Penn (left) founded Pennsylvania in 1681. He is also known for establishing good relations with the Delaware Indians.

William Penn was granted a charter for the land between New York and Maryland in 1681. King Charles II was in debt to William Penn's father. The king had borrowed a large amount of money. The charter was given as payment for what the king owed.

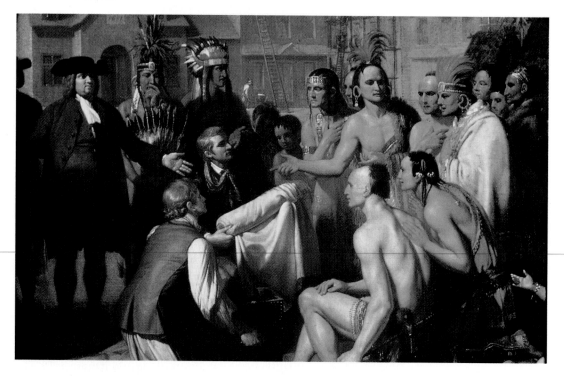

William Penn was a Quaker. He believed in the equality of all people. He gave the colonists of Pennsylvania two important individual rights: freedom of religion and the right to elect public officials. Philadelphia, a city in Pennsylvania, later came to be known as the City of Brotherly Love.

Delaware

In 1682, the Duke of York granted William Penn a region known today as Delaware. This gave Pennsylvania **access** to the Atlantic Ocean. Dutch, Swedes, and Finns settled in that area. The region was controlled by Pennsylvania and divided into three separate areas. This area was called the "Three Lower Counties." It became one colony—Delaware—in 1704.

Access
Ability to obtain or make use of something

New Jersey

Part of the land claimed by the Duke of York was a region called New Jersey. Two nobles, friends of the duke, were interested in the region. East Jersey and West Jersey were established to please these friends. For many years, problems related to the government of the regions continued. Finally, in 1702, the two regions were made into one single colony. It was called New Jersey.

Georgia

Conditions in England had gotten worse under the strict rule of King George II. People were sent to overcrowded prisons for minor crimes. James Oglethorpe, a wealthy businessman, asked to be granted a colony where the poor and unfortunate could settle when they left prison. He was given the land between South Carolina and Florida. The British were worried that the Spanish in Florida would move northward. This could cause serious problems for the British. The land given to Oglethorpe would prevent the Spanish from moving northward. This area was named Georgia. The colonists arrived in what is now Savannah, Georgia, in 1733.

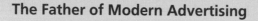

The Father of Modern Advertising

John Houghton was doing very well as a businessman in the late seventeenth century. His drugstore—they called it an apothecary shop in those days—was flourishing. He also sold coffee, tea, chocolate, and books. In addition, he reviewed books and operated a publishing company.

Houghton was an enterprising man. Why not publish a newspaper to advertise his merchandise, he thought. And why not sell advertising space to his fellow merchants as well? In 1692, his newspaper became the first to emphasize advertising. It also was the first newspaper to insist on advertising ethics. Many merchants did not let a little thing like truth stand in their way when they advertised their products. Then, as today, merchants knew how to use people's emotions to sell their products. Houghton wanted to avoid false advertising, so he designed an advertising "seal of approval." The only people who could advertise in his paper had to tell the truth about their products.

SECTION 3 REVIEW Choose the best word or words in parentheses to complete each sentence. Write your answers on a separate sheet of paper.

1) Lord Calvert set up a colony in (Georgia, Maryland, New York).

2) (Roger Williams, James Oglethorpe, Thomas Hooker) settled Connecticut.

3) Carolina was divided into North Carolina and South Carolina in (1609, 1663, 1729).

4) An owner of a colony was called a (governor, king, proprietor).

5) Pennsylvania was settled by (George Calvert, William Penn, James Oglethorpe).

What do you think ?

Do you think most Maryland colonists liked the Toleration Act? Why or why not?

★**Emigrate**
To leave for another place or country

Estimate
To make a guess based on some facts

Expansion
To spread out or increase in size

★**Indentured servant**
Person who came to the colonies under a contract to work for someone without pay for a certain time

Minority
Group of people that is a smaller part of a population

Refuge
Protection or shelter

Settlement of the thirteen colonies took place between 1607 and 1733. The number of colonists coming to America was slowly increasing. Poor traveling conditions and concern about the American Indians slowed **expansion.** Population by the late 1600s is **estimated** to have been between 200,000 and 300,000.

At first, most of the colonists were English. Other Europeans began to **emigrate,** or move to America because of religious and political problems in their countries. America was becoming known as a place of safety and **refuge.** Germans, Irish, Dutch, French, Swedes, and Scotch-Irish were among the growing population. The English majority was rapidly becoming a **minority.** The desire for freedom brought many people to America.

What Was Colonial Life Like?

American life was taking shape. Farmers cleared the land and planted crops. Merchants sold and shipped goods. The early colonial society had a wealthy class, a middle class, and a lower class. The wealthy class was merchants or large planters. Farmers, shopkeepers, artisans, and teachers were the middle class. The lower class was unskilled workers, **indentured servants** (someone who works as part of a contract), or slaves. Laws regarding slavery were first made in Massachusetts in 1650. Nine more colonies made such laws by 1715.

Many of the colonists were farmers.

Estimated Population of American Colonies 1630-1740

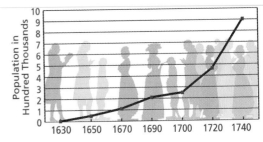

Houses were usually wood. A fireplace provided warmth and was used for cooking. Sparks from the fireplace or chimney could cause a fire that might destroy the house. Furnishings were plain and sturdy. Mattresses were canvas bags filled with straw. Homemade candles provided light. The food was rather simple. Corn was often used to make bread. Meat or wild game was cooked with vegetables in a large iron pot. With no refrigeration, food could not be stored very long. Meat was salted or smoked to preserve it. Vegetables could be dried or pickled. Some fruits could be stored in cool, dry cellars.

Generally, the health of the early colonist was poor. Little was known about the cause and treatment of diseases. Sometimes an **epidemic,** a widespread disease, would occur.

What Were the Three Colonial Regions?

The northern or New England colonies included New Hampshire, Massachusetts, Rhode Island, and Connecticut. Farms were small in the New England colonies. This was because of the rocky soil and long, cold winters. Clusters of small towns were established as interest in certain jobs grew. Shipbuilding, lumbering, fishing, trading, and ironworks grew steadily.

The southern colonies were Maryland, North Carolina, South Carolina, Georgia, and Virginia. These colonies had broad lowlands, fertile

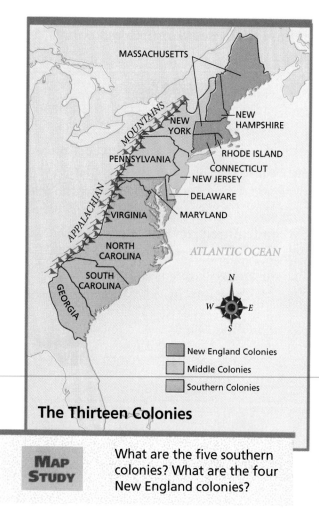

The Thirteen Colonies

MAP STUDY
What are the five southern colonies? What are the four New England colonies?

An Early Form of Labor

Indentured service was a common form of labor in colonial times. In the 1600s, there were more indentured servants than slaves in the southern colonies.

An indentured servant would come to the colonies from Europe. To pay for the trip, a servant would work for someone in the colonies. Most indentured servants had to work anywhere from four to seven years. Servants had harsh working conditions.

Many Europeans were forced to be indentured servants. People were sometimes kidnapped and sold as servants.

★Indigo
Plant used to make dye

farmlands, and a much warmer climate. The southern settlers were spread out over a large area. Plantations produced "money crops" such as rice, tobacco, and **indigo,** which was a plant used to make dye. Slave labor was introduced and used by wealthy plantation owners.

The middle colonies included New York, New Jersey, Pennsylvania, and Delaware. The climate was a mixture of both the northern and southern conditions. The colonies in the central part of colonial America served as the link between the northern and southern regions. Grains such as corn and wheat soon became important crops. The middle colonies were called the "bread colonies" because they produced large amounts of grain.

SECTION 4 REVIEW Write the correct ending for each sentence on a separate sheet of paper.

1) The American colonies were established over a period of . . .

2) Farms were small in New England because . . .

3) Crops in the South included . . .

4) Plantation owners encouraged the use of . . .

5) The middle colonies could be described as . . .

What do you think 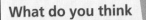 **?**

What do you think would be the most difficult part about being a colonist? Why?

The Mayflower Compact

Pilgrims wrote the Mayflower Compact on board ship on November 11, 1620. It is recognized as the first agreement for self-government ever composed and signed in America. Forty-one male adults signed the document.

"In the name of God, Amen. We whose names are underwritten, the Loyal Subjects of our dread Sovereign Lord, King James, by the Grace of God, of Great Britain, France and Ireland, King, Defender of the Faith, &

Having undertaken, for the Glory of God, and the Advancement of the Christian Faith, and the Honor of our King and Country, a voyage to plant the first colony in the northern Parts of Virginia; do by

these Presents, solemnly and mutually in the Presence of God and of one another, covenant and combine ourselves together into a civil Body Politic, for our better Ordering and Preservation, and Furtherance of the Ends aforesaid; And by virtue hereof to enact, constitute, and frame, such just and equal Laws, Ordinances, Acts, Constitutions and Offices, from time to time, as shall be thought most meet and convenient for the General good of the Colony; unto which we promise all due Submission and Obedience.

In Witness whereof we hereunto subscribed our names at Cape Cod the eleventh of November, in the reign of our Sovereign Lord, King James of England, France and Ireland . . . and of Scotland . . . . Anno Domini, 1620."

Source Reading Wrap-Up

1) The Pilgrims wound up in New England. Where had they planned to go?

2) What countries did King James rule over?

3) What was the purpose of this agreement?

4) What kinds of laws did the Pilgrims want to make?

5) What was the importance of this document for future government of America?

★ Jamestown colony was established in May 1607. The colony formed a general assembly, named the House of Burgesses, in 1619.

★ The Pilgrims reached the shore of what is now Cape Cod in 1620. There they wrote the Mayflower Compact. It stated that the Pilgrims agreed to obey laws created by the majority. They later formed a settlement in Plymouth.

★ The Puritans landed in Boston in 1630. Within a few years, nearly ten thousand colonists came to this settlement.

★ Lord Calvert established a colony in what is now St. Marys City, Maryland, on the shores of the Chesapeake Bay, in 1634.

★ Roger Williams settled Providence, Rhode Island, in 1636.

★ Thomas Hooker started a settlement in Connecticut in 1636.

★ English nobles, under a charter from King Charles II, settled Carolina in 1663. Carolina was divided into North Carolina and South Carolina in 1729.

★ The English took over a Dutch colony in 1664 and renamed it New York in honor of the Duke of York.

★ New Hampshire, formerly part of Massachusetts, was sold to the king of England in 1679. The king made New Hampshire a royal colony.

★ William Penn was granted a charter for the land between New York and Maryland in 1681. The colony was called Pennsylvania.

★ In 1682, the Duke of York granted William Penn a region known today as Delaware. The region, controlled by Pennsylvania, was divided into three counties. These became Delaware in 1704.

★ East Jersey and West Jersey united into New Jersey in 1702.

★ James Oglethorpe settled a colony in what is now Savannah, Georgia, in 1733.

★ The early colonial society was made up of a wealthy class, a middle class, and a lower class.

★ The colonies included three regions–the northern or New England colonies, the southern colonies, and the middle colonies.

Comprehension: Identifying Facts

On a separate sheet of paper, write the correct colony from the Word Bank to complete the sentences.

WORD BANK	
Connecticut	New York
Delaware	North Carolina
Georgia	Pennsylvania
Maryland	Rhode Island
Massachusetts	South Carolina
New Hampshire	Virginia
New Jersey	

1) East Jersey and West Jersey became _____.

2) Thomas Hooker started a settlement in _____.

3) _____ began as a Dutch colony.

4) Lord Calvert set up a colony in _____ in 1634.

5) Carolina became _____ and _____.

6) _____ was once divided into three separate counties.

7) King Charles II gave William Penn a charter for _____ in 1681.

8) Colonists settled in what is now Savannah, _____, in 1733.

9) Roger Williams settled Providence, _____, in 1636.

10) The Puritans first settled in _____.

11) The Jamestown colony was located in _____.

12) _____ was sold to the king of England in 1679.

Comprehension: Understanding Main Ideas

On a separate sheet of paper, write the answers to the following questions using complete sentences.

1) What two problems did the Jamestown colonists face when they first started the colony?

2) What three things affected Jamestown in 1619?

3) Who were the Pilgrims? Where did they settle?

4) Who were the Puritans? Where did they settle?

5) Which were the middle colonies? the southern? the northern?

6) How did many of the colonists make a living?

Critical Thinking: Write Your Opinion

1) The Pilgrims' Mayflower Compact represented rule by majority. Do you think rule by majority works? Why or why not?

2) Do you think you would have liked living in colonial times? Why or why not?

Test Taking Tip   When a teacher announces a test, listen carefully. Write down the topics that will be included. Write down the names of any specific readings the teacher says to review.

Chapter 4

A Struggle for Power

1700–1763

The 1700s in America involved more change for the colonists and Great Britain. The colonists began to appreciate doing things for themselves even though Great Britain wanted to control the colonies. At the same time, problems developed with the American Indians and the French over land to the west. In this chapter, you will learn about these struggles for power.

Goals for Learning

▶ To describe colonial trade practices

▶ To identify the problems over land that developed between the French and British

▶ To describe how well the French and British were prepared for war

▶ To identify the major battles of the French and Indian War

▶ To explain how the French and Indian War affected control of land and power in the colonies

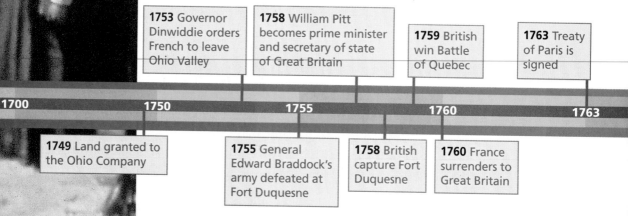

1753 Governor Dinwiddie orders French to leave Ohio Valley

1758 William Pitt becomes prime minister and secretary of state of Great Britain

1759 British win Battle of Quebec

1763 Treaty of Paris is signed

1700   1750   1755   1760   1763

1749 Land granted to the Ohio Company

1755 General Edward Braddock's army defeated at Fort Duquesne

1758 British capture Fort Duquesne

1760 France surrenders to Great Britain

Complex
Something that has many details or parts

Cultural
Having to do with the arts

★**Delegate**
A person elected to serve in government

★**Independence**
Ability to take care of oneself

★**Legislature**
Group of people elected to make laws

Responsibility
The need to complete duties or tasks

Colonists took pride in what they did. Clearing the land, building homes, and producing goods were important developments. Farming became people's main work. Families raised crops and animals for their food. Most farm families made their own clothes, furniture, and tools. The colonists were showing their ability to take care of themselves, or **independence.** With independence came a love of freedom and a strong sense of **responsibility.**

As more and larger towns were built among the farms, colonists started sharing news and ideas with their neighbors. They held town meetings to pass laws, to set taxes to help their schools, and to select **delegates,** which were people who served in their **legislatures.** A legislature is a group of people elected to make laws. They started working together to provide goods and services. Libraries and newspapers were started. Colonial writers, painters, and musicians added much to the **cultural** life of the people. The colonists became aware of their own progress, which was separate from the advances of the countries from which they had come. However, they came to realize that in order to grow, they needed to trade beyond the shores of America.

What Was Mercantilism?

As the lives of the colonists became more **complex,** their need to trade with other countries increased. However, Great Britain would not allow the colonies to trade with whomever they wished. Laws had been passed earlier to control colonial trade.

Writing About History

In your notebook, write a personal letter as if you are a colonist living in America in the 1700s. Write to a family member who lives in Europe. Explain what your daily routine is like and whether you like your life as a colonist.

The practice of **regulating** colonial trade for the profit of the home country was called **mercantilism.** Great Britain was not the only country that practiced mercantilism. France, the Netherlands, Spain, and Austria also used this policy to profit from their settlements in America. Great Britain intended to make a profit from the trading the American colonies did. The American colonies did not want controls that would benefit the British. They set out to find ways to trade on their own.

The shipping business was an important part of colonial trade.

★Mercantilism
The practice of regulating colonial trade for the profit of the home country

Regulate
To govern or direct according to a rule

John Peter Zenger and Freedom of the Press

When New York publisher John Peter Zenger printed articles against the royal governor in 1734, he was arrested. He was pronounced not guilty, because he was telling the truth, even though he was printing articles against the government. This case established the idea of freedom of the press in America.

SECTION 1 REVIEW Write answers to these questions on a separate sheet of paper using complete sentences.

1) How did farm families get their food, clothing, furniture, and tools?

2) How did the colonists exchange news and ideas?

3) Why did the colonists need to trade with other countries?

4) What is mercantilism?

5) Which countries practiced mercantilism?

What do you think ?

Why do you think freedom and independence were so important to the colonists?

Enforce
To make sure something is done according to a law

★**Triangular trade**
Trade between Africa, the West Indies, and New England

Unite
To join together as a single unit

A trade triangle was formed among Africa, the West Indies, and New England. This **triangular trade** was outside of British control, so it made more money for the colonials. Trade continued until Great Britain began to **enforce** the laws for colonial trade.

The increasing colonial businesses and trade gave more jobs and opportunities to the settlers. A spirit of independence was growing. Many colonists lost the feeling that they were living in British colonies. People from different countries—Sweden, the Netherlands, Germany, and Ireland—were increasing in number. They felt no need to be led by Great Britain. Freedom provided a better life and a desire for more independence.

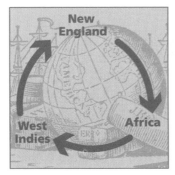

Triangular trade

Who Were the Victims of Triangular Trade?

Countless American Indians were victims of Europeans who claimed tribal lands and forced them from their homes. With the growth of the colonies, American Indians were pushed farther and farther west.

The other group harmed for the gain of the European colonists was Africans. As part of the triangular trade involving Africa, people from that continent were treated as property, not human beings. Millions of Africans were captured from their native lands and brought to America. Many colonists who needed free labor for their farms and plantations did not allow these people any rights. Millions of Africans died as a result of triangular trade. It would be many years before enslaved Africans could **unite** and move toward justice.

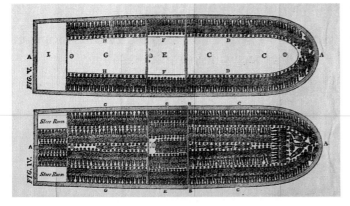

This diagram shows the crowded conditions enslaved Africans faced on ships bound for America.

What Were the Navigation Acts?

Great Britain decided to start enforcing the Navigation Acts that were passed in 1660 and 1663. The purpose of the acts was to regulate colonial trade. Problems developed as the settlers refused to accept Great Britain's strict control.

Most American merchants continued to trade with other countries. British officials in the colonies were often paid to look the other way. More new laws were passed, including the Woolens Act in 1699, the Hat Act in 1732, and the Iron Act in 1750. The Molasses Act, passed in 1733, was Great Britain's direct response to triangular trade. This law added a tax to items such as molasses that were imported from the West Indies. The threat of fighting back, or **rebellion,** and the hope for freedom were growing.

★Rebellion
A group fighting another group that is in power

SECTION 2 REVIEW Write answers to these questions on a separate sheet of paper using complete sentences.

1) What was triangular trade?

2) How did triangular trade affect American Indians?

3) How did triangular trade affect Africans?

4) What were the Navigation Acts

5) How did Americans react to the Navigation Acts?

What do you think ?

Why do you think Europeans treated the American Indians and African slaves so poorly?

★Frontier
A region with little population

Despite their problems with Great Britain, the colonies continued to grow. Settlers were moving westward, developing the **frontier.** Adventurous colonists saw an opportunity to go beyond the Appalachian Mountains. Westbound settlers faced danger because the region was already occupied by the American Indians and the French. Nevertheless, they began to go west in great numbers. The fertile land in the Ohio Valley was perfect for farming. The French, however, refused to give up the vast area claimed by their forefathers.

Both France and Great Britain had made claims to the Ohio Valley. In 1749, King George II of Great Britain granted 200,000 acres of land to the Ohio Company. After this grant was made, the French challenged the British. They staked their claims with lead markers. King Louis XV of France ordered forts built along the rivers to protect these claims.

What Problems Developed Over Land Claims?

The issue of land ownership still had not been resolved. In 1753, Governor Dinwiddie of Virginia sent a message to the French. He ordered them to leave the Ohio Valley and to recognize the British claim to the land. George Washington carried the message. He was a twenty-one-year-old major in the Virginian Army. The French received him with proper respect, but did not accept the British order to leave.

Washington was again sent into the Ohio Valley in 1754. This time, he commanded a troop of soldiers. He had orders to drive the French away from one of their forts—Fort Duquesne. The French, however, had increased the number of soldiers in their army. They greatly outnumbered Washington's force. Shots were exchanged, and the young leader had no choice but to retreat. In that brief battle, Washington showed his courage and leadership ability. The French were determined to keep control of the region.

What Was the Albany Plan of Union?

The colonists knew that the problems with land ownership could start a war between France and Great Britain. Delegates from seven colonies met in Albany, New York. The purpose of the Albany Congress was to secure an **alliance** with the Iroquois. An alliance is an agreement that joins groups of people or countries together. The other purpose was to discuss a plan to form a **union**. A union is a group of territories joining together under one government. Delegate Benjamin Franklin proposed a plan modeled after the Iroquois League. The union could create and collect taxes, maintain an army, control trade with the American Indians, and pass other laws.

Science

History in Your Life

The Work of Benjamin Franklin

To many people in the 1700s, Benjamin Franklin represented the creative spirit of America. He was an amateur scientist, inventor, successful printer, writer, and statesman. Franklin won international respect for himself and his new nation.

Franklin was the first to suggest the idea of daylight saving time. He invented bifocals—eyeglasses that have lenses with parts for reading and for distance. He invented a stove that improved home heating while using less fuel than other stoves did. In one experiment, he attached a metal key to a kite that he flew during a thunderstorm. The experiment demonstrated the electrical nature of lightning. Soon thereafter Franklin invented the lightning rod, which helps prevent fires started by lightning strikes. Many of his scientific inventions and ideas are still a part of our everyday lives.

The plan was turned down. Even the threat of a war did not convince the delegates the union was a good idea. They feared their individual freedoms would be lost. Though this first attempt to create a colonial government was unsuccessful, it was still important. Franklin's Albany Plan of Union had set the stage for great things to come in the future.

How Did the British and the French Match Up?

The threat of a war between Great Britain and France still existed. If a war broke out, each of the two countries would have certain advantages and disadvantages.

Great Britain had the advantage of more people. Almost one and a half million colonists had settled the new land. Great Britain could use the colonies for support and to **recruit** men to fight the war. Unfortunately, the British colonies were not politically united. Therefore, Great Britain would have to deal with each of the thirteen individually.

France's main disadvantage was that it had fewer people. About 65,000 French colonists were widely scattered over a large area. France's major settlements were Montreal and Quebec in what is now Canada. A big advantage, however, was that French colonies had only one controlling government. The colonists were expected to obey the decisions of the king of France, including an order to fight the war.

The French were familiar with the hard life on the Ohio Valley frontier. They enjoyed a good relationship with the American Indians developed through years of fur trading. French men married American Indian women and adopted their way of life. Many French soldiers also learned frontier warfare from the American Indians.

Benjamin Franklin

How Did the British Prepare for War?

In 1754, Major General Edward Braddock was **appointed** commander in chief of the British army in America. He was regarded as one of Great Britain's finest officers. Soon after his arrival, Great Britain sent two new **regiments** of soldiers to join him. The British expected that war would break out at any moment. The fight would later be known as the French and Indian War. The American Indians and the French were allies in this war. They fought together against the British.

SECTION 3 REVIEW Decide if each statement below tells about the British or the French. Write *British* or *French* beside each number on a separate sheet of paper.

1) Granted 200,000 acres of land in the Ohio Valley to the Ohio Company

2) Forced George Washington to retreat from Fort Duquesne

3) Lived among the American Indians

4) Had almost one and a half million colonists

5) Had fewer settlers

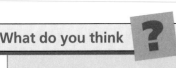

What do you think ❓

Who do you think was better prepared for a war—the French or the British? Why?

Ambush
To carry out a surprise attack

Survivor
Someone who has lived through a dangerous event

General Braddock had very little respect for American Indians as warriors. George Washington was serving under Braddock. He suggested that General Braddock prepare for a very different kind of battle. The general would not listen to Washington.

Fort Duquesne was an important French fort. The British needed to capture the fort in order to drive the French out of the Ohio Valley.

Braddock led his army of British and colonial troops toward Fort Duquesne in 1755. However, hiding behind rocks and trees, 72 French, 146 Canadians, and 637 American Indians **ambushed** them outside the fort. General Braddock died in this surprise attack, as did many of his men. Washington gathered the **survivors** and struggled back to safety.

General Braddock and many of his men were killed in a surprise attack near Fort Duquesne.

The British went on to lose battles at Fort Oswego and Fort William Henry in New York. They lost many men in failed attacks on Crown Point and Fort Ticonderoga. They failed, too, at an attempt to capture Louisbourg, a French naval base in Nova Scotia. The colonists, upon seeing many of their friends die at the hands of the French, lost confidence in the proud British army. Many of them wanted to fight their own war, without the British to give the orders.

Who Was William Pitt?

King George II was aware that France could win the war. If this happened, France would claim all the land to the Mississippi River. He needed to make some changes. In 1758, King George appointed William Pitt as prime minister and secretary of state of Great Britain.

Pitt offered words of encouragement to the colonists. This brought him greater cooperation from colonial legislatures. He sent troops and supplies from Great Britain, and he appointed only the finest officers. Together, Great Britain and the colonies formed an army of 50,000. This new army had more soldiers than all the French soldiers in the New World. The colonists gained confidence in the British leadership. They were prepared to fight the enemy and win the war.

Then and Now

If you had a toothache in the 1700s, your only choice was to have the tooth pulled. Nothing was available to relieve your toothache or the pain when your tooth was pulled. In Colonial America, a wigmaker might have pulled your tooth with some fierce-looking instrument. After your tooth was gone, you would remain toothless. There was no way to replace lost teeth then.

Today, you and your dentist have choices. Cavities can be filled or caps or crowns put on teeth. Nerves in a painful tooth can be removed without pulling the tooth. Now dentists avoid pulling teeth unless absolutely necessary. If you must have a tooth pulled, it can be replaced with a bridge, dentures, or implants. You can have pain relief during any of these processes.

SECTION 4 REVIEW On a separate sheet of paper, write *True* if the statement is true or *False* if the statement is not true.

1) General Braddock greatly respected the American Indians as soldiers.

2) General Braddock was killed near Fort Duquesne.

3) William Pitt was made prime minister of France in 1757.

4) William Pitt made several changes.

5) The colonists did not like William Pitt.

What do you think ?

Why do you think General Braddock was defeated by the American Indians and the French?

★Reinforcements
Additional soldiers used to back up an army

★Stronghold
A place, such as a military base, that is well protected from attack

★Treaty
An agreement to end fighting

The British colonial army returned to Louisbourg and defeated the French. General John Forbes also led several thousand colonial soldiers against Fort Duquesne in 1758. Upon seeing this army approach, the French set the fort afire and fled. The capture of Fort Duquesne was an important turning point in the war.

What Were the Final Stages of the War?

The British, under James Wolfe, destroyed a French fleet of **reinforcements** about to leave France. Reinforcements are additional soldiers. Sir William Johnson and Iroquois braves captured Fort Niagara for the British. General Amherst captured two French forts, Carillon and St. Frederick, and renamed them Fort Ticonderoga and Crown Point.

The British needed one major victory to force the French to surrender. The **stronghold** of the French was Quebec, Canada. A stronghold is a place that is well protected from attack. General Louis Montcalm, the French leader, was sure his position was protected by its high cliffs.

James Wolfe and his fleet of ships traveled up the St. Lawrence River to attack Quebec.

Wolfe led a fleet of ships up the St. Lawrence River to Quebec. He discovered a path that led up the cliffs to the plains above. They fought the battle at daybreak on September 13, 1759. The British won. Montcalm and Wolfe each were wounded and died. France surrendered in 1760.

What Happened After the War?

The Treaty of Paris was signed in 1763. A **treaty** is an agreement to end fighting. France gave Great Britain the land east of the Mississippi River, except New Orleans. The area of Louisiana west of the Mississippi and New Orleans, which France had claimed, went to Spain. Great Britain got the territory of Florida from Spain in exchange for Cuba. France kept two islands south of Newfoundland and some islands off the West Indies.

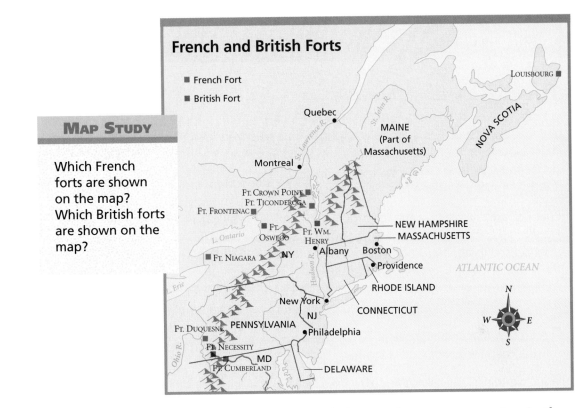

French and British Forts

- ■ French Fort
- ■ British Fort

LOUISBOURG ■

Quebec

MAINE
(Part of
Massachusetts)

NOVA SCOTIA

Montreal

FT. CROWN POINT
FT. TICONDEROGA
FT. FRONTENAC

FT. OSWEGO
FT. WM. HENRY

NEW HAMPSHIRE
MASSACHUSETTS

L. Ontario

FT. NIAGARA
NY
Albany
Boston
Providence

ATLANTIC OCEAN

L. Erie

RHODE ISLAND

New York
CONNECTICUT

FT. DUQUESNE
PENNSYLVANIA
NJ

Philadelphia

FT. NECESSITY

MD
FT. CUMBERLAND
DELAWARE

N
W E
S

MAP STUDY

Which French forts are shown on the map? Which British forts are shown on the map?

After the war, Great Britain was the strongest nation in the world. It would have to look to the colonies for higher taxes to pay for the war. Now that the French were no longer a threat to them, however, the colonists would not have to depend on Great Britain for protection.

SECTION 5 REVIEW Write answers to these questions on a separate sheet of paper using complete sentences.

1) What did the French do to Fort Duquesne?

2) Why were the British victories at Fort Duquesne and Quebec important?

3) How did General Wolfe attack Quebec?

4) What was the Treaty of Paris?

5) What land did Britain gain after the war?

What do you think ❓

How might the United States be different today if the British had lost the French and Indian War?

Poor Richard's Almanac

In 1733, the first edition of Poor Richard's Almanac *was printed. Benjamin Franklin wrote and published it every year until 1758. The Almanac was a huge success.*

Poor Richard's Almanac is fun to read. Franklin used many stories and sayings that are still used today. Many of the sayings in the Almanac were wise words of Franklin. Additional sayings were gathered in his travels. A sample of those sayings follows:

■ A Brother may not be a Friend,
But a Friend will always be a Brother.

■ A child thinks 20 Shillings and 20 years can scarce ever be spent.

■ The learned Fool writes his Nonsense in better Language than the unlearned; but still 'tis Nonsense.

■ He that sows Thorns, should never go barefoot.

■ You may delay, but Time will not.

■ Great Modesty often hides great Merit.

Poor Richard (Franklin) wrote on many subjects. Among those subjects were hints about health, money, friends, beauty, evil deeds, personal pleasures, and human matters.

The paragraph below is a sample of one of his lessons to learn.

I know, young Friend, *Ambition* fills your
Mind,
And in Life's Voyage is th' impelling Wind;
But at the Helm let sober Reason stand,
And steer the Bark with Heav'n-directed
Hand;
So shall you safe *Ambition's* Gales receive,
And ride securely, tho' the Billows heave;
So shall you shun the giddy Hero's Fate,
And by her Influence be both good and
great.

Source Reading Wrap-Up

1) Who wrote *Poor Richard's Almanac?*

2) What made *Poor Richard's Almanac* so popular then and now?

3) Of the proverbs (sayings) listed, which one do you like best and why?

4) What do you think was the message Benjamin Franklin intended when he wrote about Ambition?

5) How do you think Franklin's words are wise?

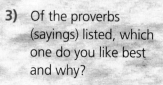

Poor Richard, 1733:
AN
Almanack
For the Year of Christ
1733,
Being the First after LEAP YEAR:

By RICHARD SAUNDERS, Philom.

PHILADELPHIA:
Printed and sold by B. FRANKLIN, at the New
Printing-Office near the Market.

CHAPTER SUMMARY

★ Colonists began to show their sense of independence and responsibility in the 1700s. However, Great Britain wanted to regulate colonial trade for its own profit. This practice was called mercantilism.

★ Trading between the West Indies, Africa, and New England formed what is known as triangular trade. This trading was done independently from Great Britain. Africans and American Indians suffered from this trading practice.

★ Great Britain began enforcing the Navigation Acts passed in 1660 and 1663. The purpose of the acts was to regulate trade between the colonies and other countries. Great Britain passed a number of other laws related to trade. Most American merchants paid little attention to these laws.

★ Problems developed in 1649 between Great Britain and France over land claims in the Ohio Valley. George Washington was sent into the Ohio Valley in 1754 with soldiers to drive the French away from Fort Duquesne. Shots were exchanged, and Washington was forced to retreat. In 1755, American Indians and the French defeated General Braddock's army at Fort Duquesne. The British continued to lose a number of battles.

★ In 1758, King George appointed William Pitt as prime minister and secretary of state of Great Britain. Pitt sent troops to the colonies and formed an army of 50,000.

★ The British captured Fort Duquesne in 1758. The British later won more key battles, including the Battle of Quebec in 1759. France surrendered in 1760.

★ The Treaty of Paris was signed in 1763. France gave Great Britain all of the land east of the Mississippi River, except New Orleans. The area of Louisiana west of the Mississippi and New Orleans, which France had claimed, went to Spain. Great Britain got Florida from Spain in exchange for Cuba. France kept only two small islands south of Newfoundland and some islands off the West Indies.

Comprehension: Identifying Facts

On a separate sheet of paper, write the correct word or words from the Word Bank that matches each sentence below.

WORD BANK	
Battle of Quebec	mercantilism
Edward Braddock	Navigation Acts
Fort Duquesne	Ohio Valley
Fort Niagara	Treaty of Paris
George Washington	triangular trade
James Wolfe	William Pitt
Louis Montcalm	

1) Fort captured by the British in 1758

2) Became prime minister and secretary of state of Great Britain in 1758

3) Was sent to drive the French away from Fort Duquesne in 1754

4) Land that caused disputes between the French and British

5) Signed after the French and Indian War

6) Battle that forced France to surrender

7) Led the British attack on Quebec

8) Trade between Africa, the West Indies, and New England

9) French leader at the Battle of Quebec

10) British general who was killed at Fort Duquesne

11) British laws to regulate trade between the colonies and other countries

12) Practice of regulating colonial trade for the profit of the home country

13) Fort captured by Sir William Johnson

Comprehension: Understanding Main Ideas

On a separate sheet of paper, write the answers to the following questions using complete sentences.

1) How well were the British prepared for war?

2) How well were the French prepared for war?

3) Why was the Battle of Quebec important?

4) Who gained what land from the Treaty of Paris?

5) How did Great Britain's power change after the war?

Critical Thinking: Write Your Opinion

1) Though they hadn't achieved complete independence, the colonists began to appreciate feeling free to do things without outside controls. How are people independent today?

2) The French and Indian War was fought mostly because of land rights. What other things do you think cause war?

Test Taking Tip When studying for a test, review any tests or quizzes you took earlier that cover the same information.

SKILLS LESSON

Unit 2 Maps

To read a map, you need to understand its symbols. Most maps have a key, or legend, that explains the symbols.

☐ New England Colonies
☐ Middle Colonies
☐ Southern Colonies

Some maps are drawn exactly to scale. You can use the scale to find the actual distances on a map.

0   100   200   300 Miles

N W E S compass rose

Most maps show direction. A compass rose shows at least the four major directions–north, east, west, and south. Some compass roses also show northeast, southeast, northwest, and southwest. Some maps show direction only by using an arrow with the letter N to show the direction of north.

Many maps have lines of longtitude and latitude. Vertical (up and down) lines are longitude. Horizontal (across) lines are latitude. Zero degrees longitude goes through Greenwich, England. Zero degrees latitude is at the equator–the widest part of the globe.

0° Longitude
0° Latitude

There are many different kinds of maps. Each kind of map provides a different kind of information. Here are some examples of maps and what they show:

Physical map–Shows the roughness of Earth's surface, including mountains, rivers, and plains

Elevation map–Shows different heights of land above the level of the sea

Political map–Shows borders between countries and states or states and counties

Climate map–Shows different kinds of climates, including, hot, dry, cold, and wet

Natural resources map–Shows where natural resources such as minerals, oil, and natural gas are in an area

Choose the kind of map you would use to answer each question.

1) Which states have a hot, dry climate?

2) What country shares the northern border of the United States?

3) Where is the Charles River located?

4) Where is the most oil in the United States located?

5) Does North Carolina include any land at an elevation of 5,000 or more feet?

★ Jamestown colony was established in May 1607.

★ The Pilgrims formed a settlement in Plymouth in 1620.

★ The Puritans landed in 1630.

★ Lord Baltimore established a colony in 1634.

★ Roger Williams settled Providence, Rhode Island, in 1636.

★ Thomas Hooker started a settlement in Connecticut in 1636.

★ English nobles settled Carolina in 1663.

★ The English renamed a Dutch colony New York in 1664.

★ New Hampshire became a colony in 1679.

★ William Penn was granted a charter for the land between New York and Maryland in 1681. The colony was called Pennsylvania. In 1682, the Duke of York granted Penn a region known today as Delaware.

★ East Jersey and West Jersey united into New Jersey in 1702.

★ James Oglethorpe settled a colony in what is now Georgia in 1733.

★ Colonists showed independence and responsibility in the 1700s.

★ Enslaved Africans and American Indians suffered from triangular trading.

★ American merchants ignored Great Britain's trade laws around 1660.

★ Problems developed in 1649 between Great Britain and France.

★ In 1757, British troops were sent to the colonies.

★ France surrendered to the British in 1760.

★ The Treaty of Paris was signed in 1763. Land was divided among Great Britain, Spain, and France.

"O thus be it ever when freemen shall stand
Between their lov'd homes & the war's desolation!
Blest with vict'ry and peace may the heav'n rescued land
Praise the power that hath made & preserv'd us a nation!
Then conquer we must, when our cause it is just,
And this be our motto—"In God is our trust,"
And the star-spangled banner in triumph shall wave
O'er the land of the free & the home of the brave."

Francis Scott Key, "The Star-Spangled Banner," verse 3, 1814

Revolution and the New Nation

1763–1815

You probably find facing challenges is easier when you work together with others. If you were a colonist in the struggling new nation, you would need to cooperate. How would you work together to protect your new nation's freedom against threats from other nations? How would you band together to establish your government? How would you unite to defend your nation in wars?

In this unit you will learn about many challenges facing the young nation. You will learn how colonists protected the nation's independence. You will learn how they united to form a government. You will learn how the United States defended itself against other nations after it gained independence.

Chapter 5: A New Nation Begins to Grow: 1763-1775

Chapter 6: The American Revolution: 1775-1783

Chapter 7: A Government Is Formed: 1783-1791

Chapter 8: Political Parties Develop: 1788-1809

Chapter 9: The Young Nation Goes to War: 1809-1815

5

1763–1775

After the French and Indian War, Great Britain tightened its control over the colonies. The British began a series of actions against the colonies that the colonists did not welcome. In this chapter, you will learn what the British did to the colonists and how the colonists reacted.

Goals for Learning

▶ To explain the purpose of the Proclamation of 1763

▶ To identify the taxes the British placed on the colonists and how the colonists protested them

▶ To explain what caused the Boston Tea Party

▶ To describe the actions taken by the First Continental Congress

▶ To explain what occurred at Lexington and Concord

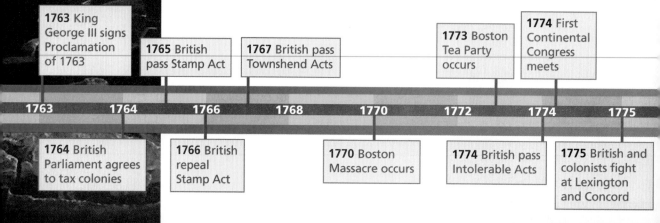

1763 King George III signs Proclamation of 1763

1765 British pass Stamp Act

1767 British pass Townshend Acts

1773 Boston Tea Party occurs

1774 First Continental Congress meets

1763   1764   1766   1768   1770   1772   1774   1775

1764 British Parliament agrees to tax colonies

1766 British repeal Stamp Act

1770 Boston Massacre occurs

1774 British pass Intolerable Acts

1775 British and colonists fight at Lexington and Concord

> **Relationship**
> *Two or more things or groups connected in some way*

British control of America was firmly established with the Treaty of Paris. However, the real hold that Great Britain had on the colonies was weak. New and different laws were passed in an effort to control trade. Colonial merchants and shippers found other ways of getting around those laws. Then new events affected the **relationship** between Great Britain and the colonies.

What Was the Proclamation of 1763?

The first problem was caused by an event that took place in the spring of 1763. Great numbers of colonists settled in the Ohio Valley, west of the Appalachian Mountains. An Ottawa chief, Pontiac, knew that more American Indian land was in

danger of being lost to British settlers. Chief Pontiac organized several American Indian nations and attacked colonial forts with some success.

To avoid further trouble with the American Indians, King George III signed the Proclamation of 1763. This act ordered all settlers to leave the Ohio Valley and return to the established colonies. It did not allow any more people to make new settlements west of the Appalachians. It said that no traders could enter the area without approval of the king.

Chief Pontiac led a rebellion of American Indians against colonial forts beginning in 1763.

The colonists were opposed to the new law. They had fought in the long French and Indian War. Now the law was saying that no one could go west. Many colonists felt that the king didn't really care about protecting them from the American Indians. They felt its real purpose was to prevent them from developing the new land. They also felt that they could fight their own battles with the American Indians. The Proclamation of 1763 was the first of several new controls to be forced on the colonies.

What Was Taxation Without Representation?

The next problem was the British debt from the French and Indian War. Supplies, ships, and soldiers had been very expensive. Some money had been raised by increasing taxes of people in Great Britain. The government had to find a way to pay off the debt without taxing the British taxpayers too much. In 1764, Parliament, the government of Great Britain, agreed that it had the right to tax the colonies in exchange for protection from all enemies. The colonists disagreed with this policy, saying they did not need any British help to protect themselves. As subjects of Great Britain, the colonists had no right to object to its rulings. Nevertheless, many felt this taxation without colonial agreement, or "taxation without representation," could not be **tolerated.** They began talking about a war over taxation.

What New British Policies Were Started?

George Grenville became prime minister of Great Britain in 1763. He decided it was necessary to get more money from the American colonies. The Sugar Act was passed in 1764. This act raised the tax on sugar, cloth goods, and other articles from any place other than Great Britain. The Currency Act, also passed in 1764, made it illegal for the colonies to print their own money. The Quartering Act was passed in 1765. This act demanded that the colonies provide housing and goods for all British soldiers in America. The Stamp Act was passed in 1765. The purpose of the act was to enable the government to tax **legal** and business papers used in America. It also taxed such items as playing cards and dice. Special stamp agents were appointed to sell the stamps and collect the taxes.

The colonists protested the Stamp Act. One way they protested was to **tar and feather** tax collectors. They covered the tax collectors with tar and then with feathers. Colonists burned legal papers and refused to pay the taxes. Also, they tried to force the removal of the Stamp Act by **boycotting** all British goods.

Riots took place in Boston as the colonists protested the Stamp Act of 1765.

★Repeal
To remove something, especially a law

A boycott occurs when a person, country, or group refuses to deal with another person, country, or group. Parliament decided to remove, or **repeal,** the tax in 1766.

The repeal of the Stamp Act pleased the colonists. The good feeling, however, did not last long. Shortly thereafter, Parliament passed the Declaratory Act. This act stated that Great Britain had control over the colonies in all cases.

SECTION 1 REVIEW Write answers to these questions on a separate sheet of paper using complete sentences.

1) Why did the British decide to tax the colonists?

2) Why did the colonists protest the Proclamation of 1763?

3) What was the attitude of the king toward the colonists?

4) Why did the colonists feel that taxation was unfair?

5) What was the Stamp Act and when was it passed?

What do you think **?**

Do you think Great Britain had the right to tax the colonists? Why or why not?

Finance
Having to do with money

Revenue
Money gained from something

Charles Townshend was appointed minister of **finance** in 1766. This put him in charge of finance for Great Britain. Like others before him, Townshend had little interest in the colonies. However, he saw them as a good source of **revenue** for Great Britain. Townshend was responsible for a new set of tax laws.

What Were the Townshend Acts?

The Townshend Acts were passed in 1767. These acts reduced the colonists' freedom to govern themselves. New taxes were placed on many items important to the colonists, including glass, paper, and tea. Protests became stronger than before. The colonists agreed to boycott British goods. Trade soon slowed down greatly.

The boycott hurt the British. It also caused serious problems for the colonial merchants. Many people lost their jobs in American ports where trade was important. For many people, it became harder to make a living and easier to be angry at the British.

What Fight Did Samuel Adams Lead?

Boston, the largest city in New England, soon became the center of action against this new British taxation policy. Samuel Adams, a member of the Massachusetts legislature, organized town meetings in Boston. A group called the Sons of Liberty, first set up in 1765 to protest the Stamp Act, took charge of the city. Great Britain sent extra regiments of troops to Boston to protect tax collectors. Fights broke out between soldiers and towns-people. By the beginning of 1770, about 4,000 British soldiers were in Boston. The soldiers were in daily contact with 16,000 Bostonians under Samuel Adams.

The Mason-Dixon Line

Two men, Charles Mason and Jeremiah Dixon, set up the boundary between Maryland and Pennsylvania between 1763-1767. This boundary is called the Mason-Dixon Line. After Mason and Dixon set up the boundary, it became a symbol of the division between the North and the South.

What Was the Boston Massacre?

One evening early in March of 1770, a crowd gathered near a group of British soldiers. The crowd began throwing stones and snowballs at the soldiers. The soldiers then fired a round of shots into the crowd. The first to fall was a free African, Crispus Attucks. A few colonists were killed, and several were wounded.

News of the Boston Massacre, as it was called, spread throughout the colonies. The people of Boston demanded that the British soldiers be removed from the city. The governor of Massachusetts agreed to remove the soldiers to prevent more trouble. The same day, all of the Townshend taxes were repealed except for the tax on tea. Great Britain had lost a good deal of money due to the boycotts. It was believed that the tax on tea was kept mainly as a symbol of the British right to rule.

This engraving by Paul Revere shows what the Boston Massacre may have looked like.

This diagram shows the area where the Boston Massacre took place. It shows the British soldiers (near the Custom House) and the places where four of the five killed colonists fell.

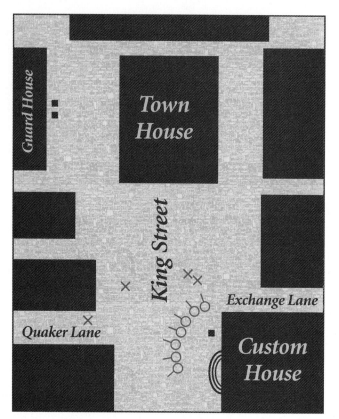

How Did the Colonists Organize and Protest?

The colonies steadily lost much of their earlier freedom. British governors, chosen by the king, could do as they pleased. They became very strict. Samuel Adams encouraged the leaders of cities to meet and talk about what to do about the British.

The committees wrote strong statements of American rights and complaints. The statements were given out all over the colonies. This helped to bring the colonists together in opposing their common enemy, the British.

Neither King George III nor Parliament took the colonists seriously. The king looked upon the colonies as weak and certainly as no match for the mighty British army and navy.

Writing About History

Research the Boston Massacre. Then write a first person account in your notebook about what happened at the Boston Massacre as if you were really there. Talk about how the event changed you as a person.

Phillis Wheatley was the first acknowledged African poet in America. A native of Africa, she was born around 1753. At age eight, she was kidnapped and taken on a slave ship to Boston. There she was purchased by a wealthy tailor as a servant for his wife. Unlike most enslaved Africans, Wheatley was allowed to learn to read and write English. She studied Greek mythology, history, and poetry. At age thirteen she wrote her first poem, "To the University of Cambridge in New England." Her first book was published when she was twenty. Despite her early reputation, she was very poor and practically unknown when she died at only age thirty.

SECTION 2 REVIEW On a separate sheet of paper, write the letter of the description in Part 2 that matches a name in Part 1.

Part 1

1) Charles Townshend

2) Samuel Adams

3) Boston Massacre

4) George III

5) Crispus Attucks

Part 2

a) killed in Boston Massacre

b) minister of finance for Great Britain

c) British soldiers shot into a crowd of colonists

d) Great Britain's king

e) led protests in Boston

What do you think ?

Do you think Samuel Adams was right to organize protests that often ended up in fights? Why or why not?

Cargo
Objects or goods carried in a ship or some other form of transportation

Competitor
A company that sells or buys the same goods or services as another company

★Duty
Tax placed on certain goods brought into a certain place

Impose
To establish a rule or law, such as a tax, on a group with less power

The British-controlled East India Trading Company sold tea. The company had to pay a tax to Great Britain on the tea before shipping it to other places. It could not afford to pay the tax, yet it would be ruined if it did not sell the tea.

What Was the British Tea Tax?

Frederick North, Great Britain's prime minister, came up with a plan. He wanted to ship the tea to America and then force the colonies to pay a **duty.** A duty is a tax placed on goods brought into a certain country or region. Lord North expected his plan to save the East India Trading Company from financial disaster and to bring in more revenue for Great Britain.

The colonists refused to pay this tax. They were afraid that soon all British merchants would pay no tax. As a result, the American **competitors** would go out of business. Samuel Adams organized the tea merchants who agreed to cancel all orders for tea. The colonists wanted to keep the tea from being unloaded to make sure that no tax would be paid.

Lord North and the king had clearly underestimated the strong feelings of the colonists. Adams made it clear the colonists would not accept a tax **imposed** without colonial consent.

What Was the Boston Tea Party?

A ship carrying tea arrived in Boston's harbor in early December 1773. The British governor of Boston was determined to have the tea unloaded and to collect the taxes. Adams was equally determined to keep the tea from being unloaded. A group of colonists dressed as Mohawk indians boarded the ship on the night of December 16, 1773. They promised not to harm the ship if the **cargo** was made available to them. The captain agreed, and the Boston Tea Party began.

Ban
To disallow something

Outrage
Anger

Resistance
The act of opposing something

Respond
To do or say something in return

Similar
Alike in some ways

More than 300 chests containing 90,000 pounds of tea were dumped into the harbor. The large crowd was sure that no spies were close at hand to observe the "party." **Similar** incidents took place in other cities. In Charleston, South Carolina, the tea was allowed to rot in damp cellars. In Annapolis, Maryland, the ship carrying tea was burned. The colonial **resistance** to British taxation had spread throughout the colonies.

The Boston Tea Party was a protest against the British Tea Tax.

How Did the British React to the Tea Party?

Some colonists did not agree with the actions taken in Boston, Charleston, and Annapolis. Many felt that dumping tea, burning a ship, and allowing tea to rot were not proper ways to protest. Some merchants even offered to pay for the tea that had been destroyed. **Outraged** by the events, the king and Parliament paid no attention to these loyal colonists.

The British **responded** to the colonists' actions by passing the Intolerable Acts in 1774. These acts allowed Great Britain to close the port of Boston to all trade, **ban** town meetings, and house British troops in people's homes.

Then and Now

LODGING

If you were a man in colonial times, you might go to a local tavern for business, social, or political gatherings. As a woman then, however, you might be a tavern keeper but not a customer. As a colonial traveler, you would get on or off stagecoaches at taverns. On a journey, you could get a good meal and lodging at a tavern. You might share a room and even a bed with more than one stranger. Sharing a bed in winter was practical because it kept you warm after the fire went out. You could expect an uncomfortable bed. Linens were not changed often because they were expensive. Today, you expect a comfortable bed and fresh sheets and towels daily. You expect a private room in a motel or hotel. You DON'T expect the proprietor will assign two or more strangers to the same room.

*Province
A part of a country or region

The acts said that British soldiers accused of breaking the law would be tried in Great Britain. Parliament also passed the Quebec Act. This act extended the Canadian **province** of Quebec into the Ohio Valley. A province is a part of a country or region. The act forced the colonists to stay to the east. The British intended to test how badly the colonists wanted to govern themselves.

SECTION 3 REVIEW Write answers to these questions on a separate sheet of paper using complete sentences.

1) What plan did Frederick North have?

2) Why did the colonists object to Frederick North's plan?

3) When and why did the Boston Tea Party take place?

4) Did all of the colonists approve of what happened at the Tea Party? Why?

5) How did the British respond to the Tea Party?

What do you think ?

Why do you think the Intolerable Acts said that British soldiers accused of crimes would be tried in Great Britain and not in the colonies?

★Convention
A formal meeting called for a special purpose

Debate
An argument or discussion among persons or a group

★Patriot
Someone who loves his or her own country

Submission
The act of giving up on something

Unify
To join together as a group or whole

The British actions against Boston increased the colonists' need to be more **unified** against the king. Samuel Adams wanted to find ways to bring about more changes. Earlier protests had brought changes. He decided that a meeting, or congress, of representatives from all the colonies should be held.

Why Did the First Continental Congress Meet?

Adams invited all the colonies to a **convention** in Philadelphia. A convention is a formal meeting called for a special purpose. This Continental Congress would help to bring about a better understanding of possible actions against the king. The meeting was called a Continental Congress because the British referred to Americans as Continentals.

All of the colonies except Georgia elected delegates to the Congress. Fifty-six outstanding men attended, including George Washington, Patrick Henry, Samuel Adams, John Adams, and John Jay. These **patriots** were well educated and were leaders in their colonies. A patriot is someone who loves his or her own country.

The Continental Congress was held in Carpenter's Hall in Philadelphia in September of 1774. The delegates **debated** important issues for seven weeks. They agreed that a Declaration of Rights should be adopted and sent to the king. The Declaration made it clear that taxation by the British would be unacceptable to the colonies. The Congress also agreed to boycott British goods. This boycott was to be strictly enforced by select committees. Another Continental Congress would be held on May 10, 1775, if the king rejected the Declaration of Rights.

The king and Parliament became furious when they received this declaration. They replied that the colonists, should they resist, would be crushed into **submission.**

Colonial minutemen were called to battle when word got out that British soldiers were coming.

★Minutemen
A group of men trained to be soldiers and who agreed to gather at a minute's notice

A few British leaders warned Parliament that changes needed to be made. The king and Parliament refused to listen to these men.

What Happened at Lexington and Concord?

American leaders Samuel Adams, John Hancock, and Patrick Henry were sure that the colonists would have to fight for freedom. A group of men had to be trained to be soldiers since the colonists had no organized army. They were called **minutemen** because they agreed to gather at a minute's notice and become soldiers.

General Gage, the military governor of Massachusetts, became aware of the colonists' plans. He had ordered a regiment under Major Pitcairn to seize all military supplies, including a gunpowder supply, stored at Concord. They had also been instructed to travel to Lexington and capture the rebel leaders.

The patriots learned about the British plans. Paul Revere and William Dawes warned the colonists of their attack by riding through Massachusetts on horseback. Revere was

The British reached Lexington first. Even though British troops later fought minutemen at Concord, most of the fighting took place at Lexington.

The First Theater in America

Fine Arts

History in Your Life

Pennsylvania was one of the thirteen British colonies when David Douglass built the Southwark Theatre in 1766. It was the first permanent theater in America. Located in Philadelphia, the Southwark was constructed of brick and wood. Oil lamps lighted its earliest productions. On April 24, 1767, Douglass presented the first professionally produced play by an American-born playwright—Thomas Godfrey's *The Prince of Parthia*.

When the Revolutionary War ended, Congress passed laws against "play acting." Theater director Lewis Hallam skirted the laws by presenting what he called "moral lectures." The Southwark's American Company of Comedians dominated American theater until it was disbanded in 1805. The Southwark closed in 1817 and was torn down in 1912. Still, it had launched a thriving tradition of regional and local theater throughout America.

captured by the British and Dawes was forced to flee toward Lexington. However, Samuel Prescott, a third rider, continued the journey to Concord. He warned colonists that the British were approaching. The colonists rushed to meet the British at Lexington.

Major Pitcairn reached Lexington on April 18, 1775. He was surprised to find about 70 armed minutemen waiting for him. Both sides fired shots and a number of people were injured or killed. These shots were later to be described as "the shots heard 'round the world." The war with Great Britain was about to begin.

SECTION 4 REVIEW Write answers to these questions on a separate sheet of paper using complete sentences.

1) What was the purpose of the First Continental Congress?

2) How could the delegates at the Congress best be described?

3) What action did the Continental Congress take?

4) Who were minutemen?

5) What did Paul Revere, William Dawes, and Samuel Prescott do?

What do you think ?

Do you think the colonists or the British were better prepared for war? Why?

The Stamp Act

The road toward independence in the United States was long. As the colonies grew in size and economic power, they became more valuable to England. The British passed many acts to control trade with the colonies. These acts made the colonists increasingly angry. The colonists rebelled when the Stamp Act was passed in 1765. They refused to pay the tax. The colonists were unified in their outrage, and they reacted in violent opposition.

"For every skin or piece of vellum or parchment, or sheet or piece of paper, on which shall be engrossed, written or printed, any declaration, plea, replication, rejoinder, demurrer, or other pleading, or any copy thereof, in any court of law within the British colonies and plantations in America, a stamp duty of three pence.

. . . And for and upon every pack of playing cards, and all dice, which shall be sold or used . . . the several stamp duties following (that is to say)

For every pack of such cards, the sum of one shilling.

And for every pair of such dice, the sum of ten shillings.

For every such pamphlet and paper being larger than half a sheet, and not exceeding one whole sheet . . . a stamp duty of one penny, for every printed copy thereof.

For every almanack or calendar, for any one particular year, or for any time less than a year, which shall be written or printed on one side only of any one sheet, skin, or piece of paper parchment, or vellum . . . a stamp duty of two pence."

Source Reading Wrap-Up

1) Why did England want to hold on to the American colonies?

2) When was the Stamp Act passed?

3) In your judgment, which of the taxed items listed would disturb the colonists the most?

4) The Stamp Act was removed in 1766. Why was this a great victory for the colonists?

5) How would you feel about the Stamp Act if you were a colonist at this time?

★ King George III signed the Proclamation of 1763, which ordered all settlers to leave the Ohio Valley. The colonists were strongly opposed to the new law.

★ In 1764, the British Parliament agreed that it had the right to tax the colonies in exchange for protection from all enemies. The colonists disagreed with this policy.

★ The British passed the Stamp Act in 1765. This enabled the British government to tax all legal and business papers used in America and other items. The colonists protested the Stamp Act. Parliament repealed it in 1766.

★ The British passed the Townshend Acts in 1767. These acts reduced the colonists' freedom to govern themselves. The acts included new taxes on many items important to the colonists, including glass, paper, and tea. The colonists agreed to boycott British goods.

★ In 1770, a crowd of people threw stones and snowballs at a group of British soldiers. The soldiers shot into the crowd, killing and wounding several colonists. This became known as the Boston Massacre. Crispus Attucks, an African, was the first person killed in the event.

★ A group of colonists dressed as Mohawk people boarded a ship carrying tea on the night of December 16, 1773. They dumped over 90,000 pounds of tea into Boston Harbor. This became known as the Boston Tea Party. Similar incidents took place in other cities.

★ The king and Parliament passed the Intolerable Acts in 1774. These acts allowed Great Britain to close the port of Boston to all trade, ban town meetings, and house British troops in people's homes. They also said that British soldiers accused of breaking the law would be tried in Great Britain.

★ The First Continental Congress met in 1774 and wrote the Declaration of Rights. It agreed to meet in 1775 if Great Britain rejected the declaration.

★ The British fought a small group of American minutemen at Lexington and Concord in 1775. Many people were injured or killed.

Comprehension: Identifying Facts

On a separate sheet of paper, write the correct word from the Word Bank to complete the sentences.

WORD BANK	
Boston Massacre	Lexington and Concord
Boston Tea Party	Proclamation of 1763
Currency Act	Quebec Act
Declaration of Rights	Stamp Act
	Sugar Act
Declaratory Act	Townshend Acts
Intolerable Acts	

1) The _____ ordered all settlers to leave the Ohio Valley and return to the established colonies.

2) The _____ raised the tax on sugar and cloth goods.

3) The _____ enabled the British government to tax legal and business papers used in America.

4) The _____ stated that the British had control over the colonies in all cases.

5) The _____ placed new taxes on many items important to the colonists, including glass, paper, and tea.

6) The _____ extended the Canadian province of Quebec into the Ohio Valley.

7) British soldiers fired into a crowd of people in an event called the _____.

8) A group of colonists dressed as Mohawks dumped British tea into a harbor in an event called the _____.

9) The _____ made it illegal for the colonies to print their own money.

10) The _____ allowed Great Britain to close the port of Boston to all trade, ban town meetings, house British troops in people's homes, and require that British soldiers accused of any unlawful act be tried in Great Britain.

11) The First Continental Congress wrote the _____.

12) British soldiers and American minutemen fought at _____.

Comprehension: Understanding Main Ideas

On a separate sheet of paper, write the answers to the following questions using complete sentences.

1) What did Chief Pontiac do?

2) What was the purpose of the Proclamation of 1763?

3) What caused the Boston Tea Party?

4) What action did the First Continental Congress take?

5) Who were minutemen?

6) What happened at Lexington and Concord?

Critical Thinking: Write Your Opinion

1) The colonists showed many ways to protest against the British. Some ways were violent and some were nonviolent. What are some nonviolent ways to protest that are used today? Which one do you think is most effective? Why?

2) How could a country fight for freedom yet enslave other people?

| Test Taking Tip | Studying together in small groups and asking questions of one another is one way to review material for tests. |

6

1775–1783

Lexington and Concord were the first of many battles between the colonists and the British. The colonists were determined to win their independence. The British were just as determined to keep the colonies under their control. The result was war—the American Revolutionary War—which lasted for over eight years. In this chapter, you will learn about what happened in that war.

Goals for Learning

▶ To explain what events immediately followed Lexington and Concord

▶ To identify what actions the Second Continental Congress took

▶ To describe why the Declaration of Independence was written

▶ To explain the strengths and weaknesses of the colonists and the British

▶ To explain how the Battle of Saratoga was a turning point in the war

▶ To explain how the colonists won the war

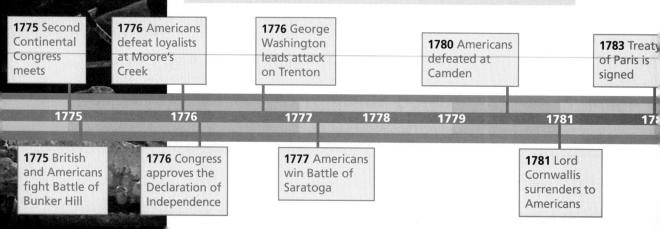

1775 Second Continental Congress meets

1776 Americans defeat loyalists at Moore's Creek

1776 George Washington leads attack on Trenton

1780 Americans defeated at Camden

1783 Treaty of Paris is signed

1775　　1776　　1777　　1778　　1779　　1781　　178

1775 British and Americans fight Battle of Bunker Hill

1776 Congress approves the Declaration of Independence

1777 Americans win Battle of Saratoga

1781 Lord Cornwallis surrenders to Americans

Disarm
To take weapons away from someone

★**Militia**
An organized group of citizens who serve as soldiers in times of war

News of the Lexington and Concord incidents spread rapidly throughout the colonies. The colonists became upset when they heard that British soldiers burned houses and fired upon innocent people. They were proud of the courage the minutemen showed in trying to prevent the British from reaching Lexington and Concord. The British did not capture Samuel Adams or John Hancock. The colonists had proved they were equal to the British and could fight for their rights.

Meanwhile, the British had seized a store of gunpowder in Virginia. Colonists were sure the British intended to **disarm** them completely. They knew they couldn't let that happen. Thus, the colonists prepared for possible attacks. They seized military supplies in New York intended for British soldiers. They prevented ships from trading with Great Britain or any of its colonies. New Jersey, Pennsylvania, the Carolinas, and Maryland worked to increase their **militia.** A militia is an organized group of citizens who serve as soldiers in times of war. The colonies were working together for a common cause—freedom.

Which British Forts Did the Americans Seize?
Massachusetts was the first colony to take military action. The leaders wanted to protect their own people. Beyond that, they thought they must take control of two major British strongholds—Fort Ticonderoga and Fort Crown Point. These forts, at the entrance to Canada, contained a large amount of military supplies.

Ethan Allen and his Green Mountain Boys of Vermont seized both forts without a shot being fired. The British, who were not prepared to fight, surrendered quickly. In this important victory, the colonists obtained badly needed cannons and a huge supply of ammunition.

When Did the Second Continental Congress Meet?

On May 10, 1775—the same day that Fort Ticonderoga was seized—the Second Continental Congress began in Philadelphia. A new delegate named John Hancock was chosen as its president. The only other new delegates were Thomas Jefferson of Virginia and Benjamin Franklin of Pennsylvania. Franklin had just returned from Great Britain after **resigning** his duties as colonial agent there.

Many colonists who wanted some peaceful way to settle the problem sent a **petition** to the king. A petition is a written paper asking for a right or benefit from someone in power. Their petition stated that they were still loyal to the king but would not accept unfair British laws. The king did not change any policies.

The Americans now had to choose between giving in to the king and fighting a war for freedom. As they had shown at Boston, Lexington, and Concord, they were not afraid to stand up to the British.

SECTION 1 REVIEW Write the answers to these questions on a separate sheet of paper using complete sentences.

1) How did the colonists react to Lexington and Concord?

2) How did the colonists prove they were equal to the British army?

3) What did the colonists do to prevent being disarmed?

4) Why was capturing Fort Ticonderoga and Fort Crown Point important for the colonists?

5) What peaceful way to solve the problem with the British did some colonists try?

What do you think ❓

Why do you think the king did not do anything in response to petitions from the colonists?

★**Commander**
Someone who controls an army or some other military group

Interfere
To enter into or take part in other people's business

Loyalty
The act of being faithful to someone

★**Pardon**
An official statement forgiving someone of something

Plea
The act of asking for something

★**Postmaster**
Person who runs the post office

Congress knew it would have to create some form of central government. After many days of debate, the delegates agreed that Congress had the power to do certain things. Congress had the power to provide for protection against future British attacks. It could declare war. It would not **interfere** in the private matters of the colonies. Each colony wanted to protect the personal freedoms of its people.

The delegates moved to organize an army. Several leaders were considered as the possible chief **commander.** A commander is a leader of a military group. One member of Congress stood out as the best choice. A vote was taken, and George Washington was officially made commander in chief of the American army. They sent out a **plea** to the colonies for troops and money to pay for the war effort.

While the war itself was beginning, Congress took other steps as a central, unified governing body. It set up a colonial post office, naming Benjamin Franklin as its **postmaster.** A postmaster runs the post office. Congress sent agents to other countries to ask for their help. It organized a navy to attack approaching British ships. It reopened ports to trading with any country but Great Britain.

How Was Boston Recovered?

After the fighting at Lexington and Concord, thousands of minutemen had been waiting in camps around Boston. The governor of Boston, General Gage, issued an order that put Boston under complete control of the British army. Gage also offered **pardons** to all colonials who would pledge their **loyalty** to the king. A pardon is an official statement forgiving someone of something. The pardon did not apply to John Hancock or Samuel Adams. No one came forward to accept a pardon.

Colonial and British losses were heavy at the Battle of Bunker Hill.

General Gage knew he had to protect the area in Boston known as Dorchester Heights. He planned to arm Bunker Hill and Breed's Hill against colonial attack. The colonials learned of Gage's plan and quickly responded. American soldiers worked all through the night to fortify Breed's Hill. The hill became the Americans' first line of defense.

On June 17, 1775, British warships in Boston Harbor opened an attack on Breed's Hill and Bunker Hill. The British expected an easy victory. The colonial soldiers held their ground.

British general William Howe led another attack. With little gunpowder, the Americans held their fire until the British were very close. The British suffered great losses and retreated. There was another British attack, and then the colonials retreated. The British captured Breed's Hill and Bunker Hill. The losses were heavy on both sides, including several British officers. After the battle, one British general said, "One more victory like this one, and we will have lost the war."

Two weeks after this battle, called the Battle of Bunker Hill, General Washington reorganized and drilled the troops. The following spring, the Americans seized Dorchester Heights.

Then and Now

Did you know that the first known wartime submarine attack occurred during the Revolutionary War? David Bushnell, a college student at Yale, had designed a one-person submarine. It was powered by a hand-held propeller. As you might expect, when Bushnell tried to sink a British warship in New York Harbor in 1776, his mission failed.

U.S. Navy submarines today are very different from Bushnell's. They are at least 300 feet long and require 150 crew members. They have atomic-powered engines and carry torpedoes and guided missiles. Today, submarines find their targets by sending out sound waves that bounce off enemy ships.

The Press and the American Revolution

Isaiah Thomas was an editor, a printer, and one of the leaders in the colonial "underground." The underground was printers, publishers, and editors who convinced the colonists to revolt against the British. Thomas's newspaper stories and a cartoon helped people decide to fight for independence.

Thomas started as an apprentice printer at age six to help support his widowed mother. At seventeen, he and his former boss founded the newspaper, *The Massachusetts Spy*. Across the top of his paper he drew a cartoon of a divided snake facing a dragon. The divided snake represented the colonies. The dragon represented Great Britain. Underneath the snake was the slogan, "Join or Die."

Thomas was one of the men who flashed the signal light from Old North Church to warn that the British were coming. The next day he watched the first battle in the Revolutionary War and wrote a story about it.

So the British wouldn't shut him down, Thomas had to smuggle his newspaper out of Boston. He moved to Worcester, Massachusetts, and became the leading publisher of the time.

The Americans brought in cannons captured at Fort Ticonderoga. Now they could control the harbor below. General Howe viewed his position as hopeless. Quietly the British army and many people loyal to the British made their way to Halifax, Nova Scotia. They left Boston to the Americans.

SECTION 2 REVIEW Write the answers to these questions on a separate sheet of paper using complete sentences.

1) What task did Congress give to George Washington?

2) What task did Congress give to Benjamin Franklin?

3) Why did Congress send out a plea to the colonists?

4) What did General Gage offer to colonists who pledged loyalty to the king?

5) Why did the colonists fortify Breed's Hill?

What do you think ?

What did the British general mean when he said after Bunker Hill, "One more victory like this one, and we will have lost the war"?

Invade
To attack or take over something

Location
The place where something is positioned

★Loyalist
American who supported the king of Great Britain

Orator
One who is good at public speaking

★Statesman
Someone who knows and practices government ideas

Congress learned in late 1775 that the British were forming an army in Canada. They became concerned that the British could **invade** New York from the North. Congress agreed to a plan to capture Montreal and Quebec. They hoped that American troops would receive help from the French colonists in Quebec.

General Richard Montgomery led the march to Montreal and captured the city. From Montreal, he led troops to Quebec, meeting Colonel Benedict Arnold and more troops along the way. Because of its **location,** Quebec was not an easy city to capture. The Americans lost the battle. General Montgomery was killed, and Colonel Arnold was severely wounded.

The failed attack on Canada was offset by a victory in North Carolina. Americans defeated British **loyalists** at Moore's Creek, North Carolina, in February 1776. Loyalists were Americans who supported the king. The victory was important for two reasons. First, the loyalists' desire to fight was greatly decreased. Also, the good news of victory raised the spirits of the Americans. Not long after that victory, the Americans were successful in turning back a naval attack on Charleston, South Carolina.

What Was the Declaration of Independence?

Richard Henry Lee of Virginia made a speech to Congress in June 1776. He stated, "these United Colonies are, and of right ought to be free and independent states." Separating from Great Britain was a big step for the colonists to take. Many still hoped that Great Britain would cooperate. Samuel Adams of Massachusetts and Patrick Henry of Virginia knew the British would not change their policy of strict colonial control. Henry was an **orator** and **statesman.** A statesman is someone who knows and practices government ideas. To both men, the war had already begun. Henry voiced his opinion loud and clear: "Separate and fight! The war has already begun!"

Patrick Henry, addressing the Virginia Assembly, called for war.

A committee was formed to write a formal letter to announce the decision that Congress reached. Thomas Jefferson wrote the **document** and presented it to Congress in late June of 1776. After some debate and a few changes, the Declaration of Independence was approved. Jefferson considered many facts when writing the Declaration. Even though Jefferson owned enslaved Africans, one point he wanted to include was the end to slavery. However, some southern and northern delegates disagreed. They refused to sign the Declaration if the slave **clause** remained. To save the Declaration, Jefferson removed the clause. As of July 4, 1776, the thirteen colonies considered themselves to be free states. Next, the states would have to unite and form a government in order to fight the British.

The Declaration of Independence was signed in this building—Carpenter's Hall—in Philadelphia, Pennsylvania.

The Declaration of Independence can be found in Appendix A of this textbook.

SECTION 3 REVIEW Choose the best word or name in parentheses to complete each sentence. Write your answers on a separate sheet of paper.

1) Congress was concerned that the British could invade (New York, Montreal, Quebec) from the North.

2) (Richard Henry Lee, Samuel Adams, Richard Montgomery) captured Montreal.

3) The Americans defeated the (American Indians, loyalists, British) at Moore's Creek.

4) (Patrick Henry, Thomas Jefferson, Samuel Adams) wrote the Declaration of Independence.

5) Some delegates refused to sign the Declaration of Independence if the (slave, freedom, independence) clause remained.

What do you think ?

Why do you think the Declaration of Independence was an important step for the Americans?

★Revolution
The act of overthrowing and replacing a government

At the beginning of the **Revolutionary** War, there were clear differences between the British and colonial forces. Key strengths and weaknesses helped decide the outcome of the war.

How Did the British Take New York City?

George Washington moved several thousand American soldiers to New York. He was sure the British would try to take control of the New York harbor. If the British were successful, the colonies would be split into two parts and greatly weakened.

British general William Howe and his brother, Admiral Richard Howe, arrived on Staten Island in the New York harbor in late July 1776. General Washington had been correct, and he was prepared to defend the city. Meanwhile, King George III offered one last chance for peace.

General Howe announced that all crimes against Great Britain would be pardoned if the people would surrender. The king's offer angered the Americans.

General Howe prepared his large army for battle. They attacked with full force. The Americans were driven off Long Island.

Colonial Strengths and Weaknesses

Strengths	Weaknesses
• Had a strong leader in George Washington	• Had little money and depended on other countries for supplies
• Were used to frontier life and using firearms	• One third of Americans were British loyalists
• Had military experience from the French and Indian War	• Had a weak navy
• Were fighting for their independence on their own soil	

British Strengths and Weaknesses

Strengths	Weaknesses
• Had well-trained soldiers, expert leaders, and the finest equipment	• Were not used to frontier style of American warfare
• Had a powerful navy	• Had to fight far from home
• Could pay other countries to fight for them	• Were fighting with France, Spain, and the Netherlands at the same time
• Had help from British loyalists	

The British hanged Nathan Hale when they captured him in Long Island.

★Hessian
A soldier paid by the British to fight the Americans

★Siege
An event in which an army prevents people in a fort or city from leaving; this is done to attempt to capture the fort or city

Nathan Hale was a young former teacher who had proved himself at Boston and now in this **siege** at New York. A siege is an army preventing people in a fort or city from leaving. This is done to attempt to capture the fort or city. Hale offered to go behind the enemy lines on Long Island to gain information for General Washington. Unfortunately, he was caught and ordered by General Howe to be hanged. According to legend, as he was about to die, he said, "I only regret that I have but one life to lose for my country."

The Americans were forced beyond New York City. George Washington realized that he could not win the battle. He led a retreat across the Hudson River. This prevented the remaining members of his army from being captured or killed.

Washington led a surprise attack on Trenton, New Jersey, on December 25, 1776. He guided his troops through a blinding storm across the ice-clogged Delaware River. He defeated a group of soldiers called **Hessians.** The Hessians had been hired by the British to fight the Americans.

A Push Toward Freedom

In January of 1776, Thomas Paine wrote a pamphlet titled "Common Sense." Paine had recently come to the colonies from Great Britain. In the pamphlet, he pointed out how foolish it was for a small island 3,000 miles away to be controlling an entire continent. The pamphlet helped start the push for independence in the colonies.

The Nail-Making Machine

Researchers believe that the first nails were made in the Middle East about five thousand years ago. Nail making was a slow process for many hundreds of years. The handmade nails had squared, tapered sides. They often split the wood pieces they were to hold together. Thus, to avoid using any nails at all, carpenters learned to use wooden pegs or fitted interlocking pieces.

In the 1700s, American inventors worked on a nail-making machine. Ezekiel Reed patented the first one in 1786. His machine made better nails than those hammered by hand or cut from large sheets of iron. Unfortunately, his nails were too expensive for wide use. Within a decade, Jacob Perkins improved on Reed's invention. Perkins's machine cut and put heads on nails in one operation. Soon the price of nails dropped from twenty-five to eight cents a pound. Nails are now a common item in our everyday life.

Washington and his men went on toward Princeton, New Jersey. One week later, they defeated three enemy regiments at Princeton. At this time when Americans needed hope, the two victories were of great importance.

SECTION 4 REVIEW On a separate sheet of paper, write *True* if the statement is true or *False* if the statement is not true.

1) General Washington was sure the British would try to take Richmond.

2) William Howe was a British general.

3) Washington ordered Nathan Hale to be hanged.

4) Washington led a retreat from New York across the Princeton River.

5) The British paid Hessians to fight the Americans.

What do you think ?

Why do you think the British paid the Hessians to fight rather than use their own soldiers?

Compromise
A settlement of differences in which each side gives up some of its demands

Isolate
To set apart from others

Proposal
A suggestion for others to consider

★**Three-pronged attack**
An attack in three separate places against an enemy

The British wanted to **isolate** New England from the other colonies. If the British controlled New York, this could be done. General Howe planned a **three-pronged attack** in October 1777. A three-pronged attack is an attack in three separate places against an enemy. The plan was carefully laid out: General John Burgoyne would march from Canada. Colonel Barry St. Leger would attack from the East. General Howe would reinforce from the South. The British intended to destroy the American army once and for all.

This plan, however, proved to be a total failure. Colonel St. Leger was met with great resistance and could not make much progress. General Howe did not send reinforcements as planned. Instead, he sent his army to attack Philadelphia. At Saratoga, the Americans met General Burgoyne and defeated his army. He surrendered to Horatio Gates, the American general.

News of the Saratoga defeat shocked the British. They wondered what they could do to make peace with the colonials. The king's earlier **proposal** to pardon and forgive the New York colonists had not been accepted. The Americans were demanding complete self-government. A peaceful **compromise** was no longer possible.

Writing About History

Find information about a battle in the Revolutionary War. Then write an article in your notebook about the battle as if you are a newspaper journalist. Explain who fought the battle, where it was fought, and why it was significant.

The British defeat at Saratoga caused a debate in France. Benjamin Franklin had asked the French for both military help and money. The French were not willing to provide aid. They thought the American army was weak and would lose to the British. After the American victory at Saratoga, however, the French decided to help the colonies.

Conditions were difficult for the American army at Valley Forge.

What Happened at Valley Forge?

Washington tried to keep Howe's army from taking Philadelphia. However, Washington was badly defeated at Brandywine. When Howe's men moved into Philadelphia, Washington struck again. This time the Americans were stopped at Germantown. Washington retreated with his surviving men, setting up winter quarters at Valley Forge. It was a bitter winter. The troops suffered many hardships such as poor shelter, no warm clothes, small amounts of food, and irregular pay. Despite the situation, Washington was able to keep his troops together.

General Howe was called to Great Britain in the spring of 1778 to explain why he had not won the war. Meanwhile, Howe's replacement, Henry Clinton, was on his way to Philadelphia. Upon arriving, he immediately **evacuated** the troops. France was sending a fleet of ships to aid the Americans.

Evacuate
To move away from a dangerous area

What Victories Did the Americans Win?

Wanting to concentrate British strength in one area, Clinton moved his troops on to New York. Washington and his men left Valley Forge to follow the British army. In a battle at Monmouth, the Americans almost succeeded in defeating the British. Clinton's army managed to escape to New York. There, Washington and his men contained the British for most of the rest of the war.

Meanwhile, the British had persuaded the American Indians to attack American settlements on the western frontier. In response, Virginia Governor Patrick Henry sent George Rogers Clark into the Ohio Valley to stop these raids. Clark was an experienced frontiersman who knew the region well. He marched his soldiers through the wilderness. Clark captured the British forts at Kaskaskia, Cahokia, and Vincennes. His outstanding leadership and courage helped the Americans control the West.

SECTION 5 REVIEW Complete the sentences below using words from the Word Bank. Write your answers on a separate sheet of paper.

WORD BANK		
Clinton	Saratoga	Vincennes
Howe	Valley Forge	

1) General Washington set up winter quarters at _____.

2) General _____ planned a three-pronged attack.

3) The Americans defeated the British at _____.

4) General _____ led the British army at Monmouth.

5) The Americans captured a British fort at _____.

What do you think **?**

Why do you think General Howe's three-pronged attack failed?

Convict
To find someone guilty of a crime

★**Traitor**
Someone who turns against his or her own country

Before the French fleet came to America's aid, the colonists had only a few warships. They had a few small merchant vessels that had been fitted with guns. The French ships brought military supplies from Europe. They attacked British ships on their way to the colonies. By the end of the war, they had captured or destroyed over 700 British vessels.

American Captain John Paul Jones became a naval hero. He successfully raided many towns along the coast of Great Britain. He also scored a naval victory in a battle with the British warship *Serapis* in September of 1779. Jones's ship was sinking, and the British ordered him to surrender. His reply was, "I have not yet begun to fight!" He captured the *Serapis* and sailed it to safety. This victory still stands as an example for the present-day United States Navy.

What Did Benedict Arnold Do?

Benedict Arnold had fought in the battles of Quebec and Saratoga. He had shown strong military ability and courage. General Washington appointed him to command West Point, the strongest and most important fort in America. However, Arnold felt that he was not getting enough credit. He plotted to turn West Point over to Great Britain. In return, he was promised a high British army rank.

Plans for the takeover were to be delivered to Arnold by John André, a major in the British army. On the way, Major André was stopped by three men and searched. They found the plans he had hidden in his boot heel. Major André was tried, **convicted** as a spy, and hanged. Benedict Arnold escaped to Great Britain, where he spent his remaining years in shame as an American **traitor**. A traitor is someone who turns against his or her own country.

Inland
A region of land that is far away from the coast

Lure
To draw in someone or something by hinting of gain

Occupy
To take control of a place

Redeem
To release from blame for something by doing something else better

★Sharpshooting
The ability to shoot a gun with great success

How Were the British Defeated?

The British captured the ports of Savannah and Charleston. In 1780, an American army fell to these determined British at Camden, South Carolina. However, a force of militiamen skilled at frontier **sharpshooting** beat the British back at Kings Mountain, North Carolina. Sharpshooting is the ability to shoot a gun with great success.

General Nathaniel Greene **lured** the British Army, led by Lord Cornwallis, **inland** in North Carolina. Greene's army weakened the British army. Greene then recaptured most of the inland positions previously **occupied** by the British.

Lord Cornwallis invaded Virginia in an effort to **redeem** himself. However, the Americans pushed him back. Cornwallis moved his men north to Yorktown, Virginia. There he hoped the British navy would provide him with supplies and protect his position.

Washington decided to move to the South for a surprise attack. Count Francois Joseph Paul de Grasse intended to move his French fleet up into the Chesapeake Bay. With Count de Grasse controlling the bay and Washington attacking from the North, Cornwallis had no way to escape.

Cornwallis tried to retreat to the West. There he was cut off by a young French officer, the Marquis de Lafayette. The British fought hard, but they had too few men. On October 19, 1781, Cornwallis surrendered.

When Great Britain's Lord North heard of the defeat of Cornwallis, he reportedly said, "It is all over." Lord North was removed from his office. The new government was prepared to make peace and give in to the Americans' demands for independence. The war had come to an end.

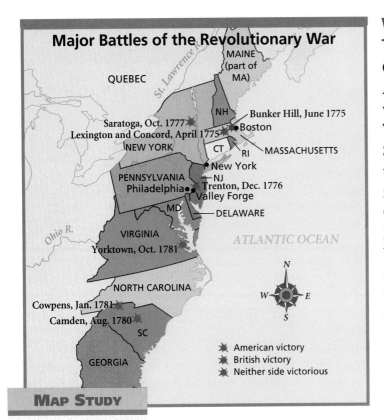

Major Battles of the Revolutionary War

QUEBEC

MAINE (part of MA)

NH

Saratoga, Oct. 1777
Lexington and Concord, April 1775

Bunker Hill, June 1775
Boston

NEW YORK

CT
RI
MASSACHUSETTS

New York

PENNSYLVANIA
Philadelphia

NJ
Trenton, Dec. 1776
Valley Forge

MD

DELAWARE

Ohio R.

VIRGINIA
Yorktown, Oct. 1781

ATLANTIC OCEAN

NORTH CAROLINA

Cowpens, Jan. 1781
Camden, Aug. 1780

SC

GEORGIA

American victory
British victory
Neither side victorious

St. Lawrence R.

N
W   E
S

MAP STUDY

What are five battles shown on this map? Which battles did the Americans win?

What Was the Treaty of Paris?

Great Britain recognized America's independence with the signing of the Treaty of Paris on September 3, 1783. The treaty established the new nation's boundaries— Canada on the North, the Mississippi River on the West, and Florida on the South. Great Britain was forced to return Florida to Spain. France gained nothing.

SECTION 6 REVIEW Choose the best word in parentheses to complete each sentence. Write your answers on a separate sheet of paper.

1) John Paul Jones was a(n) (British, American, French) sea captain.

2) (John Paul Jones, Benedict Arnold, Nathaniel Greene) was a traitor.

3) The British captured (North Carolina, Savannah, Kings Mountain).

4) Lord Cornwallis surrendered at (Charleston, Camden, Yorktown).

5) The Treaty of Paris set the American boundary to the West as (the Mississippi River, Canada, Florida).

What do you think

Which American leader do you think did the most to win the Revolutionary War? Why?

"Common Sense"

Author Thomas Paine met Benjamin Franklin in London in 1774. At Franklin's encouragement, Paine traveled to America where he began writing and publishing. His writings helped to move the colonists toward declaring independence from Britain. Here is a selection from Paine's pamphlet called "Common Sense."

"It is repugnant to reason . . . that this continent can longer remain subject to any external power. . . . The utmost stretch of human wisdom cannot, at this time, compass a plan short of separation, which can promise the continent even a year's security. Reconciliation is now a fallacious dream.

As to government matters, it is not in the power of Britain to do this continent justice: The business of it will soon be too weighty, and intricate, to be managed with any tolerable degree of convenience by a power so distant from us, and so very ignorant of us; for if they cannot conquer us, they cannot govern us. To be always running three or four thousand miles with a tale or a petition, waiting four or five months for an answer, which when obtained requires five or six more to explain it in, will in a few years be looked upon as folly and childishness—There was a time when it was proper, and there is a proper time for it to cease. . . .

To talk of friendship with those in whom our reason forbids us to have faith . . . is madness and folly. Every day wears out the little remains of a kindred between us and them, and can there be any reason to hope, that as the relationship expires, the affection will increase, or that we shall agree better, when we have ten times more and greater concerns to quarrel over than ever? . . .

O ye that love mankind! Ye that dare oppose, not only the tyranny but the tyrant, stand forth! Every spot of the old world is overrun with oppression. Freedom hath been hunted round the globe. Asia and Africa have long expelled her—Europe regards her like a stranger, and England hath given her warning to depart. O! Receive the fugitive, and prepare in time an asylum for mankind."

Source Reading Wrap-Up

1) Why was it inconvenient to have Britain, a distant power, govern the colonies?

2) Why was talk of friendship with Britain "madness and folly"?

3) What was the problem with the "old world"?

4) Paine called freedom a "fugitive" that has "been hunted round the globe." Name one example he gave for that.

5) Why do you think Paine named the pamphlet "Common Sense"?

CHAPTER SUMMARY

★ On May 10, 1775, the Second Continental Congress met in Philadelphia. John Hancock was chosen as its president. Congress decided it could declare war and that it would not interfere in the private matters of the colonies. Congress chose George Washington as commander in chief of the American army.

★ On June 17, 1775, British warships in Boston Harbor opened an attack on Breed's Hill and Bunker Hill. The British later won the battle, but only after heavy losses. The battle was called the Battle of Bunker Hill. The next spring, the Americans captured Dorchester Heights above Boston, forcing the British to leave Boston to the Americans.

★ In late 1775, General Richard Montgomery captured Montreal. From Montreal, he led troops to Quebec, meeting Colonel Benedict Arnold and more troops along the way. The Americans lost at Quebec. General Montgomery was killed.

★ The Americans defeated British loyalists at Moore's Creek, North Carolina, in February 1776.

★ Thomas Jefferson wrote the Declaration of Independence and presented it to Congress in 1776. Congress approved it after removing a slavery clause.

★ The British drove the American army from New York in July 1776. General Washington then led a surprise attack on Trenton, New Jersey, on December 25, 1776. He guided his troops through a storm across the Delaware River and defeated Hessian soldiers.

★ General Howe planned a three-pronged attack in October 1777. The plan was intended to defeat the Americans all at once. The plan failed. The Americans defeated the British at Saratoga.

★ After being pushed back by the Americans at Virginia, Britain's Lord Cornwallis moved his army to Yorktown. After heavy fighting, the British surrendered on October 19, 1781.

★ Great Britain signed the Treaty of Paris on September 3, 1783. The treaty established the new nation's boundaries—Canada on the North, the Mississippi River on the West, and Florida on the South. Great Britain was forced to return Florida to Spain. France gained nothing.

Comprehension: Identifying Facts

On a separate sheet of paper, write the correct word or words from the Word Bank to complete the sentences.

WORD BANK	
commander	petition
Declaration of Independence	postmaster
Hessians	Second Continental Congress
loyalist	statesman
militia	three-pronged attack
pardon	traitor

1) A _____ is a group of citizens who serve as soldiers in times of war.

2) An official statement forgiving someone of something is called a _____.

3) The _____ chose John Hancock as its president.

4) A written paper asking for a right or benefit from someone in power is called a _____.

5) The Second Continental Congress chose George Washington to be _____ of the American army.

6) The Second Continental Congress made Benjamin Franklin the _____.

7) The British hired _____ to fight against the Americans.

8) Thomas Jefferson wrote the _____.

9) General Howe wanted to defeat the Americans at once with a _____.

10) A _____ was an American who supported the king of Great Britain.

11) Benedict Arnold was a _____.

12) Someone who knows and practices government ideas is a _____.

Comprehension: Understanding Main Ideas

On a separate sheet of paper, write the answers to the following questions using complete sentences.

1) What events immediately followed Lexington and Concord?

2) Why did the Congress write the Declaration of Independence?

3) What strengths did the Americans have during the Revolutionary War?

4) What strengths did the British have during the Revolutionary War?

5) Why was the Battle of Saratoga a turning point of the war?

6) What finally won the war for the Americans?

Critical Thinking: Write Your Opinion

1) How do you think the Revolutionary War was different from the French and Indian War?

2) The French got nothing from the war. Why do you think they helped the Americans?

Test Taking Tip Before you begin a test, look it over quickly. Try to set aside enough time to complete each section.

A Government Is Formed

1783–1791

A new nation was born when the Treaty of Paris was signed in 1783. British control was no longer a problem, for America had won its independence. Now America had to form a government that would act as a unit for all of the states. Forming this new government of many different types of people would not be a simple task. In this chapter, you will learn how the government was formed.

Goals for Learning

▶ To explain the Articles of Confederation

▶ To identify the problems the government faced under the Articles of Confederation

▶ To explain why the Constitutional Convention was held

▶ To identify the differences between the New Jersey Plan and the Virginia Plan

▶ To list the compromises made at the Constitutional Convention

▶ To explain the differences between the Federalists and Anti-Federalists

▶ To describe the purpose of the Bill of Rights

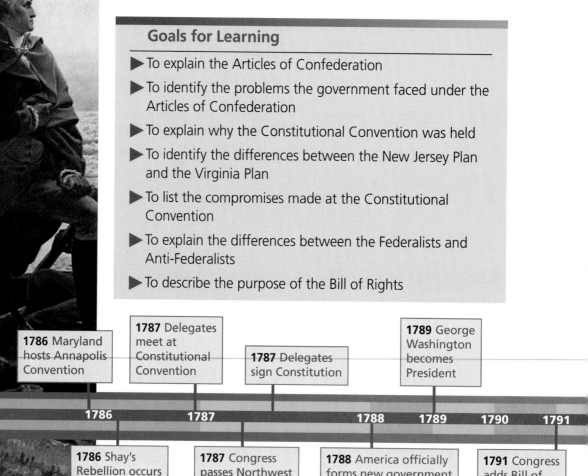

1786 Maryland hosts Annapolis Convention

1787 Delegates meet at Constitutional Convention

1787 Delegates sign Constitution

1789 George Washington becomes President

| 1783 | 1786 | 1787 | 1788 | 1789 | 1790 | 1791 |

1786 Shay's Rebellion occurs

1787 Congress passes Northwest Ordinance

1788 America officially forms new government

1791 Congress adds Bill of Rights to Constitution

During the Revolutionary War in 1781, the states adopted the Articles of Confederation. The articles set up a government with limited power over each state. During the war, the states had been willing to unite against the British. After the war, the Articles of Confederation caused problems.

What Problems Did the Western Lands Cause?

Pioneers had begun to settle in the West long before the war started. A pioneer is one of the first persons to settle in a territory. They ignored the fact that the land already belonged to American Indians. Sometimes, two states claimed the same area. This made it difficult for settlers to get help fighting the American Indians or Spanish in the southern regions. Steps to solve the problem of overlapping claims included a workable system of land **ownership.** In 1784, Thomas Jefferson developed a plan for a **temporary** government of western lands. This plan would later lead to the Northwest Ordinance of 1787.

What Trade Problems Did the Americans Face?

Americans had depended upon trade with Great Britain for many years. After the war, Great Britain closed its ports to American shippers. British merchants, though, continued to send their goods to the United States. They could sell the goods for less than the American **manufacturers** could. Americans had to find new trading partners to survive.

What Problems Developed With the Spanish?

The Spanish controlled Florida, New Orleans, and the land west of the Mississippi River. They did not take the Treaty of Paris seriously. Americans were not welcome in the southern region. Spain would not permit them to ship goods from New Orleans. Because they could not use New Orleans, western settlers had to travel by land. The route was slow and costly. The United States was too weak to force the Spanish to change their policy.

Manufacturer
A company that makes something to sell to the public or to other companies

Ownership
The act of owning something, such as land or a house

★**Pioneer**
One of the first to settle in a territory

Temporary
Something that is to be used only for a short time

Approve
To accept or agree on something

★Import
A good brought in from a foreign country

Dispute
A quarrel between people or groups

Interstate
An action that occurs between two states, such as trade

★Tariff
A tax on goods leaving or entering some place

How Was the Government Out of Control?

The government of the thirteen states was weak and ineffective under the Articles of Confederation. Nine of the thirteen states, each having one vote, had to give their **approval** before Congress could act. If a change in the Articles was proposed, all thirteen states had to agree on it. Each state, no matter how large its population, had only one vote in Congress. Larger states felt that this practice was unfair.

Congress had no power to create and collect taxes or place duties on **imports.** An import is a good brought in from a foreign country. Congress had to ask the states to give it money. Less and less money was coming in, but the debt was increasing.

To add to the problem, states were printing their own money. Paper money often lost its value. Sometimes it would not be accepted either within the state or between states. Some people thought that if more money was printed, the problem would be solved. Without gold to back it, though, the money would be worthless.

Congress also lacked the power to regulate trade among states. States began to treat each other as separate countries. They added **tariffs**—a tax on goods leaving or entering some place—to keep out other states' goods. The tariffs caused a decrease in **interstate** trade. This encouraged Americans to buy British goods instead of American goods.

There were also no national courts. State courts could not settle **disputes** among states. All of these were serious problems that the central government was unable to solve.

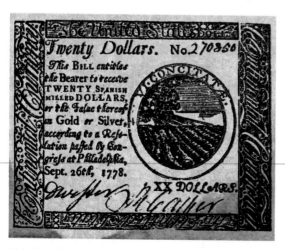

This is what a twenty dollar banknote looked like in 1778.

Noah Webster: A Household Name

Noah Webster was a man of many parts. He started his career as a lawyer and teacher. He also was recognized as a great editor. His love of words took over as he developed a three-part grammar book and started a dictionary. He was a careful observer of the weather and became well respected for his weather predictions. In addition to all this, Webster found time to be a translator, historian, economist, scientific farmer, and politician.

Webster became interested in politics when he was lobbying the state legislature to reform copyright laws. He wanted to protect authors such as himself. Webster identified himself with the Federalist party. He became one of the party's most influential voices. He defended President George Washington against the smear attacks of opposing politicians. His positive picture of Washington had a lot to do with Washington becoming known as the "Father of Our Country."

After Webster tired of politics, he went back to work on his dictionary. Webster's dictionary made his name a household word then and now.

SECTION 1 REVIEW On a separate sheet of paper, write *True* if the statement is true or *False* if the statement is not true.

1) When the Revolutionary War ended, the states were willing to give up their rights.

2) The Articles of Confederation was the first American plan of government.

3) Moving westward was not a problem for the Americans.

4) Some states printed their own money.

5) Tariffs helped interstate trade.

What do you think **?**

What do you think was the most difficult problem facing the Americans after the Revolutionary War? Why?

Commercial
Something linked to business or buying and selling

Host
A person or group who provides a place for guests to do something

Not everyone agreed with the Articles of Confederation. Business owners, merchants, shippers, manufacturers, and bankers wanted a stronger government. They could not protect themselves from the practices of stronger foreign countries and from unfair laws that Great Britain passed. The weak American government could do nothing to help these groups. Constant disputes among the states only increased the difficulties.

Why Was the Annapolis Convention Held?

Maryland and Virginia were having a dispute over **commercial** rights on the Potomac River. Delegates from these two states met at George Washington's home in Mount Vernon and worked out many of the problems. Due to the success of the Mount Vernon Conference, James Madison proposed a convention to which delegates from all the states would be invited in 1786. The Annapolis Convention was not successful because only five states sent delegates. Even Maryland, the **host** state, did not send a representative. Alexander Hamilton of New York

MAP STUDY

In which state is Annapolis located? What river serves as the boundary between Maryland and Virginia?

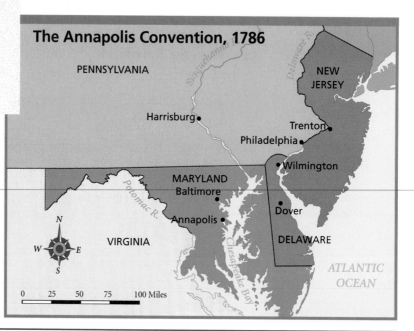

The Annapolis Convention, 1786

Shay's Rebellion was proof that a strong central government was needed.

proposed a convention for 1787. The main business would be forming a stronger government.

What Was Shay's Rebellion?

Any doubt about the need for a strong central government ended after a rebellion against the government of Massachusetts in the winter of 1786. Farmers were upset by low farm prices and high state taxes. Many of them were afraid they would lose their farms. They gathered under former army captain Daniel Shay. Shay's Rebellion closed courthouses and almost captured a storehouse of weapons. The group grew to include over 2,000 farmers. The rebellion lasted for several months.

What Happened at the Constitutional Convention?

The Articles of Confederation had succeeded in doing some good things. It had led the Americans through the war and the signing of the Treaty of Paris. It had kept the thirteen states together during a difficult time, and it provided for the peaceful settlement of western land. Now, however, it was time to create a stronger, more forceful government.

The delegates met in May of 1787 at Independence Hall in Philadelphia. All states but Rhode Island were represented at this meeting. The meeting was called the Constitutional Convention. Fifty-five of the most respected Americans were present. Among these were George Washington, James Madison, and Edmund Randolph of Virginia; John Dickinson of Delaware; Benjamin Franklin of Pennsylvania; Alexander Hamilton of New York; and William Paterson of New Jersey. Both Thomas Jefferson and John Adams were in Europe at the time and were absent from the convention. Most of the delegates were lawyers, while some were farmers and merchants.

Secrecy
The act of keeping something private

Session
A meeting or a series of meetings

At the start of the convention, it was decided that all the **sessions** were to be held in **secrecy.** The delegates wanted to be able to debate freely. They could even change their minds about some very serious subjects. The delegates felt that their heated debates need not be shared with the public.

The delegates chose George Washington to lead the convention. He was recognized as an intelligent, well-educated person and a great military leader. The delegates also greatly respected him. The delegates' choice proved to be a wise one because the convention needed a strong leader.

SECTION 2 REVIEW Write the answers to these questions on a separate sheet of paper using complete sentences.

1) What was wrong with the Articles of Confederation?

2) Why was the Annapolis Convention a failure?

3) Why did the delegates meet at the Constitutional Convention?

4) Why were the Constitutional Convention meetings held in secrecy?

5) Why did the delegates choose George Washington to lead the Constitutional Convention?

What do you think **?**

What problems do you think occur when a government is weak?

Exist
Something that is in place or operating

Guarantee
An agreement to protect something, such as property

The original purpose of the Constitutional Convention was to adjust the Articles of Confederation. However, there were too many details to be worked out. It soon became clear that the delegates needed to develop a completely different system of government.

What Were the Virginia and New Jersey Plans?

One plan for a new government was presented by Edmund Randolph of Virginia. His plan included a much stronger central government and greater control by the larger states. The proposal became known as the "large-state plan," or Virginia Plan. It called for representatives based on population.

The plan was to establish a congress to make laws, a separate government branch to enforce the laws, and a court system to **guarantee** justice under the law. Congress, the lawmaking branch, was to be divided into two parts. Legislators in the lower house would be elected by the people. Members of the upper house would be chosen by the members of the lower house. The Virginia Plan, as Randolph saw it, was very democratic. It provided for government by the people.

After two weeks of heated discussion of the Virginia Plan, William Paterson of New Jersey presented another plan. The New Jersey Plan, or "small-state plan," provided for a system of government much like the one that already **existed.** Under this plan each state was to have an equal vote in the government. The states would have much more control of the government.

Why Was a Compromise Needed?

The delegates examined each plan and expressed their points of view. As the summer temperatures soared, so did the tempers of the delegates. The debate became so strong that at times some delegates were ready to quit and call the convention a failure.

Handwriting in the 1700s was quite different from most handwriting today. Look at this letter written by Abigail Adams to her husband, John Adams. Notice the way she formed an *s*. Some of her *s*'s look like a modern *f*. See how her *d* slants to the left. Following the writing style of her time, Abigail capitalized many common nouns. Today we do not capitalize words such as *ladies, men, husbands,* and *code of laws.* Abigail spelled *favorable* with a *u*— a spelling still used in England.

Wise old Benjamin Franklin, at age eighty-one, calmed everyone down. The much younger delegates respected him and listened to his humorous but intelligent remarks. Washington's strong sense of reason encouraged the delegates to be willing to compromise.

Deadlock
A situation where two or more groups are unable to agree on something

The **deadlock** between the larger states and smaller states dragged on. The key issue was the amount of power the central government should have and how much power large and small states would continue to hold. A special committee was formed to try to work out a compromise.

SECTION 3 REVIEW Decide if each statement tells about the New Jersey Plan or the Virginia Plan. Write *New Jersey Plan* or *Virginia Plan* beside each number on a separate sheet of paper.

1) Presented by Edmund Randolph

2) States had equal votes

3) Congress was to make laws

4) Presented by William Paterson

5) Stronger central government

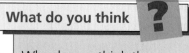

What do you think

Why do you think the amount of power state and central governments should hold caused such a debate?

★Bill
A proposal for a new law

★Justice
A judge who serves on the Supreme Court

★Legislative branch
The branch of government that makes laws

Runaway
Someone who is trying to escape

The Compromise Committee presented its report to the convention. It proposed a **legislative branch** made up of two houses—the House of Representatives and the Senate. These groups would make laws. The committee proposed that the House of Representatives would be made up according to the population of each state. The states with more people would have more representatives. This pleased the members who supported the Virginia Plan. The committee suggested the Senate have two representatives from each state, regardless of its population. This pleased the delegates who supported the New Jersey Plan. Each house would be equal except that all **bills** dealing with money would be started in the House of Representatives. A bill is a proposal for a new law. The delegates accepted the plan, called the "Great Compromise," on July 16, 1787.

What Other Compromises Were Made?

Other problems needed to be worked out. Southern states wanted slaves to be represented in the population count but not in taxation. Northern states protested. A compromise permitted three out of every five slaves to be included in the population and taxation count of the southern states. This plan is known as the Three-Fifths Compromise.

Other problems for the southern states involving slaves included **runaway** slaves. The committee proposed that all slaves who had run away be returned to their owners. Many in the South feared that Congress would try to control the number of slaves brought into the South. The committee ruled, however, that Congress could not affect the slave market until the year 1808.

Trade was of great concern to all states. The Compromise Committee recommended that Congress regulate trade between states and foreign countries. Duties would not be allowed between states. Tariffs would be permitted on goods coming to the United States from foreign countries.

The First Chief Justice

The Supreme Court has eight judges, called **justices**. Justices hear court cases from lower courts. The Supreme Court also has a chief justice who leads the other justices. John Jay of New York became the first chief justice in 1789. He served for five years.

Southern farmers were pleased. Under this plan, their **exports** to foreign countries would not be taxed. An export is a good sent to another country. Another very important part of the rulings was that states would not be allowed to print their own money. The ruling called for the central government to print money.

What Are the Executive and Judicial Branches?

The delegates decided that a President would be elected as the head of the **executive branch** of the government. The executive branch would enforce the laws. The President would serve a four-year term and would be responsible for choosing a group of **advisers.** An adviser is a person who gives information, advice, or help.

The Supreme Court would serve as the highest court in the country. The Supreme Court and lower courts would be part of the **judicial branch.** This branch would **interpret** the laws.

The three branches of government set up by the Constitution—the executive, legislative, and judicial branches—are still in place today. The delegates felt the branches provided for a separation of powers. The power would not rest in any one branch. The power is given to the **federal government** by the states. A federal government is one that is divided between central and state governments.

The United States Federal Government	
Legislative Branch—makes laws	
House of Representatives: Made up according to the population of each state	**Senate:** Two representatives from each state, regardless of its population
Judicial Branch—interprets laws	
Supreme Court: Highest court in the country	**Other courts:** Hear most court cases
Executive Branch—enforces laws	
President: Head of the executive branch	**Advisers:** Give information, advice, or help to the President

The delegates signed the Constitution in 1787. George Washington, leader of the convention, is standing by the flags.

What Was the Northwest Ordinance?

During the debate over the Constitution, one important law was created. For many years, control of land east of the Mississippi River and north of the Ohio River had caused serious problems among the states. Based on Thomas Jefferson's plan of 1784, Congress passed the Northwest Ordinance in 1787. This law stated that the area would become three to five new states as soon as the population became large enough.

Who Signed the Constitution?

The Constitution did not please all of the delegates even though many felt the Compromise Committee had done a good job. On September 17, 1787, the delegates signed the Constitution with the hope that the states would approve it. The delegates' work was done. It was up to the states to decide if the Constitution was acceptable as the law of the land.

SECTION 4 REVIEW On a separate sheet of paper, write the correct word from the word bank to complete each sentence.

WORD BANK
bill
executive
federal
judicial
legislative

1) The _____ branch interprets laws.

2) A _____ government is divided between central and state governments.

3) The _____ branch enforces the laws.

4) A _____ is a proposal for a new law.

5) The _____ branch makes the laws.

What do you think ?

Is it necessary or important to have three branches of government? Why or why not?

★**Anti-Federalist**
One who felt that the Constitution gave the central government too much power

Circulate
To pass something from person to person or place to place

Essay
A piece of writing addressing a subject from a personal point of view

★**Federalist**
One who supported the Constitution

★**Ratify**
To approve something

Supreme
To the highest degree

The people needed to decide whether to accept the Constitution. Each of the thirteen states elected delegates to debate the issues and decide whether to approve the Constitution. When nine of the thirteen states approved, or **ratified** the Constitution, it would become the **supreme** law of the land.

Not everyone supported the Constitution. Under the new plan, the power of the central government would increase. There was concern that the government would be too strong and would take away some of the freedoms that people enjoyed. People did not quite know what the Constitution could do.

Who Were the Federalists and Anti-Federalists?

As the discussions continued in the states, two groups developed. Those who supported the Constitution were called **Federalists.** Those who felt that the Constitution gave the central government too much power were called **Anti-Federalists.** They feared that state governments would be destroyed and taxes would be increased. Farmers felt the Constitution favored other businesses. The Anti-Federalists thought that the Constitution did not provide for protection of personal freedoms.

The approval of the Constitution seemed unlikely. The Federalists—led by Alexander Hamilton, James Madison, and John Jay—fought hard for its ratification. The three men published a series of **essays** called the *Federalist Papers.* They explained what the Constitution really meant. The papers were **circulated** throughout the states. Support for the Constitution increased when George Washington agreed to serve as the first President if he was called upon to do so. The Constitution would probably not have been approved without the outstanding leadership of Hamilton, Madison, Jay, and Washington.

The U.S. Census

After the Constitution was ratified, an accurate measure of the country's population was needed. The number of seats for a state in the House of Representatives was to be proportionate to its population. The U.S. Bureau of the Census was immediately established. It was to measure our population every ten years. The Bureau conducted the first census in 1790, counting 3.9 million people. At that time, the Constitution requested that the number of slaves and women be reduced by three-fifths.

The Bureau has counted the population every ten years since then. The twenty-first census in 1990 counted more than 248 million Americans. The Bureau now gathers information on race, gender, age, religion, occupation, and more. Census figures are still used to allot seats in Congress. They are also used to allot funds for social service programs, determine school district boundaries, and plan road and mass transit systems.

How Was the Constitution Ratified?

The first state to ratify was Delaware in 1787, followed by Pennsylvania and New Jersey. In 1788, Georgia and Connecticut ratified the Constitution. Massachusetts ratified it in February of 1788 with the support of John Hancock. Maryland and South Carolina followed. New Hampshire was the ninth state to approve the Constitution. When that state ratified in June of 1788, the United States officially had a new government. Without the support of New York and Virginia, however, the government would be at a serious disadvantage.

James Madison and John Marshall led the Federalists at the Virginia convention. Patrick Henry and George Mason led the Anti-Federalists. Both sides were evenly matched. On June 25, 1788, Virginia ratified the Constitution.

Alexander Hamilton led the Federalists in New York. The news that Virginia had ratified the Constitution helped Hamilton. On July 26, 1788, by a vote of thirty to twenty-seven, New York became the eleventh state to approve the Constitution.

The last two states to ratify were North Carolina and Rhode Island. On November 21, 1789, North Carolina voted to approve the Constitution. It was not until May 29, 1790, that Rhode Island gave its approval. All thirteen states had democratically approved the new form of government.

Unanimous
When all sides agree

The new government began to take shape even before some states had ratified the Constitution. George Washington was elected President in April of 1789 by **unanimous** consent. John Adams, who had received the second largest number of votes, became Vice President.

Why Was the Bill of Rights Added to the Constitution?

Some states did not like the Constitution because it did not clearly spell out personal freedoms. In 1789, it was suggested that provisions for such freedoms be added to the original document. In 1791, Congress adopted ten **amendments** to the Constitution. An amendment is a change. These became known as the Bill of Rights. The amendments provided for personal freedoms as follows:

★Amendment
A change

Assemble
To gather together

★Civil lawsuit
A court case involving private rights

Bill of Rights

- **First Amendment**
  Americans' rights to practice any religion, to express themselves in speech or writing, to give opinions in newspapers, books, and other printed materials, to **assemble** peacefully in public places, and to petition the government

- **Second Amendment**
  The right to bear arms

- **Third Amendment**
  Protection from having to house soldiers

- **Fourth Amendment**
  Protection from having your home searched

- **Fifth Amendment**
  Provides that certain steps be taken if someone is charged with a crime

- **Sixth Amendment**
  The right to a fair trial

- **Seventh Amendment**
  Civil lawsuits, court cases involving private rights, may be brought to a jury trial if it involves a sum of $20 or more

- **Eighth Amendment**
  The right to fair punishment

- **Ninth Amendment**
  The rights maintained by the people

- **Tenth Amendment**
  The rights maintained by the states and the people

JOHN FITCH: 1743–1798

John Fitch distinguished himself as the inventor of steamboats. Remarkably, Fitch accomplished this with almost no funds, political influence, or mechanical ability. In 1785, he obtained a fourteen-year monopoly to build and operate steamboats on the waters of several states. In 1787, he launched his 45-foot boat on the Delaware River. Steam-powered paddles moved the boat. Fitch launched the boat before an assembled audience of delegates to the Constitutional Convention. In 1790, he began regular runs across the Delaware River. On these runs he transported passengers between Philadelphia and Trenton, New Jersey. Fitch was also a silversmith, clock maker, and surveyor.

Seventeen other amendments have been added since the original Bill of Rights. You will learn about these amendments in later chapters. The Constitution can be found in Appendix B of this textbook. The Bill of Rights and the amendments can be found in Appendix C.

SECTION 5 REVIEW On a separate sheet of paper, write the letter of the description in Part 2 that matches a term in Part 1.

PART 1

1) Federalists
2) Anti-Federalists
3) Bill of Rights
4) amendment
5) Constitution

PART 2

a) A change
b) Supreme law of the land
c) Supported the Constitution
d) Felt the Constitution gave the central government too much power
e) First ten amendments to the Constitution

What do you think ?

How fair do you think the original Constitution was to women and groups such as enslaved Africans?

The Northwest Ordinance

In 1784, Thomas Jefferson wrote an early draft of what became the Northwest Ordinance. The Northwest Ordinance was enacted in 1787. It set forth the rules for the development of the area north of the Ohio River and east of the Mississippi. It was one of the most important parts of the Articles of Confederation. It clarified the way in which territories could become states.

"Be it ordained by the United States in Congress assembled, that the said territory, for the purposes of temporary government, be one district, subject, however, to be divided into two districts, as future circumstances may . . . make it expedient . . . .

Be it ordained . . . that there shall be appointed . . . by Congress, a governor for a term of three years . . . [and] . . . a secretary for a term of four years. . . . There shall also be appointed a court to consist of three judges.

The governor and the secretary . . . shall adopt . . . laws of the original States . . . .

The following articles shall be [a] compact between the original States and . . . the . . . territory . . . .

Art. 2 The inhabitants of the . . . territory shall be entitled to . . . a trial by jury, a proportionate representation . . . in the legislature, and of judicial proceedings according to . . . common law. . . . No cruel or unusual punishments shall be inflicted.

Art. 3 Schools and the means of education shall forever be encouraged. . . . The utmost good faith shall always be observed toward the Indians; their lands and property shall not be taken without their consent. . . .

Art. 5 There shall be formed in the . . . territory, not less than three nor more than five states; [and the boundaries of said States shall be fixed by federal guidelines] . . . . Whenever any of the said states have sixty thousand free inhabitants, it shall be . . . admitted to the Congress . . . on an equal footing with the original States in all respects.

Art. 6 There shall neither be slavery nor involuntary servitude in said territory."

Source Reading Wrap-Up

1) Congress appointed five people for the territory. What were their positions?

2) In what ways did the Northwest Ordinance protect the rights of citizens in the territory?

3) What did the Ordinance say about Indians and their land and property?

4) How many inhabitants did a territorial state need before it could be admitted to Congress?

5) How did the Northwest Ordinance control the spread of slavery?

★ After the Revolutionary War, Americans had trouble settling to the West, experienced difficulties with trade, and had problems with the Spanish. The government under the Articles of Confederation was out of control.

★ Delegates met in Annapolis, Maryland, in 1786 to work out some of the problems. The convention was a failure because so few delegates attended.

★ In 1786, Daniel Shay led a rebellion to protest low farm prices and high state taxes. The rebellion, called Shay's Rebellion, lasted for several months.

★ Delegates met at the Constitutional Convention in Philadelphia in 1787 to create a plan for a stronger central government. Two plans were discussed: The Virginia Plan favored a strong central government and more power to the larger states. The New Jersey Plan favored equal power between the states. The delegates agreed on a compromise.

★ The delegates decided that three out of every five slaves would be included in the population and taxation count of the southern states. This plan is known as the Three-Fifths Compromise. They also agreed that Congress could not affect the slave market until 1808.

★ The Constitution set up three branches of government: the executive, legislative, and judicial.

★ Congress passed the Northwest Ordinance in 1787. This law stated that the area east of the Mississippi River and north of the Ohio River would become three to five new states as soon as the population became large enough.

★ The delegates signed the Constitution on September 17, 1787. Those who supported the Constitution were called Federalists. Anti-Federalists were those who felt that the Constitution gave the central government too much power. America officially had a new government by 1788.

★ George Washington was elected the first President in 1789.

★ Congress added the Bill of Rights to the Constitution in 1791. These are the first ten amendments to the Constitution. They protect individual rights.

Comprehension: Identifying Facts

On a separate sheet of paper, write the correct term from the Word Bank to complete each sentence.

WORD BANK	
Anti-Federalist	judicial branch
bill	legislative branch
executive branch	New Jersey Plan
export	pioneer
Federalist	tariff
federal	Virginia Plan
import	

1) A tax on goods leaving or entering some place is called a _____.

2) A good sent to another country is called an _____.

3) The _____ favored equal state rights.

4) The President belongs to the _____.

5) The Senate and the House of Representatives belong to the _____.

6) An _____ felt that the Constitution gave the central government too much power.

7) The _____ favored the larger states.

8) A good brought in from a foreign country is called an _____.

9) A person who supported the Constitution was called a _____.

10) The Supreme Court belongs to the _____.

11) A government that is divided between central and state governments is a _____ government.

12) A _____ is a person who settles land that has not been settled before.

13) A _____ is a proposal for a new law.

Comprehension: Understanding Main Ideas

On a separate sheet of paper, write the answers to the following questions using complete sentences.

1) What were the Articles of Confederation?

2) What powers did the government lack under the Articles of Confederation?

3) What was the purpose of the Constitutional Convention?

4) What was the Three-Fifths Compromise?

5) What was the purpose of the Bill of Rights?

Critical Thinking: Write Your Opinion

1) It took a long time for the Constitution to be created and ratified. Why do you think it needed to take so long?

2) What do you think would have happened if the Federalists had not worked so hard to support the Constitution? Why?

Test Taking Tip | Always read directions more than once. Underline words that tell how many examples or items you must provide.

1788–1809

The United States was well on its way to a lasting government when the states ratified the Constitution. The next thirty years saw the first three Presidents take office. The American political system also came to be during this period. In this chapter, you will learn about the first three Presidents and the first political systems.

Goals for Learning

▶ To explain what Washington accomplished as President

▶ To list the parts of Alexander Hamilton's financial plan

▶ To describe what happened during President Adams's term

▶ To explain what happened in the election of 1800

▶ To describe what Jefferson accomplished as President

▶ To describe the Louisiana Purchase and why it was significant

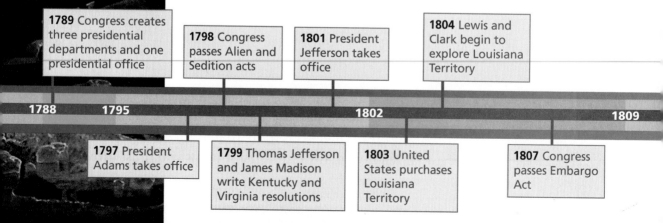

1789 Congress creates three presidential departments and one presidential office

1798 Congress passes Alien and Sedition acts

1801 President Jefferson takes office

1804 Lewis and Clark begin to explore Louisiana Territory

1788   1795   1802   1809

1797 President Adams takes office

1799 Thomas Jefferson and James Madison write Kentucky and Virginia resolutions

1803 United States purchases Louisiana Territory

1807 Congress passes Embargo Act

The first cabinet was (from left) Henry Knox, Thomas Jefferson, Edmund Randolph, Alexander Hamilton, and President Washington.

★Cabinet
A group of advisers to the President

Permanent
Lasting a long time or forever

★Treasury
A place where money is stored; the government department that handles money

The Constitution became law on June 21, 1788. It did not provide for a body of presidential advisers. Congress created three departments and one office in 1789. The heads of each department would help the President make decisions.

President Washington appointed four advisers: Thomas Jefferson from Virginia was named Secretary of State; Alexander Hamilton from New York, Secretary of the Treasury; Henry Knox from Massachusetts, Secretary of War; and Edmund Randolph from Virginia, Attorney General. This group was called the **cabinet.** A cabinet is a group of advisers to the President. It was established as a **permanent** part of the American government. Washington's early decision to form a cabinet shows how he thought a democratic government should work. He chose people whom he knew and trusted to be members of his cabinet.

What Was Alexander Hamilton's Financial Plan?

The United States was in debt because of the long, costly war and the weakness of the Articles of Confederation. The **treasury,** a place where money is stored, was empty. Congress had passed the Tariff Act of 1789, but the money collected was not enough to pay the amount owed. The states also had large debts. To gain the respect of nations across the ocean, the United States would have to pay off this debt. In addition, the treasury needed money to run the government.

The task of getting the country out of debt was put into the hands of Alexander Hamilton, Secretary of the Treasury. Hamilton recommended that several important financial measures be taken.

Hamilton's Financial Plan

- Pay the $10-million debt to foreign nations.

- Pay the $40 million owed to people who had lent money to the government during the war.

- Have the central government take on the debts that the states were left with from the war.

Hamilton's plan was not popular with many in Congress. The idea of paying off the debts of the states was especially unpopular with southern states. These states had paid off most of their debts, while the northern states still had large amounts of unsettled debts. However, Jefferson and Madison of Virginia offered to help Hamilton gain the support of Congress. They wanted to see a southern location chosen as the nation's capital instead of New York. Hamilton agreed to work toward getting a site on the Potomac River near Virginia. With the help of Jefferson and Madison, Hamilton's plan passed in Congress. The District of Columbia, now our nation's capital, was established.

In order to decrease the debt to people who had lent money to the government, Hamilton suggested giving them **bonds** that would pay **interest** over a period of time. A bond is a document that is proof of money owed. Interest is money paid to someone who lends money.

FEDERAL HALL

George Washington was officially made President in this building, Federal Hall, in New York City, the nation's capital at the time. The capital later became the District of Columbia.

Industry
Related to business and manufacturing

Hamilton also helped organize the First Bank of the United States as a safe place for funds collected as taxes. He set up the United States mint where the first American coins were put into use. Hamilton gave the country a sound financial plan.

Under Hamilton's plan, the government was able to pay off its debts. Taxes raised enough money to keep the government working. Trade increased and **industry** grew. The people of other countries and Americans gained a greater respect for the United States government.

SECTION 1 REVIEW On a separate sheet of paper, write *True* if the statement is true or *False* if the statement is not true.

1) Congress created three departments and one office in 1789.

2) George Washington appointed five advisers when he became President.

3) Alexander Hamilton's financial plan was not popular with many in Congress.

4) Hamilton's financial plan did not include paying off foreign debt.

5) Hamilton helped to organize the First Bank of the United States.

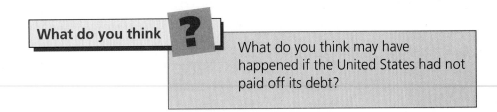

What do you think ?

What do you think may have happened if the United States had not paid off its debt?

Affairs
A person or group's day-to-day business

Disagreement
A quarrel over something

Neutral
A person or group that does not side with any particular person or group

★**Political party**
A group that represents a certain political belief

Alexander Hamilton's financial plan played a large part in the development of **political parties.** A political party is a group that represents a certain political belief. Those who supported his plans formed the Federalist party. Thomas Jefferson and James Madison were among those who felt that states should have more power to run their own **affairs.** These men helped form the Democratic-Republican party. The new party supported stronger state government. The Federalist party wanted a much stronger central government.

The Federalists generally received their strongest support from wealthy merchants and bankers. Farmers, laborers, and small shopkeepers usually backed the Democratic-Republicans. Many people thought Washington was a Federalist, although he never sided with either party. He often warned that having opposing parties could lead to further **disagreement.** Most of the leaders during Washington's presidency and that of the next President, John Adams, were Federalists.

Why Did Washington Want Neutrality?

President Washington had other concerns besides the nation's debt and the newly formed political parties. France declared war against Great Britain in 1793. Because the French had helped the Americans during the Revolutionary War, they expected some help in return. The United States was in no condition to fight another war so soon, because the military was very weak and the country was so far in debt. Washington felt it was unwise to plunge into another war. Hamilton wanted the United States to help Britain. Jefferson felt that the Americans should help France. After careful thought, the President chose to remain **neutral.** The needs of the United States had to come first.

What Problems Developed in the Western Lands?

Great Britain and Spain continued to interfere with Americans as they moved westward. The British sold firearms and whiskey to the American Indians in the North.

Alexander Hamilton

The American Indians were fighting to protect their land, which the settlers also claimed. War was likely if the British continued to cause trouble.

President Washington could not risk a war with the British and the American Indians. There had to be a peaceful settlement with the British. John Jay was sent to London in 1794 to discuss a treaty. He got the British to agree to leave their forts that were built on American soil. Americans would pay their debts to Britain and the British would repay American shippers for cargo that had been seized.

Jay's Treaty, as it was called, was not very popular with Congress. It did not protect American ships bound for France from being seized by the British. However, President Washington urged its approval in order to maintain peace with Britain.

What Agreement Did Spain and America Reach?

After Jay's Treaty had been approved, the President needed to act on the problem with Spain. The Spanish controlled the Mississippi River as well as New Orleans, which the Americans needed for a trade route. Spain also controlled a section of Florida that Americans occupied. Surprisingly, Spain agreed to permit free **navigation** on the Mississippi in 1795. This opened the port of New Orleans. In addition, the disputed west Florida territory was turned over to the United States.

How Did Washington Contribute to America?

President Washington agreed to serve a second term as President, although his health was failing. He was tired after so many years of **public service.** Public service is any job or effort done for the good of the people. The country, however, still needed him as its leader.

Contribute
To add to or take part in something

Emerge
To come into being

As differences in political ideas **emerged** near the end of Washington's second term, two separate political parties were taking shape. Washington was unsure how to handle the increasing arguments about how the government should be run. Tired and longing for his Virginia home, he refused to serve a third term. Washington died two years later at the age of 67.

The **contributions** George Washington made to the growth of the United States of America were many. As the first President of a new nation, he had no example to follow. Everywhere, there seemed to be some problem that needed his guidance. He chose excellent advisers and put the country on its feet financially and politically. Washington kept the young country out of European wars. George Washington is called the "Father of His Country" because of these many contributions.

SECTION 2 REVIEW Write the answers to these questions on a separate sheet of paper using complete sentences.

1) Why did George Washington want to keep the country out of the war?

2) Why did American settlers in western lands call for action against the British?

3) Why did Americans need to use the Mississippi River and New Orleans?

4) What did John Jay's treaty do?

5) Why is George Washington called the "Father of His Country"?

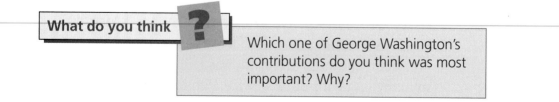

What do you think **?**

Which one of George Washington's contributions do you think was most important? Why?

★Candidate
A person who has been selected to run for a political office

John Adams had served for eight years as Vice President. The Federalists chose him to be their **candidate** for the next President. A candidate is a person who has been selected to run for a political office. Adams was well educated and experienced in government. He had been present at the First and Second Continental Congress, and he was a signer of the Declaration of Independence. He had helped achieve peace with Britain with the Treaty of Paris in 1783. Like Washington, he was strongly against any change in the power of the central government. He was known to be a stubborn man with very strong opinions.

Democratic-Republicans backed Thomas Jefferson of Virginia in his bid for the presidency. When the election of 1796 was held, Adams won, but not by much. With sixty-eight electoral votes to Adams's seventy-one, Thomas Jefferson became Vice President. This put Adams in a difficult position. He, as President, was a loyal Federalist. He favored a strong central government, whereas his Vice President was a supporter of strong state governments.

What Was the XYZ Affair?

Several European countries were at war with France when John Adams took office in 1797. The American policy of neutrality angered the French. Also, the signing of Jay's Treaty had led France to think that America was allied with Great Britain. The French began to seize American ships that carried supplies to the British.

President Adams wanted to avoid a war. He sent a group to work out a deal with France. Three secret French agents known as X, Y, and Z refused to cooperate with the delegates unless the United States gave them a large amount of money. The delegates rejected the demands for money and reported the demands to Congress. This became known as the XYZ Affair.

First Lady Abigail Adams supported women's rights. She wanted her husband, John Adams, to press for more freedom for women in America. He would not.

In preparation for war with France, Congress set up the Department of the Navy in order to build a stronger sea force. During the next two years, the U.S. Navy fought several battles against France, capturing eighty French ships while losing only one of their own. Finally, in 1800, the French signed an agreement to stop interfering with American merchant ships. However, France refused to pay any earlier shipping losses. Many Americans were not pleased by the agreement and wanted the government to take much stronger action.

John Adams was not a popular President. He was an honest man and a loyal American, but he was also considered to be **arrogant** and narrow minded. He would not compromise on issues. There was evidence of his unpopularity. For example, newspapers often did not support his policies. In addition, many foreigners coming to the United States joined the opposing party.

What Did the Alien and Sedition Acts Do?

The Federalists decided to take action to preserve their control. Congress, controlled by the Federalists, passed a series of harsh laws called the Alien and Sedition acts in 1798. Under the Alien Act, **immigrants** had to wait fourteen years before they could become United States citizens. An immigrant is a person who comes to live in a new country. The waiting period had been five years. In addition, **aliens** could be **deported** or put into prison if they were judged to be dangerous. An alien is someone who lives in one country but is a citizen of another. To deport means to send someone away from a country.

The Sedition Act made it a crime for anyone to speak out, write, or print articles against the government. Those who did and were convicted had to pay a fine of $5,000 and serve up to five years in prison.

★Constitutional
*Something that
follows the ideas
set forth in the
Constitution*

★Resolution
*An expression of
opinion or intent
voted on by a
group*

The Federalists' actions caused great excitement and became a major issue in the election of 1800. Immigrants feared they might be deported. Democratic-Republican writers were fined for their comments. Many people thought these laws went against the Constitution. The Constitution provided for freedom of the press and freedom of speech. The Federalists were trying to become more powerful by weakening those who disagreed.

Why Were the Kentucky and Virginia Resolutions Written?

Thomas Jefferson and James Madison, in response to the Alien and Sedition Acts, wrote the Kentucky and Virginia **resolutions** in 1799. A resolution is an expression of opinion or intent voted on by a group. The legislatures of those two states passed the resolutions. The writers stated that the Alien and Sedition Acts were not **constitutional**—the acts did not follow what was set forth in the Constitution. The states had created the national government, and limited its powers to those written in the Constitution. States did not have to obey acts that were not constitutional.

A Smallpox Vaccine

In 1796, English physician Edward Jenner discovered a way to prevent smallpox. He called his technique *vaccination* after the Latin word *vacca* for "cow." In America, outbreaks of smallpox had been destructive, especially among American Indians, to whom the disease was previously unknown. Thus, Jenner's discovery was greeted with enthusiasm. Harvard medical professor Benjamin Waterhouse gave the first U.S. vaccinations less than a year after Jenner's discovery. In 1802, the Boston Board of Health began the first systematic program to vaccinate against smallpox. Today, smallpox has been virtually wiped out in the United States. Most children are vaccinated before they start school. Medical researchers now have developed other vaccines to protect people against diseases such as measles and polio.

Health

History in Your Life

What Happened in the Election of 1800?

The election of 1800 was the first real contest between Democratic-Republicans and the Federalists. Although the Democratic-Republican party was formed before the election of 1796, its competition with the Federalist party did not develop until 1800.

★Elector
A person who is chosen to vote for the President and Vice President

★Electoral college
A group of people chosen to elect the President and Vice President

★Running mate
A candidate who runs for office with a candidate who is running for another position

The Federalists supported John Adams. Adams selected Charles Pinckney to be his **running mate** for Vice President. A running mate is a candidate who runs for office with a candidate who is running for another position. Thomas Jefferson was the Democratic-Republican candidate for President. His ideas appealed to farmers, small business owners, and ordinary workers. The Democratic Republicans chose Aaron Burr of New York as Jefferson's running mate. Jefferson did not like Burr, but Burr was popular in New York. Jefferson felt Burr could help win votes in the North.

An unusual problem came up with this election. The Constitution called for an **electoral college.** This was a group of people called **electors** who were chosen to elect the President and Vice President. The Constitution stated that each elector was to vote for any two candidates. When the votes were counted, Thomas Jefferson and Aaron Burr had seventy-three electoral votes each. Adams had sixty-five votes, and Pinckney, sixty-four. The Constitution said the person with the highest number of votes would become the President. The person with the second highest votes would become Vice President. Because the vote was tied, the House of Representatives then had to decide the election.

How Did Hamilton Influence Congress?

Congress found it difficult to choose between Jefferson and Burr. The Federalists wanted to elect Burr. His political views were closer to the Federalists than those of Thomas Jefferson. Alexander Hamilton, a Federalist, helped come up with the final outcome of the election. Hamilton had very little regard for Jefferson's political ideas, but he thought even less of Burr. In Hamilton's opinion, Burr could not be trusted. Hamilton was able to swing the vote in Jefferson's favor. Thomas Jefferson became President, and Aaron Burr became Vice President. The Democratic-Republicans had gained control of both the executive and the legislative branches of the government.

Would you be surprised to know that the first political parties in the United States developed over a disagreement? They differed over how much power the federal government should have. Federalists wanted to increase the government's power. Anti-Federalists wanted to weaken the government's power.

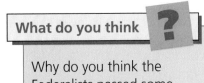

Did you know that today's two major political parties developed from these first parties? Under Thomas Jefferson, the Anti-Federalists became the Republican party. They emphasized the democratic process. Later they became the Democratic-Republican party and finally were called the Democratic party.

The Federalists became known as National Republicans. Later they were called Whigs. This party was weak until 1841 when it took a strong stand against slavery. The Whigs developed into today's Republican party.

To prevent such a tie from happening in the future, Congress passed the Twelfth Amendment to the Constitution in 1804. This stated that electors would vote separately for President and Vice President.

What Did the Federalists Accomplish?

Although the Federalist Party was defeated in the election of 1800, members of this party had helped establish the country. They had put the Constitution into effect and helped the country recover from debt. They had helped build trade with other countries, and kept America out of war with France and Great Britain.

SECTION 3 REVIEW On a separate sheet of paper, write *True* if the statement is true or *False* if the statement is not true.

1) John Adams served for eight years as Vice President under George Washington.

2) Adams won the election of 1796 by a very large number of votes.

3) Jefferson and Adams were both Federalists.

4) The Sedition Act made it a crime for anyone to speak out, write, or print articles against the government.

5) Aaron Burr won the election of 1800 and became President.

What do you think ?

Why do you think the Federalists passed some unconstitutional laws?

Thomas Jefferson was a rich landowner from Virginia. Despite his wealth, he did not dress in fancy clothes. Many thought he was untidy and not very friendly. He had been the author of the Declaration of Independence. He had a different approach to government. He believed that the government could do only what the Constitution allowed.

What Did Jefferson Do as President?

Jefferson was sworn in as President, or **inaugurated**, in the District of Columbia in 1801. In his speech to accept the presidency, called an **inaugural address**, he strongly urged all political parties to join together for the good of the country. Jefferson knew that progress would continue only if the people were united.

Other events during Jefferson's term include:

John Marshall

Before he left office, John Adams appointed John Marshall as the new chief justice of the Supreme Court. Under Marshall's guidance, the Supreme Court tried a number of cases that strengthened the "checks and balances" among the three branches of the federal government.

- The Alien and Sedition acts ended. People imprisoned under those acts were released, and charges against them were removed from the records.

- The time a person needed to live in America before becoming a citizen was lowered to five years.

- The remaining federal debt was lowered.

- The United States Military Academy at West Point was established.

- Slaves could no longer be imported into the United States (although approximately 25,000 more Africans who became enslaved were imported illegally by 1860).

- America bought the Louisiana Territory.

What Was the Louisiana Purchase?

After the French and Indian War, France had surrendered some land west of the Mississippi to Spain. In 1800, Spain had been forced to return the land, known as Louisiana, to France. Jefferson was troubled by the move. New Orleans was an important port for international trade. America had an agreement with Spain that it could bring in goods to New Orleans. Two years after France and Napoleon Bonaparte took control of the region, this agreement was withdrawn. This prevented eastern trade.

President Jefferson sent James Monroe to Paris, France, in 1803 to buy as much of Florida and New Orleans as he could for $10 million. Robert Livingston, American **ambassador** to France, was already **negotiating** with Napoleon in Paris. An ambassador is a representative from a country who works out problems with another country. Napoleon offered to sell the Louisiana region for $15 million. America would **acquire** 828,000 square miles for roughly four cents an acre. Jefferson turned to Congress for approval of the purchase. Congress approved, and the Louisiana Territory became part of America on December 20, 1803. This is known as the Louisiana Purchase.

Acquire
To gain something by purchasing or taking it

★**Ambassador**
A representative from a country who works out problems with another country

Negotiate
To work out a deal

Resource
A thing of value, often found in nature, that can be used to do or make something

Why Was the Louisiana Purchase Important?

The Louisiana Territory doubled the size of America, which controlled the entire Mississippi River and could use the port of New Orleans. America had gained **resources** in the fertile Louisiana land. In time, the Louisiana Territory would be divided into all or parts of fifteen additional states: Louisiana, Arkansas, Missouri, Iowa, Minnesota, North and South Dakota, Nebraska, Kansas, Oklahoma, Colorado, Wyoming, Texas, New Mexico, and Montana.

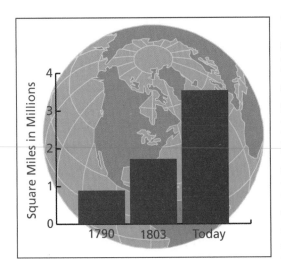

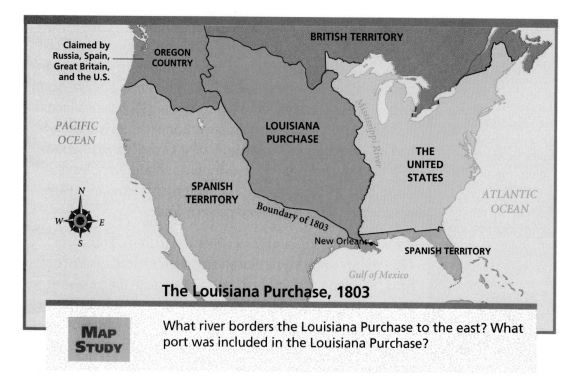

The Louisiana Purchase, 1803

MAP STUDY

What river borders the Louisiana Purchase to the east? What port was included in the Louisiana Purchase?

SECTION 4 REVIEW Choose the best word or name in parentheses to complete each sentence. Write your answers on a separate sheet of paper.

1) (John Adams, Thomas Jefferson, James Monroe) was inaugurated as President in 1801.

2) In 1800, Spain had been forced to return the land west of the Mississippi, known as Louisiana, to (Great Britain, France, the United States).

3) The United States bought the Louisiana Territory for ($20, $10, $15) million.

4) (Napoleon Bonaparte, Great Britain, James Monroe) sold the Louisiana Territory to the United States.

5) The state of (Missouri, Florida, Montana) was not included in the Louisiana Purchase.

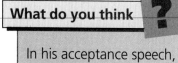

What do you think

In his acceptance speech, Jefferson called for all political parties to work together. Why do you think he said this?

Sacajawea with Lewis and Clark

Jefferson wanted to know as much as possible about what the United States had gained in the Louisiana Purchase. In 1804, he sent Meriwether Lewis and William Clark to explore the unknown northern regions.

Beginning at St. Louis, the two men journeyed northwest to the source of the Missouri River. They crossed the Rocky Mountains into Oregon Country, where they followed the Columbia River to the Pacific Ocean. They were guided by a Shoshone woman, Sacajawea.

Lewis and Clark brought back information to Jefferson about the peoples, wildlife, and lands of the Oregon Country. Many years later, the findings of Lewis and Clark would help America make a claim to that area.

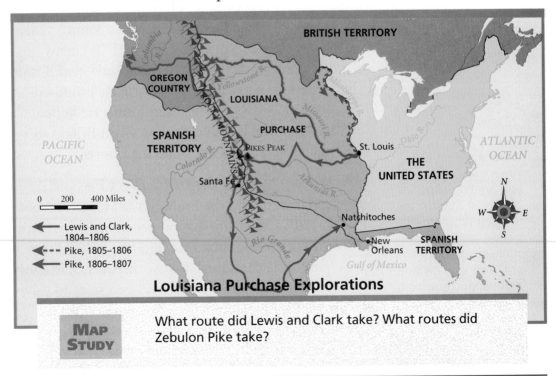

BRITISH TERRITORY

OREGON COUNTRY

LOUISIANA

PURCHASE

SPANISH TERRITORY

PACIFIC OCEAN

PIKES PEAK

Santa Fe

St. Louis

THE UNITED STATES

ATLANTIC OCEAN

Natchitoches

New Orleans

SPANISH TERRITORY

Gulf of Mexico

0 200 400 Miles

← Lewis and Clark, 1804–1806
◄--- Pike, 1805–1806
← Pike, 1806–1807

Louisiana Purchase Explorations

MAP STUDY

What route did Lewis and Clark take? What routes did Zebulon Pike take?

In 1805 and 1806, Zebulon Pike explored the northern regions of the Louisiana Purchase, seeking the source of the Mississippi River. In 1806 and 1807, he led an expedition to the Southwest. He followed the Arkansas River to the Rockies, and reached Pikes Peak in Colorado. However, this expedition was cut short when he traveled into Spanish territory where he was jailed for a time in what is now New Mexico.

How Did Jefferson Avoid War?

During Jefferson's second term as President, Great Britain and France were again at war. Napoleon's army was in full force and had conquered all his enemies except Great Britain. The United States was neutral and traded freely with France and Great Britain. American businesses **prospered** as ships carried supplies to both countries. Neither France nor Great Britain looked favorably upon America trading with its enemy. Jefferson believed the oceans were neutral and that ships could move freely. The British and French, however, had a different point of view.

Both countries set up **blockades.** A blockade is something that prevents goods or people from entering a country. Each country forbade other countries to trade with its enemy.

Thomas Jefferson knew that France and Great Britain both needed supplies from America. He proposed that all American ships stay home. He hoped this would force France and Great Britain to allow American ships into their ports.

Why Was the Embargo Act Passed?

Congress passed the Embargo Act on December 22, 1807. Under this act, no American ships could trade with foreign nations. Jefferson called this act a "peaceable **coercion.**" If it worked, it would show the world that war is not always necessary to solve problems. American merchants did not like the Embargo Act. For one and a half years, American trade fell apart. Many shippers chose to disobey

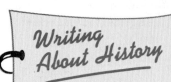

Writing About History

Write a speech to Americans as if you are President Jefferson. Explain the difficult problems the nation faces and offer some suggestions for solving them. Include an introduction, body, and conclusion in your speech.

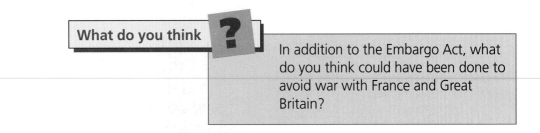

MIGUEL HIDALGO Y COSTILLA: 1753–1811

Mexican Independence Day is September 16. On that day in 1810, Miguel Hidalgo y Costilla rang the bell of his church in the village of Dolores. A priest and revolutionary, Hidalgo gathered his people and shouted his famous "grito de Dolores" (cry of Dolores). Mexico began its war of independence against Spain with that cry. Hidalgo led thousands of Indians and peasant warriors, overtaking several cities. A few months later, Spanish forces defeated and executed him. In yearly celebrations of Independence Day, the president of Mexico rings a bell in Mexico City and repeats the "grito de Dolores."

the law. Jefferson realized that the Embargo Act had been a failure. President Jefferson signed a law repealing the Embargo Act in March of 1809, only a few days before he left office.

SECTION 5 REVIEW Write the answers to these questions on a separate sheet of paper using complete sentences.

1) What did Lewis and Clark do?

2) What did Zebulon Pike do?

3) What did President Jefferson do to avoid war?

4) What was the Embargo Act?

5) What did the Embargo Act do to U.S. trade?

What do you think ?

In addition to the Embargo Act, what do you think could have been done to avoid war with France and Great Britain?

Prevention of Slave Trade

By the beginning of the 1800s, the slavery issue was already beginning to divide the nation. Northern antislavery forces had exerted sufficient pressure on Congress. In 1807, legislation was passed to discontinue the import of people from Africa for enslavement. These paragraphs are from that legislation.

"Be it enacted, by the Senate and the House of Representatives of the United States of America in Congress assembled, that from and after the 1st day of January, 1808, it shall not be lawful to import or bring into the United States or the territories thereof, from any foreign kingdom, place, or country, any Negro, mulatto, or person of color with intent to hold, sell, or dispose of such Negro, mulatto, or person of color as a slave, or to be held to service or labor.

Section 2. And it be further enacted, that no citizen or citizens of the United States, or any other person, shall, from and after the 1st day of January, in the year of Our Lord 1808, for himself, or themselves, or any other person whatsoever, either as master, factors, or owner, build, fit, equip, load, or otherwise prepare any ship or vessel, in any port or place within the jurisdiction of the United States, nor shall cause any ship or vessel to sail from any port or place within the same, for the purpose of procuring any Negro, mulatto, or person of color from any foreign kingdom, place, or country, to be transported to any port or place whatsoever within the jurisdiction of the United States, to be held, sold, or disposed of as slaves, or to be held to service or labor."

Source Reading Wrap-Up

1) Some people were involved in actually buying slaves. What other activity regarding slave trade does this legislation refer to?

2) In your own words, explain what activities this legislation made illegal.

3) Is any punishment named for those who broke this law?

4) From what you know of America in the early 1800s, explain whether you think this law was strictly obeyed.

5) How might this law have been made more effective?

★ Congress created three departments and one office in 1789. President Washington appointed four advisers. This group, called the cabinet, became a permanent part of the American government.

★ Alexander Hamilton created a financial plan to get the country out of debt. The plan was a success.

★ Hamilton's financial plan helped form political parties. Those who supported his plan formed the Federalist party. Another party, the Democratic-Republican party, felt that states should have more power to run their own affairs.

★ France declared war against Great Britain in 1793. France asked America to help fight the war. America was in no condition to fight another war so soon. President Washington kept the country neutral.

★ John Adams became President in 1797. He was not a popular President.

★ Several European countries were at war with France in 1797. France seized American ships. President Adams wanted to work out a deal with France. France's agents, called X, Y, and Z, refused to deal unless they were paid. The U.S. Navy fought several sea battles with the French.

★ Congress passed the Alien and Sedition acts in 1798.

★ Thomas Jefferson and James Madison wrote the Kentucky and Virginia resolutions in 1799 in response to the Alien and Sedition acts.

★ The election of 1800 resulted in a tie between Thomas Jefferson and Aaron Burr. The House of Representatives decided to make Jefferson President and Burr Vice President. Congress passed the Twelfth Amendment to the Constitution in 1804 to prevent such a tie from happening again.

★ President Jefferson wanted to buy the Louisiana Territory to give the United States access to New Orleans. Napoleon Bonaparte of France sold the entire region to the United States for $15 million in 1803.

★ Jefferson sent Meriwether Lewis and William Clark to explore the Louisiana Territory in 1804.

★ Congress passed the Embargo Act on December 22, 1807. Under this act, no American ships could trade with foreign nations. The Embargo Act made trade fall apart in America for over a year.

Comprehension: Identifying Facts

On a separate sheet of paper, write the correct word from the Word Bank to complete the sentences.

WORD BANK	
Alien Act	Jay's Treaty
cabinet	Kentucky
elector	Louisiana Purchase
electoral college	political party
Embargo Act	Sedition Act
immigrant	XYZ Affair

1) _____ got the British to leave their forts that were built on American soil.

2) The _____ involved three secret French agents who refused to cooperate with American delegates unless the United States gave them money.

3) The group of advisers who help the President is called a _____.

4) The _____ involved the United States buying land from the French.

5) The _____ is a group of people chosen to elect the President and Vice President.

6) A person who comes to live in a new country is called an _____.

7) Immigrants had to wait fourteen years before they could become United States citizens under the _____.

8) The _____ and Virginia resolutions were written in response to the Alien and Sedition Acts.

9) The _____ made it a crime for anyone to speak out, write, or print articles against the government.

10) A person who is chosen to vote for the President and Vice President is called an _____.

11) A _____ is a group that represents a certain political belief.

12) Under the _____, no American ships could trade with foreign nations.

Comprehension: Understanding Main Ideas

On a separate sheet of paper, write the answers to the following questions using complete sentences.

1) List three things Washington accomplished as President.

2) Which debts were to be paid off through Alexander Hamilton's financial plan?

3) What two events happened during President Adams's term?

4) Why was the election of 1800 unlike other elections?

5) List three events that happened during Jefferson's term.

6) What was the Louisiana Purchase? How did the United States benefit from it?

Critical Thinking: Write Your Opinion

1) What makes the job as President of the United States so difficult?

2) American Indians were left out of negotiating the Louisiana Purchase. Why do you think that was so?

Test Taking Tip If you don't know the answer to a question, put a check beside it and go on. Then when you are finished, go back to any checked questions and try to answer them.

1809–1815

The first three U.S. Presidents made it clear that the nation was not ready for another war. However, the troubles with France and Great Britain continued. Something had to be done to solve the problems. President James Madison was next in line to try to find a solution. In the end, the young country was forced into another war—the War of 1812. In this chapter, you will learn what caused this war and its outcome.

Goals for Learning

▶ To describe President Madison and his policies

▶ To list the causes of the War of 1812

▶ To identify the battles fought during the War of 1812

▶ To describe the outcome of the War of 1812

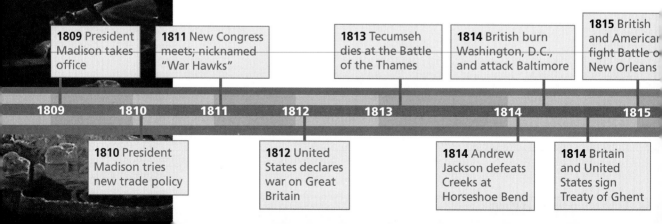

1809 President Madison takes office

1811 New Congress meets; nicknamed "War Hawks"

1813 Tecumseh dies at the Battle of the Thames

1814 British burn Washington, D.C., and attack Baltimore

1815 British and American fight Battle o New Orleans

| 1809 | 1810 | 1811 | 1812 | 1813 | 1814 | 1815 |

1810 President Madison tries new trade policy

1812 United States declares war on Great Britain

1814 Andrew Jackson defeats Creeks at Horseshoe Bend

1814 Britain and United States sign Treaty of Ghent

Aggressive
Forceful

Restriction
An act of limiting or preventing something

James Madison, the Democratic-Republican candidate from Virginia, became the fourth President in 1809. Madison was a quiet, intelligent man. He had many years of political experience. He became President just after the Embargo Act was repealed. He faced the challenge of finding a new policy for peace.

What New Policy Did Madison Propose?

President Madison tried to continue the neutral policy of Jefferson. In 1810, Madison proposed a new policy that permitted foreign trade. Madison wanted to bring back trade lost under the Embargo Act. His policy called for either France or Great Britain to stop its **restrictions** against American ships. If they did, America would refuse to trade with the other country.

Napoleon of France took advantage of Madison's proposal. He planned to use the United States against his British enemy. Britain's revenues would be greatly decreased with American ports closed to British goods. In August of 1810, Napoleon stated that France would accept American trade and would not seize American ships on the high seas.

Technology *History in Your Life*

Robert Fulton's Steamboat

In 1807, Robert Fulton built the first commercially workable steamboat. He used a steam-powered engine made in England and an unusual set of wheel-shaped paddles from another American inventor. On August 17, 1807, his new ship—*The Clermont*—sailed the Hudson River from New York to Albany in thirty-two hours. It was the forerunner of many commercial steamboats. Those boats carried grain from western farms down the Ohio and Mississippi rivers to the Gulf of Mexico. From the Gulf, the grain could easily be shipped to large ports on the east coast and in Europe. These ships helped to open up America's newly acquired western territories, enabling settlements there to thrive.

What Brought America Closer to War?

Important changes took place in 1811. The new Twelfth Congress included young, **aggressive** members. They wanted changes in policy. They did not like the way Great Britain was treating the United States. They became known as the "War Hawks."

Henry Clay was a member of Congress from Kentucky and a good speaker. Clay was chosen to lead the House of Representatives. Clay was only 34 years of age, but he had great **influence.** He and his followers were tired of American Indian raids on the frontier and blamed the British. The War Hawks wanted to put an end to the American Indian **conflict.** They also wanted to make sure there was freedom on the seas. War would result if other countries denied America that right. Meanwhile, the British continued to seize American ships and sailors as before. The British took nearly 1,000 vessels. Additionally, the French captured more than 500 American ships. At that time, both Great Britain and France were enemies of the United States.

The British had been an enemy since colonial days. Anti-British feelings existed from that time. Americans did not have these feelings toward the French. France had helped America during the Revolutionary War. Jefferson looked upon France as a friend. Madison had similar feelings toward the French. Unfortunately, he trusted Napoleon; he did not know that Napoleon only wanted to use America in his war against the British.

King Kamehameha I

Other things were happening in the world during this time. Far to the West in the Pacific, King Kamehameha I ruled the Hawaiian Islands from 1795 to 1819. Also known as "Kamehameha the Great," he conquered and united all of the Hawaiian Islands under his rule.

SECTION 1 REVIEW Write the answers to these questions on a separate sheet of paper using complete sentences.

1) Explain the trade policy that President Madison proposed.

2) How did Napoleon use the United States?

3) Describe the War Hawks.

4) What changes did the War Hawks want to make?

5) What did the Americans think of the British?

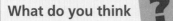

What do you think **?**

Do you think the War Hawks were right or wrong to feel the way they did toward Britain? Explain your answer.

★**Cash crop**
A crop that can be sold

★**Speaker of the House**
Leader of the House of Representatives

The first three Presidents—Washington, Adams, and Jefferson—had kept the country out of war. Each was certain that a war would destroy the young nation. By the time Madison became President, twenty years had passed since the Constitution established the new government. America was a new land with bold ideas.

The country's population had grown from about four million to more than seven million by 1810. The area of the United States had doubled in size. New England was rapidly developing industries, southern states were producing valuable **cash crops,** and slavery was increasing. A cash crop is a crop that can be sold. The frontier was being pushed farther west.

The new breed of Americans had only faint memories of colonial America. They felt the time had come for the United States to take action, and the War Hawks led the way. At the same time, Great Britain agreed to Madison's earlier offer to reopen trade between the two countries. Unfortunately, Madison was unaware of this decision.

What Were People's Attitudes Toward the War?

Henry Clay led the House of Representatives as **Speaker of the House.** He and John C. Calhoun of South Carolina saw British-owned Canada as an easy target. They thought that Canada could be defeated in just a few weeks. The War Hawks continued to stir up public opinion so that President Madison would have no choice but to declare war on Great Britain. With all the war talk, it was difficult to work toward a peaceful settlement.

The northern states, led by the Federalists, strongly opposed a war with Great Britain. But others saw several reasons for war against the British. The British had seized American ships and sailors, interfered with trade, and closed their ports to American goods.

Tecumseh tried to start a confederacy against settlers.

Tecumseh, chief of the Shawnees, tried to **organize** an American Indian **confederacy** against western settlers. A confederacy is a group that has formed an alliance. Many Americans were certain that the British would supply the American Indians with arms from Canada.

★Confederacy
A group that has formed an alliance

Organize
To put together in some kind of order

★Regular army
A state or country's official army

Why Wasn't the United States Prepared for War?

The **regular army** of the United States was poorly trained and very small. This was the nation's official army. It had less than 10,000 soldiers. The generals were old and had little or no experience in real war situations. Over the thirty-year period since the Revolutionary War, the army had become less and less important. The country could not pay for a big, well-trained army because it had no money to support it.

Media in History

Frontier Newspapers: How the West Was Won

In each frontier town, one of the first business people to set up shop was the newspaper publisher. Part of this was a result of the Congressional Act of 1814. It said all federal laws must be printed in two newspapers in each state and territory. This meant good business for newspapers.

Frontier newspapers were often crude. Many were only two or four pages, but they were well read. Editors encouraged readers to write columns. These articles encouraged a lot of community discussion. People got excited about causes. Sometimes angry dissenters burned down newspaper offices.

Western settlers set themselves apart from the rest of the United States. They only wanted the government to step in when they needed help to fight the American Indians. Because settlers regarded the "Indian problem" as serious, the frontier newspapers encouraged the War of 1812. The British in Canada were supplying gunpowder to the Indians. Thus, the western settlers wanted to flush out the British. The western congressmen elected Henry Clay Speaker of the House. This was a strong signal to the United States that the West was a powerful force in American politics.

MOTHER ELIZABETH SETON: 1774–1821

Mother Elizabeth Seton was the first native-born American to be declared a saint. Born Elizabeth Ann Bayley, she married William M. Seton in New York in 1794. The couple had five children. After her husband died in 1803, Elizabeth became a nun. Called Mother Seton, she founded the Daughters of Charity in 1809. She started the first private religious school and the first Roman Catholic orphanage in the United States. On September 14, 1975, the Roman Catholic Church made her Saint Elizabeth Ann Seton. Her feast day is celebrated on January 4.

America's navy was also not in shape for war. It had only sixteen warships. The United States would be no match for the powerful Britain, which had the largest navy in the world. Even with these disadvantages, talk of war still continued.

At the same time, America's foreign trade had almost come to a complete standstill. Trade brought in money for the government through tariffs. Now, without the revenue from tariffs, America had no money to fight a war.

SECTION 2 REVIEW On a separate sheet of paper, write *True* if the statement is true and *False* if the statement is not true.

1) Henry Clay was Speaker of the House of Representatives.

2) The War Hawks thought that Canada could not be defeated.

3) The northern states opposed a war with Great Britain.

4) Tecumseh wanted to start a confederacy against western settlers.

5) The American regular army was strong and ready for a war.

What do you think ?

Why do you think the United States was not ready for a war?

President Madison asked Congress to declare war against Great Britain on June 1, 1812. Both the House of Representatives and the Senate approved the request. Both votes were very close. Madison did not have the popular support he needed to fight a war. However, Congress declared war on June 19, 1812. They were unaware that Britain had decided to reopen trade with the United States.

The presidential election of 1812 was a contest between the War Hawks and those for peace. The War Hawks supported Madison, and those for peace supported DeWitt Clinton of New York. The vote was close, but Madison's re-election was clearly a victory for those who favored the war with Great Britain. Many well-off shippers thought the United States should wait it out with Britain rather than participate in what they called "Mr. Madison's War."

Which Early Battles Were Fought?

On land, American soldiers had very little success. Each of the three attempts in 1812 to invade Canada resulted in defeats. One defeat was at Detroit, where the Northwest Indians under Tecumseh joined the British. The following year a group invaded York (now Toronto), but held it for only a short time. A later attempt at taking Montreal was also a failure. The War Hawks' earlier claims of an easy victory in Canada had been wrong.

In the first year of the war, the American warship *Constitution* captured British ships along the Atlantic coast. After one battle, the ship earned the nickname "Old Ironsides" because cannonballs bounced off its sides. The American navy destroyed 1,500 British merchant ships during the early days of the war. In time, however, the larger British navy brought America under control by sea. It created a blockade, which stopped all shipping to and from the United States.

The American warship *Constitution* defeated the British warship *Guerrière* in 1812. After this battle, *Constitution* was nicknamed "Old Ironsides."

Which Battles Did the Americans Win?

In 1813, the Americans under Captain Oliver Hazard Perry built a fleet of small ships with timbers from a Pennsylvania forest. Then, in a fierce battle, they defeated a British naval fleet on Lake Erie. The victory was important because it stopped a possible British invasion of the Ohio Valley and gave Americans control of Lake Erie.

Two other American victories were of special importance following Perry's naval triumph in 1813. General William Henry Harrison defeated a British and American Indian force in the Battle of the Thames in Canada. Tecumseh, the Shawnee leader, was killed in that battle. The death of Tecumseh put an end to his plans to organize the American Indians against the settlers. It also put an end to the cooperation between the American Indians and the British. General Harrison became famous from this battle.

Andrew Jackson defeated the Creeks at Horseshoe Bend early in 1814. General Jackson's victory forced the American Indians to sign a treaty that opened up Georgia and present-day Alabama to American settlers. Jackson had become a hero, but his fame was just beginning to grow.

When 11,000 British troops invaded New York in 1814, they were sure that the Americans would be no match for them. However, in the Battle of Lake Champlain, the tiny American fleet **outmaneuvered** the heavily armed British ships and defeated them completely. The British returned to Canada after giving up hope of capturing New York.

Outmaneuver
To move more quickly or better than an enemy

The British attacked Washington, D.C., in 1814. They burned the capitol building and the White House.

What Happened at Washington, D.C., and Baltimore?

In August of 1814, a British fleet landed about 4,000 soldiers close to Washington, D.C. The well-trained soldiers marched on to the capital. In a few hours, the capitol building and the President's home, called the White House by some, were set on fire. Other buildings were also burned. It was a crushing loss for the Americans.

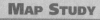

MAP STUDY

Where was Fort McHenry located? Which side advanced from Canada?

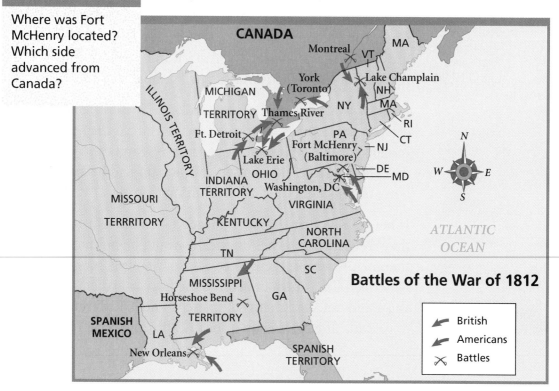

Battles of the War of 1812

- British
- Americans
- Battles

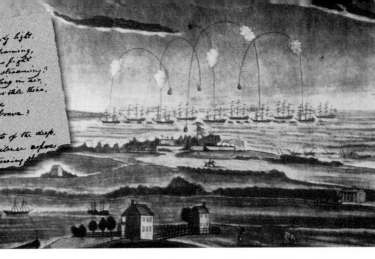

Francis Scott Key wrote a poem (above) about the Battle of Fort McHenry (right). The poem later became America's national anthem.

Anthem
A song or hymn of praise or gladness

The British navy sailed northward and shelled Fort McHenry, in an attempt to capture Baltimore. Fort McHenry guarded the entrance into Baltimore's harbor. Shells exploded all through the night. Francis Scott Key, a Washington lawyer, watched the battle. He wrote a poem that was later titled "The Star-Spangled Banner." The poem was set to music and became the American national **anthem** over 100 years later.

SECTION 3 REVIEW Choose the best name in parentheses to complete each sentence. Write your answers on a separate sheet of paper.

1) (Oliver Hazard Perry, William Henry Harrison, Tecumseh) defeated a British naval fleet on Lake Erie.

2) (Francis Scott Key, Andrew Jackson, DeWitt Clinton) defeated the Creeks at Horseshoe Bend.

3) (Andrew Jackson, Oliver Hazard Perry, Tecumseh) was killed at the Battle of the Thames.

4) The War Hawks supported (President Madison, DeWitt Clinton, Oliver Hazard Perry) for President in the 1812 election.

5) A lawyer named (DeWitt Clinton, Andrew Jackson, Francis Scott Key) wrote the "Star-Spangled Banner."

What do you think **?**

Why do you think the American Indians were willing to fight on the side of the British?

Confusion
The act of being mixed up

Possession
An object belonging to someone

Restore
To put something back or give something back to its owner

By the end of 1814, both sides wanted peace. The war had not gone well for either Great Britain or the United States. Great Britain already had a large war debt from the war with France. Increased spending and continued loss of trade revenues made the war very unpopular. The British also remembered from the Revolutionary War that Americans could fight a long war if necessary. The British people pressed for settlement. They were tired of heavy taxes and so many wars.

For Americans, the war had started in **confusion.** It was poorly organized and had mixed support. During the war, trade was nearly ruined and many people had been put out of work, especially in the northern states. It was clear that the war had failed.

What Happened at the Treaty of Ghent?

During the summer of 1814, American representatives met with British representatives in Ghent, Belgium. Talks went on for weeks before a settlement was reached. The Treaty of Ghent was signed in December. It stated only that "all territory, places, and **possessions** whatsoever taken by either party from the other during the war . . . shall be **restored.**" The war was declared a tie.

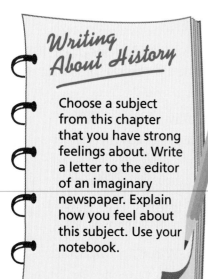

Writing About History

Choose a subject from this chapter that you have strong feelings about. Write a letter to the editor of an imaginary newspaper. Explain how you feel about this subject. Use your notebook.

What Happened at the Battle of New Orleans?

A battle was fought in 1815 at New Orleans after the Treaty of Ghent. News of the treaty had not yet reached New Orleans. The troops in the New Orleans area were led by Andrew Jackson. His small frontier army faced 8,000 of Britain's best soldiers. When the fighting ended, 2,000 British soldiers had been killed or wounded. American losses were fewer than 100. The victory was celebrated as "the surrender of the British." Jackson's fame and popularity spread throughout the land.

War of 1812 Statistics

Began: June 12, 1812
Ended: January 14, 1815
American deaths: 2,260
Americans wounded: 4,505
Cost for Americans: $89 million

What Were the Results of the War?

The War of 1812 is often called the Second Revolutionary War. Though America had declared its independence in 1776, British feelings toward their former colony had remained unchanged until the War of 1812. The British began to respect the United States as a nation. America's strong showing in the war had helped it win the respect of countries around the world.

The war gave more Americans a sense of **nationalism.** Nationalism is a sense of loyalty to one's country. Americans wanted to make the nation grow and **prosper.** During the war, manufacturing in America was given a boost as the need to be **self-sufficient** had grown.

The possibilities for safe westward expansion were changed because of forced movements of the American Indians. Once again the American Indians were victims of the European settlers.

SECTION 4 REVIEW Write the answers to these questions on a separate sheet of paper using complete sentences.

1) Why did the United States want to see an end to the war?

2) Why did Great Britain want to see an end to the war?

3) Who won the War of 1812?

4) What did the Treaty of Ghent state?

5) How did the United States benefit from the war?

★Nationalism
A sense of loyalty to one's country

Prosper
To succeed

Self-sufficient
Able to do something without help

What do you think **?**

Do you think the War of 1812 was necessary for the United States?

Speech by Tecumseh

Shawnee Chief Tecumseh worked to unite American Indians against white settlers. Settlers were rapidly taking land and forcing Indians out. Unless Indians united, they would have no land of their own. Americans respected Tecumseh. He was intelligent and an excellent speaker. Tecumseh gave this speech in 1810 in a meeting with Indiana Governor Harrison.

"I am a Shawnee. My forefathers were warriors. Their son is a warrior. From them I only take my existence; from my tribe I take nothing. . . . I would. . . ask [Governor Harrison] to tear the treaty and to obliterate the landmark. . . . The being within . . . tells me that once . . . there was no white man on this continent. That it then all belonged to red men, children of the same parents, placed on it by the Great Spirit that made them, to keep it, to traverse it, to enjoy its productions, and to fill it with the same race. Once a happy race. Since made miserable by the white people, who are never contented, but always encroaching. The . . . only way . . . to stop this evil, is for all the red men to unite in claiming a common and equal right in the land, as it was at first . . . for it never was divided, but belongs to all for the use of each . . . .

The white people have no right to take the land from the Indians, because they had it first; it is theirs . . . . All red men have equal rights to the unoccupied land . . . . There cannot be two occupations in the same place. The first excludes all others. It is not so in hunting or traveling; for there the same ground will serve many . . . but the camp is stationary, and that is occupancy. It belongs to the first who sits down on his blanket or skins which he has thrown upon the ground; and till he leaves it no other has a right."

Source Reading Wrap-Up

1) Who was Tecumseh and what did he try to do?

2) What did Tecumseh want Governor Harrison to do?

3) Whom did Tecumseh blame for American Indians no longer being a happy race?

4) Why did Tecumseh say that white people had no right to take American Indians' land?

5) Tecumseh did not object to white people hunting and traveling over the land. What did he say was a problem?

CHAPTER SUMMARY

★ James Madison became the fourth President in 1809. He started a new trade policy in 1810 with France and Great Britain. The policy said if either country stopped its trade restrictions against the United States, America would refuse to trade with the other country.

★ The Twelfth Congress met in 1811. Many members of Congress wanted to put an end to the American Indian conflict and wanted freedom on the seas. This group was nicknamed the "War Hawks."

★ The War Hawks, Henry Clay, and John C. Calhoun began to persuade the public that war with Britain was necessary.

★ Federalists in the northern states opposed a war. The United States military was not prepared for a war.

★ Congress declared war on Britain on June 19, 1812.

★ The Americans won battles at Lake Erie, the Thames River, and Horseshoe Bend. Tecumseh, an American Indian leader who had organized a confederacy, was killed at the Battle of the Thames.

★ The British attacked and burned Washington, D.C., and then attacked Baltimore.

★ By 1814, both sides wanted peace. They signed the Treaty of Ghent to end the war. However, news of the treaty had not reached New Orleans, where one final battle was fought and won by the Americans. The war was declared a tie.

★ The United States benefited from the war because it won the country the respect of other countries. The war increased feelings of nationalism, and cleared the way for westward expansion.

Comprehension: Identifying Facts

On a separate sheet of paper, write the correct word or name from the Word Bank to complete the sentences.

WORD BANK	
Andrew Jackson	Henry Clay
Battle of Lake Champlain	James Madison
Battle of New Orleans	Oliver Hazard Perry
Battle of the Thames	Tecumseh
Constitution	Treaty of Ghent
DeWitt Clinton	War Hawks
Fort McHenry	William Henry Harrison
Francis Scott Key	

1) Those who wanted peace during the election of 1812 supported _____.

2) The fourth President of the United States was _____.

3) The _____ were members of Congress who wanted changes in policy.

4) A small American fleet outmaneuvered heavily armed British ships at the _____.

5) A Shawnee chief named _____ organized an American Indian confederacy.

6) The Speaker of the House named _____ wanted America to attack Canada.

7) The Creeks were defeated by _____ at Horseshoe Bend.

8) A general named _____ defeated an American Indian and British force at the Battle of the Thames.

9) An American warship called the _____ was nicknamed "Old Ironsides."

10) A lawyer named _____ wrote the "Star-Spangled Banner."

11) The _____ was fought after the Treaty of Ghent was signed.

12) _____ guarded the entrance into Baltimore's harbor.

13) A captain named _____ defeated a British naval fleet on Lake Erie.

14) Tecumseh was killed at the _____.

15) The _____ ended the War of 1812.

Comprehension: Understanding Main Ideas

On a separate sheet of paper, write answers to the following questions using complete sentences.

1) What kind of person was President Madison? What trade policy did he introduce?

2) What were three causes of the War of 1812?

3) What did the War of 1812 do for the United States?

Critical Thinking: Write Your Opinion

1) The War of 1812 shows Congress's power to declare war. Do you think it is right for Congress to have this power?

2) How do you think the War of 1812 was different from the Revolutionary War?

Test Taking Tip When you are reading a test question, pay attention to words that are emphasized in bold type or in capital letters. Those words will help you decide how best to answer the question.

Unit 3 *Graphs and Charts*

A graph is a figure that shows relationships between numbers. Types of graphs are bar, line, and circle graphs. **Use a graph to compare numbers and percents.**

Here are examples of a simple bar graph and a simple circle graph. Each compares the number of Revolutionary War battles won by the Patriots and the Redcoats in 1777.

Revolutionary War Battles Won in 1777

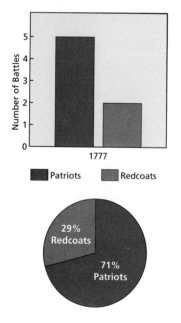

A chart is a way to put information together so it is clear. The information can be put in rows (across) and columns (up and down). **Use a chart to organize information.**

The chart in the next column gives more information about major Revolutionary War battles in 1777.

Major Revolutionary War Battles of 1777

Name of Battle	Place of Battle	Winner	
		Patriots	Redcoats
Bennington	Vermont	X	
Brandywine	Pennsylvania		X
Freeman's Farm (1st Battle)	New York	X	
Freeman's Farm (2nd Battle)	New York	X	
Germantown	Pennsylvania		X
Princeton	New Jersey	X	
Saratoga	New York	X	

The first column names the battles. The second column tells where the battles were fought. The Xs in the third or fourth column tell which side won each battle. For information about one particular battle, read across the row. Study the chart to answer the questions.

1) How many major battles were fought in 1777?

2) In which state did the most battles occur?

3) Which two battles were fought in the same location?

4) Which side won the most battles?

5) Read this information. Use it to make a chart showing which states were added between 1791 and 1814.

By 1790, all thirteen of the original colonies had signed the U.S. Constitution. They became the first thirteen states. Five states were added within the next twenty-five years. Vermont was added in 1791. Kentucky followed in 1792. Tennessee was added in 1796. Ohio became a state in 1803. Louisiana was admitted in 1812.

★ In 1764, the British Parliament agreed to tax the colonies. The colonists protested.

★ The Boston Massacre occurred in 1770.

★ Colonists dumped tea into Boston Harbor on December 16, 1773.

★ The First Continental Congress met in 1774.

★ On May 10, 1775, the Second Continental Congress decided it could declare war.

★ Colonists had several battles with the British in 1775 and early 1776.

★ Congress approved the Declaration of Independence on July 4, 1776.

★ The Revolutionary War ended at Yorktown, Virginia, on October 19, 1781.

★ The states adopted the Articles of Confederation in 1781.

★ In 1783, the Treaty of Paris established the new nation's boundaries.

★ The Constitutional Convention created a plan for a stronger central government in 1787.

★ George Washington was elected the first President in 1789.

★ Congress added the Bill of Rights to the Constitution in 1791.

★ Alexander Hamilton's successful financial plan helped form political parties.

★ France declared war against England in 1793. The United States stayed neutral.

★ John Adams became President in 1797, and Thomas Jefferson became President in 1801.

★ France sold the Louisiana Territory to the United States for $15 million.

★ James Madison became President in 1809.

★ Congress declared war on Britain on June 19, 1812, to end the American Indian conflict. The Treaty of Ghent ended the war.

"While the republic has already acquired a history world-wide, America is still unsettled and unexplored. . . . We live only on the shores of a continent even yet, and hardly know where the rivers come from which float our navy. The very timber . . . of which our houses are made, grew but yesterday in a wilderness where the Indian still hunts and the moose runs wild."

–Henry David Thoreau, "Ktaadn," 1848

Expansion and Reform

Unit 4

1816–1850

Have you heard the expression "growing pains"? America was feeling growing pains between 1816 and 1850. The population was increasing. Industries were growing and multiplying. Disagreements over issues were more numerous. Slavery especially was becoming an issue that divided people. Americans had to adapt to many changes as the nation experienced the pain of growth.

In this unit you will learn about westward growth of the United States. You will learn about growing industries and new inventions. You will learn about border disputes. You will learn about disagreements and the changing political scene in the first half of the 1800s.

Chapter 10: A New Spirit of Expansion: 1816-1824

Chapter 11: Political Changes Take Place: 1825-1838

Chapter 12: America Becomes More Democratic: 1825-1858

Chapter 13: The Country Grows Larger: 1841-1850

1816–1824

With the War of 1812 behind it, the United States was on its way to expansion. At the same time, industry and farming began to thrive in the North and the South. The country also began to address the issue of slavery and problems with bordering European colonies. James Monroe was chosen to lead the way as the next President. In this chapter, you will learn about westward expansion, problems of slavery, and some of the issues facing President Monroe.

Goals for Learning

▶ To identify how settlers moved west and the problems they faced

▶ To explain which industries developed in the North and in the South

▶ To describe the Era of Good Feelings

▶ To describe how slavery caused problems

▶ To explain the Missouri Compromise

▶ To describe the Monroe Doctrine

▶ To explain what happened in the election of 1824

1817 President Monroe takes office

1819 Spanish and Americans sign Adams-Onís Treaty

1820 Congress accepts Missouri Compromise

1823 President Monroe announces Monroe Doctrine

1816   1818   1820   1822   1824

1818 Andrew Jackson invades Seminole country

1820 President Monroe wins re-election

1822 South Carolina authorities execute Denmark Vesey and others

1824 House of Representatives chooses John Quincy Adams as President

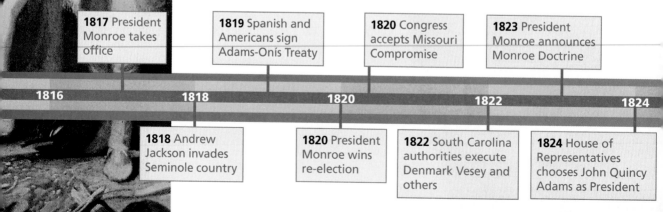

James Monroe, a Democratic-Republican, was elected President by an electoral vote of 183 to 34 in 1816. He was helped by the fact that President Madison, also a Democratic-Republican, was more popular at the end of his second term than he had been earlier. Now, after so many victories by the Democratic-Republicans, the Federalists were finished as a political party. President Monroe took office in 1817.

How Was the Country Expanding?

Between 1790 and 1820, the population of the United States increased from about four million to nearly ten million. In the frontier states, the number of persons grew from 100,000 to well over two million during that time. The country was rapidly expanding. Its shape was changing, too. The western state of Indiana was admitted to the Union in 1816. Mississippi became a state in 1817, Illinois in 1818, and Alabama in 1819. At that point, the United States had twenty-two states, an increase of nine since the Constitution was ratified by the thirteen original states.

Many settlers moved westward in covered wagons along the Ohio River route to Indiana, Illinois, northern Kentucky, and western Tennessee. The government built the Cumberland Road leading from Maryland through Virginia in 1818. This popular route was later extended across Ohio into Indiana and Illinois. When the Erie Canal was completed in 1825, New Englanders could choose yet another all-water path toward the West. This water route and the many rivers leading west became regular paths for almost seventy steamboats in common use by 1820.

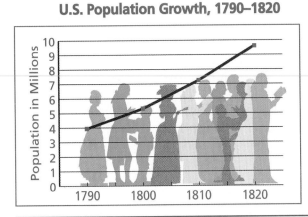

U.S. Population Growth, 1790–1820

What does this graph show? About how much did the population increase from 1790 to 1820?

How Were Westerners Different?

Settlers of the western states were not like the earlier American colonists. The western frontier was both lonely and dangerous. It was necessary for settlers to help and protect one another. Everyone was equal. Unlike that in the eastern states, the way of life on the frontier was difficult and required hard work. Westerners were fiercely independent. Many of them had been dissatisfied with their lives on the east coast, while some were new immigrants from Europe who wanted a fresh, independent start. Love of freedom and pride in the United States were most important to them. This new American spirit of nationalism grew and was a main part of life in the frontier states. Henry Clay of Kentucky brought that new spirit to the United States Congress.

There were four problems that the western states had to face: more roads were needed to improve transportation; land prices had to be inexpensive and regulated by the central government; **loans** from banks had to be available to farmers; and markets for farm goods had to be protected by the government.

Why Was Farming Ideal in the South?

Americans found conditions in the South to be ideal for farming. They took advantage of the long **growing season,** plenty of rainfall, and broad, fertile **lowlands.** The South produced crops that could be sold to other states and European countries. Crops such as cotton, rice, sugar, tobacco, indigo, and **hemp** were all big profit crops. Hemp is a plant with a tough fiber that is used for making rope. Cotton is a plant that is used to make material for clothing.

Little manufacturing was done in the South. Most of the products needed by the southern states had to be bought from European countries. Tariffs added to European products resulted in higher prices for goods that the South needed.

This poster (left) announced the sale of African slaves in the 1800s. The number of African slaves increased after the cotton gin (right) was invented.

Why Was Cotton Important in the South?

Eli Whitney invented the cotton gin in 1793. The "gin," as it was called, separated the seeds from cotton by machine rather than by hand. Cotton was not **profitable** before the gin because of the labor involved to remove the seeds. Even though African slaves had been bought and used for many years, the production of cotton was rather limited.

Profitable
Able to bring in money above operating costs

Cotton production was less than 100,000 bales in 1799. By 1810, production was up to nearly 200,000 bales. The amount was nearly 400,000 by 1820. The crop became known as "King Cotton," or white gold. Cotton became so profitable that cotton growing spread westward. More land was being used to raise more cotton. The number of African slaves also increased. Cotton was king of the South, and slavery became increasingly important there. Slave labor cost almost nothing and was needed for the increased cotton crops.

Writing About History

Research the cotton gin. Then in your notebook, write an advertisement for it. Explain what it does, its benefits, and other information that would help sell the machine. Draw a picture of the gin to show how it works.

Which Industries Developed in the North?

The industrial development of the northern states began early in colonial days. Fishing, shipbuilding, trading, and ironworks were all important to the Northern states. There was little farming because of the cold Northern winters and the rocky land. Manufacturers in the northeast wanted the government to keep European products out of the country as American industries grew. They were concerned that they would have trouble competing against British products, which were less expensive to buy.

The North did benefit from the success of the cotton crop in the South. Cotton mills in the North turned the raw cotton into thread. One Massachusetts merchant, Francis Lowell, built a new type of water-powered spinning machine and loom. The cotton thread was made into cloth and the cloth into articles of clothing. These factories, as well as factories making countless other items, grew throughout the northern states. Knowledge of manufacturing brought to America from Europe was helping create better products in a shorter amount of time.

Different political points of view were being developed as three separate regions took shape—the western frontier states, the southern states, and the northern New England states.

SECTION 1 REVIEW Write the answers to these questions on a separate sheet of paper using complete sentences.

1) What special problems did the western states face?

2) How were westerners different?

3) Why was farming good for the southern states?

4) Why did cotton production increase so much after the cotton gin was invented?

5) How did the North benefit from cotton?

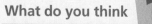

What do you think **?**

Why do you think people living on the frontier needed to be independent?

Sectional
Related to the interests of a region

James Monroe was very much aware of the growing **sectional** differences within the country. He kept these differences in mind when he chose his cabinet. His choice for Secretary of State was John Quincy Adams, the son of John Adams, from Massachusetts. The choice greatly pleased New Englanders. John C. Calhoun of South Carolina was appointed Secretary of War. William Crawford of Georgia was named Secretary of the Treasury. Monroe had considered Henry Clay of Kentucky for a cabinet position. Clay refused, however, because he wanted to remain as Speaker of the House of Representatives. President Monroe's selections resulted in a well-balanced cabinet that represented all sections of the nation.

What Was the Era of Good Feelings?

James Monroe's two terms were called the "Era of Good Feelings." In the election of 1816, the Democratic-Republicans defeated the Federalists with very little trouble. The electoral vote was 183 to 34. In 1820, Monroe won all the electoral votes except one. Some believe William Plumer of New Hampshire voted for John Quincy Adams so that George Washington would be the only President elected unanimously. There was no party to go against the Democratic-Republicans in the election of 1820. This was one sign of the unity found during the Era of Good Feelings.

What Problems Did America Have With Spanish Florida?

Trouble along the Georgia-Florida boundary had increased over the years. Plantation owners in Georgia complained that the Seminole crossed the border and attacked American families. According to some Georgians, the Seminole captured slaves and took them to Spanish Florida. Others complained that Spanish officials encouraged slaves to escape across the border.

Tuko-See-Mathla was a Seminole chief in the 1820s.

Because of the border problems, Andrew Jackson was ordered into the area. In early 1818, General Jackson gathered a fighting force of 1,000 troops. He led an invasion into Seminole country and Spanish Florida. Jackson and the troops easily took over the Spanish stronghold at St. Marks. They then captured the Spanish post in Pensacola, Florida. The Spanish protested Jackson's use of strong military force.

In 1819, the Adams-Onís Treaty was signed. Under the terms of the treaty, the Spanish gave all of Florida and other claims east of the Mississippi to the United States in exchange for $5 million, which was used to pay a debt to American citizens. The United States gave up its claim to Spanish Texas. Once again, General Andrew Jackson was the hero of the nation.

JOHN ROSS: 1790–1866

Cherokee leader John Ross was born of a Scottish father and a Cherokee mother. He was called Coowescoowe, or "the egret," in Cherokee. Well educated and articulate, he spent his life trying to resolve the deep conflicts between American Indians and the colonists. Ross worked for the U.S. government as a young man, fighting alongside Andrew Jackson in the War of 1812. Later, as a Cherokee chief, he opposed the U.S. government. He won a U.S. court case against the state of Georgia, which tried to seize Cherokee land. The court's decision was ignored. After a hard struggle to keep their land, Ross had to give up and lead the Cherokee to Oklahoma. This journey was known as the "Trail of Tears." He helped to write a constitution for a united Cherokee nation. Ross was elected chief of the new nation, but the Cherokee never achieved the unity he had hoped for.

How Did Slavery Become an Issue?

Missouri was located in the cotton-growing region and wanted to be admitted as a **slave state.** A slave state was one that could practice slavery. As of 1819, there were eleven slave states and eleven **free states.** Free states could not practice slavery. Power in the Senate was balanced between the North and the South. The addition of Missouri as the twelfth slave state would upset the balance of power. Congress had to consider this problem before deciding whether to let Missouri enter the Union as a state that allowed slavery. Also, the legislators would have to decide whether to allow slavery in new western states as far north as Missouri.

Missouri would be the first slave state west of the Mississippi River. Northerners feared slavery would spread throughout the entire Louisiana region. They thought if Missouri joined the Union as a slave state, more would follow. Congress would be unable to stop the spread of slavery.

Southern states had a different point of view. If Missouri was admitted as a free state, Congress would be able to destroy the slave system in all the states. Northerners spoke out strongly against slavery. The antislavery **movement** was of great concern to owners of cotton plantations in the South. The Missouri problem was beginning to heat up, as two sections with strong views debated the issue. Control of the Senate by northern or southern states would determine future government policies.

Cotton plantations such as this one thrived in the South.

Authorities
Persons in command of something

Execute
To put to death

Revolt
A rebellion

★Statehood
The condition of being a state

How Did Maine and Missouri Become States?

The debate went on for several months. Then, by chance, Maine asked to be admitted to the Union in December of 1819. Its constitution contained a clause that did not allow slavery. There was no question that Maine would be a free state. Maine's admission provided a possible solution to the problem. During these debates, Henry Clay of Kentucky was the Speaker of the House of Representatives. Clay, a strong leader who came to be known as "The Great Compromiser," had to satisfy both sides.

A compromise was proposed. First, the requests for becoming a state, or **statehood,** by Maine and Missouri were combined. Missouri was to be allowed to enter the Union as a slave state. Maine would join as a free state. With twelve slave states and twelve free states, there would still be a balance of power in the Senate. In addition, slavery would not be allowed in any new states north of 36 degrees 30 minutes north latitude in the Louisiana Territory. Missouri was the only state to which this law did not apply.

This Missouri Compromise, as it was called, was approved by Congress March 3, 1820. Henry Clay's influence had made the approval possible. The issue of slave states and free states was worked out for the time being.

The Missouri Compromise had made southern plantation owners think that slavery was "safe" in the South. Then one of many damaging events took place in Charleston, South Carolina, in 1822. Having heard of a possible **revolt** by the slaves of that city, the **authorities** prepared for trouble. A group of 9,000 people led by freed slave Denmark Vesey had planned to attack several South Carolina cities. However, Vesey and thirty-five other people were **executed** before any revolt could take place. This event led to stronger laws to control the movement and education of freedmen and slaves.

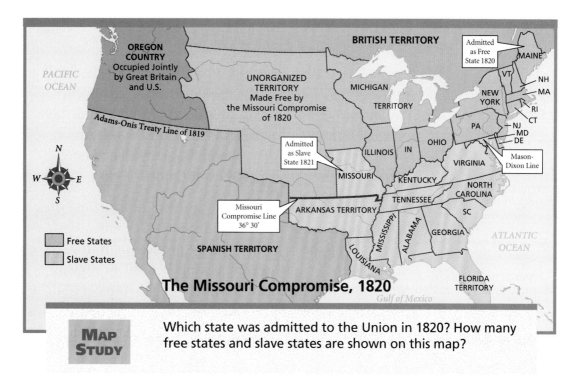

The Missouri Compromise, 1820

MAP STUDY Which state was admitted to the Union in 1820? How many free states and slave states are shown on this map?

SECTION 2 REVIEW On a separate sheet of paper, write *True* if the statement is true or *False* if the statement is not true.

1) James Monroe's political party was the Democratic-Republican party.

2) Spain owned Florida in 1818.

3) General Andrew Jackson led an invasion of Florida in 1818.

4) Missouri was a free state.

5) Denmark Vesey and thirty-five people were executed in South Carolina in 1822.

What do you think ❓

Why do you think slavery was beginning to cause problems in the United States?

Agreement
An arrangement as to the course of action

★Doctrine
A statement of a certain government policy

Joint declaration
To declare something as a group

Besides the trouble in Florida and the issue of Missouri's admission as a slave state, James Monroe faced another serious problem during his presidency. At that time, there still were European colonies in North and South America. The British, Dutch, Spanish, and Russians all had land claims from the early days of exploration.

These European colonies saw what revolutions could do. They could become free and independent countries by overthrowing their governments. America did it in 1776, and the French overthrew their king in 1789. European colonies on the American continent began to rebel against their governments. European monarchies now had to calm the revolts to get back control or lose their American colonies.

The monarchies agreed to send powerful armies and fleets to take back control of the colonies in North and South America. The British did not take part in the **agreement.** Trade with those colonies was very profitable for the British. Any change would mean less trade. The United States, as well, desired to protect those markets because of the profits of trade.

What Proposal Did the British Make?

George Canning was the British foreign secretary. He suggested that the United States and Great Britain make a **joint declaration** warning all European monarchies to keep out of the affairs of Latin America. President Monroe discussed the matter with Thomas Jefferson and James Madison. Both agreed that the proposal was a good one. John Quincy Adams, Secretary of State, did not agree. He was able to show Monroe that the United States should act alone. The President took his advice and created the statement of policy that became known as the Monroe **Doctrine.** A doctrine is a statement of a certain government policy.

What Was the Monroe Doctrine?

James Monroe announced his famous doctrine in his yearly message to Congress in December of 1823. He said that any attempt by a European power to extend its influence in any part of the **Western Hemisphere** would be considered dangerous to the peace and safety of the United States.

President Monroe was not alone in dealing with problems with European nations. His wife, Elizabeth (above) took part in foreign relations with France.

The Monroe Doctrine received widespread approval by Americans. The British, however, were not pleased with it because it was not a joint declaration. Other countries in Europe did not consider the **proclamation** to be important. The doctrine, adopted in 1823, would not be tested for many years to come. The main point, however, is that when that time came, the Monroe Doctrine could be used.

Sequoyah and a Different Form of Writing

Sequoyah was a Cherokee scholar. He invented a new writing system for the Cherokee language around 1821. His system was comprised of eighty-six symbols. Some symbols were English letters but without the same English sounds. Sequoyah's symbols represented all the Cherokee sounds. Thus, Sequoyah enabled Cherokees to become the first American Indian tribe to read and write in their own tongue. Throughout the 1820s, he personally taught thousands of Cherokees to read and write. Parts of the Bible and the first American Indian newspaper, *The Cherokee Phoenix,* were printed in Cherokee. Sequoyah's accomplishment helped unite Cherokees and made them leaders among other tribes. His intelligence and unshakable pride in his culture were inspiring.

Literature

History in Your Life

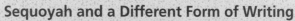

Agricultural
Having to do with raising crops or animals for food or profit

Qualified
Fit for a given purpose

The United States had become three distinct regions—the freedom-loving West, the rapidly industrializing North, and the **agricultural** South. Each region had a different political point of view, representing different needs. By 1824, sectional politics had produced five presidential candidates. The influence of the South, as led by a series of politicians from Virginia, was declining. The West and the North were becoming more and more influential.

The New England states nominated John Quincy Adams of Massachusetts. He was serving as Secretary of State under President Monroe. Adams, whose father was the second President of the United States, had a broad background in politics. John Q. Adams was clearly a **qualified** candidate.

The West nominated Henry Clay of Kentucky and Andrew Jackson of Tennessee. Clay had experience in government and had been Speaker of the House of Representatives. Clay appeared to have an excellent chance to win. No man since George Washington was as popular as Jackson. His military successes in Louisiana, Tennessee, and Florida made Americans proud. He was sure to be a strong candidate.

The South supported William Crawford of Georgia. All four men were well known as strong nationalists, with similar views as to what direction the growing country should take.

None of the four candidates received a majority of the votes, however. According to the Twelfth Amendment to the Constitution, the House of Representatives had to choose a President from the three who had the most votes. Henry Clay did not want Andrew Jackson to win. He did not like Jackson's political ideas. He strongly believed that John Q. Adams would be a better choice. Clay managed to get enough members of the House of Representatives to support Adams. Adams was chosen to be President. A few days later, President Adams announced that Henry

The First Free School for the Deaf

Thomas Hopkins Gallaudet started the first free school for the hearing impaired in America. It was formed in Hartford, Connecticut, in 1817. Gallaudet's two sons also worked with the hearing impaired. His oldest son, Thomas Gallaudet, founded the Gallaudet Home for aged deaf-mutes and the St. Ann's Church for Deaf-Mutes. His other son, Edward Miner Gallaudet, opened a school for deaf-mutes, now called Gallaudet University, in Washington, D.C.

Clay would serve as his Secretary of State. It seemed that Adams and Clay had made an agreement. Jackson was angry and felt that he should have been the President. He promised to win the next election.

SECTION 3 REVIEW Write the answers to these questions on a separate sheet of paper using complete sentences.

1) What was the purpose of the Monroe Doctrine?

2) Why were the European monarchies concerned about their colonies in North and South America?

3) What were the three regions of the country?

4) Why did the House of Representatives have to choose the President in 1824?

5) How did Henry Clay help to determine the final outcome of the election of 1824?

What do you think ?

Why do you think the Monroe Doctrine was important?

The Monroe Doctrine

President James Monroe saw signs of possible trouble as European colonies in the Americas moved toward independence. The stronger European countries might try to use force and interfere in the Western Hemisphere. In 1823, President Monroe set forth the Monroe Doctrine. Although the doctrine was not regarded as important then, it served our country well over the years that followed.

"The American continents, by the free and independent condition which they have assumed and maintain, are henceforth not to be considered as subjects for future colonization by any European powers. . . .

In the wars of the European powers in matters relating to themselves we have never taken any part, nor does it comport with our policy so to do. It is only when our rights are invaded or seriously menaced that we resent injuries or make preparation for our defense.

We owe it therefore, to candor and to the amicable relations existing between the United States and those powers to declare that we should consider any attempt on their part to extend their system to any portion of this hemisphere as dangerous to our peace and safety. With the existing colonies or dependencies of any European power we have not interfered and shall not interfere. But with the Governments who have declared their independence and maintained it, and whose independence we have, on great consideration and on just principles, acknowledged, we could not view any interposition for the purpose of oppressing them, or controlling in any other manner their destiny, by any European power in any other light than as the manifestation of an unfriendly disposition toward the United States.

Our policy in regard to Europe . . . is not to interfere in the internal concerns of any of its powers . . . ."

Source Reading Wrap-Up

1) Why did President Monroe say that future European colonies would no longer be possible in the Americas?

2) The United States did not interfere in European affairs. In return, what did President Monroe expect European countries to do?

3) When would it be necessary for the United States to take action against a European power?

4) Write one statement from the doctrine that shows President Monroe wanted the United States and European countries to continue to be friendly.

5) The Monroe Doctrine pointed out that any act of force in the Western Hemisphere by a European power would be considered a threat to the security of the United States. Why is that a special point to make?

★ President Monroe took office in 1817. His election victory finished the Federalists as a political party.

★ Between 1790 and 1820 the population of the United States increased by six million people. Much of this population increase was on the frontier. Settlers moved west on wagons and by water routes. These people were very independent and had a strong sense of nationalism. However, they wanted more roads, better land prices, loans for farmers, and protection of markets for farm goods.

★ Farming, especially cotton farming, thrived in the South. Industries such as shipbuilding, trading, and ironworks thrived in the North.

★ The Era of Good Feelings was used to describe President Monroe's two terms. However, America experienced problems with Spanish Florida, as Seminoles attacked Americans. Andrew Jackson led troops into Spanish Florida in 1818 and captured St. Marks and Pensacola. This led to the Adams-Onís Treaty in 1819, which gave Florida to America. The United States gave up Spanish Texas.

★ Slavery became an issue in 1819 when Missouri tried to enter the Union. This would have upset the balance of power between free states and slave states in Congress. In 1820, the Missouri Compromise solved the problem by letting both Maine, a free state, and Missouri, a slave state, enter the Union. However, slavery was still a problem, as several people, including a freed slave named Denmark Vesey, were executed in South Carolina for planning a slave revolt.

★ President Monroe announced the Monroe Doctrine in 1823. This policy stated that any attempt by a European power to extend its influence in any part of the Western Hemisphere would be considered a threat to the peace and safety of the United States.

★ John Quincy Adams became President in the election of 1824. The House of Representatives chose him because none of the candidates received a majority vote.

Comprehension: Identifying Facts

On a separate sheet of paper, write the correct term or name from the Word Bank to complete the sentences.

WORD BANK	
Adams-Onís Treaty	Henry Clay
Andrew Jackson	James Monroe
cotton	John Quincy Adams
cotton gin	Missouri Compromise
Denmark Vesey	Monroe Doctrine
Era of Good Feelings	slave state
free state	William Crawford
hemp	

1) _____ is a plant used to make material for clothing.

2) James Monroe's two terms as President were called the _____.

3) The _____ was used to separate cotton seeds.

4) A _____ does not practice slavery.

5) A _____ practices slavery.

6) _____ led troops into Seminole country in 1818.

7) The _____ gave Florida to the United States.

8) A freed slave named _____ was executed for planning a revolt in South Carolina.

9) _____ is used to make rope.

10) _____ took office as President in 1817.

11) The _____ made Maine and Missouri part of the Union.

12) The South supported _____ in the election of 1824.

13) _____ was known as "The Great Compromiser."

14) The _____ stated that any attempt by a European power to extend its influence in any part of the Western Hemisphere would be considered a threat to the peace and safety of the United States.

15) The House of Representatives chose _____ as President in 1824.

Comprehension: Understanding Main Ideas

On a separate sheet of paper, write the answers to the following questions using complete sentences.

1) What problems did the western settlers face?

2) Which industries developed in the North and in the South?

3) What problems did slavery cause in this time period?

Critical Thinking: Write Your Opinion

1) Do you think the Missouri Compromise was a good compromise? Why or why not?

2) Of the three sections of the United States—North, South, or West—which one would you have chosen to live in? Why?

Test Taking Tip | If you do not know the meaning of a word in a question, read the question to yourself, leaving out the word. Then see if you can figure out the meaning of the word from its use in the sentence.

Political Changes Take Place

1825–1838

The United States saw many political changes with the next three Presidents—John Quincy Adams, Andrew Jackson, and Martin Van Buren. New political parties were formed. People in the nation's three regions became more divided on their government needs. In this chapter, you will learn about these political changes in the United States.

Goals for Learning

▶ To list the three regions of the United States in the early 1800s and describe the main interests of each region

▶ To explain why the Tariff of 1828 caused problems for the federal government

▶ To describe the ways in which Andrew Jackson was different from Presidents before him

▶ To describe the rebellion led by Nat Turner and explain its importance

▶ To explain why the American Indian relocation west of the Mississippi is known as the "Trail of Tears"

▶ To describe major events in the struggle for Texas independence

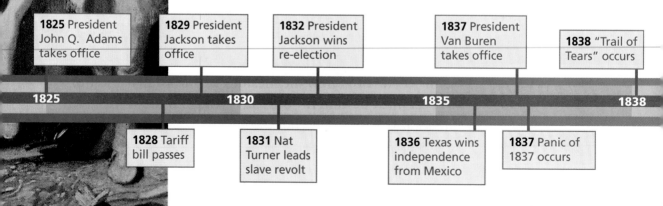

1825 President John Q. Adams takes office

1829 President Jackson takes office

1832 President Jackson wins re-election

1837 President Van Buren takes office

1838 "Trail of Tears" occurs

1825   1830   1835   1838

1828 Tariff bill passes

1831 Nat Turner leads slave revolt

1836 Texas wins independence from Mexico

1837 Panic of 1837 occurs

★Campaign
A group of activities connected to getting elected to office

Capable
Having the ability for a task

Domestic
Related to one's own country

John Quincy Adams got off to a bad start as President when he took office in 1825. Many people felt that Adams had made a deal in order to win the election. Though Adams was **capable** and experienced in government, he was thought to be unfriendly. Right from the beginning, he was not a popular President.

By 1824, the three regions of the country had become even more different. President Adams did not consider the three parts separately. He believed that the job of the central government was to lead the country as a whole.

Why Was the Tariff of 1828 Passed?

A bill passed in 1828 imposed tariffs on imported goods to protect American industries. The tariff was intended to raise prices of products made in foreign countries. Foreign products would be more expensive than **domestic** items. Americans would be more likely to buy cheaper U.S. goods.

The South did not like the tariff system. People in the South were farmers—not manufacturers. The tariffs raised the cost of the products they needed. Northerners depended on industry and wanted even higher taxes on imported goods.

Passing the bill caused three things to happen. First, Adams became more disliked. Second, Andrew Jackson gained popularity. Third, John C. Calhoun of South Carolina became a very separate leader of the South.

Who Won the Election of 1828?

As early as 1825, Andrew Jackson began his election **campaign.** A campaign is a group of activities connected to getting elected to office. Jackson, Senator Martin Van Buren of New York, and other members of Congress separated from the Democratic-Republican party and formed the Democratic party. Members of Adams's party became the National Republicans.

The National Republican party chose, or **nominated,** John Q. Adams for a second term. The Democratic party nominated Jackson. Jackson won the election. Westerners were excited by his victory. Thousands of Americans attended Jackson's inauguration.

What Was the Spoils System?

When Jackson took office in 1829, he believed that government work required no special experience. The person only needed to support the proper American ideas and be a loyal supporter of the party. Some government workers who had not supported Jackson were fired. Jackson gave government jobs to loyal supporters. This practice became known as the **spoils system.**

How Did Jackson Set Up His Cabinet?

"Old Hickory," as President Jackson was called, was a man of the average people. Instead of turning to his cabinet for advice, he called upon his friends. When his friends visited the White House, they entered through the kitchen to avoid attention. These unofficial advisers became known as Jackson's "Kitchen Cabinet."

Jackson considered it his duty to carry out the wishes of the people. Most of the American people trusted him.

BORN TO COMMAND.

KING ANDREW THE FIRST.

This cartoon, titled "King Andrew the First," made fun of President Jackson. Some people felt his style as President was like that of a powerful king.

SECTION 1 REVIEW On a separate sheet of paper, write *True* if the statement is true or *False* if the statement is not true.

1) John Quincy Adams was a popular President.

2) The South and the West did not like the tariff system.

3) Andrew Jackson was a National Republican.

4) The practice of giving government jobs to friends and supporters is known as the spoils system.

5) The "Kitchen Cabinet" was Jackson's official cabinet.

What do you think **?**

Do you think the spoils system is a good system? Why or why not?

Nat Turner and his confederates planned a revolt against slave owners.

In 1831, an enslaved African from Virginia named Nat Turner set out to free all slaves in America. His master had allowed Turner to learn to read. Having become a preacher at an early age, Turner wanted to end slavery. He and a group of his followers killed about sixty slave owners and their families across Virginia. When they were stopped, Turner and about twenty of the others were hanged. After the revolt, however, more than 100 innocent enslaved Africans were killed by fearful masters.

The revolt led by Nat Turner was the most serious slave revolt in American history. The white southerners realized more than ever that the Africans were not about to remain enslaved without a fight. For the slaves, the name Nat Turner came to represent the courage to fight **oppression** by whatever means necessary. Oppression is unfair or cruel actions by one group against a group with less power.

★**Oppression**
Unfair or cruel actions by one group against a group with less power

Fine Arts

History in Your Life

Spirituals

Spirituals make up much of our American folk song heritage. Originally they were part of African-American worship in the South. During early slavery days, African slaves had to worship in the fields as they worked. They blended Psalms and hymns their masters sang with music many had learned in Africa. Their singing style was very much their own. In 1801, Richard Allen compiled *A Collection of Spiritual Songs and Hymns* for the black church.

He was the first African American to present a collection of these songs. By the early 1800s, jubilant "call and response" songs were common. In these, one singer calls out short phrases and everyone answers. Other spirituals were slow "sorrow songs." Examples are "Nobody Knows the Trouble I've Seen," "Were You There?" and "Sometimes I Feel Like a Motherless Child." Today spirituals can be heard in concert halls and in worship of many faiths.

What Problems Developed Over Tariffs?

The South and the West had strongly opposed the tariff act passed under Adams in 1828. It raised the prices of the manufactured goods they needed. Northerners, however, wanted even higher taxes on imports so their goods would cost less than imports. A new tariff act was passed in 1832 that lowered some of the tariffs. Neither the North nor the South was pleased.

The protective tariff continued to cause problems during Jackson's term. Vice President John C. Calhoun, a southerner, found himself in a difficult position. He depended upon the political support of plantation owners, yet he disliked speaking against the President. He proposed that a state be able to decide whether a law was acceptable. The state could turn down a law it thought to be unfair. The South Carolina legislature, in turn, passed the Ordinance of Nullification. In this act, the people of this state declared that the tariff laws did not apply to them. They said that federal officials would not get the duties from their state, and forced collection would cause South Carolina to withdraw from the Union.

Jackson was a strong supporter of states' rights. He also loved his country. Jackson sent a message to South Carolina, making his position clear. All states would have to obey the laws if the country were to remain a Union. No one state would be permitted to challenge the unity of the country.

SECTION 2 REVIEW Write the answers to these questions on a separate sheet of paper using complete sentences.

1) What did Nat Turner do?

2) What is oppression?

3) Why did northerners want higher taxes on imports?

4) What was the Ordinance of Nullification?

5) What position did President Jackson take with South Carolina?

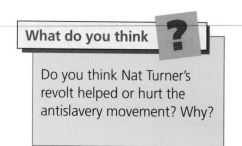

What do you think ?

Do you think Nat Turner's revolt helped or hurt the antislavery movement? Why?

Abolish
To get rid of something

Expire
To come to an end

Renew
To make something new again, such as a charter that has come to an end

★**Veto**
The power given to the President to turn down a bill

Andrew Jackson believed that all citizens should have the right to vote and that slavery should be **abolished.** Also, he was in favor of improving schools, working conditions, and the treatment of prisoners. There is little doubt that President Jackson wanted Americans to have more influence on government and an improved quality of life.

The Bank of the United States had a twenty-year charter that had been granted by President James Madison in 1816. In 1832, the president of the Bank asked for the charter to be **renewed.** This date was four years before the charter **expired.** Congress passed the bill granting the new charter to the Bank of the United States.

President Jackson did not like the Bank and did not want to renew its charter. In his opinion, the Bank of the United States and other banks, governed by a wealthy few, favored the rich and powerful people. He felt the Bank was not democratic and should be destroyed. President Jackson **vetoed** the bill when it was presented to him. A veto is the power given to the President to turn down a bill.

Media in History

The Penny Press

Until 1833, generally only the rich read newspapers. At six cents a copy, newspapers were expensive.

In 1833, Benjamin Day found a way to print 4,000 copies in an hour. He made the *New York Sun* a best-seller for just a penny a copy. He employed young boys to sell the newspapers. Their "Extra! Extra! Read all about it!" sales pitches brought in a lot of pennies.

Day didn't bore people with a lot of political news. Instead he appealed to the masses by writing short gossip items about local people and events. Because of Day's success, many other journalists began imitating his formula. The era of the Penny Press was a turning point in American journalism.

The First Bank of the United States was in Philadelphia.

Deposit
To put money into a bank

Issue
A topic of discussion or debate

Presidents before Jackson had rarely used the veto. They let Congress decide the issues. As President, Jackson believed he should make the important decisions. He used the veto to control Congress. Jackson set an example for Presidents who followed him. They appreciated the value of the veto power.

How Did Jackson Win the Election of 1832?

In 1831, Henry Clay was nominated as the National Republican candidate for President. Clay had supported the renewal of the charter for the Bank of the United States in 1832. He made the Bank veto into an election **issue.** Clay was confident he would win the election.

Jackson continued to speak out against the Bank during his campaign. Jackson won the election by a large number of votes. Jackson received 219 electoral votes, and Clay got 49. It was a crushing defeat for Clay.

President Jackson took his re-election as public approval of this Bank policy. He continued to destroy the Bank by removing all government funds from it. He **deposited** the money into smaller banks. Jackson's enemies called these banks "pet banks." Jackson was successful in reducing the power of the Bank of the United States.

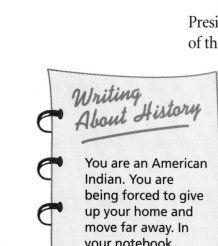

Writing About History

You are an American Indian. You are being forced to give up your home and move far away. In your notebook, write a sentence or two about this. Explain how you feel.

What Was the Trail of Tears?

Jackson went to Congress for help to decrease the fighting among settlers and American Indians. He asked that land west of the Mississippi be set aside for American Indians. The Indian Removal Act of 1830 provided for moving American Indian peoples remaining east of the Mississippi to this land.

The "Trail of Tears" was the forced removal of thousands of American Indians.

Many groups of American Indians were forced to give up their **homeland.** The largest movement took place in the Old Southwest in 1838. It included the Choctaws, Cherokees, Chickasaws, Creeks, and Seminoles. So many of these people died during the difficult trip that the journey became known as the "Trail of Tears." Very few American Indians remained east of the Mississippi River. Some Seminoles were still in Florida, and the Sauk and Fox people were in the upper Northwest Territory.

Homeland
Land that a person or group came from originally

SECTION 3 REVIEW Choose the best word or name from the Word Bank to complete each sentence. Write your answers on a separate sheet of paper.

WORD BANK

Andrew Jackson

Henry Clay

Bank of the United States

Trail of Tears

veto

1) President Jackson did not like the _____ and did not want to renew its charter.

2) A _____ is the power given to the President to turn down a bill.

3) In 1831, _____ was nominated as the National Republican candidate for President.

4) _____ believed that all citizens should have the right to vote and that slavery should be abolished.

5) Many American Indians died during the _____.

What do you think ?

Do you think you would have liked Andrew Jackson as President if you were living in the 1830s? Why or why not?

★Dictator
A person ruling a country with total control

Mission
A church

Back in the middle of the 1820s, President John Quincy Adams was willing to pay $1 million for the Mexican territory that is now Texas. A few years later, President Jackson offered to pay $5 million for the land. In both cases, Mexico refused to sell.

Mexicans encouraged Americans to move into the territory. The area was well suited to cotton growing, so many planters brought their slaves to establish large cotton plantations. By 1835, 20,000 Americans were living there. The Mexicans asked only that these people obey their laws.

In time, the Texans, as they called themselves, refused to obey the laws of Mexico. Texans declared their territory independent of Mexico. They appointed Sam Houston as commander-in-chief of the Texan army.

What Happened at the Alamo and Goliad?

Antonio López de Santa Anna was president and **dictator** of Mexico. A dictator is a person ruling a country with total control. He organized 4,000 men and led them to San Antonio in February of 1836. Santa Anna was met by a small army of Texans, led by Colonel William Travis. Santa Anna ordered the colonel to surrender. Instead, Colonel Travis moved his men into the Alamo, a rebuilt **mission.** They used the Alamo as a fort. After many days of fighting, the Texans in the Alamo were defeated. Santa Anna made sure that every one of the Texans was killed. Among the dead were two famous westerners, Jim Bowie and Davy Crockett.

The Texans lost the battle at the Alamo in 1836.

Santa Anna then moved his army to the town of Goliad. The Texans were defeated again. Santa Anna had lost many soldiers in the two battles. Nevertheless, he intended to defeat Sam Houston and win the war.

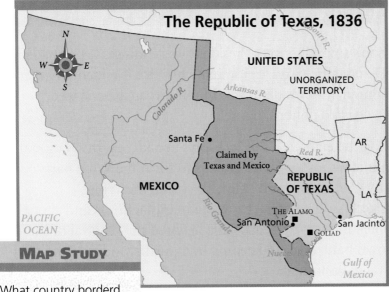

The Republic of Texas, 1836

UNITED STATES

UNORGANIZED TERRITORY

Arkansas R.

Colorado R.

Santa Fe

Claimed by Texas and Mexico

Red R.

AR

MEXICO

REPUBLIC OF TEXAS

LA

Rio Grande

PACIFIC OCEAN

THE ALAMO

San Antonio

GOLIAD

San Jacinto

Nueces R.

Gulf of Mexico

MAP STUDY

What country borderd the Republic of Texas to the West? Where was the Alamo located?

How Did Texas Win Its Independence?

Sam Houston ordered his Texan army to retreat slowly as Santa Anna pushed forward to the San Jacinto River. "Remember the Alamo!" and "Remember Goliad!" were the Texans' battle cries as they attacked and defeated the Mexican army.

Santa Anna, who had been taken prisoner, agreed to give Texas its independence. In October 1836, the new nation elected Sam Houston as its first President. Texas became the Republic of Texas.

SECTION 4 REVIEW Choose the best name from the Word Bank to complete each sentence. Write your answers on a separate sheet of paper.

WORD BANK

Davy Crockett

Colonel William Travis

John Quincy Adams

Sam Houston

Santa Anna

1) _____ was willing to pay $1 million for Texas.

2) The leader of the Texans at the Alamo was _____.

3) The leader of the Texan army that defeated Santa Anna was _____.

4) _____ was the president and dictator of Mexico.

5) _____ was a famous westerner killed in the Alamo.

What do you think ❓

Why do you think the Texan army used the battle cries "Remember the Alamo" and "Remember Goliad"?

★**Depression**
A period of financial difficulties experienced by an entire country

Jackson's second term as President was ending. He persuaded the Democratic party to nominate his Vice President, Martin Van Buren, for President. Van Buren was an experienced, well-educated political figure.

During the eight years of Jackson's presidency, the National Republicans joined other groups to form the Whig party. Led by Henry Clay and Daniel Webster, the Whigs' strongest support came from the manufacturers and shippers in the Northeast. They favored the renewal of the national bank charter, keeping high tariffs, and a strong central government.

Then and Now

If you were a student in 1825, you probably would have gone to school only through eighth grade. You would have studied only the three Rs—reading, writing, and 'rithmetic. If your parents wanted you to have more schooling, you might have attended a private academy. Many families could only send children to school for a few weeks a year. Your family might have needed your help in a factory or the fields. Most schools were only a one-room building then.

You can thank Horace Mann, the father of modern education, for a free high school education for everyone. Owing to his efforts, free high schools were a national law by 1875. Today students attend school nine months a year through age 16. Most Americans now receive a high school education.

Van Buren told voters that he would follow the same approach that Jackson had used to govern the country. A vote for Van Buren was a vote for Jackson. Van Buren won the election. He had the largest popular vote. Van Buren had 170 electoral votes, and three Whig candidates had a total of 113.

What Caused the Panic of 1837?

Trouble was waiting for President Van Buren when he took office in 1837. The United States entered a **depression,** called the Panic of 1837. A depression is a period of financial difficulties experienced by an entire country. Many of the smaller banks that Jackson had favored over the Bank of the United States had become careless. They had used paper money that was not backed by gold or silver. Some had given loans to people who never paid them back. When word of the problems got out, people rushed to the banks to take out money deposited before the panic. However, there was no money in those banks.

SARAH GRIMKÉ: 1792–1873
ANGELINA GRIMKÉ: 1805–1879

The Grimké sisters were daughters of a judge from Charleston, South Carolina. They became outspoken about ending slavery, and they favored women's rights. After they moved to Philadelphia and became Quakers, they began publishing antislavery papers. They later gave public lectures against slavery. Some other antislavery people thought the lectures were inappropriate behavior for women. The Grimkés responded by publishing essays calling for equal rights for women and enslaved people. The sisters remained committed to the antislavery and women's rights movements, which both blossomed during their lifetimes. They insisted that their parents leave them equal shares of the family's slaves, whom they freed as soon as possible. In New Jersey, they established one of America's first racially mixed schools.

Unemployment
The state of not having work

Many banks failed as a result of this panic. Prices fell on farm products and manufactured goods. Factories and mills closed. New work on roads and canals came to a halt. **Unemployment** spread, especially in the Northeast. This depression lasted for several years. Van Buren was unable to solve most of the problems it created.

SECTION 5 REVIEW Write the answers to these questions on a separate sheet of paper using complete sentences.

1) Where did the Whigs' strongest support come from?

2) What did Martin Van Buren tell voters?

3) What problem did President Van Buren face when he took office?

4) What is a depression?

5) What happened as a result of the Panic of 1837?

What do you think ?

How would you feel if you were living during a depression?

A Message From the Alamo

On February 23, 1836, Texas was fighting for independence from Mexico. Texans tried to stop the Mexican army under President Antonio López de Santa Anna at San Antonio. At the Alamo, a tiny mission, 187 Texans fought 4,000 Mexican soldiers. In this letter, Colonel William Barrett Travis sent word to his fellow citizens.

"Fellow Citizens and Compatriots:

I am besieged by a thousand or more Mexicans under Santa Anna. I have sustained a continued bombardment for twenty-four hours and have not lost a man. The enemy have demanded a surrender at discretion; otherwise the garrison is to be put to the sword if the place is taken. I have answered the summons with a cannon shot and our flag still waves proudly from the walls.

I shall never surrender or retreat.

Then, I call on you in the name of liberty, or patriotism, and of everything dear to the American character to come to our aid with all dispatch. The enemy are receiving reinforcements daily and will no doubt increase to three or four thousand in four or five days. Though this call may be neglected, I am determined to sustain myself as long as possible and die like a soldier who never forgets what is due to his own honor and that of his country. Victory or death!"

Source Reading Wrap-Up

1) On what date was the letter written?

2) After a nonstop day-long bombardment, how many men had Travis lost?

3) Under what circumstances was Travis willing to surrender?

4) What did Travis say would happen if the Texans were defeated without a surrender?

5) Why do you think Travis said "this call may be neglected"?

12) _____was the name of the party formed during Jackson's presidency.

Comprehension: Understanding Main Ideas

On a separate sheet of paper, write the answer to each question using complete sentences.

1) Why were southern slave owners concerned about Nat Turner's rebellion even though it lasted less than a week?

2) Why did the Tariff of 1828 cause problems for the federal government?

3) What are three ways in which President Jackson was different from the Presidents who came before him?

4) What were the three regions of the United States in the early 1800s and what were their main interests?

5) What was Jackson's main reason for forcing the American Indians to move west?

6) Why did the American Indian relocation become known as the "Trail of Tears?"

Critical Thinking: Write Your Opinion

1) The Tariff of 1828 affected different sections of the country in different ways. Describe how you would feel if you were a farmer in the South. What arguments would you use to convince the government that the tariff was unfair to you?

2) Why do you think that Nat Turner led a rebellion even though the army and militia were against him?

Test Taking Tip To prepare for a test, study in short sessions rather than one long session. In the week before the test, spend time each day reviewing your notes.

12

1825–1858

The last chapter explained how the U.S. political system changed in the early 1800s. However, many other things changed the nation in the early to middle 1800s. This was a time of growth in industry. Many inventions changed the way Americans did things. Immigrants came to America to seek a better way of life. Education and literature helped to shape the nation's culture. In this chapter, you will learn how inventions, education, literature, and the growth of industry changed the nation.

Goals for Learning

▶ To identify major inventions and how they contributed to the growth of industry

▶ To describe the developments and changes in land and water transportation

▶ To list three major developments in communication and to explain their importance

▶ To describe how immigration contributed to population growth

▶ To identify the contributions of several early American educators and writers to American culture

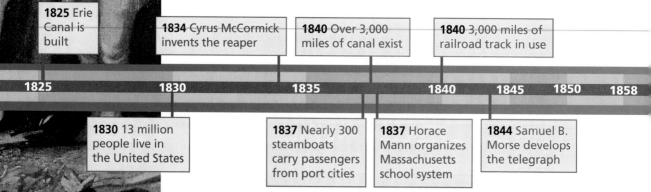

1825 Erie Canal is built

1834 Cyrus McCormick invents the reaper

1840 Over 3,000 miles of canal exist

1840 3,000 miles of railroad track in use

| 1825 | 1830 | 1835 | 1840 | 1845 | 1850 | 1858 |

1830 13 million people live in the United States

1837 Nearly 300 steamboats carry passengers from port cities

1837 Horace Mann organizes Massachusetts school system

1844 Samuel B. Morse develops the telegraph

Mechanic
Someone skilled in working with machines

Memorize
To remember what has been learned

Rural
Relating to places well outside of cities

★**Textile**
Fabric or cloth

The growth of industry in the United States was slow. There was not a good market for manufactured items. Between 1790 and 1840, about ninety percent of the American people lived in **rural** regions. Farmers had little money to spend and most of the manufactured goods were not necessary things for them. Merchants made little profit from sales to farmers.

American manufacturers would not compete with British industry. Great Britain had many more years' experience at producing most goods. In many cases, American factories could not make things as well or as inexpensively. People in the United States found British items easy to obtain at good prices. In addition, American cities did not have enough workers. The West continued to attract settlers who could not pass up the cheap, fertile land. As the country expanded, cities remained small.

Money for starting a factory was difficult to get. Bankers were not eager to lend money to would-be manufacturers because the risk of failure was so high. Without a loan, most people could not afford to buy equipment or materials.

How Did Industries Begin to Grow?

The United States began to change into an industrial giant in 1790. The roots of this change go back to Samuel Slater. Born in Great Britain, he became a skilled **mechanic.** He accepted an offer to go to America. The British law would not permit anyone to take machinery out of the country. Nor would the British allow any plans to leave the country that showed how the machines were built. While still in Great Britain, Slater **memorized** the parts of a machine he was using in a cotton factory. Later, in Rhode Island, he gained the financial support of Moses Brown. Slater was able to build a **textile** machine from memory. Textile is fabric or cloth. With the aid of Eli Whitney's cotton gin, the textile industry was changed during a few years in the 1790s.

Cyrus McCormick's reaper improved farming in the 1830s.

Americans were able to produce a good product faster and cheaper than ever before. They could begin to compete with other industrial nations.

In addition to inventing the cotton gin, Eli Whitney helped develop the idea of using **interchangeable parts** in manufacturing. Manufacturer John Hall used many of Whitney's ideas to **mass produce** rifles. To mass produce means to make great amounts of a product very fast. In time, others were using the same ideas to produce clocks, sewing machines, stoves, and countless other products.

A method of burning coal as a fuel in making iron was developed in the 1830s. Demand for iron in manufacturing was very high. As American industry became able to make its own iron, industries that made machines, farm tools, rails, and parts of railroads cars grew very quickly.

Early farming equipment was very simple and crude. Plows were made out of wood and could break easily. Every step in the crop-growing process was done by hand. In 1834, Cyrus McCormick invented a machine that could harvest grain. His new machine—the reaper—made farming possible on a much bigger scale. Shortly thereafter, John Deere invented the steel plow, which helped farmers to convert the hard prairie sod into usable farm land.

> **Interchangeable parts**
> *Parts of a machine that can be used with other machines*
>
> ★**Mass produce**
> *To make great amounts of product very fast*

SECTION 1 REVIEW Write the answers to these questions on a separate sheet of paper using complete sentences.

1) Why was industry slow to get started?

2) Why were factories slow to get started?

3) How was Samuel Slater able to build his textile machine?

4) How did the textile industry change?

5) What did Cyrus McCormick's reaper do?

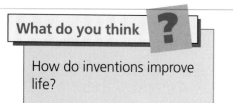

What do you think ❓

How do inventions improve life?

Early land transportation was slow and expensive. Raw materials had to be sent to factories, yet high shipping costs made the factories' products too expensive to buy. In the 1790s, a **turnpike** was built in Pennsylvania to improve transportation. A turnpike is a road that travelers pay to use. The Cumberland Road, in use since 1811, now spread to the West for nearly 600 miles. Wagons and stagecoaches could travel along this road at speeds of about ten miles an hour.

★Turnpike
A road that travelers pay to use

What Water Transportation Developed?

Transporting goods by water was slow, backbreaking, and expensive. Men using long poles could push a boat at the rate of one mile an hour.

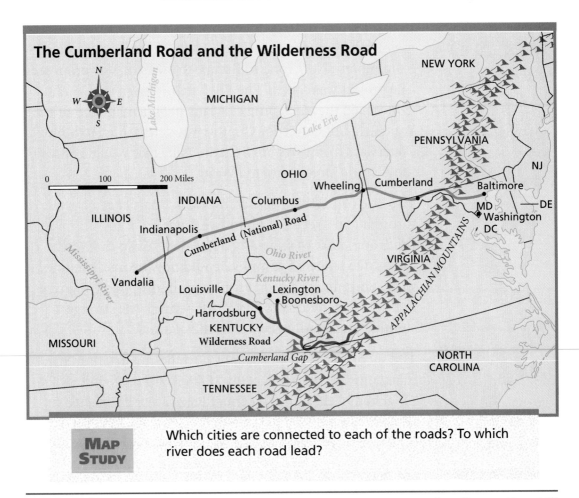

The Cumberland Road and the Wilderness Road

MAP STUDY
Which cities are connected to each of the roads? To which river does each road lead?

Robert Fulton traveled from New York City to Albany, New York, in a steam-powered boat in 1807. His small ship, the *Clermont*, covered 150 miles in thirty-two hours—about four and a half miles an hour. The steam engine was fueled by wood. Many people laughed at him and called his boat "Fulton's Folly," but his steamboat made faster water transportation possible. By 1820, sixty steamboats were carrying people up and down the Mississippi and the rivers joining it. Water transportation became the least expensive way to travel and ship goods. By 1837, nearly 300 steamboats carried passengers from port cities of Pittsburgh, Cincinnati, Louisville, St. Louis, Vicksburg, and Natchez.

Why Were Canals Built?

Along with new roads and river travel, canal building soon developed. A canal is a human-made waterway used for transportation or to connect to a natural waterway. The first major canal was the Erie Canal. In 1816, the idea of a canal from Albany, New York, to Buffalo, New York, was proposed. The project was called "The Big Ditch." Governor De Witt Clinton led the canal project. Many people made fun of the Big Ditch, but Governor Clinton was determined to build it. Waterways from New York City to Lake Erie would connect the Atlantic Ocean with the West.

The Erie Canal was finished by 1825. Boats could move through it at speeds of up to five miles an hour. Shipping times and costs were greatly decreased. A trip that once took three weeks to complete could now be made in one week. Shipping costs for a ton of grain dropped from one hundred to ten dollars. New York became the strongest shipping and trading center in the country.

The success of the Erie Canal led to the construction of many more canals. In fact, by 1840, 3,000 more miles of canal had been built. The Great Lakes were connected by canal to many rivers in the Northeast. Some canals led up to the Appalachian Mountains, where rail cars brought canal boats to canals on the opposite side.

Early locomotives were simple. They became more advanced as the popularity of railroads increased.

Commerce
Having to do with buying or selling goods

Communication
The act of sending and receiving information

★**Locomotive**
A vehicle that rides on rails and has an engine for pulling railroad cars

★**Telegraph**
A device that uses coded signals to send communications over a wire

How Did Railroads Change the Nation?

Steamboats, roads, and canals improved transportation, but not as much as the railroads did. The first railroad in America to carry passengers was the Baltimore and Ohio Railroad. It ran a distance of thirteen miles. At first, horse-drawn cars were used on the tracks. Soon, **locomotives** replaced the horses, beginning with Peter Cooper's *Tom Thumb*. A locomotive is a vehicle that rides on rails and has an engine for pulling railroad cars. Gradually, more railroads were built. Better tracks were developed. Railroads were far better than any other kind of transportation. People and freight could now travel by land in all directions. Though trains were uncomfortable and not very safe, they were faster than anything else. By 1840, 3,000 miles of railroad track were in use on various lines.

How Did Communication Improve?

There was a growing need for better, faster means of **communication.** In 1844, Samuel B. Morse developed the **telegraph,** the first of three important improvements in communication. The telegraph used coded signals to send communications over a wire. This invention brought about major changes for industry, transportation, and **commerce.**

Cyrus Field successfully laid an underwater telegraph cable from Newfoundland to Ireland in 1858. The cable was placed on the floor of the Atlantic Ocean. The cable stretched a distance of about 3,000 miles. This **transatlantic** cable connected America with Europe. Several years passed before it worked right, but the cable improved communication.

What Was the Pony Express?

The pony express also improved communication. Mail took weeks to get across the country before this postal system was started. Horse-drawn stagecoaches ran regularly, but they were unable to go very fast. The pony express could run mail from St. Joseph, Missouri, to Sacramento, California, in just ten days. The distance was about 2,000 miles. Lightweight, young riders rode their horses as fast as they could go. Every ten miles or so, a fresh horse was ready. Despite all kinds of weather and danger from attacks by American Indians and bandits, the riders raced across the country. This postal system was used for only eighteen months. The pony express came to an end when the telegraph was introduced to California in 1861.

Pony express riders carried mail from Missouri to Sacramento.

In 1840, you would have traveled from New York to Illinois by stagecoach. You would have traveled on narrow, muddy, unpaved roads. You might have held your breath when the horses and coach crossed bridges. Many bridges were mere planks and poles laid across the water. After only five miles, you would stop at a tavern for lunch. After another five miles, you would have to stop for supper and a night's lodging. Your trip from New York to Illinois by stagecoach would have taken almost three months.

One way you can make that trip today is by car. You can travel at sixty-five miles an hour on paved four-lane interstate highways. You might stop to buy gas and eat lunch in a restaurant. At night, you might stay in a motel. Traveling about eight hours a day, you can make the trip in about two days. If you need to get there quickly, you can arrive in about two hours on a jet.

SECTION 2 REVIEW On a separate sheet of paper, write *True* if the statement is true or *False* if the statement is not true.

1) Robert Fulton invented the telegraph.

2) The Erie Canal was finished by 1825.

3) By 1840, there were 30,000 miles of railroad track in the United States.

4) Cyrus Field stretched transatlantic telegraph cable 3,000 miles from Newfoundland to Ireland.

5) The pony express was used to carry mail.

What do you think **?**

Why do you think many people laughed at Robert Fulton's steam-powered boat?

Population Increase, 1790–1850

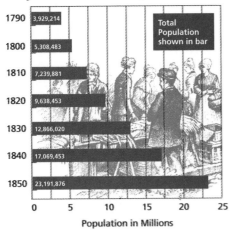

Year	Total Population shown in bar
1790	3,929,214
1800	5,308,483
1810	7,239,881
1820	9,638,453
1830	12,866,020
1840	17,069,453
1850	23,191,876

Population in Millions

What was the population in 1820? By how much did the population grow between 1820 and 1830?

In 1790, the U.S. population was nearly four million. By 1820, it had more than doubled. In 1830, thirteen million people were living in the United States. Immigrants contributed to the growth of the nation during that forty-year period. Most of the population growth, though, was due to the high birthrate in America at that time.

Where Did Early Immigrants Come From?

The number of immigrants to America from Europe remained rather small from 1790 until 1820. Aware of the great risks and high death rate, many people hesitated to make the long voyage across the Atlantic Ocean. However, about 50,000 immigrants arrived in the United States each year during that period. Most of these immigrants came from England, Ireland, Wales, and Scotland. The desire for a better life overcame any fears they may have had about the long three-month journey to America.

By 1830, newer and faster sailing ships were being used. The transatlantic trip now took two weeks instead of two to three months. Even though the trip was still dangerous and uncomfortable, the cost was much lower. More people could now afford to go to America. The Irish and Germans, especially, had reasons for leaving their countries.

The potato crop was nearly a total failure in Ireland in 1846. Most of the Irish depended on potatoes as their major source of food. Hunger and **starvation** spread throughout Ireland. Many Irish people had no choice. They had to leave their homeland. By 1850, nearly one and a half million Irish people were living in the United States.

Starvation
Suffering from lack of food

People from Germany also sought refuge in America. They left their country to escape unpleasant political conditions. Germany also had a crop failure, though it was not as serious as the one in Ireland. Many Germans made the journey across the Atlantic Ocean. By the year 1850, about four million German people had come to the United States.

★Melting pot
A nation where several groups of people belonging to different races or cultures live together

The Irish and the Germans were the first to come to the United States in large numbers. Later, people from every part of the world found their way to this country. With so many different cultures, the United States became known as the **melting pot** of the world. A melting pot is a nation where several groups of people belonging to different races or cultures live together. Problems developed because of differences in language and customs. As time passed, however, the immigrants were able to make a new home for themselves in the United States.

SECTION 3 REVIEW Choose the correct word in parentheses to complete each sentence. Write your answers on a separate sheet of paper.

1) In (1790, 1820, 1830) thirteen million people were living in the United States.

2) The (Irish, British, Scottish) depended on potatoes for food.

3) The (Irish, British, Germans) left their country because of unpleasant political conditions.

4) By 1850, (two, four, eight) million Germans had come to the United States.

5) A melting pot is a nation of several races and (cultures, countries, states).

What do you think ?

Why do you think a country that is a melting pot can have problems?

Standards
Guidelines that a person or group must follow

Tutor
A person who has been paid to teach another person

Not every child in the new nation had an opportunity to attend school. Many people believed that education was intended only for those who could pay for it. Wealthy families paid private **tutors** to teach their young children. Academies and colleges were established for educating older children.

Public education was not a popular idea. Children of working-class families were needed at home. They had many chores to do. Before the 1800s, a few public schools did exist, but the quality of education was poor. Schools were small, and children of all ages were grouped together in the same class. Teachers in general were not well educated. They could read and write, but they had no special training.

During the presidency of Andrew Jackson, more people had gained the power to vote in national elections. More Americans were coming to realize that education was important so that people could vote wisely. Many states began to adopt **standards** for school systems. Training schools for teachers were established and money was provided for better books and school buildings.

What Educational Changes Began?

Working-class people in New England became aware of the importance of education. Their children needed to go to school if they were to have a better life. Much earlier, Thomas Jefferson had said that a democracy calls for an educated people. Andrew Jackson had also favored education for all children.

Country schoolhouses like this one were common in the 1800s.

Reference book
A book, such as a dictionary, used to find information

Horace Mann reorganized the Massachusetts school system in 1837. Schools were placed under state control to be supported by taxes. All children had to attend. Mann, who was in charge of education for the state, stated that all schools had to have the same program of studies. The subjects taught were on a higher level than those in the early schools. Teachers had to be trained before they could teach. Similar plans were introduced in Rhode Island and Connecticut.

Another member of the Massachusetts school system, Noah Webster, wrote a series of readers, spellers, and grammar books. These books provided a standard of learning for American schoolchildren. His two-volume **reference book,** *An American Dictionary of the English Language,* was first published in 1828. It became widely used in schools across the country. Despite the efforts of Mann, Webster, and other educators, however, only one white child in six attended a public school in the early part of the nineteenth century.

SECTION 4 REVIEW Write the answers to these questions on a separate sheet of paper using complete sentences.

1) Why did not every child have an opportunity to attend school?

2) Why was the quality of education poor before the 1800s?

3) Why did people begin to feel that education was important?

4) What did Horace Mann do?

5) Why were Noah Webster's books important for education?

McGuffey's *Readers* were used in schools beginning in 1836. They were used to educate students until the books stopped being sold in 1927.

What do you think **?**

How do you think education has changed since the 1800s?

Bravery
The ability not to be afraid when facing danger

★Classic
A book that has lasting value or meaning

At first, colonists lived in America much as they had in Great Britain. They held on to the old customs that they had brought from their homeland. The South, the western frontier, and New England were all different from Great Britain. Unlike the original colonists, Americans did not know or care about the Great Britain of the past. During the 200 years between the settling of Jamestown and the election of President Jefferson, the nation had found its own culture. Writers and artists of that time period recorded life in America.

Which Writers Contributed to American Literature?

Before this time, Benjamin Franklin was one of the few American writers whose works were popularly read. However, between 1815 and 1860, many writers described the America they knew in books, stories, and poems. Tales of adventure and **bravery** in the growing country became **classics.** A classic is a book that has lasting value or meaning. People all over the world began to take an interest in the spirit of this bold new land.

John James Audubon

John James Audubon came as a young man from France to Mill Grove, Pennsylvania. His hobby since boyhood was observing and sketching birds. Audubon later pursued his hobby full time. In 1827, he displayed drawings entitled "The Birds of America" in Edinburgh. Audiences loved them. Audubon quickly became internationally known. With great detail, his pictures showed birds in their natural environments. Over eleven years, he created 435 hand-colored plates with 1,065 life-size figures of 489 distinct species. Publishers printed his drawings and text written with William MacGillivray. Some of the species he illustrated have become extinct. His drawings are now the best record of those species. Among conservationists his name is still prominent. The National Audubon Society publishes field guides and sponsors wildlife preservation projects.

Science

History in Your Life

JAMES FENIMORE COOPER: 1789–1851

Novelist James Fenimore Cooper, the first great American novelist, wrote tales of adventure. He wrote about the American Revolution and the French and Indian War. Cooper also wrote about adventures on the high seas, the frontiers, and the plains. His best-known novels are the five *Leatherstocking Tales.* Some of these are *The Last of the Mohicans* (1826), *The Pioneers* (1823), and *The Deerslayer* (1841). The tales feature Natty Bumppo, whom the Indians call Leatherstocking. Bumppo is an inventive frontiersman who lives close to nature with his brave American Indian friends. Cooper was deeply patriotic but was criticized for his upper class views. He became disenchanted with American democracy. Cooper believed a small, landed upper class group should govern the country.

One early American writer, Washington Irving, was successful with tales such as "The Legend of Sleepy Hollow" and "Rip Van Winkle." In 1851, Herman Melville wrote *Moby Dick,* while Nathaniel Hawthorne published *Twice-Told Tales* in 1837 and *The Scarlet Letter* in 1850. Edgar Allan Poe wrote several frightening stories, including "The Fall of the House of Usher" in 1839 and "The Murders in the Rue Morgue" in 1841. Poe also wrote a number of poems such as "The Raven."

Some American poets wrote about the vast opportunity in America, while many attacked the serious problems in the country. Emily Dickinson wrote about love and death. Henry David Thoreau focused on the peace and beauty in nature, while Walt Whitman wrote about freedom and those who fought for it.

Prose
The ordinary form of spoken or written language

Henry Wadsworth Longfellow wrote poetry and **prose,** including works such as "Paul Revere's Ride" and "Poems on Slavery" that looked at history and current events. Ralph Waldo Emerson wrote about life and what it meant to be a human being. During this period, he became very active in the antislavery campaign.

John Greenleaf Whittier had become an established writer. Mobs often attacked him because he was secretary of the American Anti-Slavery Society. Writers such as James Russell Lowell and Oliver Wendell Holmes also used their poetry to attack slavery, which they considered to be an evil practice.

Which Other Writers Attacked Slavery?

Several other writers helped to bring attention to the slavery issue during this time. Harriet Beecher Stowe of New England wrote a book called *Uncle Tom's Cabin* in 1852. She described the terrible conditions under which slaves had to live. Thousands of copies of the book were sold in the United States and in Europe. *Uncle Tom's Cabin* added to the movement to abolish slavery.

In 1857, poor southerner Hinton R. Helper wrote *The Impending Crisis in the South.* This book carried the message that the evil of slavery was ruining the South. He described the South as poor, especially due to its lack of industry. Its people were not educated and far behind the rest of the country. This book upset a lot of people, especially those in the South.

In 1831, William Lloyd Garrison published a newspaper called *The Liberator.* His point of view was clear: slavery must be stopped. Garrison was liked by some people, but others thought him to be much too **violent.** Equally important were the contributions made by an ex-slave, Frederick Douglass. Douglass bought his freedom after escaping from Maryland.

Media in History

A Person of Many Contradictions

People either loved or hated Horace Greeley. His *New York Tribune* printed lots of political opinion in a day when other newspapers featured crime and gossip. He believed that a newspaper could gain mass readership without sensational stories.

Greeley wrote passionately about what he believed in. He stood behind every word he wrote, believing honesty was the best policy. He did not talk down to the common person.

"Go West, Young Man" was Greeley's newspaper slogan. It encouraged many to seek a new life on the frontier. Greeley's editorials against slavery won many believers. He crusaded for the rights of women. He helped to organize the Republican party and elect Abraham Lincoln as President. Later Greeley himself ran unsuccessfully for President. Historians believe he was too much a person of principle to be a politician. Everyone respected him—no one could control him.

★Abolitionist
A person who wanted slavery stopped

Douglass was self-taught and became an excellent speaker and writer. When he settled in Rochester, New York, Douglass published an antislavery newspaper called *The North Star.* Douglass tried to help in the fight against slavery through his speeches and writings. Both Garrison and Douglass were **abolitionists.** An abolitionist was a person who wanted slavery stopped.

Writing About History

Write an antislavery poem. Describe a slave's longing for freedom, the conditions slaves had to live with, or other themes authors and poets wrote about at the time. Write the poem in your notebook.

How Did Other Countries View American Literature?

For many years after America was established, the Europeans did not view the nation as being well developed. More than a thousand years old, European nations thought that the "young" America could produce no great literature. However, by the middle of the nineteenth century, Americans were proving that their stories were rich and exciting. The United States was becoming a storyteller to the world.

SECTION 5 REVIEW On a separate sheet of paper, write the correct name from the Word Bank that matches each sentence below.

WORD BANK

Emily Dickinson

Frederick Douglass

Harriet Beecher Stowe

Herman Melville

William Lloyd Garrison

1) *Moby Dick* was written by _____.

2) _____ wrote about love and death.

3) _____ wrote *Uncle Tom's Cabin.*

4) A newspaper called *The Liberator* was published by _____.

5) _____ published an antislavery newspaper called *The North Star.*

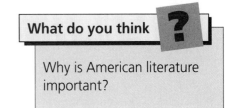

What do you think

Why is American literature important?

"Slavery As It Is"

As a student in 1834, Theodore Dwight Weld organized abolitionists in Oberlin, Ohio. Two years later, Oberlin College became the first college to admit African Americans. Weld married Angelina Grimké, another abolitionist, in 1838.

In 1839, he published American Slavery As It Is. *The pamphlet documented the evils of slavery based on testimony of such witnesses as Frederick Douglass. Harriet Beecher Stowe partly based* Uncle Tom's Cabin *on the pamphlet. It is considered second only to Stowe's book in its influence on the antislavery movement. By the time of his death in the late 1800s, Weld had become known as "the greatest Abolitionist."*

This passage is from the introduction to American Slavery As It Is.

"We will prove that the slaves in the United States are treated with barbarous inhumanity; that they are overworked, underfed, wretchedly clad and lodged, and have insufficient sleep; that they are often made to wear round their necks iron collars armed with prongs, to drag heavy chains and weights at their feet while working in the field, and to wear yokes, and bells, and iron horns . . . that they are often hunted with bloodhounds and shot down like beasts . . . that they are whipped and beaten till they faint, and sometimes until they die . . . that they are maimed, mutilated, and burned to death. All these things, and more, and worse, we shall prove. Ready, we know whereof we affirm, we have weighed it well; more and worse WE WILL PROVE."

Source Reading Wrap-Up

1) What word did Weld use to describe how slaves were housed?

2) What were two things slaves were made to wear?

3) What were two things Weld claimed was done to slaves?

4) How did Weld intend to prove the things he said?

5) Weld was a white man. Why do you think he fought so hard on behalf of the slaves?

CHAPTER SUMMARY

★ Samuel Slater brought designs for British textile machines to America. He built new machines in America and contributed to the growth of the textile industry in New England.

★ Eli Whitney invented the cotton gin, which contributed to the growth of the textile industry. Whitney also helped develop the idea of interchangeable parts in manufacturing and the concept of mass production.

★ Cyrus McCormick and John Deere invented machines that had major effects on farming.

★ The Cumberland Road, originally built in 1811, led to a system of roads and highways that spread westward for nearly 600 miles.

★ In 1807, Robert Fulton's steamboat made water transportation faster. By 1837, there were 300 steamboats carrying passengers and cargo on the Mississippi River and the rivers that joined it.

★ Canals allowed goods to be shipped quickly and cheaply. The Erie Canal was completed in 1825 and connected Buffalo, New York, to Albany, New York. By 1837, the Northeast had a network of thousands miles of canals and rivers.

★ Railroads began to provide another means of transportation. Steam locomotives could move people and freight faster than any other transportation. By 1840, there were over 3,000 miles of railroad lines in the United States.

★ Samuel B. Morse developed the telegraph in 1844. In 1858, Cyrus Field laid a transatlantic telegraph cable that connected North America with Europe.

★ The pony express carried the mail from St. Joseph, Missouri, to Sacramento, California.

★ From 1790 to 1830, the U.S. population grew from four million to thirteen million people.

★ Early immigrants to America came from Great Britain, Wales, Scotland, and Ireland. The second wave of immigrants came from Ireland and Germany.

★ Public education grew in the 1800s. Horace Mann did much to reform the Massachusetts school system.

★ Washington Irving, Edgar Allan Poe, and Emily Dickinson were among many writers who contributed to American literature.

Comprehension: Identifying Facts

On a separate sheet of paper, write the words or names from the Word Bank to complete each sentence.

WORD BANK		
education	Noah Webster	steamboat
Erie Canal	pony express	telegraph
Europe	potato	grain
Germany	railroads	
John Deere	*The Scarlet Letter*	

1) The steel plow, which allowed hard prairie sod to be farmed, was invented by _____.

2) The _____ ran from St. Joseph to Sacramento in about ten days.

3) Cyrus McCormick invented a mechanical reaper to harvest _____.

4) The first dictionary of American English was written by _____.

5) In 1825, the _____ ran from Albany to Buffalo.

6) Samuel B. Morse developed the _____, which made communication possible over long distances.

7) Nathaniel Hawthorne's famous book, _____, was set in colonial times.

8) Horace Mann tried to make people understand the importance of _____ for all children.

9) A failed _____ crop caused many immigrants to come to the United States from Ireland.

10) Robert Fulton's _____ was known as "Fulton's Folly."

11) Political unrest in _____ led many of its citizens to immigrate to America.

12) _____ were the fastest kind of transportation for passengers and freight.

13) Cyrus Field laid a telegraph cable from America to _____.

Comprehension: Understanding Main Ideas

On a separate sheet of paper, write the answer to each question using complete sentences.

1) Why did Governor De Witt Clinton want the Erie Canal to be built?

2) Why was making iron important to American industry?

3) What background did Frederick Douglass have that made him such a powerful speaker on the evils of slavery?

4) How could the pony express travel such a long distance in such a short time?

Critical Thinking: Write Your Opinion

1) Of all the inventions that you studied in this chapter, which one do you think was the most important? Explain your reasons.

2) Fewer than one out of every six children went to school in 1820. Today almost all children go to school. Why is going to school important?

3) Explain the route you would have taken from Philadelphia to St. Louis in 1837. Tell which means of transportation you would take on each section of the trip and describe what it would be like.

| Test Taking Tip | Look over a test before you begin answering questions. See how many parts there are. See what you are being asked to do on each part.

The Country Grows Larger

1841–1850

The country became much larger in the 1840s. This was the result of compromises with other countries over territory. It was also the result of a war with Mexico. Yet another cause of this expansion was the discovery of gold in California. Presidential elections were also changing. In this chapter, you will learn about these and other changes in the United States in the 1840s.

Goals for Learning

▶ To identify ways that presidential campaigns changed

▶ To discuss the concept of Manifest Destiny

▶ To describe the boundary conflicts with Great Britain over Maine and the Oregon Country

▶ To explain the reasons for the Mexican War

▶ To describe events of the California gold rush

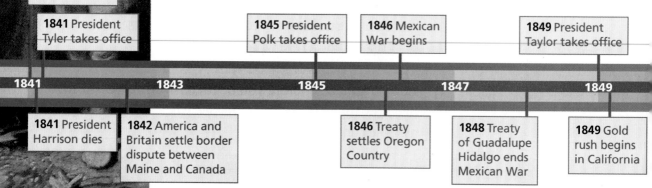

1841 President Harrison takes office

1841 President Tyler takes office

1845 President Polk takes office

1846 Mexican War begins

1849 President Taylor takes office

| 1841 | 1843 | 1845 | 1847 | 1849 |

1841 President Harrison dies

1842 America and Britain settle border dispute between Maine and Canada

1846 Treaty settles Oregon Country

1848 Treaty of Guadalupe Hidalgo ends Mexican War

1849 Gold rush begins in California

Recall from Chapter 11 that Martin Van Buren became President in 1837. When President Van Buren ran for re-election in 1840, the Whigs again nominated William Henry Harrison as their candidate. At age sixty-eight, Harrison was still remembered for his great victory against the American Indians at Tippecanoe in 1811. The Whigs chose John Tyler as their candidate for Vice President. "Tippecanoe and Tyler, too!" became the **slogan** of the Whig party.

Slogan

A word or phrase used to explain a stand or goal

What New Election Methods Were Used?

The Democrats made fun of William Henry Harrison. They said he lived in a log cabin and sat on the porch all day drinking hard cider, a kind of alcohol. Actually, Harrison lived in a very large house on 3,000 acres of land.

Whigs used posters such as this one to win votes for William Henry Harrison and to announce rallies.

The Whigs decided to use the log cabin and hard cider story to help their candidate win the election. They held big parades with a log cabin mounted on a wagon. They passed out leaflets describing Harrison as a man of the people, an old fighter, and a great hero. In addition, they organized political meetings and painted large **billboards** with pictures of Harrison and Tyler. This was the first election campaign to use these new ways of winning votes. These ways worked, for Harrison easily won the election. In addition, the Whig Party gained control of the Congress.

Billboard
A large sign used to advertise something

What Happened to President Harrison?

Harrison took office in 1841. Weary and worn out from the election, Harrison came down with a cold. His condition grew worse, and on April 4, 1841, he died. He had been the President for only one month. Harrison was the first President to die in office. Vice President John Tyler then became President.

Formerly a U.S. Senator, Tyler had been a faithful Democrat. Although he had switched to the Whig party, he held on to his belief in states' rights and a weak central government. As a result, he often came into conflict with Congress during his presidency.

SAMUEL F. B. MORSE: 1791–1872

Samuel F. B. Morse first was recognized as a painter and a founder of the National Academy of Design. He is better known today, however, as the inventor of the first successful electric telegraph. In effect, the telegraph made electricity visible. It also enabled immediate communication of messages over long distances. With his Morse code—an alphabet of dots and dashes—messages could be sent by telegraph. The first telegraphic message was sent by Morse in 1844 from Washington, D.C., to Baltimore, Maryland. It was the famous greeting, "What hath God wrought!" Later he experimented with underwater cable telegraphy. He was also involved in introducing the daguerreotype, an early type of photograph, in the United States.

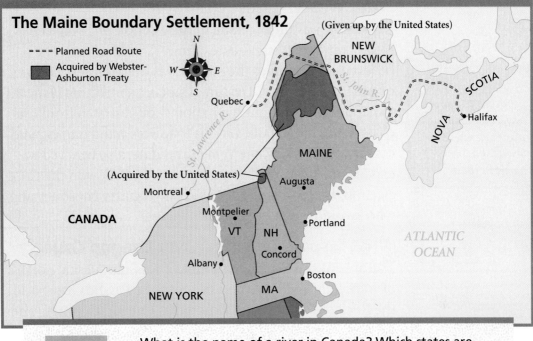

The Maine Boundary Settlement, 1842

- - - - Planned Road Route
Acquired by Webster-Ashburton Treaty

(Given up by the United States)

NEW BRUNSWICK

St. John R.

SCOTIA

NOVA

Halifax

Quebec

St. Lawrence R.

MAINE

(Acquired by the United States)

Augusta

Montreal

Montpelier

VT   NH

Portland

ATLANTIC OCEAN

CANADA

Concord

Albany

Boston

NEW YORK

MA

MAP STUDY What is the name of a river in Canada? Which states are shown on the map?

How Were Canadian Boundaries Still a Dispute?

The United States and Great Britain were still disputing over the location of the boundary between Maine and Canada. By 1842, the disagreement nearly turned into a war. British Lord Ashburton met with Secretary of State Daniel Webster to try to work out a compromise.

The land in question covered 12,000 square miles. Both countries wanted the whole area. However, after many talks, a compromise was reached. Lord Ashburton said he would accept 5,000 square miles if the boundary did not block a road planned to go from Halifax, Nova Scotia, to Quebec. The United States received a large part of land, which included the fertile Aroostook Valley. Then, as a part of the same agreement, the British adjusted the boundary of what is now northeastern Minnesota. The United States gained control over an area that was later found to contain rich iron ore on the Mesabi Range.

What Was Manifest Destiny?

Expansion was the big issue in the election of 1844. The Democratic party candidate, James K. Polk of Tennessee, believed expansion to the Pacific was the **Manifest Destiny** of America. Manifest Destiny is a belief something is meant to happen. He thought the nation should stretch from one coast to the other. Polk and his followers wanted to expand quickly. Henry Clay, the Whig candidate, also believed in expansion. He wanted to expand slowly. Polk won the close election. He took office in 1845. The country chose a man who favored quick expansion.

What Dispute Occurred Over Oregon Country?

The area of the Northwest south of Russian Alaska, north of Mexican California, and between the Pacific Ocean and the Rocky Mountains was known as Oregon Country. The United States and Great Britain signed a temporary treaty in 1818 allowing settlement of the area by both countries. Then land-hungry Americans began to move into the region. Many of them had packed all of their belongings into crowded covered wagons in hope of a better life on the fertile Oregon land.

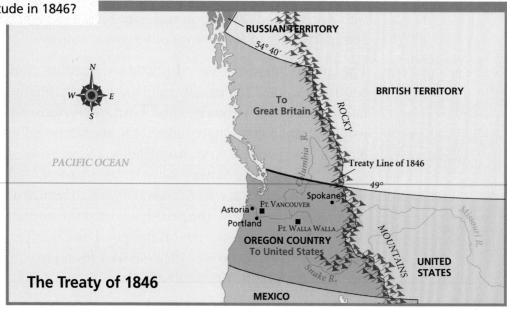

The Treaty of 1846

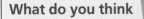
The Works of Edgar Allan Poe

Many regard Edgar Allan Poe (1809–1849) as one of the most brilliant, original writers in American literature. Poe struggled to make a living during the 1830s and 1840s. He published his writings and worked as a magazine editor and critic. A complicated, tormented man, some believe he eventually died of alcoholism. Poe is remembered for such eerie poems as "The Raven" and "Annabel Lee." He is also remembered for short stories like "The Fall of the House of Usher." Poe established a tradition of American horror stories. Filmmakers and writers like Stephen King carry on that tradition today. Poe is also considered one of the creators of the modern detective story. Examples of his detective stories are "The Murders in the Rue Morgue" and "The Masque of the Red Death." Poe never enjoyed much commercial success from his writing. However, millions of people today enjoy reading his work.

As the American population of Oregon Country grew, America and Great Britain disputed the boundary of American Oregon. In his election speech, President Polk had promised to take American Oregon as far north as 54 degrees 40 minutes north latitude, using the slogan "fifty-four forty or fight." After the two sides debated the issue, the British agreed to 49 degrees latitude as the northern boundary of America. President Polk felt this was a fair compromise, and he wanted to keep America out of yet another war with Great Britain. In the Treaty of 1846, the United States accepted the southern part of Oregon Country. Great Britain took the northern part, with 49 degrees north latitude as the boundary.

SECTION 1 REVIEW Write the answers to these questions on a separate sheet of paper using complete sentences.

1) How was the election of 1840 different from other elections?

2) What happened to President Harrison?

3) How did Britain and America settle boundary disputes over the Maine and Canadian boundary?

4) What is Manifest Destiny?

5) What was Oregon Country?

What do you think ?

Why do you think Americans felt it was so important to expand U.S. territory?

When Santa Anna surrendered to Sam Houston in the War of Texas Independence in 1836, he had agreed that the Rio Grande River was the boundary between Mexico and Texas. Later, he said the boundary was the Nueces River, which gave Texans far less territory. Texans would not accept the new Mexican boundary.

The Republic of Texas became part of the United States in 1845. Texas was the twenty-eighth state to join the Union. Slavery was allowed in Texas. Many Americans were against the state joining the Union because of this slavery issue. However, the border dispute was a more pressing problem. After Texas joined the Union, some people feared there would be a war with Mexico.

President Polk was eager to settle the Texas boundary dispute with Mexico. At the same time, he wanted to see if that country would sell California to America. He thought that Mexico, which needed money, would be willing to sell the land. The President sent John Slidell to Mexico City in 1845. As Polk's personal representative, Slidell could offer up to $25 million as payment for California. The Mexican officials refused to see him. This **insult** to the United States was not taken lightly by President Polk.

Insult
An action that upsets others

What Was the Mexican War?

Polk ordered General Zachary Taylor to advance his army beyond the Nueces River toward the Rio Grande in January of 1846. The Mexican army remained quiet. February and March passed; there was still no action. Finally, on April 25, 1846, Mexican troops crossed the Rio Grande and killed many of General Taylor's soldiers. The United States, in turn, declared war with its southern neighbor on May 13, 1846. This was the beginning of the Mexican War.

Polk still wanted to extend the United States to the Pacific coast. He ordered American troops to invade California.

General Winfield Scott was known as "Old Fuss and Feathers."

The leaders, General Stephen W. Kearny, Commodore John D. Sloat, and Army officer John C. Fremont, had very little trouble defeating the Mexicans. Meanwhile, Zachary Taylor fought his way into Mexico. "Old Rough and Ready," as he was called, won a major victory for the Americans at Buena Vista.

In early 1847, General Winfield Scott led a charge on Mexico City. Scott was an expert in preparing for battles. Because of his complete attention to every last detail, he was known as "Old Fuss and Feathers." At that time, many believed he was the country's most capable general. In September, Scott and his troops captured Mexico City.

How Did the Mexican War End?

Mexico, which had a new government, finally was ready to make peace. President Polk had sent Nicholas P. Trist to negotiate a treaty. In 1848, the Treaty of Guadalupe Hidalgo was presented to Congress. In the treaty, Mexico would turn over California and all the land between Texas and California. Mexico also agreed that the Rio Grande was the southern boundary of Texas. The United States paid Mexico $15 million for the land. Many Americans felt that all of Mexico should have been turned over to the United States. Polk suggested that the treaty be accepted. Congress agreed to the treaty in 1848. The United States now stretched from coast to coast.

Writing About History

Research a battle fought during the Mexican War. Then write a first person account of what it was like. Write it in your notebook.

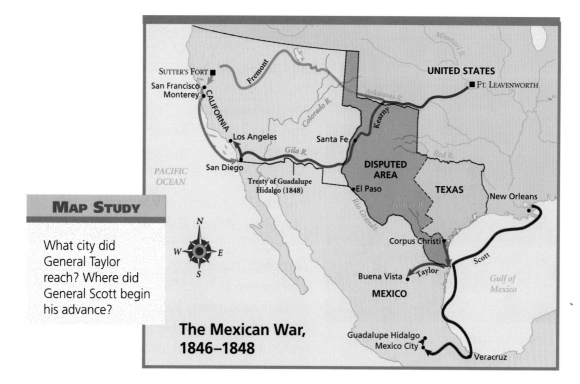

The Mexican War, 1846–1848

MAP STUDY

What city did General Taylor reach? Where did General Scott begin his advance?

SECTION 2 REVIEW Choose the best name in parentheses to complete each sentence. Write your answers on a separate sheet of paper.

1) (President Polk, Zachary Taylor, Winfield Scott) wanted to settle the border dispute with Mexico.

2) President Polk sent (Steven W. Kearny, Winfield Scott, John Slidell) to Mexico to offer payment for California.

3) (John C. Fremont, Zachary Taylor, Winfield Scott) won a major victory for the Americans at Buena Vista.

4) (Zachary Taylor, Winfield Scott, Steven W. Kearny) captured Mexico City.

5) (Winfield Scott, Zachary Taylor, John C. Fremont) was known as "Old Rough and Ready."

What do you think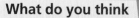

Do you think all of Mexico should have been turned over to America after the war? Why or why not?

Sources of U.S. Territorial Expansion

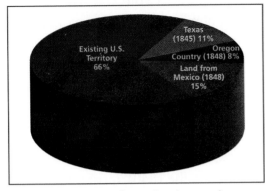

What percentage of U.S. land came from Oregon Country? What percentage of U.S. land came from Mexico in 1848?

In addition to the expansion of the United States, President Polk had other goals for the future of the country. He wanted to lower tariffs and government spending. During his four-year term as President, Polk got what he wanted. Between 1845 and 1848, the United States added more than a million square miles of land. Also, tariffs were lowered, and there was less government spending. However, even with his successes in office, President Polk refused to run for a second term.

What Happened in the Election of 1848?

Americans were excited about the victory over Mexico and about the land that had been added. New land, however, meant new problems. The biggest problem was the possible spread of slavery into the western region.

Slavery was the most important issue in the election of 1848. However, the Whigs and the Democrats took limited stands on it. Both parties were not sure how such a stand would affect the success of their candidates in the election.

The Whigs nominated General Zachary Taylor. Taylor was a hero, having won an important victory at Buena Vista during the Mexican War. Taylor was a southerner and would get strong support from slave states. The Democrats nominated Lewis Cass, a northerner from Michigan.

Many Democrats who did not want Cass broke away and formed the Free Soil party. The Free Soilers chose Martin Van Buren as their candidate for President. The new party favored free speech, free labor, and free men.

Then and Now

Where did you or your ancesters come from? What conditions had to be faced? In 1850, for example, Irish immigrants faced difficult times. Without money to travel west, they settled in New York slums. As Catholics, they were not welcomed by Protestant Americans. They took low-paying jobs in factories or as housekeepers. Still, many Irish were able to send money to family members in Ireland who were even poorer than the immigrants.

In 1850, most immigrants came from Europe. Today, most immigrants come from Asia or Mexico. In 1850, any healthy European was welcome. Today, immigration is strictly controlled. Immigrants must be accepted before coming. However, once in the United States, poor immigrants can receive welfare. They must go through several steps before becoming U.S. citizens.

Zachary Taylor won the election. He received 163 electoral votes; Cass had 127. The Democrats lost the popular vote, too. The Free Soilers took votes that would have gone to Cass. The issue of slavery decided the election by splitting the Democratic party. Taylor took office in 1849.

How Did California Become Important?

Before the 1840s, most inhabitants of California were Spaniards and American Indians. Swiss-American settler John A. Sutter was one of the first to gain success in California. He owned a large amount of land in a valley north of San Francisco. He built a big fort that travelers used on their way into California. Sutter also grew wheat and corn and had large numbers of cattle, sheep, and horses. He had this "kingdom" all to himself for most of the 1840s. However, his way of life changed a lot after an event that took place in 1848.

One day, a man who worked for Sutter collected a small sack of nuggets and dust he believed was gold. He showed the sack to Sutter. They intended to keep the find a secret. However, by 1849, the message had spread throughout the land, and people came from every direction.

Towns were formed as laborers, miners, farmers, merchants, **professional** people, and other **fortune seekers** rushed to California. The Forty-Niners, named for the year of the gold rush, used every means of transportation possible to reach the gold country. Prices for supplies and services greatly increased. Crime became a major problem. As the output of gold rose to $50 million in 1850, over 100,000 new people

Fortune seeker
One who is looking for financial gain

Professional
A person who is skilled or trained to do a task

Miners, or "Forty-Niners," labored over the California land in search of gold. Most of them ended up with nothing.

had moved to California. Some of those who joined the rush struck it rich, but most of them ended up with nothing.

In only slightly more than a year's time, the population of California had increased by over ten times. Cities had sprung up in many regions of the western land. Almost overnight, it had grown to look like a part of the United States. Then, in 1850, California applied for statehood. That same year it became the thirty-first state.

SECTION 3 REVIEW On a separate sheet of paper, write *True* if the statement is true or write *False* if the statement is not true.

1) President Polk wanted to raise tariffs and increase government spending.

2) Slavery was the most important issue in the election of 1848.

3) Martin Van Buren won the election of 1848.

4) John A. Sutter was one of the first people to find gold in California.

5) Most people seeking gold in California ended up finding nothing.

What do you think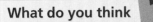

Why do you think the gold rush brought so many people to California?

Seneca Falls Declaration

In 1848, the Seneca Falls Convention was held in New York. It was led by Elizabeth Cady Stanton and Lucretia Mott. Delegates adopted the Declaration of Sentiments and Resolutions. The declaration is considered to be one of the first documents calling for equal rights for women.

"When, in the course of human events, it becomes necessary for one portion of the family of man to assume among the people of the earth a position different from that which they have hitherto occupied, but one to which the laws of nature and of nature's God entitle them, a decent respect to the opinions of mankind requires that they should declare the causes that impel them to such a course.

We hold these truths to be self-evident: that all men and women are created equal.

The history of mankind is a history of repeated injuries and usurpations on the part of man toward woman, having in direct object the establishment of an absolute tyranny over her. To prove this, let facts be submitted to a candid world .... Now, in view of this entire disenfranchisement of one-half of the people of this country, their social and religious degradation, in view of the unjust laws above mentioned, and because women do feel themselves aggrieved, oppressed, and fraudulently deprived of their most sacred rights, we insist that they have immediate admission to all the rights and privileges which belong to them as citizens of the United States. . . .

Resolve, therefore, that being invested by the Creator with the same capabilities and the same consciousness of responsibility for their exercise . . . and this being a self-evident truth growing out of the divinely implanted truth of human nature, any custom or authority adverse to it, whether modern or wearing the hoary sanction of antiquity, is to be regarded as a self-evident falsehood, and at war with mankind."

Source Reading Wrap-Up

1) What does this declaration say women are entitled to?

2) The second paragraph is similar to the beginning of the Declaration of Independence. What words have been added to make if different from the Declaration of Independence?

3) What does the third paragraph say about the history of men's treatment of women?

4) The last paragraph says a truth of human nature is that women are invested with the same capabilities and responsibilities as men. What does it say about any authority that disagrees with that?

5) How wise do you think it was for these women to make this declaration?

★ William Henry Harrison ran for President and used new campaign methods, including leaflets, billboards, and the slogan "Tippecanoe and Tyler, too!" Harrison died one month after he became President. He was the first President to die while in office.

★ A dispute arose between Great Britain and America over the northern boundary of Maine. A compromise was reached that gave land to both Great Britain and America.

★ President Polk promoted the idea of Manifest Destiny. He said that the United States was meant to control the lands and people from the Atlantic coast to the Pacific coast.

★ Great Britain and America disagreed about the boundaries for Oregon Country in the Northwest. America wanted the boundary to be at 54 degrees 40 minutes north latitude. A compromise reached in 1846 set the boundary at 49 degrees north latitude.

★ Texas became a state in 1845, but there were questions about the border between Texas and Mexico. Polk ordered American troops to advance to the Rio Grande River. The United States declared war on Mexico in May of 1846.

★ After American troops captured Mexico City, the Mexicans made peace with the United States. The Treaty of Guadalupe Hidalgo in 1848 ended the Mexican War and gave America the California territory.

★ President Polk accomplished his goal of Manifest Destiny and added more than a million square miles of land to the United States during the four years he was President.

★ Slavery was the biggest issue of the 1848 presidential election. Zachary Taylor, a southerner and hero of the Mexican War, won the election.

★ In 1848, gold was discovered on land in California owned by John Sutter. The discovery led to the largest movement of people in U.S. history.

★ During the gold rush of 1849, the population of California increased by over ten times. Many people grew rich by mining gold, but many more grew rich by selling supplies to the Forty-Niners–the people who came to California to search for gold.

★ In 1850, California applied for statehood and became the thiry-first state.

Comprehension: Identifying Facts

On a separate sheet of paper write the words from the Word Bank to complete each sentence.

WORD BANK

billboards	Minnesota
California	Texas
"Fifty-four forty or fight"	thirty-first
gold rush	"Tippecanoe and Tyler, too!"
John Sutter	twenty-eighth
John Tyler	William Henry Harrison
Manifest Destiny	Zachary Taylor

1) _____ was a phrase used by President James Polk to encourage the United States to expand from coast to coast.

2) President _____ was known as "Old Rough and Ready" because of his leadership in the Mexican War.

3) Gold was discovered on land owned by _____ in California.

4) The first President to die in office was _____.

5) The "Forty-Niners" helped increase the population of _____.

6) _____ was a very strong supporter of states' rights.

7) Texas was the _____ state to join the Union.

8) In 1850, California became the _____ state.

9) The _____ was one of the major events of 1849.

10) _____ was a slogan about a dispute over the borders of Oregon Country.

11) Harrison's campaign slogan was _____.

12) Settlers in _____ decided to give up their independence and become a state in 1845.

13) Harrison used _____ to tell people about his qualifications for President.

14) The United States gave up part of Maine, but gained a portion of what is now _____.

Comprehension: Understanding Main Ideas

On a separate sheet of paper, write the answer to each question using complete sentences.

1) Why did Great Britain dispute the northern boundary of Maine?

2) How did President Polk fulfill his dream of Manifest Destiny?

3) What were two main reasons for the Mexican War?

4) How far south into Mexico did the United States army go during the Mexican War?

Critical Thinking: Write Your Opinion

1) Harrison's presidential campaign used slogans and billboards to tell people about him. How important is advertising in today's presidential races?

2) Many people sold everything they owned so that they could go to California to search for gold. Do you think these people made good decisions? Why or why not?

| Test Taking Tip | When you don't know the answer for a question, put a check mark by it. After you have answered the questions you know, come back and try to answer the questions you have marked. |

As you study history, you will read many facts. Sometimes people write books about history in which they state their opinions. You need to be able to tell the difference between fact and opinion.

A fact can be proved true or false.

> The Cumberland Road stretched from Cumberland to Vandalia.

An opinion is someone's judgment, belief, or way of thinking about something. Look for words that tell how someone felt. An opinion is more than just a fact.

> Travel on the Cumberland Road was difficult.
>
> Travel on the Cumberland Road was easy.

Decide which of the two sentences in items 1–4 is fact and which is opinion. Explain your answer.

1) The cotton gin was the best invention of the 1800s.

The cotton gin enabled cotton production to increase.

2) A poll is an organized method of asking people what they think about a candidate.

Polls are not always correct.

3) Between 1790 and 1810, the population of the United States doubled.

Immigrants to the United States faced many hardships.

4) President Polk said that because Mexico needed money, it would be willing to sell California to the United States.

Mexican officials refused to meet with President Polk's personal representative.

5) Write a statement of fact and a statement of opinion about slavery.

★ James Monroe became President in 1817.

★ By 1820, the U.S. population increased by six million.

★ Farming thrived in the South. Industry thrived in the North.

★ The Adams-Onís Treaty gave Florida to America in 1819.

★ Slavery became an issue in 1819.

★ President Monroe announced the Monroe Doctrine in 1823.

★ Congress chose John Quincy Adams as President in 1824.

★ The country was split on the Tariff of 1828.

★ Andrew Jackson was elected President in 1828.

★ Nat Turner led a slave revolt in 1831.

★ Jackson asked Congress to set aside land for American Indians.

★ Texans won independence from Mexico in 1836.

★ Martin Van Buren became President in 1837.

★ The Panic of 1837 resulted in a depression and many bank failures.

★ Many machines helped industry and farming grow.

★ By 1837, 300 steamboats provided transportation on rivers.

★ The Erie Canal opened in 1825.

★ Railroads became the fastest means of transportation.

★ The telegraph expanded communication.

★ By 1830, the U.S. population grew to thirteen million.

★ The second wave of immigrants came from Ireland and Germany.

★ Public education grew in the 1800s.

★ President Henry Harrison died in office.

★ The United States declared war on Mexico in 1846.

★ President James Polk's Manifest Destiny added land to the United States.

★ Slavery was the big issue in the 1848 election.

★ In 1848, gold was discovered in California.

"*I can anticipate no greater calamity for the country than the dissolution of the Union. It would be an accumulation of all the evils we complain of, and I am willing to sacrifice everything but honor for its preservation.*"

–Robert E. Lee

Civil War and Reconstruction

1850–1877

Has your family ever had a difference so strong that it became divided? Differences over slavery and states' rights were growing strong in the United States around 1850. Divisions between the North and the South grew until the country split apart. The split caused the country to enter a four-year civil war. Even individual families were divided, with members fighting against each other on opposite sides. When the war ended, the country had to bind up its wounds, heal its divisions, and rebuild.

In this unit you will learn about many differences over the issue of slavery. You will learn about events that led the United States into a war within itself. You will learn about the damage the war did to individuals, families, and the nation. You will learn what the nation did to reunite and rebuild.

Chapter 14: The Slavery Problem Grows: 1850–1854

Chapter 15: The Country Separates: 1854–1861

Chapter 16: The Civil War: 1861–1865

Chapter 17: Reconstruction: 1865–1877

1850–1854

Slavery in the United States continued to cause many problems. The North and the South, and now the newly created West, debated the issue around the nation and in Congress. Short-term solutions began to appear. However, people were beginning to see that the issue was dividing the nation. In this chapter, you will learn how the issue of slavery became the main concern of the nation.

Goals for Learning

▶ To describe the various issues faced by the North and the South concerning slavery

▶ To explain the significance of the Compromise of 1850

▶ To describe the Underground Railroad and how it worked

▶ To explain the importance of cotton to the United States

▶ To explain the Fugitive Slave Law

▶ To describe the Kansas-Nebraska Act

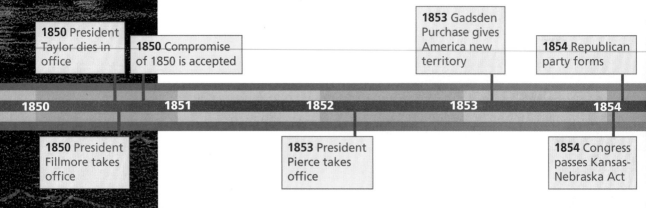

1850 President Taylor dies in office

1850 Compromise of 1850 is accepted

1853 Gadsden Purchase gives America new territory

1854 Republican party forms

| 1850 | 1851 | 1852 | 1853 | 1854 |

1850 President Fillmore takes office

1853 President Pierce takes office

1854 Congress passes Kansas-Nebraska Act

Theodore Weld

Exaggerate
To overstate the truth

Since the 1830s, abolitionists had campaigned against slavery. Leaders such as William Lloyd Garrison used antislavery newspapers to try to sway opinion in the country. Theodore Weld and his wife, the former Angelina Grimké, traveled all over the country speaking and organizing new abolitionist groups in different cities. Countless others helped enslaved Africans escape to freedom.

Southerners felt the abolitionists were trying to harm their way of life. In most cases, the white people of the South needed slave labor for their plantations and businesses. They felt the abolitionists were unfairly **exaggerating** how poorly the enslaved Africans were treated. Southern writers wrote that free Africans in the North were treated worse than enslaved Africans in the South who worked on the plantations. They claimed that free Africans had no political rights, low-level jobs, and poor living conditions. Enslaved Africans, on the other hand, were given food, clothing, and shelter by their owners.

Many northerners needed goods from southern businesses. They felt the abolitionists caused problems for them in their dealings with the South. Even others who may have opposed slavery believed that the abolitionists did more to harm the country than to improve it. Despite these difficulties, over 200,000 Americans were members of abolitionist groups throughout the northern states by 1850.

What New Debate Started in Congress?

Between 1836 and 1848, six new states had been added to the Union, bringing the total number of states to thirty. The balance of free states to slave states was at fifteen each. However, when California sought admission to the Union as a free state, tempers once again flared.

Southerners were certain that the antislavery states in the North would gain control of the country. Southern leaders wanted to protect their rights. They felt that the South should not have to change. The southern **economy** depended on slavery.

What Compromise Helped the Slavery Issue?

Three of America's most experienced leaders helped to bring a temporary settlement to the slavery issue. Daniel Webster, Henry Clay, and John C. Calhoun had spent many years in public service. All of them were well-respected leaders.

Stephen Foster

Stephen Foster wrote dozens of songs that illustrated the spirit of the United States in the mid-1800s. He wrote "Oh! Susannah" during the gold rush. Some of his other songs are "Camptown Races," "Beautiful Dreamer," and "Swanee River." Although most of Foster's songs were about the South, he visited it only once, briefly, in 1852.

Webster and Calhoun debated the slavery issue in Congress. Webster wanted the country to stay united. Calhoun was from South Carolina. He felt slavery should be allowed to continue, yet he didn't want it to destroy the country.

Henry Clay proposed a compromise. President Taylor, who opposed the spread of slavery, would not permit any compromise. The situation changed, though, when Taylor died suddenly in July of 1850 after only sixteen months in office.

The Sewing Machine

Primitive sewing machines were invented in France and England in the 1700s but were difficult to use. Many tailors and seamstresses feared they would lose their living if the machines became popular. American Walter Hunt invented the "practical lock stitch" sewing machine in 1832. Again, people who sewed by hand reacted so negatively that it failed. In the 1840s in Boston, Elias Howe developed an improved lock stitch machine. However, he was unable to sell his machine in America or England. Finally, in 1852, using Howe's needle design, Isaac Merrit Singer developed and successfully marketed a sewing machine. Key to his success were female salespeople who sold the machines on installment or credit plans. By 1860, the Singer Manufacturing Company was the world's largest producer of sewing machines. Singer sewing machines are still made today.

Consumer Science

History in Your Life

Vice President Millard Fillmore became President. Unlike Taylor, he favored a compromise. He believed that an agreement could be worked out. After nine months of debate, the Compromise of 1850 was accepted by the North and the South. The compromise was much better for the North than for the South.

A Closer Look at the Compromise of 1850

The compromise agreed to:

1. allow California to become a free state.

2. allow additional western territories such as Utah and New Mexico to decide for themselves if they wanted to allow slavery when they joined the Union.

3. abolish slave trade in the District of Columbia.

4. allow Texas to sell its claim on New Mexico for $10 million.

5. create a new law, called the **Fugitive** Slave Law, to help slave owners recapture their runaway slaves.

Fugitive
One who is fleeing from danger or from being kept against one's will

---

SECTION 1 REVIEW On a separate sheet of paper, write *True* if the statement is true or write *False* if the statement is not true.

1) Southerners felt abolitionists were exaggerating the abuse of African-American slaves.

2) Northerners did not depend on the South for business.

3) The South depended on slavery for its economy.

4) Daniel Webster and John C. Calhoun debated the slavery issue in Congress.

5) President Fillmore would not compromise on the slave issue.

What do you think ?

Do you agree that the North benefited more by the Compromise of 1850? Why or why not?

★Conductor
A person who helped free slaves by using the Underground Railroad

Network
A system that is linked together in some way

Under the Fugitive Slave Law, the federal government could be called upon to settle fugitive slave cases. People in the North had to return runaway enslaved people to owners. Anyone caught helping enslaved people would be fined. According to the law, only the owner's word was needed to prove an African was enslaved. Clearly, this law challenged any African's right to freedom.

Slave owners thought this law was fair. Northerners, though, chose to ignore the law completely. Abolitionist efforts to help enslaved people to escape were not slowed down.

How Did the Underground Railroad Help Enslaved People?

The Underground Railroad developed to help enslaved people escape slavery. The Underground Railroad was not really a railroad at all. It was a secret escape route to help enslaved people reach free states. Antislavery **conductors** were people who helped to hide enslaved Africans as they moved from station to station. "Stations" were homes of people who hid the enslaved Africans during the day and

MAP STUDY

In what direction are most of the Underground Railroad routes going?

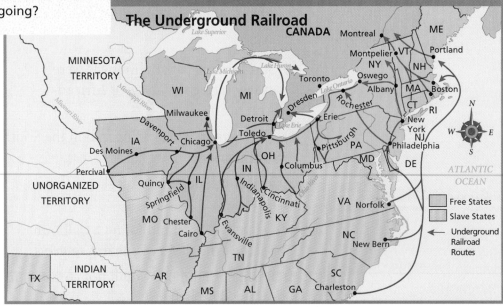

The Underground Railroad

Sojourner Truth (above)

Frederick Douglass (top left)

The Underground Railroad helped many enslaved Africans escape slavery. (top right)

sent them to other homes at night. This secret **network** went from the South to the North and into Canada. Formerly enslaved Africans Frederick Douglass, Sojourner Truth, and Harriet Tubman spoke out against slavery. They helped many people take advantage of the Underground Railroad.

How Did Cotton Control the Nation?

After the invention of the cotton gin, southern plantation owners began to receive large profits. Cotton was sold both in the United States and to other countries. It was an important raw material for the textile industry in the North. Cotton made up more than half of the total exported products of the United States. Cotton was not just another crop; it was the big moneymaker of the country.

Unfortunately, the South had made little progress over the years. The rich plantation owners prevented changes by controlling the state governments. Southerners closed themselves off to the major changes that came to the rest of the country. They got angry when people spoke out against slavery. They felt that their way of life was being threatened.

The majority of southerners did not own enslaved Africans. Most of the people in the South were farmers who did all of their own work. Southerners did not think that slavery was wrong; they considered the practice to be good for both enslaved Africans and plantation owners.

What Did Franklin Pierce Do as President?

Franklin Pierce, a Democrat from New Hampshire, became President in 1852. He took office in 1853. Pierce was not against slavery even though he was from a northern state. He chose Jefferson Davis to be his Secretary of War.

As one of his first projects, Pierce sent James Gadsden, the United States minister to Mexico, to work out the purchase of land in the Southwest in 1853. A strip of land, which now makes up part of New Mexico and Arizona, cost $10 million. With this purchase, called the Gadsden Purchase, the United States was free to build a railroad to southern California. The permanent southwest boundary between the United States and Mexico was set.

WORD BANK

Franklin Pierce

Fugitive Slave Law

Gadsden Purchase

Sojourner Truth

Underground Railroad

SECTION 2 REVIEW On a separate sheet of paper, write the correct word or name from the Word Bank to complete each sentence.

1) The _____ made people in the North return runaway enslaved Africans.

2) The _____ helped free enslaved Africans.

3) _____ was a former enslaved person who spoke out against slavery.

4) _____ became President in 1852.

5) The _____ was the purchase of land that now makes up Arizona and New Mexico.

What do you think ?

Why do you think most southerners who did not own enslaved Africans did not think slavery was wrong?

The population of California was growing well beyond the 100,000 who lived there at the time it became a state. Each month thousands more people were making their way to the West. Travel by covered wagon took two months or more. Sailing around South America was long and dangerous. Something had to be done to make the trip easier and faster.

Many towns and cities throughout the East were connected by railroads. Farmers used the railroad to bring their **produce** to market. Businesses used the railroads to ship their goods. People traveled safely and quickly by railcar. If the country was going to grow, a railroad from coast to coast was necessary.

Produce
Fruits or vegetables

Congress discussed possible routes for the railroad. The railroad could go:

1. from Chicago to the Oregon coast,
2. from Chicago to St. Louis to San Francisco,
3. from New Orleans to San Diego, or
4. from Memphis to Los Angeles.

This cartoon of Stephen Douglas as a gladiator expressed his firm stand on issues.

Congress could not agree on a route. Southerners wanted to build a railroad from New Orleans to San Diego. Northerners were against a southern route. They feared southerners would move west and take their slaves with them.

What Did Stephen Douglas Do?

The northerners, led by Senator Stephen Douglas, wanted to build a railroad from St. Louis or Chicago to California. This route, however, would go through Nebraska. Nebraska was not an organized territory.

★Popular sovereignty
Power of the people to decide something, especially whether to become a free state or a slave state

Tension
Uncomfortable feelings toward another person or group

"The Little Giant," as Douglas was called, introduced a bill to allow Nebraska to become a territory. This action brought up the slave state issue. According to the Missouri Compromise of 1820, Nebraska would organize as a free territory. The boundary line for free states was at 36 degrees 30 minutes north latitude.

Stephen Douglas and others suggested a compromise. Douglas wanted to repeal the 1820 law. He wanted to organize the territories of Kansas and Nebraska. His bill also allowed the voters in the territories to decide whether each would become a free state or a slave state. This was called **popular sovereignty.**

Congress passed the Kansas-Nebraska Act in 1854. Passing this bill caused many conflicts between political parties. **Tension** between the slave states and free states was at an all-time high. The slavery issue was hurting the country.

How Did the Republican Party Form?

A group of Free Soilers, northern Whigs, and Democrats met in 1854 and formed the Republican party. Their main problem with the existing parties was that they did not take a clear stand on slavery. Gaining most support from the North, the new party wished to repeal the Kansas-Nebraska Act and the Fugitive Slave Law.

GEORGE CATLIN: 1796–1872

George Catlin was a painter who dedicated himself to painting pictures of American Indians. He lived among them and learned their languages. Catlin made more than 500 paintings of people from fifty different tribes. His paintings and the books he wrote about his experiences recorded many sides of their daily lives. Today, most of his paintings are in a special wing of the National Gallery of Art in Washington, D.C.

This George Catlin painting shows a Mandan Bull Dance.

Uncle Tom's Cabin Ignites Slavery Issue

Harriet Beecher Stowe's novel *Uncle Tom's Cabin* was like a match being ignited. Stowe organized it as an argument against slavery. She told of the patient enslaved African Uncle Tom, the saintly white child Eva, and the cruel slave driver Simon Legree. Her descriptions of abused slaves showed what happens to people who are treated as objects rather than persons. The book gave a sense of reality to the cruel system of slavery. In the North, it started a great wave of hatred toward slavery. In the South, it outraged people. No novel before or since has had such a deep effect on Americans. It is a controversial book even today.

After the book was published in 1852, imitations appeared. "Uncle Tom" plays, poetry, and songs became popular. The book gave rise to artifacts like cards, figurines, plates, silverware, and needlepoint. Traveling shows called "Tom Troupes" did skits about enslaved Africans' culture. Sometimes characters were shown being reunited in cardboard heavens.

SECTION 3 REVIEW Write the answers to these questions on a separate sheet of paper using complete sentences.

1) Why were railroads needed for travel to the West?

2) Which routes for a railroad were discussed?

3) Which railroad route did the northerners favor?

4) Which railroad route did the southerners favor?

5) Which groups formed the Republican party?

Writing About History

Research how railroads are still used today. In your notebook, write a report explaining how they are used. Include other information you find.

What do you think ?

Which railroad route would you choose if it were up to you? Why?

Daniel Webster's Speech to the Senate

After serving as an outspoken member of Congress during the 1820s, Daniel Webster became the leader of the Whig party. He served as Secretary of State under Presidents Harrison and Polk. Webster believed that the unity of the country was more important than the abolition of slavery. After a return to the Senate in the mid 1840s, he went on to endorse the Compromise of 1850. As a result, he lost the support of many party members who strongly opposed slavery. The following passage is from one of Webster's speeches to the Senate in 1850.

"Secession! Peaceable secession! Sir, your eyes and mine are never destined to see that miracle. The dismemberment of this vast country without convulsion! The breaking up of the fountains of the great deep without ruffling the surface! Who is so foolish—I beg everybody's pardon—as to expect to see any such thing? . . .

Is the great Constitution under which we live here—covering this whole country—is it to be thawed and melted away by secession as the snows on the mountain melt under the influence of a vernal sun—disappear almost unobserved and die off? No, sir! No sir! . . . . I see it as plainly as I see the sun in heaven—I see that disruption must produce such a war as I will not describe, in its twofold characters.

Peaceable secession! Peaceable secession! The concurrent agreement of all the members of this great republic to separate! . . . Where is the line to be drawn? What states are to secede? What is to remain American? What am I to be? An American flag no longer? Where is the flag of the republic to remain? Where is the eagle still to tower? Or is he to cower, and shrink, and fall to the ground?"

Source Reading Wrap-Up

1) To what does Webster compare the Constitution?

2) Why do you think Webster repeated the phrase "peaceable secession" so often?

3) Why did Webster think that a war over secession was inevitable?

4) Webster named two main issues on which Congress was unlikely to agree regarding secession. What was one of them?

5) Do you agree with Webster's method of speaking? Explain why or why not.

CHAPTER SUMMARY

★ The abolitionist movement continued to grow.

★ Southerners believed that the end of slavery would mean the end of their way of life. The South's economy depended on the free labor of enslaved Africans.

★ As new states were added to the United States, Congress had to decide whether they would be free states or slave states. Many northerners did not want slavery to spread and opposed adding new slave states. Southerners believed that there should be an equal number of slave and free states.

★ The Compromise of 1850 was the most important act of Congress in this period. The compromise allowed California to enter the Union as a free state. It also set out rules for the addition of future free and slave states, abolished slave trade in the District of Columbia, and established the Fugitive Slave Law.

★ The Fugitive Slave Law stated that northerners had to return runaway slaves to their southern owners. The law challenged the right to freedom of almost all enslaved Africans and freemen.

★ The Underground Railroad was a secret escape route for enslaved Africans who were seeking freedom. People helped the runaways by hiding them from authorities. The routes ran northward to Canada.

★ Many former enslaved Africans were active in the abolitionist movement and with the Underground Railroad. Among the most famous were Sojourner Truth, Frederick Douglass, and Harriet Tubman.

★ Manufacturing textiles involved both the North and the South. Cotton from the South was the raw material for the mills of the North. Cotton and fabrics were the largest export of the United States.

★ In 1853, the Gadsden Purchase added the final piece of land to the United States. America purchased the strip of land, which is now in New Mexico and Arizona, for $10 million.

★ The country needed to establish a railroad route from the east coast to the west coast. Choosing a route for the railroad caused new problems between free and slave states.

★ The Kansas-Nebraska Act allowed voters in the territories to decide if they would be admitted to the United States as a free state or a slave state.

Comprehension: Identifying Facts

On a separate sheet of paper, write the words from the Word Bank to complete each sentence.

WORD BANK		
abolitionists	free states	slave states
Compromise of 1850	Fugitive Slave Law	textiles
cotton	Gadsden Purchase	Underground Railroad
the District of Columbia	Harriet Tubman	
	Kansas-Nebraska Act	William Lloyd Garrison

1) The _____ said that anyone helping a runaway enslaved African would be fined.

2) Many senior statesmen, including Henry Clay and John C. Calhoun, worked on the _____.

3) _____ published an abolitionist newspaper.

4) The _____ was used to help enslaved Africans escape to freedom.

5) The most important export from the South was _____.

6) _____ was a famous "conductor" on the Underground Railroad.

7) People who actively worked to end slavery were called _____.

8) California was admitted to the Union as one of the _____.

9) The _____ were concerned that abolitionists wanted to ruin their way of life.

10) Crops from the South provided the raw materials to make _____ in the North.

11) Under the Compromise of 1850, _____ would not have slavery.

12) The _____, proposed by Stephen Douglas, was very unpopular with slave states.

13) A piece of land in the Southwest became U.S. territory with the _____.

Comprehension: Understanding Main Ideas

On a separate sheet of paper, write the answer to each question using complete sentences.

1) Why was cotton so important for both the South and the North?

2) What impact did the railroad have on the Kansas-Nebraska Act?

3) Which part of the Compromise of 1850 affected California the most?

4) Why did southerners feel that abolitionists were wrong?

5) What was the purpose of the Fugitive Slave Law?

Critical Thinking: Write Your Opinion

1) Do you think the Compromise of 1850 was fair to both free and slave states? Explain the reasons for your answer.

2) Both sides felt very strongly about the slavery issue and had a difficult time compromising. Think of an issue today that divides how people think. Compare this issue to the abolitionist movement. How are they alike? How are they different?

Test Taking Tip If you have to choose the correct ending to a sentence, combine the first part of the sentence with each ending. Then choose the one that best completes the statement.

1854–1861

The issue of slavery was still not solved. It continued to cause problems. People began to use violence to try settle the problem. The nation was entering a very difficult period of time. Eventually, a presidential election caused the country to separate. In this chapter, you will learn the reasons why several states left the Union.

Goals for Learning

▶ To explain why Kansas's statehood was an issue for proslavery and antislavery forces

▶ To identify the importance of the Dred Scott Case

▶ To explain the importance of the Lincoln-Douglas debates

▶ To describe John Brown's raid on Harper's Ferry

▶ To explain the importance of the election of 1860

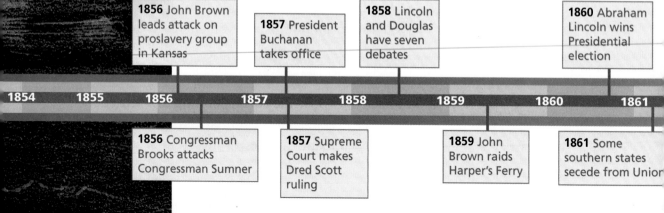

1856 John Brown leads attack on proslavery group in Kansas

1857 President Buchanan takes office

1858 Lincoln and Douglas have seven debates

1860 Abraham Lincoln wins Presidential election

| 1854 | 1855 | 1856 | 1857 | 1858 | 1859 | 1860 | 1861 |

1856 Congressman Brooks attacks Congressman Sumner

1857 Supreme Court makes Dred Scott ruling

1859 John Brown raids Harper's Ferry

1861 Some southern states secede from Union

Vow
To promise to do something

Nebraska's long, cold winters did not appeal to proslavery plantation owners. The climate was not good for growing cotton. Kansas, on the other hand, was farther south and was the target of settlers who favored slavery.

Abraham Lincoln: A Little-Known Attorney

In Peoria, Illinois, former U.S. Representative Abraham Lincoln gave a speech in response to the Kansas-Nebraska Act. He spoke out against slavery and the act itself. He **vowed** to return to politics to see what could be done to end slavery once and for all.

What Caused Fighting in Kansas?

Proslavery and antislavery supporters wanted to claim land in Kansas before it was admitted to the Union. People from New England moved to Kansas with the help of the New England Emigrant Aid Society. They brought with them boxes of guns disguised as boxes of Bibles. Southerners came from Alabama, Georgia, and North Carolina. They were also prepared to fight. Kansas became a battleground for the two groups. The territory became known as "Bleeding Kansas."

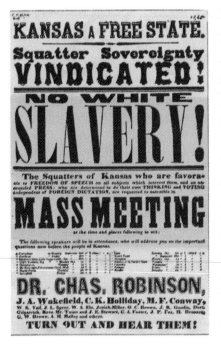

This poster announced an antislavery meeting in Kansas.

The time came to organize a territorial government in Kansas. An election was to be held; the settlers would vote for legislators. Just before the election, Missouri's senator, David R. Atchison, became the leader of a group of people whose job was to go into Kansas and vote for proslavery candidates.

Proslavery candidates won the election. They quickly formed a government and wrote a constitution. Antislavery people were angry with the outcome. They formed their own government. Kansas now had two governments, each claiming to be the legal government.

HARRIET TUBMAN: c. 1820–1913

Harriet Tubman was an African American and a bold abolitionist. Born into slavery in Maryland around 1821, she worked as a field hand. She never learned to read or write. In 1849, she escaped to Philadelphia. From there, she made many dangerous rescue missions into the South. She eventually led more than 300 other slaves to freedom through the Underground Railroad. During the Civil War, Tubman served the Union Army in South Carolina as a nurse, a scout, and a spy. Sarah Bradford wrote the story of Tubman's life and work in her book *Scenes in the Life of Harriet Tubman.*

A group of proslavery men raided Lawrence, Kansas. Antislavery forces populated Lawrence. The invaders burned buildings and one man was killed. In response to this action, abolitionist John Brown and a small band of men attacked a proslavery group at Pottawatamie Creek in 1856, killing five proslavery settlers. These and a number of other attacks caused 200 deaths and over $2 million in property damage by the end of that same year. It was unlikely that the slavery issue would be settled peacefully.

SECTION 1 REVIEW Write the answers to these questions on a separate sheet of paper using complete sentences.

1) Why was Nebraska not good for plantations?

2) Why did proslavery and antislavery supporters want to claim land in Kansas?

3) What did antislavery people do when proslavery people formed a government in Kansas?

4) What act of violence did the proslavery people commit?

5) What act of violence did the antislavery people commit?

What do you think ❓

Why do you think control over the state of Kansas was so important?

An unusual event took place in May of 1856. Senator Charles Sumner of Massachusetts made a speech against slavery. In his speech, he insulted Senator Andrew Butler of South Carolina. Sumner also made several **belittling** remarks about the state of South Carolina. His name-calling brought applause from the northern senators.

Belittling
Insulting

SOUTHERN CHIVALRY — ARGUMENT *versus* CLUB'S.

Congressman Preston Brooks struck Congressman Charles Sumner several times with a cane in 1856.

Sumner's remarks upset Senator Butler's nephew, Preston Brooks. Brooks was a member of the House of Representatives. A few days later, Brooks walked up to Sumner's desk and struck the senator several times with a cane. Sumner was seriously hurt by the hard blows to his head. It took him almost three years to return to his place in the Senate. Even intelligent leaders were turning to violence and were unable to use common sense when dealing with the slavery problem.

Who Won the Election of 1856?

Slavery was the major issue of the election of 1856. There was still trouble in Kansas, and the country seemed to be slowly heading toward war.

Technology
History in Your Life

Otis and the Elevator

In 1852, Elisha G. Otis invented a safety device to prevent the fall of an elevator car if its support cable broke. The following year, the daring Otis demonstrated his new device. He stood in an elevator car while its cable was chopped with an ax. Before this, elevators had been fairly unfamiliar devices. They were used only in factories to lift heavy objects one floor at a time. Otis had demonstrated that elevators could be made safe enough to lift people. Thus, he began what became a large industry. He patented the first passenger elevator in 1857 and a steam-powered elevator in 1861. His new elevators paved the way for a new era in architecture. The Otis safety elevator made possible the modern skyscrapers that now define skylines of cities worldwide. The Otis Elevator Company is still a large elevator manufacturer.

The Democrats nominated James "Old Buck" Buchanan of Pennsylvania. Buchanan had not been involved in the Kansas dispute. The Democrats considered Old Buck to be a safe choice.

The Republicans chose John C. Fremont of California. Fremont had been an army leader during the Mexican War. He also was a well-known explorer.

The number of immigrants in the United States had increased between the years 1820 and 1850, as more people looked to America as a land of new hope. Many people feared that foreigners would take over the country. They formed the American party to stop the wave of new immigrants. Millard Fillmore was their candidate.

James Buchanan won the election. He received 174 electoral votes to Fremont's 114. Only eight electoral votes went to Fillmore. Even though the Republicans lost the election, they showed strength. The Republicans were **optimistic** about the 1860 election. President Buchanan took office in 1857.

How Did the Dred Scott Case Affect Slavery?

President Buchanan hoped the slavery issue would finally be **resolved.** However, two days after Buchanan took office, the Supreme Court made a **ruling** in 1857 that heated the issue. A ruling is a decision of a court case. This ruling was about the freedom of an enslaved African named Dred Scott. It would be of great importance in the election of 1860.

Dred Scott had been enslaved in Missouri. His master, Dr. John Emerson, took him to live in the free state of Illinois. Later, they moved to Wisconsin, which was a free territory. Then they returned to Missouri where Emerson died five years later. Scott **sued** for his freedom on grounds that he had lived in a free territory. To sue is to bring legal action against a person to settle a difference. Scott claimed he was **entitled** to be a free man. The case reached

Dred Scott

Writing About History

You are a Supreme Court justice ruling on the Dred Scott case. In your notebook, explain your decision.

the Supreme Court. Chief Justice Roger Taney of Maryland gave the Supreme Court's decision.

According to Taney, a majority of the justices had ruled that Scott had no right to sue for his freedom—he was enslaved and not a citizen. Scott's freedom was denied because he was enslaved now in a slave state. The Supreme Court declared that the Missouri Compromise violated the Constitution and therefore was not legal. Taney said that slaves were property and could be taken anywhere. The court's decision made it possible to extend slavery into all territories. The decision shocked the country. Northerners feared that it opened the door to the spread of slavery throughout the entire nation.

WORD BANK

Charles Sumner

Dred Scott

James Buchanan

Preston Brooks

Roger Taney

SECTION 2 REVIEW On a separate sheet of paper write the names from the Word Bank to complete each sentence.

1) A former slave from Missouri named _____ was the subject of a Supreme Court case in 1857.

2) _____ struck Charles Sumner several times with a cane.

3) The Supreme Court justice who gave the Dred Scott ruling was _____.

4) _____ insulted Senator Andrew Butler of South Carolina.

5) The winner of the election of 1856 was _____.

What do you think ?

How do you think it was possible for two members of Congress to be involved in an act of violence as Preston Brooks and Charles Sumner were?

Forbid
To use power to prevent something from occurring

Opponent
A person who takes an opposite position in an event such as a debate or contest

In 1858, Abraham Lincoln ran for the U.S. Senate. His **opponent** was Stephen Douglas. Douglas was thought to be unbeatable, but Lincoln did not think so. Although Lincoln had served two years as a U.S. Representative, he was not well known. He challenged Douglas to a series of seven debates.

Douglas welcomed the opportunity to debate Lincoln. Douglas was an excellent speaker. Lincoln was not a good speaker. The two men were different in another way. Douglas was very short—barely over five feet tall. Lincoln was six feet, four inches tall.

During the debates, Lincoln reminded Douglas that the policy of popular sovereignty permitted a territory to **forbid** slavery. The Dred Scott decision, however, stated that a territory could not ban slavery. Which, Lincoln asked, did Douglas prefer? Douglas said that the people in a given state should be able to forbid slavery in spite of the Dred Scott decision. Douglas's response made many southerners angry.

Lincoln had a way of saying things that made people listen. During the seven debates, Lincoln did very well against Douglas. Lincoln lost the Senate election to Douglas, but his popularity increased. People began to call him "Honest Abe." Douglas realized that debating Lincoln had been a mistake.

Abe Lincoln's popularity increased during the Lincoln-Douglas debates of 1858.

Politicians today reach voters through debates and ads on television and radio and in newspapers. In the 1850s, politicians did not have radio or television. Congressional candidates traveled throughout their state. They gave what became known as stump speeches, because they often stood on tree stumps to address the people. Universities or towns hosted the seven Lincoln-Douglas debates. Each debate included hour-long speeches by both men. Ninety-minute replies followed the speeches. Each candidate ended with a thirty-minute summary. Today the League of Women Voters hosts presidential debates. Now debates usually last an hour and are on most networks.

What Happened at Harper's Ferry?

John Brown took action again as disputes over slavery continued. Brown believed that enslaved Africans must be freed, even if violence was necessary. He had a plan to seize the U.S. **arsenal** at Harper's Ferry, Virginia (now in West Virginia), and take the guns and **ammunition.** An arsenal is a place used to make or store military weapons. He hoped to arm the enslaved and lead them in a revolt against their masters.

Brown captured the arsenal in 1859. Colonel Robert E. Lee was sent with marines to stop Brown. The marines captured Brown. He was tried for **treason** and found guilty. Treason is a crime involving an attempt to overthrow the government.

He was hanged at Charlestown, Virginia (now in West Virginia), in December of 1859. Before his death, he wrote, "I, John Brown, am now quite certain that the crimes of this guilty land will never be purged away but with blood. I had, as I now think, mainly flattered myself that without very much bloodshed it might be done."

The raid at Harper's Ferry increased the tension between the North and the South. Northerners were shocked by the violence. Southerners believed there would be more bloodshed by abolitionists.

★Treason
A crime involving an attempt to overthrow the government

Ammunition
Bullets, gunpowder, and other things used with guns or other weapons

★Arsenal
A place used to make or store military weapons

John Brown is shown here kissing a child before being hanged.

SECTION 3 REVIEW On a separate sheet of paper, write *True* if the statement is true or *False* if the statement is not true.

1) Douglas would not debate Lincoln.

2) Lincoln was not a good speaker.

3) Lincoln did well in the debates.

4) John Brown was unable to capture an arsenal at Harper's Ferry.

5) Brown was hanged for his actions at Harper's Ferry.

What do you think ?

Why do you think people liked Abe Lincoln?

The election of 1860 offered four new presidential candidates. Their campaigns reflected the bitter divisions of the country.

Why Did the Democratic Party Split?

The Democratic party could not agree on issues and on a presidential candidate. They split into two groups. The northern delegates chose Stephen Douglas as their candidate. He supported popular sovereignty. The southern delegates selected John C. Breckinridge of Kentucky, a supporter of slavery.

What Issues Did the Republicans Support?

★Platform
A statement of ideas, policies, and beliefs of a political party in an election

The Republican party nominated Abraham Lincoln as the presidential candidate. The Republican **platform**, which is a statement of ideas, policies, and beliefs of a political party in an election, stated:

1. Slavery would not be allowed in new territories.
2. Slave states could make decisions about slavery within their own borders.
3. Free land would be available for farming in the territories.
4. Higher tariffs would be imposed.
5. No state would be permitted to leave the Union.

Popular Vote, Election of 1860

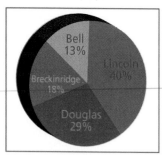

Bell 13%
Lincoln 40%
Breckinridge 18%
Douglas 29%

Who received the most votes? Who received the least?

What New Political Party Was Formed?

Another group, called the Constitutional Union party, also nominated a candidate for President. This new party was made up of former Whig and American party members. They believed that the nation would be kept at peace if everyone cooperated. John Bell of Tennessee was chosen as their candidate.

What Were the Election Results?

Lincoln won the election by nearly 500,000 votes. Before the election, some southern states had decided

> ★Secede
> *To leave a group or organization*

to leave the Union if Lincoln won. By February 1, 1861, South Carolina, Mississippi, Florida, Alabama, Georgia, Texas, and Louisiana had voted to **secede,** or leave the Union.

Union (free) states
Union (slave) states
Slave states seceding Dec. 1860–Feb. 1861
Slave states seceding April–May 1861
West Virginia—separated from Virginia 1861, admitted to Union 1863

The Secession of the Southern States

MAP STUDY Which states left the Union? How many free states were there?

SECTION 4 REVIEW On a separate sheet of paper, write *True* if the statement is true or *False* if the statement is not true.

1) The Democratic party split into two groups.

2) The Republican party was against slavery.

3) The Republican party believed the nation would have peace if everyone cooperated.

4) The Republican party nominated Stephen Douglas as their presidential candidate.

5) The Democratic party nominated John Bell as their presidential candidate.

> **What do you think** ❓
>
> Why do you think the Republican party did not want any state to leave the Union?

The Dred Scott Decision

In 1857, Chief Justice of the Supreme Court Roger Taney heard the case of Scott versus Stanford. Scott was enslaved to a Missouri doctor who had moved to Illinois and Wisconsin. In both of those states, slavery was outlawed. Following their return to Missouri, his owner died. Scott sued the doctor's widow for his freedom. Scott was successful in a Missouri circuit court. However, he had been claimed as the property of a New Yorker. Thus, the case ended up before the Supreme Court. He was denied his freedom by a seven to two vote. This is part of the statement by Chief Justice Taney.

"Now . . . the right of property in a slave is distinctly and expressly affirmed in the Constitution. The right to traffic in it, like an ordinary article of merchandise and property, was guaranteed to the citizens of the United States, in every State that might desire it, for twenty years. And the Government in express terms is pledged to protect it in all future time, if the slave escapes from his owner. . . . And no word can be found in the Constitution which gives Congress a greater power over slave property, or which entitles property of that kind to less protection than property of any other description. The only power conferred is the power coupled with the duty of guarding and protecting the owner in his rights.

Upon these considerations, it is the opinion of this court that the Act of Congress which prohibited a citizen from holding and owning property of this kind in the territory of the United States north of the line therein mentioned, is not warranted by the Constitution, and is therefore void; and that neither Scott himself, nor any of his family, were made free by being carried into this territory; even if they had been carried there by the owner, with the intention of becoming a permanent resident. . . ."

Source Reading Wrap-Up

1) What rights did Chief Justice Taney claim he was defending?

2) The Missouri Compromise forbade slavery north of a certain line. In what way does this statement refer to it?

3) What responsibility did the federal government have to the slaves?

4) What did Chief Justice Taney say about Scott's freedom?

5) How fair do you think Chief Justice Taney's decision is?

★ As Kansas moved toward statehood, it was unclear if it would be a slave state or a free state. The residents of the territory were to vote one way or the other.

★ People from both sides of the slavery issue moved to Kansas to help swing the vote their way. The proslavery people won the election and violence broke out.

★ By the election of 1856, the country was becoming more separated by the issue of slavery.

★ James Buchanan of Pennsylvania won the election for President. He had not been involved in the Kansas dispute.

★ The Supreme Court made an important ruling concerning slavery in the Dred Scott Case. Dred Scott was an enslaved African who filed a suit that said he should be free because he had lived in a free state. The court said that enslaved people were property and could be taken anywhere. Many people in the North were upset by the decision. They thought it meant slavery could expand into all states.

★ Abraham Lincoln ran for the U.S. Senate in 1858. He ran against the popular Stephen Douglas.

★ Lincoln and Douglas held a series of debates in which Lincoln showed his great wisdom and leadership style. Although he lost the election for Senate, Lincoln's popularity grew.

★ A radical abolitionist, John Brown, attacked an army arsenal at Harper's Ferry, Virginia. Brown wanted to arm enslaved Africans and lead them in a revolt.

★ John Brown was captured and hanged for treason. His actions and death increased the tensions between the North and the South.

★ The Democratic party split into two separate parties. The issue that divided them was slavery.

★ Lincoln ran for President in 1860 as the Republican candidate. The Republican platform stressed opposition to slavery and said that no state could leave the Union.

★ Soon after Lincoln won the election, several southern states voted to leave the Union and form a new country.

Comprehension: Identifying Facts

On a separate sheet of paper, write the words from the Word Bank to complete each sentence.

WORD BANK	
Abraham Lincoln	"Honest Abe"
arsenal	James Buchanan
Bibles	John Brown
"Bleeding Kansas"	property
David R. Atchison	Robert E. Lee
decision	Stephen Douglas
Dred Scott	Union

1) After his debates, Lincoln became known as _____.

2) _____ was an abolitionist who believed only violence could end slavery.

3) The winner of the 1856 election was _____.

4) _____ was an enslaved African who sued for his freedom because he had lived in free states.

5) Because of the violence there, the territory south of Nebraska became known as _____.

6) The Supreme Court's _____ in the Dred Scott Case angered many northerners.

7) The Republican candidate for President in 1860 was

_____.

8) Lincoln debated with _____ in the 1856 Senate race.

9) The Supreme Court ruled in the Dred Scott Case that enslaved people were _____ and could be taken anywhere and still remain enslaved.

10) _____ led the marines who captured John Brown during his raid on Harper's Ferry.

11) John Brown captured the army's _____ to steal weapons for a slave revolt.

12) Abolitionists brought guns into Kansas in boxes that said they were boxes of _____.

13) After Lincoln was elected President, several states voted to leave the _____.

14) _____ went to Kansas to help the proslavery group with the election.

Comprehension: Understanding Main Ideas

On a separate sheet of paper, write the answer to each question using complete sentences.

1) Why was the election in Kansas so important?

2) How did Lincoln make himself look so good in the debates with Douglas?

3) Why did John Brown attack people at Pottawatamie Creek in Kansas?

4) What was a major issue in the election of 1860?

Critical Thinking: Write Your Opinion

1) Why do you think the Supreme Court decided against Dred Scott?

2) How important are the debates between candidates before presidential elections?

Test Taking Tip   Read the test directions twice. Sometimes they will give you a hint. For example, the directions may remind you to look for the best answer.

1861–1865

Aﬅer several states left the Union, it was clear that the nation was in trouble. Very little could be done to prevent a war. Though President Lincoln tried to avoid war when he took office, the Civil War began in 1861. In this chapter, you will learn how the war started, which battles were fought, and how it came to an end.

Goals for Learning

▶ To explain the events leading to the Civil War

▶ To explain the Emancipation Proclamation

▶ To describe the major events of the Civil War

▶ To identify important people and their role in the Civil War

▶ To describe the effect of the Civil War on the United States

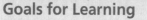
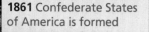

1861 Confederate States of America is formed

1862 Confederates win the Seven Days Battle

1861 Confederates attack Fort Sumter

1863 Lincoln issues the Emancipation Proclamation

1864 Lincoln is re-elected President

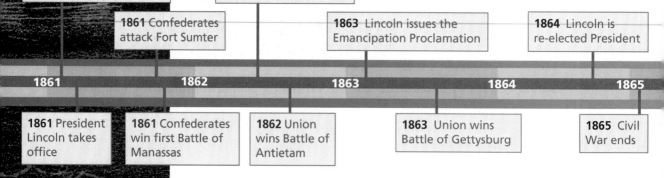

| 1861 | 1862 | 1863 | 1864 | 1865 |

1861 President Lincoln takes office

1861 Confederates win first Battle of Manassas

1862 Union wins Battle of Antietam

1863 Union wins Battle of Gettysburg

1865 Civil War ends

During Buchanan's last four months as President, seven states left the Union. Buchanan did nothing to stop them. Although he was a northerner, he agreed with the southern states. He maintained that the North had caused the problems that led to secession. He proposed that the North should return all runaway enslaved people, while all the new territories should be opened to slavery. Buchanan thought the southern states would then rejoin the Union.

Senator John Crittenden of Kentucky offered a compromise. He suggested that the Constitution be changed to allow slavery in all new territories. He also suggested that any state north of 36 degrees 30 minutes north latitude could vote to enslave people or not. Crittenden thought the southern states would be pleased with this plan and return to the Union. He hoped the slavery issue would finally be settled.

Jefferson Davis

Members of the Senate discussed the compromise, but they reached no agreement. Abraham Lincoln, leader of the Republican party, felt that slavery must be stopped forever. Senator Crittenden's plan for compromise was turned down.

What New Government Did the Southern States Form?

In February of 1861, the southern states met in Montgomery, Alabama, and formed the government of the Confederate States of America. They drew up a constitution that said that each state would be independent, that slavery would be protected, and that Confederate states would pay no federal tariffs. Jefferson Davis was chosen to serve as President of the Confederacy. Montgomery was its first capital.

What Did the Seceded States Do?

Near the end of Buchanan's presidency, the seceded states took over most of the federal properties inside their borders. These included forts and arsenals filled with large supplies of weapons. The South claimed many post offices and customhouses as well as the large supply of coins at the New Orleans Mint.

Fort Sumter in South Carolina was commanded by Major Robert Anderson. The newly formed southern government expected the North to turn the fort over to the South. President Buchanan did not agree with South Carolina's **request.** Instead, he sent a ship of supplies and food to troops at the fort. Confederates fired upon the vessel, forcing it to turn back. Afterward, Buchanan did nothing more to help the troops in Fort Sumter nor in any other federal properties in the South.

Request
The act of asking for something

What Happened When President Lincoln Took Office?

On March 4, 1861, Lincoln became President. He faced a very serious situation. Under the Constitution, no state had the right to leave the Union and form a separate government. Lincoln's first challenge as President was to bring the South back into the Union peacefully.

When Lincoln was sworn in as President, his inaugural address was about peace. He stressed that he did not intend to stop slavery in states where it was already in use. However, he wanted to see all federal properties in the South returned to Union control and all tariffs paid.

Abraham Lincoln

LUCY STONE: 1818–1893

Lucy Stone became an unyielding pioneer in women's rights and was active in abolishing slavery. She grew resistant to the male-controlled society she knew as a youth. With rare expressiveness, she lectured widely on women's rights. She was one of the first Massachusetts women to earn a college degree. Stone may have been the country's first married woman to retain her family name. She helped to organize the first national convention on women's rights. Stone and her husband established the American Woman Suffrage Association in 1869. In 1870, she founded *Woman's Journal*, which promoted women's right to vote.

★**Civil war**
A war between groups within the same country

Lincoln wanted the Union to be preserved. He appealed to the southern states to return to the Union without bloodshed. Lincoln made it clear, though, that any warlike action that the South took would lead to a **civil war.** A civil war is a war between groups within the same country.

SECTION 1 REVIEW On a separate sheet of paper write the name from the Word Bank to complete each sentence.

WORD BANK

Abraham Lincoln

Jefferson Davis

John Crittenden

President Buchanan

Robert Anderson

1) _____ thought the southern states would rejoin the Union if the North returned all runaway enslaved people.

2) Fort Sumter was commanded by _____.

3) A compromise that would have allowed slavery in new territories was proposed by _____.

4) The Confederacy chose _____ as its President.

5) The first challenge facing _____ was to get the Union back together.

What do you think **?**

Do you think Lincoln's policy toward the Confederacy was good? Why or why not?

President Lincoln received a message from Fort Sumter in March of 1861. Food and supplies were running out. More men were needed, too. Major Anderson would have to surrender the fort unless immediate action was taken. President Lincoln would not let Fort Sumter surrender to South Carolina.

In early April, President Lincoln sent a message to the governor of South Carolina. He told him that a ship carrying food was being sent to the fort. Jefferson Davis told General Beauregard, the Confederate commander in South Carolina, to order Major Anderson to surrender the fort. Major Anderson refused to surrender. On April 12, 1861, Confederates attacked Fort Sumter. Major Anderson and his men fought for nearly two days before they were forced to surrender.

Confederates attacked Fort Sumter in 1861. This was the first battle of the Civil War.

The news of the attack on Fort Sumter spread quickly. Thousands joined the Union army when Lincoln called for volunteers. Four more states, Virginia, North Carolina, Arkansas, and Tennessee, joined the Confederacy. Eleven states had left the Union.

Richmond, Virginia, became the new Confederate capital. Virginia organized a large, well-trained army led by good generals. Virginia would serve as a solid line of **defense** for the rest of the Confederacy. The states farthest north in the Confederacy were much stronger and better prepared for war than those in the deep South. The Confederate attack on Fort Sumter was the beginning of a bloody civil war.

Defense
Protection against attack

What Advantages Did Each Side Have?

With twenty-three states, the Union had a larger population than the Confederacy. Only eleven states were in the Confederacy. The South had only twenty-nine percent of the population of the North and the South combined. The North had most of the country's factories and industrial labor force. In addition, the North had more money to pay for a war.

The Confederates were united against those who wanted to destroy their way of life. Southerners were fighting to defend their land and their rights. The Confederacy had some excellent military leaders, including General Robert E. Lee. The southern men were more familiar than the northerners with firearms, the outdoors, and horses. Also, the fighting broke out on southern soil. In 1861, as the war began, the South had a definite military advantage.

General Robert E. Lee

What Was the North's Plan?

The war was expected to last only a few months. General Winfield Scott, "Old Fuss and Feathers" of the Mexican War, was the commander of the Union army. Scott was still thought to be an excellent leader. He called his plan for winning the war the "Anaconda Plan." An anaconda is a large snake that crushes its prey to death. Scott planned to crush the enemy. His plan called for:

1. a blockade of the South to stop all imports and exports,
2. capturing Richmond, Virginia, the new capital of the Confederacy, and
3. stopping all shipping on the Mississippi River.

Writing About History

Write a short story or poem about the Civil War. Describe a battle, how a person not fighting in the war is affected, how an enslaved person would view the war, or a similar topic. Write the poem or story in your notebook.

If the plan was successful, the South would be crushed and forced to surrender. Many looked upon the plan as too slow and not forceful enough.

President Lincoln ordered a blockade of all the southern states that had seceded. He cut off the seaports of the South. The Confederates were unable to ship cotton from their harbors. They needed to trade cotton for guns and ammunition from Europe. The blockade decreased the amount of supplies coming into the South.

The blockade was an important part of the Union's war plan. Some people said that with trade cut off, the South would choke to death. The South had very little industry and could not produce the materials needed to fight a war.

What Was the South's Plan?

The southerners took a different approach. They planned to let the North come to them. In addition, the South counted on the North losing interest in the war. Southerners also thought that at some point Europe would break the Union blockade to get the cotton that it needed.

SECTION 2 REVIEW Write the answers to these questions on a separate sheet of paper using complete sentences.

1) What did the attack on Fort Sumter cause?

2) What happened in Virginia after the attack on Fort Sumter?

3) What were two advantages the North had during the Civil War?

4) What were two advantages the South had during the Civil War?

5) Why did the North form a blockade of the South?

What do you think ?

Who do you think was more prepared for the Civil War— the North or the South? Why?

The new recruits for the Union army were in Washington, D.C., being trained. Scott ordered General Irvin McDowell to lead 35,000 of these inexperienced soldiers. He led them twenty-five miles to Manassas Junction near a stream called Bull Run in northern Virginia. Despite their inexperience in battle, northerners were certain that their soldiers would defeat the southern "rebels," as they were called. They were so certain that many people traveled down from Washington to watch the battle.

Camped on the banks of Bull Run, the Confederates were ready for the attack. On July 21, 1861, the battle began. At first, the Union army seemed to be winning. But then Confederate troops under General Thomas "Stonewall" Jackson arrived. The Union army was defeated. They fled back to Washington in panic.

The defeat shocked the North. They realized that the war would be a long one. Northerners were eager for a victory. They urged another attack. Northern newspapers had headlines that read, "Forward to Richmond!"

Stonewall Jackson

When the Union seemed to be winning the first Battle of Manassas, a Confederate general, trying to get his men to fight on, pointed to General Thomas J. Jackson. "Look at Jackson's brigade. It stands like a stone wall. Rally behind the Virginians!" This is how Jackson came to be known as "Stonewall."

General "Stonewall" Jackson

Who Became the New Union Leader?

In November of 1861, General Winfield Scott retired. He was seventy-five years old. It was time for a younger general to take charge. President Lincoln chose General George B. McClellan as chief of the Union armies. McClellan was thirty-five years of age and a **veteran** of the Mexican War. A veteran is an experienced or former member of the armed forces. He graduated second in his class at West Point.

McClellan was good at organizing an army and training new soldiers for battle. He was a very cautious leader. Before going into another battle, McClellan drilled his men over and over. Finally, in the spring of 1862, McClellan was ready to face the Confederate troops in Richmond.

What Happened in the Western Campaign?

The Confederate forts in western Tennessee were important in the Union plan to defeat the South. In February of 1862, Union General Ulysses S. Grant and the navy's **gunboats,** or armed ships used for battle, captured Fort Henry. This was the Confederate stronghold on the Tennessee River. Grant continued up the Cumberland River to capture Fort Donelson near Nashville. Under the direction of Admiral David G. Farragut, the Union also gained control of most of the Mississippi Valley. However, complete control was needed in order to stop the Confederacy from using the river.

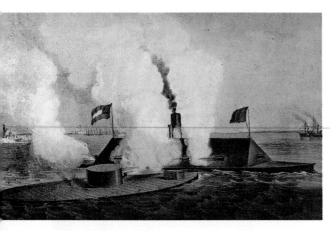

The *Monitor* and the *Merrimac* battled at Hampton Roads channel in Virginia.

What Happened Between the *Monitor* and the *Merrimac?*

On March 8, 1862, the Confederates raised a sunken Union ship, the *U.S.S. Merrimac,* and renamed it *Virginia.* The Confederates then covered the vessel with iron plates so it could not be damaged by cannonballs. This kind of ship was called an **ironclad.** The North also had an ironclad ship, called the *Monitor.*

Mathew Brady, Civil War Photographer

Many Civil War photographs bear the name of Mathew B. Brady. When we see so many, we assume he was everywhere during the war. Actually, he took few, if any, of the estimated 3,500 pictures that bear his name.

Brady had photography studios in New York and Washington, D.C. He liked to take pictures of famous people. When the war began, Brady decided to take pictures of the troops in the battlefields. Because his eyesight was failing, he hired a large group of assistants to take the pictures. He directed his photographers from Washington but took credit himself for all the pictures. Many of his photographers became angry and quit.

As a businessman, Brady did not do well either. He invested $100,000 in the Civil War project. He figured the government would pay top dollar for his photographs. But the government was not interested. Brady went broke. A few years later he died—alcoholic, alone, and forgotten in a hospital charity ward.

After he died, some of the photographs were placed in the National Archives. In this way his name lives on in history.

The two ships had a battle in March of 1862. The Confederates wanted to break the northern blockade. Neither ship won the battle. The Confederates, however, did use the *Merrimac* to prevent McClellan's army from approaching Richmond on the James River. The Confederates later destroyed the *Merrimac* to keep it from falling into the hands of the North. The *Monitor* sank off the coast of North Carolina. The *Merrimac* and the *Monitor* were the first ironclad ships to be used in battle.

Who Won the Seven Days Battles?

McClellan led his troops toward Virginia. Confederate Generals Robert E. Lee and Stonewall Jackson were ready for the attack on Richmond. They let McClellan get within a few miles of Richmond before attacking. There was heavy fighting at many different locations for seven days. For this reason, the battle was called the Seven Days Battles. From time to time, each side seemed to be winning. However, knowing his army was **outnumbered**, McClellan retreated after the seven days.

Outnumber
To have more people than an opponent in a battle

Who Won Battles at Manassas, Antietam, and Fredericksburg?

In late August of 1862, a second battle was fought at Manassas (Bull Run). The Confederate army again defeated the Union soldiers.

General Lee changed his plan from defense to offense. He prepared to attack northern states. Confederate soldiers marched into Maryland. On September 17, 1862, General McClellan and his Union army of the Potomac blocked Lee at Sharpsburg, Maryland, on Antietam Creek. The Battle of Antietam turned out to be one of the bloodiest battles of the war. At the end of the fighting, Lee was forced to retreat. McClellan did not follow Lee into Virginia. For this reason Lincoln removed McClellan as a Union leader, replacing him with General Ambrose Burnside.

Fallen soldiers were a common sight on September 17, 1862. Over 4,800 soldiers died that day during the Battle of Antietam.

General Burnside took the Union army to Fredericksburg, Virginia. Positioned on a line of hills, the Confederates defended the city. The Union army made a strong attempt to charge the hills, but their efforts failed. More than 12,000 Union soldiers were killed. General Burnside resigned. General Joseph Hooker replaced him.

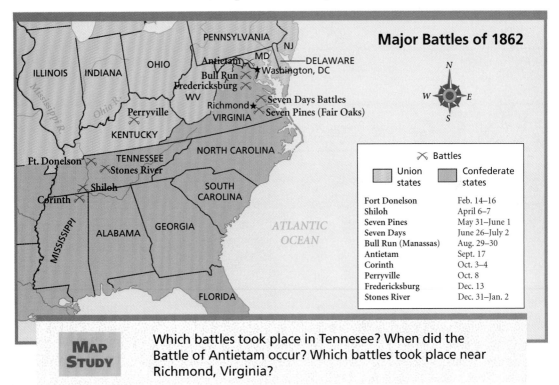

Major Battles of 1862

Battles	
Fort Donelson	Feb. 14–16
Shiloh	April 6–7
Seven Pines	May 31–June 1
Seven Days	June 26–July 2
Bull Run (Manassas)	Aug. 29–30
Antietam	Sept. 17
Corinth	Oct. 3–4
Perryville	Oct. 8
Fredericksburg	Dec. 13
Stones River	Dec. 31–Jan. 2

MAP STUDY Which battles took place in Tennesee? When did the Battle of Antietam occur? Which battles took place near Richmond, Virginia?

SECTION 3 REVIEW On a separate sheet of paper, write *True* if the statement is true or *False* if the statement is not true.

1) The Union army won the second Battle of Manassas.

2) General Grant captured Fort Henry.

3) The Confederates destroyed the *Merrimac*.

4) The Union won the Seven Days Battles.

5) General Lee and the Confederate army attacked Maryland.

What do you think **?**

How does the battle of the *Monitor* and the *Merrimac* show that the Civil War was a different kind of war from wars in the past?

President Lincoln knew that the victory at Antietam had been important. He issued a warning to the Confederate States. He said he would free all the enslaved people in those states if the states did not return to the Union by January 1, 1863. The fighting southern states did not think he would do it. To their surprise, on the first day of January in 1863, President Lincoln declared that all enslaved people in the seceded states were free. This was called the Emancipation Proclamation.

President Lincoln read the Emancipation Proclamation to his cabinet in 1862.

The proclamation applied only to those states that had left the Union. Although the Emancipation Proclamation did not abolish slavery completely, it was a major step. Northerners cheered the proclamation.

What Did Many Runaway Enslaved People Do?

Many enslaved people had run away and joined the Union army even before the Emancipation Proclamation. By the end of the war, nearly 180,000 former enslaved people had **enlisted** in the army and fought against the Confederacy. To enlist means to join the armed forces. Twenty-three African soldiers won the Medal of Honor for bravery. Several regiments of Africans were formed. They took part in many major battles. The first African group from a free state was called the 54th Massachusetts Volunteers.

★Enlist
To join the armed forces

The Fourth Colored Infantry was one of many African regiments to serve in the Civil War.

What Happened at Chancellorsville and Gettysburg?

General Joseph Hooker had intended to keep an army at Fredericksburg to keep General Lee busy. He hoped to attack Chancellorsville at the same time. Meanwhile, General Lee had heard of the planned attack. He left a small army at Fredericksburg, and went on to meet Hooker at Chancellorsville. Lee's and General Jackson's soldiers easily defeated a much larger Union army. During the battle, Stonewall Jackson was accidentally shot and wounded by his own men. He died eight days later. Lee had lost his most important general.

General Lee's original plan had been to fight a defensive war. He would wait and be ready. Now, though, the war was not going well for the South in the western states. Lee thought about sending soldiers to win back the West. On the other hand, he felt one major victory in the North would bring an end to the war.

Lee decided to attack the North. He made his way into Pennsylvania with an army of about 65,000 well-trained soldiers. General George G. Meade's Union army in Pennsylvania numbered almost 85,000. The two armies prepared for battle near the quiet town of Gettysburg.

Today we usually think of hot-air balloon rides as recreation. Did you know that hot-air balloons were used during the Civil War? The Union army sent men up in hot-air balloons to observe Confederate troop movements. The men signaled information to officers on the ground. Officers used this information to direct Union troop movement and cannon fire.

Today, the United States detects military activities from satellites revolving around Earth in space. Directed from control centers in the United States, the satellites gather secret information. With special cameras, the satellites photograph a target on Earth. Then they send images back to Earth. These images show whether countries are building or disarming weapons according to treaties.

Then and Now

On July 1, 1863, Lee attacked. The battle continued for three days, with each side having the advantage from time to time. Lee made a desperate strike on the third day. He sent General George Pickett with 13,000 soldiers to charge the Union line. The line moved back, but it did not break. Slowly, Meade's army forced the Confederates back.

The South lost the battle, and Lee retreated to the Potomac River. The losses on both sides had been very heavy. Gettysburg was the turning point of the war. Although the South continued to fight after this battle, they had little possibility of winning.

The Union won the Battle of Gettysburg in 1863.

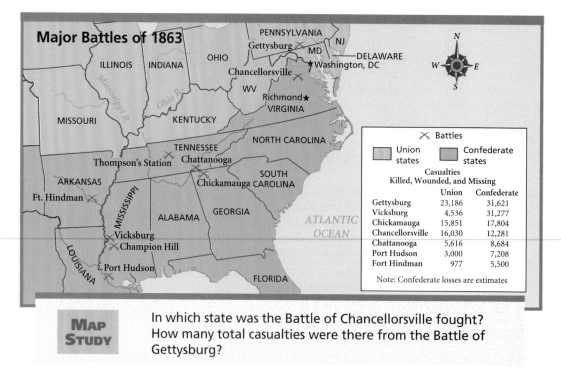

Major Battles of 1863

Battles		
Union states		Confederate states

Casualties
Killed, Wounded, and Missing

	Union	Confederate
Gettysburg	23,186	31,621
Vicksburg	4,536	31,277
Chickamauga	15,851	17,804
Chancellorsville	16,030	12,281
Chattanooga	5,616	8,684
Port Hudson	3,000	7,208
Fort Hindman	977	5,500

Note: Confederate losses are estimates.

MAP STUDY In which state was the Battle of Chancellorsville fought? How many total casualties were there from the Battle of Gettysburg?

The Gettysburg Address

Four months after the Battle of Gettysburg, President Lincoln **dedicated** a national cemetery for those who died there. His dedication speech, known as the Gettysburg Address, was short, but effective. The speech told of the grief President Lincoln felt for the soldiers who died there. It also expressed his feeling that the men fighting in the Civil War were fighting for a good cause—to protect the nation and democracy. A famous line from the address explains this idea: "…that this nation, under God, shall have a new birth of freedom—and that government of the people, by the people, for the people, shall not perish from the earth."

This second page of manuscript from the Gettysburg Address shows Lincoln's actual words.

Dedicate
To hold a ceremony as a way to honor a place or person

SECTION 4 REVIEW Choose the best word or name in parentheses to complete each sentence. Write your answers on a separate sheet of paper.

1) The (Gettysburg Address, Emancipation Proclamation, Medal of Honor) declared that slaves were free in the states that had seceded.

2) General (Robert E. Lee, Stonewall Jackson, Joseph Hooker) wanted to keep an army at Fredericksburg and attack Chancellorsville.

3) General (George G. Meade, Robert E. Lee, Stonewall Jackson) was wounded at a battle fought at Chancellorsville.

4) General (George G. Meade, Robert E. Lee, Joseph Hooker) forced the Confederates back at Gettysburg.

5) The Union army won a battle at (Fredericksburg, Chancellorsville, Gettysburg).

What do you think ?

Why do you think so many Africans were willing to fight in the Civil War?

Admiral David Farragut and the Union navy had attacked New Orleans, at the mouth of the Mississippi. They forced the Confederacy to surrender there. General Grant, under General Halleck of the army in the West, had scored many victories in the Mississippi River Valley. These victories included Shiloh, Perryville, and Murfreesboro in Tennessee.

As Lee retreated from the Battle of Gettysburg, he learned that Vicksburg, Mississippi, also had been captured by General Grant. The loss of Vicksburg meant that the entire Mississippi River was controlled by the Union army. As Grant moved eastward, the North took all the Confederate States except Georgia, North Carolina, South Carolina, and Virginia.

Grant was now the commander in chief of all the Union armies. On May 4, 1864, he forced his way toward Richmond. Even though his losses were heavy, he pressed on. Grant wanted to destroy the South so they could no longer fight. This would include destroying the cotton industry, railroads for transporting goods, and seaports for receiving goods from Europe.

Admiral David Farragut's Union navy enabled Union forces to capture New Orleans.

Lee realized that he was fighting a Union general who would not retreat, despite his losses. Lee's army was getting smaller with each battle. There was still hope for the South, though. President Lincoln was seeking re-election, and his defeat could lead to a settlement.

Who Won the Election of 1864?

In 1864, the Republicans nominated Lincoln for a second term. Civil War veteran George McClellan was the Democrats' choice for President. His party stood for bringing an end to the war. Before the election, the Union scored victories on land and sea. The sudden change in events ruined the chances of the Democrats. Lincoln won easily.

How Did General Sherman Advance His Army?

Under General Grant's orders, General William Sherman led an army of 100,000 men into Atlanta, Georgia. Confederate General John Hood tried to stop the Union troops, but he was forced to retreat. On September 2, 1864, General Sherman captured Atlanta. He continued his march to Savannah and then on to the sea.

General Sherman and about 60,000 Union troops set out from Atlanta. They had only the supplies each soldier could carry. Sherman commanded his troops to destroy everything in sight. His army cut a fifty-mile–wide path through Georgia. Sherman's troops destroyed bridges, barns, **livestock,** railroads, and crops. On December 21, 1864, the Union army captured Savannah.

Livestock
Animals used for food or profit

General Sherman marched northward to join General Grant at Richmond in the spring of 1865. Phillip Sheridan, another Union general, was closing in quickly from the West. General Lee was in a difficult situation. In one last desperate move, the Confederate leader marched his men westward. Sheridan's troops surrounded Lee near Appomattox Court House in Virginia. Lee asked for the terms of surrender, to avoid even more losses on both sides.

General Sherman's army destroyed everything that could be used by the Confederacy in Georgia.

Major Battles of 1864–1865

ILLINOIS
INDIANA
OHIO
MD
DELAWARE
★ Washington, DC
Winchester
Cedar Creek
Wilderness
WEST VIRGINIA
Spotsylvania
VIRGINIA
Richmond ★
Petersburg
APPOMATTOX COURT HOUSE ■
ATLANTIC OCEAN
Sailor's Creek
Five Forks
KENTUCKY
NORTH CAROLINA
Nashville
TENNESSEE
SOUTH CAROLINA
Kenesaw Mountain
Atlanta
MISSISSIPPI
ALABAMA
GEORGIA
Mississippi R.
Ohio R.

N
W E
S

✕ Battles
Union states
Confederate states

MAP STUDY

Where did most of the battles take place in 1864?

How Did the War End?

General Lee met General Grant to discuss the terms of surrender on April 9, 1865. General Lee knew he must agree with Grant's conditions. If not, his army would be attacked. Grant respected General Lee as a military leader. He knew that Lee had fought bravely.

Grant's terms of surrender were generous. The Confederate soldiers would be allowed to keep their horses and mules. Officers could also keep their pistols. All other military guns and supplies were to be turned over to the Union. General Lee was pleased with the terms and agreed to them. The war was over. Confederate President Jefferson Davis was later arrested and placed in prison for two years. The Union had been saved, and the slavery question was finally settled.

General Grant and his officers met with General Lee at a house in Appomattox Court House, Virginia. General Lee agreed to surrender.

The McLean House

General Lee and General Grant ended the Civil War by meeting in a house owned by a Confederate officer, Major Wilmer McLean. McLean had offered his own house as the meeting site. The house, pictured to the right, still stands today in Virginia at the Appomattox Court House National Historic Park.

Rebuild
To build something again

What Were the Losses From the War?

The losses from the war were very high. It claimed more American lives than any other war before it. The fighting damaged property, too. Sherman's march alone was estimated to have caused over $100 million in damages. The South would need a **rebuilding** program to get back to normal.

Civil War Statistics		
	Union	Confederacy
Soldiers served	2,213,400	1,003,600
Battle deaths	110,000	94,000
Wounded	275,000	226,000
Deaths by disease	224,000	60,000

SECTION 5 REVIEW Write the answers to these questions on a separate sheet of paper using complete sentences.

1) How was the loss at Vicksburg harmful to the Confederacy?

2) What was Grant's plan for winning the war?

3) Why was the election of 1864 important?

4) How did General Sherman's army destroy the South?

5) Why was General Lee forced to surrender?

What do you think ❓

The Civil War resulted in a huge loss of life and damage to property. What other things do you think the war affected?

Lee's Surrender

A fifteen-year-old boy ran away from home to enlist in the Union army in 1862. He used a false name and claimed he was eighteen. After sixteen months of fighting, the boy was injured. He transferred to a different company as a bugler. That change brought the Yankee bugler to Appomattox Court House on April 9, 1865. His company was escorting General Grant. He saw Robert E. Lee ride up on his horse, Traveler. General Lee had come to surrender to Ulysses S. Grant to end the Civil War. Seventy-five years later, in January 1940, the bugler wrote this memory of the day.

"It was not difficult to recognize the famous commander of the Army of Northern Virginia. He measured up fully to my expectations, and those expectations were rather elaborate. Though I was only a lad of eighteen, I had been in sixteen battles during three years, and had come to have a wholesome esteem for the Johnny Rebs and their leader. He had become a sort of legendary figure. . . .

What a brave pair of thoroughbreds Lee and Traveler were! That horse would have attracted attention anywhere. General Lee's uniform was immaculate and he presented a superb martial figure. But it was the face beneath the gray felt hat that made the deepest impression on me.

I have been trying to find a single word that describes it, and I have concluded that 'benign' is the adjective I am after; because that means kindly and gracious. There was something else about him that aroused my deep pity that so great a warrior should be acknowledging defeat.

There we were, a group of eager troopers in blue, and a lone orderly in gray. General Lee came from the house, his soldierly figure erect, even in defeat. We stiffened up and gave him a salute and the man in gray courteously returned it. At the moment his soul must have been heavy with sorrow, but he could return the salute of Yankee troopers. Soldiers do not carry hatred; they leave that to the stay-at-homes."

Source Reading Wrap-Up

1) Why did the bugler say it was easy to recognize General Lee?

2) What did the bugler feel toward General Lee?

3) What are three words the bugler used to describe General Lee?

4) The last paragraph refers to the colors blue and gray. What do those colors refer to?

5) How do you feel toward General Lee after reading this passage?

CHAPTER SUMMARY

★ The Confederate States of America was formed in February 1861 after seven states left the Union. Later, four more states joined the Confederacy.

★ Abraham Lincoln became President on March 4, 1861. He wanted to unite the country again.

★ Fort Sumter, a Union fort in South Carolina, was captured by the Confederacy in April 1861. This action was the beginning of the Civil War.

★ The Union established a blockade to prevent the South from selling cotton to European customers. Money from cotton would go toward buying military supplies.

★ The Union had a larger population, more factories and workers, and more money to pay for supplies, but not everyone was committed to the war.

★ The Confederacy had strong military leaders and people were fighting to maintain their way of life.

★ Lincoln appointed George McClellan as the commander of the Union army. Robert E. Lee led the Confederate army.

★ The Confederate army won many of the major battles in the early part of the war.

★ After the bloody Battle of Antietam, Lincoln removed General McClellan. Lincoln appointed Ambrose Burnside as the head of the army in 1862.

★ Lincoln issued a warning to the Confederate States. He said that if they did not return to the Union, he would free enslaved people in those states. Lincoln issued the Emancipation Proclamation on January 1, 1863.

★ The Battle of Gettysburg was fought in July of 1863. It was the worst battle of the war and lasted three days. Won by the Union, it was the turning point of the war.

★ General Grant became the head of the Union army in 1864.

★ President Lincoln was re-elected in 1864.

★ In 1864, General William Sherman led Union soldiers on a march through Georgia, destroying everything along the way.

★ Lee surrendered to Grant on April 9, 1865, ending the Civil War.

Comprehension: Identifying Facts

On a separate sheet of paper, write the words from the Word Bank to complete each sentence.

WORD BANK		
Ambrose Burnside	Fort Sumter	Robert E. Lee
Antietam	Gettysburg	Stonewall Jackson
Appomattox Court House	Gettysburg Address	Vicksburg
blockade	Jefferson Davis	William Sherman
Emancipation Proclamation	John Hood	

1) _____ was the Confederate general whose troops tried to defend Atlanta from Union attack.

2) The battle at _____ lasted for three days and was the turning point of the war.

3) One of the bloodiest battles of the war was fought in Maryland on _____ Creek.

4) General _____ commanded the Confederate army.

5) The troops of _____ cut a path of destruction fifty miles wide through Georgia.

6) After General Grant captured _____, the Union controlled the entire Mississippi River.

7) The Civil War began with the attack on _____.

8) _____ and his troops helped the Confederacy to win the Battle of Manassas in July of 1861.

9) President Lincoln gave the _____ at the dedication of a national cemetery.

10) To prevent the South from selling cotton and buying military goods, the Union formed a _____ of the Confederacy's ports.

11) _____ replaced General McClellan as the head of the Union army.

12) The _____ freed enslaved people in the Confederate States on January 1, 1863.

13) Lee signed the surrender to Grant in Virginia at _____.

14) The President of the Confederate States of America was _____.

Comprehension: Understanding Main Ideas

On a separate sheet of paper, write the answer to each question using complete sentences.

1) What was the purpose of the Union blockade?

2) What happened that helped Lincoln win re-election in 1864?

3) What were the terms of Lee's surrender to Grant?

4) What was no longer an issue after the Civil War was over?

Critical Thinking: Write Your Opinion

1) Many of the soldiers who fought in the Civil War were teenagers. What do you think of the idea of teenagers fighting in a war?

2) Lee considered Grant's terms of surrender to be generous. If you had been Grant, what would your terms of surrender have been?

Test Taking Tip Look for specifics in each question that tell you in what form your answer is to be. For example, some questions ask for a paragraph, and others may require only one sentence.

Reconstruction

1865–1877

The bloody war between the North and South had ended. Slavery was over once and for all. The nation needed to heal its wounds. Both the North and the South had changed during the war. The South lay in ruin and had to be rebuilt. The period of Reconstruction was a time of political turmoil. Some members of Congress tried to punish the South. Formerly enslaved Africans fought to keep their freedom. They became voters and landholders. By the end of Reconstruction, however, much of their freedom became limited. The wounds of the war could not be healed by politicians who looked out for their own interests. In this chapter, you will learn about Reconstruction in the South.

Goals for Learning

▶ To explain the problems of Reconstruction

▶ To explain the three new amendments to the Constitution

▶ To explain the changes in the North and the South after the Civil War

▶ To describe the presidencies of Johnson and Grant

▶ To describe the problems free African Americans faced

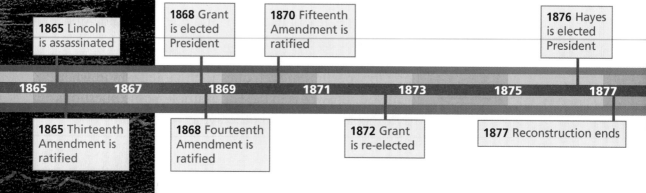

1865 Lincoln is assassinated

1868 Grant is elected President

1870 Fifteenth Amendment is ratified

1876 Hayes is elected President

| 1865 | 1867 | 1869 | 1871 | 1873 | 1875 | 1877 |

1865 Thirteenth Amendment is ratified

1868 Fourteenth Amendment is ratified

1872 Grant is re-elected

1877 Reconstruction ends

Amnesty
A pardon granted by the government

★Assassination
The killing of a politically important person

Oath
A pledge that promises loyalty to a government or other cause

Abraham Lincoln began his second term as President as the war was ending. In his inaugural address, Lincoln expressed his hopes for rebuilding the Union. He wanted all Americans to forget the war as soon as possible. He put together a plan to rebuild the nation.

The President's plan said a state could rejoin the Union when ten percent of its voters took an **oath** to support the Union. He offered **amnesty,** or pardon, to southerners. This would allow the states to rejoin the Union as quickly as possible. New state governments could be formed, but the ban on slavery would have to be obeyed. Lincoln knew that Congress had different ideas about the South. Many in Congress did not agree with Lincoln's plan. However, Lincoln felt that he had the power to proceed without the approval of Congress.

On the evening of April 14, 1865, Lincoln attended a play at Ford's Theater in Washington, D.C. John Wilkes Booth went to the box where Lincoln was sitting and shot the President in the back of the head. Booth had supported the southern cause. Lincoln died the next morning. A few days after the **assassination,** soldiers killed Booth. President Lincoln did not live to see his plans carried out. His death delayed rebuilding in the South.

John Wilkes Booth assassinated President Lincoln at Ford's Theater. The poster (above left) shows the program performed the night of the assassination.

What Were the Problems in the South?

In the South, the damage from the war had been great. Countless farms and large plantations were ruined. Confederate money was worthless. As a result, many

Richmond, Virginia, was one of many areas in the South ruined by the Civil War.

formerly wealthy people had no funds. They could not rebuild. Most banks, also victims of the failed Confederate cause, had closed. Roads throughout many southern states had become blocked with rubble from the war. Many bridges had been destroyed. Even the railroad tracks had been damaged during efforts to slow down shipments of troops and supplies.

The South had few police, no judges, and no courts. Some groups of desperate people tried to take the law into their own hands. None of the southern states had an established government to take care of the hard times that lay ahead. Among the homeless and the unemployed were the formerly enslaved people who had to find a way to support themselves.

What Was Reconstruction?

★Reconstruction
Rebuilding of the South after the Civil War

Reconstruction—the rebuilding of the South—was now in the hands of the new President, Andrew Johnson. Although he had served as Vice President to Lincoln, Johnson was not well liked by many members of Congress. A Democrat, former governor of Tennessee, and representative in Congress, Johnson had been a senator at the outbreak of the war. He had remained loyal to the Union even though he had strong ties to the South.

President Johnson tried to follow Lincoln's Reconstruction plan. He pardoned most southerners who took an oath. He appointed temporary governors in many states to help them re-form their governments and elect new representatives to Congress.

★Black Codes
Codes that prevented African Americans from owning certain kinds of land, voting, and working certain skilled jobs

★Freedmen
Formerly enslaved people

★Radical
Extreme

Within a few months, most of these states had reorganized and ratified the Thirteenth Amendment, which abolished slavery. By the end of 1865, Johnson announced that all of the southern states but Texas were readmitted to the Union. Congress did not agree.

Congress met in December 1865. Members of Congress called the **"Radical** Republicans" opposed the Reconstruction plan. A person who is radical is extreme. The Radical Republicans wanted to punish the former Confederate States for the trouble they caused the nation. The Radicals refused to recognize the newly formed southern governments or the recently elected representatives from them. They did not accept the states back into the Union.

Some newly established state governments in the South had adopted **"Black Codes."** These laws only applied to African Americans. Under the Black Codes, former slaves, now called **freedmen,** were restricted from voting, owning certain kinds of land, and working certain skilled jobs. Many members of Congress felt that the Black Codes proved that the southern states did not intend to end slavery.

SECTION 1 REVIEW Write the answers to these questions on a separate sheet of paper using complete sentences.

1) Under Lincoln's plan, how could states come back into the Union?

2) Who assassinated Abraham Lincoln?

3) What was the South like after the Civil War?

4) What was the importance of the Thirteenth Amendment?

5) What was the name of the group that was against Reconstruction?

What do you think ?

Do you think African Americans were really free in the South? Why or why not?

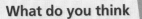

★**Agency**
An organization set up by the federal government

★**Due process**
The formal process of justice carried out in a court of law

★**Lawsuit**
A case brought before a court of law

In readmitting states to the Union, Johnson allowed voting rights to white men in the South. He made no effort to give such rights to the freedmen. Southern whites, who blamed Republicans for the war, were strongly Democratic. The freedmen, on the other hand, were pro-Republican, because President Lincoln had helped them gain their freedom. Republicans in Congress were eager to win African Americans' votes. Northern business leaders were happily back into successful business deals. They did not want a Democratic South to start lowering tariffs again.

Congress began to put its own reconstruction plan into effect by passing the Civil Rights Act of 1866. Put into effect over President Johnson's veto, this act was intended to reverse the Black Codes. Under this law, African Americans were allowed to own property, to bring **lawsuits,** and to marry legally. A lawsuit is a case brought before a court of law. Shortly afterward, Congress proposed the Fourteenth Amendment. The amendment made the Bill of Rights cover all Americans, including whites and African Americans. It said that no state shall "deprive any person of life, liberty, or property without **due process** of law; nor deny to any person equal protection of the laws." Due process is the formal process of justice carried out in a court of law. The Fourteenth Amendment did not apply to American Indians.

Tennessee was the only southern state that accepted the Fourteenth Amendment and was readmitted to the Union. The other Confederate States rejected the amendment and were not readmitted.

What Was the Freedmen's Bureau?

Congress had started the Freedmen's Bureau in 1865 as a temporary **agency** to help formerly enslaved people and some white southerners. One of the first programs of the Freedmen's Bureau was to establish hospitals to aid southern African Americans injured in the war.

In 1866, with the Freedmen's Bureau Bill, Congress enlarged the agency. It was extended to help freedmen to find jobs and give them food, clothing, and shelter until they found jobs. Freedmen and their children were given opportunities to go to school. Agents of the Freedmen's Bureau tried to help protect the **civil rights** of the African Americans. Civil rights are basic human rights given to all people.

★Civil rights
Basic human rights given to all people

What Was the Reconstruction Act of 1867?

In March of 1867, Congress passed the first of four Reconstruction acts over the veto of the President. The first act stated that the ten states that had not returned to the Union would be put under military rule by the federal government. The South was then divided into five sections. In order to be readmitted to the Union, states had to hold constitutional conventions with delegates elected by all men—white and African American. Congress had to approve a state's constitution and the state had to accept the Fourteenth Amendment before it could rejoin the Union. By 1870, all ten southern states were readmitted to the Union.

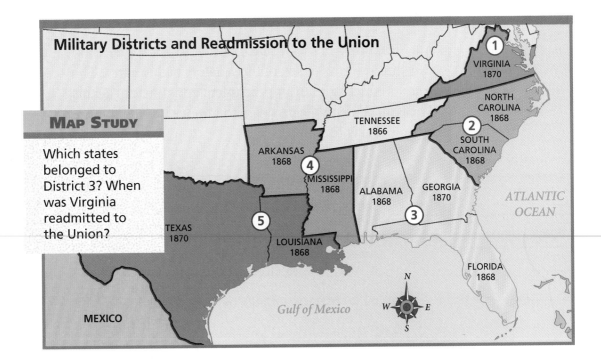

Military Districts and Readmission to the Union

MAP STUDY

Which states belonged to District 3? When was Virginia readmitted to the Union?

VIRGINIA 1870
NORTH CAROLINA 1868
TENNESSEE 1866
SOUTH CAROLINA 1868
ARKANSAS 1868
MISSISSIPPI 1868
ALABAMA 1868
GEORGIA 1870
TEXAS 1870
LOUISIANA 1868
FLORIDA 1868
ATLANTIC OCEAN
MEXICO
Gulf of Mexico

" THE MOST UNKINDEST CUT OF ALL."

REJECTED SUITOR (deserted in his hour of need)—" Oh! misery! must I lose thee too?"

A newspaper printed this cartoon of President Johnson during his impeachment trial.

★Impeach
To remove a President from office because of misconduct

Misconduct
Wrongdoing by someone holding a political or business position

Override
To reject or not accept

Why Did Congress Try to Impeach Johnson?

Johnson tried to veto a number of bills passed by Radicals in Congress. Congress was able to **override** his veto. In 1867, Congress passed the Tenure of Office Act. This act required approval from the Senate before the President could fire an appointee. Believing that the act limited the President, Johnson vetoed it. Congress overrode the veto.

President Johnson then fired one of his cabinet members, Edwin Stanton. Stanton sided with the Radicals. Some powerful senators were very upset. They wanted to **impeach** Johnson, which means that he would be charged with **misconduct** and removed from office. The House of Representatives did impeach Johnson. The Senate then had to decide if the charges were proper.

A trial was held in the Senate. In order to reach a decision, two-thirds, or thirty-six, of the senators had to agree. The vote was thirty five for impeachment and nineteen against. The Radical Republicans failed to remove President Johnson by only one vote.

Seward's Icebox

Secretary of State William Seward learned that Russia wanted to sell its Alaska territory. He planned to buy this land. Most Americans laughed at the idea. They called Alaska "Seward's Icebox" because it was so cold. On March 30, 1867, Seward signed a treaty that gave Alaska to the United States. The purchase price was $7.2 million, which is about two cents an acre!

Writing About History

Write a song about this time period. The song could focus on a certain event covered in the chapter or on a feeling people had at that time. Write the song in your notebook.

Unfortunately, Johnson had lost much support during these problems. For the remainder of his presidency he was unable to do anything further to promote the Reconstruction efforts he favored.

Who Won the Election of 1868?

In 1868, the Republicans chose General Ulysses S. Grant to be their candidate. Grant had no political experience, yet he was well known for leading the Union army in the Civil War. The Democrats chose former New York Governor Horatio Seymour as their candidate. Many felt that Grant had saved the Union, so now he would save the country. Grant won the election in a very close popular vote. About 450,000 African Americans had voted for Grant. Political parties became aware that African Americans were important to the outcome of an election.

WORD BANK
Andrew Johnson
Democrats
Fourteenth Amendment
Radical Republicans
Ulysses S. Grant

SECTION 2 REVIEW On a separate sheet of paper write the words from the Word Bank to complete each sentence.

1) The House of Representatives voted to impeach ________.

2) The ________ said that African Americans had "equal protection of the laws."

3) Most of the southern whites were ________.

4) ________ created their own Reconstruction plan.

5) ________ was elected President in 1868.

What do you think ?

What sorts of things would a President have to do for you to vote for impeachment?

★**Carpetbagger**
Northerner elected to political office in the South who took advantage of people; carried belongings in carpetbags

Corruption
Using wrong or unlawful ways for financial gain

★**Scalawag**
White southerner who controlled the new politicians who had little government knowledge

When Congress passed the Reconstruction Acts, it provided for political reorganization of the South. Under the acts, the right to hold office was taken away from men who had been political leaders of the Confederacy. Other southerners, however, were allowed to be legislators. During the thirteen years that followed, a total of sixteen African Americans served in Congress.

Who Were the Scalawags and Carpetbaggers?

In some states, such as South Carolina, white southerners put African Americans in state offices. In general, formerly enslaved Africans had little knowledge of government. They did what they were told to do. White southerners who controlled the new politicians were called **scalawags.**

Some northerners looked to the South for opportunity. They traveled to the southern states looking for jobs. Others from the North wanted to help the cause of the freedmen, either as teachers or school administrators. Still other northerners were elected to political office in the South. They took advantage of the people and made money through **corruption.** Many of these northerners carried their belongings in bags made from carpet material. They became known as **carpetbaggers.**

Carpetbaggers took advantage of people and carried belongings in bags made of carpet material.

THE MAN WITH THE (CARPET) BAGS.
The bag in front of him, filled with others' faults, he always sees. The one behind
filled with his own faults, he never sees.

What Happened to the Plantations?

The Civil War brought many changes to the South, particularly to the old plantation system. Plantations could no longer use slave labor. Large plantation owners now paid wages to their former enslaved people. Even though the wages were low, they decreased the profits of the plantation owners.

Many of the large plantations were divided into smaller pieces of land for **tenant farmers**. In this situation, landowners rented their land to owners of small farms. Usually, the tenant farmer paid a set amount of rent. He sold his crops to pay the landowner. Sometimes he might use crops to pay his rent. No matter how he paid it, the farmer ended up with less than the landowner.

Some large landowners let formerly enslaved people have land to farm. In return, the owner would get a large share of the crop. The owner provided the seed, tools, food, and general supplies to the farmer. The crop was payment for the supplies the farmer had received. These farmers were known as **sharecroppers.** Slavery had ended, but sharecropping was not much better. The owner sold the crops at a high price and paid the sharecropper a lower price. The sharecropper never stopped owing money. His debt got bigger and bigger. A new form of slavery had begun.

In sharecropping and tenant farming, the freedmen had a place to live and a chance to do the work they knew. Neither practice was good for the farmer. Even though they worked hard, the farmer and his family remained poor.

The Works of Mark Twain

"Mark Twain" was a humorous author and lecturer in the late 1800s. Born Samuel Clemens, he found his pen name while working as a Mississippi riverboat pilot. The call "Mark twain!" meant the water was two fathoms deep and thus safe to travel on. Twain's first notable tale was "The Celebrated Jumping Frog of Calaveras County." He wrote many other short stories and novels. His most famous novels are *The Adventures of Tom Sawyer* (1876) and *The Adventures of Huckleberry Finn* (1884). Twain created memorable characters in American literature and realistic portraits of nineteenth-century life. Twain's later works are gloomier than his early works. His writing sometimes reflected the prejudice of his time. As a result, many people today are uncomfortable with his work. Nonetheless, his books have been loved for their colorful pictures of childhood and humorous insight into human folly.

Literature

History in Your Life

Cotton remained a major crop throughout the South, as were tobacco and rice. After the war, pecans, peanuts, corn, wheat, fruits, and vegetables were planted. This gave the South several different kinds of crops. They no longer had to depend on just cotton, tobacco, and rice.

What Were Other Changes in the South?

People discovered iron ore, coal, and limestone in various parts of the South. This led to the creation of a strong iron and steel industry. Birmingham, Alabama, became a major steel-producing center. In other cities, lumber mills provided a good deal of the nation's building material. Mills to produce cotton cloth were built. Railroads, roads, and new industries spread throughout the South. Towns and cities got larger. Progress was beginning to take shape in the once rural South.

★Segregate
To separate by race

Before the war, the South had paid little attention to public education. Those who could afford it sent their children to private schools. During Reconstruction, states began to require public education for children. Schools were **segregated,** which meant white and African-American children attended separate schools. Unfortunately, this practice of segregation continued for many years.

P. B. S. PINCHBACK: c. 1837–1921

Captain Pinckney B. S. Pinchback fought for the Union in the Civil War. He served as a member of General Richard Butler's Corps d'Afrique. During Reconstruction, he became lieutenant governor of Louisiana. Governor Henry C. Warmouth was impeached in 1872. Pinchback thus became the first African-American governor. He served only forty-two days in that position. Within the next year, he was elected as both a Republican representative and senator to Congress. However, opposing Democrats feared his outspoken fight for African-American rights. Some claimed he broke laws to become elected. As a result, Pinchback was never seated as a representative or senator. In the years that followed, he published a weekly newspaper. He also kept fighting to end segregation and violence against African Americans.

Magazines Gain Popularity

The earliest magazines in America were journals of political opinion. From the colonial period until after the Civil War, magazines came and went. They were expensive, and most magazines did not last long. In 1879, Congress lowered postal rates for magazines to encourage more people to read. Congress wanted to improve the nation's education.

Magazine publishers borrowed the techniques of the Penny Press. They created easy-to-read magazines for the masses. This mass circulation helped to build a strong advertising base.

Editors used muckraking journalism to expose political or social injustices. Muckraking is the practice of exposing misconduct of a well-known person. This practice helped to establish investigative journalism. People also looked forward to reading the serial fiction stories that ran for several issues.

Many people regularly read magazines like *McClure's*, *Munsey's*, and *The Saturday Evening Post*. Later, *Look* and *Life* became popular with their photography features. When television came along in the late 1940s, people lost a lot of their interest in magazines.

SECTION 3 REVIEW   On a separate sheet of paper, write *True* if the statement is true or *False* of the statement is not true.

1) Tenant farmers owned the land they farmed.

2) Carpetbaggers often took advantage of southerners.

3) After the Civil War, cotton was the only crop southern farmers grew.

4) Sharecroppers became very wealthy.

5) A strong iron and steel industry developed after the war.

What do you think **?**

Would you choose to be a tenant farmer or sharecropper? Why or why not?

★**Grandfather clause**
A clause that stated that any adult African-American male could vote if his grandfather was a registered voter on January 1, 1867

★**Suffrage**
The right to vote

In February 1870, the Fifteenth Amendment gave African-American men the right to vote. Regardless of race, color, or previous slavery, every male citizen could vote. **Suffrage,** or the right to vote, had been given to all citizens except women and American Indians. Southerners opposed the new amendment. They were concerned that African Americans could decide the outcome of an election. Most northerners were not concerned because the African-American population was small.

Some southern states prevented African Americans from voting. African Americans were told that they could not vote because they could not read or did not understand the Constitution. Voting laws were passed that contained a **grandfather clause.** Any adult male could vote if his grandfather was a registered voter on January 1, 1867. Because no African American was allowed to vote before that date, all freedmen were prevented from voting. By the end of the nineteenth century, most African Americans had lost the right to vote in the ex-Confederate southern states.

The Fifteenth Amendment gave African-American men the right to vote for the first time in history.

African Americans faced other problems. Whites organized secret groups such as the **Ku Klux Klan.** The Klan wanted to keep African Americans from voting, to punish the scalawags, and to make the carpetbaggers leave the South. They used violence to scare their victims. Sometimes the violence led to murder. African Americans were most often the target of their attacks.

What Problems Did Grant Have?

President Grant had very little training in political matters. He found that being President was very different from serving as a general. He appointed his friends to government jobs and trusted that they would be honest. Although Grant was an honest man, many of his friends were not. His **administration** was hurt by several **scandals.** Grant's friends tried to get rich by using the power of their government offices. In 1872, Grant was elected for a second term.

These Ku Klux Klan members were captured during an uprising in 1868.

Administration
The period of time a President is in office

★Ku Klux Klan
A secret group against African Americans

Scandal
A disgraceful event

Shortly after President Grant began his second term, the country went into a depression. Businesses and factories began to shut down. Thousands of workers lost their jobs. Many families had no money to buy food. This depression lasted for almost four years. During this time the Republicans lost many seats in Congress.

Then and Now

Think what a subway ride was like in 1870 when Alfred Beach built America's first subway. It ran under Broadway in New York City and extended only 312 feet. The luxurious car held twenty passengers and was "shot" through a tunnel like a cannonball. The tunnel was decorated with wall paintings. This was intended only as a demonstration subway. When Beach was unable to get city approval to expand the system, it failed.

Have you ridden on today's subways? Many large cities have them. New York City's subway is about 230 miles long—the second longest system after London's. Opened in 1904, New York's subway is powered by electricity. About five million people ride the New York subway every day.

How Did Reconstruction End?

Northerners had grown tired of high taxes. They wondered how much longer Reconstruction could go on. Ten years had passed. Many northerners had lost interest in the problems of the South. They felt it was time to forget about the war. Grant's two terms had been full of corruption. The election of 1876 called for a President who could restore the people's trust in the government.

The Republicans chose Rutherford B. Hayes, the governor of Ohio, as their candidate. He was an honest man. The Democrats chose Samuel J. Tilden, the governor of New York, as their candidate. Tilden won the popular vote, but neither candidate won a majority of electoral votes. An Electoral Commission decided the election. Twenty electoral votes were in dispute.

Hayes made a political deal. He told southern Democratic leaders that he would end Reconstruction if they would support him. With southern support, the House of Representatives agreed with the Electoral Commission's decision to make Hayes President. Hayes took office in March of 1877. Within a few months all federal troops left the southern states. Reconstruction had come to an end.

★Centennial
A 100th year celebration

The country celebrated its **centennial** in 1876. A centennial is a 100th year celebration. A Centennial Exposition was held in Philadelphia to show the achievements of the young

nation. Americans were becoming masters of science and industrial development. A great nation had risen from the wilderness. It was strong and ready to face the next 100 years.

The country still had social and political problems. Some Americans still did not get along with African Americans. Freedmen continued to fight for the rights they felt they deserved. African-American voters helped elect two African-American senators and fifteen African-American representatives between 1865 and 1877. Both senators were from Mississippi. Those members of Congress proved to be good politicians.

After Reconstruction, southern state governments began denying African Americans social equality and the right to vote. The gains achieved during Reconstruction quickly vanished. In some states, conditions for African Americans were not much better than they had been before the Civil War.

SECTION 4 REVIEW On a separate sheet of paper write the word or words in parentheses that correctly complete each sentence.

1) A secret society called the (Ku Klux Klan, Radical Republicans) used violence to prevent African Americans from voting.

2) The presidency of (Hayes, Grant) was marked by corruption.

3) After Reconstruction, most African Americans (lost, gained) most of their rights.

4) The United States celebrated its centennial in (1865, 1876).

5) When federal (carpetbaggers, troops) left the South, Reconstruction ended.

What do you think ❓

Grant chose friends to fill important government posts. If you were President, how would you choose people to fill posts?

Advice to African-American Students

W. E. B. Du Bois argued that African Americans need good schools and a good education. In a letter, he once advised a student not to leave school.

"There are in the United States today tens of thousands of [young African-American women] who would be happy beyond measure to have the chance of educating themselves that you are neglecting. If you train yourself as you easily can, there are wonderful chances of usefulness before you: you can join the ranks of 15,000 Negro women teachers, of hundreds of nurses and physicians, of the growing number of clerks and stenographers, and above all the host of homemakers.

Ignorance is a cure for nothing. Get the very best training possible and the doors of opportunity will fly open before you as they are flying before thousands of your fellows. On the other hand every time a black person neglects an opportunity, it makes it more difficult for others of the race to get such an opportunity. Do you want to cut off the chances of the boys and girls of tomorrow?"

From: Herbert Aptheker, *A Documentary History of the Negro People in the United States*

Source Reading Wrap-Up

1) Why does Du Bois urge the student to stay in school?

2) What does Du Bois say happens to African Americans who neglect to get a good education?

3) What do you think Du Bois meant when he said that "ignorance is a cure for nothing." Do you agree? Why?

4) Du Bois warned the student about neglecting the opportunity for education. He said that neglecting the opportunity would "cut off the chances of the boys and girls of tomorrow." What do you think he meant by that?

5) Du Bois named some careers that were open to African-American women at that time. How do you think careers have opened up for all women since then?

★ John Wilkes Booth assassinated Abraham Lincoln on April 14, 1865, at Ford's Theater in Washington, D.C. Andrew Johnson became President.

★ The war ruined the former Confederate States. Plantations, roads, bridges, and railways were destroyed. President Johnson appointed temporary governors in many southern states to help them form new governments.

★ Some northerners punished the former Confederate States by refusing to recognize newly elected officials.

★ Congress set up the Freedmen's Bureau in 1865 to help formerly enslaved people and some white southerners find jobs and to provide medical help, clothing, food, and shelter.

★ Some southern governments adopted "Black Codes" that prevented freedmen from owning certain kinds of land, voting, and working certain skilled jobs. The Civil Rights Act of 1866 allowed freedmen to own property, marry, and bring lawsuits.

★ The Fourteenth Amendment to the Constitution, which gave African Americans equal protection under the law, was ratified in 1868. Ratified in 1870, the Fifteenth Amendment gave African-American men the right to vote.

★ In 1867, Congress passed the first of four such Reconstruction acts. It divided the South into five sections and put them under military rule. It also required the southern states to create new constitutions that had to be approved by Congress.

★ Because of a dispute over the powers of the President, Congress tried but failed to impeach Andrew Johnson.

★ Scalawags were white southerners who controlled new politicians, particularly African-American politicians. Carpetbaggers were northern politicians in the South who took advantage of people.

★ Most southern plantations were divided into smaller pieces of land. Landowners farmed their land using tenant farmers and sharecroppers.

★ Ulysses S. Grant was elected President in 1868. His two terms as President were marked with corruption and problems.

★ Rutherford B. Hayes was elected President in 1877. Hayes made a deal with southern congressmen that he would end Reconstruction and remove federal troops from the South.

Comprehension: Identifying Facts

On a separate sheet of paper, write the words from the Word Bank to complete each sentence.

WORD BANK		
Andrew Johnson	Fourteenth Amendment	Ku Klux Klan
Exposition		Reconstruction
Civil Rights Act of 1866	Freedmen's Bureau	sharecroppers
	impeachment	tenant farmers
Fifteenth Amendment	John Wilkes Booth	Ulysses S. Grant

1) The _____ to the United States Constitution gave African-American men the right to vote in elections.

2) The first_____ act divided the South into five regions and placed federal troops there to maintain order.

3) _____ was Lincoln's Vice President and became President after Lincoln died.

4) The _____ was an agency that was supposed to help formerly enslaved people and some white southerners find jobs.

5) African Americans were given equal protection under law by the _____.

6) Most _____ were freedmen who were allowed to farm the land by giving much of their harvest to landowners.

7) Americans celebrated the nation's centennial with a Centennial_____ in Philadelphia, Pennsylvania.

8) The Congress tried to get rid of President Johnson by holding hearings and voting on _____.

9) Abraham Lincoln was shot to death by _____, who supported the southern cause.

10) A secret organization, the _____, was formed to keep African Americans from voting and living free under the Constitution.

11) Congress passed the _____ before the Fourteenth Amendment was ratified.

12) _____ was elected President because people thought that he had saved the Union during the Civil War.

13) _____ rented their farms from landowners.

Comprehension: Understanding Main Ideas

On a separate sheet of paper, write the answer to each question using complete sentences.

1) What was the South like right after the Civil War ended?

2) What did "Radical Republicans" in Congress want to do to the South? Why?

3) Why did Congress establish the Freedmen's Bureau?

4) How did the plantation system change after the Civil War?

5) What were some of the problems that Grant faced as President?

Critical Thinking: Write Your Opinion

1) Ulysses S. Grant had been a capable general during the Civil War and was a hero of the North. Grant was not a very good President. Do you think that it is a mistake to elect military heroes to be President? Why or why not?

2) Do you think the Freedmen's Bureau was a good idea? Why or why not?

Test Taking Tip | Try to answer all questions as completely as possible. When asked to explain your answer, do so in complete sentences.

Looking for causes and effects will help you better understand what you read. An effect is something that happens as a result of a cause. One cause may have several effects. To determine causes and effects, ask these questions:

Why did the event happen? (cause)

What made the event happen? (cause)

What happened as a result of the event? (effect)

What cause triggered an event?

What is the effect of that event?

Here is an example of one cause and effect that led to the Civil War:

Cause: Political parties and other groups disagreed over states' rights.

Effect: Southern states seceded from the Union.

Here are more causes and effects that led to the Civil War. Read each pair of sentences. Decide which statement is the cause and which is the effect. Rewrite each sentence on your paper. Label it with *cause* or *effect*.

1) A depression occurred in 1857, with a sharp decline in prices.

Economic differences between the North and the South widened.

2) The proslavery principle expanded in the South.

Chief Justice Roger Taney's decision denied Dred Scott his freedom.

3) The tragedy of "bleeding Kansas" opened sectional divisions in the country that could not be resolved.

The Kansas-Nebraska Act was passed.

4) The Democratic party was split in its views on slavery.

Abraham Lincoln was elected President.

5) Extremist politicians, editors, and reformers created divisions between the North and South primarily through the slavery issue.

Divisions between the North and South deepened until they burst into war.

★ Congress had to decide whether new states would be free or slave states.

★ The Compromise of 1850 settled some slavery issues. The Fugitive Slave Law challenged the right to freedom of almost all enslaved people and freemen.

★ The Gadsden Purchase added the final piece of land to America.

★ Choosing a railroad route from coast to coast caused problems between free and slave states.

★ The Kansas-Nebraska Act allowed territorial voters to decide if their state would be free or slave. Proslavery people won in Kansas Territory, and violence began.

★ In the Dred Scott Case, the Supreme Court ruled that slaves were property no matter where they were taken.

★ Abolitionist John Brown's actions increased tensions between North and South.

★ The Democratic party split over slavery. The Republican platform opposed slavery and secession. Republican Presidential candidate Abraham Lincoln won in 1860.

★ Several southern states left the Union and formed the Confederate States of America in February 1861.

★ The Confederacy captured Fort Sumter, a Union fort, in April 1861. This capture began the Civil War.

★ Robert E. Lee led the Confederate Army. It won many early battles.

★ In 1863, Lincoln freed the slaves with the Emancipation Proclamation.

★ The worst battle was at Gettysburg in July 1863. The Union won. It became the turning point.

★ Lincoln was re-elected in 1864. Lee surrendered to Ulysses S. Grant on April 9, 1865.

★ Lincoln was assassinated on April 14, 1865.

★ The war ruined the South.

★ Congress set up the Freedmen's Bureau in 1865.

★ Amendment Fourteen gave formerly enslaved people equal protection under the law. Amendment Fifteen gave African-American men voting rights.

★ The Reconstruction Act of 1867 limited the South.

★ Grant became President in 1868. Rutherford B. Hayes became President in 1877, and ended Reconstruction.

"In after years, when I passed as an American among Americans, if I was suddenly made aware of the past that lay forgotten . . . suddenly reminded of what I might have been,—I thought it miracle enough that I, Mashke, the granddaughter of Raphael the Russian, born to a humble destiny, should be at home in an American metropolis, be free to fashion my own life, and should dream my dreams in English phrases."

–Mary Antin, *The Promised Land*, 1912

Development of Industrial America

1862–1900

America has been a land of frontiers. During the last part of the 1800s, America expanded on many frontiers. Settlers headed to the western frontier, claiming lands of American Indians and their ancestors. On the industrial frontier, huge and powerful industries developed. On the frontier of cities, populations grew at an astounding rate with millions of immigrants. And with all this growth came increasing numbers of new problems to solve.

In this unit you will learn about the western frontier and what happened to American Indians. You will learn about rapid growth of industries and inventions. You will learn how cities grew with waves of immigrants. You will learn about labor and political reforms resulting from the growth.

Chapter 18: Settling the Western Frontier: 1862–1890

Chapter 19: Becoming an Industrial Giant: 1870–1900

Chapter 20: A Nation of Cities: 1882–1900

Chapter 21: A New Spirit of Reform: 1872–1897

Settling the Western Frontier

1862–1890

The end of the Civil War turned more attention toward the West. The "last frontier," as it was called, was a land of freedom and adventure. It was a place where pioneers could find an opportunity for a better life. From 1862 to 1890, settlers took up the challenge to tame the nation's last frontier. In this chapter, you will learn how the United States expanded westward.

Goals for Learning

▶ To explain where in the West pioneers traveled and how they got there

▶ To describe why and how the transcontinental railroad was built

▶ To describe what kinds of people lived on the frontier and what life was like for them

▶ To explain the problems that occurred between the United States and the American Indians in the West

▶ To list the western lands that became part of the United States

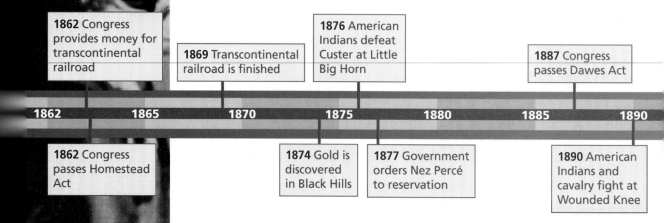

1862 Congress provides money for transcontinental railroad

1869 Transcontinental railroad is finished

1876 American Indians defeat Custer at Little Big Horn

1887 Congress passes Dawes Act

| 1862 | 1865 | 1870 | 1875 | 1880 | 1885 | 1890 |

1862 Congress passes Homestead Act

1874 Gold is discovered in Black Hills

1877 Government orders Nez Percé to reservation

1890 American Indians and cavalry fight at Wounded Knee

★**Stagecoach**
A horse-drawn coach that was used for transporting people or mail

Transcontinental
Extending across a continent

★**Wagon train**
A large number of wagons traveling together

The Great Plains was a vast stretch of land between the Missouri River and the Rocky Mountains. During the 1840s and 1850s, European settlers passed up this area on their way to the rich lands of Oregon and the gold in California. The flat, dry Great Plains seemed useless to them.

Beginning in 1858, many Americans traveled westward by **stagecoach** from St. Louis. A stagecoach is a horse-drawn coach that was used for transporting people or mail. St. Louis was the western end of the railroad at that time. The three-week journey over mountains and deserts was a difficult one. Travelers were under constant danger of attack by robbers or American Indians. American Indians often saw the settlers as invaders. At the same time, most shipments of supplies from the East traveled by long ox-drawn **wagon trains.** A wagon train is a large number of wagons traveling together. Communication improved in 1861, with the completion of the telegraph. The appeal of the western frontier grew stronger to many Americans in the East.

How Was the Transcontinental Railroad Built?

In 1862, Congress provided money for the construction of the **transcontinental** railroad. The time had come to link the far western parts of the country to the East. Two companies were chosen to build the railroad. The Central Pacific Railroad started in the West at Sacramento, California, and was built eastward. The Union Pacific Railroad started at Omaha, Nebraska, and was built westward.

European and Chinese immigrants were hired to build the transcontinental railroad.

Work on the railroad increased after the Civil War ended in 1865. The Union Pacific Railroad hired thousands of war veterans, many of whom were Irish. The work was hard and dangerous. Many workers were killed in accidents and American Indian raids. Because of difficult working conditions and the loss of workers, only a few miles of track were laid each day.

Chinese immigrants on the west coast worked for the Central Pacific Railroad. They worked very hard, and progress was very slow because the land was so mountainous. Tunnels had to be blasted. Sometimes it took all day to go just a few feet.

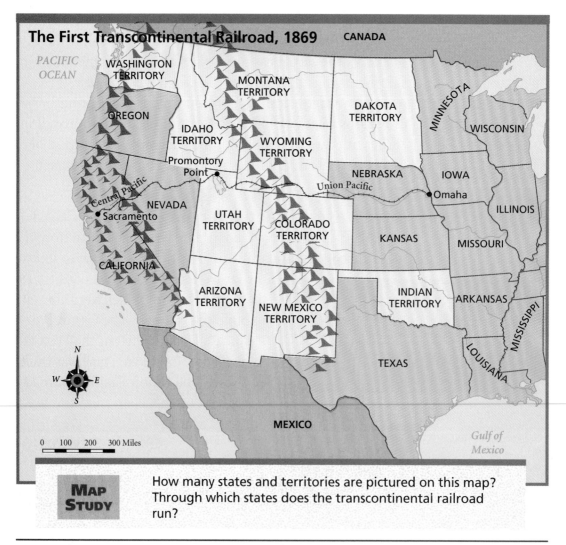

The First Transcontinental Railroad, 1869

MAP STUDY

How many states and territories are pictured on this map? Through which states does the transcontinental railroad run?

A chief of the friendly Chiricahua Apaches, Cochise was falsely accused of seizing a rancher's child in 1861. Cochise declared he was innocent, but the U.S. Army put him in prison. He escaped, and fighting followed. Thus the Apache Wars began. Cochise led his warriors on raids against American troops and European settlers. The raids nearly drove the settlers from Arizona. In 1871, General George Crook forced Cochise to surrender. With a peace treaty in 1872, the United States accepted Cochise's request to live peaceably on a reservation. He lived on the reservation along Apache Pass until his death in 1874.

(Cochise's picture was never taken for religious reasons. Therefore, no picture appears with his biography.)

In May of 1869, the two railroads met at Promontory Point, Utah. The Central Pacific Railroad had laid more than 700 miles of track. The Union Pacific laid more than 1,000 miles of track. A golden spike was driven into the final link of the track. The news of the completed transcontinental railroad went out on the telegraph to the country. Now, settling the Great Plains was more appealing to many Americans.

WORD BANK

Central Pacific

Great Plains

St. Louis

Union Pacific

Utah

SECTION 1 REVIEW On a separate sheet of paper write the word from the Word Bank to complete each sentence.

1) The _____ was land between the Missouri River and the Rocky Mountains.

2) The _____ Railroad started at Omaha, Nebraska, and was built westward.

3) The _____ Railroad started in the West at Sacramento, California, and was built eastward.

4) The Union Pacific and Central Pacific railroads met at Promontory Point, _____.

5) The western end of the railroad in 1858 was _____.

What do you think **?**

Why do you think many immigrants were willing to work on the railroad?

Cowhand
A person who tends cattle

★Prospector
A person who searches an area for gold, silver, or other minerals

Miners, farmers, and people who tended cattle, or **cowhands** as they were called, were important in settling the western frontier. These groups lived different lives and faced different problems. Each had its own interest in the frontier as they searched for gold, built cattle ranches, or claimed land for family farms.

How Did Mining Start in the West?

Gold was discovered near Pikes Peak, Colorado, just before the start of the Civil War. Silver and gold were found in Nevada. Miners and **prospectors** traveled many miles to these places. A prospector is a person who searches an area for gold, silver, or other minerals. During the 1860s, gold was also discovered in Montana, Idaho, and Wyoming. The mining boom felt throughout this Rocky Mountain region was similar in many ways to the California gold rush of 1849.

Most miners never became rich. Individual prospectors could not compete with the special equipment that large mining companies brought to the mountains. These machines were faster than the pick, pan, and shovel methods that individual miners used. Many of those who had traveled westward in search of gold settled down as farmers or ranchers. Others became loggers, taking advantage of the rich timber resources.

The lack of law and order in many mountain areas during this gold rush was similar to that in California in 1849. Many former miners grouped together to form city governments. They elected sheriffs to help provide them and their families with some law and order. As their lives became more civilized, the settlers in cities on the former frontier developed some pride in their new homes.

What Was Cattle Country?

Settlers in Texas discovered that large herds of longhorn cattle were running wild. This kind of cattle had been brought to America many years earlier by Spanish settlers. The Texans rounded up the cattle and raised the animals for beef, hides, and other goods. Texas became an important ranching area. Cattle were easy to raise in the grasslands of the Great Plains.

Ranchers wanted to bring their cattle to Chicago and many eastern cities. They could make more money if the cattle were sold in these areas. The ranchers' main problem was a lack of transportation. However, this problem was solved with the development of the railroad system. Then the grasslands were linked to America's major cities.

Ranchers Borrowed Mexican Ways

Cattle ranchers learned many of their ways of doing things from Mexican ranchers. Mexicans developed the western saddle with a special horn on the front for looping a rope. Cattle ranchers used the western saddle. Branding cattle was a Mexican way of ranching used before the American cowhand arrived. Branding is a way of marking cattle.

Cowhands guided cattle to the holding pens near railroads. Before moving the cattle, every calf was branded with the special mark of its owner. Some cattle were moved over 1,000 miles. The Chisholm Trail was a widely used route.

The herd traveled ten to fifteen miles a day. A cattle drive took more than two months. During that time cowhands usually spent as many as eighteen hours a day in the saddle. The cowhands' main jobs were to prevent a **stampede** and to protect the cattle from thieves. A stampede is a wild rush of cattle.

Cow towns were a welcome sight to tired cowhands. Cow towns had many **saloons** and gambling houses. A saloon was a public building where people gathered to drink or gamble. The only law in cow towns was provided by United States marshals such as Wild Bill Hickock. It was a difficult job, for a marshal had to cover a large territory. Law and order developed as the frontier became more settled.

Cowhands like these spent as many as eighteen hours per day in the saddle during cattle drives.

What Was the Homestead Act?

In 1862, Congress had passed the Homestead Act. This act made it very easy for pioneers to own land. Settlers were given 160 acres of land provided they agreed to live on it for five years. This offer brought many farmers, factory workers, and immigrants to the Great Plains.

What Problems Did Plains Farmers Face?

Pioneers who owned land under the Homestead Act were called **homesteaders.** These people faced difficulties that were unknown to the farmers east of the Mississippi River. Eastern farmers were used to good land, plentiful water, and good supplies of wood. The plains farmers found the ground hard to plow, and there was little rain. In many areas, trees for building materials and fuel could be found only on the riverbanks.

★**Homesteader**
A pioneer who owned land under the Homestead Act

★**Sod**
Thickly matted grass and roots

Farmers soon learned that **sod,** which is thickly matted grass and roots, could be used in place of wood as building material. Brick-like chunks of sod were cut from the ground. They were piled one on top of the other to build the walls of a house. Trees from riverbanks formed the roof, which was then covered with sod. A sod house kept a farm family cool in the summer and warm in the winter.

Barbed Wire

After the Civil War, pioneers moved rapidly into the West. Farmers claimed land and raised crops. Cowhands drove huge herds of cattle onto open range to graze. To keep cattle from trampling their crops, farmers needed practical fencing. In 1867, Lucien Smith patented an artificial thorn hedge. This was wire stretched between fence posts with short metal spikes, or barbs, twisted onto it. In 1868, Michael Kelly invented a twisted double-strand wire to hold barbs. In 1874, Illinois farmer Joseph Glidden improved the production process by locking the barbs into place. At first, the barbed wire did not prevent some problems. Cowhands cut farmers' fences so cattle could graze freely. Sometimes cowhands fenced off watering holes or barricaded a rival's cattle trails. The fences did keep cattle off railroad tracks, however, simplifying expansion of railroads to the West.

Industrial
Technology

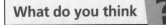
History in Your Life

There was enough water on the plains for farming, but it was underground. New inventions made it possible to drill deep wells into the Earth. Farmers then pumped water to the surface by using wind-powered devices called **windmills.** Farmers also used a dry farming method. Part of the land remained unplanted each year so that the area could absorb rainwater.

★Windmill
A wind-powered device used to pump water from a well

SECTION 2 REVIEW Write the answers to these questions on a separate sheet of paper using complete sentences.

1) What did many of the people who set out to search for gold end up doing?

2) Why did ranchers want to bring their cattle to Chicago and eastern cities?

3) What were cow towns like?

4) What was the Homestead Act?

5) How did farmers build their houses?

What do you think ❓

Do you think being a cowhand was really like it seems on television and in books? Why or why not?

The Cheyenne, Comanche, Blackfeet, and the seven tribes of the Sioux nations lived on the open plains. They were called the Plains Indians. Their way of life depended on the buffalo. The treatment of buffalo herds brought them into direct conflict with European settlers.

The Plains Indians were hunters and nomads. They followed the constantly moving buffalo herds. They ate the meat, used the hides for clothing and shelter, and made the bones into tools.

How Were American Indian Ways Destroyed?

Some army and government officials thought that killing the buffalo would force the American Indians to settle in one place. Farmers and ranchers wanted the buffalo out of their way. Others killed the buffalo so that they could sell the hides. Between 1865 and 1875, millions of buffalo were killed. William F. Cody got the name "Buffalo Bill" after he killed more than 4,000 buffalo in eighteen months.

Buffalo hides were very valuable for making high-quality leather products. Buffalo robes were popular in winter. By 1889, only 541 buffalo survived in the United States. As the buffalo herds disappeared, the American Indians lost their independence. They were forced to find another way to live.

Why Were American Indians Moved to Reservations?

The settlers and the U.S. government thought that the American Indians were in the path of progress. With little understanding of American Indians, government officials felt that the nations should settle in one place. The government signed treaties with the American Indians. According to these treaties, the American Indians would stay within certain boundaries. The remaining land would be used for the European settlers and railroads. In return, the government would teach the American Indians to

Lacrosse, a soccer-like sport, came from American-Indian ways. American Indians like this group of Sioux played the game.

★Reservation
Land set aside by the government for the American Indians

become farmers. Most nations, feeling that they had little choice, moved to a government **reservation.** A reservation is land set aside by the government for the American Indians. Some American Indians, however, chose to fight.

By the mid-1870s, after many battles and much bloodshed, most American Indians agreed to live on a reservation. These reservations were in New Mexico, Arizona, and the territories of Dakota and Wyoming. The government told the American Indians that their way of life would be protected.

What Happened When Gold Was Discovered?

The government's reservation policy was tested in 1874 when gold was discovered in the Black Hills of what is now South Dakota. This land was holy to the Sioux. They believed the Great Spirit was present in these hills. The United States government had promised that the Black Hills would belong to the Sioux forever.

Government troops tried to protect these hills for the American Indians, but the number of prospectors who wanted gold was too great. It was clear that the government could not keep its word. Chiefs Sitting Bull and Crazy Horse gathered more than 2,000 Sioux and Cheyenne warriors together. They decided to defend their lands.

Colonel George Armstrong Custer and his Seventh Cavalry met this force at the Little Big Horn River in Montana on June 25, 1876. Custer and about 210 members of his troops were killed. The only survivor was an officer's horse named Comanche.

Chief Joseph

The defeat of Custer shocked the country. The American Indians had won a great victory. However, Custer's Last Stand, as it was called, would be the last big victory for the Plains Indians. They eventually surrendered to government troops because of lack of food and ammunition.

Custer's defeat forced the government to move all American Indians onto reservations. In the summer of 1877, the government ordered the Nez Percé to a small reservation in Idaho. Settlers took their horses when the Nez Percé were leaving their homes. Angry warriors raided European settlers. The Nez Percé tried to escape to Canada to avoid any more bloodshed.

About 750 Nez Percé fled. Chief Joseph led them. They traveled 1,500 miles in seventy-five days. The weather was cold, and they did not have blankets. Little food was available. Many died along the way.

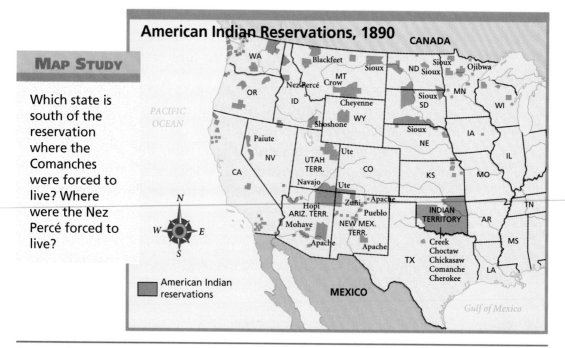

American Indian Reservations, 1890

MAP STUDY

Which state is south of the reservation where the Comanches were forced to live? Where were the Nez Percé forced to live?

American Indian reservations

Writing About History

Write a speech in your notebook as if you are an American Indian chief addressing your people. Talk about a problem your people face, such as being forced to live on a reservation or losing the buffalo herd.

Misunderstanding
Failure to understand

The Nez Percé were thirty miles from the Canadian border. Chief Joseph urged his people to surrender. He told them he was tired of fighting. "Hear me, my chiefs," he said, "I am tired; my heart is sick and sad. From where the sun now stands I will fight no more forever."

What Did Chief Red Cloud Do?

In 1870, Chief Red Cloud of the Oglala Sioux wanted to inform the government officials of the problems of the Plains Indians. He spoke at a meeting in Washington, D.C., and told the audience about broken treaties, dishonest government agents, fear, and **misunderstanding.** Red Cloud wanted the President of the United States, whom he called the Great White Father, to understand that he wanted peace.

SECTION 3 REVIEW Choose the best word or name in parentheses to complete each sentence. Write your answers on a separate sheet of paper.

1) (Colonel Custer, Buffalo Bill, Red Cloud) was defeated at Little Big Horn.

2) The Nez Percé were led by Chief (Sitting Bull, Joseph, Red Cloud).

3) In 1877, the U.S. government ordered the (Cheyenne, Sioux, Nez Percé) to a reservation.

4) Chief (Crazy Horse, Joseph, Red Cloud) spoke at a meeting in Washington, D.C.

5) Gold was discovered in (the Black Hills, Montana, Canada) in 1874.

What do you think ❓

What do you think Chief Joseph meant when he said, "I will fight no more forever"?

The American people became aware of what had happened to the American Indians living on the western frontier. In 1881, Helen Hunt Jackson published *A Century of Dishonor,* a detailed history of how the American Indians were mistreated. Her book was sent to every member of Congress.

Why Was the Dawes Act Passed?

Congress passed the Dawes Act in 1887. The purpose of the law was to turn the American Indians into independent farmers. Their lands were divided into family-size farms. Any American Indians who accepted land would be made citizens of the United States. They could not sell their land for twenty-five years. The Dawes Act attempted to protect the American Indians from being cheated. In many cases, however, the American Indians were cheated by land-hungry European settlers. In some cases, even government agents took advantage of them. It was not until 1924 that all American Indians were made citizens.

What Happened at Wounded Knee?

A religious movement known as the Ghost Dance developed in 1890. Some American Indians believed that performing this dance would protect them from soldiers' bullets, bring back the buffalo herds, remove settlers from their lands, and bring back their former way of life.

The Ghost Dance frightened the settlers. An army was sent to prevent violence. The Seventh Cavalry arrived to arrest and disarm several hundred Ghost Dance followers from different tribes at Wounded Knee, South Dakota, on December 28, 1890.

The Seventh Cavalry killed hundreds of Sioux on this site at Wounded Knee, South Dakota.

Western States Admitted to the Union, 1864–1912	
1864 Nevada	1890 Idaho
1867 Nebraska	1890 Wyoming
1876 Colorado	1896 Utah
1889 North Dakota	1907 Oklahoma
1889 South Dakota	1912 New Mexico
1889 Montana	1912 Arizona
1889 Washington	

The next day, the cavalry tried to disarm the Ghost Dance followers. Someone fired a shot. It is not known who fired. The soldiers turned their guns on the followers and killed or wounded about 290 men, women, and children. Twenty-five soldiers were also killed. This massacre at Wounded Knee ended the fighting between the United States government and the American Indians of the western plains.

Which Western Lands Became States?

People had moved into most areas of the western frontier. By 1890, for the first time in American history, there was no frontier line. The frontier had been conquered. Thirteen states were created from these vast western lands between 1864 and 1912.

SECTION 4 REVIEW On a separate sheet of paper write *True* if the statement is true or *False* if the statement is not true.

1) The purpose of the Dawes Act was to give back to American Indians their old way of living.

2) Some American Indians believed that the Ghost Dance would protect them from soldiers' bullets.

3) Ghost Dance followers killed or wounded 290 cavalry soldiers at Wounded Knee.

4) Thirteen states joined the Union between 1864 and 1912.

5) The frontier was conquered by 1890.

What do you think **?**

Why do you think the Ghost Dance was important to American Indian people?

"The Laws"

In the late 1800s, thousands immigrated to America from Europe and Asia. Chinese-American writer Maxine Hong Kingston has examined immigrants' right to belong in America. In her book China Men, *Kingston included laws against Chinese immigration.*

"The United States . . . and . . . China . . . recognize the . . . right of man to change his home and allegiance, and . . . the advantage of free . . . emigration of their citizens . . . from the one country to the other. . . . Article V of the Burlingame Treaty, signed in Washington, D.C., July 28, 1868. . . .

1868 . . . the year 40,000 miners of Chinese ancestry were Driven Out. The Fourteenth Amendment, adopted in that same year, said that naturalized Americans have the same rights as native-born Americans, but in 1870 the Nationality Act specified that only 'free white' and 'African aliens' were allowed to apply for naturalization. Chinese were not white. . . .

1878: California . . . prohibited Chinese from entering. . . . New state laws empowered cities . . . to confine them . . . or to throw them out. Shipowners . . . were to be fined for . . . transporting them. . . . [Chinese] were barred from attending public schools. The only California fishermen forced to pay fishing and shellfish taxes were the Chinese . . . they were prohibited from owning . . . real estate. They could not apply for business licenses. Employers could be fined . . . for hiring them. No Chinese could be hired by . . . governments. . . . No Chinese . . . could testify in court 'either for or against a white man' . . . . Federal courts declared some of the state and city laws unconstitutional. . . . The . . . laws were reenacted in another form.

1880: The Burlingame Treaty was modified . . . . the immigration of Chinese laborers to the United States would be 'reasonably limited.' In return . . . the American government promised to protect Chinese from lynchings.

1881: The Burlingame Treaty was suspended for . . . twenty years. . . . In protest . . . China ordered scholars studying in the United States to return home. . . ."

From: Maxine Hong Kingston, "The Laws," in *China Men*, 1980

Source Reading Wrap-Up

1) What did the Nationality Act of 1870 say?

2) How did the U.S. government offer to protect the Chinese?

3) The Burlingame Treaty was suspended for twenty years. How did the Chinese respond?

4) How did the United States never really abide by the original Burlingame Treaty?

5) Which do you think was the most unreasonable law or event in the passage? Why?

★ The Great Plains stretched between the Missouri River and the Rocky Mountains.

★ In 1862, Congress provided money for the transcontinental railroad. The railroad was finished in 1869. It was built by two companies—the Union Pacific Railroad and the Central Pacific Railroad.

★ Miners, farmers, and cowhands were the first Europeans to settle the West. Miners were drawn to gold discoveries in Nevada, Montana, Idaho, Wyoming, and Colorado. Cowhands and cattle ranchers raised cattle for beef, hides, and other goods. The Homestead Act of 1862 encouraged farmers and homesteaders to settle land in the West.

★ The Plains Indians were nomads. Their way of life was changed forever when farmers, ranchers, and others killed off the buffalo herd. Many American Indians were moved to reservations. The U.S. government promised American Indians that their way of life would be protected.

★ When gold was discovered in 1874 in the Black Hills, a holy land for the Sioux, the government's policy to protect the American Indians was tested. Gold prospectors wanted to make claims on the land.

★ Government troops tried but could not protect the Black Hills region for the American Indians. In the end, the American Indians chose to protect their land. Colonel Custer and about 210 members of the U.S. Cavalry fought and lost a battle against the Sioux and the Cheyenne at Little Big Horn in 1876.

★ Congress passed the Dawes Act in 1887. This act tried to protect American Indians. However, settlers still cheated American Indians.

★ In 1890, the Seventh Cavalry was sent to prevent violence between settlers and American Indians over the Ghost Dance. The soldiers ended up killing or wounding about 290 men, women, and children at Wounded Knee.

★ Thirteen states were added to the United States between 1864 and 1912.

Comprehension: Identifying Facts

On a separate sheet of paper, write the correct word or words from the Word Bank to complete the sentences.

WORD BANK		
Black Hills	Great Plains	Red Cloud
Central Pacific	Homestead Act	Union Pacific
Colonel Custer	Joseph	Wounded Knee
Dawes Act	Plains Indians	
Ghost Dance	prospector	

1) The _____ Railroad laid over 1,000 miles of railroad track.

2) Chinese immigrants worked for the _____ Railroad.

3) Gold discovered in the _____ region tested the government's reservation policy.

4) The _____ was land between the Missouri River and the Rocky Mountains.

5) The _____ had their way of life taken away when the buffalo were killed off.

6) The _____ was passed to turn the American Indians into farmers.

7) A _____ was a person who searched for gold, silver, or other minerals.

8) Chief _____ spoke at a meeting in Washington, D.C.

9) The _____ made it easier for pioneers to settle land.

10) Chief _____ urged his people to stop fighting.

11) Some American Indians believed in a religious movement known as the _____.

12) _____ was defeated at Little Big Horn.

13) U.S. soldiers killed or wounded about 290 men, women, and children at _____.

Comprehension: Understanding Main Ideas

On a separate sheet of paper, write the answers to the following questions using complete sentences.

1) Where in the West did pioneers travel? How did they get there?

2) Why was the transcontinental railroad built?

3) What three kinds of people lived on the frontier? What did each do?

4) How was the Plains Indians' way of life destroyed?

5) During what time period did many western states enter the Union? How many western states entered the Union during this time?

Critical Thinking: Write Your Opinion

1) What do you think would be a good title for a book describing what happened to the Plains Indians? Why?

2) Do you think you would have liked living on the frontier? Why or why not?

Test Taking Tip When you read test directions, try to restate them in your own words. Tell yourself what you are expected to do. That way, you can make sure your answer will be complete and correct.

19

1870–1900

In the early 1800s, most Americans were farmers or small shop owners. Manufacturing in small factories was done mostly in areas of the Northeast. During the Civil War, the need for war supplies, farm equipment, and machines of all types increased. Following the completion of the railroads after the war, the transportation of people and materials between the two coasts made manufacturing in all parts of the country easier. Tariffs on imports were making American-made products more valuable. As the population continued to grow, so did the demand for more and better products. Industry became common. In this chapter, you will learn more about how industry increased in the United States.

Goals for Learning

▶ To describe how Andrew Carnegie developed the steel industry

▶ To describe the development of the petroleum industry

▶ To explain the new ways in which businesses were organized

▶ To list new inventions that changed the world

1870 John D. Rockefeller starts Standard Oil Company of Ohio

1876 Thomas Edison starts lab in Menlo Park

1877 Thomas Edison invents phonograph

| 1870 | 1872 | 1874 | 1876 | 1878 | 1880 | 1882 | 1900 |

1873 Andrew Carnegie enters steel industry

1876 Alexander Graham Bell invents telephone

1883 Brooklyn Bridge opens

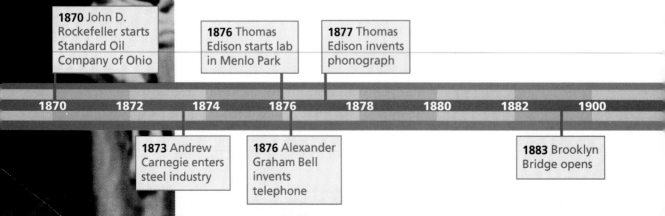

★Entrepreneur
A person who starts and organizes a business

Flexible
The ability to move or twist easily

Method
A way of doing something

★Petroleum
A liquid that can be made into fuel

Purify
To make something pure

People all over America began discovering and using the country's many natural resources—coal, iron, lumber, and **petroleum.** Petroleum is a liquid that can be made into fuel. As ways of doing things were improved and machines were invented, new industries were formed. A large flow of immigrants gave these industries an eager labor force.

Strong business leaders took part in American industries. Andrew Carnegie and John D. Rockefeller were **entrepreneurs.** An entrepreneur is a person who starts and organizes a business. They used the opportunities of this new industrial age. These men played an important part in starting the nation's steel and oil industries.

How Did Andrew Carnegie Develop the Steel Industry?

Andrew Carnegie

Andrew Carnegie realized that most bridges in the country were made from wood. One day he saw men building a bridge out of iron instead of wood. He organized the Keystone Bridge Company to build iron bridges for railroad companies.

Soon Carnegie realized that iron was not the best product with which to build bridges. Iron would rust, and it was not very strong. It cracked and broke when bent. He needed to find another material to make bridges. He knew steel, which is **purified** iron, was very strong and **flexible.** However, steel was very expensive to produce in large amounts.

Back in the 1850s, two men had developed an inexpensive way of making large amounts of steel. William Kelly, an American, discovered a **method** of making iron into steel. Meanwhile, in England, Henry Bessemer had developed a similar method. They had both discovered that the impurities in iron could be "burned off" by blowing cold air through heated iron.

While visiting England, Carnegie learned about how this method worked. He returned to America and entered the new steel industry in 1873. He built the first steel plant in the country close to Pittsburgh. Carnegie made steel for railroad tracks that cost half as much as iron tracks and were much stronger.

How Did Steel Become an Important Building Material?

Inexpensive steel rapidly changed America. The longest **suspension bridge** in the world at the time, the Brooklyn Bridge in New York, was opened in 1883. A suspension bridge is a large bridge supported by wires or chains attached to tall towers. It was a wonderful example of modern **engineering.** Tall buildings built on steel supports began to appear. They rose ten to twenty stories high. This height seemed so great that people called them **skyscrapers.** Soon steel was used to make such things as pins, nails, washtubs, and barbed wire for fences.

Agricultural and Industrial Workers

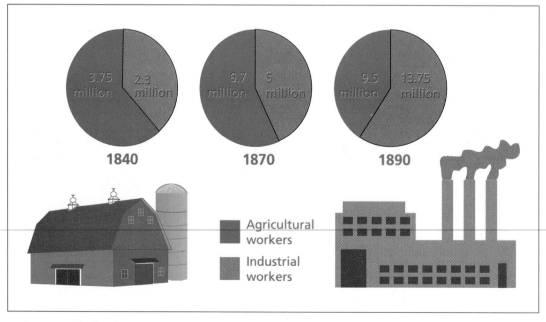

1840   1870   1890

3.75 million   2.3 million   6.7 million   5 million   9.5 million   13.75 million

Agricultural workers

Industrial workers

By how much did the number of industrial workers increase between 1840 and 1890? How many agricultural workers were there in 1870?

Carnegie's steel company produced most of the steel in the United States. He retired a very rich man in 1901. He was very generous with his money. Carnegie funded libraries, colleges, medical research, and many other projects. He gave away more than $350 million in his lifetime.

The Brooklyn Bridge

Until the 1880s, New Yorkers used a ferry to cross the East River from Manhattan to Brooklyn. In 1867, a bridge was designed and a company was chartered to build it. John A. Roebling, a pioneer in suspension bridge design, created the Brooklyn Bridge plan. He died before the bridge was built. Roebling's son, Washington, supervised construction, which began in 1869. When the bridge opened on May 24, 1883, it was hailed as the "eighth wonder of the world." With a main span of 1,595 feet, it was the world's longest bridge. It also was the first suspension bridge to use steel wire cables. Four main cables nearly sixteen inches thick are hung from two massive 275-foot granite towers. Foundations seventy-eight feet below water level support the towers. The bridge cost $15 million. In 1964, the Brooklyn Bridge was declared a national historic site. Its six traffic lanes and its sidewalks make crossing the East River easy.

Industrial Technology

History in Your Life

New York's Brooklyn Bridge opened in 1883. The bridge is a national historic site today.

The Pen Is Mightier Than the Sword

Thomas Nast proved that the pen is mightier than the sword. Nast was an inspired cartoonist. His cartoons in the magazine *Harper's Weekly* captured the best and the worst of America. He exposed the dishonest politicians in the Tweed Ring in New York City.

Nast created the symbols for the two major political parties. He drew donkeys to symbolize Democrats and elephants to represent Republicans.

Unfortunately, Nast also could be very cruel. He poked fun at Horace Greeley when Greeley was running for President in 1872. Nast's cartoons are thought to have had a lot to do with breaking Greeley's spirit. Some thought the cartoons also contributed to Greeley's mental breakdown and death.

Thomas Nast's self-portrait

WORD BANK
Andrew Carnegie
Brooklyn
entrepreneur
skyscraper
William Kelly

SECTION 1 REVIEW Complete the sentences below using words from the Word Bank. Write your answers on a separate sheet of paper.

1) An _____ is a person who organizes a business.

2) The longest suspension bridge in the world at the time it opened was the _____ Bridge.

3) A _____ is a tall building.

4) _____ built the first steel plant in the country.

5) _____ discovered a way to make iron into steel.

What do you think **?**

How is steel still important today?

Refinery
A place where a good is made pure or made into other products

A stream called Oil Creek flowed through the village of Titusville, near Pittsburgh, Pennsylvania. It was called Oil Creek because of the black, sticky oil that came up to the surface from below the ground. Most people believed that oil was not very valuable. Then, in 1855, a scientist reported that half of the petroleum or "rock oil" could be made into a product that could be burned in lamps.

Edwin Drake (right front) built this oil well in Titusville, Pennsylvania.

This report caught the attention of Edwin Drake, who traveled to the small village of Titusville. After one unsuccessful attempt, Drake drilled a hole in the ground using pipes to keep the sides from falling in. From sixty-nine feet in the earth, oil began running through the pipe in August 1859. This first oil well turned out to be the beginning of America's giant oil industry.

Soon, Titusville was filled with "oil prospectors" in search of "black gold." Oil wells appeared all along Oil Creek and areas of southwestern New York. Railroad tank cars and large pipes called pipelines were built to carry the oil to **refineries.** Oil was made into different products at these refineries. Titusville became a place where fortunes could be made overnight.

What Business Did Rockefeller Start?

John D. Rockefeller traveled from Cleveland, Ohio, to Titusville to see how he and his partners could make money from the new oil business. Rockefeller decided that he was not interested in drilling for oil because it was too risky. He believed that he could make more money refining it.

Rockefeller organized and became the president of a new company, the Standard Oil Company of Ohio, in 1870. Within ten years, the company became the most powerful company in its field. The company controlled the production and price of oil throughout the country.

In the early years, most oil was refined into a fuel called **kerosene** that was used for lamps. The need for these lamps ended in about 1900, when the electric light was invented. However, the widespread popularity of the motor car in the 1900s created a new use for an oil product—gasoline.

How Did Business Change?

Before the Civil War, most businesses were owned by one person or a group of partners. These businesses usually employed a few workers. They sold their goods to local customers. This simple organization worked well for small businesses. After the Civil War, as businesses grew larger, many organized into **corporations.** These are large, organized companies owned by shareholders.

Andrew Carnegie, John D. Rockefeller, and other business leaders were **criticized** for forming large companies. The critics believed that big businesses were too powerful. They felt it was impossible for smaller businesses to compete with them. Large corporations that have little competition are called **monopolies.** Without competition from other companies selling the same product, a monopoly can charge higher prices for poorer quality products. The buyer, with no other company to turn to, has little choice but to pay that price or do without the product.

★Corporation
A large, organized company owned by stockholders

Criticize
To show disapproval

★Kerosene
A fuel used in lamps

Monopoly
A corporation that has little competition

John D. Rockefeller

How Were Corporations Important to Business Growth?

Corporations are usually a safe form of business organization. Individuals invest money into corporations. They are protected if the corporation fails. A person who invests in a corporation has limited risk, or **liability,** for the company's debts.

Money used for investment is called **capital.** A corporation allows thousands of people to invest in a business by buying shares of stock. People who own stock can make money on their investment if the company is profitable. Modern corporations like Carnegie Steel and Standard Oil raised millions of dollars by selling stock.

How Did Companies Become Larger?

Business leaders searched for new ways to organize their companies. Andrew Carnegie did not want to depend on other companies to produce his product. He relied on mining and railroad companies. He found a new, simple solution. He bought mining and transportation companies and combined them into one large company. This allowed Andrew Carnegie to control each step in making steel. This type of new business organization became known as **vertical combination.**

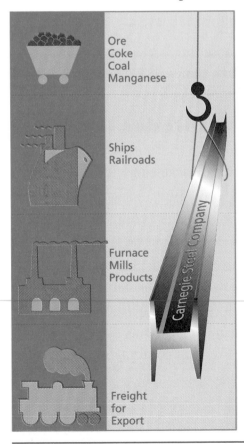

Ore
Coke
Coal
Manganese

Ships
Railroads

Furnace
Mills
Products

Carnegie Steel Company

Freight
for
Export

John D. Rockefeller was also concerned with control. He decided to get rid of competition by buying other oil refining companies. This type of organization is known as **horizontal combination.** Standard Oil Corporation became more powerful each time Rockefeller bought a new refinery.

Vertical combination allowed Carnegie to control each step in steel production.

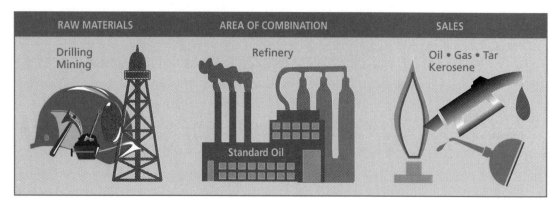

RAW MATERIALS	AREA OF COMBINATION	SALES
Drilling Mining	Refinery	Oil • Gas • Tar Kerosene
	Standard Oil	

Horizontal combination allowed Rockefeller to eliminate competition.

★Trust company
A large, powerful company that often is a monopoly

Each of these types of businesses took away competition. Carnegie Steel and Standard Oil became monopolies. They were called **trust companies.** Many kinds of trust companies developed. A trust company became a popular tool for businesses to increase their wealth. Sugar, copper, railroad, and tobacco companies were all controlled by monopolies or trusts. Trust companies could employ thousands of workers. They became giant industries that were very powerful. This changed America into an industrial nation.

SECTION 2 REVIEW Choose the best word or name in parentheses to complete each sentence. Write your answers on a separate sheet of paper.

1) The first oil well was built in (Cleveland, Titusville, Ohio).

2) (Andrew Carnegie, John D. Rockefeller, Edwin Drake) organized Standard Oil Company.

3) A (monopoly, liability, refinery) is a company that has little competition.

4) A kind of business organization that controls each step in making something is called a (trust company, horizontal combination, vertical combination).

5) A large, powerful company that often is a monopoly is called a (trust company, vertical combination, liability).

What do you think ❓

How is oil still important today?

By-product
Something produced in the process of making something else

Slaughter
To kill animals for food and other products

As the railroads were built across the nation, they helped provide the key to the success of cattle ranching. The ranchers shipped their cattle to large midwestern cities such as Chicago. In these cities, the meat-packing industry, as developed by Philip Armour, Gustavus Swift, and Nelson Morris, began to do well in the late 1890s. Cattle and hogs were **slaughtered** for meats and meat **by-products.** These products were transported to all parts of the country in refrigerated railroad cars.

Cornelius Vanderbilt

Leaders in the construction of new railroad lines in the late 1800s included Cornelius Vanderbilt and James J. Hill. Vanderbilt linked a number of short railroads in the Northeast, creating America's first great railroad system—the New York Central. His system was the first to use steel rails, steel bridges, and double tracks. James J. Hill, who became known as "The Empire Builder," developed the Great Northern Railway System to the Northwest. He encouraged immigrants to settle in that region by teaching them the newest farming methods. He founded schools and helped to start businesses that could provide different types of employment and services.

How Did Inventions Change American Society?

Americans have always been proud of their ability to invent new machines and tools. This sense of pride was never higher than after the Civil War. These were exciting years for American inventors. Some of the most important inventions used in America today were produced during this time. Many were made by Thomas Alva Edison.

Edison was known as "The Wizard of Menlo Park." A wizard is someone who is supposed to have magical powers. Edison, who never claimed to have any special powers, said his success was due to hard work.

Thomas Edison invented the phonograph.

In 1876, Edison started a research laboratory in Menlo Park, New Jersey. He brought scientists, engineers, machinists, and even clock makers together in this one place. He organized them into a team to produce things that businesses and the public could use. Edison said that his "invention factory" could turn out a minor invention every ten days and a major one every six months.

The indoor electric lightbulb was one of Edison's finest inventions. For several years, outdoor electric lights had been used in a few cities. Up until Edison's time, however, oil and gas lamps provided the only indoor lighting. After searching for two years, Edison found the solution for safe indoor electric lighting.

George Washington Carver and Booker T. Washington

The work of an African-American scientist named George Washington Carver changed farming in the South. Carver was born near the end of the Civil War. His family was enslaved. He graduated from Iowa State Agricultural College in 1894. Booker T. Washington, an African-American leader, asked Carver to join the Tuskegee Institute in Alabama two years later. At Tuskegee, Carver developed many new products from pecans, peanuts, and sweet potatoes. Because of his work, southern farmers had other cash crops to grow besides cotton.

Booker T. Washington, a son of formerly enslaved people, became a teacher and an important leader for African Americans. He started the Tuskegee Institute to train African Americans in farming, mechanics, and trades for the industrial workplace. Washington raised large amounts of money for African-American organizations, stressing his belief that African Americans should gain better jobs before seeking political and social rights. Many African-American leaders did not agree with his opinions.

The first words **reproduced** by a machine were "Mary had a little lamb." Edison spoke this line from a children's poem into his **phonograph** in 1877. Phonographs were used to reproduce sound. His improvements to Alexander Graham Bell's telephone allowed people to speak naturally instead of shouting as was necessary with Bell's early telephone. Edison invented a successful motion picture machine. He later added sound by joining it with his phonograph.

What Were Other Important Inventions?

Many important inventions came out of the 1870s and 1880s. Bell invented the telephone in 1876. George Eastman simplified the Kodak camera in 1880 so that more people could take photographs. Lewis Waterman perfected the fountain pen in 1884. Ottmar Mergenthaler invented a machine in 1884 that would make **typesetting** much easier for newspaper and book publishers all over the country. Typesetting is the method used to prepare type to be printed. Elisha Otis invented the elevator, which made the construction of skyscrapers more appealing. The first electric elevator was installed in 1889.

Alexander Graham Bell made the first long-distance call with his telephone in 1893.

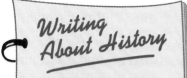

Writing About History

Research an invention that was developed between 1870 and 1900. Then write a paragraph in your notebook describing what it is used for and how it works.

Other inventors followed. Henry Ford experimented with gasoline-powered automobile engines. He developed an assembly line method for building cars cheaply. Shortly into the next century, Ford would make it possible for the average American to own an automobile.

Each of these inventors did more than create a new machine. Each invention created a new industry. These industries created new jobs for the American worker and a brighter future for the country.

Then and Now

How do you think the Wright brothers' airplane compares with a modern jet? It was the Wrights who completed the first successful flight. Look at this table to compare the two planes.

Description	Wrights' Flyer	A Boeing 747
Materials	Wood and cloth	Metal
Weight	750 pounds	775,000 pounds
Wing span	40.5 feet	196 feet
Length	21 feet	231 feet
Flight distance	120 feet	6,000 miles
Time in flight	12 seconds	15 hours
Altitude	40 feet	40,000 feet
Passengers held	1 person	400 people
Speed capacity	30 mph	600+ mph
Power source	Two propellers	Turbojet engine
Fuel storage	Less than 1 gallon	47,000 gallons

HORATIO ALGER: 1834–1899

Horatio Alger wrote more than 100 books about poor young boys who became rich and successful through honesty and hard work. His popular "rags-to-riches" stories were meant to inspire and teach young people. He also wanted to educate adults about the horrible conditions in which some children lived. An activist, Alger helped to inspire new laws against child labor. Alger disappointed his father —a Unitarian minister—when he abandoned a career as a minister and became a writer. Alger moved to New York City where he befriended many homeless orphan children. The children had come to the city after the Civil War. He often based characters in his books on children he knew.

SECTION 3 REVIEW On a separate sheet of paper, write *True* if the statement is true or *False* if the statement is not true.

1) Cornelius Vanderbilt linked a number of short railroads in the Northeast.

2) Edison invented the automobile.

3) One of Edison's first inventions was the indoor electric lightbulb.

4) A phonograph was used to take pictures.

5) Henry Ford began experimenting on gasoline engines.

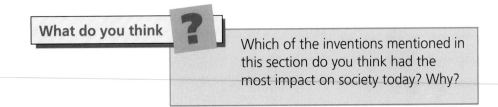

What do you think **?**

Which of the inventions mentioned in this section do you think had the most impact on society today? Why?

Queen Liliuokalani's Statement on Hawaii

With the help of U.S. marines, American business leaders attempted to take over the government of Hawaii in 1891. Queen Liliuokalani of Hawaii was unwilling to surrender the government. Still she did not want to see any battle. She issued this statement to American authorities.

"I, Liliuokalani, by the Grace of God and under the Constitution of the Kingdom, Queen, do hereby solemnly protest against any and all acts done against myself and the constitutional Government of Hawaiian Kingdom by certain persons claiming to have established a provisional government of and for this Kingdom.

That I yield to the superior force of the United States of America, whose minister, His Excellency John L. Stevens, has caused the United States troops to be landed at Honolulu and declared that he would support the said provisional government.

Now, to avoid any collision of armed forces and perhaps the loss of life, I do under this protest, and impelled by said force, yield my authority until such time as the Government of the United States shall, upon the facts being presented to it, undo the action of its representatives and reinstate me in the authority which I claim as the constitutional sovereign of the Hawaiian Islands."

From: W. D. Alexander, *History of the Later Years of the Hawaiian Monarchy*, 1896, first edition, pages 43–44.

Source Reading Wrap-Up

1) What did Queen Liliuokalani say the business leaders had established?

2) What did John L. Stevens do and say about the Hawaiian situation?

3) Why was Queen Liliuokalani giving up control of Hawaii?

4) For how long was she giving up control of Hawaii?

5) Do you think that Queen Liliuokalani's response was a wise one? Why or why not?

CHAPTER SUMMARY

★ In the second half of the 1800s, the United States began to develop new industries. Before this time, most Americans were farmers or shopkeepers.

★ Andrew Carnegie began a business that built iron bridges. Carnegie found an inexpensive method of converting iron into steel.

★ Carnegie dominated the steel industry. He became a very wealthy man and contributed to many charities.

★ Edwin Drake drilled the first oil well near Titusville, Pennsylvania. "Black gold" brought many people to Titusville to search for their fortunes.

★ John D. Rockefeller formed a corporation, the Standard Oil Company of Ohio, to refine crude petroleum into usable oil. Rockefeller's company became the most powerful in the oil business.

★ Early oil companies refined kerosene for lamps. Later they produced gasoline to be used in cars.

★ After the Civil War, companies became much larger. Large companies called corporations were started. They were owned by many investors who bought stock in the corporation and earned money from their investments.

★ Carnegie bought mining and railroad companies and combined them into one large corporation. Rockefeller tried to eliminate competition by buying other oil refining companies. These large companies were monopolies since they had little competition.

★ Cornelius Vanderbilt and James J. Hill made fortunes by constructing and running railroad systems. Railroads were important for the meat-packing industry.

★ Many inventions changed peoples' lives during this period. The inventions included Thomas Edison's indoor electric lightbulb and phonograph, Alexander Graham Bell's telephone, George Eastman's Kodak camera, and Henry Ford's gasoline-powered engines.

Comprehension: Identifying Facts

On a separate sheet of paper, write the words from the Word Bank to complete each sentence.

WORD BANK	
Andrew Carnegie	phonograph
"The Empire Builder"	railroads
engine	Standard Oil Company
George Eastman	steel
meat-packing	stock
monopoly	Titusville
Natural resources	

1) James J. Hill built the Great Northern Railway System and was known as _____.

2) _____ gave millions of dollars to fund libraries, colleges, and medical research.

3) Henry Ford helped develop a gasoline powered _____ that would later be used in automobiles.

4) _____ simplified the Kodak camera, making it possible for thousands of people to take photographs.

5) Railroads helped people like Philip Armour and Gustavus Swift develop the _____ industry.

6) A large company or corporation that has little or no competition is called a _____.

7) _____ such as coal, iron, and petroleum helped the United States to become an industrial giant.

8) Thomas Edison recited "Mary had a little lamb" on the _____, one of his inventions.

9) Cornelius Vanderbilt made his fortune building _____.

10) Rockefeller's _____ refined crude petroleum into oil and kerosene.

11) _____ is stronger and more flexible than iron.

12) Large corporations are owned by many investors who buy shares of _____.

13) "Black Gold" brought many people to _____ to seek their fortunes.

Comprehension: Understanding Main Ideas

On a separate sheet of paper, write the answer to each question using complete sentences.

1) How did Andrew Carnegie's steel company become so successful?

2) How did James J. Hill bring people to the Northwest?

3) How is a corporation organized?

4) What was Rockefeller's contribution to the oil industry?

5) How did Edison create so many inventions at his Menlo Park laboratory?

Critical Thinking: Write Your Opinion

1) What are some of the problems with becoming an industrial society?

2) Oil is one of the most highly used natural resources today. How do you think the world would be a different place today without oil?

| Test Taking Tip | Effective studying takes place over a period of time. Spend time studying new material for several days or weeks before a test. Don't try to learn new material the night before a test. |

A Nation of Cities

1882–1900

A s industry grew in the United States, so did the nation's cities. Immigrant groups and other people began to live in cities because they wanted to be close to factories. Though city life had much to offer, people living in cities faced tough working and living conditions. Many people faced discrimination. In this chapter, you will learn what it was like to live in the nation's cities.

Goals for Learning

▶ To describe working conditions in factories

▶ To explain the reasons for different immigrant groups coming to the United States

▶ To explain how immigrants and African Americans faced discrimination

▶ To describe some of the developments that made city living interesting

▶ To explain why cities had social problems

1882 Congress passes law to keep Chinese from entering America

1884 France gives America the Statue of Liberty

1890 Jacob Riis writes articles about slum housing

1882

1889

1896

1883 Supreme Court rules Civil Rights Act unconstitutional

1890 Dumbbell tenements appear in New York City

1896 Supreme Court rules "separate but equal" facilities constitutional

Dweller
Inhabitant

Specialize
To make and sell goods or services in one or two areas of business

By 1850, more than twenty-three million people lived in the United States. Twenty million of them lived on farms, in towns, and in areas smaller than towns called villages. Three and a half million (or fifteen percent) of the American people lived in cities. By 1900, this percentage of city **dwellers** had increased to forty percent.

People were drawn to cities for many reasons. Cities had exciting events. Cities had many different things to do and places to go. The main reason people moved to cities was because they could find jobs. American industry grew as more and more factories were opened in or near cities. Factories were usually built near railroad lines or a good seaport. Large factories needed many workers.

American cities usually **specialized** in one or two industries. Pittsburgh, Pennsylvania, became the nation's center for making steel. Cleveland, Ohio, became an important oil-refining city. Chicago, Illinois, grew because of the meat-packing business. Other cities like Salt Lake City, Kansas City, and San Francisco grew with the arrival of the railroad.

Railroads were a good way to move products and people from one end of the country to the other. Cities were no longer isolated from one another. Raw materials and products in one city could be shipped easily and cheaply to other cities around the nation.

Growth of Urban Population 1870–1900

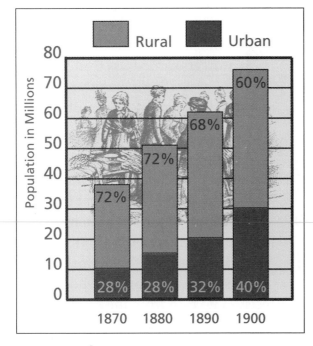

Population in Millions

Rural   Urban

- 72% (1870, Rural) / 28% (1870, Urban)
- 72% (1880, Rural) / 28% (1880, Urban)
- 68% (1890, Rural) / 32% (1890, Urban)
- 60% (1900, Rural) / 40% (1900, Urban)

1870   1880   1890   1900

ROSE SCHNEIDERMAN: 1884–1972

Rose Schneiderman was a women's labor organizer and activist. She was born in Russian Poland into a poor Orthodox Jewish family. In 1890, she came to the United States and settled in New York's Lower East Side. At age thirteen, she began working as a salesclerk. Schneiderman often worked seventy hours a week for just over $2. She organized the first women's branch of the Jewish Socialist Hat and Cap Makers' Union. She devoted much of her life to the Women's Trade Union League. Schneiderman organized garment workers' strikes and sought laws to protect the eight-hour workday and the minimum wage.

Employer
A person or company who hires someone

How Were American Workers Treated?

America's new industries needed workers. Large factories and industrial plants employed hundreds or even thousands of workers. Mass production lowered the cost of products. The success of one industry usually led to new, similar industries. Each new industry created more jobs.

Workers like these often worked long hours in poor working conditions.

Competition for these jobs was great. **Employers** did not have to pay high salaries because so many workers were available. Many workers earned less than $10.00 for a sixty-hour workweek, including only one day off.

Poor working conditions were also a problem. Powerful machines were dangerous. Most employers believed that it was the workers' responsibility to protect themselves from dangerous or unsafe working conditions. Workers who were hurt on the job received no help from the employer. Many children also worked in the factories.

floors. Later they removed lint or mended broken thread. Barefoot boys under age ten climbed onto running machines. They removed empty bobbins of thread and replaced them with filled bobbins. Child laborers worked twelve to fifteen hours a day every day but Sunday. They made only a few cents a day.

Today, U.S. laws prohibit employers from hiring children under sixteen years. However, child labor still exists in some Third World countries. Until age sixteen, American children are required to attend school. If you have a job, your working conditions are a lot different from those in the nineteenth century.

If you were a child in the nineteenth century, you might have had to work. No laws restricted child labor at the end of the nineteenth century. Some poor children did not go to school and instead went to work. Children as young as seven or eight years helped to make cloth in textile mills. They started by sweeping

Then and Now

SECTION 1 REVIEW On a separate sheet of paper, write *True* if the statement is true or *False* if the statement is not true.

1) Fewer than thirteen million people were living in the United States in 1850.

2) The main reason people moved to cities was to find jobs.

3) American cities usually specialized in one or two industries.

4) Workers received high wages for their work.

5) Employers believed it was the workers' responsibility to protect themselves from unsafe working conditions.

What do you think ?

Many children were forced to work in factories. Why was this unfair?

Advertise
To announce publicly

★Steerage
A part of a ship for passengers paying the lowest fare

The Statue of Liberty, an 1884 gift to the United States from France, stands in the harbor of New York City. The huge copper lady, holding a golden torch high above her head, provided a first look at America for millions of immigrants. They had come to America seeking liberty, jobs, and an opportunity for a better life.

Getting to the United States was very difficult for most immigrants. A ticket on a steamship often cost an immigrant family all of their savings. Most immigrants bought a ticket in **steerage.** Steerage was the lowest fare. Its passengers had to ride in the dirtiest and noisiest part of the ship far belowdecks near the engines. The conditions were unhealthy in steerage. The air was stale, and the area was crowded. There was little food, and people often became ill. Immigrants were willing to put up with the conditions to get to America.

Most of the immigrants before the 1880s came from England, Ireland, Germany, Sweden, and Norway. These people were known as "old immigrants." During the 1880s, more than one-half million "new immigrants" came from Italy, Russia, Poland, and Greece.

Immigrants came to the United States for many reasons. Many were farmers. Others came to America to escape laws that were unfair. Some came for religious freedom. Almost half of the people who came from Poland and Russia were Jewish.

The Homestead Act of 1862 offered cheap, fertile land to immigrants. American railroad companies **advertised** in Europe to attract immigrants to the American West. However, by the time most immigrants arrived in America, the best land had already been taken. Unable to move on to the western farmlands, most immigrants stayed in America's eastern and midwestern cities.

The first thing many immigrants to America saw was the Statue of Liberty.

What Problems Did Immigrants Face?

Few immigrants could speak English. Many were very poor. They had to work hard jobs. Men paved or cleaned streets. Many helped build new skyscrapers. Women found work in clothing factories.

Immigrants from Asia had settled on the west coast, yet many were denied jobs. Much of the hard work on the transcontinental railroad had been done by the Chinese. In 1882, Congress passed a law saying that no more Chinese could come to the United States.

The largest group of new immigrants came from Italy. Most of the immigrants were men. They planned to work in America for only a few years. They hoped to save their money and then return home to Italy and their families. Jewish immigrants from eastern Europe were the next largest group. Many left Europe to escape religious **prejudice.** Prejudice is a belief or action against someone because of race, sex, religion, or age. Unlike the Italians, Jewish immigrants from Russia and Poland did not plan to return to their homeland. Entire families of Jewish people had moved to America.

★Prejudice
A belief or action against someone because of race, sex, religion, or age

Some Americans did not like the new immigrants. They feared that immigrants might take jobs that Americans could have, or work at a lower wage. They disliked dealing with people who were not comfortable speaking the English language. Unfortunately, too many people had forgotten that many of their American ancestors had come to the United States as immigrants, too.

What Other Groups Faced Discrimination?

Immigrants were not the only people to experience **discrimination** at this time. Discrimination is treating people unfairly because of their race, sex, religion, or age. **Jim Crow Laws** were passed in the 1880s and 1890s. These laws separated African Americans and whites in public places. Signs saying "White Ladies Only" and drinking containers marked "White Water" and "Colored Water" began to appear in restaurants, theaters, and railroad cars. The goal of segregation was to develop "separate but equal" African American and white communities. They achieved the goal of separating the races, but African Americans were not treated equally.

★Discrimination
Treating people unfairly because of their race, sex, religion, or age

★Jim Crow Laws
Laws that separated African Americans and whites in public places

The only hope of ending Jim Crow Laws was the United States Supreme Court. Many people felt the laws were unconstitutional. The Civil Rights Act of 1875 made segregation in public places against the law. However, in 1883, the Supreme Court said the Civil Rights Act was unconstitutional. This cleared the way for more laws against African Americans. The court further ruled that the Fourteenth Amendment applied only to state governments and not to the actions of individuals. Therefore, store owners, railroad companies, and other private businesses could discriminate against African Americans or anyone else.

What Was Plessy v. Ferguson?

Louisiana passed a law in 1890 requiring railroad companies to provide "separate but equal facilities" for African American and

white passengers. Homer Plessy tested this law in 1892. This African American refused to move from the "white only" car in which he was riding. Plessy's purpose was to challenge the "separate but equal" law. He was arrested and brought before a judge named Ferguson. Plessy was found guilty.

Plessy appealed his case to the United States Supreme Court. He argued that the Louisiana law was unconstitutional. He said the Fourteenth Amendment forbids state laws that discriminate against African Americans. The Supreme Court disagreed. In 1896, the Supreme Court upheld the Louisiana law and wrote that "separate but equal" facilities were constitutional. This was a major setback for African Americans and their struggle for equal treatment before the law. This law stood until the Supreme Court overturned the Plessy ruling in 1954 when segregation in public schools was determined to be unconstitutional.

SECTION 2 REVIEW Choose the correct word in parentheses to complete each sentence. Write your answers on a separate sheet of paper.

1) The Statue of Liberty was a gift from (Sweden, France, Ireland).

2) Immigrants after the 1880s were called (old immigrants, new immigrants).

3) The largest group of new immigrants came from (Italy, Ireland, Germany).

4) Jim Crow Laws segregated (African Americans, immigrants, American Indians) from white people.

5) (Discrimination, Steerage) is treating people unfairly because of their race, sex, religion, or age.

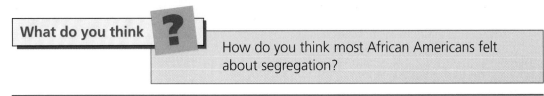

What do you think **?**

How do you think most African Americans felt about segregation?

Leisure
Something that is done for amusement

Retail
Relating to buying and selling of goods

★Streetcar
A horse-drawn or electric carriage that rides on rails and is used for transportation

★Trolley
A carriage that rides on rails and is used for transportation

Most cities provided **leisure** and entertainment. Theaters, roller skating rinks, and dance and music halls became popular. **Retail** areas included convenient stores, restaurants, and service shops. Public libraries offered all people the opportunity to escape their cares and read.

What Forms of Transportation Improved City Life?

People traveled around the city by foot or in private coaches until horse-drawn **trolleys** were invented. The trolleys carried ten to fifteen people. Horses pulled the trolleys along steel rails set into the street. These early "buses" were first used in Europe. Americans called them **streetcars.**

Transportation was improved when Thomas Edison invented a system for sending electricity in the early 1880s. The electric motor made the electric streetcar possible. Electric streetcars carried up to forty-five people. They received electricity from overhead wires. Electric streetcars were faster than trolleys.

In the late nineteenth century, streetcars helped people get around the city. The streetcars ran on rails and were pulled by horses.

Streetcar routes affected the way a city grew. Streetcar routes fanned out from the center of the city like the spokes of a wheel. Housing and businesses developed along these routes. Streetcars ran on a time schedule and were inexpensive to ride. Workers could live several miles from where they worked. Streetcars allowed people to travel easily around the city.

How Did Department Stores Begin?

At first, stores were small and specialized in a few products. Shoppers went from one store to another. Business owners later thought of putting all of these small stores into one building. It was called a department store. The new department store had hundreds of goods in one large building. Department stores became very popular. Soon every major American city had at least one department store.

F. W. Woolworth created a department store that sold a variety of products for a **fixed price.** A fixed price is a price that stays the same—there is no debate over the price. Most of the products sold in his store cost no more than five or ten cents. Woolworth's "Five and Ten Cents" store became very popular with people who had a limited **income.** He eventually built the Woolworth Building in New York City. It was the tallest building in the world for a time.

What Other Leisure Activities Were Popular?

Cities became centers for the arts. Pittsburgh, Philadelphia, Chicago, and New York built opera houses and started symphony orchestras. New museums collected paintings and sculptures. Americans could listen to the music of the great composers and see works of art from around the world.

This picture is part of a stereoscope of the Woolworth Building. A stereoscope had two pictures taken a little way apart. This made the photo look more real.

Edison's "Talking Machine"

"Mary had a little lamb" were the first words ever recorded. When Thomas Edison first heard his own voice, he was startled. He had been experimenting with a "talking machine" by using a metal cylinder with a spiral groove on it. He placed a piece of tin foil around the cylinder and casually recited the old nursery line. He had invented the first phonograph record!

The phonograph immediately became a great curiosity. Many people bought them. Prices started at $25—a lot of money at the turn of the twentieth century. A large megaphone increased the sound from the cylinder. All phonographs had to be wound by hand. There were no plug-in varieties. Later, the flat disk was invented, and cylinders became out of date.

After World War I, the phonograph industry boomed. This lasted about fifteen years, and then the bottom dropped out of phonograph sales. Radio had taken its place. Jazz was the first music to be recorded. This is the basis for the 1920s being named the Jazz Age.

Sporting events also became popular. Professional sports teams were developed. Baseball became the nation's first **spectator** sport. The National League was organized in 1876. However, baseball was a summer sport. In 1891, James Naismith of Springfield, Massachusetts, created a new indoor winter sport known as "basketball."

Spectator
One who watches an event

SECTION 3 REVIEW Write answers to these questions on a separate sheet of paper using complete sentences.

1) What forms of transportation were used in cities?

2) What was the purpose of department stores?

3) What is a fixed price?

4) What kinds of places promoted the arts in cities?

5) Which spectator sports were started at this time?

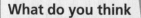

What do you think

Why do you think spectator sports were and still are important for American cities?

★**Dumbbell tenements**
Five- or six-story brick buildings that were shaped like dumbbells

Sanitation
The act of disposing of waste and keeping areas clean

★**Slum**
Area that has poor living conditions

★**Tenement**
Five- or six-story building designed to house eight to ten families

Although America's growing cities were exciting places to live, they did have many problems. Most cities had grown rapidly. Housing and **sanitation** were not very good. Living conditions became worse as more people moved into the cities.

In an attempt to create more housing, landlords in Philadelphia, Boston, and New York built special kinds of housing. They were called **tenements.** Tenements were often five- or six-story buildings. They were designed to house eight to ten families. Many people lived in the small apartments in these buildings.

By 1890, **dumbbell tenements** appeared in New York City. As many as thirty-two families lived in these five- or six-story brick buildings that were shaped like dumbbells. They were miserable places to live. People began to call these and other poor areas **slums.**

Immigrant families like this often lived in tenements. Tenements were often crowded and noisy.

The American Red Cross

Clara Barton was a volunteer nurse during the Civil War. Later she learned that the International Red Cross had been founded in Europe. She hoped to gain U.S. participation in international care of the sick and wounded during wartime. Thus, she promoted U.S. Red Cross membership at the Geneva Convention in 1864. Largely through her efforts, the United States was admitted in 1882. With friends, Barton organized the American Red Cross in 1881. She introduced its practice of providing disaster relief during peacetime. Today the American Red Cross is a private, voluntary organization with headquarters in Washington, D.C. Its nearly 3,000 local chapters focus on emergency relief and promoting public health. The chapters collect blood from donors. In emergencies, countless Americans have received blood through the Red Cross. Where disaster strikes, Red Cross volunteers help.

Health

History in Your Life

In 1890, Jacob Riis, a New York newspaper reporter, began to write articles about the lives of people living in "slum housing." His book, *How the Other Half Lives,* told the story of the lives of new immigrant families. He described buildings with dark halls that served as playgrounds for children in winter. Many tenements did not have good **ventilation.** The air was stale in the winter and very hot in the summer. Because of the large numbers of people living so close together, the buildings were very noisy. Worst of all, most of these buildings had poorly built fire escapes, which made them dangerous places to live.

Ventilation
The process of circulating fresh air in an enclosed area

How Were Cities Governed?

City governments were not prepared to deal with problems with slums. Before the Civil War, people living in cities needed few services from the government. They got their water from a city spring or private well. Volunteer fire companies provided fire protection. People disposed of their own garbage. However, in the cities a different kind of organization was needed. City governments needed a lot of practice to successfully manage large communities.

★Urban
Related to the city

City, or **urban,** problems increased during the 1880s. City officials did not know how to deal with them. Little was known about the people who lived in slums. People believed that those living in slums were poor because they had no skills or they were lazy. Religious leaders began to question this belief. They knew that something had to be done to improve the living conditions. Many religious groups were set up to help the urban poor. Examples are the Salvation Army, the Young Men's Christian Association (YMCA), and Young Women's Christian Association (YWCA).

WORD BANK

City officials

slums

tenement

urban

YMCA

SECTION 4 REVIEW On a separate sheet of paper, write the word or phrase from the Word Bank to complete each sentence.

1) A _____ is a five- or six-story building that houses eight to ten families.

2) The _____ was set up to help the urban poor.

3) Areas with poor living conditions were called _____.

4) If something is related to the city or city life, it is _____.

5) _____ did not know how to solve city problems in the 1880s.

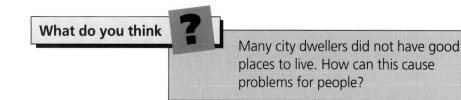

What do you think ?

Many city dwellers did not have good places to live. How can this cause problems for people?

Blanche Bruce's Speech to the Senate

Born into an enslaved family in Virginia, Blanche Bruce received his early education from his owner's son. During the Civil War, he left his master and opened a school for African Americans in Missouri. In the early years of Reconstruction, he held various Mississippi state offices. He was elected to the U.S. Senate in 1874. The passage below is from a speech Bruce made to the Senate in 1876.

"We want peace and good order at the South; but it can only come by the fullest resignation of the rights of all classes. The opposition must concede the necessity of change, not only in the temper but in the philosophy of their party organization and management. The sober American judgment must obtain in the South as elsewhere in the republic, that the only distinctions upon which parties can be safely organized and in harmony with our institutions are differences of opinions relative to policies and principles of government, and that differences of religion, nationality, or race can neither with safety nor propriety be permitted for a moment to enter into the party contests of the day.

The unanimity with which the colored voters act with a party is not referable to any race prejudice on their part. On the contrary, they invite the political cooperation of their white brethren, and vote as a unit because proscribed as such. They deprecate the establishment of the color line by the opposition, not only because the act is unwise and wrong in principle but because it isolates them from the white men of the South, and forces them, in sheer self-protection and against their inclination, to act seemingly upon the basis of a race prejudice that they neither respect nor entertain. . . .

When we can entertain opinions and select party affiliations without proscriptions, and cast our ballots as other citizens and without jeopardy to person or privilege, we can safely afford to be governed by the considerations that ordinarily determine the political action of American citizens."

Source Reading Wrap-Up

1) According to Senator Bruce, what things should determine a person's political party affiliation?

2) In the second paragraph, Senator Bruce refers to a color line established by the "opposition." Who were the opposition?

3) Why did Bruce say African Americans disapproved of the color line?

4) Senator Bruce suggests that African Americans were being encouraged to show prejudice. How?

5) Do you think Senator Bruce was speaking more to African Americans or to European Americans? Explain your reason.

★ Between 1850 and 1900, the population in cities grew from fifteen percent to forty percent.

★ Many people moved to cities to find work in industry and manufacturing.

★ Working conditions in most factories were poor. Workers were paid low wages for long hours of work. Employers showed little respect for the safety of their workers.

★ In 1884, France gave the Statue of Liberty as a gift to the United States. It was placed in New York's harbor, where it welcomed millions of immigrants.

★ In the second half of the 1800s, a majority of the immigrants came from Italy, Russia, Poland, and Greece.

★ Some immigrants came to seek their fortunes. Others, such as Jewish immigrants from eastern Europe, came to find religious freedom.

★ Many immigrants faced prejudice because they had different customs, languages, and religious values.

★ As cities grew, new developments helped people live better lives. Public transportation systems helped people get around. Department stores offered many different items in one location. Museums, concert halls, and sporting events provided leisure activities.

★ Because cities grew so rapidly, there was not enough housing. Lack of sanitation became a major problem.

★ Most city governments were not able to deal with the problems, so religious organizations such as the YMCA, YWCA, and Salvation Army were set up to help the poor.

Comprehension: Identifying Facts

On a separate sheet of paper, write the words from the Word Bank to complete each sentence.

WORD BANK	
department stores	sanitation
mass production	Statue of Liberty
meat-packing	steerage
oil-refining	streetcars
Poland	wages
prejudice	Working conditions
safety	

1) _____ in most factories were very bad because of long hours, poor air quality, and dangerous machines.

2) Workers would receive as little as $6.00 in _____ for a sixty-hour week of back-breaking work.

3) Public transportation often took the form of _____ pulled by horses and later powered by electricity.

4) Immigrant families traveled to the United States in the _____ of steamships.

5) Cities had poor _____, which caused health problems for everyone.

6) Many employers were not concerned with _____, because they believed it was the workers' problem.

7) Immigrants with different customs and who could not speak English were usually met with _____.

8) Many Jewish families from _____ came to the United States to escape religious persecution.

9) Cleveland, Ohio, became known as a center for the _____ industry.

10) The _____ industry was centered in Chicago, Illinois.

11) Large quantities of items were made in factories using a process known as _____.

12) The _____ was a gift from France.

13) F. W. Woolworth founded one of the first _____ in the country.

Comprehension: Understanding Main Ideas

On a separate sheet of paper, write the answer to each question using complete sentences.

1) What are two reasons immigrants came to the United States?

2) What problems did African Americans face?

3) Why were city governments unable to deal with the problems that population growth created?

4) Why were tenement buildings needed?

5) What was the advantage of shopping at a department store?

Critical Thinking: Write Your Opinion

1) If you had been living in Europe in the late 1800s, would you have immigrated to the United States? Why or why not?

2) Compare life in cities today with life in cities in the 1890s. How is it the same? How is it different?

| Test Taking Tip | When studying for a test, use the titles and subtitles in the chapter to help you recall the information. |

1872–1897

During the late 1800s, the United States was a modern nation filled with opportunity. The changes at this time improved the lives of many Americans. As communication, transportation, industry, and science advanced, so did American citizens. But problems remained. There was still political corruption. Working conditions remained poor. Beginning in the 1870s, people began to do something about these problems. In this chapter, you will learn how the nation worked on these reforms.

Goals for Learning

▶ To explain why reforms were needed

▶ To describe the major reforms that occurred during the period

▶ To explain how labor unions helped workers

▶ To explain the purpose of the Sherman Anti-Trust Act

▶ To describe the Populist movement

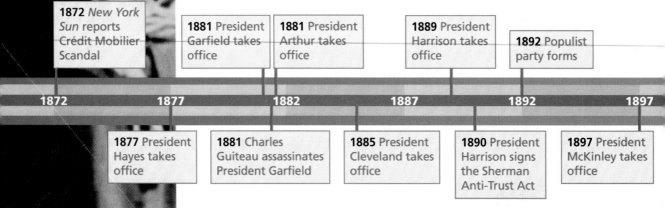

1872 *New York Sun* reports Crédit Mobilier Scandal

1881 President Garfield takes office

1881 President Arthur takes office

1889 President Harrison takes office

1892 Populist party forms

| 1872 | 1877 | 1882 | 1887 | 1892 | 1897 |

1877 President Hayes takes office

1881 Charles Guiteau assassinates President Garfield

1885 President Cleveland takes office

1890 President Harrison signs the Sherman Anti-Trust Act

1897 President McKinley takes office

Contract
A work agreement between at least two groups

★Gilded
Covered with a thin coating of gold

★Reform
A change intended to make something better

Author Mark Twain called the 1870s the "Gilded Age." He thought that American society was like a **gilded** piece of metal. Something that is gilded is covered with a thin coating of gold. Gilding covers up the original object. Twain thought many poor and powerless Americans were hidden under the control of the nation's wealthy few.

Many average American workers, certain that industrial America was hurting them, wanted change. A new spirit of **reform** began. Reform is a change intended to make something better. The people leading reform movements thought that many industrial leaders had corrupted the national and local governments for their own gain. They were becoming rich while common people suffered.

What Was the Crédit Mobilier Scandal?

The *New York Sun* newspaper published an article about the Union Pacific Railroad in 1872. The Union Pacific was one of the companies that helped build the transcontinental railroad. The article accused Union Pacific officials of making money illegally from the government through a construction company called Crédit Mobilier of America. Union Pacific had purchased the Crédit Mobilier Company. Then it gave the company **contracts** to lay railroad tracks for the federal government. Union Pacific overpaid Crédit Mobilier $50 million for laying the tracks. This way the company's records looked successful and the stock became very valuable.

RESIGNATION UNDER TRYING CIRCUMSTANCES.

President Grant thinks how it would be if all the corrupt people quit at once.

People began to question the relationship between Union Pacific and Crédit Mobilier. The head of the company, Oakes Ames, was also a congressman. He gave company stock to members of Congress to try to prevent them from **investigating**. However, Congress still investigated and found that many politicians took part in the scandal. Even Schuyler Colfax, the Vice President of the United States, was part of it. A congressional committee suggested that Ames be removed from the House of Representatives. However, he remained.

Investigate
To look into something to solve a problem or to answer a question

Grant's Struggle

General Grant won many battles during the Civil War and faced tough struggles while he was President. His most courageous battle came nine years after he left the White House. Grant was financially ruined in 1884 by a business partner who mismanaged their company. Though seriously ill, Grant wanted to give his wife financial security before he died. He worked for a year to write *Personal Memoirs of U.S. Grant*. One week after he had finished it, Grant died. The 1,231-page book sold more than 300,000 copies and earned $500,000. Ulysses S. Grant had won the last battle of his life.

Grant's administration was full of corruption in addition to the Crédit Mobilier Scandal. Grant had appointed many corrupt people to government jobs. Secretary of War William Belknap made money by cheating American Indians living on reservations. Members of the Treasury Department had received illegal payments from the whiskey companies who wanted to avoid paying tax. Even President Grant's personal secretary was in on this Whiskey Ring Scandal, as it was called. The President, without knowing it, allowed people to make millions off the government.

SECTION 1 REVIEW Write the answers to these questions on a separate sheet of paper using complete sentences.

1) What is reform?

2) What was Crédit Mobilier?

3) How did Crédit Mobilier make its money illegally?

4) What government officials were part of the Crédit Mobilier Scandal?

5) How was William Belknap corrupt?

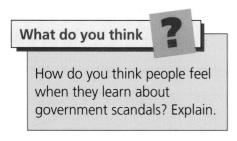

What do you think

How do you think people feel when they learn about government scandals? Explain.

★Political boss
A professional politician who controls a party or a political machine

Bribe
Payment to someone to make the person act in a certain way

★Civil service
A system in which people qualify for government jobs by passing a test

★Mugwump
A reform group that wanted to replace the spoils system with civil service

Corruption was not limited to the federal government. **Political bosses** affected many city governments. These men pretended to befriend immigrants. They offered help to poor city neighborhoods. They provided clothing, heating fuel, and food. Often they would set up social events to become known and liked among city neighborhoods. In return, they expected the people to vote for the candidates they supported.

Who Was Boss Tweed?

William Marcy Tweed was a powerful boss in New York City. Boss Tweed, as he was called, controlled a Democratic political organization known as Tammany Hall. Tweed and his friends stole millions of dollars from the city. For example, the city of New York paid one of Tweed's friends $179,729 for thirty to forty chairs and three or four tables.

This kind of behavior made reformers angry. Newspaper stories criticized the corruption. Tweed was not concerned about the stories. He thought his supporters could not read. Tweed overlooked the power of newspaper cartoons that Thomas Nast drew. Nast pictured Tweed as a crook. Nast's cartoons eventually frightened Tweed. The public's opinion of Tweed was changing. Tweed offered Nast $500,000 to leave the country for Europe. Nast refused the **bribe.** Boss Tweed was arrested for political corruption in 1871 and convicted in 1873. He died in jail in New York City.

What Did the Mugwumps Stand For?

Reformers in the Republican party criticized the spoils system, under which friends of politicians were given government positions. These reformers were called **Mugwumps.** The name came from an American Indian word meaning "chief." Mugwumps wanted to replace the spoils systems with **civil service.** Under civil service, people had to qualify for government jobs by passing a test.

Rutherford B. Hayes was elected President in 1876. The Mugwumps were disappointed that Hayes won. President Hayes surprised the reformers by investigating corruption when he took office in 1877. He found hundreds of federal workers were being paid without doing any work. He fired the people responsible and saved the country over $1 million a year.

How Did the Spoils System End?

Four years later in 1881, James Garfield became President. The new President found himself in the middle of a political fight between two Republican groups. Each group wanted Garfield to give its members government jobs. Charles

Guiteau shot President Garfield at a train station. Guiteau was angry because he did not get a government job. Garfield died three months later from the gunshot wound.

Vice President Chester A. Arthur became President after Garfield's death. President Arthur convinced Congress to pass civil service laws.

Charles Guiteau (left) killed President Garfield in 1881.

The laws made sure government jobs went to qualified people. They also prevented government workers from being fired for political reasons.

What Happened in the Election of 1884?

The Republican party did not nominate Chester A. Arthur for a second term as President. President Arthur had made many political enemies because he promoted civil service laws. The Republicans nominated James G. Blaine instead. He was the leader of a group who wanted the President to appoint friends to government jobs. The Democrats nominated New York Governor Grover Cleveland. He ran an honest campaign and would not make deals with political bosses.

Your bicycle in 1876 would have been the Ordinary. (above)

Maybe your bicycle today is one of the popular mountain bikes. (above)

You probably would have ridden the Safety bicycle in 1880 when it was invented. (left)

The campaign was rough. The Mugwumps and the Republican reformers worked to get Cleveland elected President. He won the election by about 60,000 votes. Cleveland took office in 1885.

What Happened During President Cleveland's Term?

Like the former President, Cleveland faced difficulties dealing with people who believed in the spoils system. He agreed with the Mugwumps that people should be appointed to government positions based on their skills. His appointments angered many former supporters who had expected jobs in his administration.

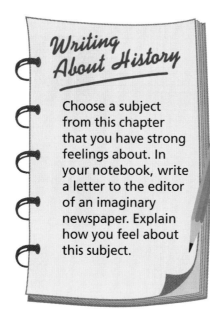

Writing About History

Choose a subject from this chapter that you have strong feelings about. In your notebook, write a letter to the editor of an imaginary newspaper. Explain how you feel about this subject.

During Cleveland's term in office, many in the federal government tried to change the way the nation's powerful railroad companies did business. These companies did not want the government to regulate their business. However, in 1887, Congress passed the Interstate Commerce Act. This law forced the railroads crossing state lines to charge customers the same fees for the same services.

In the election of 1888, President Cleveland lost to the Republican candidate, Benjamin Harrison. Harrison took office in 1889. Grover Cleveland was elected again in 1892.

SECTION 2 REVIEW On a separate sheet of paper write the word from the Word Bank to complete each sentence.

1) A reform group that wanted to replace the spoils system with civil service was called the _____.

2) A _____ is a professional politician who controls a party or a political machine.

3) _____ was arrested in 1873 for political corruption.

4) Mugwumps wanted to start _____.

5) _____ did not believe in the spoils system.

WORD BANK

political boss

Boss Tweed

civil service

Grover Cleveland

Mugwumps

What do you think ❓

Do you think civil service is fair? Why or why not?

> ★Labor union
> *An organized group of workers that seeks reforms in the workplace*

The belief in a need for reform spread beyond ridding the government of corruption. The treatment of American workers had become a growing concern. Labor leaders attempted to organize workers into groups as powerful as the big business corporations. These groups were called **labor unions.**

How Did Labor Unions Begin?

In 1869, Uriah Stevens formed the Noble Order of the Knights of Labor. This secret organization remained small until 1878 when Terrence V. Powderly became its leader. Powderly ended the secrecy and opened the union to all workers who wanted to join. Under Powderly, the union grew rapidly. Within seven years, the number of members increased from less than 50,000 to over 700,000.

A second labor union, the American Federation of Labor, began in 1886. Under Samuel Gompers's leadership, this union wanted to organize groups of skilled workers. Each different trade such as carpentry or bricklaying would have its own small union within the larger American Federation of Labor.

The two organizations were different in other ways. The Knights of Labor was interested in improving wages and working conditions. It planned to give free land to farmers. It wanted to open its own factories in which workers could share in the profits. The American Federation of Labor, on the other hand, worked mostly on labor problems. It stressed the need for an eight-hour workday, safer working conditions, and higher pay.

Samuel Gompers

★Anarchist
A person or group against all forms of government

★Strike
A kind of protest in which union workers refuse to work until their demands are met

★Strikebreaker
A nonunion worker used to replace striking union workers

How Did Labor Unions Use Strikes?

Both labor unions agreed that the most effective tool for improving conditions was the **strike.** To strike a company means that union workers refuse to work until their demands are met. Without its workers, a company would lose money. Successful strikes were not easy at first. Companies fought back. Sometimes they would not allow striking workers to return to work. The company hired nonunion workers to replace striking workers. These nonunion workers were called **strikebreakers.** Often fights broke out between the strikers and strikebreakers. Police were often called to stop fights.

A violent strike in Chicago destroyed the Knights of Labor. Seeking an eight-hour workday, almost 80,000 workers went on strike. When fights broke out on the street, police tried to break them up. Police gunfire killed several workers. A group of **anarchists,** who were against all forms of government, met at Haymarket Square to protest the workers' deaths. Someone threw a bomb that killed a policeman and one civilian. The public blamed the deaths on the Knights of Labor. Membership for the Knights of Labor decreased after the bombing.

The Chicago police (at left) fired at workers during the Haymarket Square protest.

A social worker and reformer, Jane Addams was committed to the relief of poverty in cities. In 1889, she founded Hull House, a settlement house in Chicago. Hull House offered wide-ranging services and programs to meet the needs of poor immigrants of various backgrounds. It had about forty clubs, a day nursery, a gym, a playground, and a place to give out medicine. It also had an art gallery, a theater, a music school, and classes in cooking and sewing. Addams pressured the government for various reforms. Among them were laws to protect working women, child-labor laws, and the first juvenile court. She was against war and led the fight to give women voting rights. In 1931, she was awarded the Nobel Peace Prize.

SECTION 3 REVIEW Choose the best word or name in parentheses to complete each sentence. Write your answers on a separate sheet of paper.

1) A(n) (labor union, anarchist, strikebreaker) is an organized group of workers that seeks reforms in the workplace.

2) The (American Federation of Labor, Knights of Labor) planned to give free land to farmers.

3) The (American Federation of Labor, Knights of Labor) worked mostly on labor problems.

4) (Uriah Stevens, Terrence V. Powderly, Samuel Gompers) led the American Federation of Labor.

5) A (strikebreaker, strike, labor union) is a kind of protest in which union workers refuse to work until their demands are met.

What do you think ?

What problems do you think strikers and businesses face during a strike?

Reformers had become concerned about the power of giant industries. In many cases, large companies were forcing smaller ones out of business. Small businesses were organized into trust companies. Trust companies could take away competition. The trust company became a popular way for businesses to increase their wealth. They could charge higher prices if they did not have any competition. Trusts were established in the railroad, steel, copper, sugar, coal, and meat-packing industries.

A small group of businessmen controlled large industries. Reformers believed that giving so much power to a few business leaders harmed the country. They felt the average American could not fight these powerful businesses.

How Did Congress Try to Limit Trust Companies?

Congress passed laws to correct the problem of trust companies. The Interstate Commerce Commission (ICC) was created to regulate railroads. In 1890, President Benjamin Harrison signed the Sherman Anti-Trust Act into law. This law made it illegal for large companies to form monopolies. The laws were unsuccessful. The Sherman Anti-Trust Act was used more often to **prosecute** unions on strike than against businesses. To prosecute means to charge with a crime. This outcome was the opposite of what Congress had intended.

★Prosecute
To charge with a crime

What Did the Populist Party Stand For?

The spirit of reform created a new political party called the People's or Populist party. The party, organized in 1892, represented the average American. The Populist party thought that American democracy was in danger of being destroyed by a few powerful businesses.

Farmers supported the Populist party. In the presidential election of 1892, James Weaver, the Populist candidate, received over a million votes. The Republican party began to worry about the growing power of the Populists.

How Did the 1896 Election End the Populist Party?

During the 1896 presidential campaign, the Populist party proposed many changes for the government, including the following:

1. There would be a graduated income tax plan. Taxes would increase as a person's income increased.

2. The public would own the railroad, telegraph, and telephone companies.

3. Senators would be elected by the people, not chosen by state legislatures.

4. The government would make more money available. It was hoped this would raise prices on farm products and help the economy.

The Populists thought the best way to increase the money supply was to make silver coins again. Most business owners felt only gold should be used as money. Businesses wanted to limit the supply of money to keep prices low and make it easier for big corporations to do business. President Cleveland agreed with the business owners.

Looking Backward: America in the Year 2000

In 1888, Edward Bellamy published his novel *Looking Backward*. In the novel, a man is transported through time to the year 2000. He finds that America is now run by a great trust company. All citizens attend school until they are twenty-one years of age. Then they work in the great "industrial army" until they retire. No one receives any wages in the year 2000. Everyone has an equal share of the wealth; everyone has the finest of everything.

The President of the United States is no longer elected by the vote of the people.

A group of retired, respected workers from the industrial army chooses the President. Congress passes few laws. There are no state or local governments.

Bellamy's novel was very popular. Many people treated the book as a good plan for the future. The book did have some political influence. In 1892, a Nationalist party was formed to try to achieve Bellamy's idea. This party soon joined the Populist party of factory workers and farmers who wanted to make changes in American society.

*Gold standard
A system in which gold backs a nation's money supply

In the 1896 presidential election, the Republicans nominated William McKinley, who had little concern for reforms. He supported the **gold standard.** The gold standard is a system that backs the nation's supply of money with gold. The Democratic party was split. President Cleveland wanted the gold standard. Democrats from the West and the South wanted to use silver.

William Jennings Bryan, a Democrat from Nebraska, was asked to speak at his party's convention. Bryan felt that the gold standard helped only big business. It hurt American farmers, factory workers, and small business owners. Bryan said that the supporters of the gold standard could not win because "you shall not press down upon the brow of labor this crown of thorns; you shall not crucify mankind upon a cross of gold."

One cartoon of the time called William Jennings Bryan the "Populist Paul Revere."

Bryan's "cross of gold" speech won him the Democratic nomination for President. The Populist party nominated him, too. The young man was running for President as the candidate of two political parties. He campaigned around the country. He traveled more than 18,000 miles and gave more than 600 speeches. No one before him had ever campaigned for President this way.

Popular Vote for 1896 Election

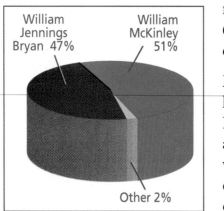

William Jennings Bryan 47%

William McKinley 51%

Other 2%

McKinley, on the other hand, remained in his home state of Ohio and rarely gave speeches. Railroad companies and banks gave large amounts of money to his campaign. Campaign workers gave out buttons and posters. These efforts worked, because McKinley won the election. He took office in 1897.

The Works of Emily Dickinson

Emily Dickinson had a reputation in Amherst, Massachusetts, as being strange for years before she died in 1886. She rarely left her house. Some said she always dressed entirely in white. After her death, friends found 1,776 poems hidden in a drawer. Dickinson had written and neatly stitched the poems into little handmade booklets. She namelessly published only seven of the poems during her lifetime. Her family allowed all of them to be published after she died. Dickinson came to be thought of as one of America's greatest poets. She had an unusual brief and symbolic style. Her poems were about such topics as death, love, and faith in God. While Dickinson traveled little, her imagination seemed to span the globe. Today millions of people have read her poems. Poets like William Carlos Williams and Adrienne Rich credited Dickinson with having a major influence on their work.

Literature
History in Your Life

The Populist movement ended with the defeat of Bryan. The spirit of reform did not end. A new group of reformers called the Progressives were middle class, well-educated people from cities. Some were Democrats. Others were Republicans. They too wanted to make changes in American society.

SECTION 4 REVIEW On a separate sheet of paper, write *True* if the statement is true or *False* if the statement is not true.

1) Small businesses were organized into trust companies to increase the companies' wealth.

2) The Sherman Anti-Trust Act made it legal for large companies to prevent others from doing business.

3) The Populist party thought that a few powerful businesses could destroy American democracy.

4) Three political parties nominated William Jennings Bryan for President.

5) William Jennings Bryan lost the election of 1896.

What do you think ❓

Why do you think so many political parties come and go as the Populist party did?

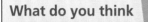

Declaration of Woman's Christian Temperance Union

A small group of Ohio women began The Woman's Christian Temperance Union (WCTU) in 1874. By 1890, membership had grown to 150,000 nationwide. The group's focus was the legal forbidding of alcoholic beverages. These people claimed alcohol was the root of many of America's problems at the turn of the century. This passage is taken from their Declaration of 1902.

"We therefore formulate and, for ourselves, adopt the following pledge, asking our sisters and brothers of a common danger and a common hope to make common cause with us in working its reasonable and helpful precepts into the practice of everyday life:

I hereby solemnly promise, God helping me, to abstain from all distilled, fermented, and malt liquors, including wine, beer, and cider, and to employ proper means to discourage the use of and traffic in the same.

To confront and enforce the rationale of this pledge, we declare our purpose to educate the young; to form a better public sentiment; to reform so far as possible, by religious, ethical, and scientific means, the drinking classes; to seek the transforming power of Divine Grace for ourselves and all for whom we work, that they and we may willfully transcend no law of pure and wholesome living; and finally we pledge ourselves to labor and to pray that all of these principles . . . may be worked out into the customs of society and the laws of the land."

Source Reading Wrap-Up

1) Women began the Woman's Christian Temperance Union. Who else besides women does the first paragraph ask for help in their cause?

2) What, if any, attempt is in this statement to make using alcohol illegal?

3) What was one purpose stated in the declaration?

4) The writers said in the last paragraph they would like to form a "better public sentiment." What do you think they meant?

5) How effective do you think the WCTU's methods were in convincing people not to drink alcohol?

CHAPTER SUMMARY

★ In 1872, the Union Pacific Railroad was found to be taking money from the government illegally. Many of the people who profited were members of Congress and business leaders. This was called the Crédit Mobilier Scandal.

★ Corruption was found in federal, state, and city governments while Ulyssess S. Grant was President.

★ William Marcy Tweed, known as Boss Tweed, controlled an organization that stole millions of dollars from New York City's government. Thomas Nast drew political cartoons that exposed Boss Tweed. Nast's cartoons helped bring Tweed to justice.

★ The Mugwumps were a group of reformers in the Republican party. They wanted to replace the spoils system with civil service.

★ Presidents Hayes, Garfield, and Arthur all worked to reform the way government jobs were performed. The civil service laws were finally passed while Arthur was President.

★ During President Cleveland's first term, the government began to regulate major industries such as the railroads.

★ The Interstate Commerce Act was passed in 1887. It regulated the way railroads could charge their customers.

★ Labor unions began to change the way workers were treated. Two of the first labor unions were the Noble Order of the Knights of Labor and the American Federation of Labor.

★ The Knights of Labor pushed for higher wages and improved working conditions. The American Federation of Labor represented skilled trades and focused on labor relations.

★ Unions used strikes as a way of improving working conditions. Many strikes turned violent.

★ The Sherman Anti-Trust Act was signed in 1890. It was created to help control monopolies. The act was not successful. The outcome was the opposite of what Congress had intended.

★ The Populist party was formed to represent the average American instead of big business. The Populists proposed many changes in the government.

Comprehension: Identifying Facts

On a separate sheet of paper, write the words from the Word Bank to complete each sentence.

WORD BANK	
American Federation of Labor	Mugwumps
Boss Tweed	Sherman Anti-Trust Act
Chester A. Arthur	strike
civil service	Thomas Nast
Crédit Mobilier	Whiskey Ring
Interstate Commerce Act	William Jennings Bryan
Knights of Labor	

1) Union Pacific Railroad was involved in the _____ Scandal.

2) _____ and his people stole millions of dollars from New York City.

3) The _____ laws required that people be qualified before they could hold a government job.

4) Samuel Gompers was one of the early leaders of the _____.

5) The _____ was one of the first laws to limit or regulate big business in America.

6) The _____ was an early labor union.

7) The _____ was a law to limit large business monopolies.

8) When labor unions wanted to change the way workers were treated, they would _____ the company.

9) The political cartoons of _____ helped put Boss Tweed in jail.

10) A group called the _____ believed that people should be appointed to government positions because of their skills.

11) The _____ was a major scandal of President Grant's administration involving even Grant's secretary.

12) _____ was the presidential candidate of the Populists.

13) Politicians did not like President _____ because he tried to do away with the spoils system.

Comprehension: Understanding Main Ideas

On a separate sheet of paper, write the answer to each question using complete sentences.

1) Why did the Knights of Labor lose members after the Haymarket Square bombing?

2) What were the main ideas of the Populist party?

3) Why was the civil service system important?

4) What was the purpose of labor unions?

Critical Thinking: Write Your Opinion

1) What is something that you would reform about the current government? Explain your answer.

2) If you could form a political party, what would be three of the things your party would stand for?

3) Do you think that large companies need to be regulated by the federal government? Why or why not?

Test Taking Tip Read test questions carefully to identify those questions that require more than one answer.

Reference materials are sources for finding different kinds of information. Here are some examples of reference materials and the kind of information you can find in them:

General information almanac: Book of recent and historic facts and figures about many subjects

Atlas: Book of maps of countries, states, and some cities

Encyclopedia: One book or a set of books with summaries and histories of many different subjects

Gazetteer: Dictionary of geographic place names and information

Newspaper: Daily or weekly publication with national, local, sports, and business news and regular features

Periodical index: Listing of magazine articles by subject and the publication in which they appear

Internet: Worldwide computer network with information on a wide variety of subjects. Includes on-line encyclopedias, newspapers, and periodicals

You could probably find the answers to all of these questions somewhere on the Internet. Name at least one other source listed above that you could use to answer these questions.

1) Where could you find the Vice Presidents who served between 1865 and 1900?

2) The Homestead Act of 1862 opened much western land to settlers. It did not, however, open land in Oklahoma, which was Indian Territory. On what date could settlers stake claims in Oklahoma?

3) In what year did Thomas Edison invent a safe indoor lightbulb?

4) What was the name of the first professional baseball team? In what year was the team formed?

5) There is a current dispute over fishing and hunting rights for an American Indian tribe in Minnesota. The Nelson Act of 1889 and 1890 took away rights originally granted in a treaty made in 1837. Where would you find the latest developments on this issue?

6) Where could you see a map of Montana with an enlargement of Great Falls?

7) Where would you find information about the Detroit River?

8) Where might you find an article about current methods of refining crude oil?

9) Where could you find last night's sports results for your local teams?

10) You can't remember where you recently read an article about public education in the 1870s. Where could you find the name and issue of the publication in which it appeared?

★ The Union Pacific and Central Pacific railroads finished the transcontinental railroad in 1869.

★ Miners, farmers, cowhands, and homesteaders settled the West.

★ Many American Indians were moved to reservations. The government promised but was unable to protect their way of life.

★ Thirteen states were added between 1864 and 1912.

★ In the second half of the 1800s, new industries began to develop. Andrew Carnegie found a method of converting iron into steel. Edwin Drake drilled the first oil well. John D. Rockefeller's Standard Oil Company of Ohio refined crude petroleum into usable oil.

★ Large companies grew into corporations. Many became monopolies.

★ Cornelius Vanderbilt and James J. Hill made fortunes with railroads.

★ World-changing inventions marked the period.

★ From 1850 to 1900, the population in cities grew from fifteen to forty percent.

★ Many people moved to cities to find work in industry and manufacturing. Working conditions in most factories were poor.

★ From 1850 to 1900, most immigrants came from Italy, Russia, Poland, and Greece. They sought their fortunes or religious freedom. Many faced prejudice because their ways were different.

★ In 1884, France gave the Statue of Liberty to the United States.

★ As cities grew, new developments made life better—transportation systems, department stores, museums, and concert halls.

★ With rapid growth, cities had problems.

★ Corruption was found in federal, state, and city governments.

★ Thomas Nast's political cartoons exposed corruption in New York.

★ Civil service laws were passed while Arthur was President.

★ The Interstate Commerce Act regulated the way railroads charged customers.

★ Labor unions began to change the way workers were treated.

★ The Sherman Anti-Trust Act was signed in 1890 to control monopolies.

★ The Populist party represented the average American.

"Over there, over there! Send the
    word, send the word over there
That the Yanks are coming, the
    Yanks are coming,
The drums rum-tumming
    everywhere.
So prepare, say a prayer,
Send the word, send the word, to
    beware.
We'll be over, we're coming over,
And we won't come back till it's
    over over there."

–George M. Cohan, 1917

The Emergence of Modern America

1898–1929

Have you noticed as you get older that you have more and bigger responsibilities? As the United States grew and developed in the early 1900s, it took on more and bigger responsibilities. As its interests expanded, the country became concerned with the affairs of other nations. It also took responsibility for its own citizens and resources in good times and bad times.

In this unit you will learn how America took wider responsibilities in the world. You will learn about American involvement in smaller wars and in World War I. You will learn how America took responsibility to give one-half of its citizens the right to vote. You will learn about America's economic crash after a period of great well-being.

Chapter 22: America Becomes a World Power: 1898–1913

Chapter 23: World War I: 1913–1920

Chapter 24: The Roaring Twenties: 1920–1929

America Becomes a World Power

1898–1913

Throughout the nineteenth century, the United States played a limited role in world affairs. Important European nations did not think of America as a world power. This changed late in the century. Confidence as a nation, new American leaders, and new world problems brought the United States into the world picture. In this chapter, you will learn how America became a world power.

Goals for Learning

▶ To explain the reasons for and outcome of the Spanish-American War

▶ To describe American expansion in the Pacific and how the United States became a stronger nation

▶ To describe the accomplishments of President Theodore Roosevelt

▶ To explain several reforms that were made during this time

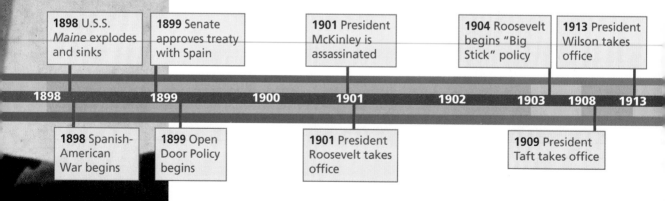

1898 U.S.S. *Maine* explodes and sinks

1899 Senate approves treaty with Spain

1901 President McKinley is assassinated

1904 Roosevelt begins "Big Stick" policy

1913 President Wilson takes office

| 1898 | 1899 | 1900 | 1901 | 1902 | 1903 | 1908 | 1913 |

1898 Spanish-American War begins

1899 Open Door Policy begins

1901 President Roosevelt takes office

1909 President Taft takes office

Before the Civil War, the United States had been working on its goal of Manifest Destiny. Once it had extended its boundaries from the Atlantic to the Pacific Ocean, attention shifted to growth of industry and business. This put America in a better position to compete with the rest of the world. During this time, Americans became confident that they could compete with the nations of Europe.

How Did America Go to War With Spain?

The only pieces of the former Spanish empire in North America were Cuba and nearby Puerto Rico in the West Indies. For many years, hundreds of thousands of people in Cuba had been victims of the unfair Spanish government there. Many Americans were living in Cuba, and many American businesses held important sugarcane industries there. These people felt that the United States should help Cubans become free of Spanish control.

Not eager to go to war with Spain, President McKinley offered to buy the island of Cuba. The Spanish refused. Then in January of 1898, he sent the battleship U.S.S. *Maine* to Cuba to protect American lives and property. But the fighting inside Cuba continued.

The battleship *Maine* exploded on February 15, 1898, and sank into the harbor of Havana, Cuba. The explosion killed 260 American sailors. The sinking of the *Maine* shocked the nation. Newspapers blamed the Spanish government.

President McKinley demanded that Spain stop the fighting in Cuba. Meanwhile, Theodore Roosevelt, Assistant Secretary of the Navy, sent Admiral Dewey and a fleet of ships to the Philippine Islands in Asia. Spain controlled these islands. Roosevelt gave Admiral Dewey orders to attack the Philippines' main harbor if war broke out as a result of the *Maine* bombing.

The U.S.S. *Maine* exploded and sank in Havana Harbor in 1898.

On April 9, 1898, Spain promised that it would stop its fighting in Cuba. Spain wanted to avoid a war with the United States. Many Americans wanted to go to war. "Remember the *Maine*" was printed on posters and buttons.

President McKinley was criticized for not punishing Spain for the sailors who died on the *Maine*. On April 11, 1898, he asked Congress for permission to use the military to stop the war in Cuba. McKinley made it clear that the United States was interested in helping Cuba gain its independence, not in taking control of it. President McKinley ignored the fact that Spain, having already agreed to stop fighting, heard of McKinley's action. Spain declared war on the United States. Congress then declared war on Spain.

SECTION 1 REVIEW On a separate sheet of paper write the word from the Word Bank to complete each sentence.

WORD BANK

Cuba

Havana

Philippine

Puerto Rico

Spain

1) The *Maine* was sunk in the harbor of _____, Cuba.

2) Spain controlled the _____ Islands.

3) American businesses held important sugarcane industries in _____.

4) Cuba and _____ were the last of the Spanish empire in North America.

5) _____ declared war on the United States.

What do you think **?**

Why do you think it was hard for Spain to maintain its empire?

The Spanish-American War lasted four months. Admiral Dewey attacked and destroyed the Spanish navy in the Philippines. At the same time, a native Filipino group revolted on land. The Spanish quickly surrendered. Future control of the islands was left unsettled, but American troops were sent to set up bases.

The biggest battle took place in Cuba. Theodore Roosevelt left his government job to help with the war. He organized a group of soldiers called the "Rough Riders." With the help of other American groups, including the all-African-American 10th Cavalry Regiment, the Rough Riders charged and captured San Juan Hill in Cuba. During this attack, the American navy under Admiral William Sampson sank all of the Spanish ships still guarding Santiago harbor.

★Armistice
A break in a war to talk peace

Spain and the United States agreed to stop fighting on August 12, 1898. They discussed how to end the war. This is called an **armistice.** On December 10, 1898, a treaty was signed that ended the war.

MAP STUDY

What city was the battleship *Maine* near when it was sunk? Where on the island of Cuba did the battle of San Juan Hill take place?

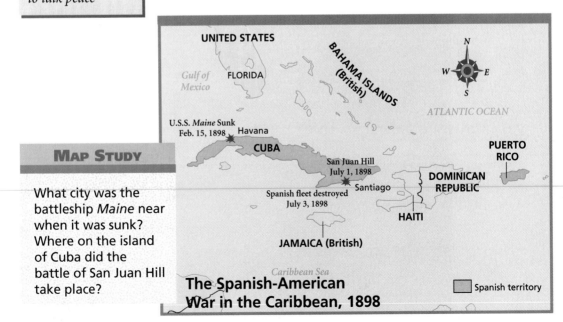

The Spanish-American War in the Caribbean, 1898

What Were the Results of the War?

The United States Senate had to ratify the treaty with Spain. Spain agreed to give Cuba its independence. The United States gained the island of Puerto Rico in the Caribbean Sea and the Pacific islands of Guam and the Philippines.

The treaty started a debate in the Senate. Some senators did not like the idea of the United States controlling foreign territories. Other senators argued the new land would make America a stronger nation; President McKinley agreed. The Senate approved the treaty in February of 1899. The United States paid $20 million to Spain for the Philippine Islands.

The people of the Philippines did not want to belong to the United States. They declared their independence. The United States sent an army to the Philippines to stop the independence movement. The United States defeated the Filipino army after three years of fighting.

The Philippine Islands provided the United States with a valuable naval base in Asia. The United States had taken the first step toward becoming a world power. Secretary of State John Hay spoke for most Americans when he said that the Spanish-American War was a "splendid little war."

Theodore Roosevelt (center, with glasses) and his Rough Riders posed at the top of San Juan Hill.

★Republic
A government in which citizens elect people to speak and act for them

What Happened to Cuba After the War?

To help the new government keep order, the United States forces remained in Cuba for four years. During this time, Cuba set up a modern educational system. New highways were built, and better sanitation was developed. Walter Reed, an American medical officer, rid the island of yellow fever, a disease that had caused problems there. In 1902, the United States withdrew from Cuba, having made an agreement with the Cuban **republic.** A republic is a government in which citizens elect people to speak and act for them. The agreement stated that America would be able to keep military bases there. It would also be able to step in if others threatened Cuba's independence.

SECTION 2 REVIEW On a separate sheet of paper, write *True* if the statement is true or *False* if the statement is not true.

1) The Spanish-American War lasted eight months.

2) Spain and the United States agreed to stop fighting on August 12, 1898.

3) The United States paid $10 million to Spain for the Philippine Islands.

4) People of the Philippines were eager to belong to the United States.

5) The United States withdrew from Cuba in 1902.

What do you think ?

When John Hay said that the Spanish-American War was a "splendid little war," what do you think he meant?

 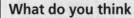

The United States continued to increase its power in the Pacific Ocean. In 1900, the Hawaiian Islands were made an American territory. The people became American citizens. These islands, in addition to the Philippines, gave America an even stronger ability to increase trade with the Far East.

America began to focus on China. China lost its independence in the nineteenth century. European countries took control of several Chinese cities, using them as trading centers. Great Britain, France, Russia, and Germany established their own government and courts in China. Japan also gained new land. America had been trading with China for years. However, now American merchants were concerned that China's trade might fall under the control of a few countries.

In 1899, Secretary of State John Hay offered a new trading policy for China. This was the Open Door Policy. Hay convinced the foreign nations in China to allow open and free trade for all countries.

MAP STUDY

When did the Hawaiian Islands become an American territory? How many islands became territories in 1898? Which ones were they?

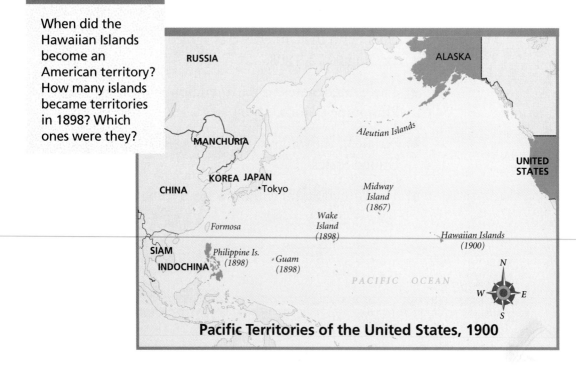

Pacific Territories of the United States, 1900

What Was the Boxer Rebellion?

Many Chinese were angry that parts of their country had been given to foreigners. They felt that something had to be done to stop what was happening. They formed political clubs and had secret meetings. Members discussed how to remove all foreigners from China. Each club had a different name, but they became known as "Boxers" because of the physical exercises many of them did.

The Boxers rebelled in the spring of 1900. European countries and Japan sent soldiers to stop the rebellion. The United States sent troops to protect its interests. The revolt of the Boxers threatened to destroy the Open Door Policy. The Boxer Rebellion, as it is called, did not last long. Foreign control of China was quickly brought back. Secretary of State Hay encouraged the countries to take no more Chinese territory. Instead, many countries imposed fines on the Chinese for damages done to their property and goods.

The United States returned a large part of this money to China. The money was used to allow Chinese students to attend American universities. This favor, along with other efforts by Americans to protect the land of native Chinese, helped bring friendly relations between the two countries for many years to come.

Chinese fighters tried to remove all foreigners from China during the Boxer Rebellion.

Ragtime and the Music of Scott Joplin

Ragtime is a unique American style of jazz written chiefly for piano. Scott Joplin became known as "the king of ragtime." The son of a formerly enslaved African, Joplin left home about age fourteen. For ten years he played piano in saloons and honky-tonks across Missouri. He settled in Sedalia, Missouri, playing piano at the Maple Leaf Club. In 1899 he published the "Maple Leaf Rag," and the sheet music sold over a million copies. Joplin wrote or collaborated on more than sixty pieces of music, including the Ragtime opera *Treemonisha* (1911). It failed to interest any serious producers during his lifetime. Joplin's music enjoyed a revival in the 1970s. *Treemonisha* won critical acclaim for its first full-scale production in 1975. The film *The Sting* (1973) used "The Entertainer" and other Joplin rags as its background music. The Advisory Board on the Pulitzer Prize awarded Joplin a special citation in 1976, sixty years after his death.

Fine Arts
History in Your Life

SECTION 3 REVIEW Write the answers to these questions on a separate sheet of paper using complete sentences.

1) What happened to Hawaiian people when the Hawaiian Islands became a United States territory?

2) Which countries established their own government and courts in China?

3) What was the Open Door Policy?

4) Why did the Boxer Rebellion start?

5) How did the United States gain friendly relations with China?

What do you think ?

Aside from improving trade with the Far East, why do you think making Hawaii a U.S. territory was important?

Abroad
Throughout the world

★**Imperialism**
The practice of taking over land to become a stronger nation

In four years' time, William McKinley had become a popular President. During his administration, the United States had gained Puerto Rico. It had set up a system to protect Cuba. America was becoming an important power in Asia. The American navy had set up a base in the Philippine Islands. China had been opened to more American trade. European nations showed they respected the United States' new power. They knew America would help protect their interests in Asia.

What Happened in the Election of 1900?

McKinley had no problem winning a second term as President in 1900. For the second time, he easily defeated the Democratic candidate, William Jennings Bryan. Bryan had tried to make **imperialism** a campaign issue. Imperialism is the practice of taking over land to become a stronger nation. The Republicans avoided bringing up the issue as much as possible. McKinley chose Theodore Roosevelt as his Vice President.

Less than one year after being re-elected, McKinley was assassinated. Theodore Roosevelt, at age forty-two, became the youngest President of the United States when he took office in 1901. He became a very powerful President. He believed in reforming America at home. He also wanted to strengthen the nation's power **abroad.** Roosevelt was a new, active leader for a new century.

This is the last photo of President McKinley (center) before he died.

President Roosevelt agreed that workers like these Pennsylvania coal miners deserved "a square deal."

What Reforms Did Roosevelt Support?

Roosevelt believed American society had many problems. He felt Americans deserved an equal opportunity to better themselves and that too many people were paid too little. American workers, said Roosevelt, must receive a "square deal."

Roosevelt wasted no time in showing that reform was important to him. In 1902, coal miners went on strike. President Roosevelt agreed with the strikers. He forced the owners to find a way to end the strike. This was the first time that the government had supported the rights of union workers.

What Political Reforms Did the Progressives Make?

A new group of reformers were the **Progressives.** The Progressives believed that America should make progress to become a better country. Progressives thought this would happen only if laws were passed to correct America's social and political problems.

Progressive reformers wanted the people to have more power in the political system. They wanted the people to choose political candidates in a **primary election.** At the time, political leaders picked the candidates. Progressives wanted to give the voters the right to approve or **reject** bills passed by state legislatures in a **referendum.** They thought that citizens should be able to suggest new laws in an **initiative.** They also believed that state and city government officials who performed poorly should be removed from office by the voters in a **recall.**

The Progressives informed the public of existing problems. Many wrote articles and books describing corruption and problems. The writers were called **muckrakers.** Lincoln Steffens wrote a book, *The Shame of Cities.* The book described problems in American city slums. *The History of Standard Oil* by Ida Tarbell explained the harsh methods John D. Rockefeller used to create his monopoly in the oil business.

The Progressives were confident the nation was ready for reform. Reformers had a President who believed as they did. Many business leaders feared Roosevelt.

How Did Roosevelt Control Big Business?

Although Roosevelt was in favor of economic growth, he did not want big businesses to harm society. He felt that to be fair in their business affairs, trusts should be broken into smaller companies. This would create competition and give less power to monopolies. He charged that trust companies went against the Sherman Anti-Trust Act.

At first Congress did not respond to the President's desire to put controls on big business. However, when the President turned to the people for support, Congress started to listen. In time, many antitrust lawsuits were brought before the Supreme Court. The Department of Commerce and Labor was created to keep an eye on business dealings. People were pleased with the efforts of President Roosevelt, who came to be known as the "trustbuster."

SECTION 4 REVIEW Choose the best word or name in parentheses to complete each sentence. Write your answers on a separate sheet of paper.

1) (William Jennings Bryan, William McKinley) won the election of 1900.

2) (Theodore Roosevelt, William Jennings Bryan) became President after McKinley was assassinated.

3) A (referendum, initiative, primary election) is the power citizens have to suggest new laws.

4) A (primary election, referendum, recall) is voting someone from office who has performed poorly.

5) A (Progressive, muckraker) was a person who wrote articles and books describing corruption and problems.

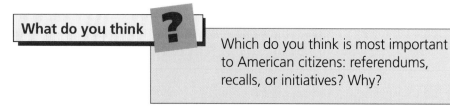

What do you think **?**

Which do you think is most important to American citizens: referendums, recalls, or initiatives? Why?

★**Conservation**
The act of protecting or limiting the use of natural resources

★**Natural resources**
Raw materials from nature, such as water and soil

During Roosevelt's administration, Congress passed many laws. They protected Americans from the sale of unhealthy meat and unsafe drugs. In 1906, Congress passed the Meat Inspection Act and the Food and Drugs Act. Government officials could inspect meat-packing plants to see if they were clean. Drug companies were required to prove their drugs were safe.

What Conservation Programs Were Started?

Before 1900, the nation's **natural resources** seemed unlimited. America had plenty of forest land, good soil, fresh water, coal, oil, and other minerals. President Roosevelt and others worried that America would run out of these resources. **Conservation** was needed to protect these resources.

Then and Now

If someone offers to sell you a medicine and claims it cures anything, will you buy it? Around 1900, newspapers were full of ads for "patent" medicines. The ads claimed the medicines could cure one or more illnesses or problems. Manufacturers never tested the medicines to prove their safety or the accuracy of the claims. The medicines were often fifty percent or more alcohol. People wanted to feel better, so they believed the claims and ordered the medicines. Sellers became rich, but the medicines did not help the buyers.

Today the Food and Drug Administration (FDA) regulates medicines. Researchers must do studies to prove a medicine does what it is supposed to do. No medicine can be on the market without FDA approval. Doctors must prescribe most medicines.

President Roosevelt appointed Gifford Pinchot to head the United States Forest Service. Pinchot was committed to protecting the nation's natural resources. He convinced President Roosevelt to add 150 million acres to the country's forest reserve and to preserve valuable mineral-rich lands for future use. In 1902, Congress passed a law that gave the federal government the power to build dams and to establish irrigation projects. Land was developed for five national parks. In 1908, the President called state governors to a national conference to discuss steps they could take to preserve resources within their states. Soon after the conference, many state governments had set up conservation groups of their own.

★Foreign policy
*The plan a
government follows
when dealing with
other nations*

What Was Roosevelt's Foreign Policy?

The plan a government follows when dealing with other nations is called **foreign policy.** The United States had three foreign policy plans. The policies involved Europe, Asia, and Latin America.

The policy toward Europe was to be neutral and isolated. The policy with Asia had more to do with settling disputes and improving trade. In 1905, Roosevelt helped Russia and Japan end a war between them. The United States set forth the Open Door Policy, which covered trade with Asia. Roosevelt also built a powerful navy. The navy protected American interests in Asia and the Caribbean Sea.

The policy toward Latin America had to do with the Monroe Doctrine. The Monroe Doctrine had stated that European nations could not start any new colonies in North or South America. Santo Domingo, the Dominican Republic of today, ran into trouble with foreign debts. President Roosevelt then added the Roosevelt Corollary. Under this addition to the Monroe Doctrine, he stated that the United States would come to the aid of any Latin American country. The United States took over temporary control of Santo Domingo's finances and saw to it that its debts to Europe were taken care of peacefully.

Why Was the Panama Canal Built?

The navy needed a fast way to move its warships from the Atlantic to the Pacific Ocean. Also, commercial shippers would benefit from having a direct route. To solve the problem, a canal needed to be built through Central America.

The shortest route for the canal was through Panama, a part of the Republic of Colombia. A group of Panamanians did not want the United States to build a canal, because they were afraid of losing control there. When the United States government offered the country $10 million for a strip of land through Panama, plus yearly rent, Colombia flatly refused.

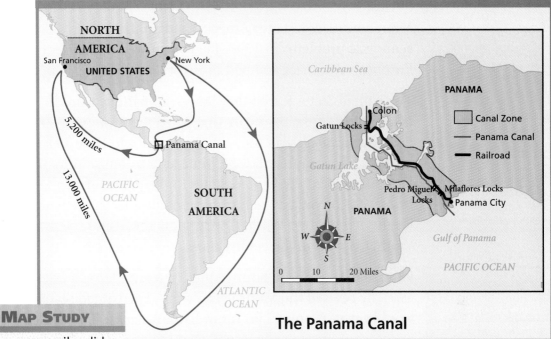

The Panama Canal

MAP STUDY

How many miles did a ship have to travel from New York to San Francisco before the Panama Canal was built?

Panama revolted against Colombia in 1903. President Roosevelt sent American battleships to help Panama. The revolt was successful. That year Panama became an independent republic. The United States paid the new Republic of Panama $10 million, plus yearly rent, for a ten-mile wide strip of land. The "Big Ditch," as the canal was called, was completed in 1914. It took ten years to build. The canal was more than fifty miles long. It cut the distance for ships traveling from New York to San Francisco by more than 7,000 miles.

The Panama Canal was a huge building project. It took ten years to finish.

What Was Roosevelt's "Big Stick" Policy?

Many countries in Latin America had political and economic problems in 1900. They borrowed money from European countries and had difficulty repaying the loans.

The United States feared that European nations would take control of the countries that owed them money. Britain, Germany, and Italy sent battleships to Venezuela in 1902. They wanted to force Venezuela to repay its loans. Venezuela asked the United States for help. President Roosevelt convinced the European nations to let the new Hague Tribunal, or World Court, settle the dispute. The World Court is in the Netherlands.

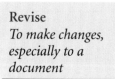

Revise
To make changes, especially to a document

Foreign battleships in South America worried Roosevelt. In 1904, he **revised** the Monroe Doctrine. The United States would act as a "police" power in Latin America. The United States would try to solve any political or economic problem in a Latin American country. The United States could use the military to bring back order to a Latin American country. This was called the "Big Stick" policy. The policy was called that because Roosevelt often used an African saying, "Speak softly and carry a big stick. . . ."

SECTION 5 REVIEW Write the answers to these questions on a separate sheet of paper using complete sentences.

1) Which laws were passed to protect Americans from unhealthy meat and unsafe drugs?

2) What steps were taken to protect America's natural resources?

3) Why did the United States want to build the Panama Canal?

4) How did the United States gain the right to build the Panama Canal?

5) What was the "Big Stick" policy?

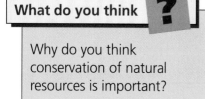

What do you think **?**

Why do you think conservation of natural resources is important?

Roosevelt enjoyed his two terms as President. He chose not to seek re-election. He said that he felt two terms as President were enough. The new President, he hoped, would continue his plan of strength abroad and reform at home. He convinced the Republican party to nominate William Howard Taft.

What Did Taft Achieve as President?

Taft and the Republican party had no trouble winning the presidency in 1908. The Democratic nominee, William Jennings Bryan, was defeated for the third time. President Taft took office in 1909. He did not enjoy being President. He had trouble working with Congress.

President Taft tried to fulfill promises that Roosevelt made. Taft ordered the breakup of the Standard Oil Trust. He demanded a restructuring of the American Tobacco Company, which had been operated much like a trust. While he was President, Congress passed the Sixteenth Amendment to give the government power to collect **income taxes.** Income tax is tax placed on money people earn.

★Income tax
Tax placed on money people earn

The Department of Labor was also set up. Laws were written to place communications companies under government control. Those who gave money to political candidates were forced to do so publicly. However, there were ongoing problems involving tariffs. At times, Taft was accused of trying to undo some of President Roosevelt's conservation plans.

W. E. B. Du Bois

W. E. B. Du Bois was a professor at Atlanta University. He published a collection of essays entitled *The Souls of Black Folk* in 1903. He said African Americans should immediately seek equal rights and opportunities. To accomplish this goal, he formed the National Association for the Advancement of Colored People (NAACP) in 1909 with Ida Wells-Barnet, an African-American reporter. Today the NAACP is over half a million members strong.

What Happened in the Election of 1912?

Despite Taft's achievements, the Progressives felt he had not supported reform. They wanted Roosevelt to run against Taft for the Republican nomination in 1912. However, the Republican party nominated Taft.

Roosevelt organized a new political party. The new Progressive party nominated Roosevelt for President. Roosevelt was confident that the American people would re-elect him. People called this new political party the Bull Moose party when Roosevelt said that he felt "as strong as a bull moose."

In 1912, the Democratic party nominated Woodrow Wilson. The Democrats were in a good position to win, because the Republican party was divided between Taft and Roosevelt. Wilson had a reform plan called the "New Freedom." He wanted to rid the country of all forms of trust companies, which he felt were bad for American democracy. He thought America would be a stronger nation if small companies could compete equally.

Theodore Roosevelt gestured with his hat to make a point during a campaign speech.

Roosevelt called his program the "New Nationalism." He believed the federal government should regulate big business. The government should be responsible for improving American society by limiting workday hours and setting a **minimum wage.** A minimum wage is the smallest amount a person can be paid to do a job. He felt that children, women, and the injured required special protection by law. Among his other wishes were an expanded conservation program and suffrage for women.

Minimum wage
The smallest amount a person can be paid to do a job

The Bull Moose party and its candidate, Theodore Roosevelt, could not get enough support. The Democrats won the 1912 election. Woodrow Wilson took office as the twenty-eighth President in 1913.

1912 Presidential Election Results		
Candidate	Popular Votes	Electoral Votes
Woodrow Wilson	6,286,214	435
Theodore Roosevelt	4,126,020	88
William Taft	3,483,922	8

SECTION 6 REVIEW On a separate sheet of paper, write *True* if the statement is true or *False* if the statement is not true.

1) William Jennings Bryan was defeated for the third time in the election of 1908.

2) President Taft enjoyed being President.

3) Congress passed the Sixteenth Amendment during the Taft administration.

4) During the election of 1912, the Republican party was divided between Taft and Wilson.

5) Roosevelt believed that big business did not need to be regulated.

What do you think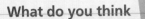

Even though Roosevelt was not elected President in the 1912 election, how do you think his ideas affected the future of America?

Speech of Booker T. Washington

Booker T. Washington was born to enslaved parents in 1856. He became a teacher and a successful founder of schools for African Americans. Washington encouraged African Americans to become skilled laborers. Because of this, many rights activists of the time thought he was promoting further enslavement to white masters. In fact, Washington desired to create peace with white people. That desire also may have separated him from his African-American peers. This passage is from a speech Washington made in 1895 to white business people in Atlanta.

"As we have proved our loyalty to you in the past, by nursing your children, watching by the sickbed of your mothers and fathers, and often following them with tear-dimmed eyes to their graves, so in the future, in our humble way, we shall stand by you with a devotion that no foreigner can approach, ready to lay down our lives, if need be, in defense of yours; interlacing our industrial, commercial, civil, and religious life with yours in a way that shall make the interests of both races one. In all things that are purely social we can be as separate as the fingers, yet one as the hand in all things essential to mutual progress."

Source Reading Wrap-Up

1) What are two key words Washington used to describe an African American's relationship to his or her master?

2) Who did Washington say could not approach the kind of devotion African Americans had to white masters?

3) How did Washington see the lives of whites and African Americans "interlacing"?

4) In what ways did he see their lives being separate?

5) How do you feel about the attitude and tone of Washington's speech?

CHAPTER SUMMARY

★ President McKinley wanted to help Cuba and Puerto Rico free themselves from Spanish rule and to expand American interests there.

★ In 1898, the U.S.S. *Maine* was sent to Cuba to protect American interests. The ship exploded in Havana harbor in February and the Spanish were blamed.

★ American Admiral Dewey's ships destroyed the Spanish fleet in the Philippines. Theodore Roosevelt led soldiers to capture San Juan Hill in Cuba. The United States and Spain signed a treaty in December. The treaty gave Puerto Rico, Guam, and the Philippines to America.

★ In 1899, America established its Open Door Policy with China. It allowed China to have free trade.

★ The Hawaiian Islands became an American territory in 1900, and its people became American citizens.

★ In 1900, the Boxer Rebellion in China failed to rid the country of foreign control. The United States established good relations with the Chinese government.

★ During the first year of his second term, William McKinley was assassinated. Theodore Roosevelt then became President. Roosevelt was a reformer and pushed for both social and political change. He served two terms as President.

★ The Progressive party established political reforms such as primary elections, referendums, initiatives, and voter recalls.

★ Congress passed laws such as the Meat Inspection Act and the Food and Drugs Act to protect the American people.

★ Roosevelt established policies for conservation and the better use of natural resources.

★ Roosevelt built a strong navy to provide defense and to show other countries America's strength.

★ America financed the building of the Panama Canal, which connected the Atlantic and Pacific oceans.

★ William Howard Taft became the next President. During his presidency, Congress passed the Sixteenth Amendment, which established an income tax. Taft's administration helped create other reforms.

★ After Taft's term, Roosevelt ran again as candidate of the Bull Moose party, but lost to Woodrow Wilson.

Comprehension: Identifying Facts

On a separate sheet of paper, write the words from the Word Bank to complete each sentence.

WORD BANK	
big stick	San Juan Hill
Boxer Rebellion	Spain
conservation	"Splendid Little War"
Panama Canal	"trustbuster"
Progressive party	William Howard Taft
recall	William McKinley
"Remember the *Maine*"	

1) Theodore Roosevelt led a group of "Rough Riders" to capture _____.

2) _____ was the call to action for the Spanish-American War.

3) President _____ was assassinated during his second term.

4) The conflict with Spain was called the _____.

5) The "Big Ditch" is what some people called the _____.

6) Theodore Roosevelt encouraged wise use, or _____, of the country's natural resources.

7) President Roosevelt used the African saying "Speak softly and carry a _____."

8) _____ ordered a breakup of the Standard Oil Trust and set up the Department of Labor.

9) Voters can remove an elected official from office with a _____.

10) The _____ took place because the Chinese wanted to be rid of foreign control.

11) _____ controlled Puerto Rico, Cuba, and the Philippines before the Spanish-American War.

12) The _____ worked for political reform, especially the way voters could make choices.

13) Early in his presidency, Roosevelt became known as the _____.

Comprehension: Understanding Main Ideas

On a separate sheet of paper, write the answer to each question using complete sentences.

1) What were two results of the Spanish-American War?

2) Who was Walter Reed and what did he do?

3) Why did some members of Congress want the United States to expand its interests in Asia?

4) What was the importance of the Panama Canal?

5) What is a primary election?

Critical Thinking: Write Your Opinion

1) Theodore Roosevelt developed five national parks. Do you think national parks are important? Explain your answer.

2) Do you think it is important for the United States to have a strong foreign policy? Why or why not?

Test Taking Tip   If you are asked to compare and contrast things in an essay test, be sure to tell how they are alike and how they are different.

World War I

1913–1920

The United States had done much to become a world power in the early part of the twentieth century. As President Wilson took over the presidency, it was time for the nation to learn the consequences of having this power. Tensions in Europe were high at this time. Soon a war like one never seen before—World War I—would affect the United States and most of Europe. In this chapter, you will learn what caused World War I and what resulted from it.

Goals for Learning

▶ To describe major successes in Wilson's presidency

▶ To explain the events that caused World War I

▶ To describe American involvement in World War I

▶ To explain the problems with the Treaty of Versailles

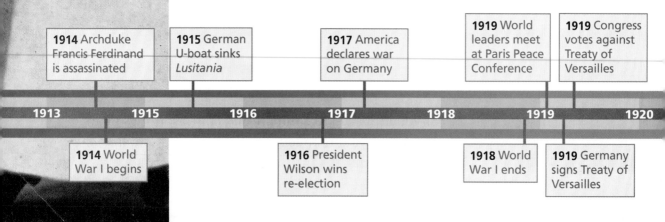

1914 Archduke Francis Ferdinand is assassinated

1915 German U-boat sinks *Lusitania*

1917 America declares war on Germany

1919 World leaders meet at Paris Peace Conference

1919 Congress votes against Treaty of Versailles

| 1913 | 1915 | 1916 | 1917 | 1918 | 1919 | 1920 |

1914 World War I begins

1916 President Wilson wins re-election

1918 World War I ends

1919 Germany signs Treaty of Versailles

President Wilson had some political experience when he became President. He had been the governor of New Jersey, during which time he was successful in fighting political bosses in that state. Wilson believed there should be legislation to improve workers' rights and change ways states voted. Wilson proved to be a strong President.

President Wilson was very skillful in getting Congress to pass the reform laws he wanted. These reform laws brought major changes to American society. Early in Wilson's administration, a new national banking system was started. It was called the Federal Reserve System. This change made it easier to put money into the economy when needed.

The Sixteenth Amendment was also ratified at this time. Though Congress passed the Sixteenth Amendment, the states still needed to ratify it. This amendment, which made income tax a law, was ratified in 1913. Before the amendment, it was unconstitutional to tax someone's personal income. Reformers wanted only wealthy Americans to pay taxes on their income. The average worker's income was too low to tax.

President Wilson achieved a great deal in a short period of time. Many Progressive reformers were pleased with Wilson's actions.

How Did War Start in Europe?

For many years, the countries of Europe had been competing for trade markets. At times, they had tried to control the same colonies in different parts of the world. Some nations wanted to get back parts of their lands lost in earlier wars. Some small countries wanted to gain their independence from larger ruling nations. Each nation tried to build the strongest army. Two alliances had been formed: One included Austria-Hungary, Germany, and Italy. The other united Great Britain, France, and Russia. Neither group trusted the other.

JIM THORPE: 1888–1953

A poll of sportswriters in 1950 declared Jim Thorpe the "greatest American athlete of the first half of this century." A native of Oklahoma, he was part Sauk and Fox Indian and part Irish. Thorpe was an outstanding college football player. Then he competed in the track and field events at the 1912 Olympic games in Sweden. He won gold medals for both the pentathlon and decathlon—the first athlete in history to do so. Thorpe later played on seven professional football teams and three major league baseball teams. He was the first president of what is now the National Football League. After his death, Thorpe was elected to the Football Hall of Fame.

Bosnia had been a part of the Austro-Hungarian Empire since 1908. However, many people in Bosnia did not want to be part of this empire. They wanted to be included in Serbia, a neighboring country. Talks of rebellion by Bosnian groups created tension within the empire. In June of 1914, the emperor of Austria-Hungary sent his nephew, Archduke Francis Ferdinand, to Sarajevo, the capital of Bosnia. He wanted to try to improve relations between Bosnia and the government of Austria-Hungary.

As a line of government cars passed through the streets of Sarajevo, a man threw a bomb at Archduke Francis Ferdinand's car. The bomb missed its target and exploded when another car passed. This wounded several people. Hours later, the Archduke went to visit the wounded people. His car slowed near a corner. Rebel Gavrilo Princip saw the Archduke, raised a pistol, and shot the Archduke and his wife. The Archduke was killed immediately and his wife died soon after.

★Emperor
The male ruler of an empire

The Austro-Hungarian **emperor,** Francis Joseph, blamed Serbia for the death of his nephew and his nephew's wife. An emperor is the male ruler of an empire. Francis Joseph had no proof that Serbia was responsible. However, one month later, on July 28, 1914, Austria-Hungary declared war on Serbia.

Allied Powers
A group of allied nations that included Great Britain, France, Serbia, Belgium, and Russia

★**Central Powers**
A group of allied nations that included Germany, Austria-Hungary, and later Turkey and Bulgaria

Chain reaction
A series of events linked to one another

Why Did Other Countries Declare War?

When Austria-Hungary declared war on Serbia, it started a **chain reaction.** Russia decided to help Serbia against Austria-Hungary. Germany decided to help Austria-Hungary defend itself against Russia. France agreed to help Russia and made plans to attack Germany. Germany then declared war on France and marched its army through Belgium to attack the French. Committed to defending Belgium and France, Great Britain declared war on Germany.

By August 14, 1914, seven European nations were at war. The **Central Powers** included Germany and Austria-Hungary and, later, Turkey (also called the Ottoman Empire) and Bulgaria. The **Allied Powers** were Great Britain, France, Serbia, Belgium, and Russia. Japan supported the Allies in hope of gaining control of Germany's Pacific colonies after the war. Italy remained neutral in the early stages of the war. Later, it broke its former alliance with Germany and Austria-Hungary to join the Allied Powers.

The war spread into most of Europe and in some parts of Africa and Asia. Even most smaller European countries took part in some way. Both sides had their defeats and victories. By 1917, the Central Powers had gained an advantage over the Allied nations.

Moments after this photo was taken, Archduke Francis Ferdinand and Archduchess Sophie were shot in Sarajevo. The killing started World War I.

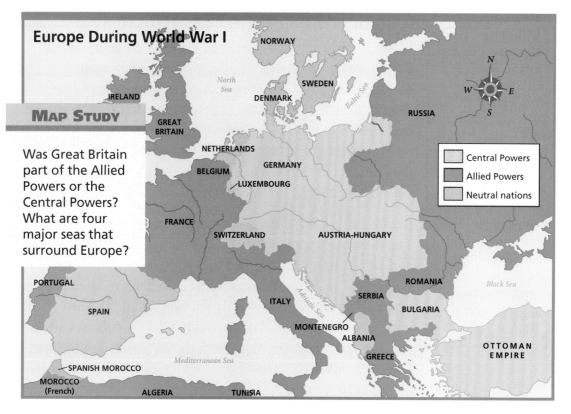

Europe During World War I

MAP STUDY

Was Great Britain part of the Allied Powers or the Central Powers? What are four major seas that surround Europe?

Legend:
- Central Powers
- Allied Powers
- Neutral nations

SECTION 1 REVIEW Choose the correct word in parentheses to complete each sentence below. Write your answers on a separate sheet of paper.

1) The (Fourteenth, Fifteenth, Sixteenth) Amendment was ratified in 1913.

2) The Federal Reserve System was a new way of (collecting taxes, banking, passing legislation).

3) Archduke (Francis Ferdinand, Gavrilo Princip, Francis Joseph) was assassinated in 1914.

4) Austria-Hungary declared war on (France, Serbia, Great Britain).

5) (Germany, Turkey, France) was part of the Allied Powers.

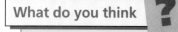

What do you think ?

Why was it possible for one event to cause a war among so many countries?

★Submarine
A ship that can travel underwater

★Torpedo
A self-propelled bomb that is shot from a tube of a submarine

President Wilson said the United States would not take sides in the war. However, American companies could sell war supplies to fighting countries. Hundreds of ships from America crossed the Atlantic Ocean and carried war supplies to France and Great Britain. Germany accused the United States of not remaining neutral.

The British navy tried to prevent Americans from trading with Germany. They stopped American ships and set up "war zones" in the Atlantic Ocean. Ships from other countries were not allowed to enter the war zone. Germany also set up a war zone around the island of Great Britain. Germany thought that it could force the British out of the war by preventing them from receiving food and war supplies. Germany said that its **submarines,** called U-boats, would sink any ships found in their war zones. A submarine is a ship that can travel underwater. President Wilson felt that the war zones were illegal. He believed that all countries should be free to sail the oceans and seas of the world.

As the Central Powers appeared to be defeating the Allied nations, many Americans were concerned about Great Britain. The enemy at the time of the Revolutionary War had become a friend to them, largely because of shared democratic practices, language, and customs. France had been an ally at the time of the Revolution. Germany, on the other hand, had become cruel in the eyes of many Americans.

What Happened When the Germans Sank the *Lusitania*?

In 1915, the *Lusitania,* a large British passenger ship, was traveling from New York to England. Off the coast of Ireland, the captain of a German U-boat spotted the ship. The U-boat fired a **torpedo** that hit the *Lusitania.* A torpedo is a self-propelled bomb that is shot from a tube of a submarine. The ship exploded and sank. Almost 1,200 people died; 128 were Americans.

The *Lusitania* before its last voyage from New York's harbor. A German torpedo sank the ship near Ireland. Many Americans turned against Germany after the ship's sinking.

Effective
Able to cause a desired result

The Birth of a Nation

The first twelve-reel film, *The Birth of a Nation*, was shown for the first time in New York City on March 3, 1915. It was a great success. However, many African Americans and other groups formed protests because the film treated African Americans poorly.

Americans were shocked and upset. Some people, including Theodore Roosevelt, called on Congress to declare war on Germany. President Wilson sent a letter of protest to the German government. Germany said that the ship was carrying war supplies as well as passengers. Britain denied that any war materials were on the ship.

The sinking of the *Lusitania* turned the American public against Germany. It was becoming more difficult for the United States to remain neutral. Germany, fearing that America would enter the war, urged its U-boat captains to be more careful in selecting ships to attack. As a result, the German war zone around Britain became less **effective.** Some ships got through to Britain with goods to continue the war against Germany.

Woodrow Wilson ran for re-election in 1916 against Charles Evans Hughes. Wilson had been a good President. Democrats and many Republicans approved of his reform program.

Fine Arts

History in Your Life

The Music of Irving Berlin

Songwriter Irving Berlin was a composer who never studied music. He could not read or write musical lines on paper. He was born in Russia in 1888. His family fled Jewish persecution in 1893. At fourteen, Berlin sang in New York's Bowery saloons and worked as a singing waiter. Early recognized as a clever lyricist, he contributed words and some melodies to many ragtime songs. His first big hit was "Alexander's Ragtime Band" in 1911. Berlin's first complete musical score was *Watch Your Step* in 1914. By 1919, he had his own music publishing company. Among his most successful shows were *The Ziegfeld Follies* (1919) and *Annie Get Your Gun* (1946). Berlin produced about 800 songs. Many of his most popular tunes are still sung today. One example is "There's No Business Like Show Business." Many Americans regard his "God Bless America" as the second national anthem.

Most Americans were pleased that the nation had stayed out of the war in Europe. The Democratic party used "He Kept Us Out of War" as Wilson's campaign slogan.

Wilson won the election. It was very close. His victory was important for the Democratic party. Woodrow Wilson was the first Democrat to be re-elected to the presidency since Andrew Jackson in 1832.

SECTION 2 REVIEW Write the answers to these questions on a separate sheet of paper using complete sentences.

1) What policy did President Wilson support when war broke out in Europe?

2) What did Germany do to try to prevent goods from reaching Great Britain?

3) What did the United States have in common with Great Britain?

4) What happened to the *Lusitania*?

5) What did Wilson do to get re-elected in 1916?

What do you think ?

Why do you think people other than soldiers are killed in wars?

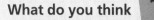

President Wilson gave a speech on January 22, 1917, to "the people of the countries now at war." He wanted the war to end. He did not want a winner or loser. Wilson wanted "peace without victory."

Standstill
Something that is not changing or improving

At the time of the President's speech, the war in Europe had been at a **standstill** for months. Both sides were worn down by nearly three years of fighting. Then Germany announced that its U-boats would sink any ship without warning in the war zone around Britain. The Germans thought that this action would force Britain to stop fighting. Germany knew the United States would probably declare war. Germany thought the war would be over before the United States sent an army to Europe.

During February and March of 1917, German U-boats torpedoed ships flying the American flag. Tension between the United States and Germany increased. Antiwar senators argued that it would be a mistake for the United States to go to war. The United States government released to the newspapers a secret letter from Germany to Mexico. In this letter, known as the Zimmermann Note, Germany asked Mexico to help Germany if Germany and the United States went to war. Germany told Mexico that if it helped to defeat the United States, Mexico would receive the states of Texas, New Mexico, and Arizona. Mexico had lost these lands to America in the 1800s.

How Did the United States Enter the War?

On April 2, 1917, Woodrow Wilson asked Congress to declare war on Germany. He said that America would fight for "peace and justice." "The world," he said, "must be made safe for democracy." On April 6, Congress declared that the United States and Germany were at war. American neutrality had ended.

When American men went to fight in World War I, large numbers of American women joined the workforce. These women are making cannon shells.

Consumer goods
Objects and things the average person buys and uses

★**Draft**
The practice of requiring people to serve in the armed forces

American factories stopped production of **consumer goods** to make war supplies. People started working longer hours to help increase the factory output. Many women now joined the American workforce to replace the men who had gone off to war. Other women joined the armed forces as nurses and office workers.

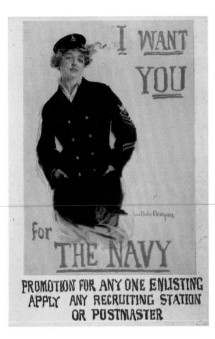

I WANT YOU for THE NAVY

PROMOTION FOR ANY ONE ENLISTING
APPLY ANY RECRUITING STATION
OR POSTMASTER

The government increased taxes and sold bonds to raise money for the war. It asked Americans to limit their use of certain food products and fuels to conserve these items for military use. Farmers used more land for growing crops to increase food production. The United States Selective Service started to **draft** young men into the army. A draft is requiring people to serve in the armed forces. The draft had not been used since the Civil War. In these ways, Americans were working to support their country in the Great War.

Posters like this encouraged people to join the armed forces.

This ship was full of doughboys who fought in Europe.

American troops arrived in Europe faster than the Germans thought possible. The first American soldiers, or "doughboys," as they were called, arrived in Europe by June 1917. By July 1918, over a million American troops were in Europe.

Large groups of American ships began to blockade German ports. They positioned **mines** to destroy enemy ships. Mines are floating bombs that explode when touched. They torpedoed many of the aggressive German U-boats that had been causing so much damage in the Atlantic.

How Did the War End?

★Mine
A bomb that floats in water and explodes when touched

In several battles in Europe, more than two million American soldiers under General John Pershing upset the German stronghold. By the fall of 1918, the Germans realized they could not win the war.

Media in History

Radio Makes It Into Prime Time

In a way, radio owes much of its success to World War I. Several inventors had spent years patenting various radio devices. Leaders among these inventors were Guglielmo Marconi, Lee De Forest, Reginald Fessenden, and Edwin Howard Armstrong. De Forest and Armstrong fought each other often in patent courts. Each claimed the other was intruding on registered patents.

When World War I began, the U.S. navy saw the military advantages of radio. The navy arranged a moratorium, or suspension, on patent suits. Thus, it was able to pool all available skills and knowledge about radio. The navy's wireless radio communications system played a big part in winning the war.

After the war, government regulation ended. A new private company—Radio Corporation of America (RCA)—got the rights to much of the navy's system. This gave RCA superiority in the young industry. Today RCA is a part of General Electric (GE), one of the world's largest electronics companies. It owns the NBC network and television stations in most of the nation's largest cities.

World War I Statistics	
American soldiers killed	116,516
American soldiers wounded	204,002
Total deaths	8,528,154
Total wounded	21,189,154
Cost to United States	$32.7 billion

The government of Germany asked the Allies for an armistice. The fighting stopped while both sides prepared to discuss how to end the war.

The German army officers and the officers of the Allied forces met in a private railroad car in France. The Great War, which later became known as World War I, had lasted more than four years. The war ended on the morning of the eleventh day, at the eleventh hour, of the eleventh month—November 11, 1918. In differing ways, the war had weakened the great powers of Europe. It had, however, increased the power of the United States.

SECTION 3 REVIEW On a separate sheet of paper, write *True* if the statement is true or *False* if the statement is not true.

1) The Zimmermann Note stated that Mexico would receive Texas, New Mexico, and Arizona if Mexico helped Germany defeat the United States.

2) Congress declared war on Germany in 1917.

3) The United States did not use a draft in the war.

4) In 1918, the Germans realized they could not win the war.

5) The power of the United States decreased after the war.

Writing About History

Find more information about American soldiers in World War I. Write in your notebook about what it was like to be an American soldier in the war.

What do you think ?

Do you think it is right for a country to use a draft to get soldiers for wars? Why or why not?

Wilson believed that if the world was to remain at peace, then the peace treaty had to be fair to all sides. Early in January of 1918, he spoke of a plan for a lasting, or permanent, peace. This plan became known as Wilson's Fourteen Points.

Five Major Ideas of Wilson's Fourteen Points

1. Secret treaties between nations would end.

2. Any nation would be free to sail in any seas and oceans of the world.

3. Nations would decrease the size of their armies and navies.

4. Boundaries of nations would be changed so people with the same language and customs could live together.

5. An organization called the League of Nations would be created to settle disputes between countries in a peaceful way.

What Happened at the Paris Peace Conference?

Conference
A meeting among a large group of people

A **conference** was held in the Palace of Versailles near Paris, France, in January of 1919. The purpose of the conference was to discuss and write a peace treaty that was acceptable to nations that fought in the war. President Wilson decided to go to the Paris Peace Conference. No President before Wilson had left the United States while in office. He wanted to make sure his League of Nations became a part of the treaty. Three other leaders who attended were David Lloyd George of Great Britain, Georges Clemenceau of France, and Vittorio Orlando of Italy. These political leaders became known as the "Big Four." Germany was not invited to attend until after the treaty was written.

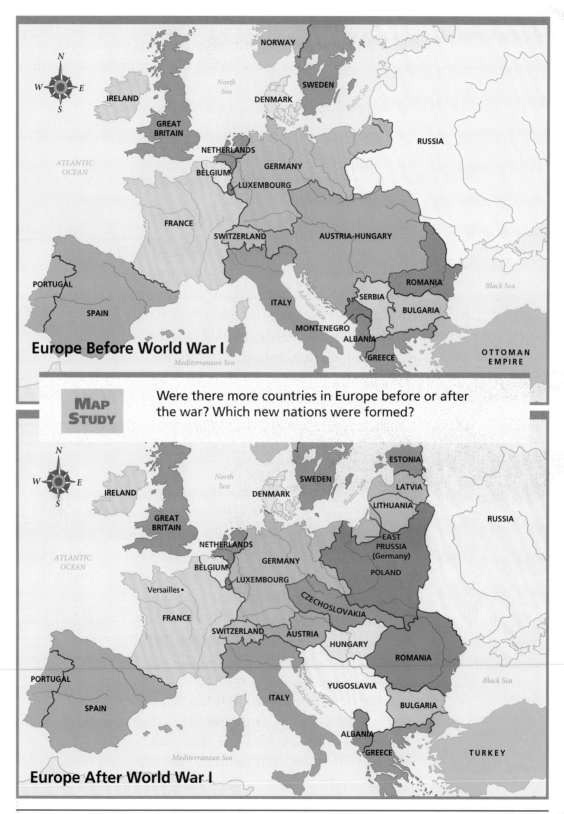

Europe Before World War I

MAP STUDY Were there more countries in Europe before or after the war? Which new nations were formed?

Europe After World War I

The Treaty of Versailles changed the map of Europe. The Austro-Hungarian Empire was broken up into Austria and Hungary. Most of the rest of the Empire was made into the new nations of Poland, Czechoslovakia, and Yugoslavia. Bosnia and Serbia became part of Yugoslavia.

President Wilson believed that the treaty did not provide the just peace he wanted. He agreed to the treaty in exchange for support of his League of Nations. Wilson thought that the League would correct the problems created by the treaty.

The treaty forced Germany to give land to France and Poland. It blamed Germany for starting the war and forced Germany to pay a huge sum of money for war damages. It took from Germany its colonies in Asia, Africa, and the North Pacific, and it demanded that the country not build a new army. The Germans were not pleased with the conditions of the treaty. However, having no other choice, Germany signed the Treaty of Versailles on July 28, 1919.

In this cartoon, the Constitution is trying to push the League of Nations off the chair.

Why Didn't Congress Ratify the Treaty?

According to the Constitution, two-thirds of the Senate must approve all treaties between the United States and another nation. The Republican senators did not like the idea of a League of Nations. According to the treaty, members of the League of Nations agreed to protect the independence and territory of each member. Republican senators thought that the United States might get drawn into a number of foreign wars, and perhaps without the approval of Congress. Some Republican senators were against the entire treaty, while others wanted parts of it rewritten. President Wilson would not make any major changes in the treaty.

President Wilson decided to take the treaty to the American people. He set out by train to carry his message across the United States. The League of Nations, he said, was the first step in making the world safe from war. Crowds of people cheered Wilson wherever he spoke. However, the Republican senators did not change their opinion of the treaty.

Wilson became ill on September 25, 1919. He canceled the rest of the tour and returned to Washington, D.C. He had a stroke, which left him unable to move the left side of his body, but still allowed him to speak clearly. He never recovered. On November 19, 1919, the United States Senate voted on the Treaty of Versailles. The treaty did not pass. The Senate voted again in March of 1920. The result was the same. It was the first time in United States history that the Senate had failed to ratify a peace treaty. The United States did not join the League of Nations. Without the United States as a member, the League of Nations was a weak organization. The Treaty of Versailles did not bring about a fair and just peace. The seeds for a second and more horrible world war had been planted. Within twenty years, the nations of the world would be at war again.

WORD BANK
Austro-Hungarian
Fourteen Points
League of Nations
Paris Peace Conference
Treaty of Versailles

SECTION 4 REVIEW On a separate sheet of paper, write the correct word from the Word Bank to complete each sentence.

1) Wilson's _____ was a plan for permanent peace.

2) The _____ took place to discuss a peace treaty acceptable to all of the nations who fought in the war.

3) The _____ changed the map of Europe.

4) The _____ was part of Wilson's Fourteen Points.

5) The _____ Empire became Austria and Hungary.

What do you think ?

Why do you think it was so important for Wilson to find a peace plan that would last forever?

Suffragette Letter

On October 16, 1917, four women picketed in front of the White House. They were picketing for women's suffrage, or right to vote. For this action they were arrested and given six-month prison sentences. Several other groups of women had also been arrested for picketing in the 1910s. None of the sentences for those groups was as long as for the group of four. The four women wrote this letter from prison to the Commissioners of the District of Columbia.

"As political prisoners, we, the undersigned, refuse to work while in prison. We have taken this stand as a matter of principle after careful consideration, and from it we shall not recede.

This action is a necessary protest against an unjust sentence: In reminding President Wilson of his preelection promises against woman suffrage, we were exercising the right of peaceful petition, guaranteed by the Constitution of the United States, which declares peaceful picketing is legal in the District of Columbia. That we have been unjustly sentenced has been well recognized—when President Wilson pardoned the first group of suffragists who had been given sixty days in the workhouse, and again when Judge Mullowny suspended the sentence for the last group of picketers. We wish to point out the inconsistency and injustice of our sentences—some of us have been given sixty days, a later group, thirty days, and another group given a suspended sentence for exactly the same action.

Conscious, therefore, of having acted in accordance with the highest standards of citizenship, we ask the commissioners of the District to grant us the rights due political prisoners."

Source Reading Wrap-Up

1) What were the women refusing to do while in prison?

2) What was the reason for their refusal?

3) The women mention two people who played a part in their dilemma. Who were they?

4) What were the women asking for?

5) How convincing do you think the women's letter was?

CHAPTER SUMMARY

★ Woodrow Wilson succeeded in having Congress pass many reform laws. During the early part of his administration the Federal Reserve System was established and the Sixteenth Amendment (income tax) was ratified.

★ In Europe, tension mounted between two groups of allied nations. Following the assassination of Archduke Francis Ferdinand in Sarajevo in 1914, war broke out in Europe. The United States remained neutral throughout the early years of the war.

★ A German U-boat sank the British passenger ship *Lusitania* in 1915. Many Americans wanted the United States to become involved in the war.

★ Following the publication of the Zimmermann Note, the United States declared war on Germany on April 6, 1917. President Wilson said that the war was to make the world "safe for democracy."

★ American factories immediately began to manufacture military supplies, and men were drafted to become soldiers.

★ By the fall of 1918 more than two million American soldiers were fighting in Europe under General John Pershing.

★ The war ended on November 11, 1918. It had weakened the great European countries but had established the United States as a major world power.

★ Wilson presented his "Fourteen Points" plan for a permanent peace in Europe. In this plan he called for the formation of the League of Nations.

★ The Treaty of Versailles officially ended World War I and redrew the boundary lines for many of the countries of Europe.

★ Many members of Congress did not like the idea of the League of Nations in the peace treaty. Wilson struggled to get the treaty approved, but Congress never approved the Treaty of Versailles. The United States did not join the League of Nations.

Comprehension: Identifying Facts

On a separate sheet of paper, write the words from the Word Bank to complete each sentence.

WORD BANK	
Allied Powers	*Lusitania*
Central Powers	submarines
Federal Reserve System	Treaty of Versailles
Francis Ferdinand	Woodrow Wilson
Germany	Zimmermann Note
League of Nations	

1) A national banking organization called the _____ was one of President Wilson's early victories.

2) Great Britain, France, Serbia, and Russia were part of an alliance called the _____.

3) The _____ alliance included Germany, Austria-Hungary, and Turkey.

4) World War I began when an assassin shot Archduke _____ and his wife in Sarajevo.

5) War zones were patrolled by German _____, called U-boats, to keep supplies from reaching Great Britain.

6) When the British ocean liner _____ was sunk, many Americans had a hard time remaining neutral.

7) _____ proposed a League of Nations as part of his plan known as the Fourteen Points.

8) Soon after newspapers published the _____, Congress declared war on Germany.

9) The _____ was a failure, partially because the United States refused to join.

10) Congress failed to approve the _____, even though Wilson tried hard to win its support.

11) _____ was not invited to attend the peace conference at the Palace of Versailles in France.

Comprehension: Understanding Main Ideas

On a separate sheet of paper, write the answer to each question using complete sentences.

1) What were two major events that occurred early in Woodrow Wilson's presidency?

2) What were the two European alliances and which countries belonged to each?

3) Why did sinking the *Lusitania* cause so much uproar?

4) What information was in the Zimmermann Note?

5) Why was Congress against the Treaty of Versailles?

6) What were three of the things that America did after it declared war on Germany?

7) Which four countries attended the peace conference at Versailles and who represented each country?

Critical Thinking: Write Your Opinion

1) After World War I, many people were against American involvement in the League of Nations. What do you think about America's involvement today in the United Nations?

2) During the early part of World War I, America remained neutral. Would it be possible for America to remain neutral today if a war broke out all over Europe?

| Test Taking Tip | When studying for a test, it may be helpful to make a timeline to help you remember the order of events. |

The Roaring Twenties

1920–1929

With World War I over, Americans were ready to return to normal. As it turned out, however, the decade of the 1920s was anything but normal and restful. The "Roaring Twenties," as the decade was called, was an exciting time for many Americans. It was full of social and cultural changes. But near its end, the decade was also a time of hardship. It was the beginning of the worst depression in American history. In this chapter, you will learn about the changes and hardships America faced in the 1920s.

Goals for Learning

▶ To describe the period known as the "Roaring Twenties"

▶ To describe how women's roles changed during the period

▶ To explain Prohibition and problems it created

▶ To describe the social and cultural developments of the period

▶ To explain the reasons for the 1929 stock market crash

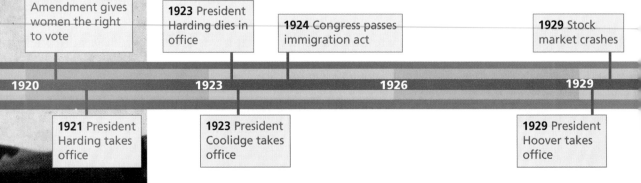

1920 Nineteenth Amendment gives women the right to vote

1923 President Harding dies in office

1924 Congress passes immigration act

1929 Stock market crashes

1920   1923   1926   1929

1921 President Harding takes office

1923 President Coolidge takes office

1929 President Hoover takes office

Association
A group working together on a common cause

Decade
A period of ten years

In 1920, the American people were tired of the tensions of reform and war. The nation had used so much energy in the last two **decades** that Americans seemed to be hoping for a rest. Average people wished the country would return to more normal times. They wanted the nation less involved in world affairs and more involved in activities at home.

What Was the Nineteenth Amendment?

In 1869, the National Woman Suffrage Association had been formed. The **association** was led by Elizabeth Cady Stanton and Susan B. Anthony. This group wanted to amend the Constitution to give women the right to vote. Over the next fifty years, the suffrage amendment was introduced in several sessions of Congress. In August of 1920, three-fourths of the states ratified the amendment. The Nineteenth Amendment gave all American women the right to vote. The long struggle had ended in victory.

What Helped Americans Return to Normal Times?

Warren G. Harding, the Republican candidate, was elected President in 1920. Harding had promised the weary voters a "return to normalcy." No one had ever heard the word *normalcy* before, because Harding had made it up.

Women struggled for almost fifty years to win the right to vote. They finally were allowed to vote starting in 1920.

Heroics
Bravery well beyond what is needed

Landslide
A majority of votes for one side

Solution
The answer to a problem

The word *normalcy* fit the feelings of the American people. They knew what Harding meant and they elected him by a **landslide.** He received more than sixty percent of the vote. This was the greatest percentage of votes ever gained by a presidential candidate, perhaps because women voted for the first time in this election. For the twelve years that followed this election, the majority of Americans voted for Republican Presidents.

Harding had been a senator from Ohio, while his Vice President, Calvin Coolidge, was the former governor of Massachusetts. After the election, Harding announced that he was not interested in "**heroics**, but healing." He was looking for quick **solutions** for the nation's problems. He took office in 1921.

What Did Harding Do as President?

During the presidency of Warren Harding, the Emergency Quota Act was passed. The law limited immigration to the United States. A new tariff act was written, raising the tax on imported goods beyond the rate set under President Wilson. A Veteran's Bureau was established to give different types of aid to ex-soldiers and their families. Government finances were organized as never before by the new Bureau of the Budget.

This cartoon shows officials in President Harding's administration trying to escape being crushed by the Teapot Dome scandal.

Generally, however, Harding was not an effective President. He was a poor judge of character in appointing people to government office. Several members of his administration were caught using their positions to make money for themselves.

The most serious scandal began in 1921. Two oil businessmen gave Secretary of the Interior Albert B. Fall $400,000. He then arranged for the oilmen to rent, at a very low price, some government oil reserves at Teapot Dome, Wyoming, and Elk Hills, California. Fall went to prison in 1929 for his crime.

Harding did not know about the dealings of the Interior Secretary until the Teapot Dome Scandal became public. This embarrassment was followed by charges of **fraud** and bribery against the Attorney General and the head of the Veteran's Bureau. Harding would not have allowed these scandals to happen if he had been able to prevent them.

Emotion
Feelings people express

Fraud
A lie or false act to steal money or something of value

President Harding died suddenly on August 2, 1923. Millions of people expressed their sorrow for his death. Harding had once said, "I cannot hope to be one of the great Presidents, but perhaps I may be remembered as one of the most loved."

What Did Coolidge Do as President?

Vice President Calvin Coolidge became the President of the United States in 1923. Coolidge was a man of few words and showed little **emotion.** One story describes how a woman told Coolidge she had bet with a friend that she could get him to say more than two words. Coolidge answered, "You lose."

Coolidge believed that "the chief business of America is business." He was a friend and supporter of the business community. He thought that government regulations to control big business were harmful to the American economy. He rejected the reform ideas of Roosevelt and Wilson. Reformers like the Progressives still fought for more government control and regulation. That fight, though, was no longer a major force in American politics.

During the election year of 1924, Coolidge seemed calm and confident about the nation's future. The economy was strong, and many people's lives were improving. Most Americans liked what they saw and voted to "keep cool with Coolidge." Coolidge was President for the next four years.

The Silent Years

During the "quiet" 1920s, there was little radio and no television. For entertainment, many people went to the "movies" to see silent films. A piano player or small orchestra in the movie theater accompanied the films. Full-length epic features like *Cleopatra*, *Ben-Hur*, and *The Ten Commandments* were popular. The most influential and popular silent film ever made was *Birth of a Nation*. Usually short comedy films preceded the main feature with stars like Charlie Chaplin and the Keystone Kops.

Silent-film stars usually had one major appeal. Douglas Fairbanks and Rudolph Valentino were romantic heroes. Mary Pickford and Lillian Gish were beautiful and innocent. Stars were often more important than the story.

The silent era suddenly ended when *The Jazz Singer*, the first "talkie," was made in 1927. Although silent movies usually were of superior quality, people stood in long lines to see talkies. Stories about singing, dancing, and laughter helped people escape from real-life troubles.

SECTION 1 REVIEW Choose the best word or name in parentheses to complete each sentence. Write your answers on a separate sheet of paper.

1) The (Seventeenth, Eighteenth, Nineteenth) Amendment gave all American women the right to vote.

2) (Calvin Coolidge, Warren G. Harding) was elected President in 1920.

3) The (Nineteenth Amendment, Emergency Quota Act) limited immigration to the United States.

4) The National Woman Suffrage Association wanted to give (African Americans, immigrants, women) the right to vote.

5) President Coolidge supported the (reformer, Progressive, business) community.

What do you think ?

Why do you think it took so long for women to gain the right to vote?

★Assembly line
A process by which a line of workers assemble something piece by piece until it is complete

Mobile
Having the ability to travel

The 1920s in American society was a period of many social changes. Industry thrived across the nation. More Americans earned higher wages, so they could afford to spend more money on goods. If they didn't have the cash, they could now buy things in monthly payments. Americans had more leisure time and more money to go out to movies or music clubs.

During the war, many American farmers had increased their production to meet a higher demand. After the war, farm prices fell and farmers had unwanted crops and expanding debts. Many of them started to consider other types of work in cities.

America became more **mobile** as a growing number of people were able to buy cars. Radios brought news and entertainment to American homes. Another invention now found in thousands of homes was the telephone. Communication by phone was helping to bring people closer.

What Was the First Widely Used Automobile?

During the 1920s, the Ford Model T automobile became the most popular way to travel. By 1916, a Model T cost about $400. Wealthy people owned most of the first automobiles. When the price of these cars dropped to about $250 by the mid-1920s, they became affordable for more Americans.

The Model T was the first mass-produced car. Henry Ford used an **assembly line** to make them. In an assembly line, a line of workers assembled the car piece by piece until it was complete. Every car was exactly alike. Henry Ford once commented that Americans could buy the Model T in "any color—as long as it's black." It had a canvas roof and no door for the driver. It had to be started with a hand crank in the front. Americans were proud to be seen in a "tin lizzie," as the Model T was nicknamed.

The assembly line made automobiles affordable for many families, like this one.

Owners found many different ways to use the Model T. Farmers, for example, used the car to pull plows, to run water pumps, and to haul hay. People made jokes about the rattling fenders and the parts that would fall out. But they kept buying the Model T until 1927 when Ford introduced the Model A.

The Model T put the nation on wheels. It became a necessary part of the lives of most Americans. The automobile gave people more choices for where they could work and live.

The federal government encouraged the building of modern highways to replace dirt roads. **Suburbs,** the new communities built outside of cities, grew rapidly. The automobile allowed Americans the freedom to travel from place to place.

How Did Women Become More Independent?

Many young American women of the 1920s were called **flappers.** The name brings to mind something not tied down that flaps in the wind. These young women refused to be "tied" to the ideas, actions, and styles of an older **generation.** Flappers cut their hair short, wore skirts cut above their knees, and painted their lips bright red.

If you were living in the 1920s, you might have decided to buy your first car. Although automobiles had been around for two decades, most people did not own one until the 1920s. Henry Ford's assembly line made cars affordable. Compare the features on a Model T with a modern family car.

Description	Model T	Modern Family Car
Average price	under $300	$15,000–$20,000
Fastest speed	40 mph	120 mph
Speed controlled by	Lever on steering wheel	Gas pedal and cruise control
Engine	4 cylinder	4, 6, or 8 cylinder
Transmission	2 gears	3 or 4 gears
Change gears	With foot pedal	Automatic
Flat tire	Repair puncture	Change tire
Assembly	By hand	With help of computers and robots

In addition to having recently won the right to vote, women gained a new independence in the 1920s. Many started to think about jobs that had been open only to men. Women began to challenge old ideas of how they should act. The changes in hair and dress styles were a clear sign that women also wanted to gain more social freedom.

Flappers wanted to show their independence. These woman are dancing the Charleston.

How Did Radio Change American Life?

By the mid-1920s, most middle-class Americans had a telephone, a radio, and a phonograph in their home. Silent movies had been popular since before World War I. The radio brought an unlimited source of free information and entertainment right into the home. By 1929, it was so popular that about ten million Americans owned radios.

The first permanent commercial radio station began broadcasting in Pittsburgh in 1920. This station reported the results of the presidential election. In 1921, baseball's World Series was heard on the radio. By 1923, there were more than 500 radio stations in the United States.

Beginning in the 1920s, the radio brought information and entertainment into millions of people's homes.

Writing About History

Find out more information about radio in the 1920s. Then write in your notebook about the similarities and differences between radio in the 1920s and radio today.

SECTION 2 REVIEW Write the answers to these questions on a separate sheet of paper using complete sentences.

1) Why did many farmers look for city jobs after World War I?

2) What process did Ford use to make the Model T?

3) What different uses did people have for the automobile?

4) Who were flappers?

5) How did radio change the American way of life?

What do you think ❓

Do you think radio is as important in people's lives today as it was in the 1920s? Why or why not?

★Composer
One who writes music

Energetic
Full of energy

Improvise
To make up as you go along

★Spiritual
A religious song

★Symphony
A long, complex musical piece

Jazz in the 1920s seemed to capture the spirit of the times. The music was "hot," **energetic,** and lively. Jazz was not played just from musical notes written on paper. Jazz songs and sounds were **improvised.**

Jazz started in the South among African-American musicians. These musicians used African rhythms, work songs, and **spirituals.** A spiritual is a religious song. By mixing these styles with European-style music, the artists created a truly original American sound.

Jazz had many forms. The earliest type of jazz was Dixieland of the South. However, by the 1920s, jazz bands could be found in most northern cities. Louis Armstrong played the trumpet with his small band in Chicago and New York. Duke Ellington started writing jazz music for big bands. As jazz became more popular, classical music **composers** picked up its sound. A composer is one who writes music. Composer George Gershwin used jazz in his **symphony** "Rhapsody in Blue" (1924) and his tone poem "An American in Paris" (1928). A symphony is a long, complex musical piece.

New dances like "the Charleston" also became popular. While doing the Charleston, young people moved freely around the dance floor. The dancers kicked their legs into the air and waved their arms above their heads. The faster the music was played, the faster they moved. Many older Americans were concerned about the effects jazz and the new dances were having on young people. One magazine wrote that the behavior of the young people was "shocking to their grandparents." Unlike people in past generations, these young people didn't care how much they shocked others.

Duke Ellington directs his big band. Ellington was a major composer and developer of jazz.

Which American Writers Produced Important Works?

Some of America's greatest writers produced important works during the 1920s. Writers tried to tell the story of what was happening in America. In *The Great Gatsby*, F. Scott Fitzgerald showed the unhappy life of a wealthy, popular man who was once a poor farm boy. Sinclair Lewis wrote about small-town life in America in *Main Street* and *Babbitt*. In *A Farewell to Arms*, Ernest Hemingway told the story of the impact World War I had on the life of an American man. Edith Wharton's *The Age of Innocence* told about the foolishness of New York high society of the late 1800s. In *Three Soldiers*, John Dos Passos wrote about the sadness of men after their return from the Great War.

The Works of Langston Hughes

James Langston Hughes was one of the most productive writers of the early 1900s. His essay "The Negro Artist and the Racial Mountain" (1926) established him as a major figure in the Harlem Renaissance. As a poet, he published two volumes of verse in the 1920s. Hughes brought the rhythms and styles of jazz and black speech into his poetry. In the Depression he wrote *Not Without Laughter*, his first novel, and short stories like "The Ways of White People." Hughes became known as a playwright when his *Mulatto* was staged on Broadway. He founded the Harlem Suitcase Theatre in 1938. During World War II, Hughes began his weekly "Simple" column in the *Chicago Defender*. It featured an African-American philosopher who talked about life, love, and race. Later in his career, he devoted time to combining drama and gospel music. An example is his *Black Nativity*.

Literature
History in Your Life

What Was the Harlem Renaissance?

An area in New York City called Harlem became a creative center for many African Americans. Writers, poets, musicians, entertainers, and students increased African-American pride. The period of the 1920s to the mid-1930s is known as the Harlem Renaissance. Writers and poets like Langston Hughes and Countee Cullen wrote about the noble past of African Americans. They also wrote of African-American dreams, disappointments, and discrimination. In his poem "Harlem," Langston Hughes posed the question of what happens to the African-American dream of equality if it continues to be put off. Would the dream, he asked, "dry up like a raisin in the sun"?

MARCUS GARVEY: 1887–1940

Marcus Garvey was a boldly determined supporter of black nationalism. He also supported black-owned businesses. He believed blacks should have their own homeland—the entire continent of Africa. Garvey spoke out against the lynchings of blacks and urged his people to strike for freedom. In 1914, he organized the Universal Negro Improvement Association in his native Jamaica. He moved the association's headquarters to Harlem in 1916. By the 1920s, it had become the largest nonreligious association in African-American history. In 1920, its first international convention brought about 25,000 delegates from twenty-five nations. Its weekly newspaper, *Negro World*, ran for fourteen years. Garvey also established two steamship lines that were owned and run by African Americans. These lines provided transportation to Africa and helped to link black businesses worldwide.

SECTION 3 REVIEW On a separate sheet of paper, write *True* if the statement is true or *False* if the statement is not true.

1) Jazz started in the South.

2) Younger people were responsible for beginning the new music and dance styles of the 1920s.

3) In *The Great Gatsby,* Ernest Hemingway told the story of the impact World War I had on the life of an American man.

4) John Dos Passos wrote a story about the sadness of men after their return from the Great War.

5) The Harlem Renaissance focused on African-American pride.

What do you think ?

The older generation did not understand the younger generation in the 1920s. Why do you think this happened? Does this still happen today? Why or why not?

> ★**Communist**
> *A person who believes in a form of government that eliminates private property*

During the 1920s, more Americans were independent and creative. They searched for fun and the good life. Still, there were problems. Many Americans were poor. The boll weevil destroyed much of southern farmers' cotton crop. Farmers in other areas still had difficulty making a living because of the low prices for crops.

What Forms of Discrimination Were Problems?

Some Americans wanted to deny equality and freedom to people who were different from them. They wanted African Americans "kept in their place." They were fearful and suspicious of immigrants. They worried about foreigners destroying American democracy. "America First" became their slogan.

A new Ku Klux Klan was formed in the South in 1915. The last time Americans had seen the Klan was during the period of Reconstruction. The new Klan feared African Americans, Jews, Catholics, and immigrants. They wanted to define an American as white, Protestant, and native born. The ideas of the Klan spread. They gained some political power and helped elect governors in two states. In 1925, Klansmen carrying American flags marched in a large parade down Pennsylvania Avenue in Washington, D.C. Behind the marchers was the symbol of American democracy, the United States Capitol. Fortunately, during the last years of the 1920s, the Klan's political power declined sharply.

In 1924, Congress passed the Immigration Act. This law limited the number of immigrants allowed into the United States from southern and eastern Europe. Immigrants from Japan were not allowed in the United States. The law was passed because it was felt that these immigrants were a threat to American democracy. Americans feared that the **communist** revolution in Russia would spread to the United States. Communists believed in a form of government that eliminated private property.

What Was Prohibition?

Crime, violence, family breakups, and child abuse were all major social problems. Reformers believed that alcohol was the root of these problems. The Eighteenth Amendment, ratified in 1919, made it illegal to sell alcohol in the United States. The ban on making and selling of alcohol was called **Prohibition.**

Because of the ban on alcohol, the 1920s also became known as "The Dry Decade." However, it really was not all that "dry." **Bootleggers** continued to make and sell liquor illegally. The public was eager to buy it. **Speakeasies,** where illegal liquor was sold, became very popular meeting places in major cities around the country.

Many Americans ignored the law. Organized crime made millions of dollars and became very powerful. Reformers may have been trying to do a good thing, but Prohibition brought a very high rise in crime. In 1933, the Twenty-First Amendment to the Constitution repealed the Prohibition amendment.

★**Bootlegger**
Someone who made or sold alcohol illegally during Prohibition

★**Prohibition**
The ban on making or selling alcohol

★**Speakeasy**
A place where liquor was sold illegally during Prohibition

WORD BANK

bootlegger
Eighteenth
Prohibition
speakeasies
Twenty-First

SECTION 4 REVIEW On a separate sheet of paper, write the word from the Word Bank to complete each sentence.

1) The _____ Amendment made it against the law to sell alcohol in the United States.

2) _____ was the name for the ban on alcohol.

3) A person who made and sold alcohol during Prohibition was called a _____.

4) Liquor was sold illegally at places called _____.

5) The _____ Amendment repealed Prohibition.

What do you think ❓

Do you think Prohibition would work if it was made a law today? Why or why not?

Solo
Done by one person

★Stock market
A market for the buying and selling of company stock

Early in the morning of May 20, 1927, a small plane called the *Spirit of St. Louis* lifted off from New York. The pilot's name was Charles Lindbergh. He headed across the Atlantic Ocean for Paris, France. Up until this time, no one had made a nonstop, **solo** flight across the Atlantic Ocean. A $25,000 prize had been offered by a New York hotel owner to the first person who could do it. Lindbergh knew that he had to stay awake and fly the plane for more than thirty hours. Paris was 3,600 miles away.

Thirty-three hours later, "Lucky Lindy" touched his plane down in Paris. Lindbergh was a perfect symbol for the nation. Americans felt that the country was strong because it was made up of people like Lucky Lindy.

Charles Lindbergh became the first person to fly a plane solo across the Atlantic Ocean.

Who Won the Election of 1928?

People paid little attention to the fact that car sales and housing construction were decreasing by 1927. Too many good things were happening. Lindbergh had reached Paris. Babe Ruth hit sixty home runs. The **stock market** was going up. The stock market is a market for the buying and selling of company stock. People were making money by buying stocks. Business was good, and people believed it would get better.

Calvin Coolidge decided not to run for re-election in 1928. The Republican party nominated Herbert Hoover. Although he had been poor as a child, Hoover worked his way through college to become a mining engineer. He was what Americans liked to call "self-made." Hoover had also been responsible for getting aid to European victims of the World War.

> ★**Soup house**
> *Place where the poor could get food*

The Democrats nominated Al Smith, the governor of New York. Republican campaign posters said, "Let's keep what we've got … Hoover and happiness, or Smith and **soup houses**." Soup houses were places where the poor could get food. In 1928, the voters picked Hoover for President. Hoover took office in 1929. The voters did not realize that they would soon get the soup houses anyway.

How Did the Stock Market Crash?

The stock market continued to rise through 1928 and most of 1929. Radio Corporation of America stock went from $94.50 a share to $505 in one year. People took their savings out of the bank and bought stocks. Many people even borrowed money to buy stocks. The price of many stocks was much higher than their true value. Many people did not seem to care. They were sure they could sell their stocks to someone else and make a profit.

On October 24, 1929, stock prices dropped sharply. There were more sellers than buyers. Five days later, on October 29, 1929, the stock market fell apart, or crashed. People tried to sell their stocks, but there were no buyers.

The United States was at the beginning of the worst economic depression in its history. The Roaring Twenties had come to a crashing end. The 1930s would be called the "Great Depression." It was a time of great struggle, when businesses failed and people lost their jobs.

SECTION 5 REVIEW Write the answers to these questions on a separate sheet of paper using complete sentences.

1) Why did Americans like Charles Lindbergh?
2) What is the stock market?
3) What were soup houses?
4) What caused the stock market to crash?
5) What was the Great Depression?

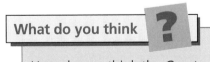

What do you think

How do you think the Great Depression changed people's attitudes?

James Weldon Johnson

James Weldon Johnson was an African-American educator, diplomat, and writer. He was a founder of the National Association for the Advancement of Colored People. In the 1920s, he was considered a primary spokesperson and interpreter of the Harlem Renaissance. This passage is from an article written in 1928 for Harper's Magazine. *It is one of many magazine articles Johnson wrote at the time.*

"All of the Negro's folk-art creations have undergone a new evaluation. His sacred music—the spirituals; his secular music—ragtime, jazz, and the work songs; his folklore—the Uncle Remus plantation tales; and his dances have received a new and higher appreciation. I dare to say that it is now more or less acknowledged that the only things artistic that have sprung from American life, and been universally recognized as American products, are the folk creations of the Negro.

But the story does not halt at this point. The Negro has done a great deal through his folk-art creations to change the national attitudes toward him; and now the efforts of the race have been reinforced and magnified by the individual Negro artist, the conscious artist. . . .

What, now, is the significance of this artistic activity on the part of the Negro and of its reactions on the American people?

I think it is twofold. In the first place, the Negro is making some distinctive contributions to our common cultural store. I do not claim it is possible for these individual artists to produce anything comparable to the folk-art in distinctive values, but I do believe they are bringing something fresh and vital into American art, something from the store of their own racial genius—warmth, color, movement, rhythm, and abandon; depth and swiftness of emotion and the beauty of sensuousness. I believe American art will be richer because of these elements in fuller quantity."

Source Reading Wrap-Up

1) In the first sentence, what does Johnson say has happened to African Americans' folk-art creations?

2) What are three specific folk-art creations from African Americans that he names?

3) In the second paragraph, what does Johnson say changed through African-Americans' folk-art creations?

4) What is one thing Johnson says African-Americans' contributions are bringing to American art?

5) Identify one element of our modern culture that was an African-American contribution from the Harlem Renaissance.

CHAPTER SUMMARY

★ The Nineteenth Amendment, which granted women the right to vote, was ratified in August of 1920. Women gained greater independence in the 1920s. Some worked outside the home and many changed their hair and clothing styles. "Flappers" were young women who showed their freedom through short hair, short skirts, and makeup.

★ President Warren Harding faced a number of scandals during his term, including the Teapot Dome Scandal in which the Secretary of the Interior sold oil rights to government land.

★ Calvin Coolidge became President when Harding died in office. Coolidge spoke little and showed little emotion. He was a supporter of business.

★ Americans had more leisure time and earned higher wages than ever before. They were able to purchase new items such as automobiles, radios, and telephones.

★ Jazz, a new style of American music, developed during this period. Louis Armstrong, Duke Ellington, and others helped make this music style popular. Along with new music came new dances like the Charleston.

★ Many of America's great writers such as F. Scott Fitzgerald, Sinclair Lewis, Langston Hughes, Edith Wharton, and John Dos Passos became famous during this decade.

★ There was a rebirth of pride in the African-American community of Harlem in New York City. Writers, musicians, and artists were part of what became known as the Harlem Renaissance.

★ African-American citizens continued to face discrimination during the 1920s. Groups such as the Ku Klux Klan spread throughout the country for a brief period. Immigrants also faced discrimination.

★ Prohibition, or a ban on making and selling alcoholic beverages, was in effect during this decade. There was much illegal activity because of Prohibition, including organized crime.

★ In May of 1927, Charles Lindbergh made the first solo transatlantic flight in his plane, the *Spirit of St. Louis.*

★ After a long period of time when stock prices were overvalued, the stock market crashed on October 29, 1929. This sent the country into the Great Depression.

Comprehension: Identifying Facts

On a separate sheet of paper, write the words from the Word Bank to complete each sentence.

WORD BANK	
bootleggers	presidential election
Charles Lindbergh	radio
Calvin Coolidge	stock market
Edith Wharton	suffrage
Langston Hughes	Teapot Dome
jazz	Warren Harding
Model T	

1) Almost everyone had a _____ in their home on which they could listen to news and entertainment.

2) Women earned the right to vote, or _____, when the Nineteenth Amendment was ratified.

3) President _____, who had faced several scandals, died in office.

4) A new form of American music called _____ developed during the 1920s.

5) _____ was a President who was known for his quiet ways and unemotional manner.

6) Harding's Secretary of the Interior sold rights to oil on government land at _____, Wyoming.

7) The great _____ crash happened in October of 1929.

8) One of the great women writers of the 1920s was _____.

9) The first commercial radio broadcasts covered the _____ in 1920.

10) _____ made the first solo airplane flight across the Atlantic Ocean in the *Spirit of St. Louis*.

11) One of the great writers of the Harlem Renaissance was _____.

12) People who sold illegal liquor during Prohibition were called _____.

13) For only $250 you could buy a _____ and travel the bumpy streets of America.

Comprehension: Understanding Main Ideas

On a separate sheet of paper, write the answer to each question using complete sentences.

1) Why was the decade called the "Roaring Twenties"?

2) What were some things that changed for women in the 1920s?

3) What was Prohibition and what problems did it cause?

4) What were four major cultural or social developments in the 1920s?

5) What was a major cause of the stock market crash of 1929?

Critical Thinking: Write Your Opinion

1) Would you have liked to live in the "Roaring Twenties"? Why or why not?

2) In the 1920s, radio brought faraway events into the homes of millions of Americans. What would you compare this with in your lifetime? Explain your choice.

Test Taking Tip	After you have completed a test, reread each question and answer. Ask yourself: Have I answered the question that was asked? Have I answered it completely?

Comparing and contrasting reveal how things are alike and how they are different. People, ideas, and events are sometimes compared and contrasted in writing. Look for words that signal comparing and contrasting when you read.

> To compare, ask: "How are these things alike?"
>
> To contrast, ask: "How are these things different?"

• To decide if things are being compared, look for words like:

> also   both   like   similar
>
> Andrew Carnegie and John D. Rockefeller were <u>both</u> industrialists.

• To decide if things are being contrasted, look for words like:

> but   however   instead
> not   only   while
>
> Andrew Carnegie's industry was steel, <u>while</u> John D. Rockefeller's industry was oil.

Decide whether each of these sentences compares or contrasts.

1) Both Theodore Roosevelt and Woodrow Wilson were U.S. presidents.

2) Roosevelt was a Progressive, while Wilson was a Democrat.

3) Roosevelt was an experienced political leader, but Wilson had been a political leader only a few years.

4) Like Roosevelt, Wilson also became a popular president.

5) Wilson, not Roosevelt, led the country through World War I.

Compare and contrast the 1910s with the 1920s. Focus on the following topics. You may write one sentence on each of the topics. Or, you may write a five-sentence paragraph on one of the topics.

6) women

7) communications

8) entertainment

9) transportation

10) international affairs

★ In 1898, America and Spain had conflicts in Cuba and the Philippines.

★ In 1899, America established its Open Door Policy with China.

★ The Hawaiian Islands became an American territory in 1900.

★ President William McKinley was assassinated in 1901. Theodore Roosevelt became President.

★ The Progressive party established political reforms.

★ Congress passed laws to protect the American people.

★ Roosevelt established policies for better use of natural resources. He built a strong navy for defense and to show America's strength.

★ America financed the building of the Panama Canal.

★ William Howard Taft became President in 1909. Amendment Sixteen established an income tax.

★ Woodrow Wilson became President in 1913. He got Congress to pass many reform laws.

★ War began in Europe in 1914. America remained neutral at first, but declared war on Germany on April 6, 1917. The war ended on November 11, 1918. It established America as a world power.

★ The Treaty of Versailles officially ended World War I and redrew European boundaries. Congress never approved the treaty.

★ In 1920, Amendment Nineteen granted women voting rights.

★ President Warren Harding faced a number of scandals during his term.

★ Calvin Coolidge became President when Harding died in office. Coolridge supported business.

★ Americans had more leisure time and earned higher wages than ever.

★ Jazz developed during the 1920s.

★ Many writers became famous during the 1920s.

★ African-American writers, musicians, and artists became part of the Harlem Renaissance.

★ African Americans, immigrants, Jews, and Catholics faced discrimination in the 1920s.

★ Prohibition prevented the sale of alcoholic beverages in the 1920s.

★ In May 1927, Charles Lindbergh made the first solo transatlantic flight.

★ The stock market crashed on October 29, 1929. The Great Depression began.

"Some went to the relief offices, and they came sadly
    back to their own people.

'They's rules—you got to be here a year before you
    can git relief. They say the gov'ment is gonna
    help. They don' know when.'

And gradually the greatest terror of all came along.

'They ain't gonna be no kinda work for three
    months.'"

–John Steinbeck, *The Grapes of Wrath*, 1939

Depression and World War II:

1930–1945

Have you noticed how hard times and difficulties can draw people together? That happened for Americans in the 1930s and 1940s. The economic crash in 1929 resulted in very hard times for many Americans during the 1930s. Many were out of work and homeless. The government established economic and social programs to help them. Americans drew together to help each other. Then in the 1940s the United States entered another world war. Americans drew together at home and overseas to support the war effort.

In this unit you will learn what Americans went through during the Great Depression. You will learn about programs that helped people through that difficult time. You will learn about events that brought about World War II. You will learn how the United States pulled together to win that war.

Chapter 25: Depression and the New Deal: 1930–1939

Chapter 26: World War II: 1939–1945

Depression and the New Deal

1930–1939

The good times of the 1920s were over when the Great Depression began. Americans spent the next decade just trying to get by. The government worked hard on plans to try to restore the country to what it had been. In this chapter, you will learn what caused the depression, the problems and hardships people faced, and what the government did to help solve the problem.

Goals for Learning

▶ To explain the factors that contributed to the Great Depression

▶ To describe conditions during the Great Depression

▶ To describe Franklin Roosevelt's "New Deal" policy

▶ To explain some of the programs of the New Deal

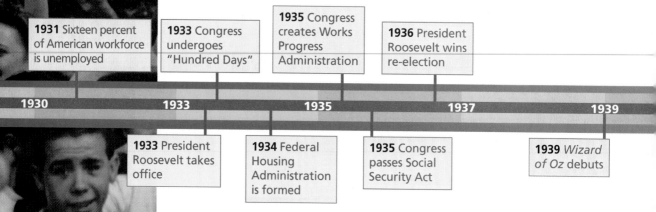

1931 Sixteen percent of American workforce is unemployed

1933 Congress undergoes "Hundred Days"

1935 Congress creates Works Progress Administration

1936 President Roosevelt wins re-election

1930   1933   1935   1937   1939

1933 President Roosevelt takes office

1934 Federal Housing Administration is formed

1935 Congress passes Social Security Act

1939 *Wizard of Oz* debuts

★Charity
A group that helps those in need

★Layoff
Letting workers go because a company cannot afford to pay them

The stock market crash of 1929 was as big a shock to President Hoover as it was to other Americans. Before the crash, the economy seemed strong. Less than four percent of American workers did not have jobs before 1929. One year later, nine percent of the workforce was unemployed.

As sales of their products decreased, American businesses were forced into **layoffs.** A layoff occurs when a company lets workers go because it cannot afford to pay them. The Ford Motor Company, for example, was forced to cut its number of workers by forty-four percent. By 1931, unemployment increased to sixteen percent. Eight million Americans could not find work. Many people lost their life savings.

President Hoover encouraged the American people to be patient. He believed the depression would end with time. He said the nation had seen hard times before, and each time the economy had bounced back.

President Hoover did not feel the federal government should have to help the unemployed. He believed state and local governments, private groups, and **charities** should help people. A charity is a group that helps those in need. According to Hoover, America was a strong democracy because Americans took responsibility for their own lives.

Although he had been President for less than a year, people blamed Hoover for causing the depression. Bitter "Hoover jokes" became popular. Empty pockets turned inside out were called "Hoover flags."

Unable to make loan payments to their banks, many people lost their homes. In many cities, homeless people built cardboard and tar paper shacks. These poorly built shelters gave some protection from bad weather. But, people living in them had to do without heat, lights, or running water. These slums became known as "Hoovervilles."

What Caused the Depression?

Several factors caused the depression. The stock market crash was only one of the causes. Businesses had grown rapidly in the 1920s. They had produced many products quickly and often faster than consumers could buy them. This **overproduction** caused big changes in many companies. As production was made to slow down, workers were laid off.

When the economy was good, people spent a lot of money. The strong economy encouraged them to buy more than they could pay for. Many people had bought things on **credit.** Credit is the practice of buying something and paying for it later. Then, when people lost their jobs, they could not pay their debts. Banks that "held paper" on unpaid loans went out of business.

Many foreign countries still in debt from the war were unable to buy products from America. In some cases, high tariffs were placed on American goods. The American economy might have grown much stronger during the 1920s if these countries had been able to buy more U.S. goods.

During the depression, breadlines helped feed the unemployed or the homeless.

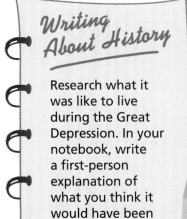

Writing About History

Research what it was like to live during the Great Depression. In your notebook, write a first-person explanation of what you think it would have been like to live during that time.

Since the end of the war, farmers had struggled with great financial difficulties. Prices for their goods had continued to go down. Many farmers were hardly able to support their families. They had little money to buy products that were necessary for survival.

How Did Americans Lose Confidence?

During the depression, the American people lost confidence in themselves and in their country. People lived in fear of tomorrow. Businesses were afraid to make new investments. Workers thought that they could lose their jobs at any time. Unemployed workers had little reason to believe that they would ever find other jobs.

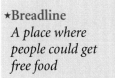

★Breadline
A place where people could get free food

Families stood in **breadlines** for free food. Homeless people slept in subways, parks, and old empty warehouses. Men who once worked regularly could be seen selling apples on the street. Across the country, Americans became very concerned about the nation's future.

SECTION 1 REVIEW On a separate sheet of paper, write *True* if the statement is true or *False* if the statement is not true.

1) Ten million Americans were unemployed in 1931.

2) President Hoover did not believe the depression would end.

3) Many people blamed the depression on President Hoover.

4) Overproduction was one of the causes of the depression.

5) People lost confidence in themselves and their country during the depression.

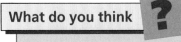

What do you think **?**

Why is confidence in yourself and your country important?

★Insurance
A plan that protects against loss in return for regular payments

★Moratorium
The legal act of delaying something

Stabilize
To bring something back to normal

Surplus
An extra amount of something

The weak economy did not improve as President Hoover had believed it would. He made plans to help the economy. Hoover proposed the following:

1. With the Agricultural Marketing Act, Congress approved $500 million to buy extra, or **surplus,** crops from farmers. Hoover hoped this act would **stabilize** farm prices. This plan was unsuccessful because the farm problem was too great. Farm prices continued to go down.

2. The Reconstruction Finance Corporation was established in 1932. This corporation loaned emergency money to banks, railroads, and **insurance** companies. Insurance is a plan that protects against loss in return for regular payments.

3. A federal public works program was established and $750 million was approved to create jobs. Some people went to work building dams, highways, and buildings. States and local communities were encouraged to establish similar programs.

4. A **moratorium** was put on payments of war debts owed to the United States. This put off payments of debts until later. Hoover hoped to ease Europe's financial problems. Then, he believed, these countries would be able to buy more products from the United States.

How Did President Roosevelt Help the Nation Recover?

Hoover's proposals for improving the economy were not enough for the American people. They wanted a change in the White House. In the 1932 election, Hoover was defeated in his attempt for re-election. In a landslide victory, Democrat Franklin Delano Roosevelt became

MARIAN ANDERSON: 1902–1993

Philadelphia-born Marian Anderson studied classical singing in Europe. She had a triumphant homecoming in 1933 with a concert at New York's Town Hall. Anderson was praised for her glorious voice, her beauty, and her dignity. She also became a symbol for African-American resistance to injustice. In 1939, she was denied permission to sing at Constitution Hall in Washington, D.C. The Secretary of the Interior fought the injustice by asking Anderson to perform at the Lincoln Memorial. She sang there the following Easter Sunday before 75,000 people. In 1955, Marian Anderson became the first African American to sing a role in the Metropolitan Opera. Thereafter, she toured twelve nations as a performing goodwill ambassador for the United States. After retiring, Anderson devoted her life to promoting civil rights.

Crisis
An event that threatens people's well-being

Recovery
The act of overcoming a problem

the new President. Roosevelt said he had a "new deal for the American people." He promised to act quickly to put the country back on its feet.

President Roosevelt took the oath of office on March 4, 1933. In a radio message, he told the American people that the economic **crisis** would not destroy the nation. He said with confidence that "the only thing we have to fear is fear itself."

Roosevelt promised a "New Deal" for "the forgotten man at the bottom of the economic pyramid." The plan covered three areas: relief, **recovery,** and reform. Roosevelt knew that many Americans were in need of immediate help. He had to find a way to get the economy to recover from its depression quickly. He believed that America's economic system had to be reformed. Basic changes were necessary to prevent another depression in the future.

What Actions Did Roosevelt and Congress Take?

Before he became President, Roosevelt said that he was willing to try different methods to end the depression. If one plan fails, he said, "admit it frankly and try another. But above all, try something."

The nation wanted action. Roosevelt acted boldly. He called Congress into special session on March 9, 1933. In the next 100 days, this Congress passed more important laws than any other Congress in American history. The period is called the Hundred Days. These actions were taken:

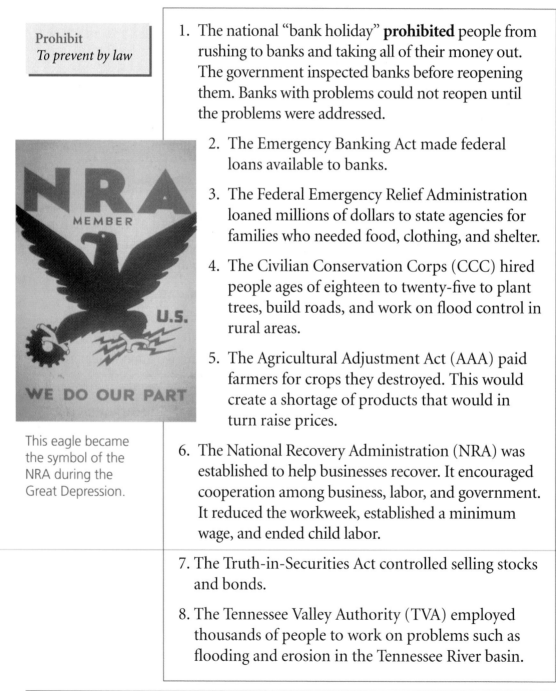

Prohibit
To prevent by law

This eagle became the symbol of the NRA during the Great Depression.

1. The national "bank holiday" **prohibited** people from rushing to banks and taking all of their money out. The government inspected banks before reopening them. Banks with problems could not reopen until the problems were addressed.

2. The Emergency Banking Act made federal loans available to banks.

3. The Federal Emergency Relief Administration loaned millions of dollars to state agencies for families who needed food, clothing, and shelter.

4. The Civilian Conservation Corps (CCC) hired people ages of eighteen to twenty-five to plant trees, build roads, and work on flood control in rural areas.

5. The Agricultural Adjustment Act (AAA) paid farmers for crops they destroyed. This would create a shortage of products that would in turn raise prices.

6. The National Recovery Administration (NRA) was established to help businesses recover. It encouraged cooperation among business, labor, and government. It reduced the workweek, established a minimum wage, and ended child labor.

7. The Truth-in-Securities Act controlled selling stocks and bonds.

8. The Tennessee Valley Authority (TVA) employed thousands of people to work on problems such as flooding and erosion in the Tennessee River basin.

Americans were hopeful that the new cooperation between businesses, labor, and the government would bring the Great Depression to an end. The Blue Eagle, the symbol for the NRA, began appearing in windows of small shops and gates of large factories. The NRA stood for the Roosevelt administration's first 100 days of efforts to end the depression.

Many unemployed laborers found work through the Works Progress Administration.

SECTION 2 REVIEW Choose the best word or name in parentheses to complete each sentence. Write your answers on a separate sheet of paper.

1) The (Reconstruction Finance Corporation, New Deal, Agricultural Marketing Act) allowed for $500 million to buy surplus crops from farmers.

2) President (Hoover, Roosevelt) promised the New Deal to Americans.

3) The (national bank holiday, Emergency Banking Act, National Recovery Administration) prohibited people from rushing to the banks to take their money out.

4) The (Agricultural Adjustment Act, Federal Emergency Relief Administration, Civilian Conservation Corps) loaned millions of dollars to state agencies.

5) The (Emergency Banking, Truth-in-Securities, Agricultural Adjustment) Act attempted to raise farm prices by cutting back production.

What do you think ?

Why do you think Congress passed more laws in this period than at any other time in American history?

★Collective
bargaining
*A way of
negotiating
between groups
of workers and
employers*

Mural
*An artistic painting
or drawing on a
wall*

During the first stage of the New Deal, the government focused on giving immediate relief to those most in need. These steps helped put the nation back on the road to economic recovery. The second stage, called the Second New Deal, tried to make economic reforms. These reforms changed the role of government in the lives of Americans.

Which Reforms Changed the Government's Role?

In April of 1935, Congress passed a $4.8 billion jobs program. It created the Works Progress Administration (WPA). Harry L. Hopkins, the head of the program, wanted to put every unemployed person to work. The WPA went on to build schools, hospitals, playgrounds, museums, and airports. Actors were hired to put on plays. Musicians were paid to give concerts. Artists were employed to paint **murals** on the walls of government buildings. Eight million Americans found work with the WPA. The jobs helped restore self-respect and confidence in American workers. The restoration of the workforce helped ease the depression. More stores opened. Factories began to hire workers as demand for their products increased.

Before the time of the New Deal, the federal government usually sided with business during labor disputes. However the new National Labor Relations Act, or Wagner Act, gave workers the right to form unions. Employers could not stop workers from forming a union. The National Labor Relations Board, a government agency, made sure the vote for a union was fair. For the first time, the United States government encouraged unions and employers to discuss wages and working conditions. Differences could be settled peacefully in a process of **collective bargaining.** This was a way of negotiating between groups of workers and their employers.

One of the most important reforms of the New Deal was the Social Security Act of 1935. Government programs took responsibility for Americans who were elderly,

*Disabled
Having a mental or physical handicap

unemployed, or **disabled**. Someone who is disabled has a mental or physical handicap. Many of the suggestions for this law were made by Secretary of Labor Frances Perkins. She was the first woman to become a member of a President's cabinet.

The Social Security Act had three parts:

Social Security Act of 1935		
Pension Benefits for the Elderly	**Unemployment Compensation**	**Disability Benefits**
Money for the pensions came from two new taxes. One tax came from the employee's pay. An equal amount came from the employer.	The employer paid an additional tax to pay unemployed workers until they found work.	Payments were made to disabled or blind Americans.

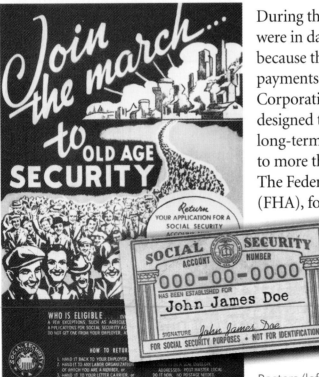

During the depression many Americans were in danger of losing their homes because they could not make their loan payments. The Home Owners Loan Corporation, established in 1933, was designed to help these people. Low-interest, long-term home loans became available to more than a million American families. The Federal Housing Administration (FHA), formed in 1934, encouraged low-cost home building and repair. It also offered banks a guarantee of repayment of loans to lower- and middle-income Americans.

Posters (left) encouraged people to support Social Security programs. A Social Security card (inset) may be applied for at birth.

Denounce
To reject or show disapproval

★Liberal
One who favors change

Overturn
To reverse

Who Won the Election of 1936?

Franklin Roosevelt was elected to a second term as President in 1936. Alf Landon, his Republican opponent, carried two states—Maine and Vermont. African Americans voted in large numbers for the Democratic party. Before this time, African Americans generally voted Republican—the party of Abraham Lincoln.

How Did the Supreme Court React to Reforms?

Roosevelt and his New Deal programs ran into problems with the Supreme Court. Most of the members of the Supreme Court believed some of the New Deal legislation was unconstitutional.

The Supreme Court declared the National Recovery Act and the Agricultural Adjustment Act unconstitutional. This declaration angered President Roosevelt. He believed that the "nine old men" on the Supreme Court stood in the way of progress. Six of the justices, who had been appointed for life, were over seventy years of age. Roosevelt decided to appoint a new justice for every justice over the age of seventy.

The six new justices, Roosevelt thought, would assure that New Deal laws would not be **overturned** by the Supreme Court. Roosevelt's decision was not well accepted. Members of Congress **denounced** it as political "court-packing." Many Americans also rejected the plan.

However, as the older justices retired, Roosevelt appointed younger, more **liberal** justices. Liberals favor change. These young justices were some of the most important justices in American history—Hugo Black, William O. Douglas, and Felix Frankfurter.

How Did Labor Unions Change?

In 1881, the American Federation of Labor (AFL) had been formed. This labor union was made up of only skilled workers. Unskilled factory workers could not belong. Therefore, they had no union to represent them. The skilled

workers were organized by **occupation.** Each occupation area formed its own union within the AFL. The AFL served as a governing body over all of the smaller unions.

The union leader, John L. Lewis, thought an industry-wide union was necessary. He felt that all workers, including factory workers, steelworkers, and autoworkers, should be admitted to one union.

Lewis formed a committee for industrial organizations within the AFL. However, the more **traditional** labor leaders were against this committee. Lewis eventually broke away and established the Congress of Industrial Organizations (CIO) in 1935.

The CIO united workers from all industries into one organization. The new union used the National Labor Relations Act to increase its number of members to six million by 1945. In 1955, the American Federation of Labor and the Congress of Industrial Organizations became one organization. It was called the AFL-CIO.

WORD BANK

American Federation

Industrial Organizations

Labor Relations

Social Security

Works Progress

SECTION 3 REVIEW On a separate sheet of paper, write the word from the Word Bank to complete each sentence.

1) The _____ Act set up programs to help the elderly, unemployed, or disabled.

2) The National _____ Act gave workers the right to form unions.

3) The _____ Administration gave people work.

4) The _____ of Labor was made up of only skilled workers.

5) The Congress of _____ united workers from all industries.

What do you think **?**

Why is it important to set up programs to protect the elderly, disabled, and unemployed?

The Great Depression affected the life of most Americans. Many people suffered great hardships. In the hard times, though, life went on. People danced to big band music called *swing*. People could escape into a theater and watch a movie for five cents. The public was eager to see a world different from its own. Hollywood provided that world through movies. The movies of the 1930s gave the American public a new world of comedy, musicals, and drama.

Orphan
A child without parents

Ginger Rogers and Fred Astaire became America's favorite dancing couple. Child star Shirley Temple usually played an **orphan** with a big heart and an optimistic outlook. Americans laughed at the crazy comedy of the Marx Brothers and their humorous adventures.

Media in History

"War of the Worlds"

It was a rainy night for most Americans on October 30, 1938. World conditions were tense as Hitler continued his invasion of Czechoslovakia. Most figured Poland would be next. In the United States, millions had their radios tuned to CBS radio's "Mercury Theater of the Air."

Then they heard a spine-tingling late news bulletin. Martians were invading America. People panicked. There were traffic jams near the announced "landing site." Thousands of calls tied up the phone lines at newspapers and radio stations. Was it true?

Orson Welles was in the hot seat. He was producing H. G. Wells's story, *The War of the Worlds*. He had broadcast repeated warnings that this was not a true event. Many had tuned in late, however, and didn't hear the warnings.

The Federal Communications Commission investigated. New regulations were passed. Fictional news bulletins were outlawed. It was clear that the power of radio could be tremendous.

The most popular book and movie of the 1930s was *Gone With the Wind*. The author, Margaret Mitchell, told the story of Scarlett O'Hara and the destruction of her family's Georgia plantation during the Civil War. The book had a **romantic** view of the American South during another period of hard times. At the end of the book, Scarlett's world had totally changed; yet she had survived. The message of the story seemed to be one that the nation in the hard times of the 1930s wanted to hear.

Romantic
Glorified

A favorite film among children in 1939 was *The Wizard of Oz*. Like many musicals and Shirley Temple movies, this film gave viewers hope that there might be a happier life "Somewhere Over the Rainbow."

Who Were Some Sports Heroes of the 1930s?

In 1936, over 5,000 athletes met in Berlin, Germany, to participate in the Olympic games. German leader Adolf Hitler hoped to prove that white German athletes were better than any other athletes. This hope was shattered by the performance of an African-American athlete named Jesse Owens. Owens won four Olympic gold medals.

Jesse Owens (left) shattered Adolf Hitler's claim that white German athletes were the best in the world. Owens won four gold medals in the 1936 Olympics in Berlin, Germany.

In 1938, Joe Louis, the heavyweight champion of the world, stepped into the boxing ring. His opponent was a German boxer named Max Schmeling. The German government published harsh words that they said came from Schmeling: "I would not take this fight if I did not believe that I, a white man, can beat a Negro." Schmeling never said these words. Joe Louis had to prove that an American could defeat a representative of Germany. Two minutes and four seconds after it began, the fight was over. Louis had won. On that night, Louis became a national hero.

Amelia Earhart

In 1928, Amelia Earhart had become the first woman passenger and logkeeper on a transatlantic flight, flying from Newfoundland to Wales. She went on to write a book about her experiences. Then, in 1932, Earhart became the first woman to fly alone over the Pacific Ocean in a round-trip flight from Hawaii to the United States. She gave talks to promote flying and to give women encouragement. In 1937, in an attempt to fly around the world, Earhart disappeared somewhere over the Pacific Ocean.

Amelia Earhart

The Development of Nylon

On May 23, 1935, Wallace H. Carothers successfully spun the first man-made fiber. A research chemist for Du Pont Laboratories, Carothers called the durable fiber "nylon." He had experimented since the late 1920s. Using a special machine, he was able to make longer molecules than ever before. Fibers made from the compounds he used could be pulled to several times their original length. Pulling made the fibers stronger and more elastic.

Du Pont introduced the first nylon product—a toothbrush with nylon bristles—in 1938. The first nylon stockings went on sale in 1939. Today nylon is made into powder, fibers, sheets, rods, and tubes. It is used to make parachutes, carpets, tires, clothing, fishing line, surgical thread, electrical equipment, and sporting goods. Plastic nylon panels replace steel on some automobiles. From clothes to cars, Americans enjoy the benefits of nylon every day.

Science
History in Your Life

SECTION 4 REVIEW Write the answers to these questions on a separate sheet of paper using complete sentences.

1) Why did people who lived during the depression like watching movies or other performances?

2) Why did people like *Gone With the Wind?*

3) What did *The Wizard of Oz* suggest about finding a happier life?

4) How did Jesse Owens spoil Adolf Hitler's hopes?

5) What did Joe Louis do?

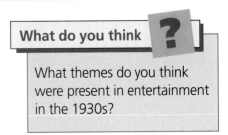

What do you think **?**

What themes do you think were present in entertainment in the 1930s?

Breadline

The impact of the depression on the lives of Americans could be seen in the nation's cities. Out-of-work men gathered in breadlines to get something to eat. A few men carried signs asking for a job. This selection concerns the life of an out-of-work man in San Francisco from December 1931 to December 1933.

"A wet and cold day in December, 1931, I was an active member of the breadline on Ritch Street in San Francisco. . . . I knew by bitter experience that it would be at least two hours before I could dip into a bowl of waterlogged stew. I was ravenously hungry, friendless, homeless, and far removed from the possibilities of obtaining a job.

It was four o'clock in the morning, and still pitch-dark, when our advance guard appeared and took up its position six abreast outside the municipal kitchen. . . . By six o'clock, when the actual feeding started, the line had reached as far as Folsom Street, when every moment brought its quota of semistarved, shabby, despairing men. . . .

During the daylight hours I roamed all over the city looking for work. Hatless, clad in overalls and heavy, hobnailed boots, peaked and hungry-looking, badly in need of a haircut, I must have been a sight. People didn't waste promises or interviews when I turned up. With a few exceptions they gave the cold shoulder. . . .

By the summer of 1932, I looked at least ten years older. My weight under normal conditions is about 170 pounds. After four months in the breadline I tipped the scales at 125. My ribs protruded like laths, and my lusterless eyes had retreated way back into dark-ringed sockets.

I didn't beg or ransack the garbage cans; nor did I rob or steal. Instead, I walked about for hours, eyes glued to the sidewalk, looking for lost coins . . . I never found. . . .

I ate and slept in the San Francisco breadline and flophouses from the first of May to the first of December, 1933. . . . My total monthly expenses amounted to seventy cents. Thirty cents went for the purchase of a daily loaf of stale bread, at a penny a loaf, the remaining forty cents kept me in tobacco. . . ."

From: Hugo Johanson, "Bread Line," *The Atlantic Monthly,* Vol. 158, No. 2 (August, 1936), pp. 164-166, 169-170, 173-174.

Source Reading Wrap-Up

1) In December 1931, where did the man find himself and why was he there?

2) What did the man do during the daylight hours?

3) What was his physical appearance?

4) By 1933, had his life improved? Why or why not?

5) By the end of 1933, what government help could this man expect?

★ Following the stock market crash of 1929, the country fell into an economic slump known as the Great Depression.

★ There were many reasons for the depression. Business had expanded too rapidly. More products were made than people could buy. Businesses laid off workers. Many people bought things on credit and when they lost their jobs, they couldn't pay their debts. There were high tariffs placed on American products. Prices for farm products continued to decline.

★ Many people were unemployed. Many were left homeless and had no way of buying food. People moved from place to place in search of work.

★ President Hoover tried helping in several ways, but most of his plans and policies failed. Most of the American people blamed Hoover for the problems of the depression.

★ Franklin Delano Roosevelt became President in 1933. He set up a number of social and economic programs called the "New Deal." Among these were the Works Progress Administration (WPA), the Civilian Conservation Corps (CCC), and the Tennessee Valley Authority (TVA).

★ The Social Security Act of 1935 set up the Social Security system to help the elderly and disabled.

★ Frances Perkins, the first woman on a President's cabinet, became Secretary of Labor under Roosevelt.

★ The labor movement grew as John L. Lewis left the American Federation of Labor (AFL) and formed the Congress of Industrial Organizations (CIO).

★ Roosevelt tried to put new justices on the Supreme Court who would support his policies, but Congress and American people objected.

★ The films and books of the period reflected the mood of the times by offering people an escape from their hardships.

★ Roosevelt's plans and policies helped bring the United States out of the Great Depression.

Comprehension: Identifying Facts

On a separate sheet of paper, write the words from the Word Bank to complete each sentence.

WORD BANK		
breadlines	Herbert Hoover	Supreme Court
Civilian Conservation Corps	Joe Louis	Tennessee Valley Authority
	New Deal	unemployment
crash	overproduction	
Frances Perkins	Social Security	Works Progress Administration

1) The _____ of the stock market was the beginning of the Great Depression.

2) During the depression, _____ was high because there were no jobs.

3) There were too many products and not enough people to buy them because of _____.

4) Soup kitchens and _____ helped feed people who had no money for food.

5) Roosevelt promised a "_____" for Americans.

6) Many people blamed President _____ for the depression.

7) _____ beat Max Schmeling in a highly publicized boxing match.

8) The _____ employed young people who planted trees, built roads, and worked on flood control.

9) The _____ Act of 1935 created programs to help the elderly, unemployed, and disabled.

10) The goal of the _____ was to put every unemployed person to work.

11) The first woman to be on a President's cabinet was Secretary of Labor _____.

12) The _____ worked on problems in the Tennessee River basin.

13) Roosevelt called the _____ "nine old men."

Comprehension: Understanding Main Ideas

On a separate sheet of paper, write the answer to each question using complete sentences.

1) What were some factors that caused the Great Depression?

2) What was life like during the Great Depression?

3) What were four programs that Roosevelt set up as part of the "New Deal?"

4) Why were the slums set up during the depression called "Hoovervilles?"

Critical Thinking: Write Your Opinion

1) Social Security was started during the Great Depression. Do you think Social Security is still important today? Explain your answer.

2) People went to the movies to escape the problems of the depression. How does television today compare with the movies during the depression?

3) If there were a massive depression today, do you think the government should step in and provide jobs? Why or why not?

| Test Taking Tip | If you don't understand the directions to a section of a test, read over the questions to see if you can figure out what you are supposed to do. If you still can't figure it out, ask the person giving the test, if possible. |

Chapter

World War II

1939–1945

President Roosevelt's plans to bring the nation out of the depression had worked. However, an even greater problem was on the horizon for the United States. After World War I, President Wilson had warned that the world might be in danger of another war in the future. As the 1930s ended, Europe was once again in trouble. A second world war, far more damaging than the first, began as Wilson had said. In this chapter, you will learn what caused World War II, how the war affected American life, and how the war ended.

Goals for Learning

▶ To explain the steps that led to World War II

▶ To describe the events at Pearl Harbor

▶ To describe what life was like in the United States during the war

▶ To explain how American involvement affected the outcome of the war

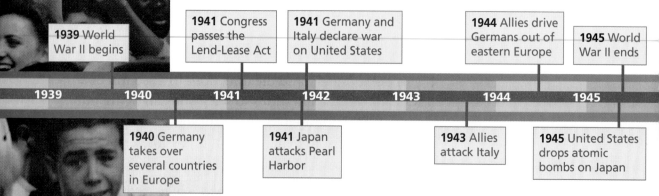

1939 World War II begins

1941 Congress passes the Lend-Lease Act

1941 Germany and Italy declare war on United States

1944 Allies drive Germans out of eastern Europe

1945 World War II ends

1939   1940   1941   1942   1943   1944   1945

1940 Germany takes over several countries in Europe

1941 Japan attacks Pearl Harbor

1943 Allies attack Italy

1945 United States drops atomic bombs on Japan

⋆**Fascist**
One who believes that the state or union is more important than the individual

⋆**Inflation**
A steady rise in prices of goods

Before and during the Great Depression in the United States, other countries around the world had a depression of their own. The social and economic problems of these different countries brought different outcomes. For example, Germany, Italy, and Japan fell under the control of dictators. The whole world would soon feel the effects of these dictators' beliefs that war might be a good solution to their nations' problems.

How Did Mussolini and Fascism Gain Support in Italy?

Benito Mussolini had controlled the Italian government since 1922. He believed that a strong leader must have full power to run the country. Under his dictatorship, other political parties were forbidden. Mussolini created the **Fascist** political party. Fascists believed the state or union was more important than the individual. They rejected the idea of democracy and personal freedom. The Fascists believed military power and war were good for a nation. Italian Fascists used the slogan: "Believe! Obey! Fight!"

How Did Hitler and Nazism Gain Support in Germany?

The German people did not understand how they lost World War I. They were upset with the strict conditions of the peace settlement. When World War I ended, Germany removed its king and established a democracy. The new Republic of Germany tried to govern its troubled nation.

The economy in Germany fell apart in 1923. **Inflation** made German paper money nearly worthless. Inflation is a steady rise in prices of goods. Prices of goods doubled daily. Germans had to carry large bags of money just to buy food for one day. Many workers lost their jobs. The democratic government of Germany was criticized for being weak. The National Socialist German Workers party, or Nazi party, opposed the German government. Adolf Hitler led the Nazis.

Hitler used his skills as a public speaker and organizer to increase the power of the Nazi party. Hitler declared that democracy was weak and could not solve the nation's problems. He added that the economic crisis was not the fault of the Germans. He blamed Germany's problems on others. He told Germans that communists and Jews were trying to destroy their government. He promised prosperity for all Germans. He preached against democracy and for hatred of the Jews.

German dictator Adolf Hitler (second from right) inspects troops.

Adolf Hitler became the **chancellor,** or chief minister of Germany, in 1933. This happened after his Nazi party had won a majority of seats in Germany's Parliament. Within months, Hitler became a dictator. He gave himself the title "der Führer." It meant "the leader." Hitler and the Nazi party quickly destroyed German democracy and individual freedoms.

★Chancellor
The chief minister in some European countries

★Citizenship
The act of belonging to a certain country

Hitler was successful in improving the German economy. German unemployment dropped. The standard of living for most Germans rose. Hitler continued a campaign against German Jews. He called them traitors. German Jews lost their **citizenship** and their jobs. Citizenship is the act of belonging to a certain country.

How Did Fascism Begin in Spain?

A civil war broke out in Spain in 1936. General Francisco Franco and his forces fought against anti-Fascists. The anti-Fascists wanted Spain to have a democratic government. The Spanish Civil War became a test for the Fascist governments of Germany and Italy. Italy sent troops to fight in Spain, and German planes bombed Spanish cities.

The communist government of the Soviet Union supported the anti-Fascists. Anti-Fascist volunteers from Great Britain, France, and the United States also fought in this war. The Americans who fought did so by their own choice, not as members of the American military. The Spanish Civil War lasted three years. The Spanish Fascist forces, supported by the governments of Italy and Germany, won in 1939. Franco became the leader of a new Fascist government.

How Did Japan Establish Control in Asia?

The worldwide depression also hurt Japan, an island nation in Asia. Japanese industries needed imported coal, oil, and iron. The depression made it difficult for nations to trade with each other. Without enough raw materials, Japan found its industries threatened.

Japan relied on imported rice to help feed its people. Unable to grow enough rice on their own, many Japanese had no food. Radical military leaders, similar to those in Germany and Italy, took control of the Japanese government. The army seized Manchuria, an area rich in coal and iron, from China. In 1937, Japan invaded China again and captured several important cities. Japan had taken its first steps to control Asia and establish a Japanese empire.

ELEANOR ROOSEVELT: 1884–1962

Eleanor Roosevelt was distinguished as a diplomat and humanitarian. She became a model for women in politics and public affairs. As First Lady when her husband Franklin D. Roosevelt was President, she exerted wide though unofficial influence. She lectured and wrote a daily newspaper column that was widely published. Active in Democratic politics, Roosevelt was a champion for the rights of women and minorities. As U.S. delegate to the United Nations, she chaired the U.N.'s Human Rights Commission. She also took a central role in drafting the U.N.'s Universal Declaration of Human Rights. Her uncle was President Theodore Roosevelt.

How Did America View the Problems in Europe?

Americans did not want to deal with the problems in Europe. During the 1930s, Americans had a much larger problem at home with the Great Depression. The New Deal programs took time to plan and put to use.

There was another reason Americans ignored problems in Europe. The memory of World War I was still fresh in their minds. Americans wanted to stay out of another foreign war. Many people felt that the United States was protected by possible attacks because of the Atlantic and Pacific oceans. Congress passed neutrality laws in 1935 and 1937. These laws prevented the sale of arms or lending money to countries at war. Throughout the 1930s, Americans watched Germany, Italy, and Japan increase in military strength.

President Roosevelt was not so certain that the United States should ignore what was going on in Europe. Beginning in 1937, he tried to keep the country aware of the problems there. For that reason, some people criticized Roosevelt. They thought he wanted to start a war.

SECTION 1 REVIEW Choose the best word or name in parentheses to complete each sentence. Write your answers on a separate sheet of paper.

1) (Hitler, Mussolini, Franco) started the Fascist party in Italy.

2) (Hitler, Mussolini, Franco) became chancellor of Germany in 1933.

3) The (anti-Fascists, Fascists) in Spain wanted a democratic government.

4) The Spanish Civil War lasted (two, three, four) years.

5) Japan invaded (Italy, Spain, China) in 1937.

What do you think ?

Why do you think some countries in Europe started to have dictators as leaders?

During the years of the Spanish Civil War, Hitler moved aggressively to expand his power in Europe. His goal was to bring the German-speaking people of Austria, Czechoslovakia, and Poland under German rule. Twice before in history, the German people had built a **reich,** or empire, in Europe. Hitler wanted to create a Third Reich.

★Reich
German empire

How Did European Leaders Give in to Hitler?

Hitler took the first step in creating a German empire in March 1938. German troops marched into Austria and declared it part of the German Third Reich. Although this action went against the Treaty of Versailles, the League of Nations did nothing to stop it. Hitler's next move was to bring three million Germans living in the Sudetenland into the Third Reich. The Sudetenland was an area of Czechoslovakia. Hitler threatened to use force. To avoid war, Neville Chamberlain, the prime minister of Great Britain, suggested that the major powers of Europe meet.

European leaders met in Munich, Germany, in 1938. Among those present were (from front left) Neville Chamberlain, Edouard Daladier, Adolf Hitler, and Benito Mussolini.

★Appeasement
Doing something to keep peace

★Synagogue
A Jewish place of worship

Chamberlain, Mussolini, Hitler, and Edouard Daladier of France met in Munich, Germany, in September 1938. Czechoslovakia was not represented. Hitler believed that the threat of war would frighten the leaders of Great Britain and France. He thought that they would give in to his demands. Chamberlain and Daladier did just that. Both leaders agreed to give Germany the Sudetenland. They felt a policy of **appeasement** was best. Appeasement is doing something to keep peace. Hitler agreed to make no more advances for territory. When Chamberlain returned to Britain, he said that the meeting in Munich had produced "peace with honor . . . peace in our time."

What Was the Holocaust?

On the night of November 9, 1938, Nazis set fire to Jewish places of worship called **synagogues.** They also broke into Jewish homes, terrorized Jewish people, and destroyed Jewish businesses. This night of terror is called "Kristallnacht," or the

German soldiers gathered this group of Jewish women and children in Warsaw, Poland, in 1943.

"Night of Broken Glass." Many Jews were killed or arrested. This was only the beginning of the terror the Jews faced.

In 1939, Germany set up death camps for the Jews as a part of Hitler's "final solution." The Nazis planned to murder every Jew whom they could find. Jews were sent by train to the death camps. Men, women, and children were killed with gas or gunfire in these camps. Many bodies were burned in large ovens.

When it became widely known in 1945 that this **Holocaust** had occurred, the world was shocked. The government of Nazi Germany had killed nearly six million innocent European Jews. In the eyes of the Germans, the Jews were **inferior** simply because of their **ethnic heritage.** For many years after the end of World War II, Nazi war criminals were hunted and brought to justice.

Why Did Germany Attack Poland?

The Treaty of Versailles, signed at the end of World War I, had given Poland a strip of land called the Polish Corridor. On this piece of land, Poland gained access to the Baltic Sea. The Germans never liked this arrangement. The Polish Corridor isolated East Prussia and the German city of Danzig from the rest of Germany. In March of 1939, Hitler demanded that Poland give back the city of Danzig in order for Germany to build a railroad through the Polish Corridor. Poland refused. Great Britain and France supported Poland. Both countries said they would go to war to defend Poland. Great Britain and France expected help from the Soviet Union in a fight against Germany.

However, Germany and the Soviet Union had signed a treaty of friendship in August of 1939. The Soviet leader, Joseph Stalin, agreed not to interfere if Germany attacked Poland. In return, Germany would give the Soviet Union the eastern half of Poland. Having gained the alliance of the Soviet Union, Hitler felt confident that he could successfully seize the Polish land.

Europe, 1938–1939

MAP STUDY

By the end of 1939, what nations had become part of the German Third Reich?

SECTION 2 REVIEW On a separate sheet of paper, write *True* if the statement is true or *False* if the statement is not true.

1) Adolf Hitler wanted to create a Third Reich.

2) Chamberlain and Daladier refused to give Hitler the Sudetenland.

3) Six million Jews were killed during the Holocaust.

4) Poland refused to give Hitler the city of Danzig.

5) Germany and the Soviet Union formed an alliance.

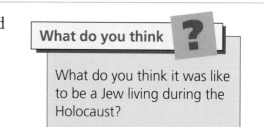

What do you think ?

What do you think it was like to be a Jew living during the Holocaust?

★Blitzkrieg
"Lightning war";
a rapid military
attack

German soldiers moved rapidly into Poland by trucks on September 1, 1939. They were supported with tanks and bombing attacks by the German air force. This new method of warfare was called **blitzkrieg,** or "lightning war." This simple act of German aggression was the beginning of World War II.

Why Did France and Britain Declare War?

Troops of the Soviet Union also attacked Poland. Great Britain and France, attempting to aid Poland, declared war on Germany. While restating his vow to remain neutral, President Roosevelt did not approve of the attack on Poland. He asked Congress to reverse its neutrality order so that the United States could sell weapons to France and Great Britain. After a long debate, the arms were made available.

A few weeks after the attack by the Soviet Union, Poland surrendered. Germany and the Soviet Union divided Poland between them. Through the winter of 1939 and 1940, there was little activity. Some people began to speak of a "phony war." The world watched and waited, however, for Hitler's next move, remembering the Nazi phrase, "Today Germany, tomorrow the world!"

Suddenly, in April of 1940, Germany attacked and defeated Denmark and Norway. The next month, Belgium, Luxembourg, and the Netherlands fell to the German army. Germany then attacked France. German soldiers broke through the French defensive line.

What Happened at Dunkirk?

More than 300,000 British, Belgian, and French soldiers were trapped between the attacking Germans and the sea. These allied troops retreated to Dunkirk, a seaport located in the north of France on the English Channel. Great Britain made a daring attempt to rescue these allied troops.

Hundreds of ships set sail from Great Britain for Dunkirk. Most of the troops were safely rescued and were in Great Britain on June 4, 1940. Six days later, Italy sided with Germany and declared war. France surrendered and requested an armistice. Hitler agreed.

What Was the Battle of Britain?

Great Britain was left alone to fight the Nazi war machine. If Great Britain was defeated, the United States would be without an ally in Europe. Prime Minister Winston Churchill spoke to the British people on June 4, 1940. He told them, "We shall defend our island, whatever the cost may be, we shall fight on the beaches . . . we shall fight in the fields and in the streets . . . we shall never surrender."

The British waited for a German invasion of their country. The German air force began around-the-clock bombing raids on Great Britain's air force bases in August of 1940. The Royal Air Force (RAF) fought back. The RAF used a new **radar** system that located incoming planes. Many German bombers were destroyed. The Germans had to change their invasion plans.

★Radar
A system used to locate objects such as planes

The German air force destroyed many buildings in London.

★Lottery
*Drawing names
to decide who is
drafted into the
military*

Security
*Methods of keeping
a place safe*

What Happened When Hitler Attacked the Soviet Union?

Hitler attacked the Soviet Union in June of 1941. He ignored their friendship treaty. This decision was a major mistake for Hitler. Great Britain, Canada, Australia, the Soviet Union, and other nations joined together to fight Germany. These countries became known as the Allies. They realized that Hitler was attempting to gain control over all of Europe.

How Did America Come Closer to War?

Most Americans still did not want the United States to enter the war. However, unlike World War I, Americans did not try to stay neutral. They became concerned about America's safety.

President Roosevelt told the American people that Great Britain needed help. Great Britain needed more weapons but did not have enough money to pay for the supplies. America had to be "the arsenal of democracy." Roosevelt proposed that the United States lend Great Britain military supplies. Congress passed the Lend-Lease Act in March of 1941. This policy was designed to keep America out of war in Europe.

Under the Lend-Lease Act, the United States government would provide weapons any country considered important to American **security.** These nations could buy, lease, exchange, or borrow equipment, arms, and supplies from the United States. During World War II, the United States provided $50 billion in lend-lease aid to the Allies.

The United States began to prepare for the chance of war. Congress approved millions of dollars to strengthen the armed forces. The Selective Service Act was passed in September of 1940. This was the first peacetime law that drafted men into the armed forces. The last draft had been during World War I. Men between the ages of twenty-one and thirty-five were selected by a **lottery** to serve one year in the military. The lottery was a drawing of names.

The United States made a trade with Great Britain and loaned it fifty small warships called destroyers. In return, Great Britain leased naval and air bases to the United States in the Western Hemisphere. These bases allowed the United States to better defend itself and to keep watch over the Panama Canal.

Media in History

World War II Songs

The World War II years were a time of intense patriotism. Everyone's life revolved around helping America win the war. Much of the popular music during this time had a fast style and was easy to dance to. The beat became known as boogie-woogie and many people began dancing the jitterbug. It was exciting and just right for a nation caught up in war.

Many songs had a war theme. Some examples are "Boogie Woogie Bugle Boy," "I'll Be Home For Christmas," "Kiss the Boys Goodbye," and "Praise the Lord and Pass the Ammunition!" Other songs with war themes are "There's a Star Spangled Banner Waving Somewhere," "The White Cliffs of Dover," and "Why Do They Call a Private a Private?"

In many ways, radio created the popularity of these songs. A weekly poll was conducted to see which songs had been played most often. Millions of people tuned in every week to the "Lucky Strike Hit Parade" to hear how the songs ranked.

SECTION 3 REVIEW Write the answers to these questions on a separate sheet of paper using complete sentences.

1) What marked the beginning of World War II?

2) Which countries did Germany capture?

3) How did the British defend themselves against German attacks?

4) What was the Lend-Lease Act?

5) What was the Selective Service Act?

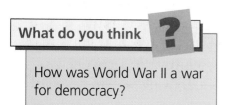

What do you think **?**

How was World War II a war for democracy?

Asset
Something of worth that someone owns

★**Axis Powers**
The alliance of Japan, Italy, and Germany in World War II

The Japanese government announced that it intended to rule all of Asia, including China. That type of control went against America's Open Door Policy. The United States had established the policy so that all nations would be allowed free trade with China. America protested Japan's actions. However, Japan continued its plan to create an empire. Japan joined Germany and Italy in an alliance. These three countries became known as the **Axis Powers.**

Japan invaded the French colony of Indochina in June of 1941. Indochina was just south of China. The United States became concerned that Japan was gaining too much land. America decided to stop selling oil and steel to Japan. Japan desperately needed oil to continue with its plan. The United States also offered a lend-lease program to China.

When Japan invaded Indochina, Roosevelt said Japan could not use money or investments it had in the United States. This is called freezing **assets.** Japan did the same thing to the United States. Trade between the two countries stopped.

Premier of Japan Fumimaro Konoye and United States Secretary of State Cordell Hull began to negotiate. The Japanese wanted to be allowed to use their assets in the United States. They also wanted to be supplied with oil. The United States wanted Japan to withdraw from China and Southeast Asia. The negotiations failed. Hideki Tojo replaced Konoye as premier.

Why Did Japan Attack Pearl Harbor?

Early on Sunday morning, December 7, 1941, 353 Japanese airplanes took off from six aircraft carriers in the Pacific Ocean. Their destination was the American naval base at Pearl Harbor, Hawaii, 220 miles away. Their mission was to destroy the American naval fleet anchored there. The Japanese thought they would be better able to conquer land in Asia if these American ships were destroyed.

Infamy
Disgraceful or lacking honor

Japan bombed ships in the harbor and planes on the ground. The surprise attack occurred at 7:55 A.M. Two hours later, the United States Pacific Fleet had lost many battleships, destroyers, and planes. The attack killed more than 2,000 Americans. Roosevelt said that December 7, 1941, was a "date that will live in **infamy**." Four days later, Germany and Italy, Japan's allies, declared war on the United States.

Japan followed up its attack on Pearl Harbor by invading the Philippine Islands and other areas in the Pacific. American and Filipino troops fought the Japanese. However, they lacked planes, tanks, and ammunition. Japan gained another victory. It now controlled the Philippine Islands.

The U.S.S. *West Virginia* and the U.S.S. *Tennessee* were among the nineteen American ships damaged or destroyed at Pearl Harbor.

Think how many plastic things are around you right now. You would have found far fewer plastics in 1941 than you do today. The manufacture of plastic boomed during World War II because silk and rubber were difficult to obtain. Inventors found ways to make tires, ropes, and parachutes from plastic. Electric radio cables were insulated with plastic.

Just think how many times a day plastic helps make your life easier. Today, plastic is everywhere, and its uses are growing. People predict that someday plastic will be used to build entire houses and vehicles. Medical advances with plastics are dramatic. Tiny plastic capsules one day may replace flawed or missing cells in people with progressive diseases like diabetes.

Then and Now

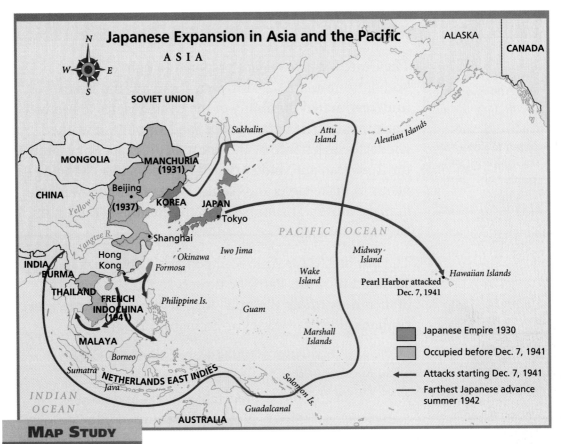

Japanese Expansion in Asia and the Pacific

Legend:
- Japanese Empire 1930
- Occupied before Dec. 7, 1941
- Attacks starting Dec. 7, 1941
- Farthest Japanese advance summer 1942

MAP STUDY

In 1930, which two countries of Asia were under Japanese control? Before 1941, which major Chinese cities did Japan control?

SECTION 4 REVIEW On a separate sheet of paper, write *True* if the statement is true or *False* if the statement is not true.

1) Japan wanted to control all of Asia.

2) All trading between Japan and America stopped.

3) America continued to supply oil to Japan.

4) Japan attacked Pearl Harbor to destroy the American fleet there.

5) The Filipinos prevented Japan from taking over the Philippines.

What do you think ?

How do you think Japan's entering the war made things worse for the Allies?

Civilian
One who is not in the military

Underestimate
To fail to guess the size, quantity, or number of something

The United States was not prepared to fight a war in both Europe and Asia. However, Germany and Japan **underestimated** the ability of the United States to produce war supplies. The nation had a good amount of workers and factories left idle by the Great Depression. For example, the American auto industry had little difficulty changing its plants to make tanks and planes. General Motors was able to make more war supplies than the combined output of Germany and Japan.

The war united the American people. It gave them a common purpose. Patriotic posters reminded Americans of their duty to "do their bit" for the war effort. American **civilians** aided the war effort in many different ways.

Careers

History in Your Life

Rosie the Riveter and the Women of World War II

When America entered World War II, most able-bodied young men left their jobs for the armed forces. More than four and a half million women took their place in support of the war effort. Evans and Loeb's sprightly song called "Rosie the Riveter" was released in 1942. The title caught on as a friendly label for all women who became manufacturing workers. The song's message hailed women's contributions on the homefront. Women worked in shipyards, steel mills, foundries, lumber mills, and aircraft and ammunition plants. They learned welding, electricity, mechanics, engineering, and chemistry. Women farmed, drove buses, wrote newspaper features, and played in the country's orchestras. Americans relied on female police officers, attorneys, and doctors. Thousands of American women also served in the military. These wartime changes helped break down forever job discrimination against women.

Millions of volunteers helped increase the supply of fresh vegetables. Parks and flower gardens were turned into "victory gardens." Victory gardens produced more than one-third of the nation's vegetables by 1943. This allowed farmers to use most of their land to grow food for the armed forces.

Raw materials were needed for American industries. America became a nation of collectors. Volunteers collected tons of newspapers, tin cans, and rubber tires. Housewives collected bacon grease for use in making ammunition. Even worn nylon stockings were collected to make gunpowder bags for the navy.

Combat
The act of fighting

Detention
The act of holding someone against his or her will

Ration
To use sparingly

Many goods were in short supply during the war. The government started to **ration** materials. Ration books contained stamps used to purchase gasoline, sugar, meat, and other products. A buyer had to pay the price for the product and a certain amount of ration stamps. Shortages even changed the style of clothes. Men's pants were made without cuffs and women's dresses were shortened because extra cloth was needed for military uniforms.

Women joined the armed forces in great numbers. They served in Europe and Asia in every role except **combat.** Millions of women replaced men in the workforce. Women learned to build planes and tanks as the men left for war. Women now had the opportunity to prove that they were as capable as any man.

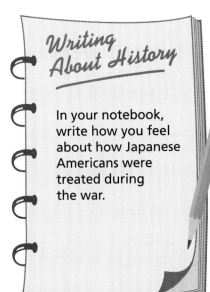

Writing About History

In your notebook, write how you feel about how Japanese Americans were treated during the war.

How Were Japanese Americans Treated During the War?

The United States feared that Japan would invade its west coast. Some citizens thought people of Japanese ancestry living in America would aid the Japanese. President Roosevelt ordered the army to move about 110,000 of these people to **detention** camps. Many Japanese Americans lost their homes and businesses. Fear, the pressure of war, and prejudice caused the nation to set aside its democratic principles. Japanese-American soldiers fought bravely in Europe while their government detained their parents and relatives.

SECTION 5 REVIEW Write the answers to these questions on a separate sheet of paper using complete sentences.

1) How was America able to produce war supplies?

2) What were victory gardens?

3) How did Americans reuse raw materials?

4) How were women involved in the war effort?

5) Why were Japanese Americans detained?

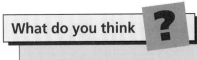

What do you think

Did detaining Japanese Americans hurt the nation? Why or why not?

Revenge
The act of getting back at someone for some wrongdoing

Despite the desire for **revenge** against Japan for Pearl Harbor, the United States decided that Hitler's Germany must be defeated first. The United States had strong ties to countries already defeated by Germany. Also, Germany seemed to be a greater threat to the Western Hemisphere than Japan did.

The only way to defeat Germany was through an Allied invasion of Europe. The Allies planned to hit Germany from the south through Italy and invade France from Britain. At the same time, the Soviet Union could move against the Germans from the east.

What Happened in the Invasion of Italy?

American, Canadian, and British troops invaded Italy in September of 1943. They captured the island of Sicily first. As Mussolini lost the island, the Italian people, tired of war, captured and executed him. The new, rebel Italian government soon surrendered to the Allied powers.

Determined to protect Germany's southern boundary, Hitler advanced toward Italy. The Allies finally captured the city of Rome on June 4, 1944. At this time, however, the Germans occupied most of northern Italy.

How Did the Allies Push the Germans Back?

The Nazis, who had known for some time that the United States was planning an invasion, prepared the coast of France. The beaches became death traps. The Nazis laid exploding mines in the water. They strung barbed wire all along the sandy shore.

General Dwight D. Eisenhower, commander of the Allied armies, landed his troops on the beaches of Normandy, France, on June 6, 1944. This was known as D-Day. It was a very tough battle. However, by night, the Allies occupied about eighty miles of the French coast. They could begin to move toward Germany.

By December of 1944, the Allies were confident that Germany's forces were trapped. But then, suddenly, the Germans **counterattacked.** The German army pushed through the Allied line. On a map of Europe, a large bulge represented Hitler's takeover of Allied territory. Led by General George Patton, the Allies counterattacked. The Germans were pushed back. The confrontation became known as the Battle of the Bulge. It was the last offensive by the German army.

What Was the Yalta Agreement?

President Roosevelt was re-elected for a fourth term in 1944. The strain of the war had taken its toll on him. He was able to cope with his polio, but the President had suffered from a number of other physical problems.

There was hope that the war against Germany would end early in 1945. Allied leaders met in February of 1945 in Yalta, a small town on the Black Sea in the Soviet Union. Roosevelt, Churchill, and Stalin agreed on a plan to follow when Germany surrendered. The plan became known as the Yalta Agreement.

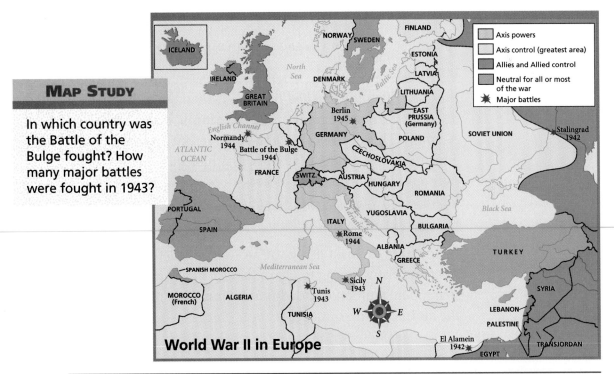

MAP STUDY

In which country was the Battle of the Bulge fought? How many major battles were fought in 1943?

World War II in Europe

*Atomic bomb
A bomb with great
destructive powers

*Bunker
An underground
shelter

The plan had several points. First, the Soviet Union agreed to enter the war against Japan. Second, Germany would be divided into four zones, each controlled by one of the Allies. Third, the Soviet Union would hold democratic elections in eastern European countries under its control. Fourth, a world organization called the United Nations would be created. The Yalta Agreement seemed reasonable at the time. However, after the war ended, parts of the agreement caused political problems between the United States and the Soviet Union.

How Did the War End?

President Franklin Roosevelt died suddenly in April of 1945. The nation was in shock. Vice President Harry S. Truman became President. On April 25, 1945, Adolf Hitler killed himself in a **bunker** in Berlin. A bunker is an underground shelter. Germany surrendered. The war in Europe was over.

The United States began to control the advance of the Japanese military. The Allies were led by American Army General Douglas MacArthur and Navy Admiral Chester Nimitz. Japan lost Guadalcanal, the Philippines, Iwo Jima, and Okinawa. Despite the losses, the Japanese refused to surrender. The Allies began to plan an invasion of Japan.

Why Were Atomic Bombs Dropped on Japan?

President Truman learned that the United States had developed a new weapon called the **atomic bomb,** or A-bomb. This bomb could end the war, but it would cause enormous loss of Japanese lives. Truman was advised that over a million American soldiers' lives would be lost if Japan was invaded on land. Such an invasion would also kill countless Japanese people.

In an effort to avoid using the atomic bomb, the President gave one last warning to Japan. Japan, however, refused to surrender. Truman decided that he must approve the use of the atomic bomb on Japan.

Hiroshima (right) was in ruin after an American plane dropped an atomic bomb on the city. The mushroom cloud (above) shows what happens when an atomic bomb goes off.

On August 6, 1945, from a plane named *Enola Gay*, the atomic bomb was dropped on the city of Hiroshima. The weapon destroyed that major Japanese city and instantly killed or wounded 130,000 people. Three days later, a second atomic bomb was dropped on the city of Nagasaki, killing or wounding 75,000 people. On August 14, 1945, Japan asked for a **cease-fire**—they wanted to end the fighting. General MacArthur accepted the formal surrender of Japan on September 2, 1945. World War II, the worst war in history, was finally over.

★Cease-fire
A call for an end to fighting

SECTION 6 REVIEW On a separate sheet of paper, write the word from the Word Bank to complete each sentence.

WORD BANK

Battle of the Bulge

D-Day

Hiroshima

Sicily

Yalta

1) Allied troops captured _____ in 1943.

2) The attack on Normandy was called _____.

3) The Germans were pushed back in the _____.

4) Allied leaders met at _____.

5) America dropped atomic bombs on _____ and Nagasaki.

What do you think **?**

World War II took millions of lives and ruined much of Europe. What do you think the world learned from the war?

Roosevelt's Four Freedoms Speech

During World War II, Americans gathered around radios to hear President Franklin Roosevelt's "fireside chats." The speeches meant much to those whose loved ones defended America overseas. Roosevelt gave this speech almost a year before America entered the war.

"As men do not live by bread alone, they do not fight by armaments alone. Those who man . . . and . . . build our defenses must have . . . an unshakable belief in the manner of life which they are defending. . . .

I have called for personal sacrifice. I am assured of the willingness of almost all Americans to respond to that call.

In the future days . . . we look forward to a world founded upon four essential human freedoms.

The first is freedom of speech and expression, everywhere in the world.

The second is freedom of every person to worship God in his own way, everywhere in the world.

The third is freedom from want, which . . . means economic understanding which will secure to every nation a healthy peacetime life for all its inhabitants . . . .

The fourth is freedom from fear . . . a world-wide reduction of armaments to such a point . . . that no nation will be in a position to commit an act of physical aggression against any neighbor . . . .

That is . . . . a definite basis for a kind of world attainable in our own time . . . . That kind of world is the very antithesis of the so-called new order of tyranny which the dictators seek to create . . . .

A good society is able to face schemes of world domination and foreign revolutions alike without fear.

Since the beginnings of our American history we have been engaged in . . . a perpetual peaceful revolution . . . which goes on steadily . . . without the concentration camp . . . . The world order which we seek is . . . free countries, working together in a friendly, civilized society."

Source Reading Wrap-Up

1) What was Roosevelt asking of the American people?

2) When did Roosevelt feel his ideas could be accomplished?

3) What were the four freedoms he named?

4) What is the world order Roosevelt said we sought?

5) Do you think Roosevelt expected America would enter another war? Why or why not?

★ Italy was ruled by Fascist Benito Mussolini. In Spain, General Franco led its Fascist government.

★ Adolf Hitler rose to power in Germany in the 1930s. In March 1938, Germany took over Austria and the Sudetenland. In September 1939, German forces invaded Poland. Following this act, France and Great Britain declared war on Germany.

★ In 1940 Germany conquered Denmark, Norway, Belgium, the Netherlands, Luxembourg, and France. Germany continued to attack Great Britain and in June of 1941 began an attack on the Soviet Union. The Allies—Australia, Canada, Great Britain, the Soviet Union and other countries—joined to fight Germany.

★ Japan began to invade portions of Indochina and formed an alliance with Germany and Italy. This group was known as the Axis Powers. On December 7, 1941, Japanese bombers launched a surprise attack on the American naval fleet anchored in Pearl Harbor in Hawaii. Four days later Japan's allies declared war on the United States.

★ America focused its military to help its allies in Europe. The first thrust was in Italy, where Mussolini's government soon fell. Germany moved quickly into Italy and stopped the Allies in Rome.

★ On D-Day, June 6, 1944, Allied troops landed in France and began an assault. Over the next months, Allied forces gained more ground against the Germans. By the end of April of 1945, Germany surrendered and the war in Europe was over.

★ During the period in which the Nazis were in power, over six million innocent European Jews were killed in concentration camps and death camps. This period, known as the Holocaust, lasted over seven years.

★ President Roosevelt died in April 1945, and Harry Truman became President.

★ Allied forces began to capture Japanese-controlled territory. The Japanese were forced back to Japan. Truman issued a final warning, but Japan refused to surrender. In an attempt to save American lives, Truman ordered the dropping of the first atomic bombs on Japan. Soon after the second bomb was dropped, Japan surrendered on September 2, 1945.

Comprehension: Identifying Facts

On a separate sheet of paper, write the words from the Word Bank to complete each sentence.

WORD BANK		
Adolf Hitler	Dwight D. Eisenhower	Pearl Harbor
Benito Mussolini		rationing
D-Day	Joseph Stalin	Third Reich
detention camps	Kristallnacht	Winston Churchill
	Lend-Lease Act	Yalta

1) _____ and his Nazi party attempted to make Germany the ruler of all Europe.

2) One of the early events in the Holocaust was called _____.

3) _____ became the Fascist dictator of Italy in 1922 and stayed in power until he was executed by the Italian people in 1943.

4) On December 7, 1941, the Japanese attacked the American fleet anchored in _____.

5) Hitler envisioned Germany as a huge empire called the _____.

6) After Hitler invaded the Soviet Union, _____ broke his agreement with Germany and joined the Allies.

7) Prime Minister _____ led Great Britain through the worst years of World War II.

8) Congress passed the _____ to help European countries fight Germany.

9) The Allied invasion of France began on June 6, 1944, which was called _____.

10) The _____ of gasoline, sugar, meat, and other products was one way Americans at home helped the war effort.

11) The American government forced thousands of Japanese Americans into _____.

12) The commander of the Allied army was _____.

13) Roosevelt, Stalin, and Churchill met in _____ to form an agreement for their roles after the war.

Comprehension: Understanding Main Ideas

On a separate sheet of paper, write the answer to each question using complete sentences.

1) Why was the German style of warfare called Blitzkrieg, or "lightning war"?

2) What did people do at home to help the war effort?

3) What events led up to the attack on Pearl Harbor?

4) How did World War II begin in Europe?

Critical Thinking: Write Your Opinion

1) At the beginning of World War II, the United States was neutral. Do you think the war would have ended sooner if America had gotten involved earlier? Explain your answer.

2) How can studying events like the Holocaust help prevent such things from happening again?

3) President Truman had the choice to drop the atomic bomb rather than invading Japan. If you had been President, what choice would you have made?

| Test Taking Tip | When taking a true-false test, look for words such as *many, some, sometimes, usually,* and *may*. These clue words may mean that the statement has exceptions. |

A table is an arrangement of figures or information in columns and rows. It allows you to organize information in a clear way. It also allows you to interpret information easily and quickly.

The United States takes a census, or counts the population, every ten years. The population table below shows the figures since 1930. It also projects the population figures for the year 2000. In addition, the table gives the percentage by which the population increased.

Population of the United States: 1930–2000		
Year	**Number**	**Increase by Percent**
1930	122,775,046	16. 1
1940	131,669,275	7.2
1950	151,325,798	14.5
1960	179,323,175	18.5
1970	203,302,031	13.4
1980	226,542,199	11.4
1990	248,718,301	9.8
2000	274,600,000	9.4

Use the table in the left column to answer these questions. You may need to do some math to get some of your answers.

1) What was the U.S. population in 1940?

2) What was the U.S. population in 1970?

3) By what number did the population increase from 1980 to 1990?

4) What was the percentage of increase between 1980 and 1990?

5) By what number is the population expected to increase from 1930 to 2000?

6) In what year did the U.S. population increase the most? the least?

7) Estimate the population for 1965.

8) Based on information in this table, predict what the population might be in the year 2010.

9) Why do you think the government takes a census every ten years?

10) Write a paragraph summarizing what you learned from the table.

★ The Great Depression followed the stock market crash of 1929.

★ Many were unemployed and homeless. They could not buy food.

★ President Hoover tried helping. Most of his plans and policies failed. Most Americans blamed Hoover for the problems of the depression.

★ Franklin Roosevelt became President in 1933. His programs helped to bring the country out of the depression.

★ The Social Security Act of 1935 set up help for the elderly and disabled.

★ John L. Lewis worked to organize labor.

★ Roosevelt tried to put justices on the Supreme Court who would support his policies. Congress and the American people objected.

★ Films and books offered an escape from people's hardships.

★ In the 1930s, Fascist Benito Mussolini ruled Italy. Francisco Franco ruled Spain's Fascist government. Nazi Adolph Hitler rose to power in Germany.

★ Germany began invading Europe in 1938. Germany invaded Poland in 1939. France and Great Britain declared war on Germany.

★ In 1940, Germany conquered Denmark, Norway, Belgium, the Netherlands, and France. It attacked Great Britain. It began attacking the Soviet Union in 1941. The Allies joined to fight Germany.

★ Japan formed an alliance with Germany and Italy called the Axis Powers. On December 7, 1941, Japan bombed the U.S. naval fleet in Pearl Harbor in Hawaii. America entered World War II the next day. Four days later the Axis Powers declared war on the United States.

★ America first helped the Allies in Europe. Allied forces gained ground against the Germans. By the end of April 1945, Germany surrendered. The war in Europe was over.

★ The Nazis killed over six million innocent European Jews in concentration and death camps. The Holocaust lasted over seven years.

★ President Roosevelt died in April 1945. Harry Truman took office.

★ Allied forces began capturing Japanese-controlled territory. Japanese forces retreated to Japan. Truman ordered the first atomic bombs dropped on Japan. After the second bomb, Japan surrendered on September 2, 1945.

"When baseball desegregated itself in 1947 on the field, the first American institution ever to do so voluntarily, baseball . . . changed how blacks and whites felt about themselves and about each other. Late . . . as it was, the arrival in the Majors of Jack Roosevelt Robinson was an extraordinary moment in American history. For the first time, a black American . . . was on a level field."

—A. Bartlett Giamatti, *Take Time for Paradise*, 1989

Postwar United States

1946–1968

Have you ever felt uneasy even when things were going well? The United States experienced both easy and uneasy times from 1945 to 1968. The nation was uneasy about communism's grip on many parts of the world. Even though America enjoyed well-being in the 1950s, a time of social unrest began at home. The unrest increased during the 1960s, but ended with positive civil rights laws. America cheered its successes in outer space during this time.

In this unit you will learn about America's efforts to stop the spread of communism. You will learn about how the nation lived through social uneasiness. You will learn about America's involvement in other wars and its place as a world leader. You will learn about its exploration of outer space.

Chapter 27: A Time of Challenge and Change: 1945–1957

Chapter 28: Support for Freedom: 1958–1968

27

1945–1957

World War II was over. The Allies defeated the Nazis and the rest of the Axis Powers. The postwar period in America and Europe was a time of recovery. New world organizations were formed to prevent such damaging wars. At the same time, a new kind of struggle between the Soviet Union and the United States was beginning. In this chapter, you will learn about this struggle and the other changes that occurred after the war.

Goals for Learning

▶ To explain the results of World War II

▶ To describe the early part of the Cold War

▶ To explain America's involvement in the Korean War

▶ To describe the United States in the decade following World War II

▶ To describe early events in the civil rights movement

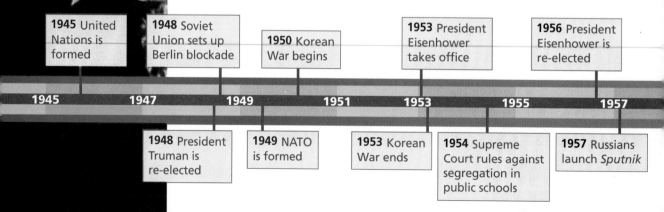

1945 United Nations is formed

1948 Soviet Union sets up Berlin blockade

1950 Korean War begins

1953 President Eisenhower takes office

1956 President Eisenhower is re-elected

| 1945 | 1947 | 1949 | 1951 | 1953 | 1955 | 1957 |

1948 President Truman is re-elected

1949 NATO is formed

1953 Korean War ends

1954 Supreme Court rules against segregation in public schools

1957 Russians launch *Sputnik*

Germans cleared rubble from the streets of Berlin, Germany, after the war.

Americans were happy that World War II had ended. Thousands celebrated in the streets of the nation's cities as their friends and loved ones returned home from the war. They waved flags, honked horns, cheered, and cried.

What Damages Did the War Cause?

The death and destruction caused by World War II was the worst in history. More than fifty-five million people died. The United States alone lost nearly 400,000 military men and women. Many millions more were seriously wounded. The bombings of Europe and Japan caused millions of civilian deaths.

The damage to cities in Europe cost well over $200 billion. Direct costs of fighting by all the countries combined was over a trillion dollars. Of that sum, America had spent $360 billion. For many years to come, the world would feel the effects of World War II.

How Did the War Change America's Role?

Americans knew that their role in the world had changed. The country could never again isolate itself from world problems. The United States was now one of the most powerful nations in the world. Not only did the nation have the power of the atomic bomb but also it had new responsibilities in the world. In the months following the end of the war, Americans were uncertain how the country should move on. However, people did know that they wanted to develop a way to keep a lasting peace.

Why Was the United Nations Formed?

Delegates from fifty nations met in San Francisco, California, in April of 1945. They created the United Nations (UN), a new world **organization.** Member countries of the General Assembly would come up with peaceful methods of settling international problems. They wanted to prevent wars better than the League of Nations had. The UN set up a Security Council. Eleven members (now fifteen) had the responsibility of keeping the peace. The United States, Great Britain, France, the Soviet Union, and China were made permanent members of the Security Council.

In response to the treatment of the Jews during World War II, the UN General Assembly declared **genocide** unlawful. Genocide is the execution of a group based on its race or political views. The assembly agreed that any country found guilty of this practice would be brought before an international court.

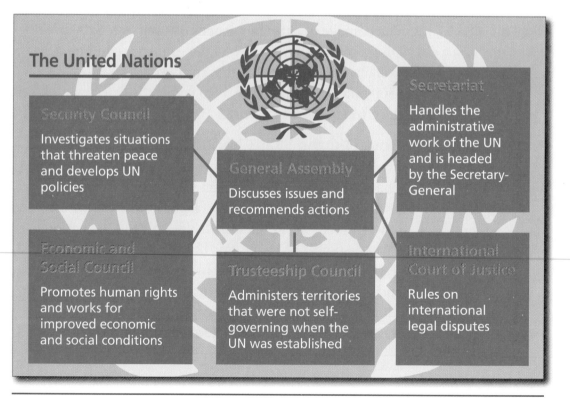

The United Nations

Security Council
Investigates situations that threaten peace and develops UN policies

Secretariat
Handles the administrative work of the UN and is headed by the Secretary-General

General Assembly
Discusses issues and recommends actions

Economic and Social Council
Promotes human rights and works for improved economic and social conditions

Trusteeship Council
Administers territories that were not self-governing when the UN was established

International Court of Justice
Rules on international legal disputes

The United Nations was soon tested with a problem in the Middle East. Palestine had been under the control of Great Britain since World War I. The Arabs and Jews wanted the British to leave. The United Nations wanted a Jewish nation and an Arab nation to be created out of Palestine. In 1948, the new nation of Israel was established. Arab nations in the Middle East objected to the creation of Israel and declared war. In 1949, the UN stopped the fighting and restored peace. The UN had passed its first test.

What Was President Truman's "Fair Deal"?

When Harry Truman became President in 1945, he had been Vice President for less than three months. Although he had spent many years in the Senate, he had very little experience dealing with the problems that faced the nation. Truman wanted to stabilize the country and work toward a lasting peace with other nations.

The months that followed the end of World War II were difficult for Truman. He faced many problems at home and abroad. Truman presented Congress with his own plan for improving the country. The program was called the "Fair Deal." It was based on the ideas of the New Deal. Truman wanted:

1. more people included in the Social Security system
2. the minimum wage increased
3. more money for education and science
4. public housing in cities

The Republicans attacked the Democrats and the Fair Deal policies. They warned the American people about the power of "big government" and the growing power of labor unions. Acting on their fear, the Republican Congress ignored Truman's veto and passed the Taft-Hartley Act in 1947. This law prevented employers from hiring only union members. Union leaders opposed this law.

Harry and Bess Truman waved from the rear platform of a train during Mr. Truman's campaign by train.

Who Won the 1948 Election?

Truman won his party's nomination in 1948, but few leaders believed he could win the election. The Democratic party was split apart over civil rights for African Americans. Truman supported civil rights. As a result, southern Democrats left the party and formed a new States' Rights "Dixiecrat" party.

Truman campaigned by train, often speaking ten times a day. The Republican party had nominated former New York Governor Thomas E. Dewey. Union workers supported Truman. African-American voters supported his stand on civil rights. Truman defeated Dewey by more than two million votes.

SECTION 1 REVIEW Choose the best word or name in parentheses to complete each sentence. Write your answers on a separate sheet of paper.

1) Over (fifty-five, sixty-five, forty-five) million people were killed in World War II.

2) The (League of Nations, United Nations) was set up in 1945.

3) The new nation of (Israel, Palestine) was established in 1948.

4) President Truman proposed the (New Deal, Fair Deal).

5) (Harry Truman, Thomas E. Dewey) was elected President in 1948.

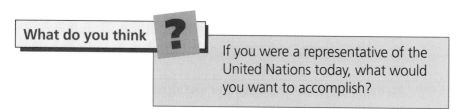

What do you think

?

If you were a representative of the United Nations today, what would you want to accomplish?

★Cold War
The disagreements between communist and noncommunist nations over economics and politics that caused tensions following World War II

Descend
To lower upon

Domination
Complete control

Even though the United States and the Soviet Union had been allies during the final days of World War II, a struggle between the two countries began soon after the war. Since the time of World War I, communists had taken control of the government of the Soviet Union. These leaders promoted the spread of communism to other countries.

What Was the Cold War?

The United States feared that the Soviet goal was world **domination** under communism. The Soviet Union opposed UN peacekeeping efforts. Western nations, including America, started to distrust the Soviet Union. This conflict was called the **Cold War**. Its weapons were mainly economics and politics. The Cold War caused each nation to stay armed just in case it became an actual war.

The Soviet Union promised to hold free elections in eastern European countries when World War II ended. This was part of the Yalta Agreement. Early in 1946, it was clear that Joseph Stalin did not plan to keep his promise. Stalin wanted the governments in eastern Europe and Germany to be communist. The United States was concerned about the spread of communism in Europe. Communism was a threat to democratic governments. Most small countries would not be able to defend themselves against communism without the help of the United States.

Winston Churchill told an audience at a college in Missouri that "an Iron Curtain has **descended** across the continent" of Europe. He said communist dictators controlled the people of eastern Europe. These dictators were supported by the powerful Soviet Union. The "Iron Curtain" stood for the military weapons that the Soviet Union used to keep control of these nations. Churchill challenged the United States. He believed that the United States had the power to stop the spread of communism before the democratic governments of Europe were threatened.

President Truman (left) and Winston Churchill believed the spread of communism should be stopped.

★Containment policy
The policy of using strength or threat of force to prevent the spread of communism

What Was the Containment Policy?

The United States believed it needed a policy to fight the spread of communism. It developed a new **containment policy.** The spread of communism was compared to water. Water flows wherever there is no resistance to it. The Soviet expansion was thought of in this way. Water can be contained by dams. Perhaps communism could be contained by applying American force wherever the Soviet Union tried to gain influence.

The new policy of containment was tested in 1947. Turkey and Greece had serious political and economic problems after World War II. The Soviet Union wanted part of Turkey's territory. Civil war had broken out in Greece. Communist forces tried to gain power in each country. In March of 1947, President Truman asked Congress for $400 million to help these countries. He said that "it must be the policy of the United States to support free peoples who are resisting . . . outside pressures. . . . If we falter in our leadership, we may endanger the peace of the world." Congress approved. Greece and Turkey were able to defeat those countries that wanted to overthrow their governments. The containment policy, now called the Truman Doctrine, had passed its first test.

What Was the Marshall Plan?

Secretary of State George C. Marshall knew that the United States had to help Europe after the war. European cities had to be rebuilt and weak economies had to be made stronger. Marshall hoped to help Europeans avoid communist takeovers. He asked the leaders of Europe to find out how much money they needed to rebuild their countries. A four-year, multibillion-dollar plan was proposed.

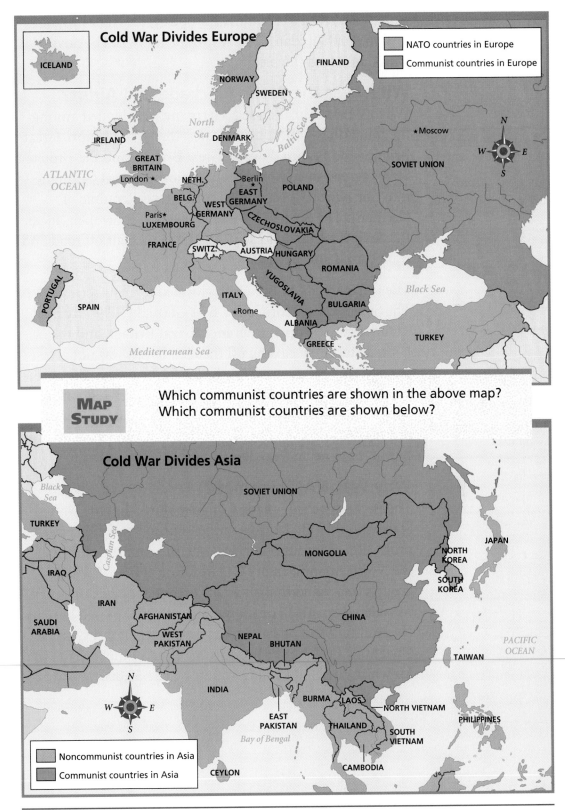

Cold War Divides Europe

NATO countries in Europe

Communist countries in Europe

ICELAND

NORWAY
SWEDEN
FINLAND

North Sea

IRELAND
DENMARK
★Moscow

GREAT
BRITAIN
London ★
NETH.
Berlin ★
POLAND
SOVIET UNION

ATLANTIC
OCEAN
BELG.
WEST
GERMANY
EAST
GERMANY
CZECHOSLOVAKIA

Paris★
LUXEMBOURG

FRANCE
SWITZ.
AUSTRIA
HUNGARY

YUGOSLAVIA
ROMANIA
Black Sea

PORTUGAL
ITALY
★Rome
BULGARIA

SPAIN
ALBANIA
TURKEY

GREECE

Mediterranean Sea

MAP STUDY Which communist countries are shown in the above map?
Which communist countries are shown below?

Cold War Divides Asia

SOVIET UNION

Black Sea
TURKEY
JAPAN

MONGOLIA
NORTH KOREA
SOUTH KOREA

IRAQ
IRAN
AFGHANISTAN
CHINA

SAUDI ARABIA
WEST PAKISTAN
NEPAL
BHUTAN
TAIWAN
PACIFIC OCEAN

INDIA
BURMA
LAOS
NORTH VIETNAM

N W E S
EAST PAKISTAN
THAILAND
SOUTH VIETNAM
PHILIPPINES

Bay of Bengal
CAMBODIA

Noncommunist countries in Asia

Communist countries in Asia

CEYLON

Caspian Sea

Congress agreed to fund the European Recovery Program, or the Marshall Plan as it came to be known. The Soviet Union opposed the program.

What Was the Berlin Blockade and Airlift?

When World War II ended, Germany was divided among the four Allies—the United States, the Soviet Union, Great Britain, and France. France, Great Britain, and the United States agreed to combine their sections of West Germany into one nation. It was called the Federal Republic of Germany. The Soviet Union objected. To show their anger, the Soviets set up a blockade in 1948. This cut off road and train traffic into Berlin.

The German city of Berlin was located in East Germany. The Soviet Union controlled East Germany. The city of Berlin was to be open to France, Great Britain, and the United States. By closing off the city, Berlin was not able to get supplies from western Europe. Three days after the blockade was set up, President Truman ordered an **airlift** of supplies to Berlin. For more than a year, planes carried tons of supplies to Berlin. Finally, the Soviet Union gave in. West Berlin remained a free, democratic city.

★Airlift
Using planes to deliver food and supplies

Why Was NATO Formed?

The Berlin blockade made Congress think that the United States should join Canada and ten European nations for the protection of one another. In 1949, the countries formed the North Atlantic Treaty Organization (NATO). This group's treaty said that an attack on one member would be considered an attack on all members. NATO would have its own military troops sent by the member nations. General Dwight D. Eisenhower was the first head of the NATO force, for which the United States volunteered 350,000 troops.

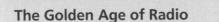

The Golden Age of Radio

Radio had seemed like magic to many people. During the Golden Age of Radio—1925 to the early 1950s—everyone wanted "a talking box" in their living room. Listeners from coast to coast could hear symphonies or the big bands. In rural areas, radio was the link to the world. Radio also made Americans more aware of the looming war in Europe. President Franklin Roosevelt used his radio "fireside chats" to unite the nation behind his New Deal programs.

People created their own mental pictures as they listened to popular mystery and action-adventure programs. Among the most successful were "Gangbusters," "Sam Spade," "Calling All Cars," and "Ellery Queen." Comedy programs such as "Fibber McGee and Molly," "Our Miss Brooks," "The Jack Benny Program," and "The Fred Allen Show" were also popular. Daytime radio had its soap operas, just as daytime television does now. Kids listened to "Jack Armstrong, the All-American Boy" and "The Lone Ranger."

The Golden Age of Radio ended in the late 1940s when television became popular.

WORD BANK

Cold War

containment policy

Marshall Plan

NATO

Soviet Union

SECTION 2 REVIEW On a separate sheet of paper, write the word from the Word Bank to complete each sentence.

1) Democratic countries tried to limit communism during the _____ .

2) _____ considers an attack on one member of its organization to be an attack on all members.

3) The _____ was a communist country.

4) The _____ was an attempt to keep communism from spreading in areas where there was little resistance.

5) The _____ was a plan to help Europe after the war.

What do you think **?**

What do you think are the dangers of a Cold War?

At the end of World War II, Japan surrendered Korea to the Allies. The country became divided into two parts. The northern section was occupied by the Soviet Union. South Korea was controlled by the United States. When the Republic of Korea was set up, America withdrew its troops and provided economic aid to the new country. However, the Soviet communists had set up the Democratic People's Republic in North Korea.

There was tension between the two Koreas. The American armies withdrew from South Korea in 1949. North Korea invaded South Korea on June 25, 1950. Two days later, the United Nations Security Council declared that North Korea was wrong. It asked for the United Nations to help South Korea. The Soviets had been boycotting the UN, so they were unable to veto this plan of action. With UN backing, President Truman ordered American troops to assist the South Koreans.

How Did Fighting Begin?

Fifteen other nations agreed to help South Korea. Still, the defense of South Korea was mainly an American responsibility. President Truman refused to call the fighting in Korea a war. Instead, Truman called it a "police action." The goal was to force North Korean troops to return to their own territory.

Armed with many modern tanks and weapons supplied by the Soviet Union and China, North Korea captured Seoul, the South Korean capital. General Douglas MacArthur, commander of the American troops, was not prepared to fight an **offensive** war. Soon only a small area in the southeast remained under UN control.

Offensive
Attacking rather than defending

MacArthur set up a defensive line at the southern port of Pusan. Then, with the aid of 50,000 more American troops, the UN forces were able to stop the North Koreans.

Writing About History

Write an essay in your notebook about whether the United States should take part in foreign wars such as the Korean War.

MacArthur and his troops were able to push the North Korean army past their own capital city toward the Chinese province of Manchuria.

Communist China had warned the UN that it would become involved if troops moved any closer to Manchuria. MacArthur told Truman that China would not enter the war. However, on November 26, 1950, 300,000 Chinese soldiers attacked the American army in North Korea. The American troops were pushed back into the South. Fortunately, by the following spring, they were able to set up a new defensive line there.

General MacArthur asked Truman for permission to bomb China. Truman feared that bombing would bring the Soviet Union into the war. When Truman refused, MacArthur asked Congress for permission. This action angered Truman. General MacArthur was challenging the power of the President. Truman fired MacArthur in April of 1951.

How Did the Korean War End?

Peace talks began in July of 1951. The two sides disagreed on the problem of prisoner exchange. The communists wanted all prisoners returned to their homeland. The United Nations wanted to give the prisoners a choice. The negotiations continued for two years. An agreement was reached in July of 1953. Prisoners had their choice. North and South Korea became two separate nations.

Both North and South Korea withdrew 1.25 miles from the final battle line. This formed a 2.5 mile neutral zone between both sides. The North Koreans and Chinese who opposed the communists in North Korea were allowed to stay in South Korea. To provide protection from any future attacks, American troops stayed in South Korea. The United States also gave further economic aid.

Salk and the Polio Vaccine

In 1943, the most well-known person with polio was President Franklin D. Roosevelt. In 1943, 1,151 deaths resulted from polio. Still more people became crippled with polio that year.

A viral infection causes polio, which is short for poliomyelitis. In severe form, polio destroys nerve cells that control skeletal muscles. It paralyzes the legs, arms, or trunk. Swallowing, talking, breathing, and heart functions can become difficult. Polio occurs most often in children.

Health

History in Your Life

In 1953, Jonas E. Salk developed a polio vaccine. After intense laboratory tests, he vaccinated Pittsburgh schoolchildren. That same year, the vaccine was tested in schools in forty-four states. It was the largest field test in history. In 1956, Salk announced that before long polio would be wiped out. He was right—1969 was the first year no one died from polio in recorded American medical history.

SECTION 3 REVIEW On a separate sheet of paper, write *True* if the statement is true or *False* if the statement is not true.

1) North Korea invaded South Korea in 1950.

2) The goal of the Korean War was to force North Korean troops to return to their own territory.

3) China was not involved in the Korean War.

4) President Truman fired General MacArthur.

5) The United States refused to give aid to South Korea after the war.

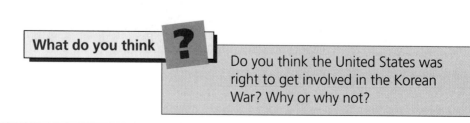

What do you think

?

Do you think the United States was right to get involved in the Korean War? Why or why not?

The Republicans argued that the Democratic party had become filled with corruption. They claimed that the Truman administration had handled the Korean War badly. "It was time for a change," the Republicans said.

In the landslide victory over Adlai Stevenson, Republican Dwight D. Eisenhower was elected President in 1952. Known as "Ike," Eisenhower was a hero of World War II. He became a popular President. He took office in 1953.

The nation's economy was doing well during most of the years Eisenhower held office. Soldiers who had returned from fighting in World War II and Korea had started families. New home construction soared, as did the need for more and better American products. During this time, the lives of most Americans improved.

★Nuclear war
War that uses atomic weapons

At home, the fear of communism and the Soviet Union still existed. The Soviet Union developed an atomic bomb. Americans were worried about a war using atomic weapons, or **nuclear war.** People built bomb shelters in their backyards. Cities set up air raid warning signals. Schoolchildren were taught to get under their desks or go to a certain place quickly when they heard air raid sirens.

This "family model" bomb shelter shows an escape opening at the top and an entrance that attached to a cellar. This kind of shelter was placed underground.

What Was McCarthyism?

Senator Joseph McCarthy used Americans' fear of communism for his own political gains. He said traitors from within America were trying to destroy the country. McCarthy became one of the Senate's most feared members. Many American educators, journalists, and entertainers lost their jobs as a result of his **accusations.** Others had their **reputations** ruined. For a long time, few politicians were willing to challenge McCarthy.

McCarthy began to investigate army officials. The Senate held televised hearings for thirty-six days in 1954. When television audiences saw McCarthy as a lying bully, they

demanded an investigation. A special Senate committee found that most of McCarthy's charges were untrue. With the help of television, the American people were able to take away much of McCarthy's power. The campaign he had used to make his accusations soon became known as **McCarthyism.**

Senator Joseph McCarthy used a map of the United States to try to prove his accusations were true.

MARGARET CHASE SMITH: 1897–1995

A Republican from Maine, Margaret Chase Smith was the first woman elected to both houses of Congress. She completed her husband's term in the House of Representatives after his death in 1940. Then Smith was elected to four more two-year terms. She next served in the Senate for twenty-five years— longer than any other woman. During the early 1950s, she spoke out against the methods of Senator Joseph McCarthy. In 1964, Smith campaigned for the Republican presidential nomination. She was the first woman ever to campaign for the presidential nomination in a major party. Smith wrote the book *Gallant Women* in 1968. The book documented the lives of independent women in American public life.

Rosa Parks

How Did the Civil Rights Movement Begin?

African Americans had fought for democracy in two world wars. Yet when they returned from those wars, they were still denied basic political and social rights. In the 1950s, many African Americans decided that the members of their race could no longer be victims.

The civil rights movement was sparked by a 1954 decision of the Supreme Court, *Brown v. the Board of Education of Topeka, Kansas.* A young African-American girl was denied the right to attend a white school. Her father sued the school board. NAACP lawyers, including Thurgood Marshall, worked very hard on this case. Marshall later became the first African American appointed to the Supreme Court. In the decision, the Supreme Court ruled that separate schools for whites and African Americans were unconstitutional. In 1954, Chief Justice Earl Warren wrote that separate can never be equal. States were ordered to end school segregation.

In December of 1955, Rosa Parks, a forty-two year-old African-American woman, got on a bus in Montgomery, Alabama. She found a seat near the front. The bus driver asked Parks to give up her seat to a white person. Rosa Parks would not. Police were called and she was arrested. Parks had not planned to challenge the law on that day. She said, "I felt it was just something that I had to do." Rosa Parks' decision not to move from her seat on a bus was the quiet beginning of a national civil rights movement.

A 26-year-old minister named Martin Luther King Jr. led a boycott of the buses in Montgomery in 1956. He helped to organize car pools to help African Americans travel around the city. He was arrested for his actions. One year later the Supreme Court ruled that segregation on public transportation was unconstitutional.

A new civil rights law was passed in August of 1957. This law made it illegal to use force to stop someone from voting. This was the first civil rights law since Reconstruction. Progress was continually challenged. The governor of Arkansas tried to prevent nine African-American children from attending an all-white school in Little Rock. The state's **National Guard** was ordered to protect this school. A national guard is a state's military force. President Eisenhower sent federal troops to help the African-American children. The governor finally backed down.

What Was Life Like in the 1950s?

American society experienced many changes in the 1950s. Jobs were available for most Americans. With the development of **automation,** factories employed thousands of people to produce countless new products. Advances in science and **technology** offered Americans better health and a higher standard of living than ever before.

Then and Now

Do you have a computer in your home or use one at school? The computer you use is a lot smaller than a computer was in the 1950s. One computer then filled an entire room. The room had to be kept cool and clean. People punched information onto cards and fed the cards into the computer. Only large businesses could afford a computer. Businesses used computers mainly to keep records and to print customers' bills and employees' paychecks.

Today businesses and schools have many computers. Many people have home computers. You may have learned how to use a computer in school. In the 1950s, you would have used a manual typewriter to prepare a report. Now you use a computer and maybe the Internet to do your homework. Maybe you send letters over e-mail. People with portable laptop computers carry them to the library, a business meeting, or even the park. Computer uses are endless.

In 1956, the federal government started a huge program to build interstate highways. The highways would connect most cities with populations over 50,000. As the roads were built, suburbs attracted more home builders.

New cars had large "fins" on their rear fenders. Some young people drove hot rods. Crew cuts were a common hairstyle for boys. Girls wore their hair in ponytails. Television was only black and white. Young children watched a puppet named Howdy Doody and his friend Buffalo Bob. Rock and roll music was new, and young

Television was black and white in the 1950s.

★Artificial satellite
A human-made object that travels in outer space and sends signals back to earth

people loved it. The term UFO (unidentified flying object) entered the average person's vocabulary.

How Was Eisenhower Re-elected?

In the election of 1956, Eisenhower was elected by an even greater landslide than in the previous election. The Democrats, however, took control of Congress. Although many Republicans considered the President to be too liberal, Americans seemed to be happy with him.

How Did the Space Race Begin?

The United States was taken by surprise when the Soviet Union launched *Sputnik* on October 4, 1957. *Sputnik* was an **artificial satellite** that traveled in outer space and sent radio signals back to earth. Everyone was concerned that a foreign country knew how to do something that the Americans did not.

The United States was developing space technology, but the Russians raced ahead. *Sputnik 2,* carrying a dog, was launched before the United States could get into space. A new battle had been added to the Cold War.

SECTION 4 REVIEW Write the answers to these questions on a separate sheet of paper using complete sentences.

1) How did Americans prepare for a nuclear war?

2) What was McCarthyism?

3) How did Rosa Parks help begin the civil rights movement?

4) How did roads improve in the 1950s?

5) How did the Russians start the space race?

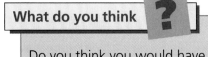

What do you think ?

Do you think you would have liked living in the 1950s? Why or why not?

The Crisis at Central High School

In 1954, the Supreme Court declared school segregation unconstitutional. In 1957, Central High School in Little Rock, Arkansas, was going to admit African-American students for the first time. Governor Orval Faubus said he could not maintain order if African-American students tried to enter. Elizabeth Eckford was one of nine African-American students who tried to integrate the school. Here are the viewpoints of Governor Faubus and Elizabeth Eckford.

"The question at issue . . . is not integration versus segregation . . . . The question now is whether . . . the head of a sovereign state can exercise his constitutional powers and discretion in maintaining peace and good order within his jurisdiction, being accountable to his own conscience and to his own people . . . .

The situation in Little Rock and Arkansas grows more explosive by the hour. This is caused for the most part by the misunderstanding of our problem by a federal judge who decreed 'immediate integration' of the public schools . . . without hearing any evidence . . . as to the conditions . . . in the community . . . ."

From: A message from Governor Faubus to President Eisenhower, September 4, 1957.

"I saw a large crowd of people standing across the street from the soldiers guarding Central. As I walked on, the crowd suddenly got very quiet. Superintendent Blossom had told us to enter by the front door. . . .

When I got right in front of the school, I went up to a guard . . . he just looked straight ahead and didn't move to let me pass him. . . . I walked until I was right in front of the path to the front door.

I stood looking at the school—it looked so big! Just then the guards let some white students go through.

The crowd was quiet . . . waiting to see what was going to happen. When I was able to steady my knees, I walked up to the guard who had let the white students in. He . . . didn't move. When I tried to squeeze past him, he raised his bayonet . . . the other guards closed in and . . . raised their bayonets. . . .

I was very frightened and didn't know what to do. I turned around and the crowd came toward me. They moved closer and closer. Somebody started yelling, 'Lynch her!'"

From: Daisy Bates, *Long Shadow of Little Rock*. New York. David McKay, 1962, 73-75.

Source Reading Wrap-Up

1) Why did Governor Faubus oppose admitting African-American students?

2) Who did Faubus think caused the crisis?

3) What did Elizabeth Eckford see when she arrived at the school?

4) How did some white guards treat her?

5) Why do you think Elizabeth Eckford risked her safety to attend a high school?

CHAPTER SUMMARY

★ The United Nations was created in San Francisco in April of 1945. The UN was established as an international organization with the responsibility of keeping peace among its member countries.

★ Distrust developed between communist and noncommunist countries. The United States did not want communism to spread beyond the countries where it was already established. The United States fought communism by supporting governments that were opposed to communism.

★ The Marshall Plan provided American aid to European countries that had suffered damage during the war.

★ The United States, France, and Great Britain flew supplies to West Berlin during a period when the Soviet Union cut off ground transportation to the city. The Berlin airlift lasted until the Soviets reopened the railroads and highways.

★ In 1949, North Korea invaded South Korea. The United States was among sixteen countries that sent troops to help South Korea. After three years of fighting, the communist North Koreans agreed to peace talks that established two separate nations.

★ Dwight D. Eisenhower, a hero of World War II, was elected President in 1952.

★ Fear of communism was widespread. Senator Joseph McCarthy used this fear to accuse hundreds of Americans of being communists or communist sympathizers. Because of McCarthy's tactics many people lost their jobs.

★ The civil rights movement grew in strength in the 1950s. The Supreme Court ruled that separate schools for whites and African Americans were unconstitutional. Martin Luther King Jr. led a boycott of buses in Montgomery, Alabama. Congress passed the Civil Rights Law in 1957.

★ During the 1950s, jobs were available for most Americans. People had money to purchase such items as televisions and new cars. Because of interstate highways, people built homes in suburbs.

Comprehension: Identifying Facts

On a separate sheet of paper, write the words from the Word Bank to complete each sentence.

WORD BANK	
Douglas MacArthur	Rosa Parks
Fair Deal	segregation
Iron Curtain	*Sputnik*
Israel	Taft-Hartley Act
Joseph McCarthy	United Nations
Joseph Stalin	West Berlin
Korea	

1) The United Nations established the country of _____ in the Middle East.

2) President Truman's economic plan was called the _____.

3) An international organization called the _____ was created in San Francisco in 1946.

4) Under the rules of the _____, employers could hire nonunion workers.

5) Winston Churchill used the term _____ to describe the division between eastern and western Europe.

6) In 1954, the Supreme Court ruled that schools must end _____.

7) _____ was the leader of the Soviet Union.

8) Truman helped establish an airlift to provide supplies to _____.

9) UN forces went to _____ to settle a dispute between the northern communists and the democratic government of the south.

10) Truman fired _____ because he went to Congress and challenged the power of the President.

11) _____ led a series of trials, trying to prove that there were communist spies working in the government and throughout the country.

12) By refusing to give up her seat on the bus, _____ helped begin the civil rights movement.

13) In 1957, the Soviet Union launched _____, an artificial satellite.

Comprehension: Understanding Main Ideas

On a separate sheet of paper, write the answer to each question using complete sentences.

1) What were some of the early events of the civil rights movement?

2) What were three results of World War II?

3) What was the United States like in the 1950s?

4) How was the United States involved in the Korean War?

5) Why was America involved in the Cold War?

Critical Thinking: Write Your Opinion

1) Senator McCarthy used the Americans' fear of communism to accuse many people falsely. Do you think this could happen today? Why or why not?

2) Television had a major effect on America in the 1950s. Do you think the Internet will have the same sort of effect? Why or why not?

| Test Taking Tip | When taking a multiple-choice test, read every choice before you answer a question. Put a line through choices you know are wrong. Then choose the best answer from the remaining choices. |

Support for Freedom

1958–1968

The 1960s in America was a time of protest. There were still many problems at home that needed to be addressed. Individual freedoms became important as never before in the nation. Yet another war—the Vietnam War—caused many of these protests. African Americans, Hispanic Americans, American Indians, and women sought to increase their rights. In this chapter, you will learn how the United States worked to gain freedom for all its citizens during the 1960s.

Goals for Learning

▶ To describe major events in the Kennedy presidency

▶ To describe developments in the civil rights movement

▶ To explain the major federal social programs of the 1960s

▶ To explain American involvement in Vietnam

▶ To explain the social and political divisions in America

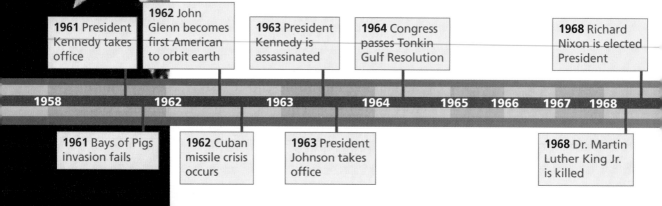

1961 President Kennedy takes office

1962 John Glenn becomes first American to orbit earth

1963 President Kennedy is assassinated

1964 Congress passes Tonkin Gulf Resolution

1968 Richard Nixon is elected President

1958   1962   1963   1964   1965   1966   1967   1968

1961 Bays of Pigs invasion fails

1962 Cuban missile crisis occurs

1963 President Johnson takes office

1968 Dr. Martin Luther King Jr. is killed

★**Atmosphere**
The gaseous layer covering the earth

★**Suborbital**
Not out of the earth's atmosphere

On January 31, 1958, the U.S. army put the first American satellite, *Explorer I*, into orbit. This was three months after the launch of *Sputnik 2*. The following October, the United States created the National Aeronautics and Space Administration (NASA).

From 1961 to 1963, the United States launched six manned Mercury spacecraft. On May 5, 1961, Alan B. Shepard Jr.

piloted *Mercury-Redstone 3 (Freedom 7)* on a fifteen-and-a-half minute **suborbital** flight. This means that the flight did not make it out of the earth's **atmosphere** and into orbit. John Glenn made history when he became the first American to orbit the earth. On February 20, 1962, Glenn orbited the earth three times in *Friendship 7*. The last Mercury mission took place in May of 1963.

Project Gemini was the code name for the United States program to launch two astronauts in a spacecraft capable of orbiting for a long time. The first two-person mission of Project Gemini took place in 1965. In the years that followed, there were nine additional Gemini flights.

John Glenn

Like most Americans in 1957, you would have been alarmed. That year the former Soviet Union had launched *Sputnik*, the first satellite, into space. Americans feared the Soviets would win the "space race" and gain military control over the United States. It took America only four months to send its own satellite into space. The space race was on. By 1963, the United States had sent several astronauts into space.

By 1990, the Cold War between the two countries was over. They no longer were competing in space. In 1996, U.S. astronauts like Shannon Lucid and Russian cosmonauts worked together in space. They met at Mir, a Russian space station. In 1997, plans were underway to build an international space station. Space exploration has come a long way since 1957.

Enthusiasm
Strong feeling of excitement

Ineligible
Not able to do something because it is against rules

Who Won the 1960 Election?

The Cold War briefly "thawed" in the late 1950s. Soviet Premier Nikita Khrushchev visited the United States in 1959 and invited President Eisenhower to visit the Soviet Union. However, Khrushchev quickly withdrew the invitation after the Soviets captured an American pilot flying far inside Soviet borders.

The 1960 presidential election grew in importance. The Republican party had controlled the White House for eight years. The Twenty-Second Amendment to the Constitution, ratified in 1951, said that a President could not serve more than two terms. Therefore, Eisenhower was **ineligible** for a third term in office. The Republicans chose Richard Nixon as their candidate. The Democrats nominated a young senator from Massachusetts—John F. Kennedy.

Known as a tough opponent of communist expansion, Nixon had gained experience in world affairs during his eight years as Vice President. Kennedy had been a member of Congress since 1946.

Kennedy and Nixon held a series of debates on national television. According to many political observers, the debates played a major role in the outcome of the election. Kennedy was young and handsome, and he remained very cool under the pressure of the televised debate.

The election was very close. Kennedy narrowly won the popular vote. He was the youngest man ever to be elected President. Kennedy was also the first President who was a Roman Catholic.

Alaska and Hawaii Become States

In 1959, Alaska and Hawaii joined the United States. They were the first states added to the nation since the admission of Arizona in 1912. Alaska is the 49th state; Hawaii is the 50th.

Kennedy took the presidential oath of office on January 20, 1961. He challenged Americans to work for the good of the nation. "My fellow Americans," he said, "ask not what your country can do for you—ask what you can do for your country." Kennedy brought a new **enthusiasm** to the American people.

Richard Nixon (left) and John F. Kennedy took part in debates on national television.

SECTION 1 REVIEW Choose the best word or name in parentheses to complete each sentence. Write your answers on a separate sheet of paper.

1) (Alan B. Shepard, John Glenn) was the first American to orbit the earth.

2) (The army, NASA, the navy) put the first American satellite into orbit.

3) The (Twentieth, Twenty-First, Twenty-Second) Amendment said a President could not be elected for more than two terms.

4) The (Republicans, Democrats) chose Richard Nixon as their candidate for President.

5) (John F. Kennedy, Richard Nixon) won the election of 1960.

What do you think **?**

Do you think presidential debates help determine the outcome of an election? Why or why not?

The communist government in Cuba was of major concern to the United States. Fidel Castro, the head of the Cuban government, had originally won support from the United States for leading a revolt against Cuba's dictator. Then, he surprised America by declaring that he was a communist. He requested help from the Soviets and received it. This communist government was only ninety miles from the Florida coastline.

The Castro government seized property owned by Americans and other countries in Cuba. The Eisenhower administration stopped all trade with Cuba except food or medicine. It encouraged anti-Castro Cuban **refugees** to invade their homeland and overthrow the government.

★Refugee
A person who flees his or her home country to seek protection

When Kennedy became President, he was asked to approve an invasion plan. Kennedy approved the plan but would not allow American troops to take part. The United States did, however, train and arm the Cuban rebels.

In April of 1961, American-supported Cubans invaded Cuba at the Bay of Pigs. The invaders thought that the Cuban people and the Cuban army would support them. They were wrong. The invasion was a complete failure. Within three days, most of the invaders were killed or captured. President Kennedy took full responsibility for the failure.

Why Was the Berlin Wall Built?

President Kennedy and the Soviet leader, Nikita Khrushchev, met in Vienna, Austria, in June of 1961. Khrushchev believed that Kennedy was too young and inexperienced to be a strong leader. Khrushchev believed that it was time to force the United States out of West Berlin. President Kennedy said that the United States would not leave the city. The Soviet Union responded by building a wall dividing the city of Berlin. The wall was between communist East Berlin and democratic West Berlin.

The Berlin Wall prevented East Berliners from leaving their section of the city.

What Was the Cuban Missile Crisis?

★Missile
A self-driven bomb

One of the most serious events of the Cold War occurred in October of 1962. The Cuban **missile** crisis almost caused a war between the United States and the Soviet Union. A missile is a self-driven bomb. The United States discovered that Cuba was secretly building missile bases. Kennedy ordered the navy to stop Soviet ships from carrying missiles to Cuba. The world watched nervously as two powerful nations challenged each other to back down. Radio and television news kept the American people informed of the situation. War appeared very possible.

Suddenly, on October 26, the Soviet ships turned around in a wide circle. They were heading back to the Soviet Union. The tension was broken.

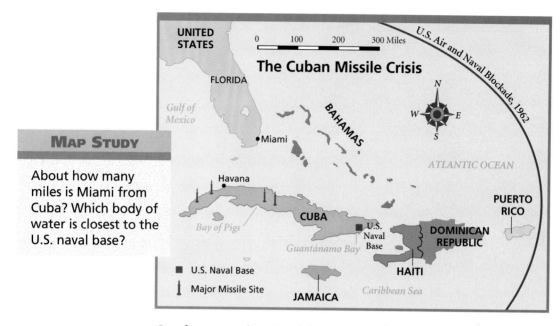

MAP STUDY

About how many miles is Miami from Cuba? Which body of water is closest to the U.S. naval base?

On the same day, President Kennedy received a letter from the Soviet Premier. Khrushchev said that he would remove the missiles from Cuba if Kennedy would promise not to invade Cuba. The Cuban missile crisis was over. President Kennedy was praised for his tough stand.

SECTION 2 REVIEW Write the answers to these questions on a separate sheet of paper using complete sentences.

1) How far was Cuba from the United States?

2) How did Kennedy try to help the Cubans?

3) What did the Soviet Union do to Berlin?

4) How did the Cuban missile crisis almost turn into a war?

5) How did people view Kennedy after the Cuban missile crisis?

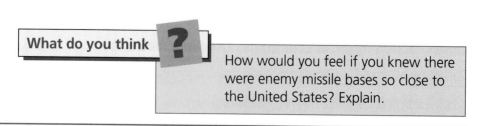

What do you think **?**

How would you feel if you knew there were enemy missile bases so close to the United States? Explain.

In the 1960s, the struggle for African-American equality moved from the courts to the streets. Segregation was still the law of the land in many parts of the country. Many African Americans were denied the right to vote. Some progress had been made during the 1950s. Yet African Americans were still treated as second-class citizens in many parts of the country.

Fulfill
To carry out something that may or may not be expected

In June of 1963, President Kennedy said, "The time has come for this nation to **fulfill** its promise . . . for equality . . . Those who do nothing are inviting shame as well as violence." The federal government tried to help end inequality and segregation for African Americans. The struggle for equality, however, still rested on Americans who risked their lives to end discrimination and segregation.

James Farmer led a sit-in in New York City.

How Did Groups Attack Segregation?

A group of African Americans and whites called "freedom riders" boarded buses and headed south. Their plan was to draw attention to segregation in the southern states. The group was led by James Farmer of the Congress of Racial Equality (CORE).

Television cameras brought the shame of segregation into the living rooms of the American people. Following the example set by Martin Luther King Jr., the freedom riders believed in peaceful protests. Yet some of their buses were burned. Many people were beaten.

Angry African Americans took part in riots in the 1960s. This riot took place in the Watts section of Los Angeles in 1965.

During 1962 and 1963, the civil rights movement caught the attention of the nation. **Riots** broke out at the University of Mississippi. A riot is a violent public disturbance. James Meredith was not allowed to attend because he was African American. A court ordered the university to admit him. The governor of the state said that he would keep Meredith out. Meredith's life was threatened. Mobs of white people protested his admission. Local police failed to keep the peace. President Kennedy sent federal troops to the university to protect Meredith. Meredith became the first African American to attend the University of Mississippi.

How Did Violence Against Protesters Increase?

Segregation in public places was still practiced in many parts of the South. African-American protesters focused their efforts on this injustice. They organized boycotts, protests, and "sit-ins." These **tactics** upset many white southerners and resulted in violence against the peaceful protesters.

★**Desegregation**
Acts to remove segregation in public places

★**Riot**
A violent public disturbance

Tactic
A method of doing something

It became clear that the federal government had to act. A national civil rights bill was sent to Congress by President Kennedy. It was known as the Civil Rights Act. Approved in 1964, the bill granted the federal government authority to speed up school **desegregation.** It protected the voting rights of African Americans. The law also required an end to segregation of public places.

What Was the March on Washington?

On August 28, 1963, more than 200,000 people gathered peacefully at the Lincoln Memorial in Washington, D.C. The March on Washington was organized by African-American leaders to show support for the passage of the

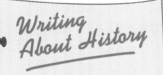

Writing About History

Research the speech Dr. Martin Luther King Jr. presented in Washington, D.C. (or see page 586 in this textbook). In your notebook, write a newspaper article about it.

civil rights bill. Participants in the march included African Americans and whites of all ages. Many waved small American flags. There were songs, prayers, and speeches. Dr. Martin Luther King Jr. spoke to the marchers of his dream for America. His speech was a challenge to the nation. It was also a message of hope.

How Was President Kennedy Assassinated?

President Kennedy began to turn his thoughts toward being re-elected. He flew to Texas to begin his campaign. On Friday, November 22, 1963, President Kennedy rode through the streets of Dallas, Texas. Riding with him were his wife and Governor John Connally of Texas and Connally's wife. The **motorcade** was moving through the streets of downtown Dallas when shots were fired.

Motorcade
A parade of cars

Governor Connally was seriously wounded. President Kennedy, who had been shot in the head and neck, was dead. A few hours later, Vice President Johnson took the presidential oath of office. Lee Harvey Oswald was arrested and accused of killing the President. Two days later on live television, Jack Ruby shot and killed Oswald. The nation was shocked that Kennedy had been assassinated.

President Kennedy (rear seat to left) rode through Dallas, Texas, before he was assassinated.

The first Peace Corps volunteers provided help to nations in Africa.

★Third World
Poor and underdeveloped countries

What Had Kennedy Achieved as President?

During President Kennedy's brief time in office, he did many things that had lasting effects. In 1961, the Peace Corps was established to improve **Third World** countries. Third World countries are poor and underdeveloped. The first Peace Corps volunteers were sent as teachers to the African nation of Ghana. Five years later, more than 10,000 Americans were serving in fifty-two countries.

When communists threatened Southeast Asia, Kennedy allowed the transport of troops and equipment to aid them. Under Kennedy, the United States, Britain, and the Soviet Union signed the Limited Test Ban Treaty, which made above-ground nuclear tests illegal. Perhaps one of his strongest moves was allocating $20 billion to NASA with a challenge to put an American on the moon by 1970.

SECTION 3 REVIEW On a separate sheet of paper, write *True* if the statement is true or *False* if the statement is not true.

1) Freedom riders planned to draw attention to segregation in the South.

2) James Meredith was against African-American rights.

3) The Civil Rights Act of 1964 allowed segregation.

4) African-American leaders organized a March in Washington to support the Civil Rights Act.

5) Jack Ruby assassinated President Kennedy.

What do you think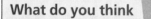

Why do you think it is important to protest peacefully?

Conservative
One who is cautious about change

Maintain
To keep in good condition

President Lyndon Johnson's vision for the future of America was similar to that of John Kennedy. Johnson challenged America to wage a "War on Poverty." The country, he felt, must provide good education for every child and minimum health care for all Americans. Certainly it must bring an end to racial injustice. In May of 1964, he gave his vision a name. He challenged the nation to build a "Great Society."

Who Won the Election of 1964?

In the 1964 election, the Democratic party nominated Lyndon Johnson for President. The Republican party nominated Senator Barry Goldwater of Arizona. There were great differences between the views of the two candidates.

Johnson felt federal programs needed to be created to improve the quality of life for every American. Goldwater, on the other hand, was very **conservative.** He felt individual states should have the final say in their policies. The federal government should not interfere.

Johnson easily won the election. He received more votes than any President before him. This election also gave the Democratic party a stronger control of Congress.

What New Laws Did Johnson Help Pass?

Robert Weaver (left) was the first African American to serve on a President's cabinet.

Johnson acted quickly to get Congress to pass laws. A Medicare Plan was passed to provide health insurance to the elderly. School districts with needy students were provided federal funds through the Elementary and Secondary School Act. Other laws attacked the problem of **maintaining** clean air and water. The Housing Act encouraged the building of low-cost housing. President Johnson appointed Robert Weaver to head the new Department of Housing and Urban Development. He was the first African American to become a member of a President's cabinet.

In 1965, President Johnson decided to expand America's role in a small country in Asia called South Vietnam. The Vietnam War became the most **divisive** conflict in the United States since the Civil War.

What Caused the Vietnam War?

After World War II, the former French territory of Vietnam was divided into two parts. North Vietnam was controlled by a communist government. South Vietnam was noncommunist. America first became involved in this area of Southeast Asia in the 1950s.

President Johnson continued the policy set forth by previous Presidents. Eisenhower had provided military weapons and economic aid to South Vietnam. Kennedy had sent military advisors. Johnson at first sent only noncombat troops to Vietnam.

In August of 1964, two American ships were attacked off the coast of North Vietnam. President Johnson asked Congress for the right "to take all necessary measures" to protect American forces in the area. This vote of Congress was called the Tonkin Gulf Resolution. Congress never declared war against North Vietnam. Johnson used the Tonkin Gulf Resolution as authority to increase American involvement in South Vietnam.

American Troops in Vietnam

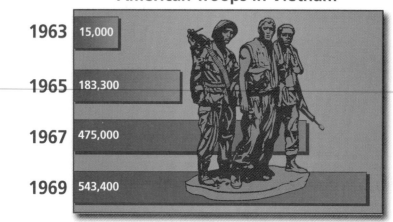

1963	15,000
1965	183,300
1967	475,000
1969	543,400

American soldiers in Vietnam had to bear harsh fighting conditions.

Replenish
To make full or complete again

The communist Vietcong continued to hold on to rural sections of South Vietnam. Even though many Vietcong groups were destroyed, they were quickly **replenished** by North Vietnamese. By the start of 1968, it was clear that the United States was not winning the war.

President Johnson set up a meeting with North and South Vietnam, the United States, and the Vietcong. The 1969 meeting was held in Paris, France, just after Johnson's presidency ended. Unfortunately, this had little effect on ending the fighting.

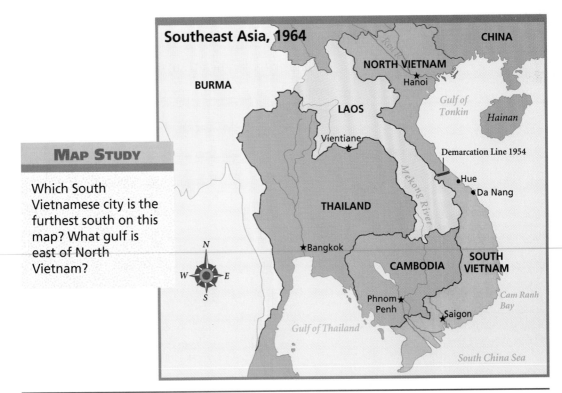

MAP STUDY

Which South Vietnamese city is the furthest south on this map? What gulf is east of North Vietnam?

Southeast Asia, 1964

CHINA

NORTH VIETNAM
★ Hanoi

BURMA

Gulf of Tonkin

Hainan

LAOS

Vientiane ✶

Demarcation Line 1954

Hue
Da Nang

Mekong River

THAILAND

N
W ✶ E
S

★ Bangkok

CAMBODIA

SOUTH VIETNAM

Cam Ranh Bay

Phnom ★ Penh

Saigon ✶

Gulf of Thailand

South China Sea

The Vietnam War

Television coverage of the Vietnam War in the late 1960s brought a new face to war. Reporters and photographers sent back filmed reports daily. The American people had never seen such a vivid picture of war. In fact, many television reports were so vivid that networks began alerting viewers first. The networks warned that the reports about to be shown might upset viewers and their children.

Media coverage was a major factor in shaping public opinion about the war. It made this one of the most disputed wars in which America had ever been involved.

WORD BANK

Barry Goldwater

Housing Act

Lyndon Johnson

Medicare

Tonkin Gulf Resolution

SECTION 4 REVIEW On a separate sheet of paper, write the word from the Word Bank to complete each sentence.

1) _____ won the 1964 election for President.

2) The Republican party nominated _____ for the 1964 election.

3) The _____ encouraged people to build low-cost housing.

4) The _____ Plan provided health insurance to the elderly.

5) Congress passed the _____ to protect American forces near North Vietnam.

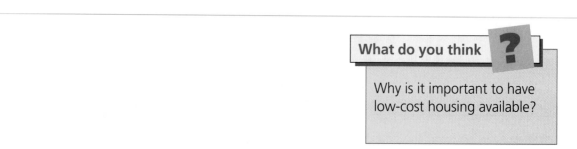

What do you think ?

Why is it important to have low-cost housing available?

★Feminist
A person who seeks the liberation of women

Liberation
Equal social or economic rights

The 1960s was a time when many Americans were committed to changing their society. The civil rights movement started a movement for Black Power. **Feminists** called for the **liberation** of women. Hispanic Americans made their problems known to the nation. The American Indian Movement (AIM) demanded better opportunities for American Indians. College students wanted more control of what they studied. Antiwar protesters wanted to end America's involvement in the war in Vietnam. Young people challenged the basic social rules of an older generation.

Who Led the Civil Rights Movement?

Martin Luther King Jr. was awarded the Nobel Peace Prize in 1964. This recognized the work of Dr. King in the civil rights movement. Under his leadership, progress had been made in gaining more equality for African Americans. The civil rights movement tried to end segregation.

Some leaders called for a new direction for African Americans. Malcolm X, a Black Muslim, encouraged African Americans to develop their own power and separate from white Americans who treated them unequally. He believed that African Americans should start their own businesses. He wanted them to begin to control their own communities.

Many Americans protested the Vietnam War.

Stokely Carmichael, an African-American leader, said African Americans needed "Black Power." He wanted them to have more than economic and political power. The Black Power movement encouraged African Americans to become interested in their history and culture. They developed a pride in their ethnic heritage.

What Was the Women's Movement?

In 1960, leaders of a new feminist, or women's, movement said that women should have the same social and economic rights as men. They believed women should be able to work in any job, including jobs that men usually held. Feminists wanted equal pay for equal jobs. The women's movement tried to gain full equality for women through the Equal Rights Amendment (ERA). The leaders of the movement wanted this amendment added to the Constitution. The Equal Rights Amendment was passed by many states but not enough to make it part of the Constitution.

What Problems Did Hispanic Americans Face?

Americans whose parents or ancestors came from Spanish-speaking countries are called Hispanic Americans. Hispanic culture—food, music, dress, and language—had had a major influence on American life. Still, in the 1960s, many Hispanic Americans were poor and had little education. Many were discriminated against. Hispanic leaders brought these problems to the nation's attention. One such leader was Cesar Chavez. He led a movement to organize Mexican-American **migrants.** These are workers who move from place to place to find work. Chavez organized the National Farm Workers Association to help Hispanic farm workers.

What Was the Youth Movement?

After World War II, millions of children were born. This was known as the **baby boom.** These children grew up during the Cold War, yet they were raised in a nation with a growing economy. America held great opportunity for them.

Cesar Chavez (right) organized a strike to gain rights for Hispanic farm workers.

CESAR CHAVEZ: 1927–1993

Labor leader Cesar Chavez devoted his time to unionizing poor migrant farm workers. Chavez was born into a Mexican-American family who became migrant farm laborers when he was ten. As a child, Chavez worked in the fields as he moved with his family. In 1962, he established the National Farm Workers Association. Migrant farm workers lived at the mercy of their employers and without protection of federal law. He organized strikes and picket lines to gain support for their cause. Chavez also organized peaceful sit-ins and marches. His efforts included a long, bitter strike against California grape growers. One of the strategies of the strike was a nationwide refusal to buy California grapes. The strike's startling success in 1970 led to the organization of farm workers' unions in different states.

★Counterculture
A culture or lifestyle that goes against the common culture

★Hippie
An extreme member of the youth culture in the 1960s

In the 1960s, the baby boom generation reached their late teens and early twenties. Many challenged the values and views of their parents. The main challenge involved the Vietnam War. Unlike their parents who had lived through World War II, many baby boomers had trouble viewing the war as a patriotic effort.

What Was the Counterculture?

Many Americans in the 1960s felt that young people were creating a **counterculture** that was very different from American society at the time. Long hair, casual clothes, beads, and headbands were the accepted styles of the counterculture. Rock music became the voice of the counterculture. Freedom from America's social rules was one theme of the youth movement. The phrase "doing your own thing" became popular. The most extreme members of the youth culture were called **hippies.**

Many other youths got very involved with their communities. They worked to clean up their environment. They became interested in politics. Many young people were part of the antiwar movement. They organized protest marches to bring attention to their causes.

What Was Woodstock?

On a weekend in August of 1969, a rock concert took place on a 600-acre farm in upstate New York. The list of performers included the biggest names in rock music. About 400,000 people attended the concert, which was billed as the Woodstock Music and Arts Fair.

There were shortages of water and food, but people shared what little they had. Although there were not many police, the crowd remained peaceful. Woodstock became national news; it was hailed for its peacefulness. Many young people suggested that Woodstock was the beginning of a new and better America. They promoted the "Woodstock Nation" as the future of America, much to their parents' concern.

The following December, about 300,000 people attended a free rock concert in Altamont, California. The joyful feelings found at Woodstock were missing at this concert. Members of a motorcycle gang hired to provide security beat a young African-American man to death. The worst fears of an older generation had been realized and the younger generation lost its dream of a "Woodstock Nation." The weekend at Woodstock had been the end of a movement, not a beginning.

SECTION 5 REVIEW Write the answers to these questions on a separate sheet of paper using complete sentences.

1) What did feminists want?

2) What did Malcolm X encourage?

3) What happened to the Equal Rights Amendment?

4) How did Cesar Chavez help Mexican-American farm workers?

5) What is a counterculture?

What do you think ?

How is the counterculture of the 1960s like youth groups today?

Throughout the 1960s, the Vietnam War grew to be a major concern for Americans. Questions arose about why the United States was involved. Americans were unsure who was winning. One day, the United States would announce a major victory in Vietnam. The next day, news reports would announce heavy losses of American troops. The public did not know what to believe. Television brought the horrors of the war directly into American homes.

Why Did Johnson Decide Not to Run for Re-election?

President Johnson was concerned about the political election. He saw the nation becoming divided into two groups—the hawks and the doves. The hawks favored war and wanted to win at all costs. The doves did not want the United States to be involved with the war.

Johnson tried to please both sides. He increased the bombing to please the hawks. At the same time, he helped start peace talks to make the doves happy.

On March 31, 1968, President Johnson spoke to the nation on television. He began with a routine talk about the war. He announced that he was going to reduce the bombings in North Vietnam. He ended his speech with a surprise. He announced that he would not seek the Democratic nomination for President.

What Happened to Martin Luther King Jr.?

Four days later, on April 4, 1968, Martin Luther King Jr. was shot to death. He had traveled to Memphis, Tennessee, to support a strike by African-American city workers. The night before his death, he spoke to his supporters. He told the audience, "I've seen the Promised Land. I may not get there with you. But I want you to know tonight that we as a people will get to the Promised Land."

It was **ironic** that a man who had preached and practiced nonviolence died as the victim of a violent act. It was also ironic that the anger that many African Americans felt at his murder led to riots and to acts of violence. Military troops were needed to control riots in many cities.

What Happened to Robert Kennedy?

Robert Kennedy's campaign for President had been gaining strength. On June 4, 1968, Robert Kennedy won the California primary. That night, he was shot by a young Jordanian Arab who did not like Kennedy's support for Israel. Two days after he was shot, Robert F. Kennedy died.

Who Won the Election of 1968?

The Democratic party nominated Vice President Hubert Humphrey as its candidate for President. The Democratic convention was held in August in Chicago. Thousands of people held antiwar protests outside of the convention site. Police broke up the protests by beating protesters with clubs. Inside the convention hall, delegates shouted angry words at each other. The Democratic party was divided and confused. Many people felt that Humphrey would continue Johnson's **controversial** policies in Vietnam. It seemed unlikely that Humphrey would be elected.

Math

History in Your Life

The Advent of Credit Cards

Credit allows a person to make purchases without cash. In America, credit plans grew quickly between 1850 and 1900. The plans allowed buyers to pay for purchases over time. In the 1920s several retail stores, hotels, and oil companies first issued credit cards to regular customers. Called "store specific," these cards could be used only with the retailer issuing them.

Modern credit cards began with the formation of Diners Club in 1950. Card holders used the same card to buy from many merchants. In 1951, Franklin National Bank of New York was the first bank to offer a card. In 1958, American Express, Carte Blanche, Bank of America, and Chase Manhattan Bank offered credit cards. In the 1980s, credit card companies had huge growth largely due to high interest charged to customers. Now nearly every American family has at least one major credit card. They use a card to buy groceries, vacations, and more.

The Republican party nominated Richard M. Nixon for President. Nixon's campaign theme was "Bring Us Together." He called for "law and order" and said he had a plan to end the war in Vietnam. He wanted "peace with honor."

George Wallace entered the presidential race as a third party candidate. He was a former Democratic governor from Alabama who had supported segregation. Wallace appealed to southern blue-collar workers. Many of these people had worked their way up without help from the federal government. They were not supportive of many federal programs.

The election was very close. Nixon received 31.8 million votes to Humphrey's 31.3 million votes. Wallace received almost 10 million votes. Nixon won the election, but he received less than fifty percent of the popular vote.

SECTION 6 REVIEW On a separate sheet of paper, write *True* if the statement is true or *False* if the statement is not true.

1) Americans were not able to tell who was winning the war in Vietnam.

2) Johnson wanted to please those who were for and against the Vietnam War.

3) President Johnson ran for re-election but lost.

4) Martin Luther King Jr. was shot to death.

5) Richard Nixon lost the election of 1968.

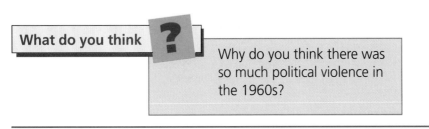

What do you think **?**

Why do you think there was so much political violence in the 1960s?

"I Have A Dream"

In 1963, more than 200,000 people marched on Washington, D.C., in a peaceful demonstration for civil rights. It was a time of unrest over civil rights in the United States. Dr. Martin Luther King Jr. delivered a speech to the marchers. The speech is considered a cornerstone of the civil rights movement. This passage is from that speech.

"I say to you today, my friends, that in spite of the difficulties and frustrations of the moment I still have a dream. It is a dream deeply rooted in the American dream.

I have a dream that one day this nation will rise up and live the true meaning of its creed: 'We hold these truths to be self-evident; that all men are created equal.'

I have a dream that one day on the red hills of Georgia the sons of former slaves and the sons of former slaveowners will be able to sit down together at the table of brotherhood.

I have a dream that one day even the state of Mississippi, a desert state sweltering with the heat of injustice and oppression, will be transformed into an oasis of freedom and justice.

I have a dream that my four little children will one day live in a nation where they will not be judged by the color of their skin but by the content of their character.

I have a dream today."

Source Reading Wrap-Up

1) What are the difficulties and frustrations to which Dr. King refers?

2) What two states does Dr. King mention in this speech?

3) What was one part of Dr. King's dream?

4) Do you think Dr. King was speaking only about the relationship between African Americans and European Americans? Explain the reason for your answer.

5) How much do you think we have progressed toward fulfilling Dr. King's dream since 1963?

★ America launched its first successful satellite into orbit in 1958. In 1961, the first of many manned space flights began with the Mercury and Gemini space programs.

★ John F. Kennedy became President in 1961. He approved a plan developed under President Eisenhower to support an invasion of Cuba by Cuban rebels to overthrow the Castro government. The invasion at the Bay of Pigs was a complete failure.

★ The Soviets built the Berlin Wall in 1961 that divided East and West Berlin.

★ The Soviet Union was providing supplies for missile bases in Cuba. U.S. ships prevented Soviet ships from reaching Cuba. Later, a deal was struck between America and the Soviet Union that ended the Cuban missile crisis.

★ African Americans and whites joined together to help end segregation. Hundreds of protest marches, sit-ins, and demonstrations were staged. In 1963, an immense march on Washington was held to urge passage of civil rights legislation.

★ During his presidency, Kennedy had created the Peace Corps and NASA and had proposed funding to help many people in poverty. President Kennedy was assassinated in Dallas on November 22, 1963. Lyndon Johnson became President.

★ President Johnson wanted to build a "Great Society." He wanted to provide education and health care for all Americans. At his urging, Congress passed legislation that created Medicare, provided federal funds for schools, and encouraged low-cost housing.

★ In 1964, Congress passed the Tonkin Gulf Resolution, which allowed Johnson to send American combat troops to Vietnam.

★ Among the social developments of the 1960s were the feminist movement, the Black Power movement, the antiwar movement, the organization of Hispanic migrants, and the youth movement.

★ Civil rights leader Martin Luther King Jr. was murdered on April 4, 1968.

★ Richard Nixon was elected President in November of 1968.

Comprehension: Identifying Facts

On a separate sheet of paper, write the words from the Word Bank to complete each sentence.

WORD BANK	
baby boom	John F. Kennedy
Bay of Pigs	Martin Luther King Jr.
Cesar Chavez	NASA
Cuban missile crisis	Peace Corps
debates	Robert Weaver
Great Society	Tonkin Gulf Resolution

1) President _____ ordered American ships to prevent Soviet ships from reaching Cuba.

2) The _____ was what President Johnson called his plan for the country.

3) Kennedy challenged _____ to put an American on the moon by 1970.

4) Kennedy started the _____, which sent American volunteers overseas to help underdeveloped nations.

5) _____ was a leader of the civil rights movement.

6) During the 1960 election campaign the Nixon-Kennedy _____ were on television.

7) America's population grew after World War II because of the _____.

8) _____ was the first African American to be on a President's cabinet.

9) _____ organized a union for farm workers in California.

10) The _____ showed that President Kennedy could stand up to the Soviet Union.

11) Cuban rebels supported by the United States tried to invade Cuba at the _____.

12) The _____ allowed President Johnson to send combat troops to Vietnam.

Comprehension: Understanding Main Ideas

On a separate sheet of paper, write the answer to each question using complete sentences.

1) What were four of the federal social programs that were passed during the 1960s?

2) Why were the Bay of Pigs invasion and the Cuban missile crisis major events in the Kennedy presidency?

3) What were three developments in the civil rights movement during this period?

4) Why did America become involved in Vietnam?

5) How did the Vietnam War cause a division in the American people?

6) Who were the "freedom riders" and what did they do?

Critical Thinking: Write Your Opinion

1) During the 1960s, young people listened to music that spoke about their society and their concerns. Is there anything similar to this today? Explain your answer.

2) Before the space program, people had never flown in space. Today space shuttles make regular flights. Would you like to go into space? Why or why not?

| Test Taking Tip | When answering multiple-choice questions, first identify the choices that you know are untrue.

Political cartoons are funny drawings about political events. The purpose of a cartoon is to make people laugh. However, cartoons also express a viewpoint about a political issue or topic. Cartoons encourage people to think about current issues. Cartoonists reveal various opinions in a drawing. They can persuade others to support their opinion through the cartoon.

Cartoons often use symbols, or objects that stand for something else. The elephant has long been a symbol of the Republican Party. The donkey is the symbol of the Democratic Party. These two animals often show up in political cartoons.

Cartoonists add labels or captions to help readers interpret the drawing. The cartoon here has three labels. They are "1964," "L.B.J.," and "Old Smoky Sauce." This cartoon was published in 1964, a presidential election year. The label "1964" is on top of a bed of hot coals. "L.B.J." is Lyndon Baines Johnson, the thirty-sixth President. LBJ was a Democrat from Texas who was campaigning for President in 1964. His opponent was Senator Barry Goldwater, a Republican from Arizona. "Old Smoky Sauce" is barbecue sauce. The cartoon shows LBJ painting Old Smoky Sauce on an elephant. He is pictured as getting ready to barbecue the Republicans in the 1964 election.

"Hang Around Till Next Fall . . . We're Planning a Big, Texas-Style Barbecue"

Study the cartoon. Then answer these questions.

1) Why is the fire labeled "1964"?

2) Why did the cartoonist dress LBJ as a cowboy?

3) What does the elephant symbolize?

4) What is the meaning of the cartoon?

5) Find a current political cartoon in your newspaper. Write what you think it means.

★ The United Nations was created in San Francisco in April 1945.

★ Distrust developed between communist and noncommunist countries. America supported anticommunist governments.

★ The Berlin airlift lasted until the Soviets reopened railroads and highways.

★ In 1949, North Korea invaded South Korea. America sent troops to South Korea. After three years, two separate nations were established.

★ World War II hero Dwight D. Eisenhower was elected President in 1952.

★ Senator Joseph McCarthy used fear of communism to accuse people of communism or communist sympathy.

★ The civil rights movement grew in the 1950s. Congress passed the Civil Rights Law in 1957.

★ During the 1950s, America was prosperous.

★ America launched its first successful satellite in 1958. The first manned space flights began in 1961.

★ John F. Kennedy became President in 1961. His plan to invade Cuba and overthrow the Castro government failed.

★ The Soviets built the Berlin Wall in 1961.

★ The Soviets supplied Cuban missile bases. U.S. ships kept Soviet ships from Cuba. A deal between America and the Soviets ended the crisis.

★ African Americans and whites joined to help end segregation. In 1963, a march on Washington was held to urge civil rights legislation.

★ President Kennedy was killed in Dallas on November 22, 1963. Lyndon Johnson became President.

★ At Johnson's urging, Congress passed laws for Medicare, school funds, and low-cost housing.

★ In 1964, the Tonkin Gulf Resolution allowed Johnson to send American troops to Vietnam.

★ The 1960s had many social movements.

★ Martin Luther King Jr. was murdered on April 4, 1968.

★ Richard Nixon was elected President in 1968. His plan ended involvement in the Vietnam War in 1973.

"It doesn't matter what you've been through, where you come from, who your parents are—nor your social or economic status. None of that matters. What matters is how you choose to love, how you choose to express that love through your work, through your family, through what you have to give to the world."

–Oprah Winfrey, commencement address at Spelman College, 1993

Contemporary United States

1968–Present

Perhaps you know how good it feels to be a peacemaker or a peacekeeper. The United States has experienced that feeling. America celebrated its 200th birthday in 1976 with the wisdom of age. Then in the 1980s and 1990s it played a role as peacemaker or peacekeeper in the troubled Middle East. America signed agreements to limit nuclear weapons. It helped other countries defend their freedom. At home, the country attempted to resolve its own social and economic struggles.

In this unit you will learn about America's role as an international peacemaker and peacekeeper. You will learn how the nation handled economic and social situations at home. You will learn about America's place in the world at the start of a new century.

Chapter 29: America in a Changing World: 1968–1980

Chapter 30: The 1980s: 1980–1989

Chapter 31: The 1990s: 1990–Present

America in a Changing World

1968–1980

The nation had been in turmoil during much of the 1960s. The Vietnam War was much of the problem. Americans were ready to see the war end. As the nation moved into the 1970s, scandals in the presidency provided a new problem at home. International issues also challenged the nation's foreign policy. In this chapter, you will learn more about the Vietnam War, about presidential scandal, and about American involvement in international issues.

Goals for Learning

▶ To explain how the Vietnam War ended and the results of the war

▶ To describe how the United States improved relations with China and the Soviet Union

▶ To describe the events of the Watergate scandal

▶ To list the problems President Ford faced

▶ To list the problems President Carter faced

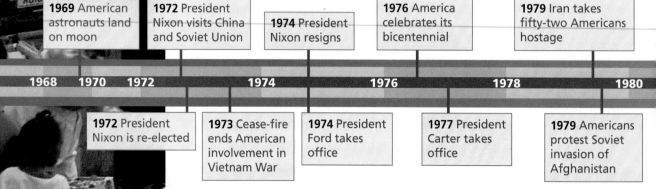

1969 American astronauts land on moon

1972 President Nixon visits China and Soviet Union

1974 President Nixon resigns

1976 America celebrates its bicentennial

1979 Iran takes fifty-two Americans hostage

1968   1970   1972   1974   1976   1978   1980

1972 President Nixon is re-elected

1973 Cease-fire ends American involvement in Vietnam War

1974 President Ford takes office

1977 President Carter takes office

1979 Americans protest Soviet invasion of Afghanistan

Collapse
Breakdown or ruin

Richard Nixon had promised to bring the troubled country together again. This was not a simple task. The first problem he faced when he took office in 1969 was to try to end the Vietnam War.

How Did Problems Continue in Vietnam?

Nixon announced a plan called Vietnamization. He planned to turn the defense of South Vietnam over to the South Vietnamese during the next three years. Americans, however, had grown impatient waiting for an end to the war.

Along the western border of South Vietnam was Cambodia. It tried very hard to remain neutral. However, its government could not prevent the Vietcong and the North Vietnamese from setting up bases on the South Vietnam border. The communists used these bases to set up attacks against the Americans and South Vietnamese. In 1970, President Nixon allowed American troops to destroy the enemy supplies in Cambodia.

The North Vietnamese and Vietcong seized control of the northeastern section of Cambodia. Some Cambodians joined forces with these armies and spread out westward and southward. They were moving toward the capital of Phnom Penh. The United States wanted to prevent the complete **collapse** of the Cambodian government. It sent Cambodia large amounts of military supplies, and American bombers gave air support to the Cambodian army.

What Happened at Kent State University?

The news of the American involvement in Cambodia caused large antiwar protests in cities around the country. Many protests took place at colleges. Feeling that these protesters were a small minority, Nixon asked for support from the "silent majority."

On May 2, 1970, a protest by students at Kent State University in Ohio ended with the burning of a school building. The governor ordered the National Guard to the university. On May 4, some students threw rocks at National Guard soldiers who then began shooting at the protesters. Four students were killed. This caused the Senate to end financial and military support for Cambodia.

What Was the First Mission to the Moon?

On July 20, 1969, American astronauts Neil Armstrong and Edwin Aldrin Jr. landed their spacecraft, the *Eagle,* on the moon. This mission, called Apollo 11, put the first astronauts on the moon. The *Eagle* stayed on the moon's surface for over twenty-one hours. About six and a half hours after landing, Armstrong took his first steps on the moon and said: "That's one small step for a man, one giant leap for mankind." Armstrong and Aldrin put the American flag on the moon and collected moon rock and soil samples. The United States went to the moon five more times before the Apollo program ended in late 1972.

How Did Vietnamization Continue?

Nixon was re-elected as President in 1972. He ran against Senator George McGovern. McGovern wanted to withdraw from Vietnam immediately. Many Democrats who refused to support such a policy voted for Nixon. Most people voted for Nixon because he was trying to remove troops from Vietnam.

In 1973, a cease-fire agreement was signed between North Vietnam and the United States. It stated that the United States would remove all troops from South Vietnam but continue to give the country military and economic aid. North Vietnam agreed to release American prisoners of war, or POWs.

American astronauts first landed on the moon in 1969.

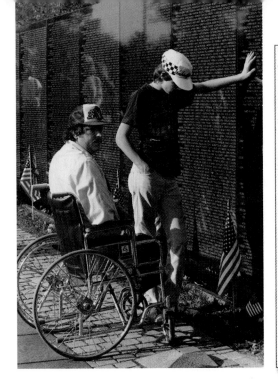

Nearly ten years after the Vietnam War ended, this wall was built to honor American soldiers killed or missing in Vietnam.

Summary of the Vietnam War

- It was the longest war in United States history.

- About 58,000 Americans were killed; about 300,000 were wounded.

- The total cost to the United States was $150 billion.

- The war caused confusion about the nation's role in world affairs.

- The War Powers Act was passed, requiring the President to explain to Congress within forty-eight hours whenever American troops were to be sent into a foreign country.

Vietnamization had been only partly successful. The South Vietnamese could not survive on their own; their army soon fell apart. The communist government of North Vietnam took over South Vietnam in April of 1975.

SECTION 1 REVIEW Write the answers to these questions on a separate sheet of paper using complete sentences.

1) What was President Nixon attempting with his Vietnamization plan?

2) Why did the United States want to help Cambodia?

3) Why did violence break out at Kent State University?

4) What did the Apollo 11 mission accomplish?

5) What became of South Vietnam once the United States stopped helping it?

What do you think ?

Do you think President Nixon was right to withdraw troops from Vietnam? Why or why not?

In the early 1950s, Chinese and American troops were enemies in the Korean War. For twenty years afterward, the relations between China and the United States had remained weak. Americans did not trade with or travel to China. The United States refused to recognize the government of the People's Republic of China. Instead, they called Taiwan the legal government of China.

Nixon wanted to relax the tensions of the Cold War. The goal was called "détente," a French word meaning relaxation. He hoped to improve relations with China and the Soviet Union. He waited until he thought these two countries would be open to his ideas. The Soviet Union and China were never close allies. Now their relationship was weakening, and they were becoming **rivals.** Nixon saw this as a good time for new negotiations.

Rival
A well-matched opponent

What Did Nixon Do in China?

Henry Kissinger, Nixon's top foreign policy adviser, secretly went to China in 1971. He met with Chinese Premier Chou En-lai. Afterward, Chou En-lai invited Nixon to come to China. When Nixon announced to the American public that he intended to visit China, many were shocked. The Soviet Union was not pleased.

Nixon went to China in February of 1972. Nixon and Chou En-lai made many efforts to settle their differences. After eight days of meetings, the two leaders announced that they agreed:

- to open up trade.
- to improve scientific and cultural relations.
- that neither country would try to dominate the Pacific.
- that the United States would recognize Taiwan as belonging to the People's Republic of China.

President Nixon (right) toured the Great Wall during his visit to China.

What Did Nixon Do in the Soviet Union?

The Soviet Union was concerned about the new relationship between the United States and China. The Soviets feared that these two countries might become allied against them. Three months after the successful meeting in China, Nixon went to Moscow. This was the first time a United States President had visited the Soviet Union in peacetime.

Nixon and Soviet President Leonid Brezhnev discussed the arms race between the two countries. They agreed to sign a treaty limiting the number of **strategic** weapons each country could have. It was called the Strategic Arms Limitation Talks (SALT). They also agreed to increase trade between the two countries and to cooperate in space exploration.

President Nixon (right) and President Brezhnev enjoyed a light moment in Moscow. Henry Kissinger signed an agreement between the United States and the Soviet Union.

The Environmental Protection Agency protects against air pollution such as this.

SECTION 2 REVIEW On a separate sheet of paper, write *True* if the statement is true or *False* if the statement is not true.

1) The United States and China had a good relationship right after the Korean War.

2) The Soviet Union and China were close allies.

3) President Nixon visited China in 1972.

4) After President Nixon visited China, the Soviets were afraid that the United States and China would become allies against them.

5) The Strategic Arms Limitation Talks (SALT) limited the number of strategic weapons the Soviets and Americans could have.

What do you think **?**

Why do you think it was important for President Nixon to meet with the Chinese and the Soviets?

Aide
One who assists

★Conspiracy
A joint act of breaking the law

Guilty
Charged with a crime or wrongdoing

★Wiretap
A device used to listen in on phone conversations

Even though Nixon was re-elected President in 1972, he was no longer in office when the fighting in Vietnam finally stopped in 1975. The political scandal known as Watergate ended his presidency.

Former Attorney General John Mitchell was chairman of Nixon's Committee to Re-elect the President (CREEP). In March of 1972, Mitchell accepted a proposal from a former FBI agent named Gordon Liddy, who wanted to spy on the Democrats. On June 17, 1972, five burglars broke into the Democratic party main office in the Watergate building. The burglars wanted to photograph documents and place devices called **wiretaps** that could be used to listen in on telephone conversations. A night watchman became suspicious and called the police, who arrested the five burglars. A White House spokesman merely called the break-in a "third-rate burglary."

How Was the Watergate Scandal Exposed?

The five burglars were convicted of **conspiracy,** burglary, and wiretapping in January of 1973. A conspiracy is a joint act of breaking the law. Later, the judge received a letter from one of the men he had convicted. This man, James McCord, admitted that he lied under oath. He said that he was pressured by the Nixon administration to plead **guilty** and to remain silent about others who were involved in the spying. During the next several months, Nixon's top **aides** and advisers H. R. Haldeman and John Ehrlichman resigned. Another aide, John Dean, was fired.

In a televised speech on April 30, 1973, President Nixon announced the resignations of his aides and the firing of Dean. He later gave permission to Attorney General Elliot Richardson to appoint Archibald Cox as special prosecutor to investigate Watergate. Meanwhile, the Senate had formed its own committee to question members of Nixon's staff. These televised hearings lasted three months.

John Dean told the Senate committee that Nixon approved paying the burglars to keep quiet. The President had committed a crime by hiding the truth. Nixon denied Dean's charges. It was one man's word against the other. During the Senate hearings, it was learned that tape recordings of White House meetings could prove whether Nixon or Dean was telling the truth. Nixon refused to give either the committee or Cox these tapes. A court order, or **subpoena,** was issued for the tapes. Nixon still refused to turn them over.

Why Did the Vice President Resign?

An unrelated scandal went on about the same time as Watergate. It involved Vice President Spiro Agnew. He was under investigation for bribery, **extortion,** and **tax evasion** during his time as Maryland governor and while he was Vice President. Extortion is stealing money by using some kind of threat. Tax evasion is failing to pay one's taxes. On October 10, 1973, Agnew resigned. Nixon nominated Congressman Gerald R. Ford of Michigan to be the new Vice President.

What Happened to President Nixon?

On Saturday, ten days after Agnew's resignation, Nixon ordered Archibald Cox to be fired. Attorney General Richardson resigned in protest because Nixon had not kept his promise of an investigation of Watergate. Nixon later fired Richardson's deputy, William Ruckelshaus. These events became known as the "Saturday Night Massacre."

The White House was flooded with phone calls and telegrams protesting Nixon's actions, while newspapers demanded that he resign. In response, Nixon handed over the subpoenaed tapes. One tape had an eighteen-minute gap. Apparently, a section of the tape had been erased. Some of the tapes Nixon promised to turn over could not be found. Meanwhile, the House Judiciary Committee was gathering **evidence** that might prove that the President should be impeached. Evidence is something that furnishes proof.

Gerald Ford was sworn in as President after President Nixon resigned.

President Nixon made another important speech on television in April of 1974. He calmly explained that stacks of notebooks on a table beside him contained typed pages of what was said on the missing tapes. The President hoped everyone would believe that he had nothing to hide.

In May, Nixon refused when asked to turn over the disputed tapes. He knew the tapes contained evidence against him. By the end of July, the House Judiciary Committee had facts that were grounds for impeachment. In response, Nixon handed over the typed records of what was included on the tapes. These records revealed the President had been involved with the Watergate cover-up from the beginning.

The only way Nixon could avoid being impeached was to resign. On August 9, 1974, Nixon resigned from office. No President in United States history had ever resigned. While he did not admit guilt, Nixon said that some of his **judgments** "were wrong."

How Did Watergate Test the Constitution?

Several people in the Nixon administration were convicted of illegal acts in the Watergate scandal. The Constitution was tested as all three branches of government met up with a constitutional crisis. How well had the system worked? Gerald Ford said on the day that he became the thirty-eighth President, "My fellow Americans, our national nightmare is over. Our Constitution works. Our great republic is a government of laws and not of men. Here, the people rule."

Judgment
The ability a person has to decide and act on something

Cable TV: The Wired Nation

It has been said that "the difference between ordinary television and cable TV is the difference between a garden hose and Niagara Falls." Cable TV expanded in the 1970s. Along with satellite delivery systems, it allowed people to choose from dozens of entertainment and informational channels. As a result, cable TV gave everyone more control over what he or she saw and heard. No longer did viewers have to be limited to the big three networks—ABC, CBS, and NBC.

The basic appeal of cable is simple. The broadcast networks must cater to a large general audience. The cable networks can offer movies without commercials, music videos, or nonstop sports twenty-four hours a day. The broadcast networks cannot offer such specialized programming.

The cable networks can zero in on special interests. Some of the popular cable networks include Cable News Network, MTV, and the Weather Channel. Others are the USA Network, Black Entertainment Television, and the Nashville Network. The noncommercial C-SPAN network covers Congress.

SECTION 3 REVIEW Choose the best word or name in parentheses to complete each sentence. Write your answers on a separate sheet of paper.

1) Five burglars broke into the Democratic party main office in the (Watergate, White House) building.

2) (H. R. Haldeman, John Ehrlichman, Archibald Cox) was a special prosecutor for the Watergate investigation.

3) Vice President (Spiro Agnew, Gerald R. Ford) resigned from office.

4) President Nixon (resigned, was impeached) from office.

5) (Spiro Agnew, Gerald R. Ford) replaced President Nixon.

What do you think ❓

You have learned about several scandals in presidencies in addition to the Watergate scandal. Why do you think there are so many scandals in presidencies?

President Ford brought a very different atmosphere to the White House. Ford was direct and good-natured. He had been a popular and hard-working congressman.

In September 1974, President Ford surprised the nation by pardoning Nixon. Ford said Nixon had suffered enough punishment. He felt the nation had to forget Watergate and move on to other matters. However, Ford was criticized for this action.

What Problems Did Ford Face?

The Ford administration was left with several problems. Inflation and unemployment were very high. People were also unhappy with the government after the Vietnam War. Ford went forward cautiously.

★Embargo
A government action that prevents certain goods from leaving a country

A new conflict broke out between Israel and its Arab neighbors in October of 1973. The United States and other countries were giving aid to Israel. Because of this aid, some Arab states put an **embargo** on oil shipments to these countries. An embargo is a government action that prevents certain goods from leaving a country. This resulted in a gas shortage. People had to wait in long lines at gas stations.

There was a shortage of home heating oil. Americans were shocked at how dependent they were on other countries.

The Organization of Petroleum Exporting Countries (OPEC) began to control prices. OPEC included several nations in the Middle East, Africa, and South America. OPEC countries raised the price of crude oil. This action drove the price of gasoline and heating oil up in the United States.

U.S. Gasoline Prices
(cents per gallon)

Year	Leaded Regular	Unleaded Regular
1973	38.8	—
1974	53.2	—
1975	56.7	—
1976	59.0	61.4
1977	62.2	65.6
1978	62.6	67.0

How Did America Celebrate Its Bicentennial?

In 1776, America had declared its independence from Great Britain. The document was dated July 4, 1776. On July 4, 1976, Americans celebrated the fact that the Declaration of Independence was 200 years old. This celebration is called a **bicentennial.**

★Bicentennial
A 200th year celebration

The celebration lasted for several months. More than 200 large sailing ships, called "tall ships," came from thirty nations. The ships docked in many east coast harbors. Queen Elizabeth of Great Britain helped celebrate the independence that had been declared against King George III, her great-great-great grandfather. She presented a six-ton bell as a gift to the nation. In the nation's capital, thirty-three tons of fireworks lit the sky around the Washington Monument.

Although America's history was being celebrated in 1976, the nation seemed happy to forget its recent past for the moment. The nation's last thirteen years had been difficult. A President and two national leaders were assassinated. A war was fought. A President and Vice President resigned. On July 4, 1976, it seemed that Americans were ready to celebrate a proud past and hope for a promising future. Two weeks later, on July 20, 1976, *Viking I* successfully landed on

Fireworks celebrated America's bicentennial.

the surface of Mars. This was a perfect example of how far America had come in 200 years.

SECTION 4 REVIEW Write the answers to these questions on a separate sheet of paper using complete sentences.

1) Why did President Ford pardon Nixon?

2) What problems did President Ford face when he took office?

3) What problems did OPEC cause for America?

4) What is a bicentennial?

5) How did Americans celebrate the bicentennial?

What do you think **?**

Why is it important to celebrate the nation's meaningful dates such as the bicentennial?

Morality
Good behavior; knowing the difference between right and wrong

July of 1976 was also the month when the Democratic party held its political convention. The Democrats nominated the little known Jimmy Carter, former governor of Georgia, for their presidential candidate. Carter campaigned very hard to get his name and ideas known to the American people. He stressed honesty, openness, trust, and **morality** in his speeches. People responded positively to his promise to restore morality in the government.

People liked Carter because he was an outsider. He was not part of the established political groups in Washington, D.C. When he accepted the nomination, he said that "1976 will not be a year of politics as usual." He said that there was a "new mood in America" in people looking for "new voices, new ideas, and new leaders." Carter promised to give the government back to the people. Senator Walter Mondale was Carter's running mate.

President Ford and Ronald Reagan, the former governor of California, ran against one another for the Republican presidential nomination. Ford won a narrow victory over Reagan at the Republican National Convention. Ford selected Senator Robert Dole as his running mate.

Who Won the Election of 1976?

The 1976 presidential election focused on such issues as the economy, the reputation of the candidates, and the desire for change. The election was extremely close. Carter won a narrow victory over Ford. Ford actually carried more states than Carter, but Carter's states had more electoral votes. Carter was the first person from the deep South to be elected President since before the Civil War.

What Changes Did President Carter Make?

Jimmy Carter wanted to bring a different style to the office of President. He wanted the American people to see him as someone like them. He wore a plain business suit to his

Writing About History

Public service advertisements are used to communicate an issue to people. Think of a way people could save energy. In your notebook, write a public service ad about your idea.

inauguration in 1977. His goal was to restore the people's confidence in their government. He was concerned with more than just style. President Carter wanted the government to provide better service at a lower cost. He reorganized the Executive Branch. He added two new departments—the Department of Energy in 1977 and the Department of Education in 1979.

The United States uses large amounts of energy. In the 1970s, Americans made up six percent of the world's population but used thirty-three percent of the world's energy. Millions of barrels of oil were imported from the Middle East. Before Carter became President, countries in the Middle East increased the price of oil and produced less of it. President Carter said that energy was a major problem for the nation. In 1978, Congress passed an energy bill that lowered the taxes for businesses that used less energy. Automotive companies were encouraged to produce smaller cars.

The energy crisis during the 1970s caused there to be long lines at gas stations. Energy guides (above) help consumers save energy.

President Carter wanted to improve the American economy. The energy crisis made it difficult for him to do that. In 1978, inflation became a serious problem. As prices went up, workers demanded higher wages. Higher wages increased the cost of doing business. Businesses had to raise prices to cover their costs. By 1979, inflation was just over eleven percent. Normal inflation was three to five percent per year.

What Problems Developed in Central America?

The government of Panama was not happy over American ownership of the Panama Canal. President Carter signed two treaties with the government of Panama in 1977. The treaties promised to give control of the Panama Canal to Panama in the year 2000. One treaty gave the United States the right to defend the Canal against any attack. Not all Americans agreed that the United States should give up control of the Panama Canal. However, the treaties created a warmer relationship between the two countries.

Other Central American countries had problems. Civil war broke out in Nicaragua, the largest country in Central America. The dictator, Anastasio Somoza, was overthrown. An independent government was established. The United States recognized this government.

Political violence broke out in 1980 in El Salvador, a tiny country in Central America. Archbishop Oscar Romero was assassinated. Later, in December, six Americans were killed. The Carter administration took away American aid to this country until an investigation was completed.

What Problems Developed With Israel?

The Middle East had had many ethnic, religious, and economic problems. The United States supported the independent state of Israel. Israel's Arab neighbors refused to recognize Israel's right to exist. They claimed that Israel's land belonged to the Arabs. Throughout the years, the Arab countries were supported by Egypt in any conflicts in which they were involved. In November of 1977, Egypt's

From left, Anwar Sadat, President Carter, and Menachem Begin shook hands after signing the peace treaty at Camp David.

president, Anwar Sadat, attempted to make peace with Israel's government.

President Carter wanted to encourage peace between these two nations. He invited Sadat and Prime Minister Menachem Begin of Israel to Camp David, the presidential retreat in Maryland. A peace treaty was signed in March of 1979. Egypt finally recognized Israel as an independent state.

Arab nations felt **betrayed** by Sadat. The treaty did not deal with Jerusalem or Palestine. These lands had been taken over by Israel during earlier wars. The Palestine Liberation Organization (PLO) continued **terrorist** acts against Israel. Terrorists are groups or individuals who use violence to make others give in to their demands. Lebanon, Israel's neighbor, was caught in the middle of this tension. Many members of the PLO were located in Lebanon. Israel bombed Lebanon several times. The United States continued to support Israel. America worked very hard to find a solution to the Palestinian problem.

Betray
To go against someone's trust

★Terrorist
Group or individual who uses violence to make others give in to its demands

MAP STUDY

What nations border Israel to the east? Where is Lebanon located?

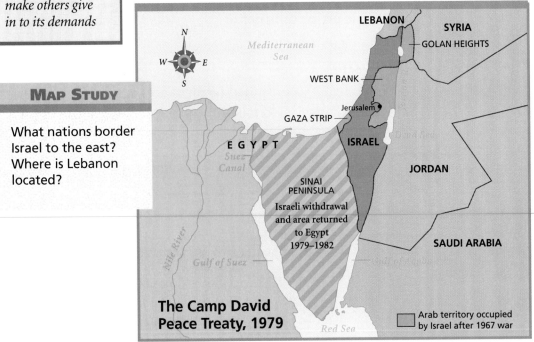

The Camp David Peace Treaty, 1979

Arab territory occupied by Israel after 1967 war

The Microwave Oven

Microwaves first caught public attention during World War II with the use of radar. Shortly after the war, scientists were able to "harness" microwaves for home cooking. In the 1950s, manufacturers introduced microwave ovens called "radar ranges." In a microwave oven, an electronic vacuum tube produces bursts of microwaves. The microwaves are scattered around the oven until they enter the food. The radiation causes molecules in the food to vibrate billions of times per second. Friction among the molecules creates the heat that cooks the food. Microwave cooking produces heat directly inside the food. A microwave oven greatly reduces the time needed to thaw frozen food and cook a meal. Regular ovens cook food gradually by heating the air surrounding it. In the 1970s, microwave oven sales rocketed. Today, most homes have a microwave oven.

WORD BANK

Anwar Sadat

Camp David

Israel

Jimmy Carter

PLO

SECTION 5 REVIEW On a separate sheet of paper, write the word from the Word Bank to complete each sentence.

1) _____ added two new departments—the Department of Energy and the Department of Education.

2) The president of Egypt was _____.

3) The prime minister of _____ was Menachem Begin.

4) A peace treaty was signed at _____ between Israel and Egypt.

5) The _____ continued terrorist acts against Israel after the Camp David talks.

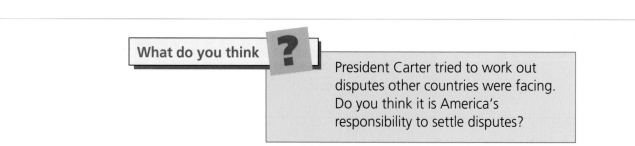

What do you think **?**

President Carter tried to work out disputes other countries were facing. Do you think it is America's responsibility to settle disputes?

The nation of Iran is an important oil-producing country in the Middle East. The United States depended on Iran's government to protect the flow of oil from the Middle East. The leader of Iran, Mohammad Reza Pahlavi, was called the Shah. He allowed his country to adopt western ways. As Shah, he wanted Iran to be a modern nation. This went against the Islamic religious beliefs of some of his people.

In 1978, the Shah began to lose his power. Public violence in the capital city of Teheran killed hundreds of people. Iranian students in the United States organized protests. The United States ordered any Americans living in Iran to leave the country.

A Moslem religious leader, the Ayatollah (meaning "reflection of God") Ruhollah Khomeini came to power in Iran. He established an Islamic republic to replace the Shah in 1979.

What Was the Hostage Crisis?

In October of 1979, President Carter allowed the Shah to come to the United States for medical treatment. This act made some Iranians angry. On November 4, hundreds of Iranians took control of the American Embassy in Iran. Sixty-six Americans were taken as **hostages.** A hostage is a person being held against his or her will by someone who wants certain demands to be met. Most of the women and all African Americans were soon released. The Iranians refused to release fifty-two remaining Americans until the United States returned the Shah and the Shah's wealth to Iran. They claimed that the Shah stole money from Iran with the help of the United States.

★Hostage
A person being held against his or her will by someone who wants certain demands to be met

The United States refused to return the Shah. President Carter sent naval ships to the area. He ordered all oil imports from Iran stopped. Still, the Iranians refused to release the hostages. Americans paid close attention to the hostage crisis in the news.

In April of 1980, President Carter sent a small group of soldiers to rescue the hostages. The mission failed. Eight soldiers died in the desert when their helicopter crashed. President Carter spent many hours trying to find a way to bring the hostages home safely. He could not find a way to do it.

Two Iranians posed with this American hostage in Teheran, Iran.

Why Did the Soviets Invade Afghanistan?

On December 27, 1979, the Middle East suffered another crisis. Soviet troop transport planes landed in Kabul, the capital of Afghanistan, in support of government groups. Two days after the invasion, President Amin of Afghanistan and his family were executed. The new president, Babrak Karmal, was friendly toward the Soviet Union.

It is believed the Soviets invaded Afghanistan because the religious unrest in the Islamic world had made its way into the Soviet Union. Invading was one way to stop this problem. President Carter protested this invasion strongly. The United States boycotted the 1980 Olympics in the Soviet Union to show disapproval of the Soviet actions. Many other countries

followed the United States' decision. The United States also stopped sending wheat and corn to the Soviet Union. The protests didn't stop the invasion. It took ten years for the Soviets to end the fighting with Afghanistan.

What Was the SALT II Treaty?

Seven years after the SALT treaty was agreed to with the Soviet Union, President Carter met with Soviet Premier Leonid Brezhnev in Vienna, Austria. In 1979, they agreed to another treaty called SALT II. This treaty was never ratified by the United States Senate. Members of the Senate felt the treaty put the United States at a military disadvantage.

President Carter shook hands with Leonid Brezhnev after agreeing to the SALT II treaty.

SECTION 6 REVIEW On a separate sheet of paper, write *True* if the statement is true or *False* if the statement is not true.

1) The Shah of Iran upset Iranians by promoting a modern nation.

2) The Shah ordered Americans living in Iran to be taken hostage.

3) President Carter allowed the Shah to come to the United States for medical treatment.

4) A small group of American soldiers rescued the hostages in Iran.

5) The Soviets invaded Afghanistan to prevent the spread of religious unrest in the Islamic world.

What do you think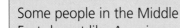

Some people in the Middle East do not like Americans. Why do you think this is so?

This Is the America We Want

In 1976, Jimmy Carter had been nominated as the Democratic candidate for President. He was full of hope and confidence. In this part of his acceptance speech for the nomination, he describes his vision for America in 1976.

"1976 will not be a year of politics as usual. It is a year of concern, and of quiet and sober reassessment of our nation's character and purpose—a year when voters have already confounded the political experts. It can be a year of inspiration and hope. And I guarantee you, it will be the year when we give the government of this country back to the people of this country.

There is a new mood in America. We have been shaken by a tragic war abroad and by scandals and broken promises at home. Our people are seeking new voices, new ideas and new leaders. . . . There is a fear that our best years are behind us, but I say to you that our nation's best is still ahead.

Our country has lived through a time of torment. It is now a time for healing. We want to have faith again! We want to be proud again! We just want the truth again! It is time for the people to run the government, and not the other way around. It is time to honor and strengthen our families, our neighborhoods, and our diverse cultures and customs. . . .

I never had more faith in America than I do today. We have an America that . . . is busy being born, not busy dying. . . . I see an America on the move again, united, a diverse and vital and tolerant nation, entering our third century with pride and confidence—an America that lives up to the majesty of our constitution and the simple decency of our people.

This is the America we want. This is the America we will have. . . ."

Source Reading Wrap-Up

1) According to Carter, how was 1976 different from past election years?

2) What did Carter say had shaken America?

3) What three things did Carter say that the American people wanted?

4) What kind of President did Carter say the nation could have?

5) In your opinion, how has President Carter's vision of America happened or not happened?

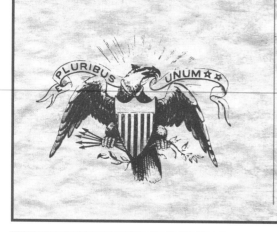

CHAPTER SUMMARY

★ In 1969 when President Nixon took office, he announced his Vietnamization plan. This plan would end American involvement in the Vietnam War and give the South Vietnamese the responsibility of defending themselves. American forces left Vietnam in 1973. The war cost many American lives. North Vietnam took over South Vietnam by 1975.

★ On July 20, 1969, American astronauts Neil Armstrong and Edwin Aldrin Jr. landed their spacecraft on the moon during the Apollo 11 mission. They were the first astronauts to land on the moon.

★ President Nixon traveled to China and the Soviet Union in 1972. This improved American relations with these countries.

★ In 1974, President Nixon resigned from office to avoid being impeached because of the Watergate scandal. Evidence had been found against him that he had been involved in a conspiracy to spy on the Democratic party in the Watergate building.

★ President Ford was met with high inflation, unemployment, and a Middle East oil embargo when he took office in 1974.

★ America celebrated its 200th birthday, or bicentennial, in 1976.

★ President Carter took office in 1977. People liked him because he seemed to be like them. He dealt with an energy crisis and problems in the Middle East and Central America during the early years of his presidency. Iran took fifty-two Americans hostage in 1979. Carter was unable to find a way to get the hostages released.

★ The United States protested the Soviet Union's invasion of Afghanistan in 1979.

★ President Carter agreed to the SALT II treaty with Soviet Premier Leonid Brezhnev in Vienna, Austria, in 1979. The U.S. Senate refused to ratify the treaty.

Comprehension: Identifying Facts

On a separate sheet of paper, write the words from the Word Bank to complete each sentence.

WORD BANK	
Afghanistan	Panama Canal
Apollo 11	Richard Nixon
bicentennial	resigned
embargo	SALT II
Gerald Ford	Spiro Agnew
Iran	Watergate
OPEC	

1) The _____ mission put the first astronauts on the moon.

2) _____ met with President Brezhnev of the Soviet Union in 1972.

3) _____ resigned as Vice President.

4) The _____ scandal involved a break-in at the Democratic party's main office.

5) Richard Nixon _____ from office to avoid being impeached.

6) _____ took over as President after Nixon left office.

7) America celebrated its _____ in 1976.

8) A treaty signed in 1977 gave the United States the right to defend the _____ against any attack.

9) _____ includes several nations in the Middle East, Africa, and South America.

10) _____ held fifty-two Americans hostage.

11) Some Arab states set up an oil _____ because the United States and other countries were giving aid to Israel.

12) The Soviets invaded _____ in 1979.

13) President Carter agreed to the _____ treaty with the Soviet Union in 1979.

Comprehension: Understanding Main Ideas

On a separate sheet of paper, write the answer to each question using complete sentences.

1) What were the effects of the Vietnam War on the American people?

2) How did President Nixon improve relations with the Soviet Union and China?

3) Why did President Nixon refuse at first to give tape recordings to the Senate committee?

4) How did an energy problem develop when Gerald Ford became President?

5) What problems did President Carter face with the Middle East?

Critical Thinking: Write Your Opinion

1) Many Americans protested the Vietnam War. If a similar war broke out today, would you protest? Why or why not?

2) If you had been an Olympic athlete in 1980, how would you have felt about the boycott of the Olympic games?

| Test Taking Tip | In a matching test, each item should be used just once. Check your answers. If you repeated an item, then another item was left out. Find the best spot for the item you left out. |

1980–1989

International and Third World problems continued in the 1980s. The Reagan and Bush administrations, the next two American presidencies, faced these problems and made sweeping changes at home. During this time, the nation experienced social problems, the successes and failures of the space program, and the end of the Cold War. In this chapter, you will learn about these and other important events that took place in the 1980s.

Goals for Learning

▶ To identify important national events that the Reagan administration faced

▶ To explain important foreign events facing the Reagan administration

▶ To describe events at the start of the Bush administration

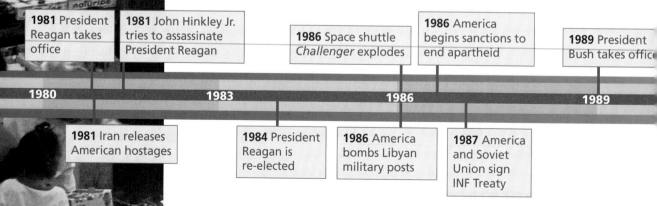

1981 President Reagan takes office

1981 John Hinkley Jr. tries to assassinate President Reagan

1986 Space shuttle *Challenger* explodes

1986 America begins sanctions to end apartheid

1989 President Bush takes office

1980   1983   1986   1989

1981 Iran releases American hostages

1984 President Reagan is re-elected

1986 America bombs Libyan military posts

1987 America and Soviet Union sign INF Treaty

Dependent
Relying on others for one's needs

Surge
To rise swiftly

The Iranian hostage crisis caused the American people to question President Carter as a leader. He lost the 1980 election to Republican Ronald Reagan. On January 20, 1981, the same day Ronald Reagan became President, Iran released the fifty-two American hostages.

Reagan was the oldest person ever to become President. He was sixty-nine years old when he took office. He was well known to the American people. Reagan had been in movies from 1937 to 1964 and had appeared on television in the 1950s and 1960s. He also had served as governor of California.

President Reagan wanted to bring back confidence to the American people. In his inaugural address, Reagan called for a "new beginning." He said the country's biggest problem was inflation. He wanted to lower taxes and decrease the power of the federal government.

How Was Reagan Almost Assassinated?

President Reagan made a speech in Washington, D.C., on his seventieth day in office. It was March 30, 1981. He included in his speech the remark, "Violent crime has **surged** ten percent." Shortly thereafter, Reagan was walking toward his car when several shots were fired by a young man named John Hinkley Jr. The President, a policeman, and two of his aides were shot. Hinkley was immediately captured. President Reagan was rushed to a hospital. He was seriously wounded, yet his courage, confidence, and good humor calmed the nation. He was back in the White House full time in a month.

What Was Reagan's "New Federalism"?

President Reagan thought that many federal programs made people too **dependent** on the government. He believed that people should take responsibility for their own lives. Community problems should be solved by volunteer groups.

In 1981, Reagan announced that he wanted to cut the 1982 federal **budget** by $33 billion. He limited money to many social programs. The only department not affected by the budget cuts was the Department of Defense. President Reagan called his plan to decrease the power of the federal government the "New Federalism."

What Was "Reaganomics"?

In an effort to get the country out of the "worst economic mess since the Great Depression," Reagan suggested many tax and budget cuts. He believed these cuts would improve the economy, decrease the size of the federal government, and decrease the expansion of social programs. The bill passed by Congress was the Economic Recovery Tax Act.

Under this plan, personal income taxes were cut by twenty-five percent over a three-year period. Business taxes were lowered through a series of benefits. Federal spending for education and the environment was cut heavily. Programs dealing with health, urban, social, and cultural issues were also cut. President Reagan's economic plan became known as "Reaganomics."

Justice Sandra Day O'Connor

Who Did Reagan Appoint to the Supreme Court?

During Reagan's presidential campaign, he promised that if a position opened on the Supreme Court, he would fill the opening with a woman. One opened several months after Reagan took office. He appointed Sandra Day O'Connor from Arizona. She became the first woman to serve on the Supreme Court.

Reagan wanted to make the Supreme Court more conservative. Justice O'Connor was his first conservative appointment to the court. Conservatives interpreted the Constitution **literally.** Conservatives charged that liberal justices found new rights in the Constitution that were not intended when it was written.

The Eruption of Mount Saint Helens

Mount Saint Helens is a volcano in Washington's Cascade Mountains. American Indians once named it "fire mountain." Before 1980, Mount Saint Helens stood 9,677 feet above sea level. In 1980, it erupted, blasting 1,300 feet off the peak and leaving a crater nearly a mile wide. Sixty-two people were killed. Damage spread over a 193-square-mile area. Hot ash started forest fires, destroying millions of trees. Temperatures near the mountaintop rose to 572 °F. Snow melted quickly, causing floods and mud slides that washed away buildings, roads, and bridges. One of the largest recorded avalanches resulted. It carried mud and debris into rivers, lakes, and valleys. Volcanic ash shot twelve miles into the sky and covered a wide area. The ash destroyed crops and killed animals, fish, and birds. Since 1980, Mount Saint Helens has been a laboratory for the U.S. Geological Survey and a huge natural "exhibit."

What Did Americans Think of Reagan?

Reagan's style as a leader was criticized. He worked a normal eight-hour business day. He gave much of the responsibility of making decisions to members of his cabinet and staff. In spite of the criticism, Reagan proved to be a popular President. He was re-elected in 1984. He defeated Walter Mondale, Carter's Vice President. Mondale chose Congresswoman Geraldine Ferraro to run as his Vice President.

What Happened to the Space Shuttle *Challenger*?

Before January 28, 1986, everyone thought that the space shuttle was a technological wonder. Twenty-four times the shuttle blasted into space and back successfully. No one thought that an accident could happen.

First Woman to Be Nominated for Vice President

Geraldine Ferraro was the first woman nominated by a major political party to run for Vice President. Ferraro, a Democrat, had served three terms in the House of Representatives. Though the Mondale-Ferraro ticket lost the 1984 election, she went on to serve on the UN Human Rights Commission.

Much had been expected of the shuttle *Challenger*. Among the crew was a high school teacher named Christa McAuliffe. She would teach lessons from space, help with scientific experiments, and after the flight, serve as a spokesperson for NASA about scientific **careers.**

The *Challenger* takeoff seemed normal. However, two rubber "O-rings" failed as a result of cold temperatures. Millions of viewers across the world watched as the *Challenger* exploded into flames just seventy-three seconds into the flight. All seven members of the crew were killed. It was the worst disaster in twenty-five years of space flight. This loss and a series of rocket failures in 1986 set back the U.S. space program for years.

SECTION 1 REVIEW On a separate sheet of paper, write *True* if the statement is true or *False* if the statement is not true.

1) President Reagan was assassinated.

2) "New Federalism" was President Reagan's plan to decrease the power of the federal government.

3) President Reagan wanted to raise taxes and expand social programs.

4) Reagan was re-elected as President.

5) The space shuttle *Discovery* exploded in 1986.

Three of the seven *Challenger* crew members are shown here shortly before liftoff. They are (from left) Greg Jarevis, Ellison Onizuka, and Christa McAuliffe.

What do you think ?

Some people feel that the space program is unnecessary, especially after an accident like the *Challenger* explosion. Do you think the space program should continue? Why or why not?

At the end of World War II, political leaders divided the world into three parts. The first group of nations were the western democracies. The second group were communist countries. The nations that were not part of either group were called the Third World. Today most nations of the Third World continue to struggle. They are not industrialized and have little power in world affairs.

The United States was concerned with problems in the Third World. The Middle East continued to be a troubled area. In Central America, Nicaragua had a communist government. The policies of South Africa troubled many Americans.

What Problems Occurred in the Middle East?

President Anwar Sadat of Egypt was assassinated in 1981. Israeli troops moved into the nation of Lebanon in 1982 to destroy the bases of the Palestine Liberation Organization (PLO). The PLO wanted a homeland for the Palestinians. The Israelis accused the PLO of being a terrorist organization.

MAYA LIN: 1959–

In 1981, 21-year-old Maya Lin's design won the commission for the Vietnam War Memorial in Washington, D.C. At that time, Lin was an architecture student. Chosen from 1,420 entries, her design was controversial. Today the memorial has become a place of healing. It is two long walls of polished granite with the names of nearly 60,000 Americans who died in Vietnam. Among Lin's other designs are the civil rights memorial in Montgomery, Alabama, and a clock in New York's Pennsylvania Station. Also an artist and sculptor, Lin says all of her work is about human thoughts and emotions. Her mother, a literature professor, and her father, dean of Fine Arts at Ohio State University, emigrated from China in the 1940s. As a child, she made pottery with her father. While Lin considers herself more American than Chinese, she regards her work as distinctly Asian.

The United States wanted a peaceful settlement in the Middle East and offered help. American marines were sent as a peacekeeping force. In October of 1983, a terrorist drove a truck loaded with **explosives** into the marine base. The truck exploded. Over 200 American soldiers died. Reagan did not remove American troops from Lebanon until several months afterward. He was looking for a long-term solution. When the troops were finally removed in February of 1984, the situation was still not settled.

Explosive
A device that explodes, such as a bomb

Rescue crews worked to help soldiers at the marine base in Lebanon that was bombed in 1983.

The trouble in the Middle East included a war between Iran and Iraq that began in 1980. The United States Navy began to protect shipping lanes in the Persian Gulf. Iranians had placed mines in the water. In May of 1987, thirty-seven sailors died when an Iraqi warplane fired a missile into the *U.S.S. Stark.*

How Did Libyan Terrorism Affect America?

In 1985, terrorist attacks at airports in Rome and Vienna killed a number of people, including many Americans. President Reagan charged Libyan leader Muammar al-Qaddafi with responsibility for the attacks. Shortly afterward, Reagan cut off trade with Libya and froze all Libyan assets in America.

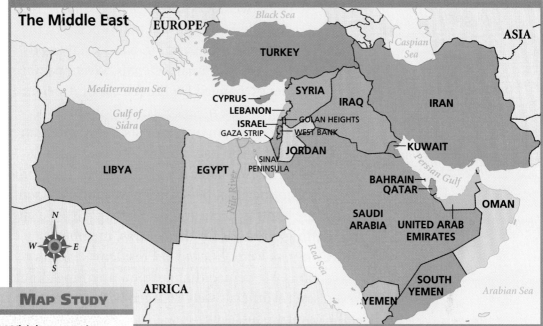

The Middle East

EUROPE
Black Sea
Caspian Sea
ASIA
TURKEY
Mediterranean Sea
Gulf of Sidra
CYPRUS
SYRIA
LEBANON
GOLAN HEIGHTS
ISRAEL
WEST BANK
GAZA STRIP
IRAQ
IRAN
LIBYA
EGYPT
JORDAN
SINAI PENINSULA
Nile River
KUWAIT
Persian Gulf
BAHRAIN
QATAR
SAUDI ARABIA
UNITED ARAB EMIRATES
OMAN
N
W   E
S
AFRICA
Red Sea
YEMEN
SOUTH YEMEN
Arabian Sea

MAP STUDY

Which countries border on Syria? Which body of water is closest to Libya?

In 1986, Qaddafi's troops fired on planes flying over international waters in the Gulf of Sidra, near Libya. The United States responded by sinking two Libyan ships and destroying one of that country's missile sites. A few weeks later, another terrorist attack killed an American soldier and injured others. Reagan ordered bombings of Libyan military posts that were thought to be training areas for terrorists.

What Was the Contra Scandal?

A communist government took power in the Central American nation of Nicaragua in 1979. The United States feared that communists would gain power in other Central American nations. In fact, Nicaragua supplied military aid to communist groups in other countries. The Reagan administration's policy was to fund a Nicaraguan group called the contras. The contras wanted to overthrow the communist government of Nicaragua. Funding the contras was controversial. Members of Congress disagreed with the White House. Congress later voted to cut off funds to the contras.

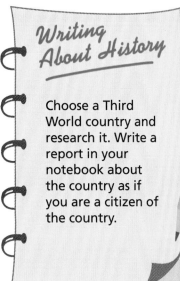

Writing About History

Choose a Third World country and research it. Write a report in your notebook about the country as if you are a citizen of the country.

In November of 1986, a magazine in the Middle East reported that officials in the Reagan administration had secretly sold weapons to Iranian officials. Weapons were being exchanged for the release of American hostages. The hostages were thought to be held in Lebanon by terrorists, yet the Reagan administration had a policy of never dealing with terrorists. Later it was discovered that some of the money that paid for the weapons was sent to the contras in Nicaragua. Having passed a law cutting off funds for the contras, members of Congress were shocked at President Reagan's actions. He denied that he knew anything about it. However, several officials were charged with attempting to cheat the government.

How Did Relations Improve With the Soviet Union?

Tensions had increased between the Soviet Union and the United States during the Carter administration. The Cold War appeared to be growing. President Reagan called the Soviet Union the "evil empire." He said the Soviets could not be trusted. The United States began the largest military buildup in peacetime. Critics said the United States should be trying to decrease its amount of military weapons. The Reagan administration argued that the nation had to be strong before any serious talks could take place.

Mikhail Gorbachev became the new leader of the Soviet Union in 1985. He wanted to make changes to improve Soviet society. He spoke of a new "openness" that allowed more criticism of Soviet society. By 1987, the relations between the Soviet Union and the United States seemed to be improving.

Gorbachev and Reagan signed a treaty to decrease the amount of nuclear weapons on December 8, 1987. Both countries agreed to destroy medium-range nuclear weapons.

President Reagan spoke with Mikhail Gorbachev in front of St. Basil's Cathedral in Moscow in 1988.

This new arms control agreement was called the Intermediate Nuclear Forces (INF) Treaty. Both nations agreed to allow government officials to inspect weapons factories to make sure that the terms of the treaty were being carried out. President Reagan said, "We can only hope that this history-making agreement will not be an end in itself but the beginning of a working relationship. . . ." In 1988, President Reagan visited the Soviet Union.

How Did America React to Apartheid?

The white government of South Africa had denied equal political and civil rights to its black population. Blacks made up over seventy percent of South Africa's population. The South African policy of racial segregation is called **apartheid.**

During the 1980s, there were protests in the United States against the policies of South Africa. Those against apartheid argued that the United States should pressure South Africa to change its policy. Others argued that the United States should not interfere in South Africa's problems.

In an effort to end apartheid in South Africa, Congress proposed a bill imposing economic **sanctions** on the country. A sanction is an action taken to force a country to do something. Under this bill, South African imports would no longer be allowed into the United States. American exports to Africa would be stopped. Also, Americans would no longer be able to invest in new South African businesses. The bill also canceled landing rights in America for all South African airlines.

★Apartheid
The South African policy of racial segregation

★Sanction
An action taken to force a country to do something

The space shuttle *Discovery* lifted off successfully in 1988. It was the first shuttle to launch after the *Challenger* disaster.

Believing that the sanctions would do too much damage to the South African economy, President Reagan vetoed the bill. However, Congress overrode his veto. The sanctions bill became law in 1986.

How Did NASA Return to Space?

For two and a half years, NASA did not send any astronauts into space. NASA spent a lot of time making sure that the shuttle would be safe. On September 29, 1988, the space shuttle *Discovery* lifted safely into space at 11:37 a.m. It carried five astronauts and the future of America's space program. The four-day flight was, above all, a test of the shuttle itself. The shuttle worked just fine. America's first step back into space was a success.

You probably know that AIDS is an incurable disease caused by the virus called HIV. You probably also know that one way the virus is spread is through HIV-infected blood. The first cases to be identified as AIDS in the United States surfaced in 1981. It was 1983 before American and French researchers discovered the virus. It took until 1985 to develop the first blood test for HIV. Before 1985, one way people got AIDS was through blood transfusions. Without the test, health workers had no way to identify blood donors with HIV. There was no way to ensure the safety of blood supplied for transfusion.

If you need a transfusion today, you can be assured that the blood has been tested for HIV. People no longer get AIDS through blood transfusions.

SECTION 2 REVIEW Choose the best word or name in parentheses to complete each sentence. Write your answers on a separate sheet of paper.

1) Over 200 American soldiers died after a bombing in (Iran, Iraq, Lebanon).

2) To make sure communism would not spread to Central American countries, the Reagan administration funded a group called the (Libyans, contras, Palestinians).

3) America bombed (Iran, Libya, Nicaragua) in 1986.

4) America and (the Soviet Union, Iran, China) signed the Intermediate Nuclear Forces (INF) Treaty in 1987.

5) Racial segregation in South Africa is called (contra, apartheid, PLO).

What do you think

How do you think apartheid is similar to problems African Americans have faced in America?

★Deficit
Debt; spending more than what is taken in

★Poll
A method of guessing the winner of elections by asking people who they plan to vote for

In the election of 1988, the Republican party chose Vice President George Bush as its candidate. The Reverend Jesse Jackson was the first African American to run for President. He ran for President in the 1984 and the 1988 elections. His efforts received much media attention. Massachusetts Governor Michael Dukakis eventually won the Democratic nomination in 1988, but Jackson's efforts were not forgotten.

On November 8, 1988, George Bush was elected President. Bush won fifty-four percent of the popular vote and 426 electoral votes compared with Dukakis' 112. On January 20, 1989, George Bush became the forty-first President of the United States.

Jesse Jackson

What Problems Did President Bush Face?

By January 1989, the United States had experienced six straight years of economic growth. This was the longest economic growth period in American history. Still, many problems faced the new Bush administration. The nation's banking industry was in deep trouble. The federal government had a large budget debt, or **deficit.** Many social problems challenged the United States.

Polls Find Out Who Will Win Elections

Political **polls** have become important in election campaigns. Most national polls ask less than 2,000 people who they will vote for in a future election. The information gained from this small group can be used to make a guess about who will win the election. Polls correctly guessed the winner of all but two presidential elections from 1952 to 1988.

The Federal Deficit, 1980–90

$3.2 trillion

$1.8 trillion

$908 million

Dollars

1980   1985   1990

One solution to the deficit problem was to collect more income taxes from the American people. However, President Bush had promised during the election campaign to hold the line against any increase in taxes. "Read my lips," he said during the campaign. "No new taxes!" By the end of 1990, fear of the growing deficit caused the Congress and the President to design a "Deficit Reduction Plan" that would increase taxes and place a limit on spending.

Media in History

Movies at Home

The videocassette recorder (VCR) brought full-length movies into people's homes. It also gave viewers control over what they watch and when they watch it.

For a time, the legality of taping shows for home use was in question. Some thought it violated copyright laws. This issue finally was settled in 1984. The Supreme Court ruled five to four that home taping was legal.

Video disc players competed with VCRs for a time, but the video disc players could not record. They could only play prerecorded programs. The public made a clear choice. It preferred the VCR because it could record, play back, and erase.

Making original movies for home viewing has become a big industry. A visit to a video store on a Friday or Saturday night shows how many people choose to watch movies at home.

What Social Problems Did Bush Face?

The budget was not the only problem facing the nation. The "quality of life" in America was a major concern. President Bush called the problem of crime and drug abuse a **"scourge."** Some people blamed the crime and drug problems on the fact that not all Americans were part of the 1980s economic boom. Several major American cities were in poor economic shape. Low-cost housing was in short supply throughout the nation.

Scourge
Widespread pain or distress

Homelessness was a common sight in the 1980s.

American cities also experienced a growing problem of homelessness. People who had no homes lived in the streets and parks of many cities. Soup kitchens increased in many American cities. These places fed hundreds of hungry people daily.

What "Firsts" Did African Americans Achieve?

In 1989 and 1990, several African Americans reached positions of power never before held by an African American. General Colin Powell was appointed by President Bush to be the Chairman of the Joint Chiefs of Staff. This position made General Powell the nation's top military officer.

In Virginia, Douglas Wilder was elected the first African-American governor of a state since Reconstruction. David Dinkins was elected the first African-American mayor of New York City. The cities of Seattle, Washington; Durham, North Carolina; and New Haven, Connecticut, all elected their first African-American mayors.

How Did Communism Begin to Fall?

In 1989, the Cold War seemed to be ending. Communism was beginning to fall. During much of the 1980s, the Soviet Union had been experiencing economic problems. The communist system had failed to provide the Soviet people with enough food. Soviet citizens demanded a more democratic voice in their government.

Communism began to show signs of falling in Europe as well. Eastern European countries under communist rule, such as Hungary, Poland, Czechoslovakia, and East Germany, began to protest communist rule. President Bush reacted to the situation in 1989 by saying, "The Cold War began with the division of Europe. It can only end when Europe is whole."

In November of 1989, for the first time, the East German government announced that its citizens could leave their country if they wished. East Germany opened its borders to the west and allowed thousands of its citizens to pass through the Berlin Wall. In time, the wall was removed completely. This was only the beginning of the many changes communist nations would see in the next few years.

SECTION 3 REVIEW Write the answers to these questions on a separate sheet of paper using complete sentences.

1) Why was it significant that Jesse Jackson ran for President in 1988?

2) What financial problems in America did the Bush administration face?

3) What were two social problems in America that the Bush administration faced?

4) What was beginning to happen to the Soviet Union in the 1980s?

5) What happened in East Germany in 1989?

What do you think ?

What do you think should be done about the problem of homelessness?

"Women Shooting for the Stars"

Stella Guerra was the Acting Deputy Assistant Secretary of the Air Force in the 1980s. She gave this speech as a tribute and encouragement to women in the armed forces. Her comments address American women even today.

"Dating back to our forebears who first stepped foot on American soil, [women] have been a part of our nation's progress. In what some have called the 'toddler years' of our country—the 1800s, we helped America take its first steps toward world prominence. We moved west, we worked in the fields tilling the soil and in the factories to produce the food and goods that our country needed to grow and prosper. . . . In the 1900s, during . . . the 'Rosie the Riveter' period, working in shipyards and steel mills, we helped our nation meet labor shortages in a time of national crisis. Afterwards, many . . . who had entered the workforce returned home—but not for long. By the midpoint of the 20th century, virtually no aspect of American society had been untouched by our eager rush into the labor force. . . .

We began to stretch, to grow, and expand our horizons. In . . . less than 50 years, our numbers in the labor force doubled. . . . In the second half of the 1970s, more of us were enrolled in college than ever before, and we began to move rapidly into business, industry, the federal sector, the teaching fields and other professions such as law and medicine. . . .

As our visions were broadened, women began to move into nontraditional areas. . . . It serves as a glistening example that in the past and in the present our hopes and dreams are interwoven into the very fiber of America. . . .

As we enter America's early adulthood we find that our hopes and dreams have been uplifted toward achievement. . . . The future holds exciting changes, challenges, and opportunities that will tax our abilities, test our skills, and require a total commitment from you and me. . . .

To meet the challenges ahead and . . . to progress, we must continue to take charge of our destinies and take responsibility for our own self-development. [No factor is more] important to our self-development . . . than self-esteem. Self-esteem comes in different doses and different degrees, and its potential is limitless."

Source Reading Wrap-Up

1) What is one contribution Guerra says women have made to America's success?

2) What years were the "toddler years"?

3) What was the "Rosie the Riveter" period?

4) What does Guerra say is most important to women's self-development?

5) How does Guerra suggest women meet the challenges ahead?

★ Ronald Reagan took office as President in 1981. Reagan introduced a plan to limit money to all departments except defense. Large budget and tax cuts were meant to strengthen the economy.

★ Reagan appointed Sandra Day O'Connor, a conservative, as a Supreme Court justice. She was the first female justice.

★ Reagan became a popular President, and was re-elected in 1984.

★ In January 1986, the space shuttle *Challenger* exploded, killing everyone on board. The disaster started a long slump in the space program.

★ Tensions eased between America and the Soviet Union when Mikhail Gorbachev and Reagan signed the INF Treaty in 1987 to reduce nuclear weapons.

★ In October 1983, American marines were in Lebanon as a peacekeeping force in the Middle East conflict between Israel and the PLO. A terrorist attack killed 200 marines. The situation was unsettled when troops left in February 1984.

★ Fearing the spread of communism from Nicaragua throughout Central America, Reagan's administration funded the contras. Congress later cut off the controversial funds.

★ Reagan's administration secretly sold weapons to Iran in 1986 in exchange for American hostages in Lebanon. The weapons money was used to fund the Nicaraguan contras, angering Congress after it had cut off funds.

★ Several Libyan terrorist attacks killed Americans in 1985. Reagan cut off trade with Libya and froze their assets. When Libya fired on American planes and made more terrorist attacks in 1986, Reagan approved bombing Libyan military posts.

★ The space program resumed in September 1988 when the space shuttle *Discovery* successfully lifted off.

★ Vice President George Bush won the 1988 presidential election.

★ Crime, drug abuse, and homelessness were social problems Bush faced. The Soviet Union and other communist countries began to challenge communism in the late 1980s.

Comprehension: Identifying Facts

On a separate sheet of paper, write the words from the Word Bank to complete each sentence.

WORD BANK		
apartheid	deficit	INF Treaty
Challenger	*Discovery*	Libya
conservative	economic	sanctions
contras	federal government	Soviet Union

1) Reagan cut funds and limited spending to make people less dependent on the _____.

2) An arms buildup was part of Reagan's hard line against the _____.

3) Explosion of the space shuttle _____ suspended the space program for more than two years.

4) The space program resumed with the launch of the space shuttle _____.

5) Reagan approved bombing military sites in _____ because of that country's terrorist attacks.

6) Mikhail Gorbachev and Reagan signed the _____ to limit nuclear weapons.

7) Sandra Day O'Connor was appointed a Supreme Court justice to make the court more _____.

8) Funds were given to the _____ because they wanted to overthrow communism in Nicaragua.

9) The United States was against South Africa's policy of _____.

10) Congress overrode Reagan's veto of the bill to impose economic _____ on South Africa.

11) A large budget _____ faced President Bush at the start of his term.

12) Severe _____ problems in the Soviet Union led the Soviet people to begin to question communism.

Comprehension: Understanding Main Ideas

On a separate sheet of paper, write the answer to each question using complete sentences.

1) What were two social problems that challenged President Bush?

2) What was one historic event that happened for African Americans in 1989 and 1990?

3) What did President Reagan say about the powers of the federal government and the states?

4) What did the United States and the Soviet Union agree to do in the treaty they made in 1987?

5) What are Third World countries?

6) Why did NASA spend so much time on the space shuttle program after the *Challenger* exploded in 1986?

Critical Thinking: Write Your Opinion

1) President Reagan wanted community problems to be solved by more volunteer efforts. In what ways do you think volunteers' efforts can be effective in solving community problems?

2) People demonstrated in the United States against South Africa's policies. How effective do you think demonstrations are in bringing about change?

| Test Taking Tip | When taking a true-false test, read each statement carefully. Write *true* only when the statement is totally true. Write *false* if part or all of the statement is false. |

The 1990s

1990–Present

World affairs continued to affect America in the 1990s. Communism in the Soviet Union ended, marking the true end of the Cold War. At the same time, the Bush administration faced a new conflict in the Middle East with the nation of Iraq. This was the beginning of several conflicts America and the next President, William Clinton, faced throughout the decade. In this chapter, you will learn about the issues at home and abroad that surfaced during the 1990s.

Goals for Learning

▶ To explain how communist rule in the Soviet Union ended

▶ To describe the causes and outcomes of the Persian Gulf War

▶ To describe the policies and attempts at reform by the Clinton administration

▶ To explain the world conflicts involving America in the 1990s

▶ To list the problems and changes that took place in America during the 1990s

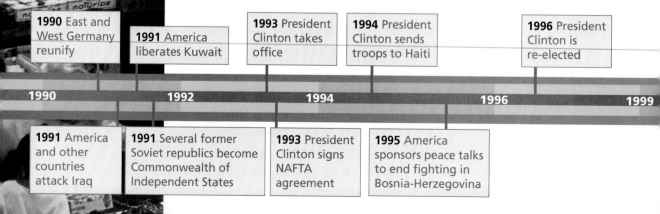

1990 East and West Germany reunify

1991 America liberates Kuwait

1993 President Clinton takes office

1994 President Clinton sends troops to Haiti

1996 President Clinton is re-elected

1990   1992   1994   1996   1999

1991 America and other countries attack Iraq

1991 Several former Soviet republics become Commonwealth of Independent States

1993 President Clinton signs NAFTA agreement

1995 America sponsors peace talks to end fighting in Bosnia-Herzegovina

Conventional
Something that is traditional or commonly used

★**Reunification**
Joining together as one country again

★**Summit**
A meeting held between or among world leaders

In early 1990, East Germany held free elections. The new government was able to come to terms with West Germany. The four World War II nations agreed to free up their ties to either half of Berlin. After a series of meetings to discuss the future of the Polish border, East and West Germany agreed on **reunification.** This means they were joined into one nation again. German reunification was made official October 3, 1990. By mid-1991, Berlin had been re-established as the capital of Germany.

What Treaties Were Signed to Reduce Arms?

In the fall of 1990, the United States, the Soviet Union, and twenty other nations signed an agreement to decrease **conventional** military forces. Known as the Conventional Forces in Europe (CFE) Treaty, the agreement set limits on military vehicles and arms in Europe. As a result of the agreement, the Soviet Union had to remove thousands of pieces of military equipment from many areas.

In Moscow in 1991, President Bush and Soviet Premier Gorbachev held a **summit.** A summit is a meeting held between or among world leaders. Both countries agreed to reduce its store of intercontinental missiles. The Strategic Arms Reduction Treaty (START) called for thirty percent fewer missile systems within seven years of the treaty. This treaty became effective in December of 1994.

How Did Communism End in the Soviet Union?

Since 1949, the Soviet Union, also called the U.S.S.R., had kept economic control of many Eastern European countries through a trade association called Comecon. However, in 1991, in an effort to cut their economic ties to the U.S.S.R., these countries broke up the association. Upon making this move, the countries looked to the west for new partnerships and financial help in reorganizing their economies.

★Glasnost
Soviet policy of open discussion of political and social issues

★Perestroika
Soviet policy of economic and government reform

President Gorbachev tried to begin changes during the 1980s with his policies of **glasnost** and **perestroika.** Glasnost was open discussion of political and social issues. Perestroika was economic and government reform. However, Soviet citizens grew more and more dissatisfied. Newspapers began to run antigovernment articles. The lack of available goods and services in the country caused many people to leave the Communist party. All across the land, voters supported candidates who replaced many of the communist leaders.

A group of staunch communists tried to overthrow Gorbachev as leader in 1990. They held him hostage while they tried to capture Boris Yeltsin, president of the Russian republic and an anticommunist. However, thousands of citizens who assembled in Moscow in protest forced the rebels to give up. Shortly thereafter, Gorbachev resigned as secretary-general of the Communist party.

MAP STUDY

How many independent states are shown on this map? Which is the largest?

The republics of the Soviet Union started to seek their independence. In December of 1991, three former Soviet republics of Russia, Ukraine, and Belarus formed the Commonwealth of Independent States.

Russia and the Commonwealth of Independent States

Former Soviet-Occupied Countries

How many former Soviet-occupied countries are shown on this map? Where is Poland located?

★Commonwealth
A group of self-governing states

A **commonwealth** is a group of self-governing states. America quickly recognized the commonwealth.

The end of the U.S.S.R. was made final by the resignation of Gorbachev as its president. President Yeltsin remained leader of the new Russian Federation. All but three of the former republics of the Soviet Union joined the commonwealth by 1995.

Countries under Soviet control began to break away in the late 1980s and early 1990s. These included Hungary, Poland, and Czechoslovakia. Within less than a year, the map of Europe had changed, and a new chapter was being written in this area's history. The democratic countries of Europe and the United States believed themselves to be the clear winners of the Cold War.

Boris Yeltsin

Internet: The Information Superhighway

The Internet started as a way to share information among scientists in the U.S. Department of Defense in the late 1960s. As it expanded through the 1970s, members of the computer industry began to participate. Finally, legislation in 1991 resulted in its mass commercialization.

Today, the Internet crosses all boundaries to bring the world to your doorstep, or rather to your computer. The World Wide Web has grown since it was started in the early 1990s. Now programs are available that act as an interface between you and the Internet. These programs are called browsers. As a result, the Internet has become user-friendly both for individuals and for business. It is called the information superhighway.

The Internet is interactive. You can "talk" with people around the world and find out information of any type. It has become a worldwide marketplace. You can buy anything from chocolate candy to automobiles to fishing lures on the Internet. You can even get a college degree on the Internet.

SECTION 1 REVIEW On a separate sheet of paper, write the word from the Word Bank to complete each sentence.

WORD BANK

Commonwealth

Glasnost

Perestroika

reunification

summit

1) All but three of the former Soviet republics became the _____ of Independent States.

2) German _____ was made official October 3, 1990.

3) A meeting between or among world leaders is called a _____.

4) _____ allowed open discussion of political and social issues.

5) _____ called for economic and government reform.

What do you think ?

How do you think America was affected by the collapse of communism in the Soviet Union?

In July of 1990, a conflict in the Middle East developed between the nation of Iraq and its small neighbor, Kuwait. President Saddam Hussein of Iraq accused Kuwait of trying to keep oil prices low and of stealing oil from Iraq's wells.

Iraq threatened Kuwait by sending more than 100,000 troops to the border of the small nation. Kuwait's whole army included only 20,000 soldiers. By the end of July, many oil-producing nations in the Persian Gulf agreed to raise the price of oil. Saddam Hussein seemed satisfied and said that he would not invade Kuwait. The crisis seemed to be ending peacefully.

What Happened When Iraq Invaded Kuwait?

On August 2, 1990, the Iraqi army invaded Kuwait. President Bush and officials discussed what the United States should do. They questioned whether Iraq should be allowed to conquer Kuwait, an independent country, and member of the United Nations. In addition, they feared that if the Iraqi army kept moving south, it could possibly conquer oil-rich Saudi Arabia. Many nations, including the United States, were concerned about having one nation control so much of an important natural resource.

On August 6, 1990, the United States and other members of the United Nations agreed to stop trading with Iraq in protest of the invasion. The United Nations said that the Iraqi army should leave Kuwait. The next day, President Bush sent American troops to protect Saudi Arabia. The military called it "Operation Desert Shield."

Many members of the United Nations agreed with the United States' actions against Iraq. On November 29, the United Nations Security Council voted 12-2 to give Iraq until January 15, 1991, to pull out of Kuwait. If Iraq failed to meet this deadline, the United States and its UN allies could use armed force.

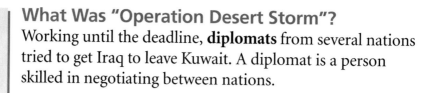
What Was "Operation Desert Storm"?

Working until the deadline, **diplomats** from several nations tried to get Iraq to leave Kuwait. A diplomat is a person skilled in negotiating between nations.

The diplomats failed. On January 17, 1991, the United States, Great Britain, France, Saudi Arabia, Kuwait, and others launched an air attack against Iraq. "Operation Desert Shield" had become "Operation Desert Storm."

For five weeks, planes rained bombs on Iraq and Iraqi forces in Kuwait. Iraq attacked Israel by launching missiles, called Scuds, into the country. Saddam Hussein thought that by doing this he could draw Israel into the war. He hoped to force the Arab nations to leave the allies and join him in a fight with Israel. Although hit with many missiles, Israel did not enter the war.

One final deadline was given to Saddam Hussein to remove his army from Kuwait. When this deadline passed, the United States and its allies launched a large ground and air attack against Iraq's huge army. The ground war lasted only four days. Many Iraqi soldiers were killed; thousands surrendered to the allies. The American and allied combat **casualties** during the war was about 370. A casualty is a person who is wounded, killed, or lost in action. Norman Schwarzkopf, commander of the allied forces, called it "miraculous." The air and land campaign against Iraq made military history. On February 27, 1991, President Bush announced to the nation, "Kuwait is liberated."

The United States and its allies used tanks and other vehicles to attack the Iraqi army.

What Challenges Remain in the Middle East?

Problems in the Middle East continue to challenge the United States. Finding a peaceful solution to the long-standing conflict between several Arab nations and Israel has troubled the world for more than four decades.

During the Persian Gulf War, Arab and western nations cooperated against a common enemy. When the war ended, President Bush felt that this cooperative spirit could be used to bring a lasting peace to the Middle East. In March of 1991, the President sent Secretary of State James Baker to the Middle East to meet with leaders. President Bush felt that the United States should help to build a "new world order" where the nations of the world seek to solve their conflicts peacefully.

SECTION 2 REVIEW   On a separate sheet of paper, write *True* if the statement is true or *False* if the statement is not true.

1) Kuwait invaded Iraq in 1990.

2) The United Nations Security Council gave Iraq until January 15, 1991, to pull out of Kuwait.

3) Saddam Hussein hoped to force Arab nations to leave the allies by attacking and starting a war with Israel.

4) The ground war against Iraq lasted four weeks.

5) Kuwait was liberated on February 27, 1991.

What do you think ?

The Persian Gulf War was caused in part over oil. Do you think it is necessary for America to be so protective of oil? Why or why not?

Republicans backed the George Bush-Dan Quayle ticket for re-election. The Democrats chose Governor Bill Clinton of Arkansas as their presidential candidate. Al Gore of Tennessee was Clinton's choice for Vice President. Texas billionaire Ross Perot ran as an independent. Although the American people were pleased with the way President Bush handled the Persian Gulf War, the tide turned during the campaign. Many Americans were concerned about the economy. The unemployment rate was at an eight-year high. A very high number of American families remained very poor.

Clinton, who stressed the need for an improved economy, won the election. He took office in 1993. Though Perot did not win, he had the best showing since third-party candidate Theodore Roosevelt ran for President in 1912.

The Democrats kept control of Congress, but the makeup of that group changed a good deal. Many longtime senators and representatives had not sought re-election. More new people were elected to Congress in 1992 than in any year

President Clinton took the oath of office in 1993. His daughter, Chelsea, (left) and his wife, Hillary Rodham Clinton, (right) were present for the ceremony.

Carol Mosely-Braun

since 1948. Many more women, African Americans, and Hispanic Americans had been elected. Among these was Carol Mosely-Braun of Illinois, who became the first African-American woman to be elected to the Senate.

What Was NAFTA?

In December of 1992, the governments of the United States, Mexico, and Canada approved the North American Free Trade Agreement (NAFTA).

Under this agreement, restrictions on investments, trade, and services among the three North American countries would be stopped completely over a fifteen-year period. The three countries now formed a giant market of goods and services. Mexico, a major importer of American goods and agricultural services, would stop its huge tariffs. The United States would also free Mexican imports of duties. The NAFTA agreement was signed into law by President Clinton in late 1993 and went into effect in January of 1994.

What Reforms Did President Clinton Attempt?

President Clinton sent a number of proposals to Congress. One proposal aimed at lowering the federal deficit by $496 billion over five years. Conservative opponents argued that it relied on high tax increases and included too few spending cuts. Several changes were made to the bill. When the bill passed in 1993, it still included plans for tax increases and budget cuts totaling $496 billion over five years.

James Brady and his wife, Sarah, attended the signing of the Brady Bill in 1993.

The Brady Bill was passed in 1993. It was named for James Brady, who was shot and permanently injured during the assassination attempt on President Reagan in 1981. This bill set up a five-day waiting period for the purchase of a handgun. It also called for a national computer network that would allow gun dealers to check on the criminal record and age of a person who wanted to buy a gun.

Congress passed the Omnibus Violent Crime Control and Prevention Act in 1994. Under this act, local governments would be given power to hire 100,000 new police officers. It also called for new state prisons to be built and communities to be given funds for crime-prevention programs. This bill also banned certain weapons and increased the number of crimes punishable by death. The costs of putting the bill into action over six years' time were to be covered by savings from the 265,000 jobs that were cut from the federal government.

Largely aided by First Lady Hillary Rodham Clinton, the President promoted huge changes in the nation's health care system. The changes were aimed at providing inexpensive medical care for all Americans. This plan called for the creation of "health alliances." It was suggested that these medical groups, through competition, would help keep costs down. Opponents of the plan argued that it would put too much burden on employers. Under this system, employers would have to pay most of their employees' insurance costs. Others believed that further tax increases would be necessary if the federal government were to take on the cost of health care for the poor. After many attempts at a compromise, Congress rejected the plan.

SECTION 3 REVIEW Write the answers to these questions on a separate sheet of paper using complete sentences.

1) What was the focus of the 1992 presidential election?

2) How did the makeup of Congress change in 1992?

3) What was the NAFTA agreement?

4) What was the Brady Bill?

5) What was the Omnibus Violent Crime Control and Prevention Act?

What do you think ?

Do you think the government should find a way to give all people health care? Why or why not?

Famine
*Widespread
starvation*

During the first years of his administration, President Clinton became involved in changes affecting many other countries. Although the United States was not directly involved in many of these, it helped to promote peace or to provide aid to these other countries.

What Happened in Somalia?

Civil war, drought, and **famine** cost thousands of lives and threatened many more in the African nation of Somalia by 1992. America and the UN sent troops to Somalia in 1992 to bring food to Somalia's starving people. However, severe American casualties forced the United States to pull out the troops by 1994. The UN pulled out its troops by 1995. While the efforts had saved millions of Somalians from starvation, the problems in that country remained.

What Middle East Peace Treaty Was Signed?

In 1993, President Clinton hosted an important summit between Israel's Prime Minister Yitzhak Rabin and Yasir Arafat of the Palestine Liberation Organization (PLO). The following year, he witnessed the signing of a peace agreement between those two leaders that ended their forty-six–year war. However, tensions remain between Israel and the PLO.

What Deal Was Made With Russia and the Ukraine?

President Clinton and Russian President Yeltsin met in Moscow in January of 1994 to discuss further ways to curb the threat of nuclear war. They agreed that neither would aim strategic weapons at territories of the other country. Clinton also convinced Ukraine President Kravchuk to take down that country's nuclear arsenal. The Ukraine did so in exchange for $1 billion in U.S. aid and a promise of American protection in case of attack.

Nelson Mandela

When Did South African Apartheid End?

In 1994, Nelson Mandela became the first black president of South Africa. Apartheid in that country came to an end. American economic sanctions had put pressure on the South African government. Upon adoption of a new constitution, the sanctions were lifted. President Clinton offered financial assistance to help strengthen the South African economy.

How Did Relations Improve With Vietnam?

More than twenty years after the Vietnam War, many Americans were still missing in action from the war. However, in 1995 President Clinton announced that there would be full diplomatic relations with Vietnam. Since then, Vietnam has released information about missing soldiers.

Persecute
To treat someone poorly or violently because of his or her religious beliefs or ethnic background

What Occurred in Bosnia-Herzegovina?

America became involved in a conflict in Bosnia-Herzegovina, part of the former Yugoslavia. Three-way fighting broke out between Croats, Bosnian Serbs, and Muslims in 1992. In 1993, America parachuted food and medicines to Muslims being **persecuted** by Serbs. Fighting continued even after a cease-fire was called in 1994. NATO began a series of air strikes against Bosnian Serbs, and UN peacekeepers were sent to the area. Bosnian Serbs

Serbian, Bosnian, and Croatian leaders met in Dayton, Ohio, in 1995 to discuss peace.

took over 350 UN peacekeepers hostage to discourage air strikes. By 1995, the warring parties agreed to a cease-fire. A peace agreement sponsored by the United States in 1995 ended fighting by 1996.

What Problems Developed With Haiti and Cuba?

President Clinton had met with removed Haitian President Jean-Bertrand Aristide in 1993. Clinton appealed to the UN for help in restoring Aristide to power. When the UN established an embargo against Haiti and threatened to invade that country, military dictator Rauol Cedras agreed to step down. However, when American and Canadian forces arrived to put Aristide back in power, the Haitian leaders refused to give up power. The UN maintained its embargo. The United States sent six warships to the coast of Haiti to enforce the embargo.

Through September of 1994, thousands of people fled Haiti in hope of gaining a better life in America. In September, however, President Clinton sent out twenty-three warships and 20,000 troops to restore the Aristide government. At the same time, Clinton sent former President Jimmy Carter to try to negotiate with the rebels in control of the country. Upon hearing of an American invasion, the Cedras dictatorship surrendered. Within a short time, Aristide was back in office in the Caribbean country.

Thousands of Cubans wanted to escape unpleasant living conditions in their homeland. Like many of the people from the nearby island of Haiti, they fled to the United States. President Clinton agreed to pick up these people and house them in holding camps in Cuba and Panama. In the fall of 1994, after negotiations with Cuba, the United States agreed to allow 20,000 Cubans per year to enter this country. Cuban officials promised to encourage citizens to remain in their homeland. In May of 1995, Clinton allowed most Cuban refugees from the holding camps to enter the United States.

MAYA ANGELOU: 1928–

Maya Angelou has had a rich career as a novelist, poet, playwright, educator, actress, and director. She is best known for her first autobiographical novel, *I Know Why the Caged Bird Sings* (1970). Angelou's writings are high spirited and faithful to black vocal rhythms. Her poetry collections include *Oh Pray My Wings Are Gonna Fit Me Well* (1975) and *Just Give Me a Cool Drink of Water 'for I Diiie* (1971). As an actress, Angelou appeared in an international tour of *Porgy and Bess*. Her work in *Look Away*, her first Broadway appearance, earned her a Tony award nomination. At William Clinton's first presidential inauguration in 1993, she read a poem she wrote for the occasion.

SECTION 4 REVIEW Choose the best word in parentheses to complete each sentence. Write your answers on a separate sheet of paper.

1) America and the UN sent troops to (Bosnia, Somalia, Haiti) in 1992 to bring food to that country's starving people.

2) President Clinton met with Russian President (Rabin, Yeltsin, Aristide) in Moscow to discuss further ways to curb the threat of nuclear harm.

3) Apartheid ended in 1994 in (South Africa, Vietnam, Haiti).

4) A peace agreement sponsored by the United States ended fighting in (Haiti, Russia, Bosnia-Herzegovina) by 1996.

5) President Clinton sent twenty-three warships and 20,000 troops to restore the Aristide government in (Haiti, Vietnam, South Africa) in 1994.

What do you think ❓

Do you think it is America's responsibility to feed starving people in other countries? Why or why not?

In 1994, the Republicans gained control of both houses of Congress for the first time since 1952. Across the country, they gained new leaders in almost thirty of the fifty states, including seven of the largest states. A new Republican plan called the "Contract With America" had been introduced. It was intended to balance the budget. Representative Newt Gingrich of Georgia introduced the plan. He went on to be chosen Speaker of the House in 1995.

Congress proposed a bill calling for a constitutional amendment for a balanced federal budget by the year 2002. The bill passed the House, but was rejected by the Senate. A second bill that called for term limits for members of Congress was defeated in the House of Representatives. A third bill, however, was passed and signed into law by President Clinton. It said that the federal government could not make demands on states unless the government provided federal money for the cost of carrying out those demands.

Many budget proposals that rose from the "Contract With America" were met with strong opposition by the President and many members of Congress. At one point, the failure to reach an agreement resulted in a partial shutdown of government offices. A compromise was reached after months of proposals and counterproposals.

What Was the Whitewater Affair?

Beginning in 1993, President Clinton and First Lady Hillary Rodham Clinton faced accusations in what became known as the Whitewater Affair. The Clintons were part owners of a company called the Whitewater Development Corporation in the 1970s. The company was backed by Madison Guaranty Savings and Loan. A federal investigation found illegal political campaign contributions, income tax fraud, and other wrongdoings to be linked to Whitewater and Guaranty Savings and Loan. The Clintons denied that they took part in the illegal acts.

In 1993, White House Counsel Vincent Foster committed **suicide.** He was the Clintons' lawyer at the time they had ownership in Whitewater. This raised further questions. Despite what seemed to be a scandal, Congressional hearings in 1995 found nothing to prove the Clintons took part in anything illegal. However, much of the American public became suspicious of the affair. A special investigation of the affair was still going on in 1997.

What Terrorism Occurred on American Soil?

Buildings on American soil were targets of major acts of terrorism in the 1990s. In 1993, after a bomb exploded in the parking garage of the World Trade Center in New York City, six people were killed and more than 1,000 were injured. The next year four men were found guilty of thirty-eight charges connected with that bombing.

A car bomb destroyed much of Oklahoma City's Federal Building in 1995.

In 1995, a car bomb exploded next to the Federal Building in Oklahoma City, Oklahoma. The collapsing walls and floors of the building killed 169 people, including nineteen children. Some 220 neighboring buildings were damaged. This was the worst terrorist bombing that had taken place on American soil. Timothy McVeigh was tried and found guilty in 1997 of charges connected with the bombing.

In 1996, President Clinton signed antiterrorism legislation. This included stiffer penalties for terrorist actions and new methods to prevent terrorism. The legislation also placed limits on death row appeals by those found guilty of terrorist acts.

What Was the Million Man March?

In October of 1995, hundreds of thousands of African-American men took part in the Million Man March in Washington, D.C. The purpose of the march was to show a sense of responsibility toward family and community. President Clinton praised the objectives of the people who participated in the rally.

What Reform Legislation Was Approved?

A number of bills first introduced in Congress right after Clinton took office were passed. A welfare reform bill passed in 1996 reduced federal help to the poor. The bill placed more responsibility for dealing with poverty on the states. Under this bill, direct federal government payments to the poor were replaced by block grants to states. These grants were to be used for the poor under federal guidelines.

A health care reform bill, barely a hint of the bill introduced years earlier, was passed. Under this bill, an American worker could keep health insurance after leaving the company that provided it. It also became illegal for insurance companies to drop customers because of a medical condition.

Upon signing a minimum wage bill in 1996, President Clinton claimed that it would enable "ten million workers to raise stronger families." The minimum wage was raised ninety cents an hour to $5.15. Additional increases were planned for future years. The bill also added tax benefits to small businesses likely to be most affected by the bill.

The Hale-Bopp Comet

"Have you seen the comet?" is a question people asked each other in the late winter and early spring of 1997. They were talking about the Hale-Bopp Comet, a comet discovered by two Americans. Hale-Bopp is named for Alan Hale and Tom Bopp, the first people to see and report it in July 1995.

A comet is a frozen ball of dirt that's part of the solar system. Usually comets stay far out in space. Sometimes a comet is thrown into orbit around the sun. When a comet warms up, gases form a cloud, or head, that can be seen from far away. A tail of exhaust trails behind the comet. The head of the Hale-Bopp Comet was about twenty-five miles wide. Its tail sometimes trailed for fifty or sixty million miles. The comet put on a "light show" in the sky for several months as it neared the earth.

The Hale-Bopp Comet was last seen 4200 years before and won't be seen again until around the year 4397. Did you see the comet in 1997?

Science
History in Your Life

What Racial Terrorism Took Place?

Over an eighteen-month period in the middle of the 1990s, ninety African-American churches in the South were destroyed by **arson**. Arson is the act of purposely setting fire to something. President Clinton promised aid to southern governors to prevent additional fires. He ordered the Emergency Management Agency to help communities make church buildings more secure and to identify suspicious activity by hate groups. People in the communities, many of them white, worked together to rebuild the churches.

Who Won the 1996 Election?

In 1996, Republicans nominated Senator Robert Dole of Kansas as their presidential candidate. Former congressman Jack Kemp was his running mate. Again, Ross Perot ran as the candidate of the independent Reform party. The **incumbent** ticket of Bill Clinton and Al Gore was the Democratic party's choice. An incumbent is a person who currently holds a certain position or office.

President Clinton was re-elected by a wide margin. He became the first Democratic President to be elected to a second term since Franklin D. Roosevelt ran over fifty years earlier.

Writing About History

Write a few paragraphs in your notebook about what you think the United States will be like in the year 2050.

What Challenges Will America Face in the Future?

Problems in Third World countries and other nations will most likely continue into the next century. As a world power, America will have to decide whether it has a responsibility to help solve these problems. It will also have to decide whether it is capable of solving these problems. It also will have to deal with problems at home.

Many issues at home remain. Saving the environment, working out civil rights issues, and lowering the national deficit are some

issues. Providing enough jobs for American citizens and keeping the economy stable are others. These are bound to be important topics in America in the next century.

Do you realize how rapidly the world's population is growing? The number of people living on Earth is exploding. Some scientists blame overpopulation for problems like pollution, famine, and global warming. The world's population is expected to increase by one billion people every twelve years. Many people think overcrowding will be the major problem in the future. They are concerned with being able to feed so many people. Look at these world population figures and estimates:

Year	Number of People
1800	1 billion
1930	2 billion
1968	3.5 billion
1990	5.3 billion
2002	6.3 billion
2014	7.3 billion

SECTION 5 REVIEW On a separate sheet of paper, write *True* if the statement is true or *False* if the statement is not true.

1) The Republican-controlled Congress wanted a constitutional amendment to achieve a balanced federal budget by the year 2002.

2) President Clinton opposed many of the ideas in the "Contract With America."

3) Arson destroyed ninety African-American churches in the South in the 1990s.

4) The Million Man March was a protest against African Americans.

5) President Clinton lost the 1996 election.

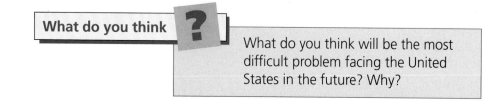

What do you think ?

What do you think will be the most difficult problem facing the United States in the future? Why?

"Favor Positive Themes"

Luis Morales is president of the Public Relations Society of America. In April 1996, he gave a speech entitled "Favor Positive Themes." Although he was speaking to business people, his message applies to all Americans.

"It seems to me that lost in the noise of political issues, lost in the . . . self-serving groups, is one issue that transcends everything else. . . . 'citizenship.'

Perhaps my own ethnic background makes me more conscious of this than most, but it does seem to me that the most pervasive issue facing us is the decline of America's traditional values. . . . We are rude, uncivil to one another, selfish to a fault, and uninterested or ignorant of our history. . . .

It is entirely within our field . . . to encourage respect and respectability and a sense of community. . . .

What can we do [to make change?] . . .

First, we can inform ourselves. Broaden our reading habits. Besides the major . . . periodicals, read some thoughtful books. . . .

We can expose ourselves to the thinking and ideas of others. . . . When we address the issues of diversity and multiculturalism, we will do so evenhandedly. We will become more aware and appreciative of the value and richness [of] a diverse society and workforce . . . .

We . . . can . . . promote a positive view of America. . . .

But we desperately need to recover our moral balance . . . . I urge you to join me in . . . regaining a sense of community, rebuilding our self-respect by respecting others. . . ."

Source Reading Wrap-Up

1) What is the issue that Morales says has gotten lost?

2) According to Morales, what is the largest overall issue facing Americans?

3) What is one thing he suggests people can do to make change?

4) What does Morales say we need to regain and rebuild?

5) How does Morales' view of citizenship agree or disagree with your view of it?

★ East and West Germany were reunified in 1990.

★ In 1990, Iraq invaded Kuwait. "Operation Desert Shield" sent American troops to protect Saudi Arabia from the Iraqi army. In 1991, America and its allies liberated Kuwait and caused severe casualties to the Iraqi army.

★ Communism collapsed in the Soviet Union in 1991. All but three of the former Soviet republics joined to form the Commonwealth of Independent States by 1995.

★ President Clinton took office in 1993. He signed the NAFTA agreement in 1993 to reduce restrictions on trade with Canada and Mexico.

★ President Clinton sent a number of proposals to Congress and promoted huge changes to the health care system. Congress rejected Clinton's initial health care plans.

★ Beginning in 1992, America experienced much foreign involvement. America improved relations with Russia, the Ukraine, South Africa, and Vietnam, and worked with Israeli and Arab leaders to form a peace agreement. It was also involved militarily in Somalia, Bosnia-Herzegovina, and Haiti.

★ Beginning in 1993, the Clintons were investigated for wrongdoings in what became known as the Whitewater Affair.

★ In 1994, Republicans gained control of Congress and implemented their plan called the "Contract With America." Among the ideas of this plan was to balance the federal budget by 2002.

★ Terrorism began to occur on American soil in 1993.

★ Welfare reform and minimum wage bills were passed in 1996.

★ In 1995, the Million Man March took place in Washington, D.C., to focus on the responsibilities of African-American men toward family and community.

★ President Clinton was re-elected President in 1996.

Comprehension: Identifying Facts

On a separate sheet of paper, write the words from the Word Bank to complete each sentence.

WORD BANK	
Bill Clinton	Million Man March
Boris Yeltsin	NAFTA
Bosnia-Herzegovina	Newt Gingrich
Brady Bill	Ross Perot
Commonwealth of Independent States	Saddam Hussein
Desert Storm	Strategic Arms Reduction Treaty
Haiti	Whitewater
Kuwait	

1) All but three of the Soviet republics formed the _____.

2) _____ was the President of Russia in 1994.

3) Iraq attacked _____ in 1990.

4) The American ground attack on Iraq was called Operation _____.

5) The _____ agreement reduced restrictions on trade among Canada, America, and Mexico.

6) The leader of Iraq during the Persian Gulf War was _____.

7) The _____ called for thirty percent fewer missile systems within seven years of the treaty.

8) The _____ focused on the responsibilities of African-American men.

9) _____ took office as President in 1993.

10) The _____ put more controls on guns in America.

11) _____ and the Republican Congress proposed the "Contract With America."

12) America sponsored a peace agreement to end fighting in _____ in 1995.

13) President Clinton sent troops to _____ to restore the Aristide government.

14) _____ was an independent candidate in the 1992 and 1996 presidential elections.

15) The _____ Affair involved accusations against the Clintons.

Comprehension: Understanding Main Ideas

On a separate sheet of paper, write the answer to each question using complete sentences.

1) What became of the Soviet Union?

2) What reforms did President Clinton attempt?

3) List two conflicts that America was involved with in the 1990s and explain what happened.

Critical Thinking: Write Your Opinion

1) What do you think should be done to stop terrorism in the United States?

2) If you were to organize a march in Washington, D.C., like the Million Man March, what would the focus of your march be? Why?

Test Taking Tip When taking a test with a short-answer section, first answer the questions you know. Then go back to spend time on the questions you are less sure of.

As U.S. citizens, we vote to elect leaders and decide certain issues. As voters, we can do several things to inform ourselves about different candidates and issues. We can read newspapers and listen to political debates on radio and TV. We can read articles about candidates in news magazines. We can become informed by reading flyers delivered to our door. We may attend political rallies at which candidates speak. We can get information from the political party of our choice. Studying a voting record on issues can show the positions of a candidate already holding office.

Qualified voters eighteen and older must first register at a city or county clerk's office. They also can register at the polls on election day. The polls are usually open from 7 A.M. to 8 P.M. Each voter is assigned a polling place in his or her district. The local newspaper usually tells people where to vote. Voters also can call the city or county clerk's office to learn their polling place. Voters who will be out of town on election day can request an absentee ballot in person or by mail. They can mark and turn in the absentee ballot ahead of the election.

At the polls, voters fill out a ballot. Election judges instruct voters on how to fill out the ballot. Different districts use various methods. Voters might have to mark Xs or complete arrows with a pen, punch holes, or pull a lever. To ensure privacy, voters make their selections in a private booth.

Election judges at each polling place count the votes at the end of election day. They deliver the count to the city or county clerk's office. Television, radio, and newspapers give election results. When all votes are counted, a winner is declared.

Before you can vote, you need to know several things. Find out the answer to these questions.

1) How long must I live in my state and district before I can vote?

2) Where do I register to vote?

3) How do I register to vote?

4) Where do I vote?

5) Where do I get an absentee ballot?

6) How do I decide who to vote for?

7) How do I fill out the ballot?

8) How are the votes counted?

9) Why do you think it is important to vote in elections?

10) Identify the day, month, and year when you can vote in a national election for the first time.

★ In July 1969, Neil Armstrong and Edwin Aldrin were the first people to land on the moon.

★ President Nixon resigned in 1974, and Gerald Ford became President.

★ America celebrated its 200th birthday in 1976.

★ Jimmy Carter became President in 1977. He signed the SALT II treaty with Leonid Brezhnev in 1979.

★ Ronald Reagan became President in 1981. He wanted to make people less dependent on the government.

★ Sandra Day O'Connor became the first female Supreme Court justice.

★ Reagan was re-elected in 1984.

★ In 1986, the space shuttle Challenger exploded.

★ Mikhail Gorbachev and Reagan signed the INF Treaty in 1987.

★ In October 1983, a terrorist attack killed 200 U.S. marines in Lebanon.

★ Libya made terrorist attacks in 1985 and 1986. U.S. planes bombed Libyan military posts.

★ The space program resumed in September 1988.

★ George Bush became President in 1989. A growing budget deficit, crime, drug abuse, and homeless people were problems he faced.

★ East and West Germany were reunified in 1990.

★ In 1990, Iraq invaded Kuwait. In 1991, U.S. and U.N. forces freed Kuwait and caused severe Iraqi casualties.

★ Communism fell in the Soviet Union in 1991. All but three of the former republics formed the Commonwealth of Independent States by 1995.

★ William Clinton became President in 1993. He signed the NAFTA agreement in 1993 to open trade with Canada and Mexico.

★ America improved relations with Russia and other countries. It worked with Israeli and Arab leaders to form a peace agreement. Peacekeeping troops went to Somalia, Bosnia-Herzegovina, and Haiti.

★ Investigation of the Clintons began in 1993 for the Whitewater Affair.

★ In 1994, Republicans gained control of Congress and formed a plan to balance the federal budget by 2002.

★ Health care reform and minimum wage bills were passed in 1995.

★ In 1995, the Million Man March in Washington, D.C., focused on African-American men's responsibilities to family and community.

★ Clinton was re-elected in 1996.

Appendices

United States History cover:

Items on the cover of this textbook are (clockwise from lower left) baseball glove, lightbulb, paper money, Susan B. Anthony dollar, bicentennial silver dollar, corn, arrowheads, Acoma Indians bowls, American flag, harmonica, sheet music, United States Constitution, Declaration of Independence, glasses, key, inkwell, spur, wheat, pocket watch, iron, campaign buttons, Purple Heart, U.S. Army pin, horseshoe, tin powder horn for gunpowder.

Appendices

Appendix A
The Declaration of Independence 670

Appendix B
The Constitution of the United States 678

Appendix C
Amendments to the Constitution 701

Appendix D
Presidents of the United States 718

Appendix E
The Fifty United States 725

Appendix F
World Atlas 738

Glossary 750

Index 768

The Declaration of Independence

La Declaración de Independencia

Adopted in Congress July 4, 1776
The Unanimous Declaration of the
Thirteen United States of America

En el Congreso, 4 de Julio de 1776
Declaración Unánime de los Trece
Estados Unidos de América

When, in the course of human events, it becomes necessary for one people to dissolve the political bands which have connected them with another, and to assume among the powers of the earth, the separate and equal station to which the laws of nature and of nature's God entitle them, a decent respect to the opinions of mankind requires that they should declare the causes which impel them to the separation.

Cuando, en el curso de los acontecimientos humanos, se hace necesario para un pueblo disolver las ligas políticas que lo han unido con otro, y asumir, entre las potencias de la tierra, un sitio separado e igual, al cual tiene derecho según las leyes de la naturaleza y el Dios de la naturaleza; el respeto debido a las opiniones del género humano exige que se declaren las causas que obligan a ese pueblo a la separación.

We hold these truths to be self-evident, that all men are created equal, that they are endowed by their Creator with certain unalienable rights, that among these are life, liberty, and the pursuit of happiness. That to secure these rights, governments are instituted among men, deriving their just powers from the consent of the governed. That whenever any form of government becomes destructive of these ends, it is the right of the people to alter or to abolish it, and to institute new government, laying its foundation on such principles and organizing its powers in such form, as to them shall seem most

Sostenemos como verdades evidentes que todos los hombres nacen iguales, que están dotados por su Creador de ciertos derechos inalienables, entre los cuales se cuentan el derecho a la vida, a la libertad y al alcance de la felicidad; que, para asegurar estos derechos, los hombres instituyen gobiernos, derivando sus justos poderes del consentimiento de los gobernados; que cuando una forma de gobierno llega a ser destructora de estos fines, es un derecho del pueblo cambiarla o abolirla, e instituir un nuevo gobierno, basado en esos principios y

likely to effect their safety and happiness. Prudence, indeed, will dictate that governments long established should not be changed for light and transient causes; and accordingly all experience hath shown that mankind are more disposed to suffer, while evils are sufferable, than to right themselves by abolishing the forms to which they are accustomed. But when a long train of abuses and usurpations, pursuing invariably the same object evinces a design to reduce them under absolute despotism, it is their right, it is their duty, to throw off such government, and to provide new guards for their future security.

Such has been the patient sufferance of these colonies; and such is now the necessity which constrains them to alter their former systems of govern-ment. The history of the present King of Great Britain is a history of repeated injuries and usurpations, all having in direct object the establishment of an absolute tyranny over these states. To prove this, let facts be submitted to a candid world.

He has refused his assent to laws, the most wholesome and necessary for the public good.

organizando su autoridad en la forma que el pueblo estime como la más conveniente para obtener su seguridad y su felicidad. En realidad, la prudencia aconsejará que los gobiernos erigidos mucho tiempo atrás no sean cambiados por causas ligeras y transitorias; en efecto, la experiencia ha demostrado que la humanidad está más bien dispuesta a sufrir, mientras los males sean tolerables, que a hacerse justicia aboliendo las formas de gobierno a las cuales se halla acostumbrada. Pero cuando una larga cadena de abusos y usurpaciones, que persiguen invariable-mente el mismo objetivo, hace patente la intención de reducir al pueblo a un despotismo absoluto, es derecho del hombre, es su obligación, arrojar a ese gobierno y procurarse nuevos guardianes para su seguridad futura.

Tal ha sido el paciente sufrimiento de estas colonias; tal es ahora la necesidad que las obliga a cambiar sus antiguos sistemas de gobierno. La historia del actual Rey de la Gran Bretaña es una historia de agravios y usurpaciones repetidas, que tienen como mira directa la de establecer una tiranía absoluta en estos estados. Para demos-trar lo anterior, presentamos los siguientes hechos ante un mundo que no los conoce:

El Rey se ha negado a aprobar las leyes más favorables y necesarias para el bienestar público.

He has forbidden his governors to pass laws of immediate and pressing importance, unless suspended in their operation till his assent should be obtained; and when so suspended, he has utterly neglected to attend to them.

He has refused to pass other laws for the accommodation of large districts of people, unless those people would relinquish the right of representation in the legislature, a right inestimable to them and formidable to tyrants only.

He has called together legislative bodies at places unusual, uncomfortable, and distant from the depository of their public records, for the sole purpose of fatiguing them into compliance with his measures.

He has dissolved representative houses repeatedly, for opposing with manly firmness his invasions on the rights of the people.

He has refused for a long time, after such dissolutions, to cause others to be elected; whereby the legislative powers, incapable of annihilation, have returned to the people at large for their exercise; the state remaining in the mean time exposed to all the dangers of invasion from without, and convulsions within.

He has endeavored to prevent the population of these states; for that purpose obstructing the laws for

Ha prohibido a sus gobernadores sancionar leyes de importancia immediata y apremiante, a menos que su ejecución se suspenda hasta obtener su asentimiento; y, una vez suspendidas, se ha negado por completo a prestarles atención.

Se ha rehusado a aprobar otras leyes convenientes a grandes comarcas pobladas, a menos que esos pueblos renuncien al derecho de ser representados en la legislatura; derecho que es inestimable para el pueblo y terrible sólo para los tiranos.

Ha convocado a los cuerpos legislativos en sitios desusados, incómodos y distantes del asiento de sus documentos públicos, con la sola idea de fatigarlos para cumplir con sus medidas.

En repetidas ocasiones ha disuelto las cámaras de representantes, por oponerse con firmeza viril a sus intromisiones en los derechos del pueblo.

Durante mucho tiempo, y después de esas disoluciones, se ha negado a permitir la elección de otras cámaras; por lo cual, los poderes legislativos, cuyo aniquilamiento es imposible, han retornado al pueblo, sin limitación para su ejercicio; permaneciendo el Estado, mientras tanto, expuesto a todos los peligros de una invasión exterior y a convulsiones internas.

Ha tratado de impedir que se pueblen estos estados; dificultando, con ese propósito las leyes de naturalización

naturalization of foreigners; refusing to pass others to encourage their migrations hither, and raising the conditions of new appropriations of lands.

He has obstructed the administration of justice, by refusing his assent to laws for establishing judiciary powers.

He has made judges dependent on his will alone, for the tenure of their offices, and the amount and payment of their salaries.

He has erected a multitude of new offices, and sent hither swarms of officers to harass our people, and eat out their substance.

He has kept among us, in times of peace, standing armies without the consent of our legislatures.

He has affected to render the military independent of and superior to the civil power.

He has combined with others to subject us to a jurisdiction foreign to our constitution, and unacknowledged by our laws; giving his assent to their acts of pretended legislation:

For quartering large bodies of armed troops among us:

For protecting them, by a mock trial, from punishment for any murders which they should commit on the inhabitants of these states:

de extranjeros; rehusando a aprobar otras para fomentar su immigración y elevando las condiciones para las nuevas adquisiciones de tierras.

Ha entorpecido la administración de justicia al no aprobar las leyes que establecen los poderes judiciales.

Ha hecho que los jueces dependan solamente de su voluntad, para poder desempeñar sus cargos y en cuanto a la cantidad y pago de sus emolumentos.

Ha fundado una gran diversidad de oficinas nuevas, enviando a un enjambre de funcionarios que acosan a nuestro pueblo y menguan su sustento.

En tiempo de paz, ha mantenido entre nosotros ejércitos permanentes, sin el consentimiento de nuestras legislaturas.

Ha influido para que la autoridad militar sea independiente de la civil y superior a ella.

Se ha asociado con otros para someternos a una jurisdicción extraña a nuestra constitución y no reconocida por nuestras leyes; aprobando sus actos de pretendida legislación:

Para acuartelar, entre nosotros, grandes cuerpos de tropas armadas:

Para protegerlos, por medio de un juicio ficticio, del castigo por los asesinatos que pudieren cometer entre los habitantes de estos estados:

For cutting off our trade with all parts of the world:

For imposing taxes on us without our consent:

For depriving us in many cases, of the benefits of trial by jury:

For transporting us beyond seas to be tried for pretended offenses:

For abolishing the free system of English laws in a neighboring province, establishing therein an arbitrary government, and enlarging its boundaries so as to render it at once an example and fit instrument for introducing the same absolute rule into these colonies:

For taking away our charters, abolishing our most valuable laws, and altering fundamentally the forms of our governments:

For suspending our own legislatures, and declaring themselves invested with power to legislate for us in all cases whatsoever.

He has abdicated government here, by declaring us out of his protection and waging war against us.

He has plundered our seas, ravaged our coasts, burned our towns, and destroyed the lives of our people.

Para suspender nuestro comercio con todas las partes del mundo:

Para imponernos impuestos sin nuestro consentimiento:

Para privarnos, en muchos casos, de los beneficios de un juicio por jurado:

Para transportarnos más allá de los mares, con el fin de ser juzgados por supuestos agravios:

Para abolir en una provincia vecina el libre sistema de las leyes inglesas, estableciendo en ella un gobierno arbitrario y extendiendo sus límites, con el objeto de dar un ejemplo y disponer de un instrumento adecuado para introducir el mismo gobierno absoluto en estas colonias:

Para suprimir nuestras cartas constitutivas, abolir nuestras leyes más valiosas y alterar en su esencia las formas de nuestros gobiernos:

Para suspender nuestras propias legislaturas y delcararse investido con facultades para legislarnos en todos los casos, cualesquiera que éstos sean.

Ha abdicado de su gobierno en estos territorios al declarar que estamos fuera de su protección y al emprender una guerra contra nosotros.

Ha saqueado nuestros mares, asolado nuestras costas, incendiado nuestras ciudades y destruido la vida de nuestro pueblo.

He is at this time transporting large armies of foreign mercenaries to complete the works of death, desolation and tyranny, already begun with circumstances of cruelty and perfidy scarcely paralleled in the most barbarous ages, and totally unworthy the head of a civilized nation.

He has constrained our fellow citizens taken captive on the high seas to bear arms against their country, to become the executioners of their friends and brethren, or to fall themselves by their hands.

He has excited domestic insurrections amongst us, and has endeavored to bring on the inhabitants of our frontiers, the merciless Indian savages, whose known rule of warfare, is an undistinguished destruction of all ages, sexes, and conditions.

In every stage of these oppressions we have petitioned for redress in the most humble terms: our repeated petitions have been answered only by repeated injury. A prince, whose character is thus marked by every act which may define a tyrant, is unfit to be the ruler of a free people.

Nor have we been wanting in attentions to our British brethren. We have warned them from time to time of attempts by their legislature to extend

Al presente, está transportando grandes ejércitos de extranjeros mercenarios para completar la obra de muerte, desolación y tirania, ya iniciada en circunstancias de crueldad y perfidia que apenas se encuentran paralelo en las épocas más bárbaras, y por completo indignas del jefe de una nación civilizada.

Ha obligado a nuestros conciudadanos, aprehendidos en alta mar, a que tomen armas contra su país, convirtiéndolos así en los verdugos de sus amigos y hermanos, o a morir bajo sus manos.

Ha provocado insurrecciones intestinas entre nosotros y se ha esforzado por lanzar sobre los habitantes de nuestras fronteras a los imisericordes indios salvajes, cuya conocida disposición para la guerra se distingue por la destrucción de vidas, sin considerar edades, sexos ni condiciones.

En todas las fases de estos abusos, hemos pedido una reparación en los términos más humildes; nuestras súplicas constantes han sido contestadas solamente con ofensas repetidas. Un princípe, cuyo carácter está marcado, en consecuencia, por todas las acciones que definen a un tirano, no es el adecuado para gobernar a un pueblo libre.

Tampoco hemos incurrido en faltas de atención con nuestros hermanos británicos. Los hemos enterado, oportunamente, de los esfuerzos de

an unwarrantable jurisdiction over us. We have reminded them of the circumstances of our emigration and settlement here. We have appealed to their native justice and magnanimity, and we have conjured them by the ties of our common kindred to disavow these usurpations, which would inevitably interrupt our connections and correspondence. They too have been deaf to the voice of justice and of consanguinity. We must, therefore, acquiesce in the necessity, which denounces our separation, and hold them, as we hold the rest of mankind, enemies in war, in peace friends.

We, therefore, the representatives of the United States of America, in General Congress, assembled, appealing to the Supreme Judge of the world for the rectitude of our intentions, do, in the name, and by authority of the good people of these colonies, solemnly publish and declare, that these united colonies are, and of right ought to be free and independent states; that they are absolved from all allegiance to the British Crown, and that all political connection between them and the state of Great Britain, is and ought to be totally dissolved; and that as free and independent states, they have full power to levy war, conclude peace, contract alliances, establish commerce, and to do all other acts and things which independent states may of right

su legislatura para extender una autoridad injustificable sobre nosotros. Les hemos recordado las circunstancias de nuestra emigración y colonización en estos territorios. Hemos apelado a su justicia y magnanimidad naturales, y los hemos conjurado, por los lazos de nuestra común ascendencia, a que repudien esas usurpaciones, las cuales, inevitablemente, llegarán a interrumpir nuestros nexos y correspondencia. Ellos también se han mostrado sordos a la voz de la justicia y de la consanguinidad. Por tanto, aceptamos la necesidad que proclama nuestra separación, y en adelante los consideramos como al resto de la humanidad: enemigos en la guerra, amigos en la paz.

En consecuencia, nosotros, los representantes de los Estados Unidos de América, reunidos en Congreso General, y apelando al Juez Supremo del Mundo en cuanto a la rectitud de nuestras intenciones, en el nombre, y por la autoridad del buen pueblo de estas colonias, solemnemente publicamos y declaramos, que estas colonias unidas son, y de derecho deben ser, estados libres e independientes; que se hallan exentos de toda fidelidad a la Corona Británica, y que todos los lazos políticos entre ellos y el Estado de la Gran Bretaña son y deben ser totalmente disueltos; y que, como estados libres e independientes, tienen poderes suficientes para declarar la guerra, concertar la paz, celebrar alianzas, establecer el comercio y para efectuar

do. And for the support of this declaration, with a firm reliance on the protection of Divine Providence, we mutually pledge to each other our lives, our fortunes, and our sacred honor.

Signed by John Hancock of Massachusetts as President of the Congress and by the fifty-five other Representatives of the thirteen United States of America:

todos aquellos actos y cosas que los estados independientes pueden, por su derecho, llevar a cabo. Y, en apoyo de esta declaración, confiando firmemente en la protección de la Divina Providencia, comprometemos mutuamente nuestras vidas, nuestros bienes, y nuestro honor sacrosanto.

New Hampshire (Nueva Hampshire)
Josiah Bartlett
William Whipple
Matthew Thornton

Connecticut
Roger Sherman
Samuel Huntington
William Williams
Oliver Wolcott

Massachusetts Bay
Samuel Adams
John Adams
Robert Treat Paine
Elbridge Gerry

Rhode Island
Stephen Hopkins
William Ellery

Pennsylvania (Pensilvania)
Robert Morris
Benjamin Rush
Benjamin Franklin
John Morton
George Clymer
James Smith

George Taylor
James Wilson
George Ross

Delaware
Caesar Rodney
George Read
Thomas M'Kean

New York (Nueva York)
William Floyd
Philip Livingston
Francis Lewis
Lewis Morris

Virginia
George Wythe
Richard Henry Lee
Thomas Jefferson
Benjamin Harrison
Thomas Nelson, Jr.
Francis Lightfoot Lee
Carter Braxton

North Carolina (Carolina del Norte)
William Hooper
Joseph Hewes
John Penn

South Carolina (Carolina del Sur)
Edward Rutledge
Thomas Heyward, Jr.
Thomas Lynch, Jr.
Arthur Middleton

Georgia
Button Gwinnett
Lyman Hall
George Walton

Maryland
Samuel Chase
William Paca
Thomas Stone
Charles Carroll of Carrollton

New Jersey (Nueva Jersey)
Richard Stockton
John Witherspoon
Francis Hopkinson
John Hart
Abraham Clark

The Constitution of the United States

Constitución de Los Estados Unidos

Preamble

We the people of the United States, in order to form a more perfect Union, establish justice, insure domestic tranquility, provide for the common defense, promote the general welfare, and secure the blessings of liberty to ourselves and our posterity, do ordain and establish this Constitution for the United States of America.

Article I
The Legislative Branch*

Congress

Section 1 All legislative powers herein granted shall be vested in a Congress of the United States, which shall consist of a Senate and House of Representatives.

The House of Representatives

Section 2 (1) The House of Representatives shall be composed of members chosen every second year by the people of the several states, and the electors in each state shall have the qualifications requisite for electors of the most numerous branch of the state legislature.

(2) No person shall be a representative who shall not have attained to the age

Preámbulo

Nosotros, el pueblo de los Estados Unidos, a fin de formar una Unión más perfecta, establecer la justicia, garantizar la tranquilidad nacional, atender a la defensa común, fomentar el bienestar general y asegurar los beneficios de la libertad para nosotros y para nuestra posteridad, por la presente promulgamos y establecemos esta Constitución para los Estados Unidos de América.

Artículo I

Sección 1 Todos los poderes legislativos otorgados por esta Constitución residirán en un Congreso de los Estados Unidos que se compondrá de un Senado y de una Cámara de Representantes.

Sección 2 (1) La Cámara de Representantes se compondrá de miembros elegidos cada dos años por el pueblo de los distintos estados y los electores en cada estado cumplirán con los requisitos exigidos a los electores de la cámara más numerosa de la asamblea legislativa de dicho estado.

* Headings and paragraph numbers have been added to help the reader. The original Constitution has only the article and section numbers.

of twenty-five years, and been seven years a citizen of the United States, and who shall not, when elected, be an inhabitant of that state in which he shall be chosen.

(3) Representatives and direct taxes shall be apportioned among the several states which may be included within this Union, according to their respective numbers, [which shall be determined by adding to the whole number of free persons, including those bound to service for a term of years, and excluding Indians not taxed, three-fifths of all other persons]. The actual enumeration shall be made within three years after the first meeting of the Congress of the United States, and within every subsequent term of ten years, in such manner as they shall by law direct. The number of representatives shall not exceed one for every thirty thousand, but each state shall have at least one representative; [and until such enumeration shall be made, the state of New Hampshire shall be entitled to choose 3, Massachusetts 8, Rhode Island and Providence Plantations 1, Connecticut 5, New York 6, New Jersey 4, Pennsylvania 8, Delaware 1, Maryland 6, Virginia 10, North Carolina 5, South Carolina 5, and Georgia 3].

(4) When vacancies happen in the representation from any state, the executive authority thereof shall issue writs of election to fill such vacancies.

(2) No podrá ser representante ninguna persona que no haya cumplido veinticinco años de edad, que no haya sido durante siete años ciudadano de los Estados Unidos y que al tiempo de su elección no resida en el estado que ha de elegirlo.

(3) Tanto los representantes como las contribuciones directas se prorratearán entre los diversos estados que integren esta Unión, en relación al número respectivo de sus habitantes, el cual se determinará añadiendo al número total de personas libres, en el que se incluye a las que estén obligadas al servicio por determinado número de años y se excluye a los indios que no paguen contribuciones, las tres quintas partes de todas las demás. Se efectuará el censo dentro de los tres años siguientes a la primera reunión del Congreso de los Estados Unidos, y en lo sucesivo cada diez años, en la forma en que éste lo dispusiere por ley. No habrá más de un representante por cada treinta mil habitantes, pero cada estado tendrá por lo menos un representante. En tanto se realiza el censo, el estado de Nueva Hampshire tendrá derecho a elegir tres representantes; Massachusetts, ocho; Rhode Island y las Plantaciones de Providence, uno; Connecticut, cinco; Nueva Jersey, cuatro; Pensilvania, ocho; Delaware, uno; Maryland, seis; Virginia, diez; Carolina del Norte, cinco; Carolina del Sur, cinco, y Georgia, tres.

(5) The House of Representatives shall choose their speaker and other officers; and shall have the sole power of impeachment.

The Senate

Section 3 (1) The Senate of the United States shall be composed of two senators from each state, [chosen by the legislature thereof,] for six years; and each senator shall have one vote.

(2) Immediately after they shall be assembled in consequence of the first election, they shall be divided as equally as may be into three classes. The seats of the senators of the first class shall be vacated at the expiration of the second year, of the second class at the expiration of the fourth year, and of the third class at the expiration of the sixth year, so that one-third may be chosen every second year; [and if vacancies happen by resignation, or otherwise, during the recess of the legislature of any state, the executive thereof may make temporary appointments until the next meeting of the legislature, which shall then fill such vacancies].

(3) No person shall be a senator who shall not have attained to the age of thirty years, and been nine years a citizen of the United States, and who shall not, when elected, be an inhabitant of that state for which he shall be chosen.

(4) Cuando ocurrieren vacancias en la representación de cualquier estado, la autoridad ejecutiva de éste ordenará celebración de elecciones para cubrirlas.

(5) La Cámara de Representantes elegirá su presidente y demás funcionarios y sólo ella tendrá la facultad de iniciar procedimientos de residencia.

Sección 3 (1) El Senado de los Estados Unidos se compondrá de dos senadores por cada estado, elegidos por sus respectivas asambleas legislativas por el término de seis años. Cada senador tendrá derecho a un voto.

(2) Tan pronto como se reúnan en virtud de la primera elección, se les dividirá en tres grupos los más iguales posible. El término de los senadores del primer grupo expirará al finalizar el segundo año; el del segundo grupo al finalizar el cuarto año y el del tercer grupo al finalizar el sexto año, de forma que cada dos años se renueve una tercera parte de sus miembros. Si ocurrieren vacancias, por renuncia o por cualquier otra causa, mientras esté en receso la Asamblea Legislativa del estado respectivo, la autoridad ejecutiva del mismo podrá hacer nombramientos provisionales hasta la próxima sesión de la asamblea legislativa, la que entonces cubrirá tales vacancias.

(3) No podrá ser senador quien no haya cumplido treinta años de edad, no haya sido durante nueve años ciudadano de los Estados Unidos y

(4) The Vice President of the United States shall be president of the Senate, but shall have no vote, unless they be equally divided.

(5) The Senate shall choose their other officers, and also a president pro tempore, in the absence of the Vice President, or when he shall exercise the office of President of the United States.

(6) The Senate shall have the sole power to try all impeachments. When sitting for that purpose, they shall be on oath or affirmation. When the President of the United States is tried, the Chief Justice shall preside: and no person shall be convicted without the concurrence of two-thirds of the members present.

(7) Judgment in cases of impeachment shall not extend further than to removal from office, and disqualification to hold and enjoy any office of honor, trust, or profit under the United States: but the party convicted shall nevertheless be liable and subject to indictment, trial, judgment, and punishment, according to law.

Organization of Congress
Section 4 (1) The times, places, and manner of holding elections for senators and representatives, shall be prescribed in each state by the legislature thereof; but the Congress may at any time by law make or alter such regulations, [except as to the places of choosing senators].

no resida, en la época de su elección, en el estado que ha de elegirlo.

(4) El Vicepresidente de los Estados Unidos será presidente del Senado, pero no tendrá voto excepto en caso de empate.

(5) El Senado eligirá sus demás funcionarios así como también un presidente pro témpore en ausencia del Vicepresidente o cuando éste desempeñare el cargo de Presidente de los Estados Unidos.

(6) Tan sólo el Senado podrá conocer de procedimientos de residencia. Cuando se reúna para este fin, los senadores prestarán juramento o harán promesa de cumplir fielmente su cometido. Si se residenciare al Presidente de los Estados Unidos, presidirá la sesión el Juez Presidente del Tribunal Supremo. Nadie será convicto sin que concurran las dos terceras partes de los senadores presentes.

(7) La sentencia en procedimientos de residencia no podrá exceder de la destitución del cargo e inhabilitación para obtener y desempeñar ningún cargo de honor, de confianza o de retribución en el gobierno de los Estados Unidos; pero el funcionario convicto quedará, no obstante, sujeto a ser acusado, juzgado, sentenciado y castigado con arreglo a derecho.

Sección 4 (1) La asamblea legislativa de cada estado determinará la fecha, lugar y modo de celebrar las elecciones de senadores y representantes; pero el

(2) The Congress shall assemble at least once in every year, [and such meeting shall be on the first Monday in December,] unless they shall by law appoint a different day.

Rules and Procedures

Section 5 (1) Each house shall be the judge of the elections, returns and qualifications of its own members, and a majority of each shall constitute a quorum to do business; but a smaller number may adjourn from day to day, and may be authorized to compel the attendance of absent members, in such manner, and under such penalties as each house may provide.

(2) Each house may determine the rules of its proceedings, punish its members for disorderly behavior, and, with the concurrence of two-thirds, expel a member.

(3) Each house shall keep a journal of its proceedings, and from time to time publish the same, excepting such parts as may in their judgment require secrecy; and the yeas and nays of the members of either house on any question shall, at the desire of one-fifth of those present, be entered on the journal.

(4) Neither house, during the session of Congress, shall, without the consent of the other, adjourn for more than three days, nor to any other place than that in which the two houses shall be sitting.

Congreso podrá en cualquier momento mediante legislación adecuada aprobar o modificar tales disposiciones, salvo en relación al lugar donde se habrá de elegir a los senadores.

(2) El Congreso se reunirá por lo meños una vez al año y tal sesión comenzará el primer lunes de diciembre, a no ser que por ley se fije otro día.

Sección 5 (1) Cada cámara será el único juez del las elecciones, resultado de las mismas y capacidad de sus propios miembros; y la mayoría de cada una de ellas constituirá un quorum para realizar sus trabajos; pero un número menor podrá recesar de día en día y estará autorizado para compeler la asistencia de los miembros ausentes, en la forma y bajo las penalidades que cada cámara determinare.

(2) Cada cámara adoptará su reglamento, podrá castigar a sus miembros por conducta impropia y expulsarlos con el voto de dos terceras partes.

(3) Cada cámara tendrá un diario de sesiones, que publicará periódicamente, con excepción de aquello que, a su juicio, deba mantenerse en secreto; y siempre que así lo pidiere la quinta parte de los miembros presentes, se harán constar en dicho diario los votos afirmativos y negativos de los miembros de una u otra cámara sobre cualquier asunto.

(4) Mientas el Congreso estuviere reunido, ninguna cámara podrá, sin el consentimiento de la otra, levantar sus

Payment and Privileges

Section 6 (1) The senators and representatives shall receive a compensation for their services, to be ascertained by law, and paid out of the treasury of the United States. They shall in all cases, except treason, felony, and breach of the peace, be privileged from arrest during their attendance at the session of their respective houses, and in going to and returning from the same; and for any speech or debate in either house, they shall not be questioned in any other place.

(2) No senator or representative shall, during the time for which he was elected, be appointed to any civil office under the authority of the United States, which shall have been created, or the emoluments whereof shall have been increased during such time; and no person holding any office under the United States, shall be a member of either house during his continuance in office.

How a Bill Becomes a Law

Section 7 (1) All bills for raising revenue shall originate in the House of Representatives; but the Senate may propose or concur with amendments as on other bills.

(2) Every bill which shall have passed the House of Representatives and the Senate, shall, before it becomes a law, be presented to the President of the United States; if he approve he shall sign it, but if not he shall return it,

sesiones por más de tres días ni reunirse en otro lugar que no sea aquel en que las dos estén instaladas.

Sección 6 (1) Los senadores y representantes recibirán por sus servicios una remuneración fijada por ley y pagadera por el Tesoro de los Estados Unidos. Mientras asistan a las sesiones de sus respectivas cámaras, así como mientras se dirijan a ellas o regresen de las mismas, no podrán ser arrestados, excepto en casos de traición, delito grave o alteración de la paz. Tampoco podrán ser reconvenidos fuera de la cámara por ninguno de sus discursos o por sus manifestaciones en cualquier debate en ella.

(2) Ningún senador o representante, mientras dure el término por el cual fue elegido, será nombrado para ningún cargo civil bajo la autoridad de los Estados Unidos, que hubiere sido creado o cuyos emolumentos hubieren sido aumentados durante tal término; y nadie que desempeñe un cargo bajo la autoridad de los Estados Unidos podrá ser miembro de ninguna de las cámaras mientras ocupe tal cargo.

Sección 7 (1) Todo proyecto de ley para imponer contribuciones se originará en la Cámara de Representantes; pero el Senado podrá proponer enmiendas o concurrir en ellas como en los demás proyectos.

(2) Todo proyecto que hubiere sido aprobado por la Cámara de

with his objections to that house in which it shall have originated, who shall enter the objections at large on their journal, and proceed to reconsider it. If after such reconsideration two-thirds of that house shall agree to pass the bill, it shall be sent, together with the objections, to the other house, by which it shall likewise be reconsidered, and if approved by two-thirds of that house, it shall become a law. But in all such cases the votes of both houses shall be determined by yeas and nays, and the names of the persons voting for and against the bill shall be entered on the journal of each house, respectively. If any bill shall not be returned by the President within ten days (Sundays excepted) after it shall have been presented to him, the same shall be a law, in like manner as if he had signed it, unless the Congress by their adjournment prevent its return, in which case it shall not be a law.

(3) Every order, resolution, or vote to which the concurrence of the Senate and House of Representatives may be necessary (except on a question of adjournment) shall be presented to the President of the United States; and before the same shall take effect, shall be approved by him, or being disapproved by him, shall be repassed by two-thirds of the Senate and House of Representatives, according to the rules and limitations prescribed in the case of a bill.

Representantes y Senado será sometido al Presidente de los Estados Unidos antes de que se convierta en ley. Si el Presidente lo aprueba, lo firmará. De lo contario, lo devolverá con sus objeciones a la cámara en donde se originó el proyecto, la que insertará en su diario las objeciones integramente y rocederá a reconsideralo. Si despúes de tal reconsideración dos terceras partes de dicha cámara convinieren en aprobar el proyecto, éste se enviará, junto con las objeciones, a la otra cámara, la que también lo reconsiderará y si resultare aprobado por las dos terceras partes de sus miembros, se convertirá en ley. En tales casos la votación en cada cámara será nominal y los votos en pro y en contra del proyecto así como los nombres de los votantes se consignarán en el diario de cada una de ellas. Si el Presidente no devolviere un proyecto de ley dentro de los diez días (excluyendo los domingos), después de haberle sido presentado, dicho proyecto se convertirá en ley, tal cual si lo hubiere firmado, a no ser que, por haber recesado, el Congreso impida su devolución. En tal caso el proyecto no se convertirá en ley.

(3) Toda orden, resolución o votación que requiera la concurrencia del Senado y de la Cámara de Representantes (salvo cuando se trate de levantar las sesiones) se presentará al Presidente de los Estados Unidos; y no tendrá efecto hasta que éste la apruebe o, en caso de ser desaprobada por él, hasta que

Powers Granted to Congress

Section 8 The Congress shall have power:

(1) To lay and collect taxes, duties, imposts, and excises, to pay the debts and provide for the common defense and general welfare of the United States; but all duties, imposts, and excises shall be uniform throughout the United States;

(2) To borrow money on the credit of the United States;

(3) To regulate commerce with foreign nations, and among the several states, and with the Indian tribes;

(4) To establish a uniform rule of naturalization, and uniform laws on the subject of bankruptcies throughout the United States;

(5) To coin money, regulate the value thereof, and of foreign coin, and fix the standard of weights and measures;

(6) To provide for the punishment of counterfeiting the securities and current coin of the United States;

(7) To establish post offices and post roads;

(8) To promote the progress of science and useful arts, by securing for limited times to authors and inventors the exclusive right to their respective writings and discoveries;

dos terceras partes del Senado y de la Cámara de Representantes la aprueben nuevamente, conforme a las reglas y restricciones prescritas para los proyectos de ley.

Sección 8 El Congreso tendrá facultad:

(1) para imponer y recaudar contribuciones, derechos, impuestos y arbitrios; para pagar las deudas y proveer para la defensa común y el bienestar general de los Estados Unidos; pero todos los derechos, impuestos y arbitrios serán uniformes en toda la nación;

(2) Para tomar dinero a préstamo con cargo al crédito de los Estados Unidos;

(3) Para reglamentar el comercio con naciones extranjeras, así como entre los estados y con las tribus indias;

(4) Para establecer una regla uniforme de naturalización y leyes uniformes de quiebras para toda la nación;

(5) Para acuñar moneda, reglamentar el valor de ésta y de la moneda extranjera, y fijar normas de pesas y medidas;

(6) Para fijar penas por la falsificación de los valores y de la moneda de los Estados Unidos;

(7) Para establecer oficinas de correo y vías postales;

(8) Para fomentar el progreso de la ciencia y de las artes útiles, garantizando por tiempo limitado a los autores e inventores el derecho exclusivo a sus respectivos escritos y descubrimientos;

(9) To constitute tribunals inferior to the Supreme Court;

(10) To define and punish piracies and felonies committed on the high seas, and offenses against the law of nations;

(11) To declare war, grant letters of marque and reprisal, and make rules concerning captures on land and water;

(12) To raise and support armies, but no appropriation of money to that use shall be for a longer term than two years;

(13) To provide and maintain a navy;

(14) To make rules for the government and regulation of the land and naval forces;

(15) To provide for calling forth the militia to execute the laws of the Union, suppress insurrections and repel invasions;

(16) To provide for organizing, arming, and disciplining, the militia, and for governing such part of them as may be employed in the service of the United States, reserving to the states respectively, the appointment of the officers, and the authority of training the militia according to the discipline prescribed by Congress;

(17) To exercise exclusive legislation in all cases whatsoever, over such district

(9) Para establecer tribunales inferiores al Tribunal Supremo;

(10) Para definir y castigar la piratería y los delitos graves cometidos en alta mar, así como las infracciones del derecho internacional;

(11) Para declarar la guerra, conceder patentes de corso y represalia y establecer reglas relativas a capturas en mar y tierra;

(12) Para reclutar y mantener ejércitos; pero ninguna asignación para este fin lo será por un período mayor de dos años;

(13) Para organizar y mantener una armada;

(14) Para establecer reglas para el gobierno y reglamentación de las fuerzas de mar y tierra;

(15) Para dictar reglas par llamar la milicia a fin de hacer cumplir las leyes de la Unión, sofocar insurrecciones y repeler invasiones;

(16) Para proveer para la organización, armamento y disciplina de la milicia y el gobierno de aquella parte de ella que estuviere al servicio de los Estados Unidos, reservando a los estados respectivos el nombramiento de los oficiales y la autoridad para adiestrar a la milicia de acuerdo con la disciplina prescrita por el Congreso;

(17) Para ejercer el derecho exclusivo a legislar en todas las materias

(not exceeding ten miles square) as may, by cession of particular states, and the acceptance of Congress, become the seat of the government of the United States, and to exercise like authority over all places purchased by the consent of the legislature of the state in which the same shall be, for the erection of forts, magazines, arsenals, dockyards, and other needful buildings; —And

(18) To make all laws which shall be necessary and proper for carrying into execution the foregoing powers, and all other powers vested by this Constitution in the government of the United States, or in any department or officer thereof.

Powers Denied Congress

Section 9 (1) The migration or importation of such persons as any of the states now existing shall think proper to admit, shall not be prohibited by the Congress prior to the year one thousand eight hundred and eight, but a tax or duty may be imposed on such importation, not exceeding ten dollars for each person.

(2) The privilege of the writ of habeas corpus shall not be suspended, unless when in cases of rebellion or invasion the public safety may require it.

(3) No bill of attainder or ex post facto law shall be passed.

concernientes a aquel distrito (cuya superficie no excederá de diez millas en cuadro) que, por cesión de algunos estados y aceptación del Congreso, se convirtiere en la sede del gobierno de los Estados Unidos; y para ejercer igual autoridad sobre todas aquellas tierras adquiridas con el consentimiento de la asamblea legislativa del estado en que radicaren, con el fin de construir fuertes, almacenes, arsenales, astilleros y otras edificaciones que fueren necesarias;

(18) Para aprobar todas las leyes que fueren necesarias y convenientes para poner en práctica las precedentes facultades, así como todas aquellas que en virtud de esta Constitución puedan estar investidas en el gobierno de los Estados Unidos o en cualquiera de sus departamentos o funcionarios.

Sección 9 (1) El Congreso no podrá antes del año 1808 prohibir la immigración de aquellas personas cuya admisión considere conveniente cualquiera de los estados existentes; pero se podrá imponer un tributo o impuesto al tal importación que no excederá de diez dólares por persona.

(2) No se suspenderá el privilegio del auto de hábeas corpus, salvo cuando en casos de rebelión o invasión la seguridad pública así lo exija.

(3) No se aprobará ningún proyecto para condenar sin celebración de juicio ni ninguna ley ex post facto.

(4) No capitation, [or other direct,] tax shall be laid, unless in proportion to the census or enumeration herein before directed to be taken.

(5) No tax or duty shall be laid on articles exported from any state.

(6) No preference shall be given by any regulation of commerce or revenue to the ports of one state over those of another: nor shall vessels bound to, or from, one state, be obliged to enter, clear, or pay duties in another.

(7) No money shall be drawn from the treasury, but in consequence of appropriations made by law; and a regular statement and account of the receipts and expenditures of all public money shall be published from time to time.

(8) No title of nobility shall be granted by the United States: And no person holding any office of profit or trust under them, shall, without the consent of the Congress, accept of any present, emolument, office, or title, of any kind whatever, from any king, prince, or foreign state.

Powers Denied the States
Section 10 (1) No state shall enter into any treaty, alliance, or confederation; grant letters of marque and reprisal; coin money; emit bills of credit; make anything but gold and silver coin a tender in payment of

(4) No se impondrá capitación u otra contribución directa, sino en proporción al censo o enumeración que esta Constitución ordena se lleve a efecto.

(5) No se impondrán contribuciones o impuestos sobre los artículos que se exporten de cualquier estado.

(6) No se dará preferencia, por ningún reglamento de comercio o de rentas internas, a los puertos de un estado sobre los de otro. Tampoco podrá obligarse a las embarcaciones que se dirijan a un estado o salgan de él, que entren, descarguen o paguen impuestos en otro.

(7) No se podrá retirar cantidad alguna del Tesoro sino a virtud de asignaciones hechas por ley; y periódicamente se publicará un estado completo de los ingresos y egresos públicos.

(8) Los Estados Unidos no concederán títulos de nobleza; y ninguna persona que desempeñe bajo la autoridad del Gobierno un cargo retribuído o de confianza podrá aceptar, sin el consentimiento del Congreso, donativo, emolumento, empleo o título, de clase alguna, de ningún rey, príncipe o nación extranjera.

Sección 10 (1) Ningún estado celebrará tratado, alianza o confederación alguna; concederá patentes de corso y represalia; acuñará moneda; emitirá cartas de crédito; autorizará el pago de deudas en otro numerario que no sea oro y plata; aprobará ningún proyecto para

debts; pass any bill of attainder, ex post facto law, or law impairing the obligation of contracts, or grant any title of nobility.

(2) No state shall, without the consent of the Congress, lay any imposts or duties on imports or exports, except what may be absolutely necessary for executing its inspection laws: and the net produce of all duties and imposts, laid by any state on imports or exports, shall be for the use of the treasury of the United States; and all such laws shall be subject to the revision and control of the Congress.

(3) No state shall, without the consent of Congress, lay any duty of tonnage, keep troops, or ships of war in time of peace, enter into any agreement or compact with another state, or with a foreign power, or engage in war, unless actually invaded, or in such imminent danger as will not admit of delay.

ARTICLE II
The Executive Branch

The President

Section 1 (1) The executive power shall be vested in a President of the United States of America. He shall hold his office during the term of four years, and, together with the Vice

condenar sin celebración de juicio, ley ex post facto o que menoscabe la obligación de los contratos, ni concederá títulos de nobleza.

(2) Ningún estado podrá, sin el consentimiento del Congreso, fijar impuestos o derechos sobre las importaciones o exportaciones, salvo cuando fuere absolutamente necesario para hacer cumplir sus leyes de inspección; y el producto neto de todos los derechos e impuestos que fijare cualquier estado sobre las importaciones o exportaciones, ingresará en el Tesoro de los Estados Unidos. Todas esas leyes quedarán sujetas a la revisión e intervención del Congreso.

(3) Ningún estado podrá, sin el consentimiento del Congreso, fijar derecho alguno de tonelaje, ni mantener tropas o embarcaciones de guerra en tiempos de paz, ni celebrar convenios o pactos con otro estado o con potencias extranjeras, ni entrar en guerra, a menos que fuere de hecho invadido o estuviere en peligro tan imminente que su defensa no admita demora.

Artículo II

Sección 1 (1) El poder ejecutivo residirá en el Presidente de los Estados Unidos de América. Este desempeñará sus funciones por un término de cuatro años y se le eligirá, junto con el Vicepresidente, quien también desempeñará su cargo por un término similar, de la siguiente manera;

President, chosen for the same term, be elected, as follows:

(2) Each state shall appoint, in such manner as the legislature thereof may direct, a number of electors, equal to the whole number of senators and representatives to which the state may be entitled in the Congress: but no senator or representative, or person holding an office of trust or profit under the United States, shall be appointed an elector.

[The electors shall meet in their respective states, and vote by ballot for two persons, of whom one at least shall not be an inhabitant of the same state with themselves. And they shall make a list of all the persons voted for, and of the number of votes for each; which list they shall sign and certify, and transmit sealed to the seat of the government of the United States, directed to the president of the Senate. The president of the Senate shall, in the presence of the Senate and House of Representatives, open all the certificates, and the votes shall then be counted. The person having the greatest number of votes shall be the President, if such number be a majority of the whole number of electors appointed; and if there be more than one who have such majority, and have an equal number of votes, then the House of Representatives shall immediately choose by ballot one of them for President; and if no person have a majority, then from the five highest on

(2) Cada estado designará, en la forma que prescribiere su asamblea legislativa, un número de compromisarios igual al número total de senadores y representantes que le corresponda en el Congreso, pero no será nombrado compromisario ningún senador o representante o persona alguna que ocupare un cargo de confianza o retribuído bajo la autoridad de los Estados Unidos.

Los compromisarios se reunirán en sus respectivos estados, y mediante votación secreta votarán por dos personas, de las cuales por lo menos una no será residente del mismo estado que ellos. Se hará una lista de todas las personas por quienes se hubiere votado así como del número de votos que cada una obtuviere. Los compromisarios firmarán y certificarán esta lista, y la remitirán sellada a la sede del gobierno de los Estados Unidos, dirigida al presidente del Senado. En presencia del Senado y de la Cámara de Representantes, el presidente del Senado abrirá todos los certificados y se procederá entonces a verificar el escrutinio. Será presidente la persona que obtuviere mayor número de votos si dicho número fuere la mayoría del número total de compromisarios designados. Si más de una persona obtuviere tal mayoría, entonces la Cámara elegirá en igual forma al Presidente de entre las cinco personas que hubieren obtenido más votos en la lista. Pero en la elección del Presidente, la votación será por

the list the said House shall in like manner choose the President. But in choosing the President, the votes shall be taken by states, the representation from each state having one vote; a quorum for this purpose shall consist of a member or members from two-thirds of the states, and a majority of all the states shall be necessary to a choice. In every case, after the choice of the President, the person having the greatest number of votes of the electors shall be the Vice President. But if there should remain two or more who have equal votes, the Senate shall choose from them by ballot the Vice President.]

(3) The Congress may determine the time of choosing the electors, and the day on which they shall give their votes; which day shall be the same throughout the United States.

(4) No person except a natural-born citizen, or a citizen of the United States at the time of the adoption of this Constitution, shall be eligible to the office of President; neither shall any person be eligible to that office who shall not have attained to the age of thirty-five years, and been fourteen years a resident within the United States.

(5) In case of the removal of the President from office, or of his death, resignation, or inability to discharge the powers and duties of the said office, the same shall devolve on the Vice President, and the Congress may by law

estados y la representación de cada estado tendrá derecho a un voto. Para este fin el quorum constará de uno o más miembros de las dos terceras partes de las representaciones de los estados, y para que haya elección será necesaria una mayoría de todos los estados. En cualquier caso, una vez elegido el Presidente, será Vicepresidente la persona que obtuviere el mayor número de votos de los compromisarios. Pero si hubiere dos o más con un número iqual de votos, el Senado, por votación secreta, elegirá entre ellas al Vicepresidente.

(3) El Congreso determinará la fecha de seleccionar los compromisarios y el día en que habrán de votar, que serán los mismos en toda la Nación.

(4) No será elegible para el cargo de Presidente quien no fuere ciudadano por nacimiento o ciudadano de los Estados Unidos al tiempo in que se adopte esta Constitución. Tampoco lo será quien no hubiere cumplido treinta y cinco años de edad y no hubiere residido catorce años en los Estados Unidos.

(5) En caso de destitución, muerte, renuncia o incapacidad del Presidente para desempeñar las funciones de su cargo, le sustituirá el Vicepresidente. En caso de destitución, muerte, renuncia o incapacidad tanto del Presidente como del Vicepresidente, el Congreso dispondrá mediante legislación quién desempeñará presidencia y tal

provide for the case of removal, death, or resignation or inability, both of the President and Vice President, declaring what officer shall then act as President, and such officer shall act accordingly, until the disability be removed, or a President shall be elected.

(6) The President shall, at stated times, receive for his services, a compensation, which shall neither be increased or diminished during the period for which he shall have been elected, and he shall not receive within that period any other emolument from the United States, or any of them.

(7) Before he enter on the execution of his office, he shall take the following oath or affirmation: —"I do solemnly swear (or affirm) that I will faithfully execute the office of President of the United States, and will to the best of my ability, preserve, protect, and defend the Constitution of the United States."

Powers of the President
Section 2 (1) The President shall be commander in chief of the Army and Navy of the United States, and of the militia of the several states, when called into the actual service of the United States; he may require the opinion, in writing, of the principal officer in each of the executive departments, upon any subject relating to the duties of their respective offices, and he shall have power to grant reprieves and pardons

funcionario ejercerá el cargo hasta que cese la incapacidad o se elija un nuevo presidente.

(6) Como remuneración por sus servicios el Presidente recibirá, en las fechas que se determinen, una compensación que no podrá ser aumentada ni disminuida durante el término para el cual se le eligió, y no reciberá durante dicho término ningún otro emolumento de los Estados Unidos ni de ninguno de los estados.

(7) Antes de comenzar a desempeñar su cargo, el Presidente prestará el siguiente juramento o promesa: "Juro (o prometo) solemnemente que desempeñaré fielmente el cargo de Presidente de los Estados Unidos y que de la mejor manera a mi alcance guardaré, protegeré y defenderé la Constitución de los Estados Unidos."

Sección 2 (1) El Presidente será jefe supremo del Ejército y de la Armada de los Estados Unidos, así como de la milicia de los distintos estados cuando ésta fuere llamada al servicio activo de la nación. Podrá exigir opinión por escrito al jefe de cada departamento ejecutivo sobre cualquier asunto que se relacione con los deberes de sus respectivos cargos y tendrá facultad para suspender la ejecución de sentencias y para conceder indultos por delitos contra los Estados Unidos, salvo en casos de residencia.

for offenses against the United States, except in cases of impeachment.

(2) He shall have power, by and with the advice and consent of the Senate, to make treaties, provided two-thirds of the senators present concur; and he shall nominate, and by and with the advice and consent of the Senate, shall appoint ambassadors, other public ministers and consuls, judges of the Supreme Court, and all other officers of the United States, whose appointments are not herein otherwise provided for, and which shall be established by law: but the Congress may by law vest the appointment of such inferior officers, as they think proper, in the President alone, in the courts of law, or in the heads of departments.

(3) The President shall have power to fill up all vacancies that may happen during the recess of the Senate, by granting commissions which shall expire at the end of their next session.

Duties of the President
Section 3 He shall from time to time give to the Congress information of the state of the Union, and recommend to their consideration such measures as he shall judge necessary and expedient; he may, on extraordinary occasions, convene both houses, or either of them, and in case of disagreement between them, with respect to the time of adjournment, he may adjourn them

(2) Con el consejo y consentimiento del Senado tendrá poder para celebrar tratados, siempre que en ellos concurran los dos terceras partes de los senadores presentes. Asimismo, con el consejo y consentimiento del Senado, nombrará embajadores, otros ministros y cónsules públicos, los jueces del Tribunal Supremo y todos los demás funcionarios de los Estados Unidos cuyos cargos se establezcan por ley y cuyos nombramientos esta Constitución no prescriba. Pero el Congreso podrá por ley, confiar el nombramiento de aquellos funcionarios subalternos que creyere prudente, al presidente únicamente, a los tribunales de justicia o a los jefes de departamento.

(3) El Presidente tendrá poder para cubrir todas las vacancias que ocurrieren durante el receso del Senado, extendiendo nombramientos que expirarán al finalizar la próxima sesión del Senado.

Sección 3 El Presidente informará periódicamente al Congreso sobre el estado de la Unión y le recomendará aquellas medidas que él estime necesarias y convenientes. Podrá, en ocasiones extraordinarias, convocar a ambas cámaras si no estuvieren de acuerdo con relación a la fecha para recesar, el Presidente podrá fijarla según lo juzgue conveniente. El Presidente recibirá a los embajadores y demás ministro públicos.

to such time as he shall think proper; he shall receive ambassadors and other public ministers; he shall take care that the laws be faithfully executed, and shall commission all the officers of the United States.

Impeachment

Section 4 The President, Vice President, and all civil officers of the United States, shall be removed from office on impeachment for, and conviction of, treason, bribery, or other high crimes and misdemeanors.

ARTICLE III
The Judicial Branch

Federal Courts and Judges

Section 1 The judicial power of the United States, shall be vested in one Supreme Court, and in such inferior courts as the Congress may from time to time ordain and establish. The judges, both of the Supreme and inferior courts, shall hold their offices during good behavior, and shall, at stated times, receive for their services, a compensation, which shall not be diminished during their continuance in office.

Jurisdiction of United States Courts

Section 2 (1) The judicial power shall extend to all cases, in law and equity, arising under this Constitution, the laws of the United States, and treaties made, or which shall be made, under their authority; — to all cases affecting ambassadors, other public ministers

Velará por el fiel cumplimiento de las leyes y extenderá los nombramientos de todos los funcionarios de los Estados Unidos.

Sección 4 El Presidente, el Vicepresidente y todos los funcionarios civiles de los Estados Unidos serán destituídos de sus cargos mediante procedimiento de residencia, previa acusación y convictos que fueren de traición, cohecho u otros delitos graves y menos graves.

Artículo III

Sección 1 El poder judicial de los Estados Unidos residirá en un Tribunal Supremo y en aquellos tribunales inferiores que periódicamente el Congreso creare y estableciere. Los jueces, tanto del Tribunal Supremo como de tribunales inferiores, desempeñarán sus cargos mientras observen buena conducta y en determinadas fechas recibirán por sus servicios una compensación que no será rebajada mientras desempeñen sus cargos.

Sección 2 (1) El poder judicial se extenderá a todo caso que en derecho y equidad surja de esta Constitución, de las leyes de los Estados Unidos, así como de los tratados celebrados o que se celebraren bajo su autoridad; a todas los casos que afecten a embajadores y otros ministros y cónsules públicos; a todos los casos de almirantazgo y jurisdicción marítima; a todas las controversias en que los Estados Unidos

and consuls; — to all cases of admiralty and maritime jurisdiction; — to controversies to which the United States shall be a party; — to controversies between two or more states; — [between a state and citizens of another state;] — between citizens of different states; — between citizens of the same state claiming lands under grants of different states, and between a state, or the citizens thereof, and foreign states, [citizens or subjects].

(2) In all cases affecting ambassadors, other public ministers and consuls, and those in which a state shall be party, the Supreme Court shall have original jurisdiction. In all the other cases before mentioned, the Supreme Court shall have appellate jurisdiction, both as to law and fact, with such exceptions, and under such regulations as the Congress shall make.

(3) The trial of all crimes, except in cases of impeachment, shall be by jury; and such trial shall be held in the state where the said crimes shall have been committed; but when not committed within any state, the trial shall be at such place or places as the Congress may by law have directed.

Treason

Section 3 (1) Treason against the United States, shall consist only in levying war against them, or in adhering to their enemies, giving them aid and comfort. No person shall be convicted of treason unless on the testimony of

sean parte; a las controversias entre dos o más estados; entre un estado y los ciudadanos de otro estado; entre los ciudadanos de diferentes estados; entre los ciudadanos del mismo estado que reclamaren tierras en virtud de concesiones hechas por diversos estados, y entre un estado o sus ciudadanos y estados, ciudadanos o súbditos extranjeros.

(2) El Tribunal Supremo tendrá jurisdicción original en todos los casos que afectaren a embajadores, ministros y cónsules públicos, y en aquellos en que un estado fuere parte. De todos los demás casos antes mencionados conocerá el Tribunal Supremo en apelación, tanto sobre cuestiones de derecho como de hecho, con las excepciones y bajo la reglamentación que el Congreso estableciere.

(3) Se juzgarán ante jurado todas las causas criminales, excepto las que den lugar al procedimiento de residencia; y el juicio se celebrará en el estado en que se cometió el delito. Si no se cometiere en ningún estado, se celebrará el juicio en el sitio o en los sitios que el Congreso designare por ley.

Sección 3 (1) El delito de traición contra los Estados Unidos consistirá solamente en tomar las armas contra ellos o en unirse a sus enemigos, dándoles ayuda y facilidades. Nadie será convicto de traición sino por el testimonio de dos testigos del hecho

two witnesses to the same overt act, or on confession in open court.

(2) The Congress shall have power to declare the punishment of treason, but no attainder of treason shall work corruption of blood, or forfeiture except during the life of the person attainted.

ARTICLE IV
The States and the Federal Government

State Acts and Records
Section 1 Full faith and credit shall be given in each state to the public acts, records, and judicial proceedings of every other state. And the Congress may by general laws prescribe the manner in which such acts, records, and proceedings shall be proved, and the effect thereof.

Rights of Citizens
Section 2 (1) The citizens of each state shall be entitled to all privileges and immunities of citizens in the several states.

(2) A person charged in any state with treason, felony, or other crime, who shall flee from justice, and be found in another state, shall on demand of the executive authority of the state from which he fled, be delivered up, to be removed to the state having jurisdiction of the crime.

incriminatorio o por confesión en corte abierta.

(2) El Congreso tendrá poder para fijar la pena correspondiente al delito de traición; pero la sentencia por traición no alcanzará en sus 4efectos a los herederos del culpable ni llevará consigo la confiscación de sus bienes salvo durante la vida de la persona sentenciada.

Artículo IV

Sección 1 Se dará entera fe y crédito en cada estado a los actos públicos, documentos y procedimientos judiciales de los otros estados. El Congreso podrá prescribir mediante leyes generales la manera de probar tales actos, documentos y procedimientos así como los efectos que deban surtir.

Sección 2 (1) Los ciudadanos de cada estado disfrutarán de todos los privilegios e immunidades de los ciudadanos de otros estados.

(2) Toda persona acusada de traición, delito grave o de cualquier otro delito, que huyere del estado en donde se le acusa y fuere hallada en otro estado, será, a solicitud de la autoridad ejecutiva del estado de donde se fugó, entregada a dicha autoridad para ser devuelta al estado que tuviere jurisdicción para conocer del delito.

(3) [No person held to service or labor in one state, under the laws thereof, escaping into another, shall, in consequence of any law or regulation therein, be discharged from such service or labor, but shall be delivered up on claim of the party to whom such service or labor may be due.]

New States and Territories

Section 3 **(1)** New states may be admitted by the Congress into this Union; but no new state shall be formed or erected within the jurisdiction of any other state; nor any state be formed by the junction of two or more states, or parts of states, without the consent of the legislatures of the states concerned as well as of the Congress.

(2) The Congress shall have power to dispose of and make all needful rules and regulations respecting the territory or other property belonging to the United States; and nothing in this Constitution shall be so construed as to prejudice any claims of the United States, or of any particular state.

Protection of States Guaranteed

Section 4 The United States shall guarantee to every state in this Union a republican form of government, and shall protect each of them against invasion; and on application of the legislature, or of the executive (when the legislature cannot be convened) against domestic violence.

(3) Ninguna persona obligada a servir o trabajar en un estado, a tenor con las leyes allí vigentes, que huyere a otro estado, será dispensada de prestar dicho servicio o trabajo amparándose en leyes o reglamentos del estado al cual se acogiere, sino que será entregada a petición de la parte que tuviere derecho al susodicho servicio o trabajo.

Sección 3 **(1)** El Congreso podrá admitir nuevos estados a esta Unión; pero no se formará o establecerá ningún estado nuevo dentro de la jurisdicción de ningún otro estado. Tampoco se formará ningún estado por unión de dos o más estados, o partes de estados, sin el consentimiento tanto de las asambleas legislativas de los estados en cuestión como del Congreso.

(2) El Congreso podrá disponer de o promulgar todas las reglas y reglamentos necesarios en relación con, el territorio o cualquier propiedad perteneciente a los Estados Unidos. Ninguna disposición de esta Constitución se interpretará en forma tal que pudiere perjudicar cualesquiera reclamaciones de los Estados Unidos o de algún estado en particular.

Sección 4 Los Estados Unidos garantizarán a cada estado de esta Unión una forma republicana de gobierno y protegerán a cada uno de ellos contra toda invasión; y cuando lo solicitare la asamblea legislativa o el ejecutivo (si no se pudiere convocar la primera), le protegerá contra desórdenes internos.

ARTICLE V
Amending the Constitution

The Congress, whenever two-thirds of both houses shall deem it necessary, shall propose amendments to this Constitution, or, on the application of the legislatures of two-thirds of the several states, shall call a convention for proposing amendments, which, in either case, shall be valid to all intents and purposes, as part of this Constitution, when ratified by the legislatures of three-fourths of the several states, or by conventions in three-fourths thereof, as the one or the other mode of ratification may be proposed by the Congress; provided [that no amendment which may be made prior to the year one thousand eight hundred and eight shall in any manner affect the first and fourth clauses in the ninth section of the first article; and] that no state, without its consent, shall be deprived of its equal suffrage in the Senate.

ARTICLE VI
General Provisions

(1) All debts contracted and engagements entered into, before the adoption of this Constitution, shall be as valid against the United States under this Constitution, as under the Confederation.

(2) This Constitution, and the laws of the United States which shall be made

Artículo V

El Congreso propondrá enmiendas a esta Constitución, siempre que dos terceras partes de ambas cámaras lo estimen necesario; o, a petición de las asambleas legislativas de dos terceras partes de los estados, convocará una convención para proponer enmiendas, las cuales, en uno u otro caso, serán válidas para todos los fines y propósitos, como parte de esta Constitución, cuando las ratifiquen las asambleas legislativas de las tres cuartas partes de los estados, o las onvenciones celebradas en las tres cuartas partes de los mismos, de acuerdo con el modo de ratificación propuesto por el Congreso; disponiéndose, que ninguna enmienda hecha antes del año mil ochocientos ocho afectara en modo alguno los incisos primero y cuarto de la novena sección del primer artículo; y que no se privará a ningún estado, sin su consentimiento, de la igualdad de sufragio en el Senado.

Artículo VI

(1) Todas las deudas y obligaciones contraídas antes de promulgarse este Constitución serán tan válidas contra los Estados Unidos bajo esta Constitución como lo eran bajo la Confederación.

(2) La presente Constitución, las leyes de los Estados Unidos que en virtud de

in pursuance thereof; and all treaties made, or which shall be made, under the authority of the United States, shall be the supreme law of the land; and the judges in every state shall be bound thereby, anything in the constitution or laws of any state to the contrary notwithstanding.

(3) The senators and representatives before mentioned, and the members of the several state legislatures, and all executive and judicial officers, both of the United States and of the several states, shall be bound by oath or affirmation, to support this Constitution; but no religious test shall ever be required as a qualification to any office or public trust under the United States.

ARTICLE VII
Ratifying the Constitution

The ratification of the conventions of nine states shall be sufficient for the establishment of this Constitution between the states so ratifying the same.

Done in convention by the unanimous consent of the states present the seventeenth day of September in the year of our Lord one thousand seven hundred and eighty-seven and of the independence of the United States of America the twelfth. In witness thereof we have hereunto subscribed our names.

ella se aprobaren y todos los tratados celebrados o que se celebraren bajo la autoridad de los Estados Unidos serán la suprema ley del país. Los jueces de cada estado estarán obligados a observarla aun cuando hubiere alguna disposición en contrario en la Constitución o en las leyes de cualquier estado.

(3) Los senadores y representantes antes mencionados, los miembros de las asambleas legislativas de los diversos estados, así como todos los funcionarios ejecutivos y judiciales, tanto de los Estados Unidos como de los diversos estados, se comprometerán bajo juramento o promesa a sostener esta Constitución; pero no existirá requisito religioso alguno para desempeñar ningún cargo o empleo, retribuído o de confianza, bajo la autoridad de los Estados Unidos.

Artículo VII

La ratificación de las convenciones de nueve estados será suficiente para que esta Constitución rija entre los estados que la ratificaren.

Dada en convención con el consentimiento unánime de los estados presentes, el día diecisiete de septiembre del año de Nuestro Señor mil setecientos ochenta y siete, duodécimo de la independencia de los Estados Unidos de América. En testimonio de lo cual suscribimos la presente.

George Washington — *President and deputy from Virginia (Presidente y Diputado por Virginia)*

Delaware
George Read
Gunning Bedford, Jr.
John Dickinson
Richard Bassett
Jacob Broom

Maryland
James McHenry
Dan of St. Thomas Jenifer
Daniel Carroll

Virginia
John Blair
James Madison, Jr.

North Carolina (Carolina del Norte)
William Blount
Richard Dobbs Spaight
Hugh Williamson

South Carolina (Carolina del Sur)
John Rutledge
Charles Cotesworth Pinckney
Charles Pinckney
Pierce Butler

Georgia
William Few
Abraham Baldwin

New Hampshire (Nueva Hampshire)
John Langdon
Nicholas Gilman

Massachusetts
Nathaniel Gorham
Rufus King

Connecticut
William Samuel Johnson
Roger Sherman

New York (Nueva York)
Alexander Hamilton

New Jersey (Nueva Jersey)
William Livingston
David Brearley
William Paterson
Jonathan Dayton

Pennsylvania (Pensilvania)
Benjamin Franklin
Thomas Mifflin
Robert Morris
George Clymer
Thomas FitzSimons
Jared Ingersoll
James Wilson
Gouverneur Morris

Attest:
William Jackson, Secretary

Amendments to the Constitution

The Bill of Rights

AMENDMENT 1
Religious and Political Freedoms (1791)

Congress shall make no law respecting an establishment of religion, or prohibiting the free exercise thereof; or abridging the freedom of speech, or of the press; or the right of the people peaceably to assemble, and to petition the government for a redress of grievances.

AMENDMENT 2
Right to Bear Arms (1791)

A well-regulated militia, being necessary to the security of a free state, the right of the people to keep and bear arms shall not be infringed.

AMENDMENT 3
Housing of Soldiers (1791)

No soldier shall, in time of peace be quartered in any house, without the consent of the owner, nor in time of war, but in a manner to be prescribed by law.

AMENDMENT 4
Search and Arrest Warrants (1791)

The right of the people to be secure in their persons, houses, papers, and

Declaración de Derechos

ENMIENDA 1

El Congreso no aprobará ninguna ley con respecto al establecimiento de religión alguna, o que prohiba el libre ejercicio de palabra o de prensa; o el derecho del pueblo a reunirse pacificamente y a solicitar del gobierno la reparación de agravios.

ENMIENDA 2

Siendo necesaria para la seguridad de un estado libre una milicia bien organizada, no se coartará el derecho de pueblo a tener y portar armas.

ENMIENDA 3

En tiempos de paz ningún soldado será alojado en casa alguna, sin el consentimiento del propietario, ni tampoco lo será en tiempos de guerra sino de la manera prescrita por ley.

ENMIENDA 4

No se violará el derecho del pueblo a la seguridad de sus personas, hogares, documentos y pertenencias, contra registros y allanamientos irrazonables,

effects, against unreasonable searches and seizures, shall not be violated, and no warrants shall issue, but upon probable cause, supported by oath or affirmation, and particularly describing the place to be searched, and the persons or things to be seized.

AMENDMENT 5
Rights in Criminal Cases (1791)
No person shall be held to answer for a capital, or otherwise infamous crime, unless on a presentment or indictment of a grand jury, except in cases arising in the land or naval forces, or in the militia, when in actual service in time of war or public danger; nor shall any person be subject for the same offense to be twice put in jeopardy of life or limb; nor shall be compelled in any criminal case to be a witness against himself, nor be deprived of life, liberty, or property, without due process of law; nor shall private property be taken for public use, without just compensation.

AMENDMENT 6
Rights to a Fair Trial (1791)
In all criminal prosecutions, the accused shall enjoy the right to a speedy and public trial, by an impartial jury of the state and district wherein the crime shall have been committed, which district shall have been previously ascertained by law, and to be informed of the nature and cause of the accusation; to be confronted with the witnesses against him; to have

y no se expedirá ningún mandamiento, sino a virtud de causa probable, apoyado por juramento o promesa, y que describa en detalle el lugar que ha de ser allanado y las personas o cosas que han de ser detenidas o incautadas.

ENMIENDA 5
Ninguna persona será obligada a responder por delito capital o infamante, sino en virtud de denuncia o acusación por un gran jurado, salvo en los casos que ocurran en las fuerzas de mar y tierra, o en la milicia, cuando se hallen en servicio activo en tiempos de guerra o de peligro público; ni podrá nadie ser sometido por el mismo delito dos veces a un juicio que pueda ocasionarle la pérdida de la vida o la integridad corporal; ni será compelido en ningún caso criminal a declarar contra sí mismo, ni será privado de su vida, de su libertad o de su propiedad, sin el debido procedimiento de ley; ni se podrá tomar propriedad privada para uso público, sin justa compensación.

ENMIENDA 6
En todas las causas criminales, el acusado gozará del derecho a un juicio rápido y público, ante un jurado imparcial del estado y distrito en que el delito haya sido cometido, distrito que será previamente fijado por ley; a ser informado de la naturaleza y causa de la acusación; a carearse con los testigos en su contra; a que se adopten medidas compulsivas para la comparecencia de

compulsory process for obtaining witnesses in his favor, and to have the assistance of counsel for his defense.

AMENDMENT 7
Rights in Civil Cases (1791)
In suits at common law, where the value in controversy shall exceed twenty dollars, the right of trial by jury shall be preserved, and no fact tried by a jury, shall be otherwise re-examined in any court of the United States, than according to the rules of the common law.

AMENDMENT 8
Bails, Fines, and Punishments (1791)
Excessive bail shall not be required, nor excessive fines imposed, nor cruel and unusual punishments inflicted.

AMENDMENT 9
Rights Retained by the People (1791)
The enumeration in the Constitution, of certain rights, shall not be construed to deny or disparage others retained by the people.

AMENDMENT 10
Powers Retained by the States and the People (1791)
The powers not delegated to the United States by the Constitution, nor prohibited by it to the states, are reserved to the states respectively, or to the people.

los testigos que cite a su favor y a la asistencia de abogado para su defensa.

ENMIENDA 7
En litigios en derecho común, en que el valor en controversia exceda de veinte dólares, se mantendrá el derecho a juicio por jurado, y ningún hecho fallado por un jurado, será revisado por ningún tribunal de los Estados Unidos, sino de acuerdo con las reglas del derecho común.

ENMIENDA 8
No se exigirán fianzas excesivas, ni se impondrán multas excesivas, ni castigos crueles e inusitados.

ENMIENDA 9
La inclusión de ciertos derechos en la Constitución no se interpretará en el sentido de denegar o restringir otros derechos que se haya reservado el pueblo.

ENMIENDA 10
Las facultades que esta Constitución no delegue a los Estados Unidos, ni prohiba a los estados, quedan reservadas a los estados respectivamente o al pueblo.

AMENDMENT 11
Lawsuits Against States (1795)

The judicial power of the United States shall not be construed to extend to any suit in law or equity, commenced or prosecuted against one of the United States by citizens of another state, or by citizens or subjects of any foreign state.

AMENDMENT 12
Election of the President and Vice President (1804)

The electors shall meet in their respective states and vote by ballot for President and Vice President, one of whom, at least, shall not be an inhabitant of the same state with themselves; they shall name in their ballots the person voted for as President, and in distinct ballots the person voted for as Vice President, and they shall make distinct lists of all persons voted for as President, and of all persons voted for as Vice President, and of the number of votes for each, which lists they shall sign and certify, and transmit sealed to the seat of the government of the United States, directed to the president of the Senate; — the president of the Senate shall, in the presence of the Senate and House of Representatives, open all the certificates and the votes shall then be counted; — the person having the greatest number of votes for President, shall be the President, if such number be a majority of the whole

ENMIENDA 11

El poder judicial de los Estados Unidos no debe interpretarse que se extiende a cualquier litigio de derecho estricto o de equidad que se inicie o prosiga contra uno de los Estados Unidos por ciudadanos de otro estado o por ciudadanos o súbditos de cualquier estado extranjero.

ENMIENDA 12

Los electores se reunirán en sus respectivos estados y votarán mediante cedulas para Presidente y Vicepresidente, uno de los cuales, cuando menos, no deberá ser habitante del mismo estado que ellos; en sus cédulas indicarán la persona a favor de la cual votan para Presidente y en cédulas diferentes la persona que eligen para Vicepresidente, y formarán listas separadas de todas las personas que reciban votos para Presidente y de todas las personas a cuyo favor se vote para Vicepresidente y del número de votos que corresponda a cada una, y firmarán y certificarán las referidas listas y las remitirán selladas a la sede de gobierno de los Estados Unidos, dirigidas al presidente del Senado; el presidente del Senado abrirá todos los certificados en presencia del Senado y de la Cámara de Representantes, después de lo cual se contarán los votos; la persona que tenga el mayor número de votos para Presidente será Presidente, siempre que dicho número represente la mayoría de todos los electores nombrados, y si ninguna

number of electors appointed; and if no person have such majority, then from the persons having the highest numbers not exceeding three on the list of those voted for as President, the House of Representatives shall choose immediately, by ballot, the President. But in choosing the President, the votes shall be taken by states, the representation from each state having one vote; a quorum for this purpose shall consist of a member or members from two-thirds of the states, and a majority of all the states shall be necessary to a choice. And if the House of Representatives shall not choose a President whenever the right of choice shall devolve upon them, [before the fourth day of March next following,] then the Vice President shall act as President, as in the case of the death or other constitutional disability of the President.

The person having the greatest number of votes as Vice President, shall be the Vice President, if such number be a majority of the whole number of electors appointed, and if no person have a majority, then from the two highest numbers on the list, the Senate shall choose the Vice President; a quorum for the purpose shall consist of two-thirds of the whole number of senators, and a majority of the whole number shall be necessary to a choice. But no person constitutionally ineligible to the office of President shall be eligible to that of Vice President of the United States.

persona tiene mayoría, entonces la Cámara de Representantes, votando por cédulas, escogerá inmediatamente el Presidente de entre las tres personas que figuren en la lista de quienes han recibido sufragio para Presidente y cuenten con más votos. Téngase presente que al elegir al Presidente la votación se hará por estados y que la representación de cada estado gozará de un voto; que para este objeto habrá quórum cuando estén presentes el miembro o los miembros que representen a los dos tercios de los estados y que será necesaria a mayoría de todos los estados para que se tenga por hecha la elección. Y si la Cámara de Representantes no eligiere Presidente, en los casos en que pase a ella el derecho de escogerlo, antes del día cuatro de marzo inmediato siguiente, entonces el Vicepresidente actuará como Presidente, de la misma manera que en el caso de muerte o de otro impedimento constitucional del Presidente.

La persona que obtenga el mayor número de votos para Vicepresidente será Vicepresidente, siempre que dicho número represente la mayoría de todos los electores nombrados, y si ninguna persona reune la mayoría, entonces el Senado escogerá al Vicepresidente entre las dos con mayor cantidad de votos que figurán en la lista; para este objeto habrá quórum con las dos terceras partes del número total de senadores y será necesaria la mayoría del número total para que la elección se tenga por hecha.

AMENDMENT 13
Abolition of Slavery (1865)

Section 1 Neither slavery nor involuntary servitude, except as a punishment for crime whereof the party shall have been duly convicted, shall exist within the United States, or any place subject to their jurisdiction.

Section 2 Congress shall have power to enforce this article by appropriate legislation.

AMENDMENT 14
Civil Rights (1868)

Section 1 All persons born or naturalized in the United States, and subject to the jurisdiction thereof, are citizens of the United States and of the state wherein they reside. No state shall make or enforce any law which shall abridge the privileges or immunities of citizens of the United States; nor shall any state deprive any person of life, liberty, or property, without due process of law; nor deny to any person within its jurisdiction the equal protection of the laws.

Section 2 Representatives shall be apportioned among the several states according to their respective numbers, counting the whole number of persons

ENMIENDA 13

1. Ni en los Estados Unidos ni en ningún lugar sujeto a su jurisdicción habrá esclavitud ni trabajo forzado, excepto como castigo de un delito del que el responsable haya quedado debidamente convicto.

2. El Congreso estará facultado para hacer cumplir este artículo por medio de leyes apropiadas.

ENMIENDA 14

1. Todas las personas nacidas o naturalizadas en los Estados Unidos y sometidas a su jurisdicción son ciudadanos de los Estados Unidos y de los estados en que residen. Ningun estado podrá dictar ni dar efecto a cualquier ley que limite los privilegios o inmunidades de los ciudadanos de los Estados Unidos; tampoco podrá estado alguno privar a cualquier persona de la vida, la libertad o la propiedad sin el debido proceso legal; ni negar a cualquier persona que se encuentre dentro de sus límites jurisdiccionales la protección de las leyes, igual para todos.

2. Los representantes se distribuirán proporcionalmente entre los diversos estados de acuerdo con su población respectiva, en la que se tomará en cuenta

in each state, [excluding Indians not taxed]. But when the right to vote at any election for the choice of electors for President and Vice President of the United States, representatives in Congress, the executive and judicial officers of a state, or the members of the legislature thereof, is denied to any of the male inhabitants of such state, being twenty-one years of age, and citizens of the United States, or in any way abridged, except for participation in rebellion, or other crime, the basis of representation therein shall be reduced in the proportion which the number of such male citizens shall bear to the whole number of male citizens twenty-one years of age in such state.

Section 3 No person shall be a senator or representative in Congress, or elector of President and Vice President, or hold any office, civil or military, under the United States, or under any state, who, having previously taken an oath, as a member of Congress, or as an officer of the United States, or as a member of any state legislature, or as an executive or judicial officer of any state, to support the Constitution of the United States, shall have engaged in insurrection or rebellion against the same, or given aid or comfort to the enemies thereof. But Congress may by a vote of two-thirds of each House, remove such disability.

Section 4 The validity of the public debt of the United States, authorized

el número total de personas que haya en cada estado, con excepción de los indios que no paguen contribuciones. Pero cuando a los habitantes varones de un estado que tengan veintiún años de edad y sean ciudadanos de los Estados Unidos se les niegue o se les coarte en la forma que sea el derecho de votar en cualquier elección en que se trate de escoger a los electores para Presidente y Vicepresidente de los Estados Unidos, a los representantes del Congreso, a los funcionarios ejecutivos y judiciales de un estado o a los miembros de su legislatura, excepto con motivo de su participación en una rebelión o en algun otro delito, la base de la representación de dicho estado se reducirá en la misma proporción en que se halle el número de los ciudadanos varones a que se hace referencia, con el número total de ciudadanos varones de veintiún años del repetido estado.

3. Las personas que habiendo prestado juramento previamente en calidad de miembros del Congreso, o de funcionarios de los Estados Unidos, o de miembros de cualquier legislatura local, o como funcionarios ejecutivos o judiciales de cualquier estado, de que sostendrían la Constitución de los Estados Unidos, hubieran participado de una insurrección o rebelión en contra de ella o proporcionando ayuda o protección a sus enemigos no podrán ser senadores o representantes en el Congreso, ni electores del Presidente o Vicepresidente, ni ocupar ningún

by law, including debts incurred for payment of pensions and bounties for services in suppressing insurrection or rebellion, shall not be questioned. But neither the United States nor any state shall assume or pay any debt or obligation incurred in aid of insurrection or rebellion against the United States, or any claim for the loss or emancipation of any slave; but all such debts, obligations, and claims shall be held illegal and void.

Section 5 The Congress shall have power to enforce, by appropriate legislation, the provisions of this article.

empleo civil o militar que dependa de los Estados Unidos o de alguno de los Estados. Pero el Congreso puede derogar tal interdicción por el voto de los dos tercios de cada cámara.

4. La validez de la deuda pública de los Estados Unidos que este autorizada por la ley, inclusive las deudas contraidas para el pago de pensiones y recompensas por servicios prestados al sofocar insurrecciones o rebeliones, será incuestionable. Pero ni los Estados Unidos ni ningún estado asumirán ni pagarán deuda u obligación alguna contraidas para ayuda de insurrecciones o rebeliones contra los Estados Unidos, como tampoco reclamación alguna con motivo de la pérdida o emancipación de esclavos, pues todas las deudas, obligaciones y reclamaciones de esa especie se considerarán ilegales y nulas.

5. El Congreso tendrá facultades para hacer cumplir las disposiciones de este artículo por medio de leyes apropiadas.

AMENDMENT 15
Right to Vote (1870)
Section 1 The right of citizens of the United States to vote shall not be denied or abridged by the United States or by any state on account of race, color, or previous condition of servitude.

Section 2 The Congress shall have power to enforce this article by appropriate legislation.

AMENDMENT 16
Income Taxes (1913)
The Congress shall have power to lay and collect taxes on incomes, from whatever source derived, without apportionment among the several states, and without regard to any census or enumeration.

AMENDMENT 17
Direct Election of Senators (1913)
(1) The Senate of the United States shall be composed of two senators from each state, elected by the people thereof for six years; and each senator shall have one vote. The electors in each state shall have the qualifications requisite for electors of the most numerous branch of the state legislatures.

(2) When vacancies happen in the representation of any state in the Senate, the executive authority of such state shall issue writs of election to fill such vacancies: provided, that the legislature of any state may empower the executive thereof to make temporary

ENMIENDA 15
1. Ni los Estados Unidos, ni ningún otro estado, podrán desconocer ni menoscabar el derecho de sufragio de los ciudadanos de los Estados Unidos por motivo de raza, color o de su condición anterior de esclavos.

2. El Congreso estará facultado para hacer cumplir este artículo mediante leyes apropiadas.

ENMIENDA 16
El Congreso tendrá facultades para establecer y recaudar impuestos sobre los ingresos, sea cual fuere la fuente de que provengan, sin prorratearlos entre los diferentes estados y sin atender a ningún censo o recuento.

ENMIENDA 17
1. El Senado de los Estados Unidos se compondrá de dos senadores por cada estado, elegidos por los habitantes del mismo por seis años, y cada senador dispondrá de un voto. Los electores de cada estado deberán poseer las condiciones requeridas para los electores de la rama más numerosa de la legislatura local.

2. Cuando ocurrán vacantes en la representación de cualquier estado en el Senado, la autoridad ejecutiva de aquel expedirá un decreto en que convocará a elecciones con el objeto de cubrir dichas vacantes, en la inteligencia de que la legislatura de cualquier estado

appointments until the people fill the vacancies by election as the legislature may direct.

(3) This amendment shall not be so construed as to affect the election or term of any senator chosen before it becomes valid as part of the Constitution.

AMENDMENT 18
Prohibition of Liquor (1919)

Section 1 After one year from the ratification of this article the manufacture, sale, or transportation of intoxicating liquors within, the importation thereof into, or the exportation thereof from the United States and all territory subject to the jurisdiction thereof for beverage purposes is hereby prohibited.

Section 2 The Congress and the several states shall have concurrent power to enforce this article by appropriate legislation.

Section 3 This article shall be inoperative unless it shall have been ratified as an amendment to the Constitution by the legislatures of the several states, as provided in the Constitution, within seven years from the date of the submission hereof to the states by the Congress.

puede autorizar a su ejecutivo a hacer un nombramiento provisional hasta tanto que las vacantes se cubrán mediante elecciones populares en la forma que disponga la legislatura.

3. No deberá entenderse que esta enmienda influye sobre la elección o período de cualquier senador elegido antes de que adquiera validez como parte integrante de la Constitución.

ENMIENDA 18

1. Un año después de la ratificación de este artículo quedará prohibida por el presente la fabricación, venta o transporte de licores embriagantes dentro de los Estados Unidos y de todos los territorios sometidos a su jurisdicción, así como su importación a los mismos o su exportación de ellos, con el propósito de usarlos como bebidas.

2. El Congreso y los diversos estados poseerán facultades concurrentes para hacer cumplir este artículo mediante leyes apropiadas.

3. Este artículo no entrará en vigor a menos de que sea ratificado con el carácter de enmienda a la Constitución por las legislaturas de los distintos estados en la forma prevista por la Constitución y dentro de los siete años siguientes a la fecha en que el Congreso lo someta a los estados.

AMENDMENT 19
Women's Suffrage (1920)

Section 1 The right of citizens of the United States to vote shall not be denied or abridged by the United States or by any state on account of sex.

Section 2 Congress shall have power to enforce this article by appropriate legislation.

AMENDMENT 20
Terms of the President and Congress (1933)

Section 1 The terms of the President and Vice President shall end at noon on the 20th day of January, and the terms of senators and representatives at noon on the third day of January, of the years in which such terms would have ended if this article had not been ratified; and the terms of their successors shall then begin.

Section 2 The Congress shall assemble at least once in every year, and such meeting shall begin at noon on the third day of January, unless they shall by law appoint a different day.

Section 3 If, at the time fixed for the beginning of the term of the President, the President elect shall have died, the Vice President elect shall become President. If a President shall not have been chosen before the time fixed for the beginning of his term, of if the President elect shall have failed to qualify, then the Vice President elect shall act as President until a President

ENMIENDA 19

1. El derecho de sufragio de los ciudadanos de los Estados Unidos no será desconocido ni limitado por los Estados Unidos o por estado alguno por razón de sexo.

2. El Congreso estará facultado para hacer cumplir este artículo por medio de leyes apropiadas.

ENMIENDA 20

1. Los períodos del Presidente y el Vicepresidente terminarán al medio día del veinte de enero y los períodos de los senadores y representantes al medio día del tres de enero, de los años en que dichos períodos habrían terminado si este artículo no hubiera sido ratificado, y en ese momento principiarán los períodos de sus sucesores.

2. El Congreso se reunirá, cuando menos, una vez cada año y dicho período de sesiones se iniciará al mediodía del tres de enero, a no ser que por medio de una ley fije una fecha diferente.

3. Si el Presidente electo hubiera muerto en el momento fijado para el comienzo del período presidencial, el Vicepresidente electo será Presidente. Si antes del momento fijado para el comienzo de su período no se hubiere elegido Presidente o si el Presidente electo no llenare los requisitos exigidos, entonces el Vicepresidente electo fungirá como Presidente electo hasta

shall have qualified; and the Congress may by law provide for the case wherein neither a President elect nor a Vice President elect shall have qualified, declaring who shall then act as President, or the manner in which one who is to act shall be selected, and such person shall act accordingly until a President or Vice President shall have qualified.

Section 4 The Congress may by law provide for the case of the death of any of the persons from whom the House of Representatives may choose a President whenever the right of choice shall have devolved upon them, and for the case of the death of any of the persons from whom the Senate may choose a Vice President whenever the right of choice shall have devolved upon them.

Section 5 Sections 1 and 2 shall take effect on the 15th day of October following the ratification of this article.

Section 6 This article shall be inoperative unless it shall have been ratified as an amendment to the Constitution by the legislatures of three-fourths of the several states within seven years from the date of its submission.

que haya un Presidente idóneo, y el Congreso podrá prever por medio de una ley el caso de que ni el Presidente electo ni el Vicepresidente electo satisfagan los requisitos constitucionales, declarando quien hará las veces de Presidente en ese supuesto o la forma en que se escogerá a la persona que habrá de actuar como tal, y la referida persona actuará con ese carácter hasta que se cuente con un Presidente o un Vicepresidente que reuna las condiciones legales.

4. El Congreso podrá preveer mediante una ley el caso de que muera cualquiera de las personas de las cuales la Cámara de Representantes está facultada para elegir Presidente cuando le corresponda el derecho de elección, así como el caso de que muera alguna de las personas entre las cuales el Senado está facultado para escoger Vicepresidente cuando pasa a el el derecho de elegir.

5. Las secciones 1 y 2 entrarán en vigor el día quince de octubre siguiente a la ratificación de este artículo.

6. Este artículo quedará sin efecto a menos de que sea ratificado como enmienda a la Constitución por las legislaturas de las tres cuartas partes de los distintos Estados, dentro de los siete años posteriores a la fecha en que se les someta.

AMENDMENT 21
Repeal of Prohibition (1933)

Section 1 The eighteenth article of amendment to the Constitution of the United States is hereby repealed.

Section 2 The transportation or importation into any state, territory, or possession of the United States for delivery or use therein of intoxicating liquors, in violation of the laws thereof, is hereby prohibited.

Section 3 This article shall be inoperative unless it shall have been ratified as an amendment to the Constitution by conventions in the several states, as provided in the Constitution, within seven years from the date of the submission hereof to the states by the Congress.

AMENDMENT 22
Limitation on Presidential Terms (1951)

Section 1 No person shall be elected to the office of the President more than twice, and no person who has held the office of President, or acted as President, for more than two years of a term to which some other person was elected President shall be elected to the office of the President more than once. But this article shall not apply to any person holding the office of President when this article was proposed by the Congress, and shall not prevent any person who may be holding the office of President, or acting as President,

ENMIENDA 21

1. Queda derogado por el presente el decimoctavo de los artículos de enmienda a la Constitución de los Estados Unidos.

2. Se prohíbe por el presente que se transporte o importen licores embriagantes a cualquier estado, territorio o posesión de los Estados Unidos, para ser entregados o utilizados en su interior con violación de sus respectivas leyes.

3. Este artículo quedará sin efecto a menos de que sea ratificado como enmienda a la Constitución por convenciones que se celebrarán en los diversos estados, en la forma prevista por la Constitución, dentro de los siete años siguientes a la fecha en que el Congreso lo someta a los estados.

ENMIENDA 22

1. No se elegirá a la misma persona para el cargo de Presidente más de dos veces, ni más de una vez a la persona que haya desempeñado dicho cargo o que haya actuado como Presidente durante más de dos años de un período para el que se haya elegido como Presidente a otra persona. El presente artículo no se aplicará a la persona que ocupaba el puesto de Presidente cuando el mismo se propuso por el Congreso, ni impedirá que la persona que desempeñe dicho cargo o que actúe como Presidente durante el período en que el repetido artículo entre envigor,

during the term within which this article becomes operative from holding the office of President or acting as President during the remainder of such term.

Section 2 This article shall be inoperative unless it shall have been ratified as an amendment to the Constitution by the legislatures of three-fourths of the several states within seven years from the date of its submission to the states by the Congress.

AMENDMENT 23
Suffrage in the District of Columbia (1961)

Section 1 The district constituting the seat of government of the United States shall appoint in such manner as the Congress may direct: A number of electors of President and Vice President equal to the whole number of senators and representatives in Congress to which the district would be entitled if it were a state, but in no event more than the least populous state; they shall be in addition to those appointed by the states, but they shall be considered, for the purposes of the election of President and Vice President, to be electors appointed by a state; and they shall meet in the district and perform such duties as provided by the twelfth article of amendment.

Section 2 The Congress shall have power to enforce this article by appropriate legislation.

desempeñe el puesto de Presidente o actúe como tal durante el resto del referido período.

2. Este artículo quedará sin efecto a menos de que las legislaturas de tres cuartas partes de los diversos estados lo ratifiquen como enmienda a la Constitución dentro de los siete años siguientes a la fecha en que el Congreso los someta a los estados.

ENMIENDA 23

1. El distrito que constituye la sede del gobierno de los Estados Unidos nombrará, según disponga el Congreso: Un número de electores para elegir al Presidente y al Vicepresidente, igual al número total de senadores y representantes ante el Congreso al que el distrito tendría derecho si fuere un estado, pero en ningún caso será dicho número mayor que el del estado de menos población; estos electores se sumarán al número de aquellos electores nombrados por los estados, pero para fines de la elección del Presidente y del Vicepresidente, serán considerados como electores nombrados por un estado; celebrarán sus reuniones en el distrito y cumplirán con los deberes que se estipulan en la Enmienda 12.

2. El Congreso queda facultado para poner en vigor este artículo por medio de legislación adecuada.

AMENDMENT 24
Poll Taxes (1964)

Section 1 The right of citizens of the United States to vote in any primary or other election for President or Vice President, for electors for President or Vice President, or for senator or representative in Congress, shall not be denied or abridged by the United States or any state by reason of failure to pay any poll tax or other tax.

Section 2 The Congress shall have power to enforce this article by appropriate legislation.

AMENDMENT 25
Presidential Disability and Succession (1967)

Section 1 In case of the removal of the President from office or of his death or resignation, the Vice President shall become President.

Section 2 Whenever there is a vacancy in the office of the Vice President, the President shall nominate a Vice President who shall take office upon confirmation by a majority vote of both houses of Congress.

Section 3 Whenever the President transmits to the president *pro tempore* of the Senate and the Speaker of the House of Representatives his written declaration that he is unable to discharge the powers and duties of his office, and until he transmits to them a written declaration to the contrary, such powers and duties shall

ENMIENDA 24

1. Ni los Estados Unidos ni ningún estado podrán denegar o coartar a los ciudadanos de los Estados Unidos el derecho al sufragio en cualquier elección primaria o de otra clase para Presidente o Vicepresidente, para electores para elegir al Presidente o al Vicepresidente o para senador o representante ante el Congreso, por motivo de no haber pagado un impuesto electoral o cualquier otro impuesto.

2. El Congreso queda facultado para poner en vigor este artículo por medio de legislación adecuada.

ENMIENDA 25

1. En caso de que el Presidente sea despuesto de su cargo, o en caso de su muerte o renuncia, el Vicepresidente será nombrado Presidente.

2. Cuando el puesto de Vicepresidente estuviera vacante, el Presidente nombrará un Vicepresidente que tomará posesión de su cargo al ser confirmado por voto mayoritario de ambas cámaras del Congreso.

3. Cuando el Presidente transmitiera al presidente pro tempore del Senado y al Presidente de Debates de la Cámara de Diputados su declaración escrita de que está imposibilitado de desempeñar los derechos y deberes de su cargo, y mientras no transmitiere a ellos una declaración escrita en sentido contrario, tales derechos y deberes serán

be discharged by the Vice President as acting President.

Section 4 Whenever the Vice President and a majority of either the principal officers of the executive departments or of such other body as Congress may by law provide, transmit to the president pro tempore of the Senate and the Speaker of the House of Representatives their written declaration that the President is unable to discharge the powers and duties of his office, the Vice President shall immediately assume the powers and duties of the office as acting President.

Thereafter, when the President transmits to the president pro tempore of the Senate and the speaker of the House of Representatives his written declaration that no inability exists, he shall resume the powers and duties of his office unless the Vice President and a majority of either the principal officers of the executive department or of such other body as Congress may by law provide, transmit within four days to the president pro tempore of the Senate and the Speaker of the House of Representatives their written declaration that the President is unable to discharge the powers and duties of his office. Thereupon Congress shall decide the issue, assembling within forty-eight hours for that purpose if not in session. If the Congress, within twenty-one days after receipt of the latter written declaration, or, if Congress

desempeñados por el Vicepresidente como Presidente en funciones.

4. Cuando el Vicepresidente y la mayoría de los principales funcionarios de los departamentos ejecutivos o de cualquier otro cuerpo que el Congreso autorizara por ley trasmitieran al Presidente pro tempore del Senado y al Presidente de Debates de la Cámara de Diputados su declaración escrita de que el Presidente esta imposibilitado de ejercer los derechos y deberes de su cargo, el Vicepresidente inmediatamente asumirá los derechos y deberes del cargo como Presidente en funciones.

Por consiguiente, cuando el Presidente transmitiera al presidente pro tempore del Senado y al Presidente de Debates de la Cámara de Diputados su declaración escrita de que no existe imposibilidad alguna, asumirá de nuevo los derechos y deberes de su cargo, a menos que el Vicepresidente y la mayoría de los funcionarios principales de los departamentos ejecutivos o de cualquier otro cuerpo que el Congreso haya autorizado por ley transmitieran en el término de cuatro días al presidente pro tempore del Senado y al Presidente de Debates de la Cámara de Diputados su declaración escrita de que el Presidente está imposibilitado de ejercer los derechos y deberes de su cargo. Luego entonces, el Congreso decidirá que solución debe adoptarse, para lo cual se reunirá en el término de

is not in session, within twenty-one days after Congress is required to assemble, determines by two-thirds vote of both houses that the President is unable to discharge the powers and duties of his office, the Vice President shall continue to discharge the same as acting President; otherwise, the President shall resume the powers and duties of his office.

AMENDMENT 26
Suffrage for 18-Year-Olds (1971)

Section 1 The right of citizens of the United States, who are eighteen years of age or older, to vote shall not be denied or abridged by the United States or by any state on account of age.

Section 2 The Congress shall have power to enforce this article by appropriate legislation.

AMENDMENT 27
Congressional Pay (1992)

No law, varying the compensation for the services of the senators and representatives, shall take effect, until an election of representatives shall have intervened.

cuarenta y ocho horas, si no estuviera en sesión. Si el Congreso, en el término de veintiún días de recibida la ulterior declaración escrita o, de no estar en sesión, dentro de los veintiún días de haber sido convocado a reunirse, determinará por voto de las dos terceras partes de ambas cámaras que el Presidente está imposibilitado de ejercer los derechos y deberes de su cargo, el Vicepresidente continuará desempeñando el cargo como Presidente actuante; de lo contrario, el Presidente asumirá de nuevo los derechos y deberes de su cargo.

ENMIENDA 26

1. El derecho a votar de los ciudadanos de los Estado Unidos, de dieciocho años de edad o más, no será negado o menguado ni por los Estados Unidos ni por ningún estado a causa de la edad.

2. El Congreso tendrá poder para hacer valer este artículo mediante la legislación adecuada.

ENMIENDA 27

Niguna ley que varíe la compensación por los servicios de los senadores y representantes entrará en vigor sino hasta que haya tenido lugar una elección de los representantes.

Presidents of the United States

1. George Washington
"Father of His Country"
Term of Office: 1789-1797
Elected From: Virginia
Party: None
Born: 1732 Died: 1799

2. John Adams
"Colossus of Debate"
Term of Office: 1797-1801
Elected From: Massachusetts
Party: Federalist
Born: 1735 Died: 1826

3. Thomas Jefferson
"Father of the Declaration of
Independence"
Term of Office: 1801-1809
Elected From: Virginia
Party: Democratic-Republican
Born: 1743 Died: 1826

4. James Madison
"Father of the Constitution"
Term of Office: 1809-1817
Elected From: Virginia
Party: Democratic-Republican
Born: 1751 Died: 1836

5. James Monroe
"Era of Good Feeling President"
Term of Office: 1817-1825
Elected From: Virginia
Party: Democratic-Republican
Born: 1758 Died: 1831

6. John Quincy Adams
"Old Man Eloquent"
Term of Office: 1825-1829
Elected From: Massachusetts
Party: None
Born: 1767 Died: 1848

7. Andrew Jackson
"Old Hickory"
Term of Office: 1829-1837
Elected From: South Carolina
Party: Democratic
Born: 1767   Died: 1845

8. Martin Van Buren
"Young Hickory"
Term of Office: 1837-1841
Elected From: New York
Party: Democratic
Born: 1782   Died: 1862

9. William H. Harrison
"Old Tippecanoe"
Term of Office: 1841
Elected From: Virginia
Party: Whig
Born: 1773   Died: 1841

10. John Tyler
"Accidental President"
Term of Office: 1841-1845
Elected From: Virginia
Party: Whig
Born: 1790   Died: 1862

11. James K. Polk
"First Dark Horse"
Term of Office: 1845-1849
Elected From: Tennessee
Party: Democratic
Born: 1795   Died: 1849

12. Zachary Taylor
"Old Rough and Ready"
Term of Office: 1849-1850
Elected From: Virginia
Party: Whig
Born: 1784   Died: 1850

13. Millard Fillmore

"Wool-Carder President"
Term of Office: 1850-1853
Elected From: New York
Party: Whig
Born: 1800   Died: 1874

14. Franklin Pierce

"Handsome Frank"
Term of Office: 1853-1857
Elected From: New Hampshire
Party: Democratic
Born: 1804   Died: 1869

15. James Buchanan

"Bachelor President"
Term of Office: 1857-1861
Elected From: Pennsylvania
Party: Democratic
Born: 1791   Died: 1868

16. Abraham Lincoln

"Honest Abe"
Term of Office: 1861-1865
Elected From: Illinois
Party: Republican
Born: 1809   Died: 1865

17. Andrew Johnson

"King Andrew the First"
Term of Office: 1865-1869
Elected From: Tennessee
Party: Republican
Born: 1808   Died: 1875

18. Ulysses S. Grant

"American Caesar"
Term of Office: 1869-1877
Elected From: Ohio
Party: Republican
Born: 1822   Died: 1885

19. Rutherford B. Hayes

"Hero of '77"
Term of Office: 1877-1881
Elected From: Ohio
Party: Republican
Born: 1822   Died: 1893

20. James A. Garfield

"Preacher President"
Term of Office: 1881
Elected From: Ohio
Party: Republican
Born: 1831   Died: 1881

21. Chester A. Arthur

"America's First Gentleman"
Term of Office: 1881-1885
Elected From: New York
Party: Republican
Born: 1830   Died: 1886

22., 24. Grover Cleveland

"Perpetual Candidate"
Term of Office: 1885-1889,
1893-1897
Elected From: New York
Party: Democratic
Born: 1837   Died: 1908

23. Benjamin Harrison

"Centennial President"
Term of Office: 1889-1893
Elected From: Indiana
Party: Republican
Born: 1833   Died: 1901

25. William McKinley

"Stocking-Foot Orator"
Term of Office: 1897-1901
Elected From: Ohio
Party: Republican
Born: 1843   Died: 1901

26. Theodore Roosevelt

"TR"

Term of Office: 1901-1909
Elected From: New York
Party: Republican
Born: 1858   Died: 1919

27. William H. Taft

"Big Chief"

Term of Office: 1909-1913
Elected From: Ohio
Party: Republican
Born: 1857   Died: 1930

28. Woodrow Wilson

"Professor"

Term of Office: 1913-1921
Elected From: New Jersey
Party: Democratic
Born: 1856   Died: 1924

29. Warren G. Harding

"Dark Horse Candidate"

Term of Office: 1921-1923
Elected From: Ohio
Party: Republican
Born: 1865   Died: 1923

30. Calvin Coolidge

"Silent Cal"

Term of Office: 1923-1929
Elected From: Massachusetts
Party: Republican
Born: 1872   Died: 1933

31. Herbert Hoover

"Grand Old Man"

Term of Office: 1929-1933
Elected From: California
Party: Republican
Born: 1874   Died: 1964

32. Franklin D. Roosevelt
"FDR"
Term of Office: 1933-1945
Elected From: New York
Party: Democratic
Born: 1882   Died: 1945

33. Harry S. Truman
"Man from Independence"
Term of Office: 1945-1953
Elected From: Missouri
Party: Democratic
Born: 1884   Died: 1972

34. Dwight D. Eisenhower
"Ike"
Term of Office: 1953-1961
Elected From: Kansas
Party: Republican
Born: 1890   Died: 1969

35. John F. Kennedy
"JFK"
Term of Office: 1961-1963
Elected From: Massachusetts
Party: Democratic
Born: 1917   Died: 1963

36. Lyndon B. Johnson
"LBJ"
Term of Office: 1963-1969
Elected From: Texas
Party: Democratic
Born: 1908   Died: 1973

37. Richard M. Nixon
"Embattled President"
Term of Office: 1969-1974
Elected From: California
Party: Republican
Born: 1913   Died: 1994

38. Gerald R. Ford
"Mr. Clean"
Term of Office: 1974-1977
Elected From: Michigan
Party: Republican
Born: 1913

39. James E. Carter
"Peanut Farmer"
Term of Office: 1977-1981
Elected From: Georgia
Party: Democratic
Born: 1924

40. Ronald W. Reagan
"Great Communicator"
Term of Office: 1981-1989
Elected From: California
Party: Republican
Born: 1911

41. George H.W. Bush
Term of Office: 1989-1993
Elected From: Texas
Party: Republican
Born: 1924

42. William J. Clinton
Term of Office: 1993-2001
Elected From: Arkansas
Party: Democratic
Born: 1946

The Fifty United States

West

Midwest

Northeast

South

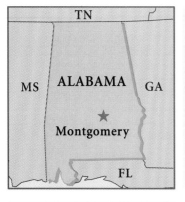

TN

MS   **ALABAMA**   GA

★
Montgomery

FL

Alabama

Capital: Montgomery
Organized as a territory: March 3, 1817
Entered Union: December 14, 1819
Order of entry: 22nd state
Motto: We dare defend our rights.
Geographic region: South
Nicknames: Yellowhammer State, The Heart of Dixie
Origin of name Alabama: May come from a Choctaw word, meaning "thicket clearers" or "vegetation gatherers"
State flower: Camellia
State bird: Yellowhammer
Largest city: Birmingham
Land area: 50,750 square miles
Land area rank: 28th largest state
Population: 4,040,587
Population rank: 22nd largest state
Postal abbreviation: AL

Canada

ALASKA

Juneau

Alaska

Capital: Juneau
Organized as a territory: 1912
Entered Union: January 3, 1959
Order of entry: 49th state
Motto: North to the Future.
Geographic region: West
Nicknames: The Last Frontier, Land of the Midnight Sun
Origin of name Alaska: Misinterpreted Aleut word, meaning "great land" or "that which the sea breaks against"
State flower: Forget-me-not
State bird: Willow ptarmigan
Largest city: Anchorage
Land area: 570,374 square miles
Land area rank: Largest state
Population: 550,043
Population rank: 49th largest state
Postal abbreviation: AK

Arizona

Capital: Phoenix
Organized as a territory: February 24, 1863
Entered Union: February 14, 1912
Order of entry: 48th state
Motto: God enriches.
Geographic region: West
Nickname: Grand Canyon State
Origin of name Arizona: From the Indian word Arizonac, meaning "little spring" or "young spring"

State flower: Saguaro cactus flower
State bird: Cactus wren
Largest city: Phoenix
Land area: 114,000 square miles
Land area rank: 6th largest state
Population: 3,665,228
Population rank: 24th largest state
Postal abbreviation: AZ

Arkansas

Capital: Little Rock
Organized as a territory: March 2, 1819
Entered Union: June 15, 1836
Order of entry: 25th state
Motto: The people rule.
Geographic region: West
Nickname: Land of Opportunity
Origin of name Arkansas: From the Quapaw Indians

State flower: Apple blossom
State bird: Mockingbird
Largest city: Little Rock
Land area: 52,075 square miles
Land area rank: 27th largest state
Population: 2,350,725
Population rank: 33rd largest state
Postal abbreviation: AR

California

Capital: Sacramento
Organized as a territory: 1847
Entered Union: September 9, 1850
Order of entry: 31st state
Motto: I have found it.
Geographic region: West
Nickname: Golden State
Origin of name California: From a book, *Las Sergas de Esplandián,* by Garcia Ordóñez de Montalvo, written about 1500

State flower: Golden poppy
State bird: California valley quail
Largest city: Los Angeles
Land area: 155,973 square miles
Land area rank: 3rd largest state
Population: 29,760,021
Population rank: Largest state
Postal abbreviation: CA

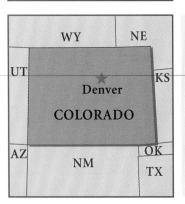

Colorado

Capital: Denver
Organized as a territory: February 28, 1861
Entered Union: August 1, 1876
Order of entry: 38th state
Motto: Nothing without Providence.
Geographic region: West
Nickname: Centennial State
Origin of name Colorado: From Spanish, meaning "ruddy" or "red"

State flower: Rocky Mountain columbine
State bird: Lark bunting
Largest city: Denver
Land area: 103,730 square miles
Land area rank: 8th largest state
Population: 3,294,394
Population rank: 26th largest state
Postal abbreviation: CO

Connecticut

Capital: Hartford
Became a colony: 1662
Entered Union: January 9, 1788
Order of entry: 5th state
Motto: He who transplanted still sustains.
Geographic region: Northeast
Nicknames: Nutmeg State, Constitution State

Origin of name Connecticut: From the Indian word *Quinnehtukqut,* meaning "beside the long tidal river"
State flower: Mountain laurel
State bird: American robin
Largest city: Bridgeport
Land area: 4,845 square miles
Land area rank: 48th largest state
Population: 3,287,116
Population rank: 27th largest state
Postal abbreviation: CT

Delaware

Capital: Dover
Became a colony: 1682
Entered Union: December 7, 1787
Order of entry: First state
Motto: Liberty and independence.
Geographic region: Northeast
Nicknames: Diamond State, First State, Small Wonder
Origin of name Delaware: From Delaware River and Bay, which were

named for Sir Thomas West, Lord De La Warr
State flower: Peach blossom
State bird: Blue hen chicken
Largest city: Wilmington
Land area: 1,982 square miles
Land area rank: 49th largest state
Population: 666,168
Population rank: 46th largest state
Postal abbreviation: DE

Florida

Capital: Tallahassee
Organized as a territory: March 20, 1822
Entered Union: March 3, 1845
Order of entry: 27th state
Motto: In God we trust.
Geographic region: South
Nickname: Sunshine State
Origin of name Florida: From the Spanish, meaning "feast of flowers"

State flower: Orange blossom
State bird: Mockingbird
Largest city: Jacksonville
Land area: 53,997 square miles
Land area rank: 26th largest state
Population: 12,937,926
Population rank: 4th largest state
Postal abbreviation: FL

Georgia

Capital: Atlanta
Became a colony: 1733
Entered Union: January 2, 1788
Order of entry: 4th state
Motto: Wisdom, justice, and moderation.
Geographic region: South
Nicknames: Peach State, Empire State of the South

Origin of name Georgia: In honor of George II of England
State flower: Cherokee rose
State bird: Brown thrasher
Largest city: Atlanta
Land area: 57,919 square miles
Land area rank: 21st largest state
Population: 6,478,216
Population rank: 11th largest state
Postal abbreviation: GA

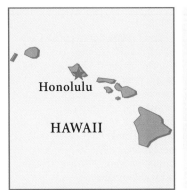

Hawaii

Capital: Honolulu
Organized as a territory: 1900
Entered Union: August 21, 1959
Order of entry: 50th state
Motto: The life of the land is perpetuated in righteousness.
Geographic region: West
Nickname: Aloha State
Origin of name Hawaii: Islands may have been named by Hawaii Loa, their traditional discoverer; may have been named after Hawaii or Hawaiki, the traditional home of the Polynesians
State flower: Yellow hibiscus
State bird: Nene (hawaiian goose)
Largest city: Honolulu
Land area: 6,423.4 square miles
Land area rank: 47th largest state
Population: 1,108,229
Population rank: 41st largest state
Postal abbreviation: HI

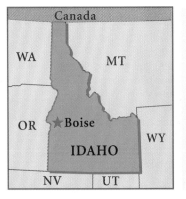

Idaho

Capital: Boise
Organized as a territory: March 3, 1863
Entered Union: July 3, 1890
Order of entry: 43rd state
Motto: It is forever.
Geographic region: West
Nicknames: Gem State, Spud State, Panhandle State
Origin of name Idaho: An invented name of unknown meaning
State flower: Syringa
State bird: Mountain bluebird
Largest city: Boise
Land area: 82,751 square miles
Land area rank: 11th largest state
Population: 1,006,749
Population rank: 42nd largest state
Postal abbreviation: ID

Illinois

Capital: Springfield
Organized as a territory: February 3, 1809
Entered Union: December 3, 1818
Order of entry: 21st state
Motto: State sovereignty, national union.
Geographic region: Midwest
Nickname: Prairie State
Origin of name Illinois: From an Indian word and French suffix, meaning "tribe of superior men"
State flower: Violet
State bird: Cardinal
Largest city: Chicago
Land area: 55,593 square miles
Land area rank: 24th largest state
Population: 11,430,602
Population rank: 6th largest state
Postal abbreviation: IL

Indiana

Capital: Indianapolis
Organized as a territory: May 7, 1800
Entered Union: December 11, 1816
Order of entry: 19th state
Motto: The crossroads of America.
Geographic region: Midwest
Nickname: Hoosier State
Origin of name Indiana: Meaning "land of Indians"
State flower: Peony
State bird: Cardinal
Largest city: Indianapolis
Land area: 35,870 square miles
Land area rank: 38th largest state
Population: 5,544,159
Population rank: 14th largest state
Postal abbreviation: IN

Iowa

Capital: Des Moines
Organized as a territory: June 12, 1838
Entered Union: December 28, 1846
Order of entry: 29th state
Motto: Our liberties we prize and our rights we will maintain.
Geographic region: Midwest
Nickname: Hawkeye State
Origin of name Iowa: Probably from an Indian word meaning "I-o-w-a, this is the place," or "the beautiful land"
State flower: Wild rose
State bird: Eastern goldfinch
Largest city: Des Moines
Land area: 55,875 square miles
Land area rank: 23rd largest state
Population: 2,776,755
Population rank: 30th largest state
Postal abbreviation: IA

Kansas

Capital: Topeka
Organized as a territory: May 30, 1854
Entered Union: January 29, 1861
Order of entry: 34th state
Motto: To the stars through difficulties.
Geographic region: Midwest
Nicknames: Sunflower State, Jayhawk State
Origin of name Kansas: From a Sioux word, meaning "people of the south wind"
State flower: Sunflower
State bird: Western meadowlark
Largest city: Wichita
Land area: 81,823 square miles
Land area rank: 13th largest state
Population: 2,477,574
Population rank: 32nd state
Postal abbreviation: KS

Kentucky

Capital: Frankfort
Became a colony: 1607, as part of Virginia
Entered Union: June 1, 1792
Order of entry: 15th state
Motto: United we stand, divided we fall.
Geographic region: South
Nickname: Bluegrass State
Origin of name Kentucky: From the Iroquoian word *Ken-tah-ten,* meaning "land of tomorrow"
State flower: Goldenrod
State bird: Kentucky cardinal
Largest city: Louisville
Land area: 39,732 square miles
Land area rank: 36th largest state
Population: 3,685,296
Population rank: 23rd largest state
Postal abbreviation: KY

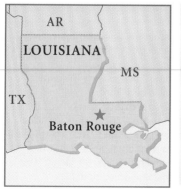

Louisiana

Capital: Baton Rouge
Organized as a territory: March 26, 1804
Entered Union: April 30, 1812
Order of entry: 18th state
Motto: Union, justice, and confidence.
Geographic region: South
Nicknames: Pelican State, Sportsman's Paradise, Creole State, Sugar State
Origin of name Louisiana: In honor of Louis XIV of France
State flower: Magnolia
State bird: Pelican
Largest city: New Orleans
Land area: 43,566 square miles
Land area rank: 33rd largest state
Population: 4,219,973
Population rank: 21st largest state
Postal abbreviation: LA

Maine

Capital: Augusta
Became a colony: 1620, as part of Massachusetts
Entered Union: March 15, 1820
Order of entry: 23rd state
Motto: I lead.
Geographic region: Northeast
Nickname: Pine Tree State
Origin of name Maine: It has been considered a compliment to Henrietta Maria, wife of Charles I of England, who was said to have owned the province of Mayne in France.
State flower: White pine cone and tassel
State bird: Chickadee
Largest city: Portland
Land area: 30,865 square miles
Land area rank: 39th largest state
Population: 1,227,928
Population rank: 38th largest state
Postal abbreviation: ME

Maryland

Capital: Annapolis
Became a colony: 1632
Entered Union: April 28, 1788
Order of entry: 7th state
Motto: Manly deeds, womanly words.
Geographic region: Northeast
Nicknames: Free State, Old Line State
Origin of name Maryland: In honor of Henrietta Maria, wife of Charles I of England
State flower: Black-eyed susan
State bird: Baltimore oriole
Largest city: Baltimore
Land area: 9,775 square miles
Land area rank: 42nd largest state
Population: 4,781,468
Population rank: 19th largest state
Postal abbreviation: MD

Massachusetts

Capital: Boston
Became a colony: 1620
Entered Union: February 6, 1788
Order of entry: 6th state
Motto: By the sword we seek peace, but peace only under liberty.
Geographic region: Northeast
Nicknames: Bay State, Old Colony State
Origin of name Massachusetts: From two Indian words, meaning "great mountain place"
State flower: Mayflower
State bird: Chickadee
Largest city: Boston
Land area: 7,838 square miles
Land area rank: 45th largest state
Population: 6,016,425
Population rank: 13th largest state
Postal abbreviation: MA

Michigan

Capital: Lansing
Organized as a territory: January 11, 1805
Entered Union: January 26, 1837
Order of entry: 26th state
Motto: If you seek a pleasant peninsula, look around you.
Geographic region: Midwest
Nickname: Wolverine State
Origin of name Michigan: From Indian word *Michigana,* meaning "great or large lake"
State flower: Apple blossom
State bird: Robin
Largest city: Detroit
Land area: 56,809.2 square miles
Land area rank: 22nd largest state
Population: 9,295,297
Population rank: 8th largest state
Postal abbreviation: MI

Minnesota

Capital: St. Paul
Organized as a territory: March 3, 1849
Entered Union: May 11, 1858
Order of entry: 32nd state
Motto: The North Star.
Geographic region: Midwest
Nicknames: North Star State, Gopher State, Land of 10,000 Lakes

Origin of name Minnesota: From a Dakota Indian word, meaning "sky-tinted water"
State flower: Showy lady slipper
State bird: Common loon
Largest city: Minneapolis
Land area: 79,617 square miles
Land area rank: 14th largest state
Population: 4,375,099
Population rank: 20th largest state
Postal abbreviation: MN

Mississippi

Capital: Jackson
Organized as a territory: April 7, 1798
Entered Union: December 10, 1817
Order of entry: 20th state
Motto: By valor and arms.
Geographic region: South
Nickname: Magnolia State
Origin of name Mississippi: From an Indian word, meaning "Father of Waters"

State flower: Flower of the magnolia or evergreen magnolia
State bird: Mockingbird
Largest city: Jackson
Land area: 46,914 square miles
Land area rank: 31st largest state
Population: 2,573,216
Population rank: 31st largest state
Postal abbreviation: MS

Missouri

Capital: Jefferson City
Organized as a territory: June 4, 1812
Entered Union: August 10, 1821
Order of entry: 24th state
Motto: The welfare of the people shall be the supreme law.
Geographic region: Midwest
Nickname: Show-Me State

Origin of name Missouri: Named after Missouri Indians; *Missouri* means "town of the large canoes"
State flower: Hawthorn
State bird: Bluebird
Largest city: Kansas City
Land area: 68,945 square miles
Land area rank: 18th largest state
Population: 5,117,073
Population rank: 15th largest state
Postal abbreviation: MO

Montana

Capital: Helena
Organized as a territory: May 26, 1864
Entered Union: November 8, 1889
Order of entry: 41st state
Motto: Gold and silver.
Geographic region: West
Nickname: Treasure State
Origin of name Montana: Latinized Spanish word, meaning "mountainous"

State flower: Bitterroot
State bird: Western meadowlark
Largest city: Billings
Land area: 145,556 square miles
Land area rank: 4th largest state
Population: 799,065
Population rank: 44th largest state
Postal abbreviation: MT

Nebraska

Capital: Lincoln
Organized as a territory: May 30, 1854
Entered Union: March 1, 1867
Order of entry: 37th state
Motto: Equality before the law.
Geographic region: Midwest
Nicknames: Cornhusker State, Beef State, Tree Planter State

Origin of name Nebraska: From an Oto Indian word, meaning "flat water"
State flower: Goldenrod
State bird: Western meadowlark
Largest city: Omaha
Land area: 76,878 square miles
Land area rank: 15th largest state
Population: 1,578,385
Population rank: 36th largest state
Postal abbreviation: NE

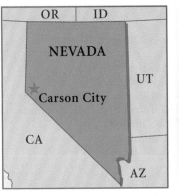

Nevada

Capital: Carson City
Organized as a territory: March 2, 1861
Entered Union: October 31, 1864
Order of entry: 36th state
Motto: All for our country.
Geographic region: West
Nicknames: Sagebrush State, Silver State, Battle Born State
Origin of name Nevada: Spanish word, meaning "snowcapped"

State flower: Sagebrush
State bird: Mountain bluebird
Largest city: Las Vegas
Land area: 109,806 square miles
Land area rank: 7th largest state
Population: 1,201,833
Population rank: 39th largest state
Postal abbreviation: NV

New Hampshire

Capital: Concord
Became a colony: 1623
Entered Union: June 21, 1788
Order of entry: 9th state
Motto: Live free or die.
Geographic region: Northeast
Nickname: Granite State
Origin of name New Hampshire: From the English county of Hampshire

State flower: Purple lilac
State bird: Purple finch
Largest city: Manchester
Land area: 8,969 square miles
Land area rank: 44th largest state
Population: 1,109,252
Population rank: 40th largest state
Postal abbreviation: NH

New Jersey

Capital: Trenton
Became a colony: 1702
Entered Union: December 18, 1787
Order of entry: 3rd state
Motto: Liberty and prosperity.
Geographic region: Northeast
Nickname: Garden State
Origin of name New Jersey: From the Channel Isle of Jersey

State flower: Purple violet
State bird: Eastern goldfinch
Largest city: Newark
Land area: 7,419 square miles
Land area rank: 46th largest state
Population: 7,730,188
Population rank: 9th largest state
Postal abbreviation: NJ

New Mexico

Capital: Santa Fe
Organized as a territory: September 9, 1850
Entered Union: January 6, 1912
Order of entry: 47th state
Motto: It grows as it goes.
Geographic region: West
Nicknames: Land of Enchantment, Sunshine State

Origin of name New Mexico: From the country of Mexico
State flower: Yucca
State bird: Roadrunner
Largest city: Albuquerque
Land area: 121,635 square miles
Land area rank: 5th largest state
Population: 1,515,069
Population rank: 37th largest state
Postal abbreviation: NM

New York

Capital: Albany
Became a colony: 1609 as a Dutch colony, 1664 as an English colony
Entered Union: July 26, 1788
Order of entry: 11th state
Motto: Ever upward.
Geographic region: Northeast
Nickname: Empire State
Origin of name New York: In honor of the English Duke of York

State flower: Rose
State bird: Bluebird
Largest city: New York City
Land area: 47,224 square miles
Land area rank: 30th largest state
Population: 17,990,455
Population rank: 2nd largest state
Postal abbreviation: NY

North Carolina

Capital: Raleigh
Became a colony: 1663
Entered Union: November 21, 1789
Order of entry: 12th state
Motto: To be rather than to seem.
Geographic region: South
Nickname: Tar Heel State
Origin of name Carolina: In honor of Charles I of England

State flower: Dogwood
State bird: Cardinal
Largest city: Charlotte
Land area: 48,718 square miles
Land area rank: 29th largest state
Population: 6,628,637
Population rank: 10th largest state
Postal abbreviation: NC

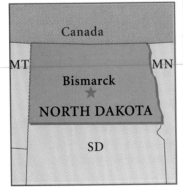

North Dakota

Capital: Bismarck
Organized as a territory: March 2, 1861
Entered Union: November 2, 1889
Order of entry: 39th state
Motto: Liberty and union, now and forever: one and inseparable.
Geographic region: Midwest
Nicknames: Sioux State, Flickertail State, Peace Garden State

Origin of name Dakota: From the Sioux tribe, meaning "allies"
State flower: Wild prairie rose
State bird: Western meadowlark
Largest city: Fargo
Land area: 68,994 square miles
Land area rank: 17th largest state
Population: 638,800
Population rank: 47th largest state
Postal abbreviation: ND

Ohio

Capital: Columbus
Organized as a territory: 1783
Entered Union: March 1, 1803
Order of entry: 17th state
Motto: With God, all things are possible.
Geographic region: Midwest
Nickname: Buckeye State
Origin of name Ohio: From an Iroquoian word, meaning "great river"

State flower: Scarlet carnation
State bird: Cardinal
Largest city: Columbus
Land area: 40,953 square miles
Land area rank: 35th largest state
Population: 10,847,115
Population rank: 7th largest state
Postal abbreviation: OH

Oklahoma

Capital: Oklahoma City
Organized as a territory: May 2, 1890
Entered Union: November 16, 1907
Order of entry: 46th state
Motto: Labor conquers all things.
Geographic region: West
Nickname: Sooner State
Origin of name Oklahoma: From two Choctaw Indian words, meaning "red people"

State flower: Mistletoe
State bird: Scissor-tailed flycatcher
Largest city: Oklahoma City
Land area: 68,679 square miles
Land area rank: 19th largest state
Population: 3,145,585
Population rank: 28th largest state
Postal abbreviation: OK

Oregon

Capital: Salem
Organized as a territory: August 14, 1848
Entered Union: February 14, 1859
Order of entry: 33rd state
Motto: She flies with her own wings.
Geographic region: West
Nickname: Beaver State
Origin of name Oregon: Unknown, but generally accepted to have been

taken from the writings of Major Robert Rogers, an English army officer
State flower: Oregon grape
State bird: Western meadowlark
Largest city: Portland
Land area: 96,003 square miles
Land area rank: 10th largest state
Population: 2,842,321
Population rank: 29th largest state
Postal abbreviation: OR

Pennsylvania

Capital: Harrisburg
Became a colony: 1681
Entered Union: December 12, 1787
Order of entry: 2nd state
Motto: Virtue, liberty, and independence.
Geographic region: Northeast
Nickname: Keystone State
Origin of name Pennsylvania: In honor of Admiral Sir William Penn,

father of William Penn, meaning "Penn's woodland"
State flower: Mountain laurel
State bird: Ruffed grouse
Largest city: Philadelphia
Land area: 44,820 square miles
Land area rank: 32nd largest state
Population: 11,881,643
Population rank: 5th largest state
Postal abbreviation: PA

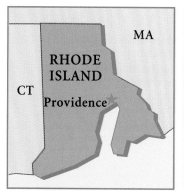

Rhode Island

Capital: Providence
Became a colony: 1636
Entered Union: May 29, 1790
Order of entry: 13th state
Motto: Hope.
Geographic region: Northeast
Nickname: The Ocean State
Origin of name Rhode Island:
From the Greek Island of Rhodes

State flower: Violet
State bird: Rhode Island Red
Largest city: Providence
Land area: 1,045 square miles
Land area rank: Smallest state
Population: 1,003,464
Population rank: 43rd largest state
Postal abbreviation: RI

South Carolina

Capital: Columbia
Became a colony: 1663
Entered Union: May 23, 1788
Order of entry: 8th state
Mottoes: Prepared in mind and resources. While I breathe, I hope.
Geographic region: South
Nickname: Palmetto State
Origin of name Carolina:
In honor of Charles I of England

State flower: Carolina yellow jessamine
State bird: Carolina wren
Largest city: Columbia
Land area: 30,111 square miles
Land area rank: 40th largest state
Population: 3,486,703
Population rank: 25th largest state
Postal abbreviation: SC

South Dakota

Capital: Pierre
Organized as a territory: March 2, 1861
Entered Union: November 2, 1889
Order of entry: 40th state
Motto: Under God the people rule.
Geographic region: Midwest
Nicknames: Mount Rushmore State, Coyote State
Origin of name Dakota: From the Sioux Indians, meaning "allies"

State flower: American pasqueflower
State bird: Ring-necked pheasant
Largest city: Sioux Falls
Land area: 75,898 square miles
Land area rank: 16th largest state
Population: 696,004
Population rank: 45th largest state
Postal abbreviation: SD

Tennessee

Capital: Nashville
Organized as a territory: 1790
Entered Union: June 1, 1796
Order of entry: 16th state
Motto: Agriculture and Commerce.
Geographic region: South
Nickname: Volunteer State
Origin of name Tennessee:
Cherokee word of unknown meaning

State flower: Iris
State bird: Mockingbird
Largest city: Memphis
Land area: 41,220 square miles
Land area rank: 34th largest state
Population: 4,877,185
Population rank: 17th largest state
Postal abbreviation: TN

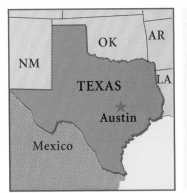

Texas

Capital: Austin
Became an independent republic: 1836
Entered Union: December 29, 1845
Order of entry: 28th state
Motto: Friendship.
Geographic region: West
Nickname: Lone Star State
Origin of name Texas: From an Indian word, meaning "friends"

State flower: Bluebonnet
State bird: Mockingbird
Largest city: Houston
Land area: 261,914 square miles
Land area rank: 2nd largest state
Population: 16,986,510
Population rank: 3rd largest state
Postal abbreviation: TX

Utah

Capital: Salt Lake City
Organized as a territory: September 9, 1850
Entered Union: January 4, 1896
Order of entry: 45th state
Motto: Industry.
Geographic region: West
Nickname: Beehive State
Origin of name Utah: From the Ute Indians, meaning "people of the mountains"

State flower: Sego lily
State bird: California gull
Largest city: Salt Lake City
Land area: 82,168 square miles
Land area rank: 12th largest state
Population: 1,722,850
Population rank: 35th largest state
Postal abbreviation: UT

Vermont

Capital: Montpelier
Became a colony: 1623, as part of New Hampshire
Entered Union: March 4, 1791
Order of entry: 14th state
Motto: Vermont, Freedom, and Unity.
Geographic region: Northeast
Nickname: Green Mountain State
Origin of name Vermont: From the French words *vert mont*, meaning "green mountain"

State flower: Red clover
State bird: Hermit thrush
Largest city: Burlington
Land area: 9,249 square miles
Land area rank: 43rd largest state
Population: 562,758
Population rank: 48th largest state
Postal abbreviation: VT

Virginia

Capital: Richmond
Became a colony: 1607
Entered Union: June 25, 1788
Order of entry: 10th state
Motto: Thus always to tyrants.
Geographic region: South
Nicknames: The Old Dominion, Mother of Presidents
Origin of name Virginia: In honor of Elizabeth, "Virgin Queen" of England

State flower: American dogwood
State bird: Cardinal
Largest city: Virginia Beach
Land area: 39,598 square miles
Land area rank: 37th largest state
Population: 6,187,358
Population rank: 12th largest state
Postal abbreviation: VA

Washington

Capital: Olympia
Organized as a territory: March 2, 1853
Entered Union: November 11, 1889
Order of entry: 42nd state
Motto: Al-Ki (Indian word, meaning "by and by").
Geographic region: West
Nicknames: Evergreen State, Chinook State

Origin of name Washington: In honor of George Washington.
State flower: Coast rhododendron
State bird: Willow goldfinch
Largest city: Seattle
Land area: 66,582 square miles
Land area rank: 20th largest state
Population: 4,866,692
Population rank: 18th largest state
Postal abbreviation: WA

West Virginia

Capital: Charleston
Became a colony: 1607, as part of Virginia colony
Entered Union: June 20, 1863
Order of entry: 35th state
Motto: Mountaineers are always free.
Geographic region: South
Nickname: Mountain State
Origin of name Virginia: In honor of Elizabeth, "Virgin Queen" of England

State flower: Rhododendron
State bird: Cardinal
Largest city: Charleston
Land area: 24,087 square miles
Land area rank: 41st largest state
Population: 1,793,477
Population rank: 34th largest state
Postal abbreviation: WV

Wisconsin

Capital: Madison
Organized as a territory: July 4, 1836
Entered Union: May 29, 1848
Order of entry: 30th state
Motto: Forward.
Geographic region: Midwest
Nickname: Badger State
Origin of name Wisconsin: French misinterpretation of an Indian word whose meaning is disputed

State flower: Wood violet
State bird: Robin
Largest city: Milwaukee
Land area: 54,314 square miles
Land area rank: 25th largest state
Population: 4,891,769
Population rank: 16th largest state
Postal abbreviation: WI

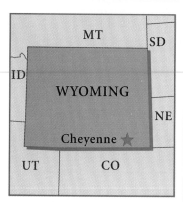

Wyoming

Capital: Cheyenne
Organized as a territory: May 19, 1869
Entered Union: July 10, 1890
Order of entry: 44th state
Motto: Equal rights.
Geographic region: West
Nickname: Equality State
Origin of name Wyoming: From the Delaware Indian word, meaning "mountains and valleys alternating"

State flower: Indian paintbrush
State bird: Meadowlark
Largest city: Cheyenne
Land area: 97,105 square miles
Land area rank: 9th largest state
Population: 453,588
Population rank: Smallest state
Postal abbreviation: WY

ARCTIC OCEAN

Beaufort Sea

Baffin Bay

GREENLAND

ICELA

Bering Sea

Gulf of Alaska

CANADA

NORTH
AMERICA

Hudson Bay

Labrador Sea

UNITED STATES OF AMERICA

NORTH
ATLANTIC
OCEAN

NORTH
PACIFIC
OCEAN

CANARY ISLANDS

MEXICO

Gulf of Mexico

THE BAHAMAS

CUBA

DOMINICAN
REPUBLIC

WESTER
SAHARA

BELIZE

HAITI

PUERTO RICO (U.S.)

MAURIT

HONDURAS

Caribbean Sea

SENEGAL

GUATEMALA

THE GAMBIA

EL SALVADOR

PANAMA

GUINEA-BISSAU

NICARAGUA

VENEZUELA

GUYANA

GUINEA

COSTA RICA

SURINAME

SIERRA LEONE

FRENCH GUIANA

LIBE

COLOMBIA

ECUADOR

SOUTH
AMERICA

PERU

BRAZIL

BOLIVIA

PARAGUAY

SOUTH
PACIFIC
OCEAN

CHILE

ARGENTINA

SO
ATLA
OC

URUGUAY

N
W E
S

FALKLAND ISLANDS (U.K.)

SOUTH GEORGIA ISLAND (U.K.)

United States Physical

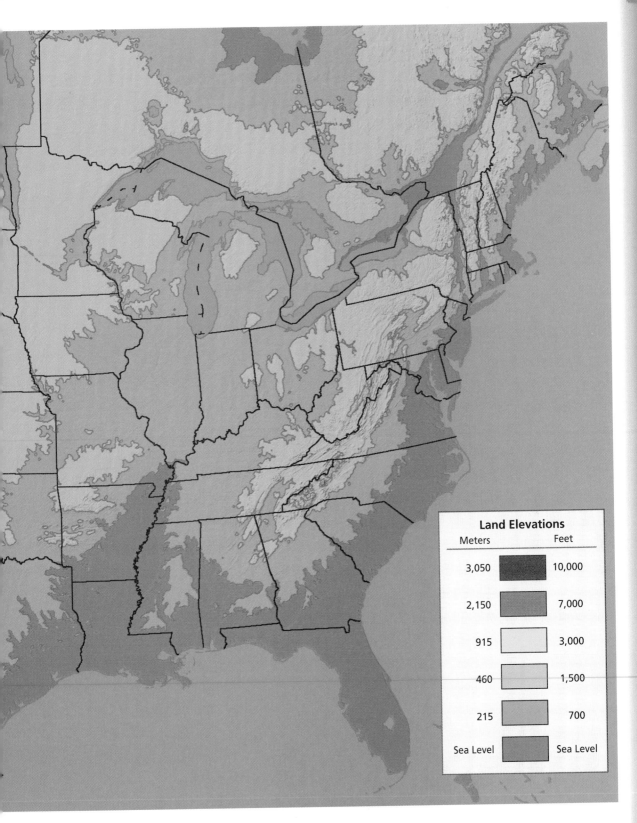

Land Elevations

Meters		Feet
3,050		10,000
2,150		7,000
915		3,000
460		1,500
215		700
Sea Level		Sea Level

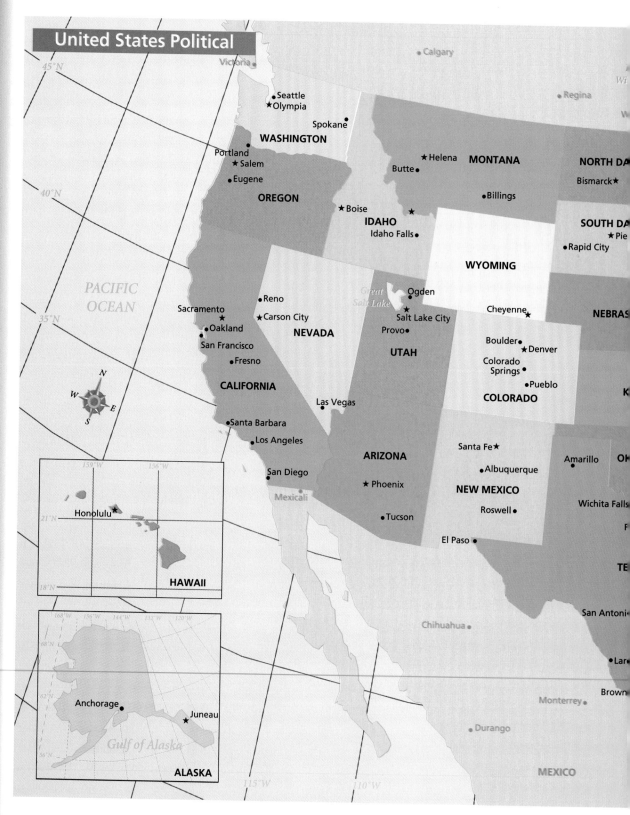

United States Political

Victoria

• Calgary

• Regina

45°N

• Seattle
★ Olympia

Spokane •

WASHINGTON

Portland •
★ Salem

• Eugene

OREGON

★ Helena   **MONTANA**

Butte •

NORTH DA

Bismarck ★

• Billings

40°N

★ Boise

IDAHO

Idaho Falls •

★

SOUTH DA

★ Pie

• Rapid City

WYOMING

**PACIFIC
OCEAN**

*Great
Salt Lake*

• Ogden

Cheyenne ★

NEBRAS

35°N

Sacramento
★

• Reno

• Oakland

San Francisco •

• Carson City

NEVADA

Salt Lake City
Provo •

★

UTAH

Boulder •
★ Denver

Colorado
Springs •

• Pueblo

COLORADO

K

• Fresno

CALIFORNIA

Las Vegas
•

Santa Fe ★

Amarillo
•

O

• Santa Barbara

• Los Angeles

San Diego •

ARIZONA

Mexicali

★ Phoenix

NEW MEXICO

• Albuquerque

Roswell •

Wichita Falls

F

• Tucson

El Paso •

TE

N
W ☉ E
S

San Antoni

159°W   156°W

21°N   Honolulu ★

Chihuahua •

• Lar

18°N

HAWAII

168°W 156°W 144°W 132°W 120°W

68°N

Brown

Monterrey •

62°N

Anchorage •

★ Juneau

Gulf of Alaska

56°N

• Durango

115°W   110°W

MEXICO

ALASKA

United States History   Appendix F   World Atlas   **743**

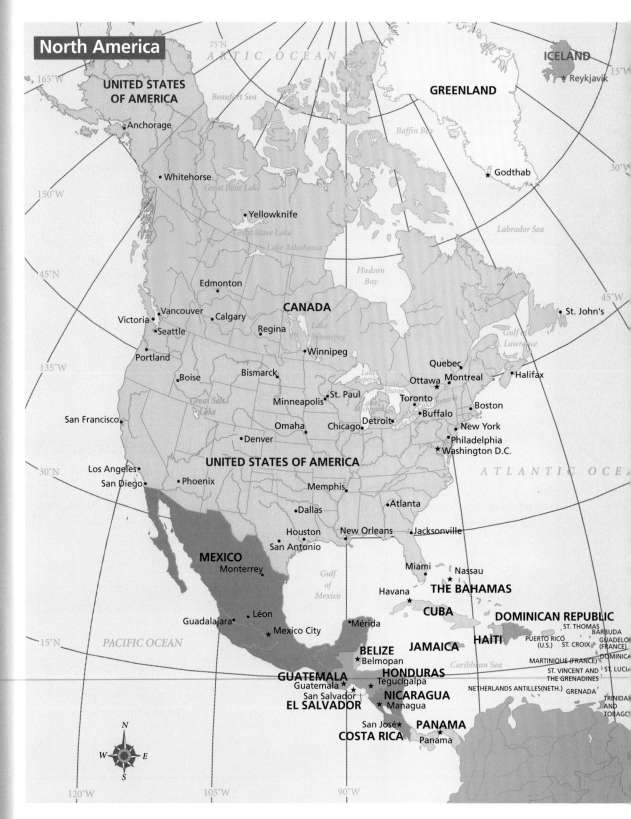

North America

ARTIC OCEAN

75°N

ICELAND

★ Reykjavík

15°N

30°W

UNITED STATES OF AMERICA

165°W

Beaufort Sea

• Anchorage

GREENLAND

150°W

• Whitehorse

Baffin Bay

★ Godthab

Great Bear Lake

45°N

• Yellowknife

Labrador Sea

Great Slave Lake

Lake Athabasca

Hudson Bay

45°N

• Edmonton

CANADA

• St. John's

Victoria • Vancouver • Calgary

• Seattle

Regina

Lake Winnipeg

Quebec

Gulf of St. Lawrence

• Halifax

Portland

• Winnipeg

Ottawa • Montreal

135°W

• Boise

Bismarck

Lake Superior

Lake Huron

Toronto

• Boston

San Francisco •

Minneapolis • St. Paul

Lake Michigan

Detroit • Buffalo

Lake Erie

Lake Ontario

• New York

Omaha

Chicago •

• Philadelphia

UNITED STATES OF AMERICA

• Denver

★ Washington D.C.

Los Angeles •

ATLANTIC OCEAN

30°N

San Diego •

• Phoenix

Memphis •

• Atlanta

• Dallas

Houston •

New Orleans •

• Jacksonville

San Antonio •

MEXICO

Miami •

• Nassau

Monterrey •

★

THE BAHAMAS

Gulf of Mexico

Havana

★

CUBA

DOMINICAN REPUBLIC

ST. THOMAS

BARBUDA

15°N

Guadalajara • • Léon

• Mérida

PUERTO RICO (U.S.)

GUADELOU (FRANCE)

PACIFIC OCEAN

★ Mexico City

HAITI

ST. CROIX

DOMINICA

BELIZE

JAMAICA

MARTINIQUE (FRANCE)

★ Belmopan

Caribbean Sea

ST. VINCENT AND

ST. LUCIA

GUATEMALA

HONDURAS

THE GRENADINES

Guatemala ★

★ Tegucigalpa

NETHERLANDS ANTILLES(NETH.)

GRENADA

San Salvador ★

NICARAGUA

TRINIDA

EL SALVADOR

★ Managua

AND TOBAGO

San José ★

PANAMA

COSTA RICA

★ Panama

N

W ● E

S

120°W

105°W

90°W

Caribbean Sea

ST. LUCIA
GRENADA

South America

Managua ★

San José ●

Panama

Barranquilla ●

Caracas ●
Valencia ●
VENEZUELA

Cúcuta ●
Medellín ●
Bogotá ●
★

Puerto Ayacucho ●

Georgetown
★ Paramaribo
GUYANA ★
SURINAME ★ Cayenne
**FRENCH
GUIANA**

COLOMBIA

Mitú ●

★ Quito
ECUADOR ● Guayaquil

Macapá ●

Belém ●

Santarém ●

Fortaleza ●
Teresina ●

**Galápagos
Islands**

Talara ●

PERU

Recife ●

Maceió ●
Aracaju ●

Salvador ●

Trujillo ●

Huánuco ●

BRAZIL

Barreiras ●

Porto Velho ●

Lima ●
Ica ●
Cuzco ●

BOLIVIA
La Paz
★
Santa Cruz ●
★ Sucre

★ **Brásilia**
● Goiânia

Iquique ●

PACIFIC OCEAN

Antofagasta ●

PARAGUAY

Rio de Janeiro ●
São Paulo ●

CHILE

★ **Asunción**

Córdoba ●

Rosario ●

ATLANTIC OCEAN

★ Santiago

URUGUAY
Buenos Aires ★
★ **Montevideo**

Concepción ●

ARGENTINA

Valdivia ●

Puerto Montt ●

Comodoro Rivadavia ●

N
W E
S

**FALKLAND ISLANDS
(U.K.)**

**SOUTH GEORGIA ISLAND
(U.K.)**

90°W   80°W   70°W   60°W   50°W   40°W

Europe

Reykjavik ★ ICELAND

Faroe Islands

NORTH ATLANTIC OCEAN

Norwegian Sea

SWEDEN

FINLAND

RUSSIA

NORWAY

Oslo ★

Gulf of Bothnia

Helsinki ★

Stockholm ★

★ Tallinn
ESTONIA

Moscow ★

Baltic Sea

★ Riga
LATVIA

North Sea

DENMARK

LITHUANIA
Vilnius ★

★ Minsk
BELARUS

Belfast ★
IRELAND

Dublin ★

★ Copenhagen

U. K.

NETHERLANDS

Amsterdam ★

Berlin ★

Warsaw ★

★ Kiev
UKRAI

London ★

Brussels ★
BELGIUM
LUX.

GERMANY

POLAND

English Channel

★ Paris

Prague ★
CZECH
REP.

Ostrava •

SLOVAKIA

Vienna ★ ★ Bratislava

MOLDOVA

Chisinau ★

FRANCE

Bern ★
SWITZERLAND

AUSTRIA

★ Budapest
HUNGARY

ROMANIA

Bay of Biscay

SLOVENIA
★ Zagreb

Belgrade ★

Bucharest ★

Monte Carlo ★
MONACO

BOSNIA AND
HERZEGOVINA

CROATIA

ITALY

★ Sarajevo
SERBIA

BULGARIA

• Varna

PORTUGAL

ANDORRA

★ Madrid

Adriatic

MACEDONIA

★ Sofia

★ Skopje

Black

Corsica

★ Rome

Anka

Lisbon •

SPAIN

Tiranë ★
ALBANIA

Aegean Sea

Sardinia

GREECE

★ Gibraltar

Balearic Islands

Tyrrhenian Sea

Athens ★

Algiers •

Ionian Sea

Rabat •

N
W E
S

Tunis •

★ Valletta
MALTA

Mediterranean Sea

Tripoli •

Alexandria •

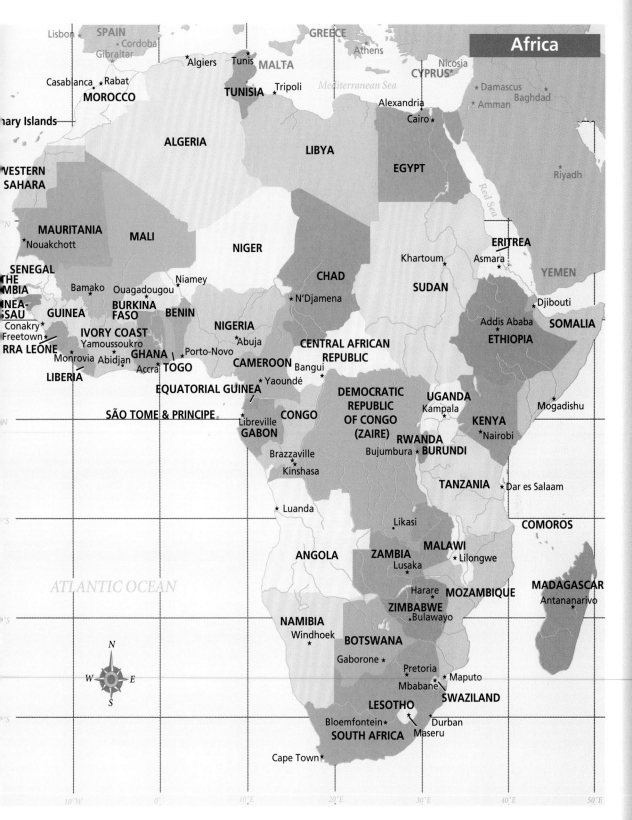

Africa

Lisbon • SPAIN
• Cordoba
Gibraltar
GREECE
Athens
Africa

Casablanca • Rabat
nary Islands
MOROCCO
*Algiers *Tunis **MALTA**
TUNISIA *Tripoli
*Nicosia
CYPRUS
*Damascus
*Amman Baghdad

Mediterranean Sea

Alexandria
Cairo *

ALGERIA
LIBYA
EGYPT
Riyadh

*N
**WESTERN
SAHARA**

MAURITANIA
*Nouakchott
MALI
NIGER
Khartoum
*Asmara
ERITREA
YEMEN

SENEGAL
**THE
MBIA**
Bamako
Niamey
CHAD
SUDAN
Djibouti

**NEA-
SAU**
Ouagadougou
**BURKINA
FASO**
*N'Djamena
Addis Ababa
SOMALIA

GUINEA
Conakry *
Freetown
RRA LEONE
BENIN
NIGERIA
*Abuja
**CENTRAL AFRICAN
REPUBLIC**
ETHIOPIA

IVORY COAST
Yamoussoukro
Monrovia Abidjan
GHANA
Accra *
Porto-Novo
TOGO
CAMEROON
Bangui

LIBERIA
EQUATORIAL GUINEA
*Yaoundé
**DEMOCRATIC
REPUBLIC
OF CONGO
(ZAIRE)**
UGANDA
Kampala
Mogadishu

SÃO TOME & PRINCIPE
Libreville
CONGO
GABON
KENYA
*Nairobi

Brazzaville
Kinshasa
RWANDA
Bujumbura *
BURUNDI

TANZANIA
*Dar es Salaam

* Luanda

* Likasi
COMOROS

ATLANTIC OCEAN
ANGOLA
ZAMBIA
Lusaka
MALAWI
* Lilongwe
MADAGASCAR
Antananarivo
*

Harare
*
MOZAMBIQUE

ZIMBABWE
.Bulawayo

NAMIBIA
Windhoek
*
BOTSWANA
Gaborone *
Pretoria
* *Maputo
Mbabane

LESOTHO
SWAZILAND

Bloemfontein*
SOUTH AFRICA
*Durban
Maseru

Cape Town*

N
W E
S

Asia and Australia

RUSSIA

RUSSIA

- Moscow

- Novosibirsk

East Siberian Sea

Sea of Okhotsk

Bering Sea

Karaganda

KAZAKHSTAN

Ulaanbaatar•

MONGOLIA

AZERBAIJAN
GEORGIA
ARMENIA
TURKEY

TURKMENISTAN
UZBEKISTAN

Black Sea

Tashkent•

KYRGYZSTAN

TAJIKISTAN

Beijing•

CHINA

NORTH KOREA
•Pyongyang
•Seoul
SOUTH KOREA

JAPAN
•Tokyo

SYRIA
Baghdad
IRAQ
ISRAEL
JORDAN

•Tehran

AFGHANISTAN

IRAN

PAKISTAN

NEPAL

BHUTAN

Chengdu•

East China Sea

P A C I F I C
O C E A N

KUWAIT
QATAR
SAUDI ARABIA

U.A.E.

OMAN

New Delhi
INDIA
Calcutta,•

Dhaka
MYANMAR
BANGLADESH
Rangoon•

TAIWAN

Hanoi•

Hong Kong

Bombay•

Vientiane•

LAOS

•Sanaa
YEMEN

THAILAND
KAMPUCHEA

Bangkok•

VIETNAM

•Manila

Red Sea

Colombo•
SRI LANKA

Phnom Penh•

BRUNEI

PHILIPPINES

•Davao

Kuala Lumpur•

MALAYSIA

Jakarta•

I N D O N E S I A

PAPUA
NEW GUINEA

Java Sea

I N D I A N   O C E A N

Arafura Sea

Port Moresby•

Timor Sea

Coral Sea

FIJI

NEW CALEDONIA

N
W   E
S

AUSTRALIA

Perth•

*Great
Australian Bight*

Adelaide•
•Canberra

Auckland•

*Tasman
Sea*

Wellington•

NEW ZEALAND

30°E   60°E   90°E   120°E   150°E   180°E

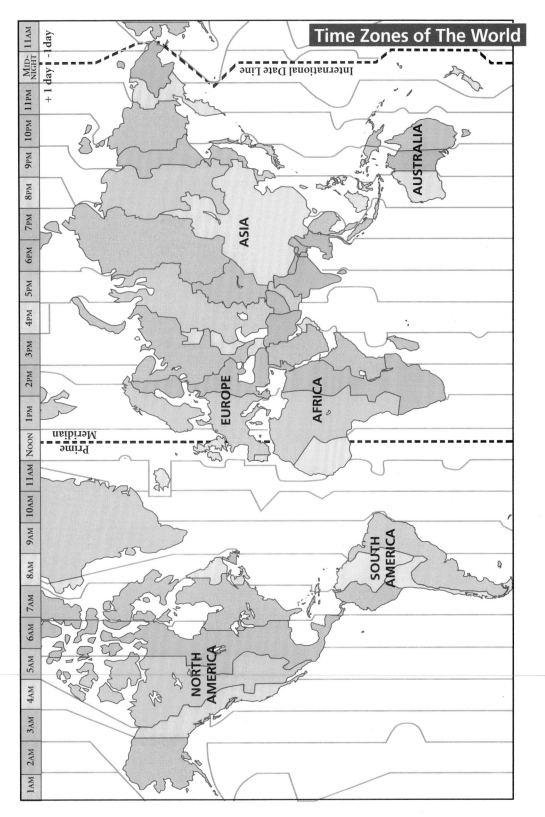

Time Zones of The World

International Date Line

Prime Meridian

1AM 2AM 3AM 4AM 5AM 6AM 7AM 8AM 9AM 10AM 11AM NOON 1PM 2PM 3PM 4PM 5PM 6PM 7PM 8PM 9PM 10PM 11PM MID-NIGHT 11AM

+ 1 day   – 1day

NORTH AMERICA

SOUTH AMERICA

EUROPE

AFRICA

ASIA

AUSTRALIA

Glossary

A

Abolish — To get rid of something (p. 221)

Abolitionist — A person who wanted slavery stopped (p. 247)

Abroad — Throughout the world (p. 432)

Access — Ability or right to enter or use (p. 67)

Accusation — A charge of wrongdoing (p. 556)

Acquire — To gain something by purchasing or taking it (p. 169)

Administration — The period during which an official serves (p. 337)

Advertise — To promote an idea or product (p. 388)

Adviser — A person who gives information, advice, or help (p. 146)

Affairs — A person or group's day-to-day business (p. 160)

Agency — An organization set up by the federal government (p. 328)

Aggressive — Forceful (p. 179)

Agreement — An arrangement as to the course of action (p. 208)

Agricultural — Having to do with raising crops or animals for food or profit (p. 210)

Aide — A person who assists (p. 601)

Airlift — Using planes to deliver food and supplies (p. 550)

Alien — Someone who lives in a country but is not a citizen of that country (p.164)

Alliance — An agreement that joins groups of people or countries together (p. 82)

Allied Powers— A group of allied nations that included Great Britian, France, Serbia, Belgium, and Russia (p. 451)

Ambassador — A representative from a country who works out problems with another country (p. 169)

Ambush — To carry out a surprise attack (p. 84)

Amendment — A change (p. 150)

Ammunition — Bullets, gunpowder, and other things fired from guns or other weapons (p. 293)

Amnesty — A pardon granted by the government (p. 325)

Anarchist — A person or group against all forms of government (p. 410)

Anthem — A song or hymn of praise or gladness (p. 187)

Anti-Federalist — A person who felt that the Constitution gave the central government too much power (p. 148)

Apartheid — The South African policy of racial segregation (p. 629)

Appeasement — Giving in to other's demands in order to keep peace (p. 518)

Appoint — To name or choose a person to do something (p. 83)

Approve — To accept or agree on something (p. 138)

Archaeologist — A person who studies the remains of past human life (p. 13)

Architect — A person skilled in designing buildings (p. 16)

Armada — Fleet of warships (p. 43)

Armistice — A break in a war to talk peace (p. 427)

Arrogant — Acting better than others (p. 164)

Arsenal — A place to make or store military weapons (p. 293)

Arson — The act of purposely setting fire to something (p. 658)

Artificial satellite — A human-made object that travels in outer space and sends signals back to Earth (p. 559)

Artisan — A skilled worker (p. 18)

Assassination — The killing of a politically important person (p. 325)

Assemble — To gather together (p. 150)

Assembly line — A process by which a line of workers assemble something piece by piece until it is complete (p. 473)

Asset — Something of worth that someone owns; a useful quality (p. 525)

Association — A group working together on a common cause (p. 469)

Astronomy — The study of space and the planets (p. 16)

Atmosphere — The gaseous layer covering the Earth (p. 565)

Atomic bomb — A nuclear bomb with great destructive powers (p. 532)

Authorities — Persons in command (p. 206)

Automation — The use of machines to do work (p. 558)

Axis Powers — The alliance of Japan, Italy, and Germany in World War II (p. 525)

B

Baby boom — The millions of babies born after World War II (p. 580)

Ban — To disallow (p. 105)

Belittling — Insulting (p. 289)

Beringia — A thousand-mile–wide land bridge that connected Siberia to Alaska (p. 13)

Betray — To go against someone's trust (p. 611)

Bicentennial — A 200th year celebration (p. 606)

Bill — A proposal for a new law (p. 145)

Billboard — A large sign used to advertise (p. 254)

Black Codes — Laws that prevented African Americans from buying land, voting, and working at jobs other than farming (p. 327)

Blitzkrieg — "Lightning war"; a rapid military attack (p. 521)

Blockade — To prevent goods or people from entering or leaving (p. 172)

Blockhouse — Building used for protection from attack; fort (p. 56)

Bond — A document that states that a given sum of money is owed; a guarantee that a sum of money will be paid at a specific time (p. 158)

Bootlegger — Someone who made or sold alcohol illegally during Prohibition (p. 481)

Boundary — A real or imaginary marker that shows what land a person owns or an outline of a country; a line that sets a limit (p. 64)

Boycott — To refuse to deal with a person, country, or group (p. 98)

Bravery — The ability not to be afraid when facing danger; courage in the face of danger (p. 244)

Breadline — A place where people could get free food (p. 495)

Bribe — Payment made to get a person to act in a certain way (p. 405)

Budget — A plan that shows how much money is available and how the money will be spent (p. 622)

Bunker — An underground shelter (p. 532)

Burial — The act of burying the dead (p. 21)

By-product — Something produced in the process of making something else (p. 375)

Cabinet — A group of advisers to the President (p. 157)

Campaign — A plan of activities done to achieve a goal; military operations to achieve a goal as part of a war (p. 217)

Canal — A human-made waterway (p. 18)

Candidate — A person who has been selected to run for a political office (p. 163)

Capable — Having the ability to do a task (p. 217)

Capital — Money used for investments; money or property used in business by an individual firm (p. 373)

Career — A permanent job or line of work (p. 624)

Cargo — Objects or goods carried in a ship or other form of transportation (p. 104)

Caribou — Large deer that live in arctic regions (p. 13)

Carpetbaggers — Northerners who went to the South after the Civil War to make money; they carried their belongings in carpet bags (p. 332)

Cash crop — Any crop that is easy to sell, such as wheat or cotton (p. 181)

Casualty — A person who is wounded, killed, or lost in military action (p. 646)

Cease-fire — A call for an end to fighting (p. 533)

Centennial — A 100th-year celebration (p. 338)

Central Powers — A group of allied nations that included Germany, Austria-Hungary, and later Turkey and Bulgaria (p. 451)

Chain reaction — A series of events linked to one another (p. 451)

Chancellor — The chief minister in some European countries (p. 514)

Charity — A group that helps those in need (p. 493)

Charter — Written agreement granting power in the name of a state or country (p. 43)

Circulate — To pass from person to person or place to place (p. 148)

Citizenship — The state of having the rights, privileges, and duties granted by a country to its citizens; act of belonging to a certain country (p. 514)

Civilian — A person who is not in the military (p. 528)

Civilization — People or country with a high level of cultural development (p. 16)

Civil lawsuit — A court case involving private rights (p. 150)

Civil rights — Basic human rights given to all people (p. 329)

Civil service — A system in which people qualify for government jobs by passing a test; the group of people who work in branches of public service concerned with all government functions outside of the armed forces (p. 405)

Civil war — A war between groups within the same country (p. 303)

Classic — A book that has lasting value or meaning; an author or book considered standard (p. 244)

Clause — A section of a document (p. 121)

Clergy — Person or group given the power by the church to perform religious tasks (p. 64)

Clovis point — A finely flaked stone spearhead (p. 14)

Coerce — To pressure a person or group to do something (p. 172)

Cold War — The disagreements between communist and noncommunist nations over economics and politics that caused tensions following World War II (p. 547)

Collapse — A breakdown or ruin (p. 595)

Collective bargaining — A way of negotiating between groups of workers and employers (p. 500)

Colony — A group of people living in a new area under rule of their native land (p. 43)

Combat — The act of fighting (p. 529)

Commander — A person who controls an army or some other group (p. 117)

Commerce — The buying or selling of goods; exchange of goods between different areas in different countries (p. 237)

Commercial — Something linked to business or buying and selling; suitable for a wide popular market (p. 140)

Commission — To appoint a person or group to do a task (p. 39)

Commonwealth — A group of self-governing states (p. 643)

Communication — The act of sending and receiving information (p. 237)

Communist — A person who believes in a form of government that eliminates private property (p. 480)

Compass — An instrument used to show direction (p. 35)

Competitor — A company that sells or buys the same goods or services as another company; a rival (p. 104)

Complex — Complicated or having many parts (p. 77)

Composer — One who writes music (p. 477)

Compromise — A settlement of differences in which each side gives up some of its demands (p. 126)

Conductor — A person who helped free slaves by using the Underground Railroad; a leader or guide (p. 276)

Confederacy — A group that has formed an alliance for some purpose; the Confederate States of America (p. 182)

Conference — A meeting among a large group of people (p. 460)

Conflict — A disagreement, fight, battle, or war (p. 180)

Confusion — A state of being mixed up, without direction (p. 188)

Conquer — To gain something by force; defeat (p. 39)

Conservation — The act of protecting or limiting the use of natural resources (p. 437)

Conservative — A person who is cautious about change (p. 575)

Conspiracy — A joint act of breaking the law; a secret plan or agreement of two or more people to do an unlawful or harmful act (p. 601)

Constitutional — Following the ideas set forth in the Constitution (p. 165)

Consumer goods — Objects or things the average person buys and uses (p. 457)

Containment policy — The policy of using strength or threat of force to prevent the spread of communism (p. 548)

Continent — Large land mass on Earth; for example, North America or Africa (p. 36)

Contract — A work agreement between at least two groups (p. 403)

Contribute — To add to or take part in (p. 162)

Controversial — Something that causes much debate and disagreement (p. 584)

Convention — A formal meeting called for a special purpose (p. 107)

Conventional — Something that is traditional or commonly used (p. 641)

Convict — To find guilty of a crime (p. 129)

Corporation — A large, organized company owned by stockholders (p. 372)

Corruption — Wrong or unlawful ways used for financial gain (p. 332)

Cotton — A plant used to make cloth (p. 20)

Counterattack — To fight back following an attack (p. 531)

Counterculture — The behavior and lifestyle of people who reject the usual values and behavior of society (p. 581)

Cowhand — A person who tends cattle (p. 352)

Credit — An agreement to buy goods or services that will be paid for at a later date; the reputation of a person or firm based on its record for paying bills when due (p. 494)

Crisis — An event that threatens people's well-being; a time of uncertainty that leads to change; a personal tragedy; a point of confrontation (p. 497)

Criticize — To show disapproval (p. 372)

Cultivate — To grow crops (p. 16)

Cultural — Having to do with the arts (p. 77)

Culture — The values, attitudes, and customs of a group (p. 13)

D

Deadlock — A situation where two or more groups are unable to agree (p. 144)

Debate — An argument or discussion among persons or a group (p. 107)

Decade — A period of ten years (p. 469)

Dedicate — To hold a ceremony as a way to honor a place or person (p. 315)

Defense — Protection against attack (p. 304)

Deficit — Debt; spending more than what is taken in (p. 632)

Delegate — A person elected to serve in government; a representative of a group (p. 77)

Democratic — Government in which the people hold power (p. 60)

Denounce — To reject or show disapproval (p. 502)

Dependent — Relying on others for one's needs (p. 621)

Deport — To send someone away from a country (p. 164)

Deposit — To put money into a bank or account (p. 222)

Depression — A period of financial difficulties experienced by an entire country (p. 226)

Descend — To lower upon; to come down from a higher place (p. 547)

Descendent — A person who comes from a specific group of people (p. 22)

Desegregation — To create racial equality by removing barriers and unfair practices (p. 572)

Destination — The place where one is going (p. 60)

Detention — The act of holding someone against his or her will (p. 529)

Dictator — A person ruling a country with total control (p. 224)

Diplomat — One skilled in negotiating between nations (p. 646)

Disabled — Having a mental or physical handicap (p. 501)

Disagreement — A quarrel (p. 160)

Disarm — To take a weapon or weapons away from someone (p. 115)

Discrimination — Unfair treatment because of a person's race, sex, religion, or age (p. 390)

Dispute — A quarrel between people or groups (p. 138)

Divisive — Something that divides or separates in a damaging way (p. 576)

Doctrine — A statement of a certain government policy or religious belief (p. 208)

Document — An official paper or piece of writing (p. 121)

Domestic — Related to one's own country; produced in one's own country (p. 217)

Domination — Complete control (p. 547)

Draft — The practice of requiring people to serve in the armed forces (p. 457)

Due process — The formal process of justice carried out in a court of law (p. 328)

Dumbbell tenements — Eight-story brick buildings that were shaped like a hand weight—larger on each end and narrower in the middle (p. 395)

Duty — Tax placed on goods brought into a place (p. 104)

Dweller — A person who lives in a certain area (p. 385)

Dwelling — A home (p. 21)

E

Economy — A system of producing, using, and distributing wealth (p. 274)

Effective — Able to cause a desired result (p. 454)

Elector — A person who is chosen to vote for the President and Vice President (p. 166)

Electoral college — A group of people elected to make the popular election of the President and Vice President official (p. 166)

Embargo — A government action that prevents certain goods from being shipped out of a country (p. 605)

Emerge — To come into being (p. 162)

Emigrate — To leave for another place or country (p. 69)

Emotion — Feelings people express (p. 471)

Empire — A large amount of territory under one ruler (p. 39)

Employer — A person or company who hires workers (p. 386)

Energetic — Full of energy (p. 477)

Enforce — To make sure something is done according to a law; to see that laws are obeyed (p. 79)

Engineering — The trade that uses scientific knowledge to plan and build objects (p. 368)

Enlist — To volunteer to join the armed forces (p. 312)

Enthusiasm — Strong feeling of excitement (p. 566)

Entitle — To give a person or group the right to do something (p. 290)

Entrepreneur — A person who starts and operates a business (p. 367)

Epidemic — An outbreak of disease (p. 70)

Equality — Having the same rights as others (p. 64)

Essay — A piece of writing that addresses a subject from a personal point of view (p. 148)

Estimate — To make a guess or judgment (p. 69)

Ethnic heritage — A person's cultural background and race (p. 519)

Evacuate — To move away from a dangerous area; to clear an area because of a threat or dangerous situation (p. 127)

Evidence — Something that furnishes proof (p. 602)

Exaggerate — To overstate the truth (p. 273)

Execute — To put to death; to complete or carry out an order or task (p. 206)

Executive branch — The branch of government that enforces laws; the branch of goverment led by the President (p. 146)

Exist — Being in place or operating (p. 143)

Expansion — A spreading out or an increase in size; becoming larger (p. 69)

Expedition — Journey made by a person or group for a certain purpose (p. 42)

Expire — To come to an end; to run out (p. 221)

Explosive — A device that explodes, such as a bomb (p. 626)

Export — A good sent to another country; a product produced in one country for sale to another country (p. 146)

Extortion — Stealing money by using some kind of threat (p. 602)

F

Famine — Widespread starvation (p. 651)

Fascist — One who believes that the state or government is more important than the individual (p. 513)

Federal government — A government that is shared between central and state governments (p. 146)

Federalist — A person who supported the Constitution; someone who believed in a strong central government (p. 148)

Feminist — A person who seeks equal rights and treatment of women (p. 579)

Finance — Having to do with money (p. 100)

Fixed price — A price that stays the same (p. 393)

Flappers — Young women in the 1920s who cut their hair short, wore skirts cut above their knees, and painted their lips bright red (p. 474)

Flexible — Able to move or twist easily (p. 367)

Forbid — To use power to prevent something; to refuse to allow something to happen (p. 292)

Foreign policy — The plan a government follows when dealing with other nations (p. 438)

Fortune seeker — One who is looking for financial gain (p. 262)

Fraud — A lie or false act to steal money or something of value (p. 471)

Free state — A state where people agreed not to practice slavery (p. 205)

Freedmen — Formerly enslaved people (p. 327)

Frontier — A region with little population; the unexplored portion of a country or settlement (p. 81)

Fugitive — A person who flees from a bad situation; a runaway (p. 275)

Fulfill — To carry out or bring to completion; to satisfy a requirement (p. 571)

G

General assembly — Group that makes laws for a larger group (p. 57)

Generation — People who live in the same time period and are about the same age (p. 474)

Genocide — The execution of a group of people based on its race or political views (p. 544)

Gilded — Covered with a thin coating of gold (p. 403)

Glacier — A large body of ice (p. 14)

Glasnost — Soviet policy of open discussion of political and social issues (p. 642)

Globe — Model of the Earth (p. 35)

Gold standard — A system in which gold backs a nation's money supply (p. 414)

Governor — Person chosen to lead a group of people within a given area, such as a colony or a state (p. 56)

Grandfather clause — A clause that stated that any adult African-American male could vote if his grandfather was a registered voter on January 1, 1867; a law that allows that a new regulation will not affect some people or groups (p. 336)

Growing season — The length of time a crop has to grow (p. 200)

Guarantee — An agreement to protect something (p. 143)

Guidance — Direction or leadership (p. 65)

Guilty — Justly charged or convicted of a crime or wrongdoing (p. 601)

Gunboat — An armed ship used for battle (p. 308)

H

Hemp — A plant with a tough fiber that is used for making rope (p. 200)

Heroics — Bravery well beyond what is needed (p. 470)

Hessian — A German soldier paid by the British to fight the Americans (p. 124)

Hieroglyphic — A system of writing that uses picture-like symbols (p. 16)

Hippie — An extreme member of the youth culture in the 1960s (p. 581)

Holocaust — The mass murder of European Jews during World War II (p. 519)

Homeland — Land that a person or group came from originally (p. 223)

Homesteader — A pioneer who owned land under the Homestead Act (p. 354)

Horizontal combination — Buying one's competition (p. 373)

Host — A person or group who provides a place for guests (p. 140)

Hostage — A person held against his or her will by someone who wants certain demands to be met (p. 613)

I

Ice Age — A period of time when much of the earth and the earth's water was frozen (p. 13)

Immigrant — A person who comes to live in a country (p. 164)

Impeach — To remove a President from office because of misconduct (p. 330)

Imperialism — Seeking to take over land to become a stronger nation; a policy of expanding the rule of a country over other foreign countries (p. 433)

Import — A good brought in from a foreign country (p. 138)

Impose — To establish a rule or law, such as a tax, on a group with less power (p. 104)

Improvise — To play an instrument without following music; to make up as one goes along (p. 477)

Inaugural address — A speech a President gives to accept the presidency (p. 168)

Inaugurate — To swear someone into office (p. 168)

Income — Money; money received from work or other sources (p. 393)

Income tax — Tax placed on money people earn (p. 441)

Incumbent — A person who currently holds a certain position or office (p. 658)

Indentured servant — A person who works for another to pay off a debt (p. 69)

Independence — Ability to take care of oneself (p. 77)

Indigo — A plant used to make dye (p. 71)

Industry — Business and manufacturing (p. 159)

Ineligible — Not able to do something because it is against rules (p. 566)

Infamy — Disgrace; lacking honor; not qualified (p. 526)

Inferior — Less advanced or lower in position; of less quality (p. 519)

Inflation — A steady rise in prices (p. 513)

Influence — The ability to convince someone of something; the ability of a person or thing to produce an effect on others (p. 180)

Initiative — The power citizens have to suggest new laws (p. 435)

Inland — A region of land that is far away from the coast; in or toward the interior of a country (p. 130)

Insult — An action that upsets others; to put down (p. 258)

Insurance — A plan that protects against loss in return for regular payments (p. 496)

Interchangeable parts — Parts of a machine that can be used with other machines (p. 234)

Interest — A fee paid to someone who lends money (p. 158)

Interfere — To enter into or take part in other people's business in an unwelcomed way (p. 117)

Interpret — To explain or tell the meaning of (p. 146)

Interstate — An action that occurs between two states, such as trade (p. 138)

Invade — To attack or take over; to enter forcefully (p. 120)

Investigate — To look into something to solve a problem or to answer a question (p. 404)

Investor — Person who lends money to a company; the investor hopes to receive more money back when the company makes money (p. 59)

Ironclad — A military ship covered in iron plates (p. 308)

Ironic — Something that is opposite of what is expected; out of keeping or place (p. 584)

Irrigation — A system of watering crops that uses canals or ditches of water (p. 20)

Isolate — To set apart from others (p. 126)

Issue — A topic of discussion or debate (p. 222)

J

Jim Crow Laws — Unfair laws that separated African Americans and whites in public places; laws that refused equal treatment to African Americans (p. 390)

Joint declaration — Something declared as a group or by several countries (p. 208)

Judgment — The ability a person uses to decide and act on something (p. 603)

Judicial branch — The branch of government that interprets laws (p. 146)

Justice — A judge who serves on the Supreme Court (p. 145)

Kachina — Spirits of an ancestor (p. 23)

Kerosene — A fuel (p. 372)

Kiva — A large underground room used for ceremonies by American Indians (p. 20)

Ku Klux Klan — A secret group that is against African Americans and other minorities (p. 337)

Labor union — An organized group of workers that seeks reforms in the workplace (p. 409)

Landslide — A majority of votes for one side (p. 470)

Lawsuit — A case brought before a court of law (p. 328)

Layoff — To let go of workers when a company cannot afford to pay them; the act of dimissing employees, especially temporarily (p. 493)

Legal — Having to do with the law (p. 98)

Legislative branch — The branch of government that makes laws (p. 145)

Legislature — Group of people elected to make laws (p. 77)

Leisure — Something that is done for amusement; free time away from work or duty (p. 392)

Liability — A risk (p. 373)

Liberal — A person who favors change (p. 502)

Liberation — Equal social or economic rights (p. 579)

Literally — Taken exactly as something is stated, written, or directed (p. 622)

Livestock — Animals used for food or profit; horses, cattle, or other useful animals kept on a farm or ranch (p. 317)

Loan — Money lent to someone that is to be repaid, usually with interest (p. 200)

Location — The place where something is positioned (p. 120)

Locomotive — A vehicle that rides on rails and has an engine for pulling railroad cars (p. 237)

Loot — To take or damage things by use of force (p. 43)

Lottery — Drawing names to decide who is drafted into the military (p. 523)

Lowland — A low or level piece of land that is below surrounding area (p. 200)

Loyalist — Americans who supported the king of Great Britain during the American Revolution (p. 120)

Loyalty — Faithfulness (p. 117)

Lure — To draw in someone or something by hinting of gain; to attract (p. 130)

Mainland — Main part of a continent (p. 39)

Maintain — To keep in good condition (p. 575)

Majority — More than half of the total (p. 60)

Manifest Destiny — A belief something is meant to happen, especially that America would own land from coast to coast (p. 256)

Manufacturer — A company that makes something to sell to the public or to other companies (p. 137)

Mass produce — To make great amounts of product; to produce goods in large quantities (p. 234)

McCarthyism — Senator Joseph McCarthy's campaign to use fear of communism for his own gains; the use of unproven accusations and unfair means to expose disloyalty (p. 556)

Mechanic — A person skilled in working with machines (p. 233)

Melting pot — A nation where people belonging to different races or cultures live together (p. 241)

Memorize — To remember what has been learned (p. 233)

Mercantilism — The practice of regulating colonial trade for the profit of the home country (p. 78)

Merchant — Buyer and seller of goods (p. 35)

Mesa — A flat-topped height (p. 20)

Mesoamerica — The area of land that includes what is now Mexico and other countries south through Costa Rica (p. 16)

Method — A way of doing something (p. 367)

Migrant — A worker who travels from place to place to work (p. 580)

Military — Having to do with armed forces (p. 18)

Militia — An organized group of citizens who serve as soldiers in times of war (p. 115)

Mine — A bomb that explodes when touched (p. 458)

Minimum wage — The smallest amount a person can legally be paid to do a job (p. 443)

Minority — A person or group of people that is a smaller part of a population (p. 69)

Minutemen — A group of men trained to be soldiers and who agreed to gather at a minute's notice (p. 108)

Misconduct — Wrongdoing (p. 330)

Missile — A self-driven bomb (p. 569)

Mission — A church (p. 224)

Misunderstanding — Failure to understand (p. 359)

Mobile — Having the ability to travel (p. 473)

Monarch — A person who rules a kingdom or territory (p. 35)

Monopoly — A corporation that has little competition (p. 372)

Morality — Good behavior; knowing the difference between right and wrong; following the ideals of good conduct (p. 608)

Moratorium — The legal act of delaying something (p. 496)

Motorcade — A parade of cars (p. 573)

Movement — A series of actions carried out to work toward a certain goal; an action or activity (p. 205)

Muckraker — A person who wrote articles and books describing corruption and problems (p. 435)

Mugwump — A reform group that wanted to replace a system of giving political jobs to friends and supporters (p. 405)

Mural — An artistic painting or drawing on a wall (p. 500)

N

National Guard — A state's volunteer military force (p. 558)

Nationalism — A sense of loyalty to one's country (p. 189)

Natural resources — Raw materials from nature, such as water and soil (p. 437)

Navigate — To travel by water (p. 161)

Negotiate — To work out a deal (p. 169)

Network — A system that is linked together in some way (p. 276)

Neutral — Not siding with any particular person or group (p. 160)

Noble — A person who is part of a society's upper or ruling class (p. 35)

Nomads — People who do not live in one place but keep moving from place to place (p. 13)

Nominate — To choose someone to do something, such as run for office (p. 218)

Nuclear war — War that uses atomic weapons (p. 555)

Orphan — A child who is without parents (p. 504)

Outmaneuver — To move better or more quickly than others (p. 185)

Outnumber — To have more people than an opponent; to have a greater number (p. 309)

Outrage — Anger (p. 105)

Overproduction — Producing too many goods (p. 494)

Override — To reject or not accept (p. 330)

Overturn — To reverse (p. 502)

Ownership — The state of owning something, such as land or a house (p. 137)

O

Oath — A pledge that promises loyalty (p. 325)

Occupation — A person's job or line of work (p. 503)

Occupy — To take control of a place; to take up space (p. 130)

Offensive — An attack; an attempt to score in a game or contest (p. 552)

Opponent — A person who takes an opposite position in an event (p. 292)

Oppression — Unfair or cruel actions by one group against a group that has less power (p. 219)

Optimistic — Having good feelings about what may happen in the future (p. 290)

Orator — One who is good at public speaking (p. 120)

Organization — A group of people working together for a common cause (p. 544)

Organize — To put together in some kind of order; to decide on a plan of action (p. 182)

P

Pardon — An official statement forgiving someone (p. 117)

Pastor — Member of the clergy (p. 65)

Patriot — Someone who loves his or her own country (p. 107)

Patroon — Dutch landowner (p. 65)

Perestroika — Soviet policy of economic and government reform (p. 642)

Permanent — Lasting a long time or forever (p. 157)

Persecute — To treat someone poorly or violently because of his or her religious beliefs or ethnic background (p. 652)

Petition — A request for a right or benefit from someone in power (p. 116)

Petroleum — A liquid that can be made into fuel (p. 367)

Phonograph — A machine used to reproduce sound (p. 377)

Pioneer — One of the first people to settle in a territory (p. 137)

Plantation — Large farm that grows huge amounts of a certain crop (p. 57)

Platform — A statement of ideas, policies, and beliefs of a political party in an election (p. 294)

Plea — Asking for something (p. 117)

Policy — Set of rules or an action plan of a person or group (p. 64)

Political— Relating to government or the way it runs (p. 45)

Political boss — A professional politician who controls a party or a political machine (p. 405)

Political party — A group that represents certain beliefs about government; a group that selects candidates for political office (p. 160)

Poll — A method of predicting the winner of an election by asking people who they plan to vote for; a method of gathering information (p. 632)

Popular sovereignty — Power of the people to decide something (p. 432)

Possession — An object belonging to someone (p. 188)

Postmaster — A person who runs a post office (p. 117)

Prejudice — A belief or action against someone because of race, sex, religion, or age (p. 389)

Primary election — An election in which the people choose candidates (p. 435)

Proclamation — An official public announcement (p. 209)

Produce — Fruits and vegetables (p. 279)

Professional — A person who is skilled or trained to do a task (p. 262)

Profitable — Able to bring in money above operating costs (p. 201)

Progressives — People who believed that America should pass laws to correct America's social and political problems (p. 435)

Prohibit — To prevent by law; to prevent from doing something (p. 498)

Prohibition — The ban on making or selling alcohol (p. 481)

Proposal — A suggestion for others to consider (p. 126)

Proprietor — Owner (p. 64)

Prose — The ordinary form of spoken or written language (p. 245)

Prosecute — To charge with a crime (p. 412)

Prospector — A person who searches an area for gold, silver, or other minerals (p. 352)

Prosper — To succeed or do well (p. 172)

Province — A part of a country or region (p. 106)

Provisions — Supplies needed for a trip or voyage (p. 62)

Public service — Any job or effort done for the good of the people, such as a government job (p. 161)

Publish — To print something, such as a book, newspaper, or magazine (p. 35)

Purify — To make pure or clean (p. 367)

Q

Qualified — Fit for a given purpose (p. 210)

R

Radar — A system used to locate objects such as planes (p. 522)

Radical — Extreme (p. 327)

Ratify — To approve (p. 148)

Ration — To use sparingly (p. 529)

Rebellion — A group fighting another group that is in power; an uprising against authority (p. 80)

Rebuild — To build again (p. 319)

Recall — The act of voting someone who has performed poorly out of office (p. 435)

Reconstruction — Rebuilding of the South after the Civil War (p. 326)

Recovery — The act of overcoming a problem (p. 497)

Recruit — To get new members for a group (p. 82)

Redeem — To release from blame (p. 130)

Reference book — A book, such as a dictionary, used to find information (p. 243)

Referendum — The right voters have to approve or not approve bills (p. 435)

Refinery — A place where a good is made pure or made into other products (p. 371)

Reform — A change intended to make something better (p. 403)

Refuge — Protection or shelter (p. 69)

Refugee — A person who flees his or her home country to seek protection (p. 568)

Regiment — Large group of soldiers (p. 83)

Regular army — Official army (p. 182)

Regulate — To govern or direct according to rules or laws (p. 78)

Reich — A German empire (p. 517)

Reinforcements — Additional soldiers used to back up an army (p. 86)

Reject — To refuse to accept (p. 435)

Relationship — Two or more things or groups connected in some way; the state of being connected or related (p. 97)

Religious — Relating to a belief in a higher being (p. 21)

Renew — To make something new again (p. 221)

Repeal — To remove or reverse something, especially a law (p. 99)

Replenish — To make full or complete again (p. 577)

Representative — A person who is given power to act for others (p. 57)

Reproduce — To copy or duplicate (p. 377)

Republic — A government in which citizens elect people to speak and act for them (p. 429)

Reputation — How a person is judged by others; the opinion others have of a person (p. 556)

Request — The act of asking for something (p. 302)

Reservation — Land set aside by the government for the American Indians; the act of setting something aside for someone (p. 357)

Reservoir — A large place used to store water (p. 22)

Resign — To give up an office or position (p. 116)

Resistance — An act of opposing something (p. 105)

Resolution — An expression of opinion or intent voted on by a group (p. 165)

Resolve — To settle a difference (p. 290)

Resource — A thing of value, often found in nature, that can be used to do or make something (p. 169)

Respond — To do or say something in return (p. 105)

Responsibility — The need to complete duties or tasks; something a person is charged with doing (p. 77)

Restore — To give something back to its owner; to repair (p. 188)

Restriction — Something that limits or prevents a limitation (p. 179)

Retail — Relating to the selling of goods (p. 392)

Reunification — Joining together as one country again (p. 641)

Revenge — The act of getting back at someone (p. 530)

Revenue — Money earned or gained from something (p. 100)

Revise — To make changes, especially to a document (p. 440)

Revolt — A rebellion (p. 206)

Revolution — Overthrow and replacement of a government (p. 123)

Riot — A violent public disturbance (p. 572)

Ritual — The actions that take place during a ceremony (p. 20)

Rival — A well-matched opponent; a person who is competing for something (p. 598)

Romantic — Glorified (p. 505)

Ruling — A decision in a court case (p. 290)

Runaway — Someone who is trying to escape (p. 145)

Running mate — A candidate who runs for office with a candidate who is running for another position (p. 166)

Rural — Relating to places outside of cities; in the country (p. 233)

S

Saloon — A public building where people gather to drink or gamble (p. 353)

Sanction — An action taken to force a country to do something (p. 629)

Sanitation — The act of disposing of waste and keeping areas clean (p. 395)

Scalawag — White southerners who controlled the new African-American politicians after the Civil War (p. 332)

Scandal — A disgraceful event (p. 337)

Scourge — A cause of widespread pain or distress (p. 634)

Secede — To leave a group or organization, such as a nation of states (p. 295)

Secrecy — Keeping something private (p. 142)

Sectional — Related to the interests of a region (p. 203)

Security — Methods of keeping peace; a state of being free from danger (p. 523)

Segregate — To separate by race (p. 334)

Self-sufficient — Able to do something without help (p. 189)

Session — A meeting or a series of meetings (p. 142)

Settlement — A place or region newly settled (p. 16)

Share — Certificate bought from a stock company that represents a certain part of ownership of the company; portion (p. 59)

Sharecropper — A farmer who pays some of his or her crops to a landowner as rent (p. 333)

Sharpshooting — The ability to shoot a gun with great success (p. 130)

Siege — An event in which an army prevents people in a fort or city from leaving (p. 124)

Similar — Alike in some ways (p. 105)

Skyscraper — A tall building (p. 368)

Slaughter — To kill animals for food and other products (p. 375)

Slavery — The practice of forcing a person or group to work without pay or rights (p. 39)

Slave state — A state that could practice slavery (p. 205)

Slogan — A word or phrase used to explain a stand or goal (p. 253)

Slum — An area with poor living conditions (p. 395)

Sod — Thickly matted grass and roots (p. 354)

Solo — Done by one person (p. 482)

Solution — The answer to a problem (p. 470)

Soup house — Place where the poor could get food (p. 483)

Speakeasy — A place where liquor was sold illegally during Prohibition (p. 481)

Speaker of the House — Leader of the United States House of Representatives (p. 181)

Specialize — To put one's efforts and skills in one or two areas of business (p. 385)

Spectator — A person who watches an event (p. 394)

Spiritual — African-American religious song (p. 477)

Spoils system — The practice of giving government jobs to loyal supporters (p. 218)

Stabilize — To bring something back to normal (p. 496)

Stagecoach — A horse-drawn coach used for transporting people or mail (p. 349)

Stampede — A wild rush (p. 353)

Standards — Guidelines that a person or group must follow; a generally accepted way of doing something (p. 242)

Standstill — Something that is not changing or improving (p. 456)

Starvation — Lack of food (p. 240)

Statehood — The condition of being a state (p. 206)

Statesman — Someone who knows and practices government ideas (p. 120)

Steerage — A part of a passenger ship that was inexpensive to ride in but was uncomfortable and unhealthy (p. 388)

Stock company — Company that is owned by people who own the company stock (p. 59)

Stock market — A market for the buying and selling of company stock (p. 482)

Strategic — Important or helpful in carrying out a plan (p. 599)

Streetcar — A horse-drawn or electric carriage that rides on rails and is used for transportation (p. 392)

Strike — A kind of protest in which union workers refuse to work until their demands are met (p. 410)

Strikebreaker — A nonunion worker used to replace striking union workers (p. 410)

Stronghold — A well-protected place (p. 86)

Submarine — A ship that can travel underwater (p. 453)

Submission — The act of giving up on something (p. 107)

Suborbital — Not out of the earth's atmosphere (p. 565)

Subpeona — A court order (p. 602)

Suburb — Community built outside of cities (p. 474)

Sue — To bring legal action against a person or company to settle a difference (p. 290)

Suffrage — The right to vote (p. 336)

Suicide — To kill oneself (p. 656)

Summit — A meeting held between or among world leaders (p. 641)

Supreme — To the highest degree (p. 148)

Surge — To rise swiftly (p. 621)

Surplus — An extra amount of something; more than what is needed (p. 496)

Survivor — A person who has lived through a dangerous event (p. 84)

Suspension bridge — A large bridge supported by wires or chains attached to tall towers (p. 368)

Symphony — A long, complex musical piece (p. 477)

Synagogue — A Jewish place of worship (p. 518)

Tactic — A method of doing something (p. 572)

Tar and feather — To cover a person with tar and then with feathers in order to punish (p. 98)

Tariff — A tax on goods leaving or entering a place (p. 138)

Tax evasion — Failing to pay one's taxes (p. 602)

Technology — The use of science to create new machines or other advances (p. 558)

Telegraph — A device that uses coded signals to send communications over a wire (p. 237)

Temporary — For a short time (p. 137)

Tenant farmer — A farmer who pays rent to a landowner for use of the land (p. 333)

Tenement — Three-or four-story buildings designed to house eight to ten families (p. 395)

Tension — Uncomfortable or unfriendly feelings between people or groups (p. 280)

Territory — Land (p. 35)

Terrorist — An individual or group that uses violence to make others give in to its demands (p. 611)

Textile — Fabric or cloth (p. 233)

Theory — A best guess; an explanation or idea that may or may not be true (p. 13)

Third World — Poor and underdeveloped countries (p. 574)

Three-pronged attack — An attack in three separate places against an enemy (p. 126)

Tobacco — A plant that some people smoke or chew (p. 24)

Tolerate — To allow (p. 98)

Torpedo — A self-propelled bomb that is shot from a tube of a submarine (p. 453)

Totem pole — A tall, colorful carved object built by American Indians that has a certain religious meaning (p. 29)

Traditional — The usual way of doing things (p. 503)

Traitor — Someone who turns against his or her own country (p. 129)

Transatlantic — Crossing the Atlantic Ocean (p. 238)

Transcontinental — Extending across a continent (p. 349)

Treason — A crime involving an attempt to overthrow or weaken the government (p. 293)

Treasury — A place where money is stored; the government department that handles money (p. 157)

Treaty — An agreement to end fighting or turmoil (p. 84)

Triangular trade — Trade between Africa, the West Indies, and New England (p. 79)

Trolley — A carriage that rides on rails and is used for transportation (p. 392)

Trust company — A large, powerful company that often is a monopoly (p. 374)

Turnpike — A road that travelers pay to use (p. 235)

Tutor — A person who has been paid to teach another person (p. 242)

Typesetting — The methods used to prepare type to be printed (p. 377)

U

Unanimous — When all sides agree; being in agreement (p. 149)

Underestimate — To fail to guess the size, quantity, or number of something (p. 528)

Unemployment — The state of not having work (p. 227)

Unify — To join together as a group or whole (p. 107)

Union — A joining together (p. 82)

Unite — To join together as a single unit (p. 79)

Urban — Related to the city (p. 397)

V

Ventilation — Circulation of fresh air in an enclosed area (p. 396)

Vertical combination — A kind of business organization that controls each step in making something (p. 373)

Veteran — A former member of the armed forces (p. 308)

Veto — The power given to the President to turn down a bill (p. 221)

Village — A small settlement (p. 20)

Violent — Severe or harmful (p. 246)

Vow — To promise (p. 287)

Voyage — The act of traveling, especially by sea (p. 36)

W

Wagon train — A large number of wagons traveling together in a row (p. 349)

Western Hemisphere — The land and oceans around North and South America (p. 209)

Windmill — A wind-powered device (p. 355)

Wiretap — A device used to listen in on phone conversations (p. 601)

Index

A

Abolitionists, 245, 247, 273, 276, 283, 288, 293, 297. *See also* Antislavery movement
Adams, Abigail, 144
Adams, John, 107, 141, 144, 149, 160, 163-64, 166, 168, 175, 181, 203
Adams, John Quincy, 213, 217-18, 220, 224, 229
Adams, Samuel, 100, 102, 104, 107-8, 115, 117, 120
Adams-Onís Treaty, 204, 213
Addams, Jane, 411
Adena, 24, 31
Advertising, 68
Advisers, 175
Afghanistan, 614, 617
Africa, 79, 89, 605
African Americans, 276, 283, 312, 328-29, 336-37, 339-41, 376, 390-91, 444, 485, 557-58, 560-61, 571-73, 634, 658, 661
Agency, 328
Agnew, Spiro, 602
Agricultural Adjustment Act (AAA), 498, 502
Agricultural Marketing Act, 496
AIDS, 628
Airlifts, 550
Alabama, 287, 199, 295
Alamo, 224-25, 228-29
Alaska, 13, 29, 330, 566
Albany Congress, 82
Albany Plan, 82
Alcohol, 481
Aldrin, Edwin, Jr., 596, 617
Alger, Horatio, 379
Alien Act, 164, 168, 175

Aliens, 164
Allen, Ethan, 115
Allen, Richard, 219
Alliance, 82
Allied Powers, 451, 459, 523, 530-32, 535, 552
Ambassadors, 169
Amendments, 150
American Anti-Slavery Society, 246
American Federation of Labor (AFL), 409, 417, 502, 509
American Federation of Labor and the Congress of Industrial Organizations (AFL-CIO), 503
American Indian Movement (AIM), 579
American Indians, 79, 81, 84, 89, 137, 161, 180, 182, 185, 222-23, 229, 253, 356-61, 363, 404. *See also* Names of individual peoples
American Red Cross, 396
American Slavery as It Is, 248
American Tobacco Company, 441
Amherst, General, 86
Amin, President, 614
Anaconda Plan, 305
Anarchists, 410
Anasazis, 21-22, 31
Anderson, Marian, 497
Anderson, Robert, 302, 304
André, John, 129
Angelou, Maya, 654
Annapolis (Maryland), 105, 153
Annapolis Convention, 140
Anthony, Susan B., 469
Antietam, 310, 312, 321
Anti-Fascists, 514-15
Anti-Federalists, 148-49, 153, 167

Antislavery movement, 205, 227, 248, 283, 303. *See also* Abolitionists
Antiwar movement, 581, 587, 595-96
Apache Wars, 351
Apartheid, 630
Apollo II, 596, 617
Appeasement, 518
Appomattox Court House, 317, 319, 320
Arafat, Yasir, 651
Archaeologists, 13, 16, 20
Architects, 16-17
Aristide, Jean-Bertrand, 653
Arizona, 283, 357, 566
Arkansas, 169, 304
Armada, 43
Armistice, 427
Armistice Day, 471
Armour, Philip, 375
Armstrong, Edwin Howard, 458
Armstrong, Louis, 477, 485
Armstrong, Neil, 596, 617
Arnold, Benedict, 120, 129, 133
Aroostook Valley, 255
Arsenal, 293
Arson, 658
Arthur, Chester A., 406, 417
Articles of Confederation, 138, 140-41, 152, 153, 157
Artisans, 18
Ashburton, Lord, 255
Assassination, 325
Assembly line, 473
Astaire, Fred, 504
Astronomy, 16, 18
Atchison, David R., 287
Atlantic Ocean, 39, 60, 453
Atomic bombs, 532-33, 535, 543, 555
Attucks, Crispus, 101, 111
Audubon, John James, 244
Australia, 523, 535
Austria, 517, 535
Austria-Hungary, 450-51

Austro-Hungarian Empire, 462
Automobiles, 378, 473-475, 528, 558, 561, 609
Axis Powers, 525, 535
Aztecs, 17-18, 31, 40, 47

B

Baby boom, 580-81
Baker, James, 647
Balboa, Vasco Núñez de, 39, 42, 47
Baltimore and Ohio Railroad, 237
Bank holiday, 498
Bank of the United States, 221-22, 226, 229
Banneker, Benjamin, 122
Barton, Clara, 396
Bay of Pigs, 568, 587
Beach, Alfred, 338
Beauregard, General, 304
Begin, Menachem, 611
Belarus, 643
Belgium, 521, 535
Belknap, William, 404
Bell, Alexander Graham, 377, 381
Bell, John, 294
Bellamy, Edward, 413
Beringia, 13
Berlin (Germany), 550, 568, 641
Berlin, Irving, 455
Berlin Wall, 568-69, 587, 635
Bessemer, Henry, 367-68
Bicentennial, 606, 607
Bicycles, 407
Big Stick Policy, 440
Bill of Rights, 150-51, 153, 328
Bills, 145
Birmingham (Alabama), 334
Birth of Nation, The, 454
Black, Hugo, 502
Black Codes, 327-28, 341

Blackfeet, 356

Black gold, 371, 381

Black Hills, 357-363

Black power movement, 579, 587

Blaine, James G., 406

Blitzkrieg, 521

Blockades, 172, 184, 306, 550

Blockhouse, 56

Blue Eagle, 499

Bonaparte, Napoleon, 169, 172, 175,
    179-80

Bonds, 158, 457

Boogie-woogie, 524

Booth, John Wilkes, 325, 341

Bootlegger, 481

Bopp, Tom, 657

Bosnia, 450, 462

Bosnia-Herzegovina, 652, 661

Boss Tweed, 405, 417

Boston
    Board of Health, 165
    Harbor, 104-5, 118, 133
    Massacre, 101, 111
    Tea Party, 104-5, 111

Bowie, Jim, 224

Bowling, 56

Boxer Rebellion, 445

Boycotts, 98-101, 107, 552

Braddock, Edward, 83-84, 89

Bradford, Sarah, 288

Brady Bill, 649

Brady, James, 649

Brady, Mathew, 309

Breadbasket, 71

Breadlines, 495, 508

Breckinridge, John C., 294

Breed's Hill, 118, 133

Brent, Margaret, 64

Brezhnev, Leonid, 599, 615, 617

British Parliament, 111

Brooklyn Bridge, 368-69

Brooks, Preston, 289

Brown, John, 288, 293, 297

Brown, Mose, 233

*Brown v. the Board of Education of
    Topeka, Kansas,* 557

Browsers, 644

Bruce, Blanche, 398

Bryan, William Jennings, 414-15, 433, 441

Buchanan, James, 290, 297, 301-2

Budget and tax cuts, 637

Buena Vista, 259, 261

Bulgaria, 451

Bull Moose party, 442-43, 445

Bull Run, 307, 310

Bunker Hill, 118, 133

Bunkers, 532

Bureau of the Budget, 470

Burgoyne, John, 126

Burial grounds, 24, 26

Burnside, Ambrose, 310-11, 321

Burr, Aaron, 166, 175

Bush, George, 632-35, 637, 641, 645-48

Bushnell, David, 118

Butler, Andrew, 289

Butler, Richard, 334

C

Cabeza de Vaca, Álvar Núñez, 46

Cabinet, 157, 175

Cables, 238

Cable TV, 604

Cabot, John, 38, 42, 47

Cahokia, 27

Calhoun, John C., 181, 191, 203, 217,
    220, 274

California, 258-59, 265, 273, 278-79, 283,
    349, 352

Calvert, Cecilius Lord, 64, 73

Cambodia, 595-96

Campaigns, 217

Camp David, 611

Canada, 29, 41, 115, 131, 181, 184, 255, 358, 535, 550, 649, 661

Canals, 18, 20, 236, 249

Candidates, 163

Canning, George, 208

Capital, 373

Careers, 528

Carmichael, Stokely, 579

Carnegie, Andrew, 367-69, 372-74, 381

Carolina, 65, 73. *See also* North Carolina; South Carolina

Carothers, Wallace H., 507

Carpenter's Hall, 107

Carpetbaggers, 332, 337, 341

Carter, Jimmy, 608-11, 613-17, 621, 653

Cartier, Jacques, 41-42, 47

Carver, George Washington, 376

Carver, John, 60

Cash crops, 181

Cass, Lewis, 261-62

Castro, Fidel, 568, 587

Casualties, 646

Catlin, George, 280

Cattle ranching, 353, 363, 375

Cayuga, 27

Cease fire, 533

Cedras, Rauol, 653

Centennial, 338

Central America, 617, 637

Central High School, 560

Central Pacific Railroad, 349-51, 363

Central Powers, 451

Chaco Canyon, 21

Challenger, 624, 637

Chamberlain, Neville, 517-18

Champlain, Samuel de, 44

Chancellors, 514

Chancellorsville, 313

Chapa Mesa, 22

Charities, 493

Charles I, 61-62, 64

Charles II, 65-66, 73

Charleston (South Carolina), 65, 105, 120, 130, 485

Charleston, the (dance), 477

Charlestown (Virginia), 293

Charter, 43, 45, 59-60, 62, 64-66, 221-22

Charts, 18, 22, 28, 42, 146, 169, 199, 261, 319, 368, 373, 374, 385, 459, 501, 544, 576, 605

Chavez, Cesar, 580-81

Chavin, 18

Checks and balances, 168

Cherokees, 27, 204, 209, 223, 229

Chesapeake Bay, 64, 73, 130

Cheyenne, 356-57, 363

Chickasaws, 223

Chief justice, 145, 168

Child labor, 379, 387

Chimu, 18

China, 35, 38, 445, 515, 525, 544, 552-53, 598-99, 617

Chippewa, 28

Chiricahua Apaches, 351

Chisholm Trail, 353

Choctaws, 223, 229

Chou En-lai, 598

Church of England, 59

Churchill, Winston, 522, 531, 547

Citizenship, 168, 514

Civilian Conservation Corps (CCC), 498, 509

Civilizations, 16-18, 20, 26

Civil lawsuits, 150

Civil rights, 329

Civil Rights Act, 328, 341, 390, 572

Civil Rights Law, 558, 561

Civil rights movement, 557-58, 561, 571-73, 579, 586-87, 659

Civil service, 405

Civil War, 303, 321

Clark, George Rogers, 128

Clark, William, 171, 175

Classics, 244, 245

Clay, Henry, 180-82, 191, 200, 203, 206, 210-11, 222, 226, 256, 274

Clemenceau, Georges, 460

Clemens, Samuel. *See* Twain, Mark

Clermont, 236

Cleveland, Grover, 406-8, 413-14, 417

Clinton, DeWitt, 184, 236

Clinton, Henry, 127-28

Clinton, Hillary Rodham, 650, 655

Clinton, William, 648-58, 654, 658

Clovis points, 14

Coal, 334, 434

Cochise, 351

Cody, William F., 356

Cold War, 547, 559, 565-66, 569, 580, 598, 628, 635, 643

Colfax, Schuyler, 404

Collective bargaining, 500

Colonies, 43-45, 55-67, 69-71, 73, 77-83

Colorado, 169

Columbia, 438-39

Columbus, Christopher, 36-38, 42, 47

Comanche, 356, 358

Comecon, 641

Comets, 657

Commanders, 117

Committee to Re-elect the President (CREEP), 601

"Common Sense," 132

Commonwealth of Independent States, 643, 661

Communism, 547-48, 552-53, 555-56, 561, 568, 577, 627, 635, 637, 642, 661

Communists, 480-81, 561, 574, 595

Compass, 35, 47

Composers, 477

Compromise Committee, 145, 147

Compromise of 1850, 274, 282-83

Computers, 558, 606, 644

Concentration camps, 535

Concord (Massachusetts), 108, 111, 115, 117

Conductors, 276

Confederacy, 182, 304-14, 316, 318, 321

Confederate States of America, 301, 321

Congress, 117, 120-21, 133, 138, 143, 145, 147, 150, 153, 157-58, 161, 163-64, 166-67, 169, 173, 175, 184, 191, 217, 221-22, 229, 259, 274, 279, 282-83, 325, 328-30, 341, 349, 360, 363, 404, 406, 412, 436-37, 445, 449, 465, 498, 500, 509, 545, 548, 556, 561, 587, 627-28, 630, 637, 649, 655, 661

Congressional Act of 1814, 182

Congress of Industrial Organizations (CIO), 503, 509

Congress of Racial Equality (CORE), 571

Connally, John, 573

Connecticut, 65, 70, 73, 149

Conservation, 437, 441, 445, 659

Conspiracies, 601

U.S.S. *Constitution*, 184

Constitution, 146-51, 149, 153, 157, 165-67, 175, 181, 291, 301-2, 462

Constitutional Convention, 141-42, 153

Constitutional Union party, 294

Consumer science, 56, 274

Containment policy, 548

Continental Congress, 107, 111, 116, 133, 163

Continents, 36

Contract With America, 655, 661

Contras, 627-28, 637

Conventional Forces in Europe Treaty (CFE), 641

Conventions, 107

Convoy, 458

Coolidge, Calvin, 470-71, 482, 485

Cooper, James Fenimore, 245

Cooper, Peter, 237

Corn, 16, 21

Cornwallis, Lord, 130, 133

Corporations, 372-73, 381
Corruption, 338, 405-6, 417, 555
Cortés, Hernando, 40, 42, 47
Cotton, 20, 200-202, 205, 224, 277, 283, 306, 316, 321, 334
Cotton gin, 201, 233-34, 249, 277
Counterattack, 531
Counterculture, 581
Cowhands, 353, 363
Cox, Archibald, 601-2
Crawford, William, 203, 210
Crazy Horse, 357
Credit, 494, 509, 584
Credit cards, 584
Crédit Mobilier Scandal, 403-4, 417
Creeks, 185, 223, 229
Crime, 262, 481, 634, 637
Crittenden, John, 301
Crocket, Davy, 224
Crook, George, 351
Crown Point, 84, 86, 115
Cuba, 37, 89, 425-29, 433, 445, 568-70, 587, 653
Cullen, Countee, 478
Cultivate, 16
Cumberland River, 308
Cumberland Road, 199, 235, 249
Currency Act, 98
Custer, George Armstrong, 358, 363
Custer's Last Stand, 358
Czechoslovakia, 462, 517-18, 635, 643

D

Daladier, Eduardo, 518
Dare, Virginia, 44
Davis, Jefferson, 278, 301, 304, 318
Dawes, William, 108
Dawes Act, 360, 363
Day, Benjamin, 221

D-Day, 530, 535
Deaf, free school for, 211
Dean, John, 601-2
Death camps, 519, 535
Debates, 147
Debates, presidential, 292, 297, 566
Declaration of American Rights, 107, 111
Declaration of Independence, 121, 133, 163, 168
Declaration of Sentiments and Resolutions, 264
Declaratory Act, 99
Deere, John, 249
Deficit, federal, 168, 632-33, 649, 659
De Forest, Lee, 458
de Grasse, Francois Joseph Paul Count, 130
Delaware, 67, 71, 73
Delaware, Lord, 56
Delegates, 77, 82, 107, 117, 140-48, 153, 163, 329, 584
Democratic government, 60
Democratic party, 167, 262, 297, 317
Democratic-Republicans, 160, 163, 165-66, 175, 203
Denmark, 521, 535
Dentistry, 85
Department of Commerce and Labor, 436
Department of Defense, 622
Department of Education, 609
Department of Energy, 609
Department of Housing and Urban Development, 575
Department of Labor, 441, 509
Department stores, 393, 399
Deport, 164
Depression, 226, 229
Desegregation, 572
Desert Shield, 645-46, 661
Desert Storm, 646
Dewey, Admiral, 425, 427, 445
Dewey, Thomas E., 546
Dickinson, Emily, 245, 249, 415

Dickinson, John, 141
Dictators, 224, 547
Diners Club, 584
Dinkins, David, 634
Dinwiddie, Governor, 81
Diplomats, 646
Disabled, 501
Discovery, 630, 637
Discrimination, 390, 480, 485, 571, 580
Diseases, 70
District of Columbia, 158, 283
Dixieland, 477
Dixon, Jeremiah, 100
Doctrine, 208
Dole, Robert, 608, 658
Dorchester Heights, 118, 133
Dos Passos, John, 478, 485
Doughboys, 458
Douglas, Stephen, 279-80, 292, 294, 297
Douglas, William O., 502
Douglass, David, 109
Douglass, Frederick, 246-48, 277, 283
Doves, 583
Draft, 457, 523
Drake, Edwin, 371, 381
Drake, Sir Francis, 42, 47
Drug abuse, 634, 637
Du Bois, W. E. B., 340, 441
Due Process, 328
Dukakis, Michael, 632
Dumbbell tenements, 395
Dunkirk (France), 521-22
Du Pont Laboratories, 507
Duties, 104, 145

E

Eagle, 596
Earhart, Amelia, 506
Earth, 39-40

East Germany, 550, 635, 641, 661
East India Trading Company, 104
East Jersey, 67, 73
Eastman, George, 377, 381
Eckford, Elizabeth, 560, 659
Economic Recovery Tax Act, 622
Economy, 659
Edison, Thomas, 375-77, 381, 392, 394
Education, public, 242-43, 249, 334, 340
Egypt, 611, 625
Ehrlichman, John, 601
Eighteenth Amendment, 481
Eisenhower, Dwight D., 530, 550, 555,
    558-59, 561, 566, 576, 587
Elector, 166
Electoral college, 166
Elementary and Secondary School Act, 575
Elevators, 289, 377
Elizabeth I, 43
Elizabeth II, 606
Elk Hills (California), 470
Ellington, Duke, 477, 485
Emancipation Proclamation, 312, 321
Embargo, 605
Embargo Act, 172-73, 175, 179
Emergency Banking Act, 498
Emergency Management Agency, 658
Emergency Quota Act, 470
Emerson, John, 290
Emerson, Ralph Waldo, 245
Emigrant Aid Society, 287
Emigrate, 69
Emperors, 450
Empires, 39
Endangered Species Act, 600
Energy, 609
Energy crisis, 610, 617
England and the English, 36, 38, 42-45,
    47, 55-57, 59, 65-67, 73, 110, 522.
    See also Great Britain
Enlist, 312
Enola Gay, 533

Entrepreneurs, 367
Environmental Protection Agency (EPA), 600
Epidemics, 70
Equal Rights Amendment (ERA), 580.
    See also Feminist movement; Womens's rights movement
Era of Good Feelings, 203, 213
Erie Canal, 199, 236, 249
Eskimo. See Inuit
Evidence, 602
Executive branch, 146, 153, 609
Expeditions, 42, 44, 62
Exploration, beginning of, 35
Explorer I, 565
Explorers, 36-42
Exports, 146, 283, 630
Extortion, 602

F

Fair Deal, 545
Fall, Albert B., 470
Far East, 35, 38-40, 47, 430
Farmer, James, 571
Farming, 20-21, 31, 77, 200, 213, 234, 249, 354-55, 363, 376, 496
Farragut, David G., 308, 316
Fascists, 513, 535
Faubus, Orval, 560
Federal budget, 661
Federal Building (Oklahoma City, Oklahoma), 656
Federal Communications Commission, 504
Federal Emergency Relief Administration, 498
Federal government, 146
Federal Housing Administration (FHA), 501

Federalist Papers, 148
Federalists, 148-49, 153, 160, 163-67, 175, 181, 191, 203, 213
Federal Republic of Germany, 550
Federal Reserve System, 449, 465
Feminist movement, 579, 580, 587.
    See also Equal Rights Amendment; Women's rights movement
Ferraro, Geraldine, 623
Fessenden, Reginald, 458
Field, Cyrus, 238, 249
Fifteenth Amendment, 336, 341
Fillmore, Millard, 275, 290
Fine arts, 22, 109, 219, 432, 455
Fireside chats, 534, 551
Fitch, John, 151
Fitzgerald, F. Scott, 478, 485
Fixed price, 393
Flappers, 474, 485
Florida, 39, 46, 47, 86, 89, 131, 137, 161, 203-4, 208, 295, 568
Food and Drug Administration (FDA), 437
Food and Drugs Act, 437, 445
Football Hall of Fame, 450
Ford, Gerald R., 602-3, 605, 608, 617
Ford, Henry, 378, 381, 475
Ford Motor Company, 473, 493
Ford's Theater, 325, 341
Foreign policy, 438
Fort Donelson, 308
Fort Duquesne, 81, 84, 86, 89
Fort Henry, 308
Fort McHenry, 187
Fort Niagara, 86
Fort Oswego, 84
Fort Sumter, 302, 304, 321
Fort Ticonderoga, 84, 86, 115-16, 119
Fort William Henry, 84
Forty-Niners, 262
Foster, Stephen, 274
Foster, Vincent, 656
Fountain of Youth, 38-39, 47

Fourteen Points, 460, 465
Fourteenth Amendment, 328-29, 341, 390-91
France, 40-41, 44, 47, 78, 81-87, 89, 126, 129, 131, 133, 160-61, 163-64, 169, 173, 175, 179-80, 188, 191, 388, 399, 430, 451, 453, 459, 462, 515, 518-19, 521-22, 530, 535, 544, 550, 561, 577, 646
Francis Ferdinand, Archduke, 450, 465
Francis Joseph I, 450
Franco, Francisco, 514-15, 535
Frankfurter, Felix, 502
Franklin, Benjamin, 82, 88, 115, 117, 126, 132, 141, 144, 244
Franklin National Bank of New York, 584
Fredericksburg (Virginia), 311, 313
Freedmen, 206, 327-29, 332-33, 339
Freedmen's Bureau, 328-29, 341
Freedom of the Press, 78
Freedom riders, 571
Free Soil party, 261-62
Free states, 205-6, 273, 280, 283, 297
Fremont, John C., 259, 290
French and Indian War, 84-87
Frontier, 81
Frontier newspapers, 182
Fugitive Slave Law, 280, 283
Fulton, Robert, 179, 236, 249, 276

G

Gadsden, James, 278
Gadsden Purchase, 278, 283
Gage, General, 108, 117-18
Gallaudet, Thomas Hopkins, 211
Garfield, James, 406, 417
Garrison, William Lloyd, 246, 273
Garvey, Marcus, 479
Gates, Horatio, 126
Gemini space program, 565, 587
General Assembly, 57, 73, 544

General Electric (GE), 458
General Motors, 528
Geneva Convention, 396
Genocide, 544
Geography, 622
George, David Lloyd, 460
George II, 65, 67, 81, 84, 89
George III, 97, 102, 111, 123
Georgia, 67, 70, 80, 149, 203, 287, 295, 316
Germany, 241, 430, 451, 453-54, 456, 458-59, 462, 465, 513-16, 518-19, 521-23, 525-26, 528, 530-31, 535, 550, 635, 641, 661
Gershwin, George, 477
Gettysburg, 315, 321
Gettysburg Address, 315
Ghana, 574
Ghost Dance, 360, 363
Gilbert, Sir Humphrey, 43
Gilded, 403
Gingrich, Newt, 655
Glaciers, 14
Glasnost, 642
Glenn, John, 565
Glidden, Joseph, 355
Globe, 35, 47
Godfrey, Thomas, 109
Gold, 38-40, 47, 55, 138, 226, 262-63, 265, 352, 357, 363, 403, 414
Golden Age of Radio, 551
Gold rush, 262, 265
Gold standard, 414
Goldwater, Barry, 575
Gompers, Samuel, 409
Gone With the Wind, 505
Gorbachev, Mikhail, 629, 637, 641-43
Gore, Al, 648, 658
Government, branches of
    executive, 146, 153, 609
    judicial, 146, 153
    legislative, 145, 153
Governors, 56-57
Grandfather clause, 336

Grant, Ulysses S., 308, 316-21, 331, 337-38, 341, 404, 417

Great Britain, 79-87, 89, 98-102, 104-9, 111, 115, 120, 123-31, 133, 137, 140, 160, 163, 172, 175, 179-81, 184, 186-88, 191, 208, 233, 240, 244, 255-57, 265, 430, 451, 453-54, 456, 515, 518-19, 521-24, 535, 544, 550, 561, 574, 606, 646. *See also* England and the English

Great Compromise, 145

Great Depression, 485, 493-95, 499, 508-9, 516, 528

Great Northern Railway System, 375

Great Plains, 349-51, 353-54, 363

Greece, 548

Greeley, Horace, 246, 370

Green Corn Ceremony, 27

Greene, Nathaniel, 130

Greenland, 29

Green Mountain Boys, 115

Greenville, George, 98

Grimké, Angelina, 227, 248, 273

Grimké, Sarah, 227

Guam, 428

Guerra, Stella, 636

Guiteau, Charles, 406

Gunboat, 308

H

Haida, 29, 31

Haiti, 653, 661

Halderman, H. R., 601

Hale, Alan, 657

Hale, Nathan, 124

Hale-Bopp Comet, 657

Hall, John, 234

Hallam, Lewis, 109

Halleck, General, 316

Hamilton, Alexander, 140-41, 148-49, 157-60, 166, 175

Hancock, John, 115-17, 108, 133, 149

Handwriting, 144

Harding, Warren, 469, 471, 485

Harlem Renaissance, 478, 484-85

Harper's Ferry (Virginia), 293, 297

Harrison, Benjamin, 408, 412

Harrison, William Henry, 185, 253-54, 265

Hat Act, 80

Hawaii, 430, 445, 566

Hawks, 583

Hawthorne, Nathaniel, 245

Hay, John, 428, 430-31

Hayes, Rutherford B., 338, 341, 406, 417

Haymarket Square, 410

Health, 165, 396, 554

Health care system, 650, 657, 661

Helper, Hinton R., 246

Hemingway, Ernest, 478

Hemp, 200

Henry, Patrick, 107-8, 120, 128, 149

Henson, Matthew, 442

Hessians, 124, 133

Hickock, Wild Bill, 353

Hidalgo y Costilla, Miguel, 173

Hidatsa, 28, 31

Hieroglyphics, 16

Highways, 558

Hill, James J., 375, 381

Hinkley, John, Jr., 621

Hippies, 581

Hiroshima, 533

Hispanics, 579-80, 587

Hispaniola, 37

History in Your Life, 22, 56, 82, 109, 125, 149, 165, 179, 209, 219, 244, 257, 274, 289, 333, 355, 369, 396, 415, 432, 455, 478, 507, 528, 554, 584, 612, 622, 657

Hitler, Adolf, 504-5, 513-14, 517-19, 521-23, 530-32, 535

HIV, 628
Hohokam, 20, 31
Holmes, Oliver Wendell, 246
Holocaust, 519, 535
Homelessness, 326, 493, 495, 509, 634, 637
Home Owners Loan Corporation, 501
Homestead Act, 354, 363, 388
Homesteader, 354
Hood, John, 317
Hooker, Joseph, 311, 313
Hooker, Thomas, 65, 73
Hoover, Herbert, 493, 496, 509
Hopewells, 24-25, 28, 31
Hopi, 23
Hopkins, Harry L., 500
Horizontal combination, 373
Horseshoe Bend, 185, 191
Hostages, 613-14, 617, 628
Hot-air balloons, 313
Houghton, John, 68
House of Burgesses, 57, 73
House Judiciary Committee, 602-3
House of Representatives, 145, 149, 166,
    175, 180, 184, 213, 289, 330
Housing, 70, 354, 395, 555, 587, 634
Housing Act, 575
Houston, Sam, 224-25, 229, 258
Howe, Elias, 274
Howe, Richard, 123
Howe, William, 118-19, 123, 126-27, 133
Hughes, Charles Evans, 454
Hughes, Langston, 478, 485
Hull, Cordell, 525
Hull House, 411
Humphrey, Hubert, 584
Hundred Days, the, 498
Hungary, 635, 643
Hunt, Walter, 274
Hunting tools, 14
Hussein, Saddam, 645-46

I

Ice Age, 13
Illinois, 199
Immigrants, 164-65, 200, 240-41, 249, 290,
    350, 354, 362, 367, 388-90, 396, 399, 405,
    478, 480, 485
Immigration Act, 480
Impeachment, 330, 603, 617
Imperialism, 433
Imports, 138, 217, 220, 470, 630, 649
Inaugural address, 168
Inaugurate, 168
Incas, 18-19, 31, 39
Income taxes, 441, 449, 633
Incumbent, 658
Indentured servants, 69, 71
Independence, 77-78
    women's, 474-75
India, 35
Indiana, 199
Indian Removal Act, 222
Indigo, 70
Indochina, 525, 535
Industrial technology, 125
Industry, 159, 202, 213, 233-34, 334, 367,
    385-86, 399, 412, 528
Inflation, 513, 617
Initiatives, 435, 445
Insurance, 496
Interest, 158
Intermediate Nuclear Forces (INF),
    Treaty 629, 637
International Red Cross, 396
International space station, 565
Internet, 644
Interstate Commerce Act, 408, 417
Interstate Commerce Commission
    (ICC), 412
Intolerable Acts, 105, 111
Inuit, 29, 31
Inventions, 375-78, 381

Investors, 59-60, 373
Iowa, 169
Iran, 613, 617, 626, 637
Iraq, 626, 645-46, 661
Iron Act, 80
Ironclad, 308
Iron ore, 334, 367
Ironworks, 234
Iroquois, 27, 82, 86
Irrigation, 20, 31
Irving, Washington, 245, 249
Isabella, 36
Israel, 605, 611, 613, 637, 646-47, 651
Italy, 35, 389, 513-16, 522, 526, 530, 535

J

Jackson, Andrew, 185, 188, 204, 210-11, 213, 217-18, 220-22, 224, 226, 229, 242
Jackson, Helen Hunt, 360
Jackson, Jesse, 632
Jackson, Thomas J., 307, 309, 313
James I, 45, 47, 59
Jamestown (Virginia), 45, 47, 55-58, 73
Japan, 430-31, 438, 451, 480, 515-16, 525-26, 528-30, 532-33, 535, 543, 552
Japanese Americans, 529
Jay, John, 107, 145, 148, 161
Jay's Treaty, 161, 163
Jazz, 394, 477, 485
Jefferson, Thomas, 115, 121-22, 133, 137, 141, 147, 152, 157-58, 160, 163, 165-69, 171-73, 175, 179-81, 208, 242, 244
Jenner, Edward, 165
Jews, 389, 515, 519, 535, 544-45
Jim Crow Laws, 390
Jitterbug, 524
Johnson, Andrew, 326-28, 330-31, 341
Johnson, James Welden, 484
Johnson, Lyndon, 573, 575-77, 583-84, 587
Johnson, William, 86

Jones, John Paul, 129
Joplin, Scott, 432
Joseph, Chief, 359
Juanita, 19
Judicial branch, 146, 153

K

Kachinas, 22, 23
Kamehameha I, 180
Kansas, 169, 280, 287-90, 297
Kansas-Nebraska Act, 280, 283, 287
Karmal, Babrak, 614
Kearny, Stephen W., 259
Kelly, Michael, 355
Kelly, William, 367
Kemp, Jack, 658
Kennedy, John F., 566, 568-74, 576, 587
Kennedy, Robert, 584
Kentucky and Virginia resolutions, 165, 175
Kerosene, 372
Key, Francis Scott, 187
Keystone Bridge Company, 367
Khomeini, Ayatollah Ruhollah, 613
Khrushchev, Nikita, 566, 568, 570
King, Martin Luther Jr., 557, 561, 571, 573, 579, 583-84, 586-87
King's Mountain, North Carolina, 130
Kingston, Maxine Hong, 362
Kissinger, Henry, 598
Kitchen Cabinet, 218
Kivas, 20
Knights of Labor, 409-10, 417
Knox, Henry, 157
Konoye, Fumimaro, 525
Korea, 552-53, 561
Korean War, 555, 598
Kravechuk, President, 651
Ku Klux Klan, 337, 478, 485
Kuwait, 645-46, 661
Kwakiutl, 29, 31

L

Labor Relations Act, 503
Labor unions, 409, 410, 412, 417, 434, 503, 581
Lafayette, Marquis de, 130
Lake Champlain, Battle of, 185
Lake Erie, 185
Landon, Alf, 501
Latin America, 438, 440
Lawsuits, 328
Layoffs, 493, 509
League of Nations, 460, 462-63, 465, 544
League of Women Voters, 292
Lebanon, 611, 625, 628, 637
Lee, Richard Henry, 120
Lee, Robert E., 293, 305, 309, 310, 313-14, 316, 318-21
Legislative branch, 145, 153
Legislators, 143, 205
Legislatures, 77, 165
Leisure activities, 393-94
Lend-Lease Act, 523
Lewis, John L., 503, 509
Lewis, Meriwether, 171, 175
Lewis, Sinclair, 478, 485
Lexington (Massachusetts), 108-9, 111, 115, 117
Liberals, 502, 559
Liberator, The, 246
Libya, 626-27, 637
Liddy, Gordon, 601
Liliuokalani, Queen, 380
Limestone, 334
Limited Test Ban Treaty, 574
Lin, Maya, 625
Lincoln, Abraham, 287, 292, 294-95, 297, 301-04, 306, 308, 310, 312, 315-17, 321, 325-28, 328, 341
Lincoln Memorial, 497, 572
Lindbergh, Charles, 482, 485
Literature, 209, 257, 333, 415, 478
Little Big Horn, 358, 363

Little Rock (Arkansas), 558, 560
Livingston, Robert, 169
Locomotives, 237
London Company, 59-60
Longfellow, Henry Wadsworth, 245
Looking Backward, 413
Lottery, 523
Louis XV, 81
Louis, Joe, 506
Louisiana, 86, 89, 169, 295
    Purchase, 169, 171-72
    Territory, 175, 206
Lowell, Francis, 202
Lowell, James Russell, 246
Loyalists, 120
Lucid, Shannon, 565
Lusitania, 453-54, 465

M

MacArthur, Douglas, 532-33, 552-53
MacGillivray, William, 244
Madison, James, 140-41, 148-49, 158, 160, 165, 175, 179-81, 184, 191, 221
Madison's War, 184
Magazines, 335
Magellan, Ferdinand, 39-40, 42, 47
Maine, 206, 255, 265
U.S.S. Maine, 425-26, 445
Mainland, 39
Malcolm X, 579
Manassas Junction, 307, 310
Manchuria, 553
Mandan, 28, 31
Mandela, Nelson, 652
Manifest Destiny, 256, 265, 425
Mann, Horace, 226, 243, 249
Manufacturing, 202, 233-34, 399
Mapmaking, 35, 47
Map studies, 14, 25-26, 36, 37, 41, 70, 87, 131, 140, 170-71, 186, 207, 225, 235,

255-56, 276, 295, 311, 314, 318, 329, 350, 358, 427, 430, 439, 452, 461, 520, 527, 531, 549, 570, 577, 611, 627, 642-43

March on Washington, 572-73

Marconi, Guglielmo, 458

Marshall, George C., 548

Marshall, John, 149, 168

Marshall, Thurgood, 557

Marshall Plan, 548, 550, 561

Maryland, 64, 70, 73, 100, 115, 140, 149

Marx Brothers, 504

Mason, Charles, 100

Mason, George, 149

Mason-Dixon Line, 100

Massachusetts, 62, 66, 69-70, 73, 115, 149, 243

Mass produce, 234

Mass production, 249, 386

Math, 149, 584

Mayans, 16-17, 30-31

Mayflower, 60

Mayflower Compact, 60-61, 72-73

McAuliffe, Christa, 624

McCarthy, Joseph, 556, 561

McCarthyism, 536

McClellan, George, 308-10, 317, 321

McCord, James, 601

McCormick, Cyrus, 234, 249

McDowell, Irvin, 307

McGovern, George, 597

McKinley, William, 414, 425-26, 428, 433, 445

McLean, Wilmer, 319

Meade, George G., 313-14

Meadowcroft Rockshelter, 13

Meat Inspection Act, 437, 445

Meat-packing industry, 381, 385

Media in History, 68, 119, 139, 182, 221, 246, 281, 309, 335, 370, 394, 458, 472, 504, 524, 551, 578, 604, 633, 644

Medicare, 575, 587

Medicines, 437

Mediterranean Sea, 35

Melting pot, 241

Melville, Herman, 245

Mercantilism, 77-78, 89

Mercury space program, 587

Meredith, James, 572

Mergenthaler, Ottmar, 377

U.S.S. *Merrimac*, 308-9

Mesabi Range, 255

Mesa Verde National Park, 22

Mesoamerica, 16-18, 20, 31

Metropolitan Opera, 497

Mexican Independence Day, 173

Mexican War, 258-59, 261, 265

Mexico, 16-17, 40, 46, 224, 228, 229, 258-59, 261, 265, 278, 649, 661

Mexico City, 258-59

Microwave ovens, 612

Middle colonies, 71, 73

Middle East, 545, 605, 613-14, 617, 625-26, 645, 647

Migrant workers, 580-81, 587

Militia, 115

Million Man March, 657, 661

Minimum wage, 443, 657, 661

Mining, 352, 363, 381, 434, 458

Minnesota, 169, 225

Minutemen, 108-9, 111, 115, 117

Mir, 565

Missiles, 569

Mississippi, 199, 295, 316

Mississippian culture, 26-28, 31

Mississippi River, 89, 131, 137, 161

Missouri, 169, 205-6, 208

Missouri Compromise, 206, 213, 280, 291

Mitchell, John, 601

Mitchell, Margaret, 505

Model T, 473-74

Mogollons, 20-21, 31

Mohawks, 27-28

Molasses Act, 80

Monarchies, 35, 208

Mondale, Walter, 608, 623

Money, 138, 146, 226, 233, 414

Monitor, 308-9
Monks Mound, 27
Monmouth, 128
Monopolies, 372, 374, 381, 417, 435
Monroe, James, 169, 199, 203, 208-10, 212-13
Monroe Doctrine, 208-9, 212, 213, 438, 440
Montana, 169
Montcalm, Louis, 86
Montezuma II, 40
Montgomery (Alabama), 301, 557, 561, 625
Montgomery, Richard, 120, 133
Montreal, 83, 120, 133
Moon, 596, 617
Moore's Creek (North Carolina), 120
Morales, Luis, 660
Moratorium, 496
Morris, Nelson, 375
Morse, Samuel F. B., 237, 249, 254
Morse code, 254
Moscow, 642, 651
Mosely-Braun, Carol, 649
Mott, Lucretia, 264
Moundville (Alabama), 27
Mount Vernon Conference, 140
Movies, 504-5, 633. *See also* Silent films
Muckrakers, 335, 435
Mugwumps, 405, 407, 417
Museums, 393
Music, 393, 582
Mussolini, Benito, 513, 518, 530, 535

Nast, Thomas, 370, 405, 417
Natchez, 28
National Academy of Design, 254
National Aeronautics and Space Administration (NASA), 565, 574, 587, 624, 630
National Archives, 309
National Association for the Advancement of Colored People (NAACP), 441, 484, 557
National Audubon Society, 244
National Bank of the United States, 159
National Farm Workers Association, 580-81
National Gallery of Art, 280
National Guard, 558, 596
Nationalism, 189, 191, 213
    black, 479
National Labor Relations Act, 500
National League, 394
National Recovery Act, 502
National Recovery Administration (NRA), 498-99
National Republicans, 167
National Socialist German Workers party. *See* Nazis
National Woman Suffrage Association, 309, 469
Natural resources, 367, 437
Navajos, 23, 31
Navigation Acts, 80, 89
Navy, United States, 164, 175, 183, 458, 626
Nazis, 513-14, 518-19, 530, 535
Nebraska, 169, 279-80, 287
Netherlands, 59, 78, 440, 521, 535
New Deal, 497, 500, 502, 509, 516, 551
New England, 59, 79, 89, 100, 181, 210, 229, 242, 244, 287
    colonies, 70, 73
New Federalism, 622
Newfoundland, 38, 41, 47
New France, 44

N

Nagasaki, 533
Nails, 125
Naismith, James, 394
Narragansetts, 65

New Freedom, 442
New Hampshire, 66, 70, 73, 149
New immigrants, 388-90
New Jersey, 67, 71, 73, 115, 133, 149
New Jersey Plan, 143, 145, 153
New Mexico, 172, 278, 283, 357
New Nationalism, 443
New Orleans, 86, 89, 137, 161, 169, 175, 188, 191, 316
New Orleans Mint, 302
Newspapers, 68, 119, 182, 221, 246
New World, 47
New York, 65-66, 71, 73, 123-24, 149, 185, 369, 388, 395
Nez Percé, 358-59
Nicaragua, 610, 625, 627-28, 637
Nimitz, Chester, 532
Ninepins, 56
Nineteenth Amendment, 469, 485
Nixon, Richard, 566, 585, 587, 595-96, 598-99, 601-3, 605, 617
Noble Order of the Knights of Labor, 409, 417
Nobles, 35, 64
Nomads, 13, 18, 28, 31, 356
Nominate, 218
Nootka, 29, 31
North, the, 202, 205, 210, 220, 273-77, 302, 305-7, 313, 316
North, Frederick, 104
North, Lord, 130
North American Free Trade Agreement (NAFTA), 649, 661
North Atlantic Treaty Organization (NATO), 550, 652
North Carolina, 41, 44, 47, 65, 70, 73, 115, 120, 130, 133, 149, 287, 304, 309, 316
North Dakota, 169
Northern Ireland, 240
North Pole, 442
North Star, The, 247
Northwest Indians, 184

Northwest Ordinance, 137, 147, 152, 153
Northwest Passage, 40-41, 47
Norway, 521, 535
Nuclear war, 555
Nuclear weapons, 629, 637, 651
Nueces River, 258
Nylon, 507

O

Oberlin College, 248
O'Connor, Sandra Day, 622-23, 637
Oglethorpe, James, 67, 73, 80
Ohio Company, 81
Ohio Valley, 81, 83-84, 89, 97, 106, 111, 128, 185
Oil, 371-74, 381, 385, 435, 470, 609, 617
Oil Creek, 371
Oil embargo, 617
Oklahoma, 169
Oklahoma City (Oklahoma), 656
Old immigrants, 388
Olmecs, 16, 31
Omaha (Nebraska), 349
Omnibus Violent Crime Control and Prevention Act, 650
Onandaga, 27
Oneida, 27
Open Door Policy, 430-31, 438, 445, 525
Open trade, 661
Oppression, 219
Ordinance of Nullification, 220
Oregon, 349
Oregon Country, 256-57, 265
Organization of Petroleum Exporting Countries (OPEC), 605
Orlando, Vittorio, 460
Osage, 30
Oswald, Lee Harvey, 573
Otis, Elisha G., 289, 377

Otis Elevator Company, 289
Overpopulation, 659
Owens, Jesse, 505

P

Pacific Northwest cultures, 29, 31
Pacific Ocean, 39, 47
Pahlavi, Shah Mohammad Reza, 613
Paine, Thomas, 124, 132
Palestine, 545
Palestine Liberation Organization (PLO),
    611, 625, 637, 651
Panama, 438-39, 610, 653
    Canal, 439, 445, 524, 610
Panic of 1837, 226-27, 229
Pardons, 117
Paris Peace Conference, 460
Parks, Rosa, 557
Parliament, 98-99, 102, 107-8, 514. *See also*
    British Parliament
Paterson, William, 141,143
Patriots, 107-8
Patroons, 65
Patton, George, 531
Pawnees, 28-29, 31
Peace Corps, 574, 587
Pearl Harbor, 525-26, 530, 535
Peary, Robert E., 442
Penn, William, 66-67, 73
Pennsylvania, 66-67, 71, 73, 100, 109, 115,
    149, 235, 313
Penny Press, 221, 335
Perestroika, 642
Perkins, Frances, 501, 509
Perkins, Jacob, 125
Perot, Ross, 648, 658
Perry, Oliver Hazard, 185
Pershing, John, 458, 465

Persian Gulf War, 645-47
Peru, 18-19
Petitions, 116
Petroleum, 367
Philip II, 43
Philippines, 428, 430, 433, 526
Phnom Penh, 595
Phonographs, 377, 394, 475
Pickett, George, 314
Pierce, Franklin, 278
Pike, Zebulon, 172
Pikes Peak (Colorado), 172, 352
Pilgrims, 59-61, 72
Pinchback, Pinckney B. S., 334
Pinchot, Gifford, 437
Pinckney, Charles, 166
Pioneers, 137
Pitcairn, Major, 108-9
Pitt, William, 84-85, 89
Pizarro, Francisco, 39
Plains Indians, 28-29, 31, 356, 358-59, 363
Plantations, 57, 71, 79, 203, 206, 224, 273,
    277-78, 333
Plastics, 526
Platform, 294
Plessy, Homer, 391
Plessy, v. Ferguson, 390-91
Plumer, William, 203
Plymouth, 73, 60
Plymouth Company, 45, 59
Pocahontas, 56
Poe, Edgar Allan, 245, 249, 257
Poland, 462, 517, 519, 521, 535, 635, 643
Polio, 554
Polish Corridor, 519
Political, 45
    boss, 405
    parties, 160, 162, 280
    reforms, 445
Polk, James K., 256-59, 261, 265
Polls, 632
Polo, Marco, 35, 47

Ponce de León, Juan, 38-39, 42, 47
Pontiac, 97
Pony express, 238, 249
Poor Richard's Almanac, 88
Popular sovereignty, 280
Population, United States, 181, 199, 240, 249, 385, 659
Populist party, 412-15, 417
Portugal, 36, 44, 78
Postmaster, 117
Potomac River, 140, 158, 314
Poverty Point, 26
Powderly, Terrence V., 409
Powell, Colin, 634
Powhatans, 56
Prejudice, 389
Prescott, Samuel, 108-9
Primary elections, 435, 445
Princip, Gavrilo, 450
Prisoners, 221
Prisoners of war, 596
Proclamation of 1763, 97, 111
Progressives, 435, 442, 445, 449
Prohibition, 481, 485
Proprietors, 64
Prosecute, 412
Prospectors, 352
Protests, 572, 595-96
Providence (Rhode Island), 73
Provinces, 106
Public Relations Society of America, 660
Public services, 161
Public transportation, 392-93, 399
Pueblos, 23, 31
Puerto Rico, 37, 425, 428, 433, 445
Puritans, 61-64, 73

Q

al-Qaddafi, Muammar, 626-27
Quakers, 67, 227
Quartering Act, 98
Quayle, Dan, 648
Quebec, 44, 83, 89, 106, 120, 129, 133
Quebec Act, 106
Quetzalcoatl, 17-18

R

Rabin, Yitzhak, 651
Radars, 522
Radical Republicans, 327
Radicals, 327, 330
Radio, 458, 475-76, 504, 534, 551
Radio Corporation of America (RCA), 458, 483
Ragtime, 432
Railroads, 237, 249, 279, 283, 316, 349-51, 363, 375, 381, 385, 403, 408, 417
Raleigh, Sir Walter, 43-44, 47
Randolph, Edmond, 141, 143, 157
Ratifies, 148-49
Reagan, Ronald, 608, 621-23, 626-30, 637, 649
Rebellions, 80
Recalls, 435
Reconstruction, 326-27, 331, 334, 338-39
Reconstruction Act, 329, 332, 341
Reconstruction Finance Corporation, 496
Red Cloud, Chief, 359
Reed, Ezekiel, 125
Reed, Walter, 429
Referendums, 435, 445
Refinery, 371
Reform, 403, 406-7, 412-15, 417, 435, 442
Reformers, 481
Refugees, 568, 653

Regiments, 83
Regular Army, 182
Reinforcements, 86
Repeal, 99
Representatives, 57
Republican National Convention, 608
Republican party, 167, 280, 417, 655
Republic of Columbia, 438
Republic of Texas, 225
Republics, 429
Reservations, 30, 351, 357-58, 363, 404
Reservoirs, 22
Resolutions, 165
Reunifications, 641
Revere, Paul, 108
Revolutionary War, 123-25, 128, 130
Revolutions, 123
Rhode Island, 64-65, 70, 149
Rice, 334
Rich, Adrienne, 415
Richardson, Elliot, 601-2
Richmond (Virginia), 304, 317
Riis, Jacob, 396
Rio Grande, 258-59
Riots, 572
Roanoke colony, 44, 47
Roaring Twenties, 468-87
Rockefeller, John D., 367, 372-73, 381, 435
Roebling, John A., 369
Rogers, Ginger, 504
Rolfe, John, 56
Roman Catholic Church, 183
Rome, 530, 535
Romero, Oscar, Archbishop, 610
Roosevelt, Eleanor, 515
Roosevelt, Franklin Delano, 496-502, 509,
    515-16, 521, 523, 525-26, 529, 531-32,
    534, 551, 554
Roosevelt, Theodore, 425, 427, 433-34,
    436-43, 445, 454, 515
Roosevelt Corollary, 438
"Rosie the Riveter," 528

Ross, John, 204
Rough Riders, 427
Royal Air Force (RAF), 522
Ruby, Jack, 573
Ruling, 290
Running mates, 166
Rural areas, 233
Russia, 330, 430, 438, 574, 643, 661.
    See also Soviet Union
Russian Federation, 643
Ruth, Babe, 482

S

Sacajawea, 171
Sacramento (California), 249, 349
Sadat, Anwar, 611, 625
Safety of workers, 399
Saint Helens, Mount, 622
St. Lawrence River, 41, 44, 47, 86, 89
St. Leger, Barry, 126
St. Louis (Missouri), 249
St. Marks (Florida), 204
St. Marys City (Maryland), 64, 73
Salk, Jonas E., 554
Saloons, 353
Salvation Army, 397, 399
Sampson, William, 427
Sanction, 630
Sanitation, 395, 399
San Juan Hill, 445
Santa Anna, Antonio López de, 224-25,
    228, 258
Sarajevo, 450
Saratoga, 126, 129, 133
Satellites, 313, 559, 565, 587,
Saturday Night Massacre, 602
Saudi Arabia, 645-46, 661
Sauk and Fox, 223
Savannah (Georgia), 73, 130, 317

Scalawags, 332, 337, 341

Schmeling, Max, 506

Schneiderman, Rose, 386

Schools, 221, 226, 242-43, 249, 340, 391, 557, 560-61, 572, 587

Schwarzkopf, Norman, 646

Science, 82, 244, 507, 657

Scotland, 240

Scott, Dred, 290-92, 296-97

Scott, Winfield, 259, 305, 307-8

Scott versus Stanford, 296

Secede, 295

Second Revolutionary War. *See* War of 1812

Secretary of Interior, 470, 485

Security Council, 544

Sedition Act, 164, 168, 175

Segregation, 334, 390-91, 557, 560-61, 571-72, 579, 587

Selective Service, 457, 523

Seminoles, 203-4, 213, 223, 229

Senate, 145, 184, 205, 282, 292, 297, 330, 398, 428, 462-63, 556, 649

Seneca, 27

Seneca Falls Convention, 264

Separatists. *See* Pilgrims

Sequoyah, 209

Serapis, 129

Serbia, 450-51, 462

Serpent Mound, 24

Seton, Mother Elizabeth, 183

Settlements, 16, 20-21, 24-25, 27-28, 44, 65-67

Seven Days Battles, 309

Seventh Cavalry, 358, 360

Seward, William, 330

Sewing machine, 274

Seymour, Horatio, 331

Sharecroppers, 333

Shares, 59

Sharpshooting, 130

Shay, Daniel, 141, 153

Shay's Rebellion, 141, 153

Shepard, Alan B., Jr., 565

Sheridan, Phillip, 317

Sherman, William, 317, 319, 321

Sherman Anti-Trust Act, 412, 417, 435

Shipbuilding, 213, 236

Siberia, 13, 31

Siege, 124

Silent films, 472, 475. *See also* Movies

Silver, 39-40, 47, 55, 226, 352, 414

Singer, Isaac Merrit, 274

Sioux, 356-57, 359, 363

Sisters of Charity, 183

Sitting Bull, 357

Sixteenth Amendment, 441, 445, 449, 465

Skyscrapers, 368

Slater, Samuel, 233, 249

Slave market, 145

Slavery, 39, 69, 79, 121, 145, 168, 174, 201, 205-6, 213, 219, 221, 229, 246-47, 258, 261-62, 265, 273-74, 276-78, 280, 283, 289-94, 297, 301-2, 318, 327

Slave states, 205-6, 273, 280, 283, 297

Slave trade, 174

Slidell, John, 258

Sloat, John D., 259

Slums, 395-97, 435, 493

Smallpox vaccine, 165

Smith, Al, 483

Smith, John, 55-56

Smith, Lucien, 355

Smith, Margaret Chase, 556

Snaketown, 20

Social problems, 481

Social Security, 500-06, 509, 575

Sod, 354

Somalia, 651, 661

Somoza, Anastasio, 610

Songs
    Civil War, 310
    World War II, 524, 528

Sons of Liberty, 100

Soup house, 483

South, the, 145, 200, 205-6, 210, 220, 229, 244, 246, 273-77, 283, 302-3, 305-8, 313-14, 316, 318, 325-26, 328-29 reshaping, 332-34. *See also* Reconstruction

South Africa, 625, 630, 652, 661

South America, 38-39, 42, 47, 279, 440, 605

South Carolina, 65, 70, 73, 115, 149, 217, 220, 229, 274, 295, 302, 304, 316, 332 Ordinance of Nullification, 229

South Dakota, 169, 360-61

Southern colonies, 70-71, 73

Southwark Theatre, 109

Soviet Union, 515, 519, 521, 523, 530, 535, 544, 547-48, 550, 552-53, 555, 559, 561, 565-66, 568-69, 587, 598-99, 614-15, 617, 628-29, 635, 637, 641-43, 661. *See also* Russia

Space exploration, 565, 587, 623-24, 630, 637

Spain, 36, 40, 43-44, 78, 86, 89, 131, 133, 137, 160-61, 169, 425-26, 428, 514-15, 517, 535

Spanish-American War, 427-28

Spanish Armada, 47

Spanish Civil War, 514-15, 517

Speakeasy, 481

Speaker of the House, 181, 182

Spice Islands, 35

Spirit of St. Louis, 482, 485

Spirituals, 219, 477

Spoils system, 218, 229, 405, 417

Sports, 394, 505-6

Sputnik, 559, 656

Stagecoaches, 239, 349

Stalin, Joseph, 519, 531, 547

Stamp Act, 98-100, 110, 111

Stampedes, 353

Standard Oil, 372-74, 381, 441

Stanton, Edwin, 330

Stanton, Elizabeth Cady, 264, 469

U.S.S. *Stark,* 626

"Star-Spangled Banner, The", 187

State courts, 138

Statehood, 206

Statesman, 120

Statue of Liberty, 388, 399

Steamboats, 175, 249

Steel industry, 367-39, 373, 381, 385

Steerage, 388

Steffens, Lincoln, 435

Stevens, Uriah, 409

Stevenson, Adlai, 555

Stock company, 59, 373

Stock market, 482-83, 485, 493-94, 509

Stone, Lucy, 303

Stowe, Harriet Beecher, 246, 248, 281

Strategic Arms Limitations Talks (SALT), 599

Strategic Arms Limitations Talks II (SALT II), 615, 617

Strategic Arms Reduction Treaty (START), 641

Streetcars, 392

Strikes, 410, 417, 434, 581

Stronghold, 86

Stump speeches, 292

Stuyvesant, Peter, 66

Submarines, 118, 453

Subpoena, 602

Suburbs, 474

Subways, 338

Sudetenland, 517-18, 535

Sue, 290

Suffrage, 336, 443, 464, 469

Sugar Act, 98

Summit, 641

Sumner, Charles, 289

Supreme Court, 145-46, 168, 290-91, 296-97, 390-91, 436, 502, 509, 557, 560-61, 622-23, 637

Suspension bridges, 368

Sutter, John, 262, 265

Swift, Gustavus, 375
Symphony, 477
Synagogues, 518

T

Taft, William Howard, 441-42, 445
Taft-Hartley Act, 545
Taiwan, 598
Talkies, 472
Tammany Hall, 405
Taney, Roger, 291, 296
Tarbell, Ida, 435
Tar and feather, 98
Tariff of 1828, 217, 220, 229
Tariffs, 138, 145, 183, 200, 217, 220, 261,
    301-2, 441, 470, 494, 509, 649
Tax, 159, 220, 457, 649-50
    evasion, 602
Taxation without representation, 98
Taylor, Zachary, 258-59, 261-62, 265,
    274-75
Teapot Dome (Wyoming), 470
    Scandal, 485
Technology, 179, 289, 355, 369, 612
Tecumseh, 182, 184-85, 190-91
Teheran, 613
Telegraphs, 237-38, 249, 254, 349
Telephone, 473
Television, 551, 556, 558, 561, 566, 571,
    578, 583, 601, 603, 604
Temple, Shirley, 504
Tenant farmer, 333
Tenements, 395-96
Tennessee, 304, 308, 316
Tennessee Valley Authority (TVA), 498, 509
Tenochtitlán, 17, 40
Tenure of Office Act, 330
Territories, 35, 44
Terrorism, 611, 626, 628, 637, 656, 661

Test Taking Tips, 33, 49, 75, 91, 113, 135,
    155, 177, 193, 215, 231, 251, 267, 285,
    299, 323, 343, 365, 383, 401, 419, 447,
    467, 487, 511, 537, 563, 589, 619, 639,
    663
Texas, 204, 224-25, 228, 229, 265, 295, 327, 353,
    456
Textile industry, 233, 249, 283, 387
Thames, Battle of the, 185, 191
Third Reich, 517
Third World, 574, 658
Thirteenth Amendment, 327
Thomas, Isaiah, 119
Thoreau, Henry David, 245
Thorpe, Jim, 450
Three-Fifths Compromise, 145, 153
Three-pronged attack, 126
Tilden, Samuel J., 338
Tippecanoe, 253
Titusville, 371-72
Tlingit, 29, 31
Tobacco, 56-58, 200, 334
Tojo, Hideki, 525
Toleration Act, 64
Toltecs, 17
Tonkin Gulf Resolution, 576, 587
Torpedo, 453
Totem poles, 29
Townshend, Charles, 100
Townshend Acts, 100-101, 111
Trade, 145, 159, 161, 169, 183, 208, 430,
    433, 438, 449, 525, 641, 649
Trail of Tears, 204, 229
Traitors, 129
Transportation. See also Automobiles;
    Highways; Railroads; Trolleys
    water, 235-36
    public, 392-93, 399
Travel, 474
Travis, William Barrett, 224, 228
Treason, 293
Treasury, 157

Treasury Department, 404
Treaty, 86
    of 1846, 257
    of Ghent, 188, 191
    of Guadalupe Hidalgo, 259, 265
    of Paris, 86, 89, 131, 133, 137, 141, 163
Triangular trade, 79-80, 89
Trist, Nicholas P., 259
Trolleys, 392
Truman, Harry S., 532, 535, 545-46, 548, 550, 552-53, 555
Truman Doctrine, 548
Trust company, 374, 412, 442
Truth, Sojourner, 277, 283
Truth-in-Securities Act, 498
Tsimshian, 29, 31
Tubman, Harriet, 277, 283, 288
Turkey, 451, 548
Turner, Nat, 219, 229
Turnpikes, 235
Tuscarora, 27
Tuskegee Institute, 376
Twain, Mark, 333, 403
Tweed, William Marcy, 405, 417
Twelfth Amendment, 167, 175, 210
Twelfth Congress, 179, 191
Twenty-First Amendment, 481
Twenty-Second Amendment, 566
Tyler, John, 253-54
Typesetting, 377

U

U-boats, 453-54, 456, 458
Ukraine, 643, 651, 661
Uncle Tom's Cabin, 246, 248, 281
Underground, Colonial, 119
Underground Railroad, 276-77, 283, 288
Unemployment, 227, 326, 493, 495, 509, 617

Union, the, 82, 205-6, 220, 229, 258, 273, 283, 287, 295, 297, 301-2, 304-14, 316-18, 321, 325, 327-29
Union Pacific Railroad, 349-51, 363, 403-4, 417
United Nations, 515, 533, 544-45, 552-53, 561, 645, 651, 661
    Human Rights Commission, 515, 623
    Security Council, 552, 645
United States
    Bureau of the Census, 149
    Department of Defense, 644
    Forest Service, 437
    Military Academy, 168
    Navy, 129
Universal Negro Improvement Association, 479
Urban areas, 395-397, 399

V

Vaccinations, 165, 554
Valley Forge, 127-28
Van Buren, Martin, 217, 226-27, 229, 253, 261, 632
Vanderbilt, Cornelius, 375-381
Venezuela, 440
Verrazano, Giovanni da, 40-42, 47
Versailles, 460
    Treaty of, 462-63, 465, 517, 519
Vertical combination, 373
Vesey, Denmark, 206, 213
Vespucci, Amerigo, 38, 42, 47
Veterans, 308
Veteran's Bureau, 470
Veto, 221-22, 330
Vicksburg (Mississippi), 316
Victory Gardens, 528
Videocassette recorder (VCR), 633
Video disc players, 633

Vietcong, 577
Vietnam, 576-77, 579, 583-84, 587, 596-97,
  601, 617, 652, 661
Vietnamization, 595-97, 617
Vietnam War, 576-78, 581, 583, 595, 597,
  605, 617, 652
  Memorial, 625
Viking I, 607
Villages, 20, 28
Virginia, 308
Virginia, 45, 115,130, 133, 140, 149, 210,
  304, 307, 309
  Company, 45, 47, 57-58
  Plan, 143, 145, 153
Volcanoes, 622
Voter recalls, 445
Voting rights, 221, 328, 336
Voyages, 36

W

Wages, 399
Wagner Act, 500
Wagon trains, 349
Wales, 240
Wallace, George, 585
Wang, An, 606
War of 1812, 182, 184-87, 189
War Hawks, 179-81, 184, 191
Warmouth, Henry C., 334
War on Poverty, 575
War of Texas Independence, 258
Warren, Earl, 557
War zone, 453-54, 456
Washington, Booker T., 376, 444
Washington, George, 81, 84, 86, 89, 107,
  117-18, 123-25, 127-30, 133, 139-42,
  144, 148-49, 153, 157, 160-63, 175, 181,
  203, 210
Washington Monument, 606

Watergate scandal, 601-3, 617
Waterhouse, Benjamin, 165
Waterman, Lewis, 377
Weaver, James, 412
Weaver, Robert, 575
Webster, Daniel, 226, 255, 274, 282
Webster, Noah, 139, 243
Weld, Theodore Dwight, 248, 273
Welfare reform, 657
Welles, Orson, 504
Wells, 355
Wells-Barnet, Ida, 441
West, the, 210, 229, 244
West Germany, 550, 641, 661
West Indies, 36-37, 47, 79-80, 86, 89, 425
West Jersey, 69, 73
West Point, 129, 308
Westward expansion, 189, 199-202
Wharton, Edith, 478, 485
Wheatley, Phillis, 103
Whigs, 167, 226, 254, 282
Whiskey Ring Scandal, 404
White, John, 44, 47
White House, 186, 218
Whitewater Affair, 655-56, 661
Whitman, Walt, 245
Whitney, Eli, 201, 233-34, 249
Whittier, John Greenleaf, 246
Wilder, Douglas, 634
Williams, Roger, 64-65, 73
Williams, William Carlos, 415
Wilson, Woodrow, 442-43, 445, 449,
  453-56, 460, 462-63, 465
  Fourteen Points, 460
Windmill, 355
Winthrop, John, 62
Wiretap, 601
Wizard of Oz, The, 505
Wolfe, James, 86
Woman's Christian Temperance Union
  (WCTU), 416
Woman's Journal, 303

Women's rights movement, 227, 264, 303, 580. *See also* Equal Rights Amendment; Feminist Movement
Women's Trade Union League, 386
Woodstock, 582
Wool Act, 80
Woolworth, F. W., 393
Woolworth Building, 393
Working conditions, 221, 386, 399, 417
Works Progress Administration (WPA), 500, 509
World Court, 440
World Trade Center, 656
World War I, 456-59
World War II, 519, 521, 523-34, 543
World Wide Web, 644
Wounded Knee, 360-61, 363
Wright brothers, 378
Writers, 244-47, 478, 505
Writing About History, 28, 44, 63, 77, 102, 126, 150, 172, 188, 201, 222, 247, 259, 281, 291, 306, 331, 359, 378, 390, 408, 429, 459, 476, 495, 529, 553, 573, 609, 630, 658
Wyoming, 169, 357

X

XYZ Affair, 163, 175

Y

Yalta Agreement, 531-32, 547
Yeltsin, Boris, 642-43, 651
York, Duke of, 66-67, 73
Yorktown (Virginia), 130
Young Men's Christian Association (YMCA), 397, 399
Young Women's Christian Association (YWCA), 397, 399
Youth movement, 580-81, 587
Yugoslavia, 462, 652

Z

Zenger, John Peter, 78
Zimmermann Note, 456, 465

Acknowledgments

Acknowledgment is made for permission to reprint the following copyrighted material.

Page 30: Reprinted with permission of Simon & Schuster from *Cabeza de Vaca's Adventures in the Unknown Interior of America,* translated and edited by Cyclone Covey. Copyright © 1961 by Macmillan Publishing Company.

Page 362: From *China Men* by Maxine Hong Kingston. Copyright © 1980 by Maxine Hong Kingston. Reprinted by permission of Alfred A. Knopf, Inc.

Page 490: From *The Grapes of Wrath* by John Steinbeck. Copyright 1939, renewed © 1967 by John Steinbeck. Used by permission of Viking Penguin, a division of Penguin Books USA Inc.

Page 540: From *Take Time for Paradise,* copyright 1989 by the estate of A. Bartlett Giamatti. Reprinted by permission of Mildred Marmur Associates Ltd. as Agent for the Estate of A. Bartlett Giamatti.

Page 560: From *The Long Shadow of Little Rock* by Daisy Bates, copyright 1986, reprinted by permission of The University of Arkansas Press.

Page 636: From a speech entitled "Women in America Shooting for the Stars: As We See Ourselves So Do We Act" by Stella Guerra. *Vital Speeches,* September 15, 1986, vol. 52, p. 726.

Page 660: From a speech entitled "Favor Positive Themes" by Luis Morales. *Vital Speeches,* July 15, 1996, vol. 62, p. 602.

Images

Unit 1
Page 10, © Richard Alexander Cooke, III; p. 11, Jacksonville Museum of Contemporary Art, Florida/SuperStock.

Chapter 1
Page 15, courtesy of J. M. Adovasio, Mercyhurst, Archaeological Institute; p. 15 (inset), © 1997 John McGrail, all rights reserved; p. 17, 24a, 24b, © Richard Alexander Cooke, III; p. 19, Joel Sartore © National Geographic Society; p. 21, © 1992 Ira Block; p. 23, © National Geographic Society; p. 23 (inset) © SuperStock; p. 27, Tom Hull, *America's Ancient Cities* © National Geographic Society; p. 29, Anne B. Keiser © National Geographic Society.

Chapter 2
Pages 36, 38, 40a, 40b, 43, 45, The Granger Collection, New York.

Unit 2
Page 52, The Bettmann Archive.

Chapter 3
Page 62, The Bettmann Archive; pp. 55, 60, 61, 69, The Granger Collection, New York; p. 57, Library of Congress; p. 64, Judy J. King; p. 66, Corbis-Bettmann.

Chapter 4
Pages 78, 80, Corbis-Bettmann; pp. 79, 83, 86, The Granger Collection, New York; p. 84, Library of Congress.

Unit 3
Page 94, The Granger Collection, New York; p. 95, SuperStock.

Chapter 5
Page 97, 105, 108a, 108b, The Granger Collection, New York; p. 99, Library of Congress; pp. 101, 103, The Bettmann Archive.

Chapter 6
Page 118, The Bettmann Archive; p. 121a, 124, 127, The Granger Collection, New York; p. 121b, © 1996, 1997 John McGrail, all rights reserved; p. 122, Photographs and Prints Division, Schomberg Center for Research in Black Culture, the New York Public Library, Astor, Lennox, and Tilden Foundations.

Chapter 7
Pages 138, 141, 147, The Granger Collection, New York; p. 144, courtesy Massachusetts Historical Society; p. 151, Judy J. King.

Chapter 8
Pages 157, 158, 164, 168, 171, The Granger Collection, New York; p. 161, Corbis-Bettmann; p. 173, Culver Pictures, Inc.

Chapter 9
Pages 180, 182, 183, 185, 187 (inset), The Granger Collection, New York; p. 186, 187, The Bettmann Archive.

Unit 4
Page 196, Corbis-Bettmann; p. 197, © 1996 Smithsonian Institute.

Chapter 10
Pages 201a, 201b, 204b, 209a, 211, The Granger Collection, New York; p. 204a, SuperStock; p. 205, The Bettmann Archive; p. 209b, Bettmann Newsphotos.

Chapter 11
Pages 218, 219, 222, 224, 227a, 227b, The Granger Collection, New York; p. 223, Woolaroc Museum, Bartlesville, Oklahoma.